TAKING SIDES

Clashing Views in

Mass Media and Society

TENTH EDITION

TAKING SIDES

Clashing Views in

Mass Media and Society

TENTH EDITION

Selected, Edited, and with Introductions by

Alison Alexander
University of Georgia

and

Jarice Hanson
University of Massachusetts at Amherst

 **Higher Education**

Boston   Burr Ridge, IL   Dubuque, IA   New York   San Francisco   St. Louis
Bangkok   Bogotá   Caracas   Kuala Lumpur   Lisbon   London   Madrid   Mexico City
Milan   Montreal   New Delhi   Santiago   Seoul   Singapore   Sydney   Taipei   Toronto

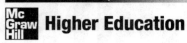

Higher Education

TAKING SIDES: MASS MEDIA AND SOCIETY, TENTH EDITION

Published by McGraw-Hill, a business unit of The McGraw-Hill Companies, Inc., 1221 Avenue of the Americas, New York, NY 10020. Copyright © 2009 by The McGraw-Hill Companies, Inc. All rights reserved. Previous edition(s) 1991–2007. No part of this publication may be reproduced or distributed in any form or by any means, or stored in a database or retrieval system, without the prior written consent of The McGraw-Hill Companies, Inc., including, but not limited to, in any network or other electronic storage or transmission, or broadcast for distance learning.

Some ancillaries, including electronic and print components, may not be available to customers outside the United States.

Taking Sides® is a registered trademark of the McGraw-Hill Companies, Inc.
Taking Sides is published by the **Contemporary Learning Series** group within the McGraw-Hill Higher Education division.

1 2 3 4 5 6 7 8 9 0 DOC/DOC 0 9 8

MHID: 0-07-351524-8
ISBN: 978-0-07-351524-3
ISSN: 94-31766

Managing Editor: *Larry Loeppke*
Production Manager: *Faye Schilling*
Senior Developmental Editor: *Susan Brusch*
Editorial Assistant: *Nancy Meissner*
Production Service Assistant: *Rita Hingtgen*
Permissions Coordinator: *Lenny J. Behnke*
Senior Marketing Manager: *Julie Keck*
Marketing Communications Specialist: *Mary Klein*
Marketing Coordinator: *Alice Link*
Project Manager: *Jane Mohr*
Design Specialist: *Tara McDermott*
Senior Administrative Assistant: *DeAnna Dausener*
Cover Graphics: *Kristine Jubeck*

Compositor: Hurix Systems Private Limited
Cover Image: Digital Vision/Getty Images

Library of Congress Cataloging-in-Publication Data
Main entry under title:
Taking sides: clashing views in mass media and society/selected, edited, and with introductions by Alison Alexander and Jarice Hanson.—10th ed.

Includes bibliographical references.
1.Mass media. 2. Information services. I. Alexander, Alison, *comp.* II. Hanson, Jarice, *comp.*
302.23

www.mhhe.com

Preface

Mass communication is one of the most popular college majors in the country, which perhaps reflects a belief in the importance of communications systems, as well as students' desires to work in one of the media or communications industries. This book, which contains 36 selections presented in a pro and con format, addresses 18 different controversial issues in mass communications and society. The purpose of this volume, and indeed of any course that deals with the social impact of media, is to create a literate consumer of media—someone who can walk the fine line between a naïve acceptance of all media and a cynical disregard for any positive benefits that they may offer.

Media today reflect the evolution of industries that have spread their reach to multiple types of media, and indeed, to more nations of the world than ever before. In the United States we have seen the impact of entertainment media on many forms of public discourse—news, politics, education, and more. We have also seen communication technologies rapidly enter the home in a number of ways: through the Internet, and personal devices such as iPods, personal digital assistants (PDAs), and cell phones. These many forms of media extend our capacities to communicate and to consume media content, and therefore, the study of media and society is very much a part of the way in which we now live our lives by blending technologies and services, public and private media uses, and public and private behaviors. In the near future, many of the technologies we use today may be subsumed by yet newer technologies, or greater use of those we already use. Film, television, radio, and print already reach us through the Internet. Traditional wired telephones may soon become a thing of the past. Since many of the issues in this volume are often in the news (or even are the news!), you may already have opinions about them. We encourage you to read the selections and discuss the issues with an open mind. Even if you do not initially agree with a position or do not even understand how it is possible to make the opposing argument, give it a try. Remember, these problems often are not restricted to only two views; there may be many, and we encourage you to discuss these topics as broadly as possible. We believe that thinking seriously about media is an important goal.

Plan of the book   This book is primarily designed for students in an introductory course in mass communication (sometimes called introduction to mass media or introduction to mass media and society). The issues are such that they can be easily incorporated into any media course regardless of how it is organized—thematically, chronologically, or by medium. The 36 selections have been taken from a variety of sources and were chosen because of their usefulness in defending a position and for their accessibility to students.

Each issue in this volume has an issue *introduction,* which sets the stage for the debate as it is argued in the YES and NO selections. Each issue concludes with a *postscript* that makes some final observations about the selections, points the way to other questions related to the issue, and offers suggestions for further reading on the issue. The introductions and postscripts do not pre-empt what is the reader's own task: to achieve a critical and informed view of the issues at stake. In reading an issue and forming your own opinion you should not feel confined to adopt one or the other of the positions presented. Some readers may see important points on both sides of an issue and may construct for themselves a new and creative approach. Such an approach might incorporate the best of both sides, or it might provide an entirely new vantage point for understanding. Relevant Internet site addresses (URLs) that may prove useful as starting points for further research are provided on the *Internet References* page that accompanies each unit opener. At the back of the book is a listing of all the *contributors to this volume,* which will give you additional information on the communication scholars, practitioners, policymakers, and media critics whose views are debated here.

Changes to this edition   The tenth edition represents a considerable revision, and the topics are perhaps more controversial than in past editions. This may be a reflection of the world in which we live—or perhaps it is a result of a greater awareness of media literacy and the impact of the media in our lives. We have edited Unit 1 to include only three issues, and have expanded other areas in which there is currently more controversy. We now call Unit 2 "A Question of Content" and broaden our scope from traditional mass media to more personal uses of questionable materials as applied in video games and alcohol advertising (Issues 4 and 5). Unit 3 has three new issues: Issue 7, "Should the White House Control the Press?", 9, "Should Images of War Be Censored?", and 10, "Is Blogging Journalism?". Unit 4 on Regulation is entirely new: 11, "Should We Still Believe in the First Amendment?", 12, "Is Big Media Business Bad for Democracy?", and 13, "Has Industry Regulation Controlled Indecent Media Content?". Unit 5 on Media Business also has three new issues: 14, "Are Legacy Media Systems Becoming Obsolete?", 15, "Does the Rise of Faith-Based Media Encourage Tolerance?", and 16, "Is Radio Dying?".

A word to the instructor   An *Instructor's Resource Guide With Test Questions* (multiple-choice and essay) is available through the publisher for the instructor using *Taking Sides* in the classroom. And a general guidebook, *Using Taking Sides in the Classroom*, which discusses methods and techniques for integrating the pro-con approach into any classroom setting, is also available. An online version of *Using Taking Sides in the Classroom* and a correspondence service for Taking Sides adopters can be found at http://www.mhcls.com/usingts/.

   Taking Sides: Clashing Views in Mass Media and Society is only one title in the Taking Sides series. If you are interested in seeing the table of contents for any of the other titles, please visit the Taking Sides Web site at http://www.mhcls.com/takingsides.

Acknowledgments   We wish to thank Nichole Altman for her continued watchful eye over the preparation of this book. Many thoughtful instructors at many institutions across the country provided feedback to help us incorporate new ideas into this edition. We also thank Keisha Hoerner for her help in preparing the Instructor's Manual, and Margaret Griffith of Temple University for her valuable assistance in researching topics and articles.

Finally we would like to thank our families and friends (James, Katie, James Jr., Torie, Frank, Dewey and Xena) for their patience and understanding during the period in which we prepared this book. And of course, we would like to thank all of our students for bringing their interests to our classrooms.

Alison Alexander
University of Georgia

Jarice Hanson
University of Massachusetts, Amherst

Contents In Brief

Contents

Critical scholar of modern mass media Professor Schiller argues that mass media institutions are key elements of the modern capitalistic world order. Media, he argues, produce economic profits and the ideology necessary to sustain a world system of exploitative divisions of social and financial resources. It is the job of the citizenry to understand the myths that act to sustain this existing state of power relationships. Professors of communication Horace Newcomb and Paul M. Hirsch in their classic article counter that television serves as a site of negotiation for cultural issues, images, and ideas. Viewer selections from among institutional choices is a negotiation process as viewers select from a wide set of approaches to issues and ideas.

W. James Potter, a professor of communication, examines existing research in the area of children and television violence. Such research is extensive and covers a variety of theoretical and methodological areas. He examines the nature of the impact of television on children and concludes that strong evidence exists for harmful effects. Jib Fowles, a professor of communication, finds the research on children and television violence less convincing. Despite the number of studies, he believes that the overall conclusions are unwarranted. Fowles finds that the influence is small, lab results are artificial, and fieldwork is inconclusive. In short, he finds television violence research flawed and unable to prove a linkage between violent images and harm to children.

Thomas Mascaro comments on the long history of examining how people of color have been portrayed in various forms of media. He makes the point that African-American women have often been stereotyped in television sitcoms, but during the seven seasons of the hit TV show, *Homicide: Life on the Streets*, African-American women were given a venue for portrayals that were more socially significant and socially relevant. Janis Sanchez-Hucles, Patrick S. Hudgins, and Kimberly Gamble conduct an analysis of many images of women of color from magazine advertising in six female or family-oriented magazines, and found that women of color were portrayed differently; in this issue, we examine African-American women in particular, but we include comments on other women of color, for further consideration.

UNIT 2   A QUESTION OF CONTENT   71

On March 21, 2000, the U.S. Congress held a hearing (106–1096) on "The Impact of Interactive Violence on Children." Among the several witnesses testifying before the committee, Dr. Craig A. Anderson provided one of the most persuasive arguments on the impact and effect of violent video games. An expert on the effect of violence in television and film, Dr. Anderson hold the position that video games prompt young people toward even more aggression and violence than do other media content. A special report in the British magazine *The Economist* discusses research that indicates that not only is there a generational divide among those who play video games, but the lack of long-term research limits what is actually known about the effects of playing video games. Citing a number of different studies about the moral impact of gaming and the skills necessary to play, this position argues that the issue of violence and aggression will pass as the critics age.

The authors of these selections take different approaches to the problem of copyright legislation in the days of digital technology. Vaidhyanathan discusses how complicated copyright law has become, but says it is still effective, because the law gives the owner of intellectual property the right to say "no." Ardito discusses the problem caused of web-based content like that published on MySpace and YouTube that often manipulates content originally created by someone else, and distributed for free. She claims that the responsibility for policing copyrighted works is cumbersome, expensive, time consuming, and ultimately unworkable; therefore, she suggests that copyright is no longer a viable law, in its present state.

John E. Calfee, a former U.S. Trade Commission economist, takes the position that advertising is very useful to people and that the information that advertising imparts helps consumers make better decisions. He maintains that the benefits of advertising far outweigh the negative criticisms. Author Dinyar Godrej makes the claim that advertising doesn't really tell us anything new about products, but instead, it acts upon our emotions to create anxiety if we don't buy products. The result then, is a culture in which we consume more than we need to, and still feel badly about ourselves. This type of consumer culture then permeates our lifestyles.

UNIT 3 NEWS AND POLITICS   133

Information has always been a weapon in the battle to frame reality. Schulman traces the efforts of military information operations (IO) to wage psychological warfare against the enemy, and outlines some ways in which this has blurred the line between providing truthful information to the public and press and conducting propaganda campaigns. Mainstream media failed in their responsibility to provide sound news and commentary for Americans to base their critical decisions about invading Iraq, according to Ryan. One reason is that journalists did not use an objective approach to executive and military information and assertions. This abdication of responsibility allowed the government and media to frame reality unchallenged.

Mass communication scholars examine the truth behind the assumption that negative campaigning has a negative impact on voters. Their experimental research study found that participants deemed negative ads fairly worthless and that such ads increased negativity about campaigns. Other potential consequences such as cynicism, efficacy, and apathy were not found. Political advertising scholars report on the lessons of their studies of negative campaign advertising. Negative ads, they argue, are more memorable. They help voters make distinctions between candidates; they influence voters. But not all negative ads are useful, and the authors help us make the distinction. Despite the revulsion that pervades public opinion toward negative ads, these authors argue that they are helpful to voters.

This study examined political coverage of the first presidential debate and the political convention on *The Daily Show* and on network nightly newscasts. The study found the network coverage to be more hype than substance, and *The Daily Show* to be more humor than substance. The amount of substantive information between the two newscasts was about the same for both the story and for the entire half-hour program. Hollander examined learning from comedy and late-night programs. National survey data were used to examine whether exposure to comedy and late-night programs actually inform viewers, focusing on recall and recognition. Some support is found for the prediction that the consumption of such programs is more associated with recognition of information than with actual recall.

UNIT 4   REGULATION   213

Maciejewski and Ozar argue that the basis of first amendment rights is in the concept of the publics' right to know. Rarely will you read an article that is so explicit in outlining its underlying premises. Outline what these authors are putting forward, in order to understand the important distinctions they make. But, ask your own questions. Do you agree with their fundamental presuppositions? Is the right to know both clear and valid? Can you derive other possible dimensions of analysis than those given? And, would you select the same possibilities to define the concept? This article outlines the importance of the right to know, locates it in natural law, and establishes, for the authors, the important parameters of the law. So why do we find so many, in the following article, willing to give up these rights when we move from the abstract concept to its operationalization in contemporary society. In contrast, the *State of the First Amendment: 2004* report reveals lackluster support for the First Amendment in general and its application to controversial cases in particular. Few know the freedoms guaranteed or care passionately about them—almost one-third feel the freedom granted under the First Amendment "goes too far." Moreover, Americans seem less supportive of freedom of the press than of any other freedoms guaranteed in our Bill of Rights.

Issue 11   Should Freedom of Speech Ever Be Restricted?   242

YES: **Eugene Volokh**, from "Freedom of Speech, Cyberspace, Harassment Law, and the Clinton," *Law and Contemporary Problems* (2000)   *244*

NO: **Edison and Jacobs Media Research**, from "Indecency Survey," *www.EdisonResearch.com* (March 2004)   *254*

Law professor Eugene Volokh examines several situations in which absolute freedom of speech would very likely conflict with the precedents that have been set in the realm of creating "hostile environment law." For example, if any offensive speech or images were transmitted in a public arena, the law would side with the more conservative approach toward restricting speech or images that would offend certain people, or that would create an uncomfortable atmosphere. Two media consulting firms collaborated on a survey of rock radio listeners to discover what might be offensive to them. The results, taken from the perspective of the audience who listens to rock, create an argument for restricting government involvement in censoring content, and a clear preference for allowing individuals to choose what they hear, or requiring parental involvement in the cases of radio content and audiences of children.

Issue 12   Has Industry Regulation Controlled Indecent Media Content?   263

YES: **Rhoda Rabkin**, from "Children, Entertainment, and Marketing," *Consumer Research* (June 2002)   *265*

NO: **James Poniewozik**, from "The Decency Police," *Time* (March 28, 2005)   *273*

Author Rhoda Rabkin strongly defends the industry system of self-censorship, and feels that any government intervention toward monitoring media content is doomed to failure. She examines a number of media forms and claims that any time there has been a question about content, the industry generally re-packages the products for different audiences and age groups. She advocates for voluntary codes of conduct over federal censorship of entertainment. James Poniewozik profiles the Parents Television Council's Entertainment Tracking System and discusses parents' complaints about contemporary television content. He discusses the FCC's present position, and some of the steps the television industry has taken to encourage parents to exercise more control over what their children watch (like the V-chip), but finds that the issues of morality and indecency have been addressed inconsistently, resulting in a wider array of viewpoints concerning indecent material.

Issue 13   Is the Use of Video News Releases Bad Journalism?   282

YES: **Trudy Lieberman**, from "Epidemic: Phony Medical News is on the Rise," *Columbia Journalism Review* (March/April 2007)   *284*

NO: **Public Relations Society of America**, from "Video News Releases: Comment of Public Relations Society of America to FCC," *Response to Request for Comment, Federal Communications Commission* (June 24, 2005)   *292*

Trudy Lieberman investigates the use of video news releases (VNRs) in newscasts that are really marketing endeavors by hospitals and health companies. Who is in control of health news? Lieberman worries that newsrooms substitute "feel good" VNRs for in-depth reporting. Can reliance on the slickly produced packages and profitable relationships formed threaten journalistic independence? In their Comment to the Federal Communications Commission, the Public Relations Society of America (PRSA) defends the production of VNRs and argues against imposing additional restrictions on their use. PRSA argues that their current code of ethics is sufficient, and that PR professionals strongly object to the use of VNRs when sponsors or financial interests are not fully disclosed.

UNIT 5   MEDIA BUSINESS   303

Issue 14   Can the Independent Musical Artist Thrive in Today's Music Business?   304

YES: **Chuck Salter**, from "Way Behind the Music," *Fast Company* (February 2007)   *306*

NO: **Eric Boehlert**, from "Pay for Play," *Salon.com* (March 14, 2001)   *313*

Chuck Salter looks at the way musical artists have had to become business people to control the branding of their "products." He examines the business model established by John Legend, and describes how today's musical artists must retain control of their brand to survive in the music industry today. Eric Boehlert describes why radio has become so bad, with regard to diversity of music, and how little opportunity there is for new artists to get their music on the air. He describes what has happened to the traditional music industry/radio alliance, and how independent record promoters have influenced both businesses.

Issue 15   Can Present Technology Support Internet Growth?   322

YES: **Spencer E. Ante**, from "Back from the Dead," *Business Week* (June 25, 2007)   *324*

NO: **David Talbot**, from "The Internet Is Broken," *Technology Review* (December 2005/January 2006)   *331*

Computer expert Spencer E. Ante claims that recent growth in new start-up firms that have learned how to compress information for the Internet, and increase options for message delivery, have created business opportunities for firms to compete in video and data delivery, resulting in a new telecom boom. *Technology Review* correspondent David Talbot claims that the problems that were originally in the Internet's architecture have only worsened, and that we need to reconceptualize a whole new structure for online communication before users get frustrated with the fragile Internet we now have.

Ted Turner, founder of CNN, argues that government protects big media, and shuts out upstarts like him. Throughout his career he has seen regulations emerge that transfer power to larger corporations, making it impossible to survive as an independent. Important people, ideas, and innovations are lost with this model. Federal Communications Commission (FCC) ex-Chairman Michael Powell, in testimony before the Senate Committee on Commercial, Science and Transportation, outlined the FCC proposal to relax ownership rules. He cites changes in the marketplace and argues that these changes will benefit the public interest through protecting viewpoint diversity, enhancing competition, and fostering localism.

Robert Kuttner discusses the future of traditional newspapers in the age of the Internet. Newspapers can make it, he argues, but only if they partner with the Internet to provide the quality journalism that is the hallmark of print, and the immediacy, comprehensiveness, and innovativeness of the best of the Internet. This requires a commitment to the process of developing a dual product that is expensive, but cannot be achieved at the expense of quality journalism. One study found that local news diminished under corporate ownership. Increasingly cross-ownerships are proposed to allow local television and newspaper outlets in a single market to be owned by a single company. As concentration increases, news departments are slashed, ultimately threatening the ability to produce quality reporting.

Journalist Simson Garfinkel discusses how today's technology has the potential to destroy our privacy. He makes the case that the government and individuals could take steps to protect themselves against privacy abuse, particularly by returning to the groundwork set by the government in the1970s and by educating people on how to avoid privacy traps. *Forbes* reporter Adam L. Penenberg discusses his own experiences with an Internet detective agency, and he explains how easy it is for companies to get unauthorized access to personal information. He specifically describes how much, and where, personal information is kept and the lack of safeguards in our current system.

Technology Review senior editor Wade Roush reflects on the way we currently use the architecture of the web. He outlines the likely scenario for the future of the Internet, with global networks connected to "smart nodes" that will be able to store all of our files, and allow us to access them from remote sites with only small, handheld devices. The improvements in technology will then lead to a more dynamic use of the web, and will make the Internet more user-friendly, as well as more secure. Author Matthew Robinson warns that no matter what technologies we have available, human beings seem interested in fewer subjects and know even less about politics and current events. He warns that even though we may call it an "information" society, there is evidence to suggest that we actually know less than in earlier years. His examples are humorous as well as sobering.

Correlation Guide

The *Taking Sides* series presents current issues in a debate-style format designed to stimulate student interest and develop critical thinking skills. Each issue is thoughtfully framed with an issue summary, an issue introduction, and a post-script. The pro and con essays—selected for their liveliness and substance—represent the arguments of leading scholars and commentators in their fields.

Taking Sides: Clashing Views in Mass Media and Society, 10/e is an easy-to-use reader that presents issues on important topics such as *Copyright Law and Intellectual Property, Fake News and Journalism, Survival of Print Newspapers, and more.* For more information on *Taking Sides* and other *McGraw-Hill Contemporary Learning Series* titles, visit www.mhcls.com.

This convenient guide matches the issues in **Taking Sides: Mass Media and Society, 10/e** with the corresponding chapters in two of our best-selling McGraw-Hill Mass Media textbooks by Baran and Rodman.

Taking Sides: Mass Media and Society, 10/e	Introduction to Mass Communication, 5/e by Baran	Mass Media in a Changing World, 2009 Updated Edition, 2/e by Rodman
Issue 1: Are American Values Shaped by the Mass Media?	**Chapter 1:** Mass Communication, Culture, and Media Literacy **Chapter 13:** Theories and Effects of Mass Communication	**Chapter 2:** Media Impact
Issue 2: Is Television Harmful for Children?	**Chapter 8:** Television, Cable, and Mobile Video **Chapter 13:** Theories and Effects of Mass Communication	**Chapter 2:** Media Impact **Chapter 9:** Television
Issue 3: Are Representations of African-American Women in Media Accurate?	**Chapter 6:** Film	**Chapter 6:** Movies **Chapter 9:** Television
Issue 4: Do Video Games Encourage Violent Behavior?	**Chapter 9:** Video Games **Chapter 13:** Theories and Effects of Mass Communication	**Chapter 1:** Introduction: Media in a Changing World **Chapter 2:** Media Impact
Issue 5: Do Copyright Laws Protect Ownership of Intellectual Property?	**Chapter 10:** The Internet and the World Wide Web	**Chapter 14:** Media Law
Issue 6: Is Advertising Good for Society?	**Chapter 1:** Mass Communication, Culture, and Media Literacy **Chapter 12:** Advertising	**Chapter 13:** Advertising
Issue 7: Are Political/Military Leaders to Blame for Misinformation in Time of War?	**Chapter 1:** Mass Communication, Culture, and Media Literacy **Chapter 13:** Theories and Effects of Mass Communication	**Chapter 11:** Electronic News **Chapter 15:** Media Ethics

Taking Sides: Mass Media and Society, 10/e	Introduction to Mass Communication, 5/e by Baran	Mass Media in a Changing World, 2009 Updated Edition, 2/e by Rodman
Issue 8: Is Negative Campaigning Bad for the American Political Process?	**Chapter 1:** Mass Communication, Culture, and Media Literacy **Chapter 13:** Theories and Effects of Mass Communication	**Chapter 2:** Media Impact **Chapter 15:** Media Ethics
Issue 9: Does Fake News Mislead the Public?	**Chapter 8:** Television, Cable, and Mobile Video	**Chapter 11:** Electronic news **Chapter 12:** Public Relations **Chapter 15:** Media Ethics
Issue 10: Should the Public Support the Freedom of the Press?	**Chapter 10:** The Internet and the World Wide Web	**Chapter 14:** Media Law
Issue 11: Should Freedom of Speech Ever Be Restricted?	**Chapter 10:** The Internet and the World Wide Web **Chapter 13:** Theories and Effects of Mass Communication **Chapter 14:** Media Freedom, Regulation, and Ethics	**Chapter 8:** Radio **Chapter 13:** Advertising **Chapter 14:** Media Law
Issue 12: Has Industry Regulation Controlled Indecent Media Content?	**Chapter 3:** Books **Chapter 6:** Film **Chapter 10:** The Internet and the World Wide Web	**Chapter 6:** Movies **Chapter 14:** Media Law **Chapter 15:** Media Ethics
Issue 13: Are Video News Releases Misused?	**Chapter 8:** Television, Cable, and Mobile Video **Chapter 11:** Public Relations	**Chapter 11:** Electronic News **Chapter 15:** Media Ethics
Issue 14: Can the Independent Musical Artist Thrive in Today's Music Business?	**Chapter 7:** Radio, Recording, and Popular Music	**Chapter 7:** Recording and the Music Industry
Issue 15: Can Present Technology Support Internet Growth?	**Chapter 10:** The Internet and the World Wide Web	**Chapter 10:** The Internet
Issue 16: Does Big Media Control the FCC?	**Chapter 7:** Radio, Recording, and Popular Music **Chapter 8:** Television, Cable, and Mobile Video	**Chapter 1:** Introduction: Media in a Changing World **Chapter 8:** Radio **Chapter 9:** Television **Chapter 14:** Media Law
Issue 17: Will Print Newspapers Survive in an Online World?	**Chapter 4:** Newspapers **Chapter 10:** The Internet and the World Wide Web	**Chapter 1:** Introduction: Media in a Changing World **Chapter 4:** Newspapers
Issue 18: Can Privacy Be Protected in the Information Age?	**Chapter 10:** The Internet and the World Wide Web	**Chapter 10:** The Internet **Chapter 15:** Media Ethics
Issue 19: Are People Better Informed in the Information Society?	**Chapter 1:** Mass Communication, Culture, and Media Literacy **Chapter 13:** Theories and Effects of Mass Communication **Chapter 10:** The Internet and the World Wide Web	**Chapter 1:** Introduction: Media in a Changing World **Chapter 2:** Media Impact **Chapter 10:** The Internet

Introduction

Ways of Thinking About Mass Media and Society

Alison Alexander and Jarice Hanson

Media are everywhere in our industrialized world today. It is likely that anyone reading this book has access to more forms of media than their grandparents could have ever dreamed of. Many readers are probably adept at multitasking—a term unheard of when this book series began. With access to telephones (both land and cell), radio, tv, films, CDs, videotapes, DVDs, personal computers and the Internet—which has the ability to transfer any of the messages formerly confined to the discrete forms just mentioned, our sense of our world, and our relationship to it, has become a complex web of real messages as well as mediated messages.

Media are often scapegoats for the problems of society. Sometimes, the relationship of social issues and media seem too obvious *not* to have some connection. For example, violence in the media may be a reflection of society, or, as some critics claim, violence in the media makes it seem that violence in society is the norm. But in reality, an important reason the media is so often blamed for social problems is because the media are so pervasive. Their very ubiquity gives them the status that makes them seem more influential than they actually are. If one were to look at the statistics on violence in the United States, it would be possible to see that there are fewer violent acts today than in recent history—but because of violences depicted in the media, through reportage or fictional representation, violence appears more prevalent.

There are many approaches to investigating the relationships that are suggested by media and society. From an organizational perspective, the producers of media must find content and distribution forms that will be profitable, and therefore, they have a unique outlook on the audience as consumers. From the perspective of the creative artist, the profit motive may be important, but the exploration of the unique communicative power of the media may be paramount. The audience also, has different use patterns, such as desires for information or entertainment, and demonstrates a variety of choices in content offered to them. Whether the media reflect society, or shape society, has a lot to do with the dynamic interaction of many of these different components.

To complicate matters, even our terms and definitions have evolved. The "mass" media have changed in recent years. Not long ago, "mass" media referred to messages that were created by large organizations for broad, heterogeneous audiences. This concept no longer suffices for the contemporary media environments. While the "mass" media still exist in the forms of radio, television, film, and general interest newspapers and magazines, many media forms today are hybrids of "mass" and "personal" media technologies that open a new realm of understanding about how audiences process the meaning of the messages. Digital technologies and distribution forms have created many opportunities for merging (or *converging*) media. Time-shifting, memory, storage of information, and truth all play important roles in the use of Internet communication, and call our attention to aspects of the communicative process that need fresh examination.

Still, most of the new services and forms of media rely, in part, on the major mass media distribution forms and technologies of television, radio, film, and print. The challenge, then, is to understand how individuals in society use media in a variety of formats and contexts, and how they make sense of the messages they take from the content of those media forms.

As we look at U.S. history, we can see that almost every form of media was first subject to some type of regulation by the government, or by the media industry itself. This has changed over the years, so that we now have a virtually unregulated media environment in which the responsibility for the content of media no longer rests with higher authorities. We, as consumers, are asked to be critical of that media which we consume. This requires that we be educated consumers, rather than relying on standards and practices of industry, or government intervention into questionable content. While this may not seem like a big problem for adult consumers, the questions and answers become more difficult when we consider how children use the media to form judgments, form opinions, or seek information.

The growing media landscape is changing our habits. The average American still spends over three hours a day viewing television, and in the average home the television is on for over seven hours a day. Politics and political processes have changed, in part, due to the way politicians use the media to reach voters. A proliferation of television channels has resulted from the popularity of cable, but does cable offer anything different from broadcast television? Videocassettes deliver feature-length films to the home, changing the traditional practice of viewing film in a public place, and video distribution via the Internet is now a practical option for anyone with transmission lines large enough to download large files. The recording industry is still reeling over the impact of MP3 and free software that allows consumers to sample, buy, or steal music on line. Communications is now a multibillion-dollar industry and the third fastest-growing industry in America. From these and other simple examples, it is clear that the media have changed American society, but our understanding of how and why remains incomplete.

Dynamics of Interaction

In recent years, the proliferation of new forms of media have changed on a global scale. In the U.S., 98% of homes have at least one traditional wired-telephone, while cell phone use continues to rise. Still, there are places in the world where traditional wired-phone lines may be limited, or where access to telephones is rare. There are some countries that have more cell phone use, per capita, than people in North America. In the U.S., over 98% of the population has access to at least one television set, but in some parts of the world, televisions are still viewed communally, or viewed only at certain hours of the day. The use of home computers and the Internet has grown annually in the U.S., with a majority of home computer users accessing their messages over high speed systems. And yet, less than half of the people of the world have access to the Web. These figures demonstrate that the global media environment is still far from equitable, and they suggest that different cultures may use the media in different ways.

But apart from questions of access and available content, many fundamental questions about the power of media remain the same. How do audiences use the media available to them? How do message senders produce meaning? How much of the meaning of any message is produced by the audience? One increasingly important question for discussion is how do additional uses of media change our interpersonal environments and human interactions?

In the early years of the 21st century, many of the institutions we have come to depend upon are undergoing massive changes. The recording industry is perhaps one of the most rapidly changing fields, with micro-radio, web-streaming, and subscription services offering different alternatives for message distribution. We have branched from the ethical and legal issues of music downloading to issues of copyright ownership and peer-to-peer file transfer protocols. Many of the industries that you've grown up with are undergoing massive changes due to new ownership rules, competition, and industry change. We can expect to continue to see threats and challenges to our traditional media systems in the future. Even the ubiquitous personal computer could become obsolete with personal desk assistants (PDAs) offering cheaper, more portable forms of computing, and the ability to store information at remote locations.

Progress in Media Research

Much of media research has been in search of theory. Theory is an organized, commonsense refinement of everyday thinking; it is an attempt to establish a systematic view of a phenomenon in order to better understand that phenomenon. Theory is tested against reality to establish whether or not it is a good explanation. For example, a researcher might notice that what is covered by news outlets is very similar to what citizens say are the important issues of the day. From such observations comes agenda setting (the notion that the media confers importance on the topics it covers, directing public attention to what is considered important).

Much of the early media research was produced to answer questions of print media because print has long been regarded a permanent record of history and events. The ability of newspapers and books to shape and influence public opinion was regarded as a necessity to the founding of new forms of governments—including the U.S. government. But the bias of the medium carried certain restrictions with it. Print media was limited to those individuals who could read. The relationships of information control and the power of these forms of communication to influence readers contributed to a belief that reporting should be objective and fair and that a multiple number of viewpoints should be available to readers.

The principles that emerged from this relationship were addressed in an often—quoted statement attributed to Thomas Jefferson, who wrote, "Were it left to me to decide whether we should have a government without newspapers, or newspapers without a government, I should not hesitate a moment to prefer the latter." But the next sentence in Jefferson's statement is equally as important, and often omitted from quotations. "But I should mean that every man should receive those papers and be capable of reading them."

Today, media research on the relationships of media senders, the channels of communication, and the receivers of messages is not enough. Consumers must realize that "media literacy" is an important concept as well. People can no longer take for granted that the media exist primarily to provide news, information, and entertainment. They must be more attuned to what media content says about them as individuals and as members of a society. By integrating these various cultural components, the public can better criticize the regulations or lack of regulation that permits media industries to function the way they do. People must realize that individuals may read or understand media content in different ways, and that different cultures act as important components of understanding messages, as well as controlling access to some forms of media.

The use of social science data to explore the effects of media on audiences strongly emphasized psychological and sociological schools of thought. It did not take long to move from the "magic bullet theory"—which proposed that media had a direct and immediate effect on the receivers of the message, and the same message intended by the senders was the same when it was "shot" into the receiver, to other ideas of limited, or even indirect means of influencing the audience.

Media research has shifted from addressing specifically effects–oriented paradigms to exploring the nature of the institutions of media production themselves, as well as examining the unique characteristics of each form of media. What most researchers agree upon today, is that the best way to understand the power and impact of media is to look at context specific situations to better understand the dynamics involved in the use of media and the importance of the content.

Still, there are many approaches to media research, from a variety of interdisciplinary fields: psychology, sociology, linguistics, art, comparative literature, economics, political science, and more. What each of these avenues of inquiry have in common is that they all tend to focus attention on individuals, families, or other social groups; society in general; and culture in the broad sense. All of the interpretations frame meaning and investigate their subjects within institutional frameworks that are specific to any nation and/ or culture.

Today's researchers question the notions of past theories and models as well as definitions of *mass* and *society*, and now place much of the emphasis of media dynamics in the perspective of global information exchange. A major controversy erupted in the early 1970s when many Third World countries disagreed with principles that sought to reify the industrialized nations' media. The New World Information Order (NWIO) perspective advanced the importance of the economic and social benefits of industrialized countries, and it noted that emerging nations had different priorities that reflected indigenous cultures, which were sometimes at odds with Western notions of a free press. The Third World countries' concern dealt with power as imposed upon a nation from outside, using media as a vehicle for cultural dependency and imperialism.

Many of the questions for media researchers in the 21st century deal with the continued fragmentation of the audience, caused by greater choice of channels and technologies for both traditional, and new communication purposes. The power of some of these technologies to reach virtually any place on the globe within fractions of a second will continue to pose questions of access to media, and the meaning of the messages transmitted. As individuals become more dependent upon the Internet for communication purposes, the sense of audience will further be changed as individual users choose what they want to receive, pay for, and keep. For all of these reasons, the field of media research is rich, growing, and challenging.

Questions for Consideration

In addressing the issues in this book, it is important to consider some recurring questions:

1. Are the media unifying or fragmenting? Does media content help the socialization process or does it create anxiety or inaccurate portrayals of the world? Do people feel powerless because they have little ability to shape the messages of media?
2. How are our basic institutions changing as we use media in new, and different ways? Do media support or undermine our political processes? Do they change what we think of when we claim to live in a "democracy"? Do media operate in the public interest, or do media serve the rich and powerful corporations' quest for profit? Can the media do both simultaneously?
3. Whose interests do the media represent? Do audiences actively work toward integrating media messages with their own experiences? How do new media technologies change our traditional ways of communicating? Are they leading us to a world in which interpersonal communication is radically altered because we rely on information systems to replace many traditional behaviors?

Summary

We live in a media-rich environment where almost everybody has access to some forms of media, and some choices in content. As new technologies and services are developed, are they responding to the problems that previous media researchers and the public have detected? Over time, individuals have improved their ability to unravel the complex set of interactions that ties the media and society together, but they need to continue to question past results, new practices and technologies, and their own evaluative measures. When people critically examine the world around them—a world often presented by the media—they can more fully understand and enjoy the way they relate as individuals, as members of groups, and as members of a society.

Internet References . . .

Communication Studies: General Communication Resources

An encyclopedic resource related to a host of mass communication issues, this site is maintained by the University of Iowa's Department of Communication Studies. It provides excellent links covering advertising, cultural studies, digital media, film, gender and media studies.

http://www.uiowa.edu/commstud/
resources/general.html

Kaiser Family Foundation

The Kaiser Family Foundation site provides articles on a broad range of television topics, including the v-chip, sexual messages, and media and children. "Generation M: Media in the Lives of 8–18 Year Olds" may be of particular interest.

http://www.kff.org

Wikipedia

This is an online encyclopedia written and edited by users. You will find useful information on many topics, and will get to watch the encyclopedia evolve through the efforts of its users. Perhaps you'll even write for it!

http://www.wikipedia.com

Writer's Guild of America

The Writer's Guild is the union for media entertainment writers. The non-member areas of their Web site have information useful for aspiring writers. Their Research Links Page is a particularly useful resource.

http://www.wga.org

Media Awareness Network

The Media Awareness Network is a Canadian site dedicated to promoting critical thinking in youth about the media. Media issues discussed include violence, stereotyping, online hate, and information privacy.

http://www.media-awareness.ca

Media and Social Issues

*D*o media reflect the social attitudes and concerns of our times, or are they also able to construct, legitimate, and reinforce the social realities, behaviors, attitudes, and images of others? Do they operate to maintain existing power structures, or are they a pluralistic representation of diverse views? The ways media help us to shape a sense of reality are complex. How much do media influence us, versus how we use media to fit our already preconceived ideas? Should concern be directed toward vulnerable populations like children? If we truly have a variety of information sources and content to choose from, perhaps we can assume that distorted images are balanced with realistic ones—but is this a likely scenario for every single person who lives in our society? Questions about the place of media within society, and within what many people call the "information age," are important for us to understand, whether we use media, or whether media use us.

- Are American Values Shaped by the Mass Media?
- Is Television Harmful for Children?
- Are Representations of African-American Women in Media Accurate?

ISSUE 1

Are American Values Shaped by the Mass Media?

YES: Herbert I. Schiller, from *The Mind Managers* (Beacon Press, 1973)

NO: Horace Newcomb and Paul M. Hirsch, from "Television as a Cultural Forum: Implications for Research," *Quarterly Review of Film Studies* (Summer 1983)

ISSUE SUMMARY

YES: Critical scholar of modern mass media Professor Schiller argues that mass media institutions are key elements of the modern capitalistic world order. Media, he argues, produce economic profits and the ideology necessary to sustain a world system of exploitative divisions of social and financial resources. It is the job of the citizenry to understand the myths that act to sustain this existing state of power relationships.

NO: Professors of communication Horace Newcomb and Paul M. Hirsch in their classic article counter that television serves as a site of negotiation for cultural issues, images, and ideas. Viewer selections from among institutional choices is a negotiation process as viewers select from a wide set of approaches to issues and ideas.

Can the media fundamentally reshape a culture? Americans are increasingly part of a culture in which information and ideas are electronically disseminated. Are media simply the conduit, the information channel, through which these ideas flow? None of the authors above would agree with that simplistic description. But they do disagree significantly on the way media influences society. Stop a moment and consider: what are the ways you feel media influence society? Groups within our society? And yourself? Currently in mass communication research, two vastly different perspectives on the impact of media on society exist. The critical/cultural perspective is advocated by Schiller, the pluralistic perspective by Newcomb and Hirsch. These articles are classic statements of the disagreements between these perspectives.

Schiller outlines the five myths that structure media content and manipulate consciousness. These myths function to reproduce the status quo and maintain existing social power structures. Despite changes in technologies and practices, Schiller argues that the ideological core of media messages remains the same. He is not alone in his concern that electronic media are negatively influencing our society. There are a number of mass communication scholars from the critical and cultural perspectives who are concerned that the power of media to shape attitude and opinions, paired with the power of media organizations to craft messages, will inevitably result in a recreation of current power structures, which inequitably divide social resources.

Newcomb and Hirsch offer the opposite interpretation. They assert that television operates as a cultural forum and is central to the process of public thinking. It is in the stories that media tell, that the nation creates, recreates and maintains its sense of self. In part, the effects of mass media on American values may be explained by examining the limits and effectiveness of popular pluralism, and the processes by which that pluralism is created and maintained. Communication, according to Newcomb and Hirsch, is dependent on shared meaning. Television is dependent upon pluralism more than many other forms of discourse. So one must consider how television is implicated in the creation of patterns of interpretation and the maintenance of sharing that defines pluralism as an effective cultural norm.

The media are so pervasive it is hard to believe they do not have important effects. Alternatively, many people do not believe that the media have personally influenced them to buy products or have harmed them, nor do they believe that the media hold a place of "prime importance" in shaping their lives. In everyday experience, many people do not consider the media as having an observable impact on them or on those around them. However, to understand how the media may shape the attitudes of individuals and of society, and how media may shape culture itself, requires that the reader stand back from his or her personal experiences in order to analyze the arguments presented on each side of this debate.

In the first selection, Schiller argues that U.S. media, through their "taken for granted" myths help structure the practices and meanings around which society takes shape. Ideology is not imposed but is systematically preferred by certain features of television, whereas other oppositional ideas are ignored or domesticated. Schiller was a powerful proponent of the theory that media is structured by the economic conditions under which it operates.

In the second selection, Newcomb and Hirsch advance a cultural forum model to understand the place of television in our society. Multiple meanings are key in understanding how television operates to provide a forum for the featuring of issues and ideas, and providing therefore a forum wherein those issues become a focus of cultural concern. Rather than concentrating on the fears of media's influence upon society, Newcomb and Hirsch push us to examine their functions.

YES

Herbert I. Schiller

The Mind Managers

Introduction

America's media managers create, process, refine, and preside over the circulation of images and information which determine our beliefs and attitudes and, ultimately, our behavior. When they deliberately produce messages that do not correspond to the realities of social existence, the media managers become mind managers. Messages that intentionally create a false sense of reality and produce a consciousness that cannot comprehend or willfully rejects the actual conditions of life, personal or social, are manipulative messages.

Manipulation of human minds, according to Paulo Freire, "is an instrument of conquest." It is one of the means by which "the dominant elites try to conform the masses to their objectives.[1] By using myths which explain, justify, and sometimes even glamorize the prevailing conditions of existence, manipulators secure popular support for a social order that is not in the majority's long-term real interest. When manipulation is successful, alternative social arrangements remain unconsidered. . . .

The permanent division of the society into two broad categories of "winners" and "losers" arises and persists as a result of the maintenance, recognition, and, indeed, sanctification of the system of private ownership of productive property and the extension of the ownership principle to all other aspects of human existence. The general acceptance of this arrangement for carrying on social activity makes it inevitable that some prosper, consolidate their success, and join the dominant shapers and molders of the community. The others, the majority, work on as mere conformists, the disadvantaged, and the manipulated; they are manipulated especially to continue to participate, if not wholeheartedly, at least positively, in the established routines. The system gives them a return adequate to achieve some marks of economic status, and manipulation leads them to hope that they might turn these routines to greater personal advantage for themselves or their children.

It is not surprising that manipulation, as an instrument of control, should reach its highest development in the United States. In America, more than anywhere else, the favorable conditions we have briefly noted permit a large fraction of the population to escape total suppression and thereby become potential actors in the historical process. Manipulation allows the appearance of active engagement while denying many of the material and *all* of the psychic benefits of genuine involvement. . . .

The means of manipulation are many, but, clearly, control of the informational and ideational apparatus at all levels is essential. This is secured by the operation of a simple rule of the market economy. Ownership and control of the mass media, like all other forms of property, is available to those with capital. Inevitably, radio- and television-station ownership, newspaper and magazine proprietorship, movie-making, and book publishing are largely in the hands of corporate chains and media conglomerates. The apparatus is thus ready to assume an active and dominant role in the manipulative process.

My intention is to identify some of these conditioning forces and to reveal the means by which they conceal their presence, deny their influence, or exercise directional control under auspices plat superficially appear benign and/or natural. The search for these "hidden processes," along with their subtle mechanics, should not be mistaken for a more common kind of investigation—the exposé of clandestine activities. Conspiracy is neither invoked nor considered in these pages. Though the idea of mind management lends itself easily to such an approach, the comprehensive conditioning carried on throughout American society today does not require, and actually cannot be understood in, such terms. . . .

Manipulation and the Packaged Consciousness

Five Myths That Structure Content

1. The Myth of Individualism and Personal Choice   Manipulation's greatest triumph, most observable in the United States, is to have taken advantage of the special historical circumstances of Western development to perpetrate as truth a definition of freedom cast in individualistic terms. This enables the concept to serve a double function. It protects the ownership of productive private property while simultaneously offering itself as the guardian of the individual's well-being, suggesting, if not insisting, that the latter is unattainable without the existence of the former. Upon this central construct an entire scaffolding of manipulation is erected. What accounts for the strength of this powerful notion?

. . . The identification of personal choice with human freedom can be seen arising side-by-side with seventeenth-century individualism, both products of the emerging market economy.[2]

For several hundred years individual proprietorship, allied with technological improvement, increased output and thereby bestowed great importance on personal independence in the industrial and political processes. The view that freedom is a personal matter, and that the individual's rights supersede the group's and provide the basis for social organization, gained credibility with the rise of material rewards and leisure time. Note, however, that these conditions were not distributed evenly among all classes of Western society and that they did not begin to exist in the rest of the world. . . .

In the newly settled United States, few restraints impeded the imposition of an individualistic private entrepreneurial system and its accompanying myths of personal choice and individual freedom. Both enterprise and myth found a hospitable setting. The growth of the former and consolidation of the latter were inevitable. How far the process has been carried is evident today in the easy public acceptance of the giant multinational private corporation as an example of individual endeavor. . . .

Privatism in every sphere of life is considered normal. The American life style, from its most minor detail to its most deeply felt beliefs and practices, reflects an exclusively self-centered outlook, which is in turn an accurate image of the structure of the economy itself. The American dream includes a personal means of transportation, a single-family home, the proprietor-operated business. Such other institutions as a competitive health system are obvious, if not natural, features of the privately organized economy. . . .

Though individual freedom and personal choice are its most powerful mythic defenses, the system of private ownership and production requires and creates additional constructs, along with the techniques to transmit them. These notions either rationalize its existence and promise a great future, or divert attention from its searing inadequacies and conceal the possibilities of new departures for human development. Some of these constructs and techniques are not exclusive to the privatistic industrial order, and can be applied in any social system intent on maintaining its dominion. Other myths, and the means of circulating them, are closely associated with the specific characteristics of this social system.

2. The Myth of Neutrality   For manipulation to be most effective, evidence of its presence should be nonexistent. When the manipulated believe things are the way they are naturally and inevitably, manipulation is successful. In short, manipulation requires a false reality that is a continuous denial of its existence.

It is essential, therefore, that people who are manipulated believe in the neutrality of their key social institutions. They must believe that government, the media, education, and science are beyond the clash of conflicting social interests. Government, and the national government in particular, remains the centerpiece of the neutrality myth. This myth presupposes belief in the basic integrity and nonpartisanship of government in general and of its constituent parts—Congress, the judiciary, and the Presidency. Corruption, deceit, and knavery, when they occur from time to time, are seen to be the result of human weakness. The institutions themselves are beyond reproach. The fundamental soundness of the overall system is assured by the well-designed instrumentalities that comprise the whole.

The Presidency, for instance, is beyond the reach of special interests, according to this mythology. The first and most extreme manipulative use of the Presidency, therefore, is to claim the nonpartisanship of the office, and to seem to withdraw it from clamorous conflict. . . .

The chief executive, though the most important, is but one of many governmental departments that seek to present themselves as neutral agents, embracing no objectives but the general welfare, and serving everyone impartially and disinterestedly. For half a century all the media joined in propagating the myth of the FBI as a nonpolitical and highly effective agency of law enforcement. In fact, the Bureau has been used continuously to intimidate and coerce social critics.

The mass media, too, are supposed to be neutral. Departures from even-handedness in news reportage are admitted but, the press assure us, result from human error and cannot be interpreted as flaws in the basically sound institutions of information dissemination. That the media (press, periodicals, radio, and television) are almost without exception business enterprises, receiving their revenues from commercial sales of time or space, seems to create no problems for those who defend the objectivity and integrity of the informational services.[3] . . .

Science, which more than any other intellectual activity has been integrated into the corporate economy, continues also to insist on its value-free neutrality. Unwilling to consider the implications of the sources of its funding, the directions of its research, the applications of its theories, and the character of the paradigms it creates, science promotes the notion of its insulation from the social forces that affect all other ongoing activities in the nation.

The system of schooling, from the elementary through the university level, is also, according to the manipulators, devoid of deliberate ideological purpose. Still, the product must reflect the teaching: it is astonishing how large a proportion of the graduates at each stage continue, despite all the ballyhoo about the counterculture, to believe in and observe the competitive ethic of business enterprise.

Wherever one looks in the social sphere, neutrality and objectivity are invoked to describe the functioning of value-laden and purposeful activities which lend support to the prevailing institutional system. Essential to the everyday maintenance of the control system is the carefully nurtured myth that no special groups or views have a preponderant influence on the country's important decision-making processes. . . .

3. The Myth of Unchanging Human Nature   Human expectations can be the lubricant of social change. When human expectations are low, passivity prevails. There can, of course, be various kinds of images in anyone's mind concerning political, social, economic, and personal realities. The common denominator of all such imagery, however, is the view people have of human nature. What human nature is seen to be ultimately affects the way human beings behave, not because they must act as they do but because they believe they are expected to act that way. . . .

It is predictable that in the United States a theory that emphasizes the aggressive side of human behavior and the unchangeability of human nature would find approval, permeate most work and thought, and be circulated widely by the mass media. Certainly, an economy that is built on and rewards private ownership and individual acquisition, and is subject to the personal and social conflicts these arrangements impose, can be expected to be gratified with an explanation that legitimizes its operative principles. How reassuring to consider these conflictful relationships inherent in the human condition rather than imposed by social circumstance! This outlook fits nicely too with the antiideological stance the system projects. It induces a "scientific" and "objective" approach to the human condition rigorously measuring human microbehavior in all its depravities, and for the most part ignoring the broader and less measurable social parameters.

Daily TV programming, for example, with its quota of half a dozen murders per hour, is rationalized easily by media controllers as an effort to give the people what they want. Too bad, they shrug, if human nature demands eighteen hours daily of mayhem and slaughter. . . .

Fortune finds it cheering, for "example, that some American social scientists are again emphasizing "the intractability of human nature" in their explanations of social phenomena. "The orthodox view of environment as the all-important influence on people's behavior," it reports, "is yielding to a new awareness of the role of hereditary factors: enthusiasm for schemes to reform society by remolding men is giving way to a healthy appreciation of the basic intractability of human nature."[4]

The net social effects of the thesis that human nature is at fault are further disorientation, total inability to recognize the causes of malaise—much less to take any steps to overcome it—and, of most consequence, continued adherence to the *status quo*. . . .

It is to prevent social action (and it is immaterial whether the intent is articulated or not) that so much publicity and attention are devoted to every pessimistic appraisal of human potential. If we are doomed forever by our inheritance, there is not much to be done about it. But there is a good reason and a good market for undervaluing human capability. An entrenched social system depends on keeping the popular and, especially, the "enlightened" mind unsure and doubtful about its human prospects. . . .

This does not necessitate ignoring history. On the contrary, endless recitation of what happened in the past accompanies assertions about how much change is occurring under our very noses. But these are invariably *physical* changes—new means of transportation, air conditioning, space rockets, packaged foods. Mind managers dwell on these matters but carefully refrain from considering changes in social relationships or in the institutional structures that undergird the economy.

Every conceivable kind of futuristic device is canvassed and blueprinted. Yet those who will use these wonder items will apparently continue to be married, raise children in suburban homes, work for private companies, vote for a President in a two-party system and pay a large portion of their incomes for defense, law and order, and superhighways. The world, except for some glamorous surface redecorations, will remain as it is; basic relationships will not change, because they, like human nature, are allegedly unchangeable. As for those parts of the world that have undergone far-reaching social rearrangements, reports of these transformations, if there are any, emphasize the defects, problems, and crises, which are seized upon with relish by domestic consciousness manipulators. . . .

4. The Myth of the Absence of Social Conflict   . . . Consciousness controllers, in their presentation of the domestic scene, deny absolutely the presence of social conflict. On the face of it, this seems an impossible task. After all violence is "as American as apple pie." Not only in fact but in fantasy: in films, on TV, and over the radio, the daily quota of violent scenarios offered the public is staggering. How is this carnival of conflict reconcilable with the media managers' intent to present an image of social harmony? The contradiction is easily resolved.

As presented by the national message-making apparatus, conflict is almost always an *individual* matter, in its manifestations and in its origin. The social roots of conflict just do not exist for the cultural-informational managers. True, there are "good guys" and "bad guys," but, except for such ritualized situations as westerns, which are recognized as scenarios of the past, role identification is divorced from significant social categories.

Black, brown, yellow, red, and other ethnic Americans have always fared poorly in the manufactured cultural imagery. Still, these are minorities which all segments of the white population have exploited in varying degrees. As for the great social division in the nation, between worker and owner, with rare exceptions it has been left unexamined. Attention is diverted elsewhere— generally toward the problems of the upward-striving middle segment of the population, that category with which everyone is supposed to identify. . . .

Elite control requires omission or distortion of social reality. Honest examination and discussion of social conflict can only deepen and intensify resistance to social inequity. Economically powerful groups and companies quickly get edgy when attention is called to exploitative practices in which they are engaged. *Variety*'s television editor, Les Brown, described such an incident. Coca-Cola Food Company and the Florida Fruit and Vegetable Association reacted sharply to a TV documentary, "Migrant," which centered on migrant fruit pickers in Florida. Brown wrote that "the miracle of *Migrant* was that it was televised at all." Warnings were sent to NBC not to show the program because it was "biased." Cuts in the film were demanded, and at least one was made. Finally, after the showing, "Coca-Cola shifted all its network billings to CBS and ABC."[5]

On a strictly commercial level, the presentation of social issues creates uneasiness in mass audiences, or so the audience researchers believe. To be safe, to hold onto as large a public as possible, sponsors are always eager to eliminate potentially "controversial" program material.

The entertainments and cultural products that have been most successful in the United States, those that have received the warmest support and publicity from the communications system, are invariably movies, TV programs, books, and mass entertainments (i.e., Disneyland) which may offer more than a fair quota of violence but never take up *social* conflict. . . .

5. *The Myth of Media Pluralism*   Personal choice exercised in an environment of cultural-information diversity is the image, circulated worldwide, of the condition of life in America. This view is also internalized in the belief structure of a large majority of Americans, which makes them particularly susceptible to thoroughgoing manipulation. It is, therefore, one of the central myths upon which mind management flourishes. Choice and diversity, though separate concepts, are in fact inseparable; choice is unattainable in any real sense without diversity. If real options are nonexistent, choosing is either

meaningless or manipulative. It is manipulative when accompanied by the illusion that the choice is meaningful.

Though it cannot be verified, the odds are that the illusion of informational choice is more pervasive in the United States than anywhere else in the world. The illusion is sustained by a willingness, deliberately maintained by information controllers, to mistake *abundance of media for diversity of content.* . . .

The fact of the matter is that, except for a rather small and highly selective segment of the population who know what they are looking for and can therefore take advantage of the massive communications flow, most Americans are basically, though unconsciously, trapped in what amounts to a nochoice informational bind. Variety of opinion on foreign and domestic news or, for that matter, local community business, hardly exists in the media. This results essentially from the inherent identity of interests, material and ideological, of property-holders (in this case, the private owners of the communications media), and from the monopolistic character of the communications industry in general.

The limiting effects of monopoly are in need of no explanation, and communications monopolies restrict informational choice wherever they operate. They offer one version of reality—their own. In this category fall most of the nation's newspapers, magazines, and films, which are produced by national or regional communications conglomerates. The number of American cities in which competing newspapers circulate has shrunk to a handful.

While there is a competition of sorts for audiences among the three major TV networks, two conditions determine the limits of the variety presented. Though each network struggles gamely to attract as large an audience as possible, it imitates its two rivals in program format and content. If ABC is successful with a western serial, CBS and NBC will in all likelihood "compete" with "shoot-'em-ups" in the same time slot. Besides, each of the three national networks is part of, or is itself, an enormous communications business, with the drives and motivations of any other profit-seeking enterprise. This means that diversity in the informational-entertainment sector exists only in the sense that there are a number of superficially different versions of the main categories of program. For example, there are several talk shows on late-night TV; there may be half a dozen private-eye, western, or law-and-order TV serials to "choose from" in prime time; there are three network news commentators with different personalities who offer essentially identical information. One can switch the radio dial and get round-the-clock news from one or, at most, two news services; or one can hear Top 40 popular songs played by "competing" disc jockeys.

Though no single program, performer, commentator, or informational bit is necessarily identical to its competitors, *there is no significant qualitative difference.* Just as a supermarket offers six identical soaps in different colors and a drugstore sells a variety of brands of aspirin at different prices, disc jockeys play the same records between personalized advertisements for different commodities. . . .

Yet it is this condition of communicational pluralism, empty as it is of real diversity, which affords great strength to the prevailing system of consciousness-packaging. The multichannel communications flow creates confidence in, and lends credibility to, the notion of free informational choice. Meanwhile, its main effect is to provide continuous reinforcement of the *status quo*. Similar stimuli, emanating from apparently diverse sources, envelop the listener/viewer/reader in a message/image environment that ordinarily seems uncontrolled, relatively free, and quite natural. How could it be otherwise with such an abundance of programs and transmitters? Corporate profit-seeking, the main objective of conglomeratized communications, however real and ultimately determining, is an invisible abstraction to the consumers of the cultural images. And one thing is certain: the media do not call their audiences' attention to its existence or its mode of operation. . . .

The fundamental similarity of the informational material and cultural messages that each of the mass media independently transmits makes it necessary to view the communications system as a totality. The media are mutually and continuously reinforcing. Since they operate according to commercial rules, rely on advertising, and are tied tightly to the corporate economy, both in their own structure and in their relationships with sponsors, the media constitute an industry, not an aggregation of independent, freewheeling informational entrepreneurs, each offering a highly individualistic product. By need and by design, the images and messages they purvey are, with few exceptions, constructed to achieve similar objectives, which are, simply put, profitability and the affirmation and maintenance of the private-ownership consumer society.

Consequently, research directed at discovering the impact of a single TV program or movie, or even an entire category of stimuli, such as "violence on TV" can often be fruitless. Who can justifiably claim that TV violence is inducing delinquent juvenile behavior when violence is endemic to all mass communications channels? Who can suggest that any single category of programming is producing male chauvinist or racist behavior when stimuli and imagery carrying such sentiments flow unceasingly through all the channels of transmission?

It is generally agreed that television is the most powerful medium; certainly its influence as a purveyor of the system's values cannot be overstated. All the same, television, no matter how powerful, itself depends on the absence of dissonant stimuli in the other media. Each of the informational channels makes its unique contribution, but the result is the same—the consolidation of the *status quo*.

Notes

1. Paulo Freire, *Pedagogy of the Oppressed* (New York: Herder and Herder, 1971), p. 144.
2. C. B. MacPherson, *The Political Theory of Possessive Individualism* (Oxford: Clarendon Press, 1962).

3.   Henry Luce, the founder of *Time, Life, Fortune, Sports Illustrated,* and other mass circulation magazines, knew otherwise. He told his staff at *Time:* "The alleged journalistic objectivity, a claim that a writer presents facts without applying any value judgment to them [is] modem usage—and that is strictly a phony. It is that that I had to renounce and denounce. So when we say the hell with objectivity, that is what we are talking about." W. A. Swanberg, *Luce and His Empire* (New York: Charles Scribner's Sons, 1972), p. 331.

4.   "The Social Engineers Retreat Under Fire," *Fortune,* October 1972, p. 3.

5.   Les Brown, *Television: The Business Behind The Box* (New York: Harcourt, Brace Jovanovich, 1971), pp. 196–203.

Horace Newcomb and
Paul M. Hirsch

 **NO**

Television as a Cultural Forum

A cultural basis for the analysis and criticism of television is, for us, the bridge between a concern for television as a communications medium, central to contemporary society, and television as aesthetic object, the expressive medium that, through its storytelling functions, unites and examines a culture. The shortcomings of each of these approaches taken alone are manifold.

The first is based primarily in a concern for understanding specific messages that may have specific effects, and grounds its analysis in "communication" narrowly defined. Complexities of image, style, resonance, narrativity, history, metaphor, and so on are reduced in favor of that content that can be more precisely, some say more objectively, described. The content categories are not allowed to emerge from the text, as is the case in naturalistic observation and in textual analysis. Rather they are predefined in order to be measured more easily. The incidence of certain content categories may be cited as significant, or their "effects" more clearly correlated with some behavior. This concern for measuring is, of course, the result of conceiving television in one way rather than another, as "communication" rather than as "art."

The narrowest versions of this form of analysis need not concern us here. It is to the best versions that we must look, to those that do admit to a range of aesthetic expression and something of a variety of reception. Even when we examine these closely, however, we see that they often assume a monolithic "meaning" in television content. The concern is for "dominant" messages embedded in the pleasant disguise of fictional entertainment, and the concern of the researcher is often that the control of these messages is, more than anything else, a complex sort of political control. The critique that emerges, then, is consciously or unconsciously a critique of the society that is transmitting and maintaining the dominant ideology with the assistance, again conscious or unconscious, of those who control communications technologies and businesses. (Ironically, this perspective does not depend on political perspective or persuasion. It is held by groups on the "right" who see American values being subverted, as well as by those on the "left" who see American values being imposed.)

Such a position assumes that the audience shares or "gets" the same messages and their meanings as the researcher finds. At times, like the literary critic, the researcher assumes this on the basis of superior insight, technique, or sensibility. In a more "scientific" manner the researcher may seek to establish a correlation between the discovered messages and the understanding of the audience. Rarely, however, does the message analyst allow for the possibility that the audience, while sharing this one meaning, may create many others that have not been examined, asked about, or controlled for.

The television "critic" on the other hand, often basing his work on the analysis of literature or film, succeeds in calling attention to the distinctive qualities of the medium, to the special nature of television fiction. But this approach all too often ignores important questions of production and reception. Intent on correcting what it takes to be a skewed interest in such matters, it often avoids the "business" of television and its "technology." These critics, much like their counterparts in the social sciences, usually assume that viewers should understand programs in the way the critic does, or that the audience is incapable of properly evaluating the entertaining work and should accept the critic's superior judgment.

The differences between the two views of what television is and does rest, in part, on the now familiar distinction between transportation and ritual views of communication processes. The social scientific, or communication theory model outlined above (and we do not claim that it is an exhaustive description) rests most thoroughly on the transportation view. As articulated by James Carey, this model holds that communication is a "process of transmitting messages at a distance for the purpose of control. The archetypal case of communication then is persuasion, attitude change, behavior modification, socialization through the transmission of information, influence, or conditioning."[1]

The more "literary" or "aesthetically based" approach leans toward, but hardly comes to terms with, ritual models of communication. As put by Carey, the ritual view sees communication "not directed toward the extension of messages in space but the maintenance of society in time; not the act of imparting information but the representation of shared beliefs."[2]

Carey also cuts through the middle of these definitions with a more succinct one of his own: "Communication is a symbolic process whereby reality is produced, maintained, repaired, and transformed."[3] It is in the attempt to amplify this basic observation that we present a cultural basis for the analysis of television. We hardly suggest that such an approach is entirely new, or that others are unaware of or do not share many of our assumptions. On the contrary, we find a growing awareness in many disciplines of the nature of symbolic thought, communication, and action, and we see attempts to understand television emerging rapidly from this body of shared concerns.[4]

⋅⊰◉⊱⋅

Our own model for television is grounded in an examination of the cultural role of entertainment and parallels this with a close analysis of television program content in all its various textual levels and forms. We focus on the collective, cultural view of the social construction and negotiation of reality, on the creation of what Carey refers to as "public thought."[5] It is not difficult to see television as central to this process of public thinking. As Hirsch has pointed out,[6] it is now our national medium, replacing those media—film, radio, picture magazines, newspapers—that once served a similar function. Those who create for such media are, in the words of anthropologist Marshall Sahlins, "hucksters of the symbol."[7] They are cultural *bricoleurs*, seeking and creating new meaning in the combination of cultural elements with embedded significance. They respond to real events, changes in social structure and organization, and to shifts in attitude and value. They also respond to technological shift, the coming of cable or the use of videotape recorders. We think it is clear that the television producer should be added to Sahlins's list of "hucksters." They work in precisely the manner he describes, as do television writers and, to a lesser extent, directors and actors. So too do programmers and network executives who must make decisions about the programs they purchase, develop, and air. At each step of this complicated process they function as cultural interpreters.

Similar notions have often been outlined by scholars of popular culture focusing on the formal characteristics of popular entertainment.[8] To those insights cultural theory adds the possibility of matching formal analysis with cultural and social practice. The best theoretical explanation for this link is suggested to us in the continuing work of anthropologist Victor Turner. This work focuses on cultural ritual and reminds us that ritual must be seen as process rather than as product, a notion not often applied to the study of television, yet crucial to an adequate understanding of the medium.

Specifically we make use of one aspect of Turner's analysis, his view of the *liminal* stage of the ritual process. This is the "in between" stage, when one is neither totally in nor out of society. It is a stage of license, when rules may be broken or bent, when roles may be reversed, when categories may be overturned. Its essence, suggests Turner,

> is to be found in its release from normal constraints, making possible the deconstruction of the "uninteresting" constructions of common sense, the "meaningfulness of ordinary life," . . . into cultural units which may then be reconstructed in novel ways, some of them bizarre to the point of monstrosity. . . . Liminality is the domain of the "interesting" or of "uncommon sense."[9]

Turner does not limit this observation to traditional societies engaged in the *practice* of ritual. He also applies his views to postindustrial, complex societies. In doing so he finds the liminal domain in the arts—all of them.[10] "The dismemberment of ritual has . . . provided the opportunity of theatre in the high culture and carnival at the folk level. A multiplicity of desacralized performative genres have assumed, prismatically, the task of plural cultural reflexivity."[11] In short, contemporary cultures examine themselves through their arts, much as traditional societies do via the experience of ritual. Ritual and the arts offer a metalanguage, a way of understanding who and what we are, how values and attitudes are adjusted, how meaning shifts.

In contributing to this process, particularly in American society, where its role is central, television fulfills what Fiske and Hartley refer to as the "bardic function" of contemporary societies.[12] In its role as central cultural medium it presents a multiplicity of meanings rather than a monolithic dominant point of view. It often focuses on our most prevalent concerns, our deepest dilemmas. Our most traditional views, those that are repressive and reactionary, as well as those that are subversive and emancipatory, are upheld, examined, maintained, and transformed. The emphasis is on process rather than product, on discussion rather than indoctrination, on contradiction and confusion rather than coherence. It is with this view that we turn to an analysis of the texts of television that demonstrates and supports the conception of television as a cultural forum.

⚜

This new perspective requires that we revise some of our notions regarding television analysis, criticism, and research. The function of the creator as *bricoleur*, taken from Sahlins, is again indicated and clarified. The focus on "uncommon sense," on the freedom afforded by the idea of television as a liminal realm helps us to understand the reliance on and interest in forms, plots, and character types that are not at all familiar in our lived experience. The skewed demography of the world of television is not quite so bizarre and repressive once we admit that it is the realm in which we allow our monsters to come out and play, our dreams to be wrought into pictures, our fantasies transformed into plot structures. Cowboys, detectives, bionic men, and great green hulks; fatherly physicians, glamorous female detectives, and tightly knit families living out the pain of the Great Depression; all these become part of the dramatic logic of public thought.

Shows such as *Fantasy Island* and *Love Boat*, difficult to account for within traditional critical systems except as examples of trivia and romance, are easily understood. Islands and boats are among the most fitting liminal metaphors, as Homer, Bacon, Shakespeare, and Melville, among others, have recognized. So, too, are the worlds of the Western and the detective story. With this view we can see the "bizarre" world of situation comedy as a means of deconstructing the world of "common sense" in which all, or most, of us live and work. It also enables us to explain such strange phenomena as game shows and late night talk fests. In short, almost any version of the television text functions as a forum in which important cultural topics may be considered. We illustrate this not with a contemporary program where problems almost always appear on the surface of the show, but with an episode of *Father Knows Best* from the early 1960s. We begin by noting that *FKB* is often cited as an innocuous series, constructed around unstinting paeans to American middle-class virtues and blissfully ignorant of social conflict. In short, it is precisely the sort of television program that reproduces dominant ideology by lulling its audience into a dream world where the status quo is the only status.

In the episode in question Betty Anderson, the older daughter in the family, breaks a great many rules by deciding that she will become an engineer. Over great protest, she is given an internship with a surveying crew as part of a high school "career education" program. But the head of the surveying crew, a young college student, drives her away with taunts and insensitivity. She walks off the job on the first day. Later in the week the young man comes to the Anderson home where Jim Anderson chides him with fatherly anger. The young man apologizes and Betty, overhearing him from the other room, runs upstairs, changes clothes, and comes down. The show ends with their flirtation underway.

Traditional ideological criticism, conducted from the communications or the textual analysis perspective, would remark on the way in which social conflict is ultimately subordinated in this dramatic structure to the personal, the emotional. Commentary would focus on the way in which the questioning of the role structure is shifted away from the world of work to the domestic arena. The emphasis would be on the conclusion of the episode in which Betty's real problem of identity and sex-role, and society's problem of sex-role discrimination, is bound by a more traditional conflict and thereby defused, contained, and redirected. Such a reading is possible, indeed accurate.

We would point out, however, that our emotional sympathy is with Betty throughout this episode. Nowhere does the text instruct the viewer that her concerns are unnatural, no matter how unnaturally they may be framed by other members of the cast. Every argument that can be made for a strong feminist perspective is condensed into the brief, half-hour presentation. The concept of the cultural forum, then, offers a different interpretation. We suggest that in popular culture generally, in television specifically, the raising of questions is as important as the answering of them. That is, it is equally important that an audience be introduced to the problems surrounding sex-role discrimination as it is to conclude the episode in a traditional manner. Indeed, it would be startling to think that mainstream texts in mass society would overtly challenge dominant ideas. But this hardly prevents the oppositional ideas from appearing. Put another way, we argue that television does not present firm ideological conclusions—despite its *formal* conclusions—so much as it *comments on* ideological problems. The conflicts we see in television drama, embedded in familiar and nonthreatening frames, are conflicts ongoing in American social experience and cultural history. In a few cases we might see strong perspectives that argue for the absolute correctness of one point of view or another. But for the most part the rhetoric of television drama is a rhetoric of discussion. Shows such as *All in the Family*, or *The Defenders*, or *Gunsmoke*, which raise the forum/discussion to an intense and obvious level, often make best use of the medium and become highly successful. We see statements *about* the issues and it should be clear that ideological positions can be balanced within the forum by others from a different perspective.

We recognize, of course, that this variety works for the most part within the limits of American monopoly-capitalism and within the range of American pluralism. It is an effective pluralistic forum only insofar as American political pluralism is or can be.[13] We also note, however, that one of the primary functions of the popular culture forum, the television forum, is to monitor the limits and the effectiveness of this pluralism, perhaps the only "public" forum in which this role is performed. As content shifts and attracts the attention of groups and individuals, criticism and reform can be initiated. We will have more to say on this topic shortly.

Our intention here is hardly to argue for the richness of *Father Knows Best* as a television text or as social commentary. Indeed, in our view, any emphasis on individual episodes, series, or even genres, misses the central point of the forum concept. While each of these units can and does present its audiences with incredibly mixed ideas, it is television as a whole system that presents a mass audience with the range and variety of ideas and ideologies inherent in American culture. In order to fully understand the role of television in that culture, we must examine a variety of analytical foci and, finally, see them as parts of a greater whole.

We can, for instance, concentrate on a single episode of television content, as we have done in our example. In our view most television shows offer something of this range of complexity. Not every one of them treats social problems of such immediacy, but submerged in any episode are assumptions about who and what we are. Conflicting viewpoints of social issues are, in fact, the elements that structure most television programs.

At the series level this complexity is heightened. In spite of notions to the contrary, most television shows do change over time. Stanley Cavell has recently suggested that this serial nature of television is perhaps its defining characteristic.[14] By contrast we see that feature only as a primary aspect of the rhetoric of television, one that shifts meaning and shades ideology as series develop. Even a series such as *The Brady Bunch* dealt with ever more complex issues merely because the children, on whom the show focused, grew older. In other cases, shows such as *The Waltons* shifted in content and meaning because they represented shifts in historical time. As the series moved out of the period of the Great Depression, through World War II, and into the postwar period, its tone and emphasis shifted too. In some cases, of course, this sort of change is structured into the show from the beginning, even when the appearance is that of static, undeveloping nature. In *All in the Family* the possibility of change and Archie's resistance to it form the central dramatic problem and offer the central opportunity for dramatic richness, a richness that has developed over many years until the character we now see bears little resemblance to the one we met in the beginning. This is also true of *M*A*S*H*, although there the structured conflicts have more to do with framing than with character development. In *M*A*S*H* we are caught in an anti-war rhetoric that cannot end a war. A truly radical alternative, a desertion or an insurrection, would end the series. But it would also end the "discussion" of this issue. We remain trapped, like American culture in its historical reality, with a dream and the rhetoric of peace and with a bitter experience that denies them.

The model of the forum extends beyond the use of the series with attention to genre. One tendency of genre studies has been to focus on similarities within forms, to indicate the ways in which all Westerns, situation comedies, detective shows, and so on are alike. Clearly, however, it is in the economic interests of producers to build on audience familiarity with generic patterns and instill novelty into those generically based presentations. Truly innovative forms that use the generic base as a foundation are likely to be among the more successful shows. This also means that the shows, despite generic similarity, will carry individual rhetorical slants. As a result, while shows like *M*A*S*H*,

The Mary Tyler Moore Show, and *All in the Family* may all treat similar issues, those issues will have different meanings because of the variations in character, tone, history, style, and so on, despite a general "liberal" tone. Other shows, minus that tone, will clash in varying degrees. The notion that they are all, in some sense, "situation comedies" does not adequately explain the treatment of ideas within them.

This hardly diminishes the strength of generic variation as yet another version of differences within the forum. The rhetoric of the soap opera *pattern* is different from that of the situation comedy and that of the detective show. Thus, when similar topics are treated within different generic frames another level of "discussion" is at work.

It is for this reason that we find it important to examine strips of television programming, "flow" as Raymond Williams refers to it.[15] Within these flow strips we may find opposing ideas abutting one another. We may find opposing treatments of the same ideas. And we will certainly find a viewing behavior that is more akin to actual experience than that found when concentrating on the individual show, the series, or the genre. The forum model, then, has led us into a new exploration of the definition of the television text. We are now examining the "viewing strip" as a potential text and are discovering that in the range of options offered by any given evening's television, the forum is indeed a more accurate model of what goes on *within* television than any other that we know of. By taping entire weeks of television content, and tracing various potential strips in the body of that week, we can construct a huge range of potential "texts" that may have been seen by individual viewers.

Each level of text—the strip as text, the television week, the television day—is compounded yet again by the history of the medium. Our hypothesis is that we might track the history of America's social discussions of the past three decades by examining the multiple rhetorics of television during that period. Given the problematic state of television archiving, a careful study of that hypothesis presents an enormous difficulty. It is, nevertheless, an exciting prospect.

●⟨◉⟩●

Clearly, our emphasis is on the treatment of issues, on rhetoric. We recognize the validity of analytical structures that emphasize television's skewed demographic patterns, its particular social aberrations, or other "unrealistic distortions" of the world of experience. But we also recognize that in order to make sense of those structures and patterns researchers return again and again to the "meaning" of that television world, to the processes and problems of interpretation. In our view this practice is hardly limited to those of us who study television. It is also open to audiences who view it each evening and to professionals who create for the medium.

The goal of every producer is to create the difference that makes a difference, to maintain an audience with sufficient reference to the known and recognized, but to move ahead into something that distinguishes his show for the program buyer, the scheduler, and most importantly, for the mass audience.

As recent work by Newcomb and Alley shows,[16] the goal of many producers, the most successful and powerful ones, is also to include personal ideas in their work, to use television as all artists use their media, as means of personal expression. Given this goal it is possible to examine the work of individual producers as other units of analysis and to compare the work of different producers as expressions within the forum. We need only think of the work of Quinn Martin and Jack Webb, or to contrast their work with that of Norman Lear or Gary Marshall, to recognize the individuality at work within television making. Choices by producers to work in certain generic forms, to express certain political, moral, and ethical attitudes, to explore certain sociocultural topics, all affect the nature of the ultimate "flow text" of television seen by viewers and assure a range of variations within that text.

The existence of this variation is borne out by varying responses among those who view television. A degree of this variance occurs among professional television critics who like and dislike shows for different reasons. But because television critics, certainly in American journalistic situations, are more alike than different in many ways, a more important indicator of the range of responses is that found among "ordinary" viewers, or the disagreements implied by audience acceptance and enthusiasm for program material soundly disavowed by professional critics. Work by Himmleweit in England[17] and Neuman in America[18] indicates that individual viewers do function as "critics," do make important distinctions, and are able, under certain circumstances, to articulate the bases for their judgments. While this work is just beginning, it is still possible to suggest from anecdotal evidence that people agree and disagree with television for a variety of reasons. They find in television texts representations of and challenges to their own ideas, and must somehow come to terms with what is there.

If disagreements cut too deeply into the value structure of the individual, if television threatens the sense of cultural security, the individual may take steps to engage the medium at the level of personal action. Most often this occurs in the form of letters to the network or to local stations, and again, the pattern is not new to television. It has occurred with every other mass medium in modern industrial society.

Nor is it merely the formation of groups or the expression of personal points of view that indicates the working of a forum. It is the range of response, the directly contradictory readings of the medium, that cue us to its multiple meanings. Groups may object to the same programs, for example, for entirely opposing reasons. In *Charlie's Angels* feminists may find yet another example of sexist repression, while fundamentalist religious groups may find examples of moral decay expressed in the sexual freedom, the personal appearance, or the "unfeminine" behavior of the protagonists. Other viewers doubtless find the expression of meaningful liberation of women. At this level, the point is hardly that one group is "right" and another "wrong," much less that one is "right" while the other is "left." Individuals and groups are, for many reasons, involved in making their own meanings from the television text.

This variation in interpretive strategies can be related to suggestions made by Stuart Hall in his influential essay, "Encoding and Decoding in the

Television Discourse."[19] There he suggests three basic modes of interpretation, corresponding to the interpreter's political stance within the social structure. The interpretation may be "dominant," accepting the prevailing ideological structure. It may be "oppositional," rejecting the basic aspects of the structure. Or it may be "negotiated," creating a sort of personal synthesis. As later work by some of Hall's colleagues suggests, however, it quickly becomes necessary to expand the range of possible interpretations.[20] Following these suggestions to a radical extreme it might be possible to argue that every individual interpretation of television content could, in some way, be "different." Clearly, however, communication is dependent on a greater degree of shared meanings, and expressions of popular entertainment are perhaps even more dependent on the shared level than many other forms of discourse. Our concern then is for the ways in which interpretation is negotiated in society. Special interest groups that focus, at times, on television provide us with readily available resources for the study of interpretive practices.

We see these groups as representative of metaphoric "fault lines" in American society. Television is the terrain in which the faults are expressed and worked out. In studying the groups, their rhetoric, the issues on which they focus, their tactics, their forms of organization, we hope to demonstrate that the idea of the "forum" is more than a metaphor in its own right. In forming special interest groups, or in using such groups to speak about television, citizens actually enter the forum. Television shoves them toward action, toward expression of ideas and values. At this level the model of "television as a cultural forum" enables us to examine "the sociology of interpretation."

Here much attention needs to be given to the historical aspects of this form of activity. How has the definition of issues changed over time? How has that change correlated with change in the television texts? These are important questions which, while difficult to study, are crucial to a full understanding of the role of television in culture. It is primarily through this sort of study that we will be able to define much more precisely the limits of the forum, for groups form monitoring devices that alert us to shortcomings not only in the world of television representation, but to the world of political experience as well. We know, for example, that because of heightened concern on the part of special interest groups, and responses from the creative and institutional communities of television industries, the "fictional" population of black citizens now roughly equals that of the actual population. Regardless of whether such a match is "good" or "necessary," regardless of the nature of the depiction of blacks on television, this indicates that the forum extends beyond the screen. The issue of violence, also deserving close study, is more mixed, varying from year to year. The influence of groups, of individuals, of studies, of the terrible consequences of murder and assassination, however, cannot be denied. Television does not exist in a realm of its own, cut off from the influence of citizens. Our aim is to discover, as precisely as possible, the ways in which the varied worlds interact.

Throughout this kind of analysis, then, it is necessary to cite a range of varied responses to the texts of television. Using the viewing "strip" as the appropriate text of television, and recognizing that it is filled with varied topics and approaches to those topics, we begin to think of the television viewer as a *bricoleur* who matches the creator in the making of meanings. Bringing values and attitudes, a universe of personal experiences and concerns, to the texts, the viewer selects, examines, acknowledges, and makes texts of his or her own.[21] If we conceive of special interest groups as representatives of *patterns* of cultural attitude and response, we have a potent source of study.

On the production end of this process, in addition to the work of individual producers, we must examine the role of network executives who must purchase and program television content. They, too, are cultural interpreters, intent on "reading" the culture through its relation to the "market." Executives who head and staff the internal censor agencies of each network, the offices of Broadcast Standards or Standards and Practices, are in a similar position. Perhaps as much as any individual or group they present us with a source of rich material for analysis. They are actively engaged in gauging cultural values. Their own research, the assumptions and the findings, needs to be re-analyzed for cultural implications, as does the work of the programmers. In determining who is doing what, with whom, at what times, they are interpreting social behavior in America and assigning it meaning. They are using television as a cultural litmus that can be applied in defining such problematic concepts as "childhood," "family," "maturity," and "appropriate." With the Standards and Practices offices, they interpret *and* define the permissible and the "normal." But their interpretations of behavior open to us as many questions as answers, and an appropriate overview, a new model of television is necessary in order to best understand their work and ours.

❦

This new model of "television as a cultural forum" fits the experience of television more accurately than others we have seen applied. Our assumption is that it opens a range of new questions and calls for re-analysis of older findings from both the textual-critical approach and the mass communications research perspective. Ultimately the new model is a simple one. It recognizes the range of interpretation of television content that is now admitted even by those analysts most concerned with television's presentation and maintenance of dominant ideological messages and meanings. But it differs from those perspectives because it does not see this as surprising or unusual. For the most part, that is what central storytelling systems do in all societies. We are far more concerned with the ways in which television contributes to change than with mapping the obvious ways in which it maintains dominant viewpoints. Most research on television, most textual analysis, has assumed that the medium is thin, repetitive, similar, nearly identical in textual formation, easily defined, described, and explained. The variety of response on the part of audiences has been received, as a result of this view, as extraordinary, an astonishing "discovery."

We begin with the observation, based on careful textual analysis, that television is dense, rich, and complex rather than impoverished. Any selection, any cut, any set of questions that is extracted from that text must somehow account for that density, must account for what is *not* studied or measured, for the opposing meanings, for the answering images and symbols. Audiences appear to make meaning by selecting that which touches experience and personal history. The range of responses then should be taken as commonplace rather than as unexpected. But research and critical analysis cannot afford so personal a view. Rather, they must somehow define and describe the inventory that makes possible the multiple meanings extracted by audiences, creators, and network decision makers.

Our model is based on the assumption and observation that only so rich a text could attract a mass audience in a complex culture. The forum offers a perspective that is as complex, as contradictory and confused, as much in process as American culture is in experience. Its texture matches that of our daily experiences. If we can understand it better, then perhaps we will better understand the world we live in, the actions that we must take in order to live there.

Notes

1. James Carey, "A Cultural Approach to Communications," *Communications 2* (December 1975).

2. Ibid.

3. James Carey, "Culture and Communications," *Communications Research* (April 1975).

4. See Roger Silverstone, *The Message of Television: Myth and Narrative in Contemporary Culture* (London: Heinemann, 1981), on structural and narrative analysis; John Fiske and John Hartley, *Reading Television* (London: Methuen, 1978), on the semiotic and cultural bases for the analysis of television; David Thorburn, *The Story Machine* (Oxford University Press: forthcoming), on the aesthetics of television; Himmleweit, Hilda et al., "The Audience as Critic: An Approach to the Study of Entertainment," in *The Entertainment Functions of Television,* ed. Percy Tannenbaum (New York: Lawrence Eribaum Associates, 1980) and W. Russel Neuman, "Television and American Culture: The Mass Medium and the Pluralist Audience," *Public Opinion Quarterly,* 46: 4 (Winter 1982), pp. 471–87, on the role of the audience as critic; Todd Gitlin, "Prime Time Ideology: The Hegemonic Process in Television Entertainment," *Social Problems* 26:3 (1979), and Douglas Kellner, "TV, Ideology, and Emancipatory Popular Culture," *Socialist Review* 45 (May–June, 1979), on hegemony and new applications of critical theory; James T. Lull, "The Social Uses of Television," *Human Communications Research* 7:3 (1980), and "Family Communication Patterns and the Social Uses of Television," *Communications Research* 7: 3 (1979), and Tim Meyer, Paul Traudt, and James Anderson, Non-Traditional Mass Communication Research Methods: Observational Case Studies of Media Use in Natural Settings, *Communication Yearbook IV*, ed. Dan Nimmo (New Brunswick, N.J.: Transaction Books), on audience ethnography and symbolic interactionism; and, most importantly, the ongoing work of The Center for Contemporary Cultural Studies at Birmingham University, England, most recently published in *Culture, Media, Language*, ed. Stuart Hall et al. (London: Hutchinson, in association with The Center for Contemporary Cultural Studies, 1980), on the interaction of culture and textual analysis from a thoughtful political perspective.

5. Carey, 1976.

6. Paul Hirsch, "The Role of Popular Culture and Television in Contemporary Society," *Television: The Critical View,* ed. Horace Newcomb (New York: Oxford University Press, 1979, 1982).

7. Marshall Sahlins, *Culture and Practical Reason* (Chicago: University of Chicago Press, 1976), p. 217.

8. John Cawelti, *Adventure, Mystery, and Romance* (Chicago: University of Chicago Press, 1976), and David Thorburn, "Television Melodrama," *Television: The Critical View* (New York: Oxford University Press, 1979, 1982).

9. Victor Turner, "Process, System, and Symbol: A New Anthropological Synthesis," *Daedalus* (Summer 1977), p. 68.

10. In various works Turner uses both the terms "liminal" and "liminoid" to refer to works of imagination and entertainment in contemporary culture. The latter term is used to clearly mark the distinction between events that have distinct behavioral consequences and those that do not. As Turner suggests, the consequences of entertainment in contemporary culture are hardly as profound as those of the liminal stage of ritual in traditional culture. We are aware of this basic distinction but use the former term in order to avoid a fuller explanation of the neologism. See Turner, "Afterword," to *The Reversible World*, Barbara Babcock, ed. (Ithaca: Cornell University Press, 1979), and "Liminal to Liminoid, in Play, Flow, and Ritual: An Essay in Comparative Symbology," *Rice University Studies*, 60:3 (1974).

11. Turner, 1977, p. 73.

12. Fiske and Hartley, 1978, p. 85.

13. We are indebted to Prof. Mary Douglas for encouraging this observation. At the presentation of these ideas at the New York Institute for the Humanities seminar on "The Mass Production of Mythology," she checked our enthusiasm for a pluralistic model of television by stating accurately and succinctly, "there are pluralisms and pluralisms." This comment led us to consider more thoroughly the means by which the forum and responses to it function as a tool with which to monitor the quality of pluralism in American social life, including its entertainments. The observation added a much needed component to our planned historical analysis.

14. Stanley Cavell, "The Fact of Television," *Daedalus* 3: 4 (Fall 1982).

15. Raymond Williams, *Television, Technology and Cultural Form* (New York: Schocken, 1971), p. 86 ff.

16. Horace Newcomb and Robert Alley, *The Television Producer as Artist in American Commercial Television* (New York: Oxford University Press, 1983).

17. Ibid.

18. Ibid.

19. Stuart Hall, "Encoding and Decoding in the Television Discourse," *Culture, Media, Language* (London: Hutchinson, in association with The Center for Contemporary Cultural Studies, 1980).

20. See Dave Morley and Charlotte Brunsdon, *Everyday Television: "Nationwide"* (London: British Film Institute, 1978), and Morley, "Subjects, Readers, Texts," in *Culture, Media, Language.*

21. We are indebted to Louis Black and Eric Michaels of the Radio-TV-Film department of the University of Texas-Austin for calling this aspect of televiewing to Newcomb's attention. It creates a much desired balance to Sahlin's view of the creator as *bricoleur* and indicates yet another matter in which the forum model enhances our ability to account for more aspects of the television experience. See, especially, Eric Michaels, *TV Tribes*, unpublished Ph.D. dissertation, University of Texas-Austin. 1982.

POSTSCRIPT

Are American Values Shaped by the Mass Media?

Television is pervasive in American life. Yet the influence of television on society is difficult to ascertain. Although these issues are as hotly debated today as they were when these articles were written, a number of things have changed since then. Newcomb and Hirsch have noted that with the passing of the network era, the notion that television serves as a site of negotiation for cultural issues, images, and ideas has shifted. The development of multiple channels now undercuts the dominance of the "big three" network era. Now the "viewing strip" is so complex as to be almost impossible to identify. The negotiation process may be much more complex than ever, as viewers select from an ever-widening set of approaches to issues and ideas. The cultural negotiation is perhaps more limited, because choices are more diverse. Similarly, alterations in programming strategies, particularly the creation of niche programming, may strain the notion of an ideological core of myths that structure content as advanced by Schiller. Yet many argue that all this additional programming is simply "more of the same." Others disagree, arguing that specialized channels and additional electronic options like the Internet open up spaces for "contested meanings" that challenge the dominant hegemonic reality. For a different take on the ways in which production of media content is influenced by corporate ownership, see Issue 14 on economics and media content.

Yet some effects of television have been dramatically illustrated. The media were instrumental in bringing together the entire nation to mourn and to respond to the events of September 11, 2001. Television's ability to bring events to millions of viewers may mean that television itself is a factor in determining events. For example, television has reshaped American politics, but it may have little influence on how people actually vote. Television is now the primary source of news for most Americans. It has also altered the ways in which Americans spend their time, ranking third behind sleep and work.

For more from Horace Newcomb, see his edited book *Television: The Critical View*, 6th ed. (Oxford University Press, 2000). Herbert Schiller was the author of several books, including *Corporate Inc, Information Inequality,* and *Networks of Power.* Authors such as Neil Postman also suggest that media shapes American values, by changing the nature of public discourse. Postman argues in *Amusing Ourselves to Death* (Viking Penguin, 1985) that television promotes triviality by speaking in only one voice—the voice of entertainment. Thus he maintains that television is transforming American culture into show business, to the detriment of rational public discourse.

ISSUE 2

Is Television Harmful for Children?

YES: W. James Potter, from *On Media Violence* (Sage Publications, 1999)

NO: Jib Fowles, from *The Case for Television Violence* (Sage Publications, 1999)

ISSUE SUMMARY

YES: W. James Potter, a professor of communication, examines existing research in the area of children and television violence. Such research is extensive and covers a variety of theoretical and methodological areas. He examines the nature of the impact of television on children and concludes that strong evidence exists for harmful effects.

NO: Jib Fowles, a professor of communication, finds the research on children and television violence less convincing. Despite the number of studies, he believes that the overall conclusions are unwarranted. Fowles finds that the influence is small, lab results are artificial, and fieldwork is inconclusive. In short, he finds television violence research flawed and unable to prove a linkage between violent images and harm to children.

Youths now have access to more violent images than at any other time in United States history, and these images are available in a diverse array of electronic sources: television, movies, video games, and music. Does such graphic, immediate, and pervasive imagery influence children's behavior and ultimately the level of violence in society? Is media a powerful force that can no longer be considered mere entertainment? Or, are Americans as a society overreacting, using media as a scapegoat for the concern over seemingly hopeless social problems?

In April 1999, after a series of similar school shootings, Columbine High School in Littleton, Colorado, was forever etched in our memory. The shootings there raised, in the most dramatic way possible, questions of how America had come to this tragedy. Did media play a role? Many would argue yes and would point to reenactments of video games, fashion choices from recent movies, imitative behaviors, and Internet discussions. Others would point to the long history of mental illness and social isolation of the perpetrators as more proximate causes.

Is media violence a threat to society? Those who would answer affirmatively might point to the content of children's viewing, arguing that it is a significant part of the socialization process and decrying the stereotypes, violence, and mindlessness of much of television fare. Others might argue that there are other negative consequences intrinsic to television viewing: the common daily fare of television themes, particularly a perception of the world as a scary place. Many would maintain that there are millions of people who watch television with no discernable negative consequences. Furthermore, they might say that there is a constellation of negative influences that seem to appear in violent individuals, a lack of proof, and an absurdity of thinking that television entertainment harms people.

Researchers began to study the impact of television on children early in television history by asking who watches, how much, and why. They analyzed what children see on television and how the content influences their cognitive development, school achievement, family interaction, social behaviors, and general attitudes and opinions. This is a large and complex social issue, so even extensive research has not provided final answers to all the questions that concerned parents and educators, professional mass communicators, and legislators have raised.

W. James Potter asserts that decades of research have led to several strong conclusions: violence is a public health problem and evidence is there to support the risks of exposure and discern the most susceptible individuals. Moreover, violent portrayals are pervasive; exposure leads to negative effects, both immediately and over the long term; and certain types of portrayals and certain types of viewers maximize the probability of negative effects. Jib Fowles disagrees. The evidence just is not that strong, he asserts, and the impact is very small when it does occur. He criticizes the methods of laboratory, field, and correlational research. Why, he asks, are such small effects considered so worthy of concern? His suspicion is that the scapegoating of media allows politicians, businesspeople, and society in general to feel they are tackling a problem without really taking any of the steps necessary to promote fundamental change.

YES

W. James Potter

On Media Violence

Overview and Introduction

Violence in American society is a public health problem. Although most people have never witnessed an act of serious violence in person, we are all constantly reminded of its presence by the media. The media constantly report news about individual violent crimes. The media also use violence as a staple in telling fictional stories to entertain us. Thus, the media amplify and reconfigure the violence in real life and continuously pump these messages into our culture.

The culture is responding with a range of negative effects. Each year about 25,000 people are murdered, and more than 2 million are injured in assaults. On the highways, aggressive behavior such as tailgating, weaving through busy lanes, honking or screaming at other drivers, exchanging insults, and even engaging in gunfire is a factor in nearly 28,000 traffic deaths annually, and the problem is getting worse at a rate of 7% per year. Gun-related deaths increased more than 60% from 1968 to 1994, to about 40,000 annually, and this problem is now considered a public health epidemic by 87% of surgeons and 94% of internists across the United States. Meanwhile, the number of pistols manufactured in the United States continues to increase—up 92% from 1985 to 1992.

Teenagers are living in fear. A Harris poll of 2,000 U.S. teenagers found that most of them fear violence and crime and that this fear is affecting their everyday behavior. About 46% of respondents said they have changed their daily behavior because of a fear of crime and violence; 12% said they carry a weapon to school for protection; 12% have altered their route to school; 20% said they have avoided particular parks or playgrounds; 20% said they have changed their circle of friends; and 33% have stayed away from school at times because of fear of violence. In addition, 25% said they did not feel safe in their own neighborhood, and 33% said they fear being a victim of a drive-by shooting. Nearly twice as many teenagers reported gangs in their school in 1995 compared to 1989, and this increase is seen in all types of neighborhoods; violent crime in schools increased 23.5% during the same period.

This problem has far-reaching economic implications. The U.S. Department of Justice estimates the total cost of crime and violence (such as child abuse and domestic violence, in addition to crimes such as murder, rape, and robbery) to be $500 billion per year, or about twice the annual budget of the Defense

Department. The cost includes real expenses (such as legal fees, the cost of lost time from work, the cost of police work, and the cost of running the nation's prisons and parole systems) and intangibles (such as loss of affection from murdered family members). Violent crime is responsible for 14% of injury-related medical spending and up to 20% of mental health care expenditures.

The problem of violence in our culture has many apparent causes, including poverty, breakdown of the nuclear family, shift away from traditional morality to a situational pluralism, and the mass media. The media are especially interesting as a source of the problem. Because they are so visible, the media are an easy target for blame. In addition, they keep reminding us of the problem in their news stories. But there is also a more subtle and likely more powerful reason why the media should be regarded as a major cause of this public health problem: They manufacture a steady stream of fictional messages that convey to all of us in this culture what life is about. Media stories tell us how we should deal with conflict, how we should treat other people, what is risky, and what it means to be powerful. The media need to share the blame for this serious public health problem.

How do we address the problem? The path to remedies begins with a solid knowledge base. It is the task of social scientists to generate much of this knowledge. For the past five decades, social scientists and other scholars have been studying the topic of media violence. This topic has attracted researchers from many different disciplines, especially psychology, sociology, mental health science, cultural studies, law, and public policy. This research addresses questions such as these: How much media violence is there? What are the meanings conveyed in the way violence is portrayed? and What effect does violence have on viewers as individuals, as members of particular groups, and as members of society? Estimates of the number of studies conducted to answer these questions range as high as 3,000 and even 3,500. . . .

Effects of Exposure to Media Violence

Does exposure to violence in the media lead to effects? With each passing year, the answer is a stronger yes. The general finding from a great deal of research is that exposure to violent portrayals in the media increases the probability of an effect. The most often tested effect is referred to as *learning to behave aggressively*. This effect is also referred to as direct imitation of violence, instigation or triggering of aggressive impulses, and disinhibition of socialization against aggressive behavior. Two other negative effects—desensitization and fear—are also becoming prevalent in the literature.

Exposure to certain violent portrayals can lead to positive or prosocial effects. Intervention studies, especially with children, have shown that when a media-literate person talks through the action and asks questions of the viewer during the exposure, the viewer will be able to develop a counterreading of the violence; that is, the viewer may learn that violent actions are wrong even though those actions are shown as successful in the media portrayal.

The effects have been documented to occur immediately or over the long term. Immediate effects happen during exposure or shortly after the exposure (within about an hour). They might last only several minutes, or they might last weeks. Long-term effects do not occur after one or several exposures; they begin to show up only after an accumulation of exposures over weeks or years. Once a long-term effect eventually occurs, it usually lasts a very long period of time.

This [selection] focuses on the issues of both immediate effects and long-term effects of exposure to media violence. . . .

From the large body of effects research, I have assembled 10 major findings. These are the findings that consistently appear in quantitative metaanalyses and narrative reviews of this literature. Because these findings are so widespread in the literature and because they are so rarely disputed by scholars, they can be regarded as empirically established laws.

Immediate Effects of Violent Content

The first six laws illuminate the major findings of research into the immediate effects of exposure to media violence. Immediate effects occur during exposure or within several hours afterward.

> *1. Exposure to violent portrayals in the media can lead to subsequent viewer aggression through disinhibition.*

This conclusion is found in most of the early reviews. For example, Stein and Friedrich closely analyzed 49 studies of the effects of antisocial and prosocial television content on people 3 to 18 years of age in the United States. They concluded that the correlational studies showed generally significant relationships ($r = .10$ to $.32$) and that the experiments generally showed an increase in aggression resulting from exposure to television violence across all age groups.

This conclusion gained major visibility in the 1972 Surgeon General's Report which stated that there was an influence, but this conclusion was softened by the industry members on the panel. . . .

Some of the early reviewers disagreed with this conclusion. . . .

In the two decades since this early disagreement, a great deal more empirical research has helped overcome these shortcomings, so most (but not all) of these critics have been convinced of the general finding that exposure to media violence can lead to an immediate disinhibition effect. All narrative reviews since 1980 have concluded that viewing of violence is consistently related to subsequent aggressiveness. This finding holds in surveys, laboratory experiments, and naturalistic experiments. For example, Roberts and Maccoby concluded that "the overwhelming proportion of results point to a causal relationship between exposure to mass communication portrayals of violence and an increased probability that viewers will behave violently at some subsequent time." Also, Friedrich-Cofer and Huston concluded that "the weight of the evidence from different methods of investigation supports the hypothesis that television violence affects aggression."

Meta-analytical studies that have reexamined the data quantitatively across sets of studies have also consistently concluded that viewing of aggression is likely to lead to antisocial behavior. For example, Paik and Comstock conducted a meta-analysis of 217 studies of the effects of television violence on antisocial behavior and reported finding a positive and significant correlation. They concluded that "regardless of age—whether nursery school, elementary school, college, or adult—results remain positive at a high significance level." Andison looked at 67 studies involving 30,000 participants (including 31 laboratory experiments) and found a relationship between viewing and subsequent aggression, with more than half of the studies showing a correlation (r) between .31 and .70. Hearold looked at 230 studies involving 100,000 participants to determine the effect of viewing violence on a wide range of antisocial behaviors in addition to aggression (including rule breaking, materialism, and perceiving oneself as powerless in society). Hearold concluded that for all ages and all measures, the majority of studies reported an association between exposure to violence and antisocial behavior. . . .

On balance, it is prudent to conclude that media portrayals of violence can lead to the immediate effect of aggressive behavior, that this can happen in response to as little as a single exposure, and that this effect can last up to several weeks. Furthermore, the effect is causal, with exposure leading to aggression. However, this causal link is part of a reciprocal process; that is, people with aggressive tendencies seek out violent portrayals in the media.

> *2. The immediate disinhibition effect is influenced by viewer demographics, viewer traits, viewer states, characteristics in the portrayals, and situational cues.*

Each human is a complex being who brings to each exposure situation a unique set of motivations, traits, predispositions, exposure history, and personality factors. These characteristics work together incrementally to increase or decrease the probability of the person's being affected.

2.1 Viewer Demographics
The key characteristics of the viewer that have been found to be related to a disinhibition effect are age and gender, but social class and ethnic background have also been found to play a part.

Demographics of age and gender.   Boys and younger children are more affected. Part of the reason is that boys pay more attention to violence. Moreover, younger children have more trouble following story plots, so they are more likely to be drawn into high-action episodes without considering motives or consequences. Age by itself is not as good an explanation as is ability for cognitive processing.

Socioeconomic status.   Lower-class youth watch more television and therefore more violence.

Ethnicity.   Children from minority and immigrant groups are vulnerable because they are heavy viewers of television.

2.2 Viewer Traits

The key characteristics of viewer traits are socialization against aggression, . . . cognitive processing, and personality type.

Socialization against aggression.   Family life is an important contributing factor. Children in households with strong norms against violence are not likely to experience enough disinhibition to exhibit aggressive behavior. The disinhibition effect is stronger in children living in households in which . . . children are abused by parents, watch more violence, and identify more with violent heroes; and in families that have high-stress environments.

Peer and adult role models have a strong effect in this socialization process. Male peers have the most immediate influence in shaping children's aggressive behaviors in the short term; adult males have the most lasting effect 6 months later. . . .

Cognitive processing.   Viewers' reactions depend on their individual interpretations of the aggression. Rule and Ferguson (1986) said that viewers first must form a representation or cognitive structure consisting of general social knowledge about the positive value that can be attached to aggression. The process of developing such a structure requires that viewers attend to the material (depending on the salience and complexity of the program). Then viewers make attributions and form moral evaluations in the comprehension stage. Then they store their comprehension in memory.

Cognitive processing is related to age. Developmental psychologists have shown that children's minds mature cognitively and that in some early stages they are unable to process certain types of television content well. . . . [U]ntil age 5, they are especially attracted to and influenced by vivid production features, such as rapid movement of characters, rapid changes of scenes, and unexpected sights and sounds. Children seek out and pay attention to cartoon violence, not because of the violence, but because of the vivid production features. By ages 6 to 11, children have developed the ability to lengthen their attention spans and make sense of continuous plots. . . .

Personality type.   The more aggressive the person is, the more influence viewing of violence will have on that person's subsequent aggressive behavior (Comstock et al., 1978; Stein & Friedrich, 1972). And children who are emotionally disturbed are more susceptible to a disinhibition effect (Sprafkin et al., 1992). . . .

2.3 Viewer States

The degrees of physiological arousal, anger, and frustration have all been found to increase the probability of a negative effect.

Aroused state.   Portrayals (even if they are not violent) that leave viewers in an aroused state are more likely to lead to aggressive behavior (Berkowitz & Geen, 1966; Donnerstein & Berkowitz, 1981; Tannenbaum, 1972; Zillman, 1971).

Emotional reaction.   Viewers who are upset by the media exposure (negative hedonic value stimuli) are more likely to aggress (Rule & Ferguson, 1986; Zillmann et al., 1981). Such aggression is especially likely when people are left in a state of unresolved excitement (Comstock, 1985). . . . In his meta-analysis of 1,043 effects of television on social behavior, Hearold (1986) concluded that frustration . . . is not a necessary condition, but rather a contributory condition. . . .

Degree of identity.   It has been well established that the more a person, especially a child, identifies with a character, the more likely the person will be influenced by that character's behavior.

Identity seems to be a multifaceted construct composed of similarity, attractiveness, and hero status. If the perpetrator of violence is perceived as *similar* to the viewer, the likelihood of learning to behave aggressively increases (Lieberman Research, 1975; Rosekrans & Hartup, 1967). When violence is performed by an *attractive* character, the probability of aggression increases (Comstock et al., 1978; Hearold, 1986). Attractiveness of a villain is also an important consideration (Health et al., 1989). . . .

2.4 Characteristics in the Portrayals

Reviews of the literature are clear on the point that people interpret the meaning of violent portrayals and use contextual information to construct that meaning.

In the media effects literature, there appear to be five notable contextual variables: rewards and punishments, consequences, justification, realism, and production techniques. . . .

Rewards and punishments.   Rewards and punishments to perpetrators of violence provide important information to viewers about which actions are acceptable. However, there is reason to believe that the effect does not work with children younger than 10, who usually have difficulty linking violence presented early in a program with its punishment rendered later (Collins, 1973).

In repeated experiments, viewers who watch a model rewarded for performing violently in the media are more likely to experience a disinhibition effect and behave in a similar manner. But when violence is punished in the media portrayal, the aggressiveness of viewers is likely to be inhibited (Comstock et al., 1978). In addition, when nonaggressive characters are rewarded, viewers' levels of aggression can be reduced.

The absence of punishment also leads to disinhibition. That is, the perpetrators need not be rewarded in order for the disinhibition effect to occur. . . .

Consequences.   The way in which the consequences of violence are portrayed influences the disinhibition effect. . . . For example, Goranson showed people a film of a prize fight in which either there were no consequences or the loser of the fight received a bad beating and later died. The participants who did not see the negative consequences were more likely to behave aggressively after the viewing.

A key element in the consequences is whether the victim shows pain, because pain cues inhibit subsequent aggression. Moreover, Swart and

Berkowitz (1976) showed that viewers could generalize pain cues to characters other than the victims.

Justification.   Reviews of the effects research conclude that justification of violent acts leads to higher aggression. For example, Bryan and Schwartz observed that "aggressive behavior in the service of morally commendable ends appears condoned. Apparently, the assumption is made that moral goals temper immoral actions. . . . Thus, both the imitation and interpersonal attraction of the transgressing model may be determined more by outcomes than by moral principles."

Several experiments offer support for these arguments. First, Berkowitz and Rawlings (1963) found that justification of filmed aggression lowers viewers' inhibitions to aggress in real life.

Justification is keyed to motives. Brown and Tedeschi (1976) found that offensive violence was regarded as more violent even when the actions themselves were not as violent. For example, a verbal threat that is made offensively is perceived as more violent than a punch that is delivered defensively.

The one motive that has been found to lead to the strongest disinhibition is vengeance. For example, Berkowitz and Alioto introduced a film of a sporting event (boxing and football) by saying that the participants were acting either as professionals wanting to win or as motivated by vengeance and wanting to hurt the other. They found that the vengeance film led to more shocks and longer duration of shocks in a subsequent test of participants. When violence was portrayed as vengeance, disinhibition was stronger than when violence was portrayed as self-defense or as a means of achieving altruistic goals.

Young children have difficulty understanding motives. For example, Collins (1973) ran an experiment on children aged 8 to 15 to see if a time lag from portrayal of motivation to portrayal of aggression changed participants' behaviors or interpretations. Participants were shown either a 30-minute film in which federal agents confronted some criminals or a control film of a travelogue. In the treatment film, the criminals hit and shot the federal agents, displaying negative motivation (desire to escape justice) and negative consequences (a criminal fell to his death while trying to escape). Some participants saw the sequence uninterrupted; others saw the motivation, followed by a 4-minute interruption of commercials, then the aggression. Both 18 days before the experiment and then again right after the viewing, participants were asked their responses to a wide range of hypothetical interpersonal conflict situations. There was a difference by age. Third graders displayed more aggressive choices on the postviewing measure when they had experienced the separation condition; sixth and 10th graders did not exhibit this effect. The author concluded that among younger children, temporal separation of story elements obscures the message that aggression was negatively motivated and punished. . . .

Realism.   When viewers believe that the aggression is portrayed in a realistic manner, they are more likely to try it in real life.

Production techniques.   Certain production techniques can capture and hold attention, potentially leading to differences in the way the action is perceived.

Attention is increased when graphic and explicit acts are used to increase the dramatic nature of the narrative, to increase positive dispositions toward the characters using violence, and to increase levels of arousal, which is more likely to result in aggressive behavior. . . .

  3. Exposure to violence in the media can lead to fear effects.

The best available review is by Cantor (1994), who defines fear effect as an immediate physiological effect of arousal, along with an emotional reaction of anxiety and distress.

  4. An immediate fear effect is influenced by a set of key factors about viewers and the portrayals.

4.1 Viewer Factors
Identification with the target.   The degree of identification with the target is associated with a fear effect. For example, characters who are attractive, who are heroic, or who are perceived as similar to the viewer evoke viewer empathy. When a character with whom viewers empathize is then the target of violence, viewers experience an increased feeling of fear.
  The identification with characters can lead to an enjoyment effect. For example, Tannenbaum and Gaer (1965) found that participants who identified more with the hero felt more stress and benefited more from a happy ending in which their stress was reduced. However, a sad or indeterminate ending increased participants' stress.

Prior real-life experience.   Prior experience with fearful events in real life leads viewers, especially children, to identify more strongly with the characters and events and thereby to involve them more emotionally.

Belief that the depicted violent action could happen to the viewer.   When viewers think there is a good chance that the violence they see could happen to them in real life, they are more likely to experience an immediate fear effect.

Motivations for exposure.   People expose themselves to media violence for many different reasons. Certain reasons for exposure can reduce a fear effect. If people's motivation to view violence is entertainment, they can employ a discounting procedure to lessen the effects of fear.

Level of arousal.   Higher levels of arousal lead to higher feelings of fear.

Ability to use coping strategies.   When people are able to remind themselves that the violence in the media cannot hurt them, they are less likely to experience a fear effect.

Developmental differences.   Children at lower levels of cognitive development are unable to follow plot lines well, so they are more influenced by individual violent episodes, which seem to appear randomly and without motivation.

Ability to perceive the reality of the portrayals.   Children are less able than older viewers to understand the fantasy nature of certain violent portrayals.

4.2 Portrayal Factors

Type of stimulus.   Cantor (1994) says that the fright effect is triggered by three categories of stimuli that usually are found in combination with many portrayals of violence in the media. First is the category of dangers and injuries, stimuli that depict events that threaten great harm. Included in this category are natural disasters, attacks by vicious animals, large-scale accidents, and violent encounters at levels ranging from interpersonal to intergalactic. Second is the category of distortions of natural forms. This category includes familiar organisms that are shown as deformed or unnatural through mutilation, accidents of birth, or conditioning. And third is the category of experience of endangerment and fear by others. This type of stimulus evokes empathy for particular characters, and the viewer then feels the fear that the characters in the narrative are portraying.

Unjustified violence.   When violence is portrayed as unjustified, viewers become more fearful.

Graphicness.   Higher levels of explicitness and graphicness increase viewer fear.

Rewards.   When violence goes unpunished, viewers become more fearful.

Realism.   Live-action violence provokes more intense fear than cartoon violence does. For example, Lazarus et al. found that showing gory accidents to adults aroused them physiologically less when the participants were told that the accidents were fake. This effect has also been found with children. In addition, fear is enhanced when elements in a portrayal resemble characteristics in a person's own life.

> *5. Exposure to violence in the media can lead to desensitization.*

In the short term, viewers of repeated violence can show a lack of arousal and emotional response through habituation to the stimuli.

> *6. An immediate desensitization effect is influenced by a set of key factors about viewers and the portrayals.*

Children and adults can become desensitized to violence upon multiple exposures through temporary habituation. But the habituation appears to be relatively short term.

6.1 Viewer Factors

People who are exposed to larger amounts of television violence are usually found to be more susceptible to immediate desensitization.

6.2 Portrayal Factors

There appear to be two contextual variables that increase the likelihood of a desensitization effect: graphicness and humor.

Graphicness.   Graphicness of violence can lead to immediate desensitization. In experiments in which participants are exposed to graphic violence, initially they have strong physiological responses, but these responses steadily decline during the exposure. This effect has also been shown with children, especially among the heaviest viewers of TV violence.

Humor.   Humor contributes to the desensitization effect.

Long-Term Effects of Violent Content

Long-term effects of exposure to media violence are more difficult to measure than are immediate effects. The primary reason is that long-term effects occur so gradually that by the time an effect is clearly indicated, it is very difficult to trace that effect back to media exposures. It is not possible to argue that any single exposure triggers the effect. Instead, we must argue that the long-term pattern of exposure leads to the effect. A good analogy is the way in which an orthodontist straightens teeth. Orthodontists do not produce an immediate effect by yanking teeth into line in one appointment. Instead, they apply braces that exert very little pressure, but that weak pressure is constant. A person who begins wearing braces might experience sore gums initially, but even then there is no observable change to the alignment of the teeth. This change in alignment cannot be observed even after a week or a month. Only after many months is the change observable.

It is exceedingly difficult for social scientists to make a strong case that the media are responsible for long-term effects. The public, policymakers, and especially critics of social science research want to be persuaded that there is a causal connection. But with a matter of this complexity that requires the long term evolution of often conflicting influences in the naturalistic environment of viewers' everyday lives, the case for causation cannot be made in any manner stronger than a tentative probabilistic one. Even then, a critic could point to a "third variable" as a potential alternative explanation.

> *7. Long-term exposure to media violence is related to aggression in a person's life.*

Evidence suggests that this effect is causative and cumulative (Eron, 1982). This effect is also reciprocal: Exposure to violence leads to increased aggression, and people with higher levels of aggression usually seek out higher levels of exposure to aggression.

Huesmann, Eron, Guerra, and Crawshaw (1994) conclude from their longitudinal research that viewing violence as a child has a causal effect on patterns of higher aggressive behavior in adults. This finding has appeared in studies in the United States, Australia, Finland, Israel, Poland, the Netherlands, and South Africa. While recognizing that exposure to violence on TV is not the only cause of aggression in viewers, Huesmann et al. conclude that the research suggests that the effect of viewing television violence on aggression "is relatively independent of other likely influences and of a magnitude great enough to account for socially important differences."

The long-term disinhibition effect is influenced by "a variety of environmental, cultural, familial, and cognitive" factors. A major influence on this effect is the degree to which viewers identify with characters who behave violently. For example, Eron found that the learning effect is enhanced when children identify closely with aggressive TV characters. He argued that aggression is a learned behavior, that the continued viewing of television violence is a very likely cause of aggressive behavior, and that this is a long-lasting effect on children.

Once children reach adolescence, their behavioral dispositions and inhibitory controls have become crystallized to the extent that their aggressive habits are very difficult to change, and achievement have been found to be related to this effect. Huesmann et al. concluded that low IQ makes the learning of aggressive responses more likely at an early age, and this aggressive behavior makes continued intellectual development more difficult into adulthood.

Evidence also suggests that the effect is contingent on the type of family life. In Japan, for example, Kashiwagi and Munakata (1985) found no correlation between exposure to TV violence and aggressiveness of viewers in real life for children in general. But an effect was observed among young children living in families in which the parents did not get along well.

8. Media violence is related to subsequent violence in society.

When television is introduced into a country, the violence and crime rates in that country, especially crimes of theft, increase. Within a country, the amount of exposure to violence that a demographic group typically experiences in the media is related to the crime rate in neighborhoods where those demographic groups are concentrated. Finally, some evidence suggests that when a high-profile violent act is depicted in the news or in fictional programming, the incidents of criminal aggression increase subsequent to that coverage.

All these findings are subject to the criticism that the researchers have only demonstrated co-occurrence of media violence and real-life aggression. Researchers are asked to identify possible "third variables" that might be alternative explanations for the apparent relationship, and then to show that the relationship exists even after the effects of these third variables are controlled. Although researchers have been testing control variables, critics are still concerned that one or more important variables that have yet to be controlled may account for a possible alternative explanation of the effect.

9. People exposed to many violent portrayals over a long time will come to exaggerate their chances of being victimized.

This generalized fear effect has a great deal of empirical support in the survey literature. But this relationship is generally weak in magnitude, and it is sensitive to third variables in the form of controls and contingencies. The magnitude of the correlation coefficients (r) is usually low, typically in the range of .10 to .30, which means that exposure is able to explain only less than 10% of the variation in the responses of cultivation indicators. . . .

The magnitude of the cultivation effect is relatively weak even by social science standards. Cultivation theorists have defended their findings by saying that even though the effect is small, it is persistent. . . .

This cultivation effect is also remarkably robust. In the relatively large literature on cultivation, almost all the coefficients fall within a consistently narrow band. Not only is this effect remarkable in its consistency, but this consistency becomes truly startling when one realizes the wide variety of measures (of both television exposure and cultivation indicators) that are used in the computations of these coefficients.

10. People exposed to many violent portrayals over a long time will come to be more accepting of violence.

This effect is the gradual desensitizing of viewers to the plight of victims, as well as to violence in general. After repeated exposure to media violence over a long period of time, viewers lose a sense of sympathy with the victims of violence. Viewers also learn that violence is a "normal" part of society, that violence can be used successfully, and that violence is frequently rewarded.

The probability of this long-term effect is increased when people are continually exposed to graphic portrayals of violence. For example, Linz, Donnerstein, and Penrod (1988a) exposed male participants to five slasher movies during a 2-week period. After each film, the male participants exhibited decreasing perceptions that the films were violent or that they were degrading to women.

Conclusion

After more than five decades of research on the effects of exposure to media violence, we can be certain that there are both immediate and long-term effects. The strongest supported immediate effect is the following: Exposure to violent portrayals in the media increases subsequent viewer aggression. We also know that there are other positive and negative immediate effects, such as fear and desensitization. As for long-term effects, we can conclude that exposure to violence in the media is linked with long-term negative effects of trait aggression, fearful worldview, and desensitization to violence. The effects process is highly complex and is influenced by many factors about the viewers, situational cues, and contextual characteristics of the violent portrayals.

Violence Viewing and Science

Examining the Research

For the moment, it is prudent not to question the forces that gave rise to the violence effects literature and have sustained it for five decades nor to tease out the unarticulated assumptions enmeshed in it. Let us begin by taking this extensive literature entirely on its own terms. What will become clear is that although the majority of the published studies on the topic do report antisocial findings, the average extent of the findings is slight—often so much so that the findings are open to several interpretations. . . .

Those who pore over the violence effects literature agree that the case against televised fantasy viciousness is most broadly and clearly made in the large number of laboratory studies, such as those done by Bandura. Overall, these studies offer support for the imitative hypothesis—that younger viewers will exhibit a tendency to act out the aggression seen on the screen. In this group of studies, many find the issue reduced to a pristine clarity, parsed of all needless complexity and obscurity, and answered with sufficient experimental evidence. What is found in this literature can be rightfully generalized to the real world, some believe, to spark a host of inferences and even policies. However, the laboratory is not the real world, and may be so unreal as to discredit the results.

The unnaturalness of laboratory studies is frequently commented on by those who have reservations regarding this research (Buckingham, 1993, p. 11; Gunter & McAteer, 1990, p. 13; Noble, 1975, p. 125), but the extent of the artificiality is rarely defined, leaving those who are unfamiliar with these settings or the nature of these experiments with little sense of what is meant by "unnatural." . . .

[In a behavioral laboratory setting] in a room with other unmet children, the child may be unexpectedly frustrated or angered by the experimenters—shown toys but not allowed to touch them, perhaps, or spoken to brusquely. The child is then instructed to look at a video monitor. It would be highly unlikely for the young subject to sense that this experience in any way resembled television viewing as done at home. . . . Most signally, at home television viewing is an entirely voluntary activity: The child is in front of the set because the child has elected to do so and in most instances has elected the content, and he or she will elect other content if the current material does not satisfy. In the behavioral laboratory, the child is compelled to watch and, worse, compelled to watch material not of the child's choosing and probably not of the child's liking. The essential element of the domestic television-viewing experience, that of pleasure, has been methodically stripped away.

Furthermore, what the child views in a typical laboratory experiment will bear little resemblance to what the child views at home. The footage will comprise only a segment of a program and will feature only aggressive actions. The intermittent relief of commercials or changed channels is missing, as are television stories' routine endings bringing dramatic closure in which everything is set right, with the correct values ascendant.

The child then may be led to another room that resembles the one in the video segment and encouraged to play while being observed. This is the room that, in Bandura et al.'s (1963) famous experiment, contained the Bobo doll identical to the one shown on the screen. Is it any wonder that uneasy children, jockeying for notice and position in a newly convened peer group, having seen a videotaped adult strike the doll without repercussions, and being tacitly encouraged by hovering experimenters who do not seem to disapprove of such action, would also hit the doll? As Noble (1975) wryly asked, "What else can one do to a self-righting bobo doll except hit it?" (p. 133). There are typically only a limited number of options, all behavioral, for the young subjects. Certainly, no researcher is asking them about the meanings they may have taken from the screened violence.

In summary, laboratory experiments on violence viewing are concocted schemes that violate all the essential stipulations of actual viewing in the real world (Cook, Kendzierski, & Thomas, 1983, p. 180) and in doing so have nothing to teach about the television experience (although they may say much about the experimenters). Viewing in the laboratory setting is involuntary, public, choiceless, intense, uncomfortable, and single-minded, whereas actual viewing is voluntary, private, selective, nonchalant, comfortable, and in the context of competing activities. Laboratory research has taken the viewing experience and turned it inside out so that the viewer is no longer in charge. In this manner, experimenters have made a mockery out of the everyday act of television viewing. Distorted to this extent, laboratory viewing can be said to simulate household viewing only if one is determined to believe so. . . .

The inadequacies of laboratory research on television violence effects are apparent in the small body of research on the matter of desensitization or, as Slaby (1994) called it, "the bystander effect." The few attempts to replicate the finding of the four Drabman and Thomas experiments (Drabman & Thomas 1974a, 1974b, 1976; Thomas & Drabman, 1975)—that children exposed to violent footage would take longer to call for the intercession of an adult supervisor—have produced inconsistent results. Horton and Santogrossi (1978) failed to replicate in that the scores for the control group did not differ from the scores for the experimental groups. In addition, Woodfield (1988) did not find statistically significant differences between children exposed to violent content and children exposed to nonviolent content. . . .

A third attempt to replicate by Molitor and Hirsch (1994) did duplicate the original findings, apparently showing that children are more likely to tolerate aggression in others if they are first shown violent footage. An examination of their results, however, does give rise to questions about the rigor of the research. This experiment was set up with the active collaboration of the original researchers and may be less of an attempt to relicate (or not) than an attempt to vindicate. Forty-two Catholic school fourth- and fifth-grade children were assigned to two treatment groups (there was no control group). As for all laboratory experiments, the viewing conditions were so thoroughly alien that results may have been induced by subtle clues from the adult laboratory personnel, especially for obedient children from a parochial school setting. Children shown violent content (a segment from *Karate Kid*) waited longer on average before requesting adult intervention than did children shown nonviolent content (footage from the 1984 Olympic games). Again, this finding could be interpreted as evidence of catharsis: The violent content might have lowered levels of arousal and induced a momentary lassitude. The findings could also have resulted from a sense of ennui: Postexperiment interviews revealed that all the children shown *Karate Kid* had seen the movie before, some as many as 10 times (p. 201). By comparison, the Olympic contests might have seemed more exciting and stimulated swifter reactions to the videotaped misbehavior. The first author was one of the laboratory experimenters; therefore, the specter of expectancy bias cannot be dismissed.

Even if desensitization were to exist as a replicable laboratory finding, the pressing question is whether or not the effect generalizes to the real world. Are there any data in support of the notion that exposure to television violence makes people callous to hostility in everyday life? The evidence on this is scarce and in the negative. Studying many British youngsters, Belson (1978) could find no correlation between levels of television violence viewing and callousness to real violence or inconsiderateness to others (pp. 471–475, 511–516). Research by Hagell and Newburn (1994) can answer the question of whether some youngsters who view heightened hours of television become "desensitized" to violence and embark on criminal lives; unexpectedly, teenage criminals view on average less television, and less violent content, than their law-abiding peers.

Reviewers of the small desensitization literature conclude there is no empirical evidence that anything like the bystander effect actually exists in real life (Gauntlett, 1995, p. 39; Van der Voort, 1986, p. 327; Zillmann, 1991, p. 124). Even George Comstock (1989), normally sympathetic to the violence effects literature, concedes about desensitization studies that "what the research does not demonstrate is any likelihood that media portrayals would affect the response to injury, suffering, or violent death experienced firsthand" (p. 275).

I now turn from the contrivances of laboratory research to the more promising methodology of field experiments, in which typically children in circumstances familiar to them are rated on aggressiveness through the observation of their behavior, exposed to either violent or nonviolent footage, and then unobtrusively rated again. Although this literature holds out the hope of conclusive findings in natural settings, the actual results display a disquietingly wide range of outcomes. Some of the data gathered indicate, instead of an elevation in aggressive behaviors, a diminishment in aggressive behaviors following several weeks of high-violence viewing. Feshbach and Singer (1971) were able to control the viewing diets of approximately 400 boys in three private boarding schools and four homes for wayward boys. For 6 weeks, half the boys were randomly assigned to a viewing menu high in violent content, whereas the other half made their selections from nonaggressive shows. Aggression levels were determined by trained observers in the weeks before and after the controlled viewing period. No behavioral differences were reported for the adolescents in the private schools, but among the poorer, semidelinquent youths, those who had been watching the more violent shows were calmer than their peers on the blander viewing diet. The authors concluded that "exposure to aggressive content on television seems to reduce or control the expression of aggression in aggressive boys from relatively low socioeconomic backgrounds" (p. 145).

Although Wood et al. (1991) report that the eight field experiments they reviewed did, overall, demonstrate an imitative effect from watching televised violence, other reviewers of this literature do not concur (Cumberbatch & Howitt, 1989, p. 41; Freedman, 1988, p. 151). McGuire (1986) comments dismissively on "effects that range from the statistically trivial to practically insubstantial" (p. 213). Most decisively, Gadow and Sprafkin (1989), themselves contributors to the field experiment research, concluded their thorough review of the 20 studies they located by stating that "the findings from the field experiments offer little support for the media aggression hypothesis" (p. 404).

In the aftermath of the thoroughgoing artificiality of the laboratory studies, and the equivocation of the field experiment results, the burden of proof must fall on the third methodology, that of correlational studies. In the search for statistical correlations (or not) between violence viewing and aggressive or criminal behavior, this literature contains several studies impressive for their naturalness and their size. Not all these studies uncover a parallel between, on the one hand, increased levels of violence viewing and, on the other hand, increased rates of misbehavior, by whatever measure. For example, for a sample of 2,000 11- to 16-year-olds, Lynn, Hampson, and Agahi (1989) found no correlation between levels of violence viewing and levels of aggression. Nevertheless, many studies do report a positive correlation. It should be noted that the magnitude of this co-occurrence is usually quite small, typically producing a low correlation coefficient of 10 to 20 (Freedman, 1988, p. 153). Using these correlations (small as they are), the question becomes one of the direction(s) of possible causality. Does violence viewing lead to subsequent aggression as is commonly assumed? Could more aggressive children prefer violent content, perhaps as a vicarious outlet for their hostility? . . . Could any of a host of other factors give rise to both elevated variables?

Following his substantial correlational study of 1,500 London adolescents, Belson (1978) highlighted one of his findings—that boys with high levels of exposure to television violence commit 49% more acts of serious violence than do those who view less—and on this basis issued a call for a reduction in video carnage (p. 526). Closer examination of his data (pp. 380–382), however, reveals that the relationship between the two variables is far more irregular than he suggests in his text. Low viewers of television violence are more aggressive than moderate viewers, whereas very high violence viewers are less aggressive than those in the moderate to high range. Moreover, "acts of serious violence" constituted only one of Belson's four measures of real-life aggression; the other three were "total number of acts of violence," "total number of acts of violence weighted by degree of severity of the act," and "total number of violent acts excluding minor ones." Findings for these three variables cannot be said to substantiate Belson's conclusion. That is, for these measures, the linking of violence viewing to subsequent aggression was negated by reverse correlations—that aggressive youngsters sought out violent content (pp. 389–392). Three of his measures refuted his argument, but Belson chose to emphasize a fourth, itself a demonstrably inconsistent measure. . . .

For the total television effects literature, whatever the methodology, the reviews . . . by Andison (1977), Hearold (1986), and Paik and Comstock (1994) are not the only ones that have been compiled. Other overviews reach very different summary judgments about this body of studies in its entirety. A review published contemporaneously with that of Andison considered the same research projects and derived a different conclusion (Kaplan & Singer, 1976). Kaplan and Singer examined whether the extant literature could support an activation view (that watching televised fantasy violence leads to aggression), a catharsis view (that such viewing leads to a decrease in aggression), or a null view, and they determined that the null position was the most judicious. They wrote, "Our review of the literature strongly suggests that the activating effects of television fantasy violence are marginal at best. The scientific data do not consistently link violent television fantasy programming to violent behavior" (p. 62).

In the same volume in which Susan Hearold's (1986) meta-analysis of violence studies appeared, there was also published a literature review by William McGuire (1986). In contrast to Hearold, it was McGuire's judgment that the evidence of untoward effects from violence viewing was not compelling. Throughout the 1980s, an assured critique of the violence effects literature [was] issued from Jonathan Freedman (1984, 1986, 1988). Freedman cautiously examined the major studies within each of the methodological categories. . . . Regarding correlational studies, he noted that "not one study produced strong consistent results, and most produced a substantial number of negative findings" (1988, p. 158). Freedman's general conclusion is that "considering all of the research—laboratory, field experiments, and correlational studies—the evidence does not support the idea that viewing television violence causes aggression" (1988, p. 158).

Freedman's dismissal of the violence effects literature is echoed in other literature reviews from British scholars, who may enjoy an objective distance on this largely American research agenda. Cumberbatch and Howitt (1989) discussed the shortcomings of most of the major studies and stated that the research data "are insufficiently robust to allow a firm conclusion about television violence as studied" (p. 51). David Gauntlett (1995) . . . analyzed at length most of the consequential studies. He believes that "the work of effects researchers is done" (p. 1). "The search for direct 'effects' of television on behavior is over: Every effort has been made, and they simply cannot be found" (p. 120). Ian Vine (1997) concurs: "Turning now to the systemic evidence from hundreds of published studies of the relationship between viewing violence and subsequent problematic behaviors, the most certain conclusion is that there is no genuine consensus of findings" (p. 138). . . .

Discourse Within Discourse

Opened up for inspection, the sizable violence effects literature turns out to be an uneven discourse—inconsistent, flawed, pocked. This literature proves nothing conclusively, or equivalently, this literature proves everything in that support for any position can be drawn from its corpus. The upshot is that, no matter what some reformers affirm, the campaign against television violence is bereft of any strong, consensual scientific core. Flaws extend through to the very premises of the literature—flaws so total that they may crowd out alternative viewpoints and produce in some amind-numbed acquiescence. Specifically, the literature's two main subjects—television and the viewer—are assumed to be what they are not.

Viewers are conceived of as feckless and vacuous, like jellyfish in video tides. Viewers have no intentions, no discretion, and no powers of interpretation. Into their minds can be stuffed all matter of content. Most often, the viewer postulated in the effects literature is young, epitomizing immaturity and malleability. This literature, wrote Carmen Luke (1990), "had constructed a set of scientifically validated truths about the child viewer as a behavioral response mechanism, as passive and devoid of cognitive abilities. The possibility that viewers bring anything other than demographic variables to the screen was conceptually excluded" (p. 281). Although there is ample evidence that the young are highly active, selective, and discriminating viewers (Buckingham, 1993; Clifford, Gunter, & McAleer, 1995; Durkin, 1985; Gunter & McAteer, 1990; Hawkins & Pingree, 1986; Hodge & Tripp, 1986; Noble, 1975), this is never the version in the violence effects literature.

Television, on the other hand, is seen as powerful, coercive, and sinister. The medium is not a servant but a tyrant. It rules rather than pleases. It is omnipotent; it cannot be regulated, switched, modulated, interpreted, belittled, welcomed, or ignored. All the things that television is in the real world it is not within the violence effects literature.

The relationship between television content and viewers, as implied in this research, is one way only, as television pounds its insidious message into a hapless audience; there is no conception of a return flow of information by which viewers via ratings indicate preferences for certain content rather than other content. The only result allowable from the viewing experience is that of direct and noxious effects. Other possibilities—of pleasures, relaxation, reinterpretations, therapy, and so on—are not to be considered. The television viewing experience, twisted beyond recognition, is conceived of in pathological terms; in fact, a large amount of the research throughout the past decades has been funded by national mental health budgets.

All these preconceptions apply before a bit of research is actually conducted. The surprising result is not that there have been worrisome findings reported but that, given these presuppositions, the negative findings were not much grander still. . . .

The war on television violence, the larger discourse, has united many allies with otherwise weak ties—prominent authorities and grassroots organizations, liberals and conservatives, and the religious and the secular. We must ask why they put aside their differences, lift their voices together, and join in this particular cause. This implausible alliance constitutes a force field that waxes and wanes throughout the decades, losing strength at one point and gaining it at another; it would seem to have a rhythm all its own. What can account for the regular reoccurrence of this public discourse denouncing television violence?

POSTSCRIPT

Is Television Harmful for Children?

Much of what we know about the effects of television comes from the study of children enjoying traditional television, but this knowledge is being challenged by the impact of emerging telecommunications technology. The Internet, cable television programming, video games, and VCRs have changed the face of television within the home. Indeed, VCRs have greatly increased the control that parents have over the material to which children are exposed at young ages and have greatly increased the diversity of content that children can be exposed to as they get older. The Internet, a 500-channel world, increasing international programming ventures, and regulatory changes will alter the way children interact with electronic media. What influence that will have is very hard to predict.

One conclusion is inescapable. There is now much more diversity of media content available, and there are many more choices for parents and children. One of the clearest findings of research on the impact of violence on child aggression is that parents, through their behavior and their positive and negative comments, can have a major influence on whether or not children behave aggressively subsequent to exposure. With choices come hard decisions for parents. The promise of television and other media can now be better fulfilled, with more choices than ever before. Alternatively, a diet of violence and mindlessness is easily found.

Although this issue concerns children, there are important developmental and social differences due to age. Young children, particularly preschoolers, are most likely to be controlled by their parents, are most likely to have difficulty understanding some of the narratives and conventions of media fare, and are arguably the most vulnerable to learning from the messages of the media to which they are exposed. The "tween" years are a transition to more adult programs and themes and are a time of great transition socially. Poised between the worlds of adulthood and childhood, the tween partakes of both, sometimes with difficult consequences. Tweens are not even considered by the media to be part of the "child" audience. Their viewing patterns are much more like those of adults, and like adults they are presumed to be cognitively able to protect themselves from the effects of violence or even advertising. So they proudly proclaim that the media have no effect on them.

The National Television Violence Study, 3 vols. (Sage Publications, 1996–1998), conducted by a consortium of professors from several universities, offers a commentary on the state of violence on American television for viewers, policymakers, industry leaders, and scholars. Robert Liebert and Joyce Sprafkin's *The Early Window: Effects of Television on Children and Youth*, 3rd ed. (Pergamon Press, 1988) is an excellent introduction to the history and issues of media effects. Judith Van Evra offers a view of existing research in *Television and Child Development,* 2d ed. (Lawrence Erlbaum, 1998). School violence has revived the debate on media violence and children, according to Paige Albiniak in "Media: Littleton's Latest Suspect," *Broadcasting & Cable* (May 3, 1999). Not only television but video games come under attack. Lieutenant Colonel Dave Grossman, a former Army ranger and paratrooper, writes about video games that teach children to kill by using the same warfare tactics used to train the military, in the *Saturday Evening Post* (July/August and September/October 1999). Many articles were written after the Columbine tragedy that implicated violent video games in the violence of U.S. society.

ISSUE 3

Are Representations of African-American Women in Media Accurate?

YES: Thomas A. Mascaro, from "Shades of Black on *Homicide: Life on the Street*; Advances and Retreats in Portrayals of African American Women," *Journal of Popular Film and Television* (Summer 2005)

NO: Janis Sanchez-Hucles, Patrick S. Hudgins, and Kimberly Gamble, from "Reflection and Distortion: Women of Color in Magazine Advertisements," in Ellen Cole and Jessica Henderson Daniel, eds., *Featuring Females* (American Psychological Association, 2005)

ISSUE SUMMARY

YES: Thomas Mascaro comments on the long history of examining how people of color have been portrayed in various forms of media. He makes the point that African-American women have often been stereotyped in television sitcoms, but during the seven seasons of the hit TV show, *Homicide: Life on the Streets*, African-American women were given a venue for portrayals that were more socially significant and socially relevant.

NO: Janis Sanchez-Hucles, Patrick S. Hudgins, and Kimberly Gamble conduct an analysis of many images of women of color from magazine advertising in six female or family-oriented magazines, and found that women of color were portrayed differently; in this issue, we examine African-American women in particular, but we include comments on other women of color, for further consideration.

One of the most common questions about media content has to do with whether media accurately represent and reflect society. There has been intense controversy about how race is portrayed in the media, and how women are portrayed as objects, rather than as individuals. Many scholars argue that racial representations in popular culture help mold public opinion and set the agenda for public discourse on race issues in the media and in society as a whole, and that images of women that capitalize on body and sexuality set up unrealistic expectations for both women and men, concerning how women should look and how they should behave. This issue examines a number of questions. Do members of an audience identify with characters portrayed? Do expressions of, and images in the media, communicate effectively about different cultures? How much can we learn about other cultures through media portrayals, or do representations feed stereotypical thinking and reinforce racial and/or cultural biases? How are images of women portrayed in the media?

For a long time, content providers have been criticized for underrepresenting or misrepresenting people of color. Starting in the 1980s, African-American actors became more of a presence in television, and the financial viability of creating programs that appealed to both black and white audiences started to turn the tide. The very successful *Cosby Show*, which debuted in 1984, is still one of the most successful television sitcoms of all times, but even this program was criticized for portraying a family that was so perfect, it defied reality.

Similarly, portrayals of all women have been criticized for presenting unrealistic body types and for representing so many women as sex objects. Actresses and female celebrities are often significantly under a healthy body weight, and women are often portrayed as sex objects, or as persons who use their sexual power when they interact with men. In these two selections, we complicate the question of racial representation in media with the difficult problem of how all women are portrayed in the media.

Professor Thomas A. Mascaro focuses on one program in particular; *Homicide: Life on the Street,* which had a seven-year run on television from 1993 to 2000. His analysis goes much further than how women were portrayed on this program, and he reflects on female/male relationships and contemporary topics to help underscore how much television has evolved in the accurate portrayal of African-American women, and the important cultural impact of how people are represented in television.

Janis Sanchez-Hucles, Patrick S. Hudgins, and Kimberly Gamble take a slightly different approach to the question of how women are portrayed. They report the results of a content analysis of how women of color were represented in six popular, contemporary magazines and find that African-American women may be more of a presence in magazines today, but that they are still primarily portrayed in stereotypical ways. We report their findings related to a number of racial groups, but we focus specifically on African-American women because as Sanchez-Hucles, Hudgins, and Gamble state, there were more representations of African-American women in the ads they studied than other women of color.

What you'll realize as you read these selections is that different forms of media may well capitalize on different stereotypes or images. How and why can one form of media be more progressive, while another form continues to draw on old stereotypes? Who are the audiences for these forms? What do they take from their viewing of these portrayals, and why can different forms of media represent women the way they do? No matter what the answers to these questions, the selections in this issue remind us that there is no one answer that fits all forms of media.

YES

Thomas A. Mascaro

Shades of Black on *Homicide: Life on the Street*; Advances and retreats in portrayals of African American women

The character Mary Pembleton broke new ground in network television drama with her realistic portrayal of a middle-class African American woman on a recurring prime-time series, *Homicide: Life on the Street* (NBC, 1993–99). As interpreted and performed by Ami Brabson, Mary Pembleton was a confident, self-sufficient, life-loving woman who managed a successful professional career. She was an affectionate, attractive, sensual, challenging, supportive spouse. She was funny, without mugging or cracking wise. She was an able, protective mother. And she was a fiercely determined survivor.

But Brabson, a Shakespearean-trained, theatrical actor who received her master's of fine arts degree from New York University's Graduate Acting Program, expressed the passion, intelligence, and commitment of Mary Pembleton with such exquisite understatement that series creators rarely brought her onto center stage, instead developing the character traits of her detective husband, Frank Pembleton (played by Brabson's real-life spouse Andre Braugher).

This sophisticated portrayal of a black woman represented a significant progressive step, but the failure to more fully develop Mary Pembleton and her family life stands as a missed opportunity by network television to give viewers believable models of the full spectrum of American culture. Despite these limitations, however, *Homicide*—as it did through its positive and varied portrayals of African American men—presented a wide range of shades and characteristics more typical of real black women than usually found in dramatic roles. Rather than relying on stereotypical characters, such as crack whores, welfare cheats, addicts, boisterous jive-talking single moms, or sexy cops with attitude, the writers, actors, and directors of Homicide presented African American women with diverse human qualities.

But there is an added element that emerges from an analysis of African American women on *Homicide*—they existed during a time, the 1990s, when network television news had abandoned the long-form documentaries that previously had dealt with complex social issues. Consequently, the storylines

From *Journal of Popular Film and Television*, Summer 2005. Reprinted by permission of the Helen Dwight Reid Educational Foundation. Published by Heldref Publications, 1319, Eighteenth St., NW, Washington, DC 20036-1802. Copyright © 2005. www.heldref.org

and performances of these black females take on greater significance as the proxy voices of real women who confront formidable daily obstacles in crime-ridden urban settings.

Waldman and Walker, in their examination of women and documentary, explain that women's history is counterhistory: "[W]omen speak and write from the margins of patriarchy". This points to a dilemma at the heart of African American media studies: "Because the interests and needs of various groups of women are always going to be different, we have grappled with the problem of securing the common goal of human rights for women while dealing with constituent interests that may be at odds". The more a minority culture strives for a common goal, the more individuals within that subculture are likely to be portrayed and received in broad strokes that dissolve personal distinctions. Individuality gives way to the struggle for social justice.

If there were no African American women on television, one social goal would be to have at least some representation. But one, two, or three black women on television do not, and cannot, represent all black women. Women, including African Americans, can achieve parity only if they have the freedom to show themselves through rich, textured portraits and in many different views of appearance, character, and action. . . .

The success of black-produced television shows in the 1980s and 1990s, including *The Cosby Show*, *A Different World*, and *The Fresh Prince of Bel Air*, "highlighted intraracial differences" and the "refreshing possibility that racial authenticity could be negotiated rather than assumed. . . . What emerged were contested narratives that challenged the very notion of 'blackness' itself".

But . . . others also write about the difficulty that African Americans experience when trying to define blackness in serious or dramatic settings. Pressure from network executives to perpetuate the black sitcom formula, and their unwillingness to support black drama or dramadies, as was the case for *Frank's Place* and *Roc*, has restricted African Americans' use of fiction to comment on reality.

This situation improved in the 1990s with the drama *Homicide: Life on the Street*. What follows is a critical examination of running characters and also African American women who appeared in single installments. The analysis shows that *Homicide* succeeded not only in expanding representations of black women in prime time but also by involving viewers with powerful stories derived from real conditions in fictional Baltimore and, by extension, other American cities.

This research is built on a foundation of literature that can be reduced to a few thematic conclusions: The appearance of black lead characters in drama is rare, compared with situation comedies; access by African Americans to the creative and management part of the television business is critical to the ownership and preservation of black culture; black women, even more than black men, continue to be underrepresented on television in storylines of consequence; and black women face a vexing web of real-life problems. *Homicide* made advances and retreats on all facets of these trends.

Recalling East Side/West Side

A useful foil for analyzing *Homicide* is the Kennedy-era single-season drama produced by David Susskind, *East Side/West Side*, which featured the first regular black lead on a prime-time dramatic series. Cicely Tyson played Jane Foster, the office secretary to George C. Scott's Neil Brock, a young, white social worker in the New York slums. Episodes of *East Side/West Side* often dealt with child abuse, the welfare syndrome, aging, addiction, crime, and race relations. On November 4, 1963, CBS aired an installment of *East Side/West Side* that was particularly powerful in its statement about unequal treatment of the races. That episode—"Who Do You Kill?"—also is a good benchmark for examining changes in television portrayals of race and judging the significance of *Homicide*.

The story features a black couple in their twenties, played by Diana Sands and James Earl Jones, living with their infant daughter in a rat-infested Harlem tenement. In one horrifying scene, a rat gets into the baby's crib and bites the girl. The father scoops up his daughter and rushes into the busy street where he tries, unsuccessfully, to hail a cab or anyone to drive him to a hospital. When the girl dies, we see the city (and the dominant culture) as insensitive to a black father in desperate need of a lift. Brock, the white social worker, is unable to appreciate the agony the parents are feeling and is powerless to help in a meaningful way. The tragedy also strains the couple's marriage; the wife begins to drink, will not leave her bed, and refuses to attend the child's funeral. At her minister's urging, and for her husband's sake, the mother finds the wherewithal to persevere.

As the following analysis will make clear, comparing *Homicide* to *East Side/West Side* shows progress in real race relations and circumstances for urban African Americans and also in televised portrayals of race. But the same comparison demonstrates the slow pace of broad social change in America and in representations of culture on television.

Homicide episode 310, "Every Mother's Son," directed by Ken Fink, bursts onto the screen. An African American boy shoots another black kid in the head at close range. The hand-held, single-camera documentary style of *Homicide* adds to the realism, drama, and uneasy feeling the crime and arrest evoke.

Although the episode introduces the desire of Mary and Frank Pembleton to have a baby, the most poignant moments deal with the black mothers of the two boys. Their losses—one through death, the other because of a prison sentence—could be experienced by any urban mother. The artistry of key scenes speaks to universal themes of parenting and the unique pains and dilemmas of African American women.

The investigation begins with the children who witnessed the shooting at a local Baltimore bowling alley. The dialogue here dramatizes a reality: Even African American kids who play innocently at bowling alleys and are not involved with gangs are victims of terror that comes "out of nowhere."

The victim is Darryl Nawls; the shooter Ronnie Sayers. The detectives, doing their unhappy but routine duty, go to tell the victim's mother that her son has been killed. They drive up to what appears to be project housing.

Jason Nawls, six or seven years old, answers the door. He is home alone. He tells the cops that his mom's at work and "there ain't no dad." Jason goes with the officers to his mother's job at a restaurant. The scene establishes the reality of a working African American mom who lacks the support of a spouse and is trying to raise children on a waitress's pay. This forces the mother to leave her children alone, unsupervised and more likely to get into trouble.

When Jason enters the restaurant and announces, "Momma. These two guys are detectives," her body language supplants dialogue. Gay Thomas, who plays Mary Nawls, is beautiful, but is not dressed in sexy garb. She wears a colorful teal-patterned sweatshirt and a lighter, flowered apron with matching headscarf. This is a subtle costuming choice with African hints, a muted form of African American pride worn with more volume by Phylicia Rashad as Clair Huxtable on *The Cosby Show* and black women on other shows.

Pembleton asks, "Are you Mary Nawls, Darryl's mother?"

"I'm his mother," she replies warily. "Where is Darryl? Is he in some kind of trouble or something?" The point-of-view camera moves closer to Mary Nawls. Pembleton clears his throat. "Has he been in some kind of accident?" she asks, as she maneuvers around the table she is setting, putting it between her and the lawman.

"Mrs. Nawls," Pembleton says, "I'm a homicide detective."

"Homicide," she restates. Then leaning on the table to support her weakening legs, she asks, "What homicide?" The camera cuts to Pembleton's partner, Tim Bayliss, and we see young Jason spinning playfully on the counter stool.

The camera cuts back to Mary Nawls and, typical of *Homicide*'s theatricality, she performs rather than explains her feelings. Pembleton tries to head off the reaction: "Miss Naw—." But she puts out her hand like a traffic cop and says. "No." She backs into the corner behind the table and repeatedly swats her arm at Pembleton as though chasing away a hectoring insect. She cowers and wails in short outbursts. She flails her arms the way the African American women did at Emmett Till's funeral in Chicago and the way African women often express agony and sorrow in international news stories. She clenches her fist; she covers her mouth. Pembleton steps closer, either to comfort her or lead her out, but, without touching him, she raises her hand again—fearful, protective, trying to create safe space. "Oh, God," she cries, "Where's my baby?" Mary Nawls then moves around the counter to wrap shielding arms around her surviving son.

There is another artistic layer woven into this scene that amplifies its impact. As Mary Nawls realizes her son has been killed, the song "Full Moon, Empty Heart" begins to play under the spoken parts. The scene continues with no dialogue—a *Homicide* trademark—as Pembleton, Bayliss, and Mary Nawls enter the morgue to identify the body of young Darryl. The coroner unzips the body bag to reveal a black adolescent with a gunshot wound to his head. Mary Nawls brushes her hand against the child's cheek, cries, and nods, affirming the worst. The camera cuts to a close-up of Jason peering in just as Mary covers his eyes with her hand.

"See this child twice stolen from me," says the singer—in this case, once by economic circumstances in which Mary Nawls was forced to work and could not be with her son and so lost him to the street, and again by gunshot.

It is a common theme for African American women who reside in impoverished urban neighborhoods.

As Pembleton and Bayliss question the shooter's mother, Patrice Sayers—played by Rhonda Stubbins-White—we see another version of life for black women. She is home caring for a sick child, David. She cannot believe the detectives' insinuations that her Ronnie may have been involved in a shooting; he is incapable of violence, she believes. He was home that morning as always and ate his usual bowl of raisin bran. His life is stable—and still the reality of the streets and a violent culture overwhelm a caring mother. "My Ronnie couldn't be involved in anything like this," she says. "He's only fourteen years old!"

Bayliss, pacing, freezes and looks at Patrice Sayers with disbelieving eyes. "He's how old?" he asks quietly.

"Fourteen," she repeats. Pembleton drops his head, rubs his shiny pate, and sighs. None of the adults wants to believe a child is capable of such an act.

When the cops corner Ronnie, he pulls his gun in a standoff with Pembleton, man to boy, gun to gun. Pembleton questions him about Darryl. But Ronnie is confused—he thought he shot a kid named Basil, who had been after him. He shot the wrong kid.

Documentary, drama, and art merge in the next scene. While Jason Nawls goes with another detective to get a soda, Darryl's mother sits on the waiting room bench. And while Ronnie consults with a court-appointed attorney, his mother also goes to the waiting room. Bayliss's facial expression mirrors our reaction at the irony of the image—two mothers, both victims of violence, momentarily ignorant of their connection.

Mary notices Patrice's tears and her futile search for tissues. She offers Patrice one of hers. The blocking of this scene—the relationship among actors, lights, and camera—is important to the analysis. Normally, dialogue is shot by cross-shooting, with the actors facing one another and the camera filming first one part of the dialogue, then the other. The editor splices the film into a conversation.

In "Every Mother's Son," however, the women are seated next to each other. Artistically, both women are on the same side of a social problem. As the camera cuts, we see two African American women as representatives of all women, but especially blacks—the two profiles represent "every mother."

The dramatic tension is riveting as the women engage in idle talk about their children. Mary, fighting tears, says her Darryl was an adventurer who wanted to join the military and see the world—her loss is our loss. Patrice returns the tissue to Mary—their tears now blended into the same cloth. "I've been to three funerals this year for Darryl's friends." Mary says. "Seems like that's how we have our socials now."

As Ronnie is led from interrogation up to processing, Patrice now reveals what Mary did not know—the assailant is Patrice's son. Mary screams, "That's the boy who killed my baby? That's the bastard that killed my son?" She lunges at the boy who is shielded by the detectives, then turns to Patrice: "That's your boy?"

In the coda to the program, Patrice visits the restaurant where Mary works. Jason is with her in the eatery, in plain sight. Patrice's David is also with his mother. Patrice has come to offer an apology and a Mass card to Mary on behalf of Darryl. The two young boys begin roughhousing. Patrice intervenes and scolds David about playing rough. "It's OK," says Mary. "Kids are kids and kids gotta play." She also notices that they like to play together. But when Patrice suggests that maybe they could get to know each other, Mary says, "And what would happen if they did that? What would happen—if they found out about each other's older brothers?"

The scene closes with a close-up of Patrice, then Mary, and the camera tilts down to Jason, held protectively by Mary, then over to David. It is the story of African American women who pay a price now for violent urban life and poverty and who are likely to pay the price again as their young sons grope their way into a threatening world.

A Natural Woman

Murphy Brown was known for her love of singer Aretha Franklin. When she had her baby out of wedlock—amidst national consternation stirred up by Vice President Dan Quayle—Murphy held the infant and quietly sang the words to a familiar Franklin song, "You make me feel like a natural woman." But on *Homicide*, the definition of a natural woman was broadened significantly by Ami Brabson in the role of Mary Pembleton.

Mary Pembleton debuted in the penultimate episode of season 1, "And the Rockets' Dead Glare." Frank has been offered a promotion to shift commander. Mary and Frank meet at a fine restaurant where Frank says, "We can't afford this place." Mary leans in and appeals softly to Frank's sense of social justice: "Don't take the job because of the money; take the job because of the job. This is an enormous honor that's been offered to you. A detective as young as you, a man of color. Think of the good you could do getting things done your way." But Frank declines the offer.

In "Partners" (episode 312), Frank turns in his badge to protest his being dragged into a political scandal involving the police commissioner and the commissioner's gay lover. This provides the writers with an opportunity to place Frank at home. Although these are fleeting glimpses, the pictures and exchanges between Frank and Mary are rich with social meaning.

Their townhouse is immaculate, with white walls and gleaming appliances in the small kitchen. Frank is washing dishes. Mary scurries in to report that she will be late due to a cocktail party after work. She wears a fetching red dress. Her hair is done in tiny braids that delicately frame her pretty face. She is putting on earrings and a necklace. The couple engages in the household patter typical of any working family.

The scene establishes Mary and Frank Pembleton as a solid, working, middle-class African American couple; Mary usually does the cooking, but this does not interfere with her professional or social life. She and Frank trust one another to be with members of the opposite sex in social settings, can afford modern conveniences, and can speak frankly about differences of opinion.

The disappointing aspect, in terms of portrayals of black professionals, also relates to its strength as a cultural message. Mary and her husband are shown in routine situations—like any American couple. As *Homicide* is a crime drama, the home scene is used for comic relief and only slightly to reveal back-story about one of the main characters. Although the portrayal of Mary Pembleton is of a strong, professional, witty, and beautiful black wife, it flashes by too quickly to have the kind of powerful social impact that an Archie and Edith Bunker had in *All in the Family* or to reveal the texture and intricacies of a white domestic couple, as interpreted by Paul and Jamie Buchman in *Mad About You*. The same can be said of prime-time dramas that aired at the same time as *Homicide*, such as *Picket Fences* or *Sisters*, which, despite their quirky styles and uneven audience ratings, offered a broader forum for white domesticity.

The intimacy of Frank and Mary is developed further in "The Gas Man" (episode 320). Bruno Kirby guest stars as Victor in this tale about a released convict imprisoned six years for knowingly installing a faulty furnace in a family's home. Frank Pembleton investigated and Victor was convicted of manslaughter. On the day Victor is released, he pledges to his hapless partner to kill Pembleton, but first he stalks the couple.

Frank appears in a bathrobe at his front door, searching for the morning newspaper. Moments later, Frank and Mary emerge dressed for work, enjoy a quick smooch, and head off in separate cars, with the criminal tailing Frank.

Later in the day, Frank rushes from the precinct office, late for an appointment, which we learn is a rendezvous with Mary at a local hotel. Mary opens the door wearing a black negligee and drags Frank inside. He emerges with a sperm sample in a plastic container, which he rushes to a fertility clinic. His sperm count is low.

Victor toys with Pembleton. He sneaks into his townhouse and opens a gas valve on the stove, which Frank discovers before turning in. Next, the villain stalks Mary, showing up in a market. He helps her with an awkward bag and pre-tends to be an arson detective. He compliments her beauty. Before he leaves, he tells Mary that if she cannot conceive, she can always adopt, which she finds very troubling: Why would he know about their difficulty conceiving?

Then Mary calls Frank to report she found all the gas valves on the stove open and a message on the answering machine from Victor. Frank orders her to remain home with police protection and goes off to confront the caller. But Frank is ambushed and held at knife-point by Victor, who, ultimately, cannot do the deed and breaks down crying on Frank's shoulder.

Mary Pembleton continued to make appearances in *Homicide* episodes through season 6, more to add texture to Frank's character than to raise her visibility. In "The Wedding" (episode 420), about Detective Meldrick Lewis's (Clark Johnson) whirlwind marriage, Mary goes into labor with her first child during the reception. In subsequent episodes, the baby serves as a prop or object of philosophical conversations between Frank and his partner, Tim, about their lives and jobs.

Then Frank has a debilitating stroke ("Work Related," episode 422). The incident and recovery naturally involve Mary to a greater extent than in earlier episodes, and she becomes more of a presence each week, especially throughout season 5. Mary is the precinct's connection to Frank, answering calls about his recovery. She bears the brunt of Frank's frustration over his infirmities.

Trouble begins after Frank returns to duty ("Diener," episode 514). Lying sleepily next to Mary, Frank is tired but satisfied to be back on the job. Mary tries to share the news that baby Olivia is learning to play peek-a-boo. When Frank dozes, Mary releases pent-up resentment, telling Frank that she wants them to see a marriage counselor. Frank replies, deflecting the problem to his wife, "OK, sweetie, if you're upset, I guess you should talk to somebody." The next morning, Frank knots his tie and tries to engage Olivia in peek-a-boo, to no avail.

These few seconds of telefilm speak volumes about social progress for African Americans. More than three decades after "Who Do You Kill?" on *East Side/West Side*, we see another black couple raising an infant in an urban environment. Only now, the room is bright, warm, and filled with a delicate lullaby playing in the background; the child is adorable, loved, and safe with two working parents who, despite some rocky moments, are solidly married and trying to work out disagreements.

From our privileged position inside a marriage counselor's office ("Valentine's Day," episode 516), we learn the kind of intimate details about an American couple that make television compelling. Frank originally met Mary in New York City, while playing volleyball (notably not basketball, thus avoiding a racial stereotype) with friends. She was with a group of her friends when he fell into her potato salad, which apparently was quite delicious. "That first moment, when she was wiping the potato salad off my face," says Frank, "I knew." They had a spiritual bond in addition to a physical attraction. . . .

The next episode, "Kaddish," is about redemption, not just for Frank but also for John Munch, a Jew who participates in the mourning prayer recited after the death of a relative. (Munch honors the death of a childhood sweetheart.) Frank tries to rebuild bridges with his partner Bayliss and by returning to morning Mass. He recalls the moment in an old case when he lost his faith in God. But he also remembers that his definition of faith then was tied to his devoted love for his wife. His epiphany clears the way for reconciliation.

Because the series is about homicide detectives and stars Andre Braugher, it stands to reason that storylines would develop Frank Pembleton's character with more depth than his spouse. But this particular storyline involved the personal family life of Frank, Mary, and their children, born and unborn, and became an ongoing opportunity to feature a middle-class couple, who happen to be African American, with all the legitimacy that other couples have enjoyed on television since its inception. It was the first time that American television viewers got to know a black woman in a dramatic series over six seasons and to see her as an equal partner with her male spouse—a natural woman for reasons other than bearing a child. . . .

African American Women Finally Make the Opening Credits

Black women appeared in prominent roles in *Homicide* from the outset of the series, most notable being Adena Watson and Mary Pembleton. In season 3, actress Gloria Reuben—who later held a starring role in NBC's hospital drama

ER—guest starred in a trilogy based on the shootings of three homicide cops. Reuben played sex-crimes detective Teresa Walker in a role that capitalized on her attractiveness but, more important, on her professionalism as a skilled cop.

The fifth season of *Homicide* established another advancement for black women with the frequent appearance of Detective Terri Stivers (played by Toni Lewis). If Stivers is not the focal point of many episodes, she remains an important televised character. She fits in, gets along with her co-workers, and is competent. Ultimately, she is a cop with a conscience. Stivers teams with Detective Lewis to investigate a series of drug-related deaths possibly linked to the sinister, oleaginous villain Luther Mahoney.

In "Deception" (episode 519), Lewis, Stivers, and Kellerman, the only white detective of the three, corner the black drug lord Luther Mahoney. But when Mahoney lowers his weapon, Kellerman executes him. During the course of several episodes, this scenario leads to a violent spree that terrorizes Baltimore and the police department. It is Stivers who finally musters the courage to cross the "blue line" when she discloses to her lieutenant, Giardello, that the shoot was not clean, which leads to Kellerman's dismissal. Absolved, Stivers takes front stage in the seventh season when she appears in the opening credits.

Also joining the cast is Michael Michele as Detective Rene Sheppard, a beautiful African American woman with fine features, fair complexion, and Miss America good looks. In the final season, the opening credits featured five black regulars: two women, including Michele, and three men. There was praise in African American studies for the arrival of Michael Michele in a lead role. But it is a stretch to interpret her appearance as an advance. Instead, the cast and show makeover for season 7 have more in common with the ABC series *NYPD Blue* than with the original *Homicide: Life on the Street*, suggesting the changes were intended to raise ratings rather than uplift the art.

When Sheppard joins the homicide police, the male detectives line up to court her (season 7, episode 101). But Sheppard is intent on making the grade as a homicide detective.

In "Shades of Gray" (episode 710), detectives Lewis and Sheppard approach the house of a witness. Lewis goes to the rear, leaving Sheppard alone in front. The subject emerges, Sheppard pulls her gun, and the man takes her weapon and beats her savagely. She recovers, and Lewis makes a dramatic stand in a local bar, demanding that his partner's weapon be returned, which it is. But Lewis's apparent loyalty to his partner is suspect. In subsequent stories, he is reluctant to team up with another woman or to take Sheppard back out on a case. It is not until the series finale, episode 722, "Forgive Us Our Trespasses," that Lewis invites Sheppard to join him on a call, after Sheppard asserts that she will not let his distrust of her interfere with doing her job.

Then, just before the series ended, *Homicide* presented an episode on street gangs involving young black girls. In "The Why Chromosome" (episode 721), Sheppard invites Laura Ballard to investigate a gang-related killing. An adolescent girl is found dead on the steps of a school; the name "Destiny" tattooed on her arm. This scenario provides a textured display of beliefs, attitudes, skin colors, and lifestyles among black women and girls—a significant departure from the one-dimensional black women seen in situation comedies.

As in "Every Mother's Son," the victim comes from a stable home. We see three daughters ranging in age from a four- or five-year-old to two teenagers, Destiny and her tough sister Crystal. A religious cross rests on the fireplace mantle. The home is neat. The children have ample possessions and wardrobe. The problems visiting this black family stem from outside—from the culture and the streets.

Ballard and Sheppard canvass the neighborhood but are stonewalled. Finally, they find Crystal in a fast-food eatery and learn that Crystal has a wicked attitude: Her father had burned her with cigarettes; she suffered scarring injuries from attacks by rival gangs, was initiating Destiny into her gang, and has no need for these cops. These are hardened street kids who talk of "bitches" and "ho's" with every breath. They have lost all civilized feeling. They are toughened survivors who feel justified in using any means necessary to fend off rival gangs and abusive men—not white people but people of their own race and community.

Through a rush of action and locker-room dialogue between Ballard and Sheppard, we learn that Destiny had been sent to infiltrate the rival gang by seducing Casper. Casper's girlfriend, Denise, the mother of his two-year-old child, learns of the rendezvous. She makes up her face as a boy, dons the orange colors of the rival gang, and kills Destiny. Crystal figures out what happened and kills Denise.

This episode illustrates the decay in urban neighborhoods, evidenced by the abuse and involvement of women in violent daily life, and also shows that Sheppard and Ballard can solve a murder case without the help of male detectives. In typical *Homicide* documentary-like fashion, however, "The Why Chromosome" comments on real-life urban problems, in this case the expansion of the criminal population to include young girls. But Sheppard's character, unlike African American women in previous episodes—namely Mary Pembleton, Mary Nawls, Terri Stivers, Teresa Walker, and others—is more of a beautiful mouthpiece than an agent of change.

Shades of Black on *Homicide: Life on the Street*

Compared with *East Side/West Side*, we see tremendous progress in how *Homicide: Life on the Street* involved all races and ethnicities in its depictions of urban America. By comparing the *East Side/West Side* episode "Who Do You Kill?" with several installments of *Homicide*, in which Frank and Mary lived in a comfortable home, enjoyed two paychecks, made future plans, and could protect their baby, we finally see cultural evidence of the eradication of the real-life scourges of Jim Crow policies that caused such lopsided social damage to African Americans.

We also see progress when we compare *Homicide* with the 1970s ABC police comedy *Barney Miller*, which took on issues of racial injustice with levity, instead of the documentary feeling of the drama. *Homicide* is *Barney Miller* with edge and attitude. Both shows presented an ethnic melange of Jews,

Puerto Ricans, Italian Americans, African Americans, Irish Americans, WASPs, men, and women. *Barney Miller,* airing on the heels of civil rights victories and amidst the country's exploration of integration, showed us what we could become and how we would have to deal with racial change. *Homicide* showed us what we have become thirty years after the Civil Rights Act of 1964—a classist society making progress in race relations but paying dearly with the lives of young people. It showed a crime-ridden society in which an absence of physical security and economic equality traps African Americans by the circumstances of their births and exacerbates, rather than assuages, human suffering.

With advances on television came retreats. The African American women who made regular appearances on *Homicide* were able to shine or come into their own in some episodes. But none achieved the prominence and richness of character development of Frank Pembleton (a black male), Tim Bayliss (a white male), or many of the other featured characters. Still, in the context of African American studies of portrayals of race on television, *Homicide* is an important show with mostly positive contributions to equality of representation of American culture.

The series premiered in January 1993 and lasted seven seasons on NBC, appearing Fridays at 10 p.m. After its first run, the series went into syndication on Lifetime—which explains, in part, the increased visibility of women in later episodes—and Court TV. It currently runs on Book TV in Canada. The first three seasons and a few episodes of later seasons have been released on DVD or are available on videotape. For those able to view the entire series, they will find a wide range of African American women more representative of real life than is typical for television characters: black women who are trustworthy with men and children, able to commiserate with one another, care about their fellow human beings, and respect black men. They are free to disagree with whites, as well as about integration, and can rise above racism. They are intelligent and gifted, sometimes make mistakes, have varying skin color, socialize with other women and men outside the workplace, and are worthy of compassion and capable of rendering the same.

In short, *Homicide: Life on the Street* obliterates the idea of a single, static image of the African American woman and paints America with a full range of colors and textures. Through its documentary origins and style, the series supplanted the decline in network television documentaries that previously had paid attention to social issues. Through its sensitive casting—in front of and behind the camera—it provided opportunities for African Americans to have vital input in the creative process, building on the gains of *Frank's Place,* which lasted only one season on CBS in 1987. . . .

Janis Sanchez-Hucles, Patrick S. Hudgins, and Kimberly Gamble  **NO**

Reflection and Distortion: Women of Color in Magazine Advertisements

A White mother and daughter stare at a showcase featuring two Asian mannequins dressed in skin-tight, short, and provocative spandex outfits; Daisy Fuentes is featured with a caption explaining boldly that she is not pregnant but she takes multivitamins, as if it is novel for a Latina to be not pregnant when taking multivitamins; ads with African American women show them advertising oversized pantyhose and shopping at discount stores; Native American women are absent from all ads.

The media are active in both reflecting and distorting the lives of people of color. What is reflected is the United States' ongoing difficulty in dealing with race in inclusive and sensitive ways. Race and ethnicity issues are often distorted because the voice or perspective of the media typically represents a majority standpoint rather than the voices and perspectives of people of color. Media portrayals of people of color both reflect and shape social perceptions. Often these images are distorted because they reflect biased and limited views. Sometimes this distortion is accidental and innocuous, but in other cases it is purposeful and harmful. This [selection] is designed to emphasize the importance the media play in supporting societal norms and standards. We demonstrate how magazine ads in particular continue to stereotype, limit, and distort women of color in ways that can be negative to how these women are perceived by themselves and others.

Women of color continue to be the most marginalized group in magazine ad representations despite changing attitudes about women and racial ethnic groups. This relative invisibility unfortunately reflects the low status they are accorded in the wider society with respect to their economic, political, and social clout. Many majority theorists have ignored research aimed at women of color, and often too few women of color in academic circles are willing or able to advance this area of scholarship. Research suggests that the journalistic workforce is 87.5% European American and 69% male.

Research has also repeatedly shown that the media have a profound impact on how individuals understand, relate, and code information. Media sources have the potential to offer effective and positive portrayals of the diverse individuals that comprise society in their role as potent socializing mechanisms. Ads can influence perceptions and create self-fulfilling prophecies by contributing to stereotypes, prejudices, and societal inequities. Specifically, advertisements have been identified as one of the most significant factors impacting society. It has been estimated that more than 184 billion ads are shown daily in newspapers and 6 billion ads appear in monthly magazines. In magazines, ads comprise 52% of the content.

Content analyses of advertisements have historically focused on gender biases relating to the lives of middle-income white females. Advertisements stereotyped these women as housewives, incapable of decision making or responsibility, dependent, decorative, and in need of male attention.

The feminist movement has been credited with moving women out of the home and into the outside world of work. However, bias continues with regard to women being more likely than men to be portrayed in decorative and sexually provocative ads.

Content analyses that have focused on race and ethnicity have consistently shown underrepresentation of these groups relative to their population. Ads have historically portrayed people of color in subservient roles and jobs unless they were in athletics or entertainment. Scholars have found continued evidence of stereotypes for African Americans with these individuals depicted as athletes and entertainers and in need of charity from others. African Americans have been the focus of inquiry more so than other groups and have been seen in magazine ads in greater numbers than other groups.

It appears that just as the feminist movement led to some amelioration of bias for women, the civil rights movement helped increase the representation of minorities and decreased some of the racial biases. A host of researchers believe, however, that the battle of end racial bias was stalled in the 1990s. The obvious racism of icons such as Aunt Jemima and Frito Bandito ended, but advertising is still largely a segregated business. Although the percentage of ethnic minorities portrayed in magazines has increased since the 1950s, there has never been accurate representation. This poor lack of representation is surprising because research has shown that using diverse ethnic minorities in ads does not have any adverse impact on majority members' use of advertised products. It is also ironic that by not being more inclusive, magazine advertising may be limiting its potential markets in today's increasingly diverse society. . . .

Only recently have researchers looked at the intersection of race and gender for individuals of color. Plous and Neptune, in their 1997 study of racial and gender bias for Whites and African Americans in magazine ads, examined fashion-oriented ads from six magazines from 1985 to 1994. During this period, they found an increase from past levels in the number of African American females featured in fashion ads in women's magazines. African American women, however, were significantly more likely to be portrayed as exotic, as predatory, and in animal prints, and both races of females were more likely than men to be shown in sexually provocative and revealing attire such as lingerie or bathing suits.

For the purpose of our research, we have adapted Plous and Neptune's 1997 methodology to look at portrayals of women of color in female and family-oriented magazines. Plous and Neptune's 1997 methodology was used because it was the only other study that had a similar focus of inquiry. Like

Plous and Neptune, we examined the content and possible messages of magazine ads. We developed a typology of categories based on content that emerged from the data and that in many cases overlapped with the categories of Plous and Neptune. We wished to explore basic questions about the representation of women of color in majority versus ethnic magazines. Our specific goals were to investigate the following research questions:

1. What are the percentages of women of color ads in majority versus ethnic magazines?
2. Are there differences in the ad focus for majority versus ethnic magazines?
3. Are there differences in how women of color are portrayed in majority ads versus ethnic magazine ads?

. . . We conducted a content analysis of six female or family-oriented magazines: *Family Circle, Cosmopolitan, Filipinas, Ebony, Essence,* and *Latin Girl.* . . .

Examination of three issues of the six magazines revealed a total of 453 ads. *Cosmopolitan* accounted for 154 ads; *Ebony,* 91; *Essence,* 114; *Family Circle,* 39; *Filipina,* 22; and *Latin Girl* 33. The total numbers of people pictured in these 453 ads were 830 people with 588 female (71 %) and 242 (29%) male. Of the total ads, 43% depicted women of color; 23%, men of color; 27%, female European Americans; 7%, male European Americans; and 0.7%, racially ambiguous females that the coders could not agree on and therefore were coded as "indeterminate female." . . .

As some of these magazines obviously target female readers, many of these magazines have high percentages of female ads (ads that feature females). The two exceptions are *Filipina* and *Ebony.* In *Filipina,* the majority of ads include both males and females. In *Ebony,* there is a more diverse distribution across ad categories, and this publication features the highest percentage of men in its ads. It is striking that no Native American women were depicted in any of the ads and only one Native American male was observed. . . .

Percentages of Women of Color in Ads in Majority and Ethnic Magazines

Ethnicity	Cosmopolitan	Family Circle	Latin Girl	Filipina	Essence	Ebony
European American	82	84	5	9	8	7
African American	10	11	7	2	86	90
Latin American	4	6	64	0	4	3
Asian American	3	0	0	89	2	0
Native American	0	0	0	0	0	0
Indeterminate	1	0	24	0	0	0

Clothes are among the top five categories for all magazines except *Filipinas* where this category is not included and *Ebony* where the percentage is only 3%. Both *Cosmopolitan* and *Essence,* which are aimed at younger female audiences, show the greatest diversity of products. *Latin Girl* is unique in having 12% of its ads focusing on education and careers; other publications do not emphasize these areas.

There were some interesting gender differences in ad portrayals. . . . Differences across gender were seen in ads for cigarettes, alcohol, automobiles, and clothing. In the ads portraying cigarettes, alcohol, and automobiles, there was more use of ads featuring both males and females. In the ads featuring cigarettes, half were of women only and half were of both men and women with no ads of men only. Of the alcohol ads, 27% featured women, 17% featured men, and 56% had both men and women. In the category of automobile ads, 35% featured men only, versus 24% with females only and 41% with males and females. In contrast, clothing ads focused heavily on women.

In what appears to be a continuation of a historical theme, all of the ethnic magazines except *Filipina* included entertainment ads whereas only one of the two majority magazines included this category and at a lower percentage than the ethnic magazines. A racial difference can also be seen in the distribution of ads for cigarettes and alcohol. Two of the three magazines that advertised both cigarettes and alcohol were the African American magazines and Blacks were featured in the majority ads as well. Perhaps it is not surprising to observe that the two African American magazines also had the lowest percentage of medical and health ads.

. . . In an attempt to assess the potential sexualization of ads, body exposure, body positioning, and clothing were also documented. The majority of ads had no or minimal body exposure. *Essence* and *Cosmopolitan* depicted the highest percentages of body exposure and *Filipina* showed the least body exposure. . . .

How Women of Color Are Portrayed in Majority Magazines

Despite the fact that women of color are typically underrepresented in majority magazines, images of these women still function to disproportionately portray them as exotic and in stereotyped ways, and they are used to advertise less socially desirable products. For example, although the European American magazine *Family Circle* did not use any ads featuring Asian women, it featured an ad with a mother and child staring at two Asian mannequins in a store window who were dressed in revealing and provocative dressy spandex outfits. This portrayal fits the all-too-familiar stereotype of sexuality, passivity, and availability that Asian American women are often placed in, and it also fetishes them as objects. Other examples of how women of color were portrayed in majority magazines include the following:

- One magazine shows an African American female cooking a turkey with a European American female offering help or instruction by proffering a baking bag;
- In one majority magazine, an African American woman is used to advertise plus-size pantyhose;
- An African American female is used in one majority magazine ad to promote shopping at Wal-Mart because "the everyday low prices are very affordable";

- Women of color are more frequently featured in majority magazines to advertise beauty products for damaged hair;
- Individual women of color and groups of individuals of color feature disproportionately in cigarette and alcohol ads;
- There is only one ad on birth control in all the ads studied, and it features women of color; and
- There were no ads featuring Native Americans.

How Women of Color Are Portrayed in Ethnic Magazines

Ethnic magazines focus on one group of ethnic women and underrepresent majority women and ethnic women who are not in their group. Women of color are more likely to be portrayed with men in ethnic magazines than in majority magazines, and there are higher percentages of males in these magazines. Part of the explanation for this may relate to the fact that both *Filipina* and *Ebony* target more of a family readership, whereas the other magazines have more of a female focus. Despite the fact that more men and couples are seen in ethnic ads, only one interracial couple was shown in all of the ads, and this occurred in one of the black magazines. This suggests some continuing discomfort with portraying interracial relationships. . . .

There appeared to be some competing themes in ethnic magazines. On the one hand, models showed somewhat more diversity in size, especially in African American magazines. This appears to suggest some healthy resistance to using only super-thin models as is often seen in majority publications. It also appears that minority magazines show a diversity of appearances and no longer focus only on lighter skinned and more anglicized-looking models. However, there also seems to be a very subtle but intransigent adherence to White beauty standards as well. In ethnic magazines women are exhorted to change their appearance by straightening or texturing their apparently unruly hair, lightening or covering up their skin, and generally conforming to the flawless appearance of models. The fact that ethnic magazines show a diversity of colors but also pay allegiance to white beauty standards suggests ambivalence in advertising messages from a racial identity development perspective. It is positive that magazine ads feature more Afrocentric-looking models but there are vestiges of perhaps a realistic reminder that White females continue to epitomize what society deems to be beautiful. . . .

Conclusions

Bias, stereotypes, and mixed messages appear to be alive and well in magazine ads. Ethnic women are still underrepresented based on their population in majority publications. Only African American females have come close to achieving proportionate representation in the majority magazines examined. It is striking to note that Native American females were not depicted at all in any of the ads. It appears that the paucity of this population group and their

broad dispersion across the United States makes them an insignificant consumer market to advertisers. Hence, they are ignored.

Despite the low representation of women of color in majority magazines, they are still portrayed in ads that are sexual or exotic or that show
them advertising less socially desirable products. It is stunning to see that
magazine ads still show such biases toward women of color. The goal of advertising is to appeal to consumers, and yet advertisers are insensitive to the
increasing numbers of ethnic women and the expanded financial markets that
these women represent. Some researchers have noted that many ethnic minority
women should be considered prime consumers because they make major
financial decisions in their families.

Because ethnic women also buy and are exposed to the ads of majority
magazines, it is long overdue for these publications to make more accurate
representations of these women. Given the power of the media, men, women,
and children of all races should not be exposed to ethnic women in ads that
disproportionately associate them with less socially desirable products such as
alcohol, in need of help for damaged hair, or dependent on advice for cooking
or finding low-budget stores. These images reinforce negative stereotypes. Furthermore, researchers have consistently noted that because of the widespread
segregation of people's social lives, most of what people learn about other
races comes from the media and not personal experiences. . . .

POSTSCRIPT

Are Representations of African-American Women in Media Accurate?

Whenever issues of race or gender are discussed, it is important to ask, What are the consequences of long-term exposure to media messages? This question leads naturally to another essential question: What are the unintended consequences of television viewing, or consuming any type of media, including advertising? And perhaps most importantly, how do matters of race, gender, and social class give us a sense of others in contemporary society?

One avenue to explore these questions would be to look at who creates the media images. It is true that there are now more African Americans who work in the television industry than in the 1980s, but at the same time, many of the magazines cited in the second selection are owned or controlled by persons of color. Why then, can we see more positive, realistic portrayals and scripts for women in television, than in the images represented in minority-owned magazines? This raises yet another important question: Was *Homicide: Life on the Street* unusual, or was it a turning point in television that supported other stronger images for African-American women today?

There are a number of excellent books and articles on these topics that would help expand your knowledge about these issues. Clint C. Wilson and Felix Gutierrez published *Minorities in the Media: Diversity and the End of Mass Communication* (Sage Publications, 1985), in which they examine how African Americans, Native Americans, Latinos, and Asians have been portrayed. Herman Gray has written about the hidden patterns that undermine equality in *Watching Race: Television and the Struggle for the Sign of Blackness* (University of Minnesota Press, 1997). In his influential 2001 book, *Primetime Blues: African Americans on Network Television*, Donald Bogle showed that African-American characters on television often provided a distorted picture of the African-American population, particularly in comedies.

There are many studies of how women are portrayed in media, including Naomi Wolf's impressive tome, *The Beauty Myth* (William Morrow, 1991, 2002), which addresses how these images result in attitudes and behaviors for both women and men in society. Susan J. Douglas' *Where the Girls Are: Growing Up Female with the Mass Media* (Three Rivers Press, 1994) deals with images that have specifically come from media.

Some recent articles on the topic include Rhea Sengupta's "Reading Representations of Black, East Asian, and White Women in Magazines for Adolescent Girls," *Sex Roles* (vol. 54, 2006, pp. 799–808); and Megan E. Williams' "The *Crisis* Cover Girl: Lena Horne, the NAACP, and Representations of African

American Femininity, 1941–1945," *American Periodicals* (vol. 16, 2006, pp. 200–218). Finally, Marian Meyers', "African American Women and Violence: Gender, Race, and Class in the News," *Critical Studies in Mass Communication* (vol. 21, June 2004, pp. 95–118) sheds important light on how African-American women are portrayed in a form of media that purports to reflect reality, but still typifies problematic portrayals of race, gender, and class.

Internet References . . .

Advertising Age

The Web site of *Advertising Age* magazine provides access to articles and features about media advertising, such as the history of television advertising.

http://adage.com

Advertising World

This site is maintained by the Advertising Department of the University of Texas and contains links to material on a variety of advertising topics and issues.

http://advertising.utexas.edu/world/index.asp

Peabody Archives, University of Georgia

Since 1941, the University of Georgia Grady College has been home to the Peabody Awards, which recognize the best of broadcast programming. This archive of winners features news, entertainment, educational, children's, and documentary programming.

http://www.peabody.uga.edu

Television News Archive, Vanderbilt University

Singe 1968, the Television News Archive has systematically recorded, abstracted, and indexed national television newscasts. This database is the guide to the Vanderbilt University collection of network television news programs.

http://tvnews.vanderbilt.edu

The Copyright Web Site

A commercial site with extensive copyright information. The digital URL listed below follows the current digital legal controversies in Internet, Web, and software. Specialized information for movie, television, and other outlets is available also on the site.

http://www.benedict.com/Digital/Digital.aspx

A Question of Content

*W*e no longer live in a world in which all of our media are directed toward mass audiences. Today we have both mass media and personal media, like videogames, iPods, and cell phones. Because people use media content in very different ways, and so much of how we make sense of media depends on our own ages and life experiences, the issue of media content that is appropriate for certain audiences takes on a new importance. In this section we deal with issues that often influence people from all ages, ethnic groups, and all walks of life—but the questions for discussion become more pointed when we consider that different audiences may perceive different things in the content of some forms of media. In this section we examine some specific aspects of using media for a sense of identity and belonging. We conclude with an issue that addresses some of the most fundamental questions about one industry that is sure to spark debate.

- Do Video Games Encourage Violent Behavior?
- Do Copyright Laws Protect Ownership of Intellectual Property?
- Is Advertising Good for Society?

ISSUE 4

Do Video Games Encourage Violent Behavior?

YES: Craig A. Anderson, from Prepared Statement to the Hearing Before the Committee on Commerce, Science, and Transportation of the United States Senate (March 21, 2000)

NO: *The Economist* Staff Writer, from "Chasing the Dream," *The Economist* (August 6, 2005)

ISSUE SUMMARY

YES: On March 21, 2000, the U.S. Congress held a hearing (106-1096) on "The Impact of Interactive Violence on Children." Among the several witnesses testifying before the committee, Dr. Craig A. Anderson provided one of the most persuasive arguments on the impact and effect of violent video games. An expert on the effect of violence in television and film, Dr. Anderson holds the position that video games prompt young people toward even more aggression and violence than do other media content.

NO: A special report in the British magazine *The Economist* discusses research that indicates that not only is there a generational divide among those who play video games, but the lack of long-term research limits what is actually known about the effects of playing video games. Citing a number of different studies about the moral impact of gaming and the skills necessary to play, this position argues that the issue of violence and aggression will pass as the critics age.

In recent years the subject of the effect of video games has joined television, film, and recorded music as a topic that provokes strong reactions among individuals who feel that some content may encourage violent, or at least aggressive behavior among young people. While there is less concern about how any type of content affects adults, most of the controversy deals with how children, adolescents, teens and young adults use controversial media content. The underlying reason for this is that younger users are assumed to have a lesser sense of moral responsibility and judgment about the relationship of media content and reality.

Even though the video game industry voluntarily rates the content of video games (as does the motion picture, television, and recording industries), many parents and critics of media violence feel that video games are a unique form of entertainment that warrants special consideration. Since the games are often played alone, on personal devices, consoles, or computers, the video game user's interaction with the game is interactive and direct. The sophistication of computer graphics have produced images that look even more realistic than ever before. The controversy became especially heated during the summer of 2005 when "Grand Theft Auto" was released and found to contain some hidden sex scenes.

The selections chosen to represent controversial views for this issue both cite evidence of research studies that have different conclusions. This raises important problems for us, as readers. How do we decide which studies to believe? How do we weigh the evidence and the credibility of the authors of differing studies? How much of our own experience informs the way we think about some of these types of issues?

As you'll see in Dr. Anderson's statement to the Congressional Committee, he is a person who has dedicated his professional life to understanding the relationship of media content and violence/aggression. He cites research studies that have been amassed over many years that unmistakenly correlate violent and aggressive behavior with children and young people who engage in media content that represents violence and aggression as a behavioral norm. And, even though he agrees that very violent video games really came to the market in the 1990s, and that the specific research findings geared toward these media are sparse, and tend to focus on short-term research rather than long-term studies, he makes a persuasive case about how previous studies for other forms of media do affect individuals' personalities.

The Special Report in *The Economist* takes a broader sociological view of video games and how they are used by different age groups. This selection considers a wider scope of video games, from the violent ones to those that take intense concentration and teach valuable skills. But here, the evidence cited regarding violence and aggression is reported to be "inconclusive." This position is indeed due in part to the desire of the video game industry to broaden appeal to the widest number of users possible, but it also reflects on the specific issue under consideration.

As you consider the evidence provided by the two positions on this issue, how do you formulate your own position? If you were a parent would you see things differently? Are video games different from any other form of traditional media content?

YES

Craig A. Anderson

The Impact of Interactive Violence on Children

Prepared Statement of Dr. Craig A. Anderson, Iowa State University, Department of Psychology, Ames, Iowa

Distinguished Senators, ladies, and gentlemen. I am Craig Anderson, Professor of Psychology and Chair of the Department of Psychology at Iowa State University. I have studied human behavior for over 25 years. My first research publication, in 1979, concerned one potential contributing factor in the outbreak of riots. My first publication on video game violence appeared in 1987. Next month, the American Psychological Association will publish a new research article on video games and violence that I wrote with a colleague of mine (Karen Dill). The article will appear in the Journal of Personality and Social Psychology, the premier scientific outlet for research in social and personality phenomena. I recently wrote the "Human Aggression and Violence" articles for both the Encyclopedia of Psychology and the Encyclopedia of Sociology.

I am very happy to be here to speak with you today about the problems of exposing people, especially young people, to interactive violence, that is, violent video games. Though there are many complexities in this realm of behavioral research, there is one clear and simple message that parents, educators, and public policy makers such as yourselves need to hear: Playing violent video games can cause increases in aggression and violence.

A second message to take away from my report is also very important: There are good reasons to expect that the effects of exposure to violent video games on subsequent aggressive behavior will be even greater than the well-documented effects of exposure to violent television and movies. I'll return to this point in moment.

TV & Movie Violence: Facts & Relevance

But first, I want to highlight some facts concerning TV and movie violence, many of which were reported to a Senate hearing last year by Professor Rowell Huesmann of the University of Michigan.

Statement to the Committee on Commerce, Science, and Transportation, United States Senate, March 21, 2000.

Fact 1.   Exposure to violent TV and movies causes increases in aggression and violence.

Fact 2.   These effects are of two kinds: short term and long term. The short term effect is that aggression increases immediately after viewing a violent TV show or movie, and lasts for at least 20 minutes. The long term effect is that repeated exposure to violent TV and movies increases the violence-proneness of the person watching such shows. In essence, children who watch a lot of violent shows become more violent as adults than they would have become had they not been exposed to so much TV and movie violence.

Fact 3.   Both the long term and the short term effects occur to both boys and girls.

Fact 4.   The effects of TV and movie violence on aggression are not small. Indeed, the media violence effect on aggression is bigger than the effect of exposure to lead on IQ scores in children, the effect of calcium intake on bone mass, the effect of homework on academic achievement, or the effect of asbestos exposure on cancer.

Why consider the TV and movie violence research literature when discussing video game violence? There are three main reasons. First, the psychological processes underlying TV and movie violence effects on aggression are also at work when people play video games. The similarities between exposure to TV violence and exposure to video game violence are so great that ignoring the TV violence literature would be foolish. Second, the research literature on TV violence effects is vast, whereas the research literature on video game violence is small. Researchers have been investigating TV effects for over 40 years, but video games didn't even exist until the 1970s, and extremely violent video games didn't emerge until the early 1990s. Third, because the TV/movie violence research literature is so mature there has been ample time to answer early criticisms of the research with additional research designed to address the criticisms. Thus, the various shoot-from-the-hip criticisms and myths created by those with a vested interest in creating and selling various kinds of violent entertainment media have been successfully tested and debunked. I'll describe some of the more popular ones in a few moments.

Video Game Violence: Scope & Research

Now, let's consider facts derived from the relatively small research literature that is specifically focused on video games.

Fact 1.   Video games are consuming a larger amount of time every year. Virtually all children now play video games. The average 7th grader is playing electronic games at least 4 hours per week, and about half of those games are violent. Even though number of hours spent playing video games tends to decline in the high school and college years, a significant portion of students are playing quite a few video games. In 1998 3.3% of men entering public universities in the United States reported playing video games more than 15 hours per week in their senior year in high school. In 1999 that percentage jumped to a full 4%.

Fact 2.   Young people who play lots of violent video games behave more violently than those who do not. For example, in the most recent study of this type exposure to video game violence during late adolescence accounted for 13–22% of the variance in violent behaviors committed by this sample of people. By way of comparison, smoking accounts for about 14% of lung cancer variance.

Fact 3.   Experimental studies have shown that playing a violent video game causes an increase in aggressive thinking. For example, in one study young college students were randomly assigned the task of playing a violent video game (Marathon 2) or a nonviolent game (Glider Pro). Later, they were given a list of partially completed words, such as mu   er. They were asked to fill in the blanks as quickly as possible. Some of the partial words could form either an aggressive word (murder) or a nonaggressive word (mutter). Those who had played the violent game generated 43% more aggressive completions than those who had played a nonviolent game.

Fact 4.   Experimental studies have shown that playing a violent video game causes an increase in retaliatory aggression. For example, in one study participants were randomly assigned to play either a violent game (Wolfenstein 3D) or a nonviolent game (Myst). Shortly afterwards, they received a series of mild provocations and were given an opportunity to retaliate aggressively. Those who had played the violent game retaliated at a 17% higher rate than those who had played the nonviolent game.

Fact 5.   Experimental and correlational studies have shown that playing violent video games leads to a decrease in prosocial (helping) behaviors.

Why Media Violence Increases Aggression & Violence

Why does exposure to violent media increase aggression and violence? There are several different ways in which watching or playing violent media can increase aggression and violence. The most powerful and long lasting involves learning processes. From infancy, humans learn how to perceive, interpret, judge, and respond to events in the physical and social environment. We learn by observing the world around us, and by acting on that world. We learn rules for how the social world works. We learn behavioral scripts and use them to interpret events and actions of others and to guide our own behavioral responses to those events. These various knowledge structures develop over time. They are based on the day-to-day observations of and interactions with other people, real (as in the family) and imagined (as in the mass media). Children who are exposed to a lot of violent media learn a number of lessons that change them into more aggressive people. They learn that there are lots of bad people out there who will hurt them. They come to expect others to be mean and nasty. They learn to interpret negative events that occur to them as intentional harm, rather than as a accidental mistake. They learn that the proper way to deal with such harm is to retaliate. Perhaps as importantly, they do not learn nonviolent solutions to interpersonal conflicts.

As these knowledge structures develop over time, they become more complex and difficult to change. In a sense, the developing personality is like slowly-hardening clay. Environmental experiences, including violent media, shape the clay. Changes are relatively easy to make at first, when the clay is soft, but later on changes become increasingly difficult. Longitudinal studies suggest that aggression-related knowledge structures begin to harden around age 8 or 9, and become more perseverant with increasing age.

The result of repeated exposure to violent scripts, regardless of source, can be seen in several different aspects of a person's personality. There is evidence that such exposure increases general feelings of hostility, thoughts about aggression and retaliation, suspicions about the motives of others, and expectations about how others are likely to deal with a potential conflict situation. Repeated exposure to violent media also reduces negative feelings that normally arise when observing someone else get hurt. In other words, people become desensitized to violence. Finally, exposure to violent media teaches people that aggressive retaliation is good and proper.

Violent Video Games vs. TV & Movies

Earlier, I said that there are good reasons to expect that violent interactive media will have an even stronger effect on aggression and violence than traditional forms of media violence such as TV and movies. These several reasons all involve differences between TV and video games that influence learning processes. The following four reasons all have considerable research support behind them, but have not yet been extensively investigated in the video game domain.

Reason 1. Identification with the aggressor increases imitation of the aggressor. In TV shows and movies there may be several characters with which an observer can identify, some of whom may not behave in a violent fashion. In most violent video games, the player must identify with one violent character. In "first person shooters," for instance, the player assumes the identity of the hero or heroine, and then controls that character's actions throughout the game. This commonly includes selection of weapons and target and use of the weapons to wound, maim, or kill the various enemies in the game environment. Common weapons include guns, grenades, chain saws and other cutting tools, cars and tanks, bombs, hands, and knives.

Reason 2. Active participation increases learning. The violent video game player is a much more active participant than is the violent TV show watcher. That alone may increase the effectiveness of the violent story lines in teaching the underlying retaliatory aggression scripts to the game player. Active participation is a more effective teaching tool in part because it requires attention to the material being taught.

Reason 3. Rehearsing an entire behavioral sequence is more effective than rehearsing only a part of it. The aggression script being rehearsed is more complete in a video game than in a TV show or movie. For example, the video game player must choose to aggress, and in essence rehearses this choice process, whereas the TV viewer does not have to make any such choices. Similarly, in video games the player must carry out the violent action, unlike the violent TV viewer. Indeed, in many video games the player physically enacts the same behaviors in the game that would be required to enact it in the real world. Some games involve shooting a realistic electronic gun, for instance. Some virtual reality games involve the participant throwing punches, ducking, and so on. As the computer revolution continues, the "realism" of the video game environment will increase dramatically.

Reason 4.   Repetition increases learning. The addictive nature of video games means that their lessons will be taught repeatedly. This is largely a function of the reinforcing properties of the games, including the active and changing images, the accompanying sounds, and the actual awarding of points or extra lives or special effects when a certain level of performance is reached.

Myths

I'd also like to comment briefly on a number of myths concerning media violence. Many of these myths have been around for years. Some come from well-intentioned sources that simply happen to be wrong; others are foisted on our society by those who believe that their profits will be harmed if an informed society (especially parents) begins to shun violent TV shows, movies, and video games.

Myth 1.   The TV/movie violence literature is inconclusive. Any scientist in any field of science knows that no single study can definitively answer the complex questions encompassed by a given phenomenon. Even the best of studies have limitations. It's a ridiculously easy task to nitpick at any individual study, which frequently happens whenever scientific studies seem to contradict a personal belief or might have implications about the safety of one's products. The history of the smoking/lung cancer debate is a wonderful example of where such nitpicking successfully delayed widespread dissemination and acceptance of the fact that the product (mainly cigarettes) caused injury and death. The myth that the TV/movie violence literature is inconclusive has been similarly perpetuated by self-serving nitpicking.

Scientific answers to complex questions take years of careful research by numerous scientists interested in the same question. We have to examine the questions from multiple perspectives, using multiple methodologies. About 30 years ago, when questioned about the propriety of calling Fidel Castro a communist, Richard Cardinal Cushing replied, "When I see a bird that walks like a duck and swims like a duck and quacks like a duck, I call that bird a duck." When one looks at the whole body research in the TV/movie violence domain, clear answers do emerge. In this domain, it is now quite clear that exposure to violent media significantly increases aggression and violence in both the immediate situation and over time. The TV/movie violence research community has correctly identified their duck.

Myth 2.   Violent media have harmful effects only on a very small minority of people who use these media. One version of this myth is commonly generated by parents who allow their children to watch violent movies and play violent games. It generally sounds like this, "My 12 year old son watches violent TV shows, goes to violent movies, and plays violent video games, and he's never killed anyone." Of course, most people who consume high levels of violent media, adults or youth, do not end up in prison for violent crimes. Most smokers do not die of lung cancer, either. The more relevant question is whether many (or most) people become more angry, aggressive, and violent as a result of being exposed to high levels of media violence. Are they more likely to slap a child or spouse when provoked? Are they more likely to drive aggressively, and display "road rage?" Are they more likely to assault co-workers? The answer is a clear yes.

Myth 3. Violent media, especially violent games, allow a person to get rid of violent tendencies in a nonharmful way. This myth has a long history and has at least two labels: the catharsis hypothesis, or venting. The basic idea is that various frustrations and stresses produce an accumulation of violent tendencies or motivations somewhere in the body, and that venting these aggressive inclinations either by observing violent media or by aggressive game playing will somehow lead to a healthy reduction in these pent-up violent tendencies. This idea is that it is not only incorrect, but in fact the opposite actually happens. We've know for over thirty years that behaving aggressively or watching someone else behavior aggressively in one context, including in "safe" games of one kind or another, increases subsequent aggression. It does not decrease it.

Myth 4. Laboratory studies of aggression do not measure "real" aggression, and are therefore irrelevant. This myth persists despite the successes of psychological laboratory research in a variety of domains. In the last few years, social psychologists from the University of Southern California and from Iowa State University have carefully examined this claim, using very different methodologies, and have clearly demonstrated it to be nothing more than a myth. Laboratory studies of aggression accurately and validly measure "real" aggression.

Myth 5. The magnitude of violent media effects on aggression and violence is trivially small. This myth is related to Myth 2, which claims that only a few people are influenced by media violence. In fact, as noted earlier the TV violence effect on aggression and violence is larger than many effects that are seen as huge by the medical profession and by society at large. Furthermore, preliminary evidence and well-developed theory suggests that the violent video game effects may be substantially larger.

For Good or Ill

I have focused my remarks on the negative consequences of exposing young people to violent video games, and on the reasons why violent video games are likely to prove more harmful even than violent TV or movies. Although this may be obvious to many, I should also like to note that many of the characteristics that make violent video games such a powerful source of increased aggression and violence in society also can be used to create video games that enhance learning of lessons that are quite valuable to society. This includes traditional academic lessons as well as less traditional but still valuable social lessons.

Caveats

Obviously, many factors contribute to any particular act of violence. There is usually some initial provocation, seen as unjust by one party or the other. This is followed by some sort of retaliatory response, which is in turn interpreted as an unjust provocation. This leads to an escalatory cycle that may end in physical harm to one or both parties. How people respond to initial provocations depends to a great extent on the social situation (most people are less likely to respond aggressively in church than they are in a bar), on their current frame of mind (those who have been thinking aggressive thoughts or who are feeling hostile are more likely to respond aggressively), and on the personality of the individual (habitually aggressive people are more likely to respond aggressively than habitually peaceful people). Short term exposure to media violence influences a person's frame of mind, and long term exposure creates people who are somewhat more aggressive habitually, but many factors contribute to current frame of mind and to habitual aggressiveness. However, even though one cannot reasonably claim that a particular act of violence or that a lifetime of violence was caused exclusively by the perpetrator's exposure to violent entertainment media, one can reasonably claim that such exposure was a contributing causal factor. More importantly for this hearing, my research colleagues are correct in claiming that high exposure to media violence is a major contributing cause of the high rate of violence in modern U.S. society. Just as important, there are effective ways of reducing this particular contributing cause. Educating parents and society at large about the dangers of exposure to media violence could have an important impact.

Unknowns

The research literature on video games is sparse. There are numerous questions begging for an answer that is simply not yet available. Just to whet your appetite, here are a few questions I believe need to be addressed by new research.

1. Does explicitly gory violence desensitize video game players more so than less gory violence? If so, does this desensitization increase subsequent aggression? Does it decrease helping behavior?
2. What features increase the game player's identification with an aggressive character in video games?
3. What features, if any, could be added to violent video games to decrease the impact on subsequent aggression by the game player? For instance, does the addition of pain responses by the game victims make players less reluctant to reenact the aggression in later real-world situations, or do such pain responses in the game further desensitize the player to others' pain?
4. Can exciting video games be created that teach and reinforce nonviolent solutions to social conflicts?

Chasing the Dream—Video Gaming

As video gaming spreads, the debate about its social impact is intensifying. Is it a new medium on a par with film and music, a valuable educational tool, a form of harmless fun or a digital menace that turns children into violent zombies? Video gaming is all these things, depending on whom you ask.

Gaming has gone from a minority activity a few years ago to mass entertainment. Video games increasingly resemble films, with photorealistic images, complex plotlines and even famous actors. The next generation of games consoles—which will be launched over the next few months by Microsoft, Sony and Nintendo—will intensify the debate over gaming and its impact on society, as the industry tries to reach out to new customers and its opponents become ever more vocal. Games consoles are the most powerful mass-produced computers in the world and the new machines will offer unprecedented levels of performance. This will, for example, make possible characters with convincing facial expressions, opening the way to games with the emotional charge of films, which could have broader appeal and convince sceptics that gaming has finally come of age as a mainstream form of entertainment. But it will also make depictions of violence even more lifelike, to the dismay of critics.

This summer [2005] there has been a huge fuss about the inclusion of hidden sex scenes in "Grand Theft Auto: San Andreas," a highly popular, but controversial, game in which the player assumes the role of a street gangster. The sex scenes are not a normal part of the game. But the offending scenes can be activated using a patch downloaded from the internet. Senator Hillary Clinton and a chorus of other American politicians have called for federal prosecutors to investigate the game and examine whether the industry's system of self-regulation, which applies age ratings to games, is working properly. Mrs Clinton accused video games of "stealing the innocence of our children" and "making the difficult job of being a parent even harder."

As a result of the furore, "Grand Theft Auto" had its rating in America changed—from "M" for mature (over-17s only) to "AO" for adults only (over-18s)—by the industry's rating board. But since most big retailers refuse to stock "AO" titles, of which very few exist, Rockstar Games, the maker of "Grand Theft Auto," is producing a new "M"-rated version without the hidden sexual material. This is merely the latest round in a long-running fight. Before the current fuss over "Grand Theft Auto," politicians and lobby groups were getting worked up over "Narc," a game that depicts drug-taking, and "25 to Life," another urban cops-and-robbers game.

Ironically, the "Grand Theft Auto" episode has re-ignited the debate over the impact of video games, just as the industry is preparing to launch its biggest-ever marketing blitz to accompany the introduction of its new consoles. Amid all the arguments about the minutiae of rating systems, the unlocking of hidden content, and the stealing of children's innocence, however, three important factors are generally overlooked: that attitudes to gaming are marked by a generational divide; that there is no convincing evidence that games make people violent; and that games have great potential in education.

Start with the demographics. Attitudes towards gaming depend to a great extent on age. In America, for example, half of the population plays computer or video games. However most players are under 40—according to Nielsen, a market-research firm, 76% of them—while most critics of gaming are over 40. An entire generation that began gaming as children has kept playing. The average age of American gamers is 30. Most are "digital natives" who grew up surrounded by technology, argues Marc Prensky of games2train, a firm that promotes the educational use of games. He describes older people as "digital immigrants" who, like newcomers anywhere, have had to adapt in various ways to their new digital surroundings.

Just getting by in a foreign land without some grasp of the local language is difficult, says Mr Prensky. Digital immigrants have had to learn to use technologies such as the internet and mobile phones. But relatively few of them have embraced video games. The word "game" itself also confuses matters, since it evokes childish playthings. "What they don't understand, because they've never played them, is that these are complex games, which take 30, 40 or 100 hours to complete," says Mr Prensky. Games are, in fact, played mainly by young adults. Only a third of gamers are under 18.

"It's just a generational divide," says Gerhard Florin, the European boss of Electronic Arts, the world's biggest games publisher. "It's people not knowing what they are talking about, because they have never played a game, accusing millions of gamers of being zombies or violent." Digital natives who have played video games since childhood already regard them as a form of entertainment on a par with films and music. Older digital natives now have children of their own and enjoy playing video games with them.

The gaming industry is trying to address the generational divide. It is producing games designed to appeal to non-gamers and encouraging casual gamers (who may occasionally play simple web-based games, or games on mobile phones) to play more. This has led to the development of games with a wider appeal. Some of them replace the usual control pad with novel input devices: microphones for singing games, cameras for dancing and action games, and even drums. In addition, the industry has started to cater more to women, who seem to prefer social simulation games such as "The Sims," and to older people, who (if they play games at all) often prefer computerised versions of card games and board games. Other promising avenues include portable gaming, mobile gaming and online downloads of simple games.

Many people enjoy gaming, but do not necessarily want to commit themselves to an epic quest that will take dozens of hours to complete.

The industry, in short, is doing its best to broaden gaming's appeal, which is of course in its own best interests. For the time being, however, the demographic divide persists, and it does much to explain the polarisation of opinion over gaming and, in particular, worries about violence. It also provides the answer to a question that is often asked about gaming: when will it become a truly mainstream form of entertainment? It already is among the under-40s, but will probably never achieve mainstream status among older people.

But aren't critics right to worry that gaming might make people violent? Hardly a week goes by in which a game is not blamed for inspiring someone to commit a violent crime. After all, say critics, acting out violent behaviour in a game is very different from passively watching it in a film. Yet surveys of studies into games and violence have produced inconclusive results, notes Dmitri Williams, who specialises in studying the social impact of media at the University of Illinois. And, in a paper on the subject published in June in *Communication Monographs,* he notes that such research typically has serious shortcomings.

For example, studies have examined only the short-term effects of gaming. There have been no studies that track the long-term effects on the players themselves. Another problem, says Mr Williams, is that it is meaningless to generalise about "game play" when there are thousands of games in dozens of genres. It is, he notes, equivalent to suggesting that all television programmes, radio shows and movies are the same. Better-designed studies that measure the long-term effects of specific types of games are needed.

They're beginning to happen. In his paper, Mr Williams describes the first such study, which he carried out with Marko Skoric of the University of Michigan. The study concentrated on a "massively multiplayer online role-playing game" (MMORPG) called "Asheron's Call 2." This type of game requires the player to roam around a fantasy world and kill monsters to build up attribute points. It is "substantially more violent than the average video game and should have more effect, given the highly repetitive nature of the violence," the researchers noted.

Two groups of subjects were recruited, none of whom had played MMORPGs before and many of whom had never played video games at all. One group then played the game for a month, for an average of nearly two hours per day. The other group acted as a control. All participants were asked questions about the frequency of aggressive social interactions (such as arguments with their spouses) during the course of the month to test the idea that gaming makes people more aggressive.

Moral Choices

Game players, it turned out, were no more aggressive than the control group. Whether the participants had played games before, the number of hours spent gaming, and whether they liked violent movies or not, made no difference.

The researchers noted, however, that more research is still needed to assess the impact of other genres, such as shoot-'em-ups or the urban violence of "Grand Theft Auto." All games are different, and only when more detailed studies have been carried out will it be possible to generalise about the impact of gaming.

But as Steven Johnson, a cultural critic, points out in a recent book, "Everything Bad Is Good for You," gaming is now so widespread that if it did make people more violent, it ought to be obvious. Instead, he notes, in America violent crime actually fell sharply in the 1990s, just as the use of video and computer games was taking off. Of course, it's possible that crime would have fallen by even more over the period had America not taken up video games; still, video gaming has clearly not turned America into a more violent place than it was.

What's more, plenty of games, far from encouraging degeneracy, are morally complex, subtle and, very possibly, improving. Many now explicitly require players to choose whether to be good or evil, and their choices determine how the game they are playing develops.

In "Black & White," for example, the player must groom a creature whose behaviour and form reflects his moral choices (get it wrong and the results can be ugly). Several games based on the "Star Wars" movies require players to choose between the light and dark sides of the Force, equivalent to good and evil. Perhaps most striking is the sequence in "Halo 2," a bestselling shoot-'em-up, in which the player must take the role of an alien. Having previously seen aliens as faceless enemies, notes Paul Jackson of Forrester, a consultancy, "suddenly you are asked to empathise with the enemy's position. It's very interesting. Games are much more complex than the critics realise."

The move away from linear narratives to more complex games that allow players to make moral choices, argues Mr Prensky, means that games provide an opportunity to discuss moral questions. "These are wonderful examples for us to be discussing with our kids," he says. Indeed, perhaps the best way to address concerns over the effects of video games is to emphasise their vast potential to educate.

Even games with no educational intent require players to learn a great deal. Games are complex, adaptive and force players to make a huge number of decisions. Gamers must construct hypotheses about the in-game world, learn its rules through trial and error, solve problems and puzzles, develop strategies and get help from other players via the internet when they get stuck. The problem-solving mechanic that underlies most games is like the 90% of an iceberg below the waterline—invisible to non-gamers. But look beneath the violent veneer of "Grand Theft Auto," and it is really no different from a swords-and-sorcery game. Instead of stealing a crystal and delivering it to a wizard so that he can cure the princess, say, you may have to intercept a consignment of drugs and deliver it to a gang boss so he can ransom a hostage. It is the pleasure of this problem-solving, not the superficial violence which sometimes accompanies it, that can make gaming such a satisfying experience.

Nobody is using "Grand Theft Auto" in schools, of course, since it is intended for adults. But other off-the-shelf games such as "Sim City" or

"Rollercoaster Tycoon," which contain model economies, are used in education. By playing them it is possible to understand how such models work, and to deduce what their biases are. (In "Sim City," for example, in which the player assumes the role of a city mayor, no amount of spending on health care is ever enough to satisfy patients, and the fastest route to prosperity is to cut taxes.)

Games can be used in many other ways. Tim Rylands, a British teacher in a primary school near Bristol, recently won an award from Becta, a government education agency, for using computer games in the classroom. By projecting the fantasy world of "Myst," a role-playing game, on to a large screen and prompting his 11-year-old pupils to write descriptions and reactions as he navigates through it, he has achieved striking improvements in their English test scores.

Another area where games are becoming more popular is in corporate training. In "Got Game," a book published last year by Harvard Business School Press, John Beck and Mitchell Wade, two management consultants, argue that gaming provides excellent training for a career in business. Gamers, they write, are skilled at multi-tasking, good at making decisions and evaluating risks, flexible in the face of change and inclined to treat setbacks as chances to try again. Firms that understand and exploit this, they argue, can gain a competitive advantage.

Pilots have been trained using flight simulators for years, and simulators are now used by soldiers and surgeons too. But gaming can be used to train desk workers as well. Mr Prensky's firm has provided simple quiz games for such firms as IBM and Nokia, to test workers' knowledge of rules and regulations, for example. For Pfizer, a drug company, his firm built a simulation of its drug-development process that was then used to train new recruits. Other examples abound: PricewaterhouseCoopers built an elaborate simulation to teach novice auditors about financial derivatives. Some lawyers are using simulators to warm up for court appearances. Convincing older executives of the merits of using games in training can be tricky, Mr Prensky admits. "But when they have a serious strategic training problem, and realise that their own people are 20-year-olds, more and more are willing to take the leap," he says.

So games are inherently good, not bad? Actually they are neither, like books, films, the internet, or any other medium. All can be used to depict sex and violence, or to educate and inform. Indeed, the inclusion of violent and sexual content in games is arguably a sign of the maturity of the medium, as games become more like films.

Movies provide one analogy for the future of gaming, which seems destined to become a mainstream medium. Games already come in a variety of genres, and are rated for different age groups, just like movies. But just how far gaming still has to go is illustrated by the persistence of the double standard that applies different rules to games and films. Critics of gaming object to violence in games, even though it is common in movies. They worry about the industry's rating model, even though it is borrowed from the movie industry. They call upon big retailers (such as Wal-Mart) not to sell AO-rated games, but seem not to mind that they sell unrated movies that include far more explicit content.

In June, Senator Charles Schumer held a press conference to draw attention to the M-rated game "25 to Life," in which players take the role of a policeman or a gangster. "Little Johnny should be learning how to read, not how to kill cops," he declared. True, but little Johnny should not be smoking, drinking alcohol or watching Quentin Tarantino movies either. Just as there are rules to try to keep these things out of little Johnny's hands, there are rules for video games too. Political opportunism is part of the explanation for this double standard: many of gaming's critics in America are Democrats playing to the centre.

Another analogy can be made between games and music—specifically, with the emergence of rock and roll in the 1950s. Like games today, it was a new art form that was condemned for encouraging bad behaviour among young people. Some records were banned from the radio, and others had their lyrics changed. Politicians called for laws banning the sending of offending records by post. But now the post-war generation has grown up, rock and roll is considered to be harmless. Rap music, or gaming, is under attack instead. "There's always this pattern," says Mr Williams of the University of Illinois. "Old stuff is respected, and new stuff is junk." Novels, he points out, were once considered too lowbrow to be studied at university. Eventually the professors who believed this retired. Novels are now regarded as literature. "Once a generation has its perception, it is pretty much set," says Mr Williams. "What happens is that they die."

Like rock and roll in the 1950s, games have been accepted by the young and largely rejected by the old. Once the young are old, and the old are dead, games will be regarded as just another medium and the debate will have moved on. Critics of gaming do not just have the facts against them; they have history against them, too. "Thirty years from now, we'll be arguing about holograms, or something," says Mr Williams.

POSTSCRIPT

Do Video Games Encourage Violent Behavior?

It may be true that there are few long-term studies of the effect of playing video games now, but this will change in time. There are many longitudinal studies of the way violence and aggression are portrayed in other forms of media. In all of these cases, it is important to consider who sponsors the research and what agenda the sponsoring agency may have. In this edition of *Taking Sides*, you will see several cases for which the attitudes or biases of the authors of certain studies should suggest a critical framework for evaluating their position.

This type of controversy also takes into consideration whether a media industry can adequately control access to questionable material through ratings systems. While ratings on the packages of many games and other content may be somewhat effective as a measure of who may have access to media content, how are those ratings enforced? Is it possible for an industry to monitor use when the bottom line is selling their product? How much regulation should be exercised from outside? Should the government take a stronger role in creating guidelines, or should the bulk of the responsibility be placed on the shoulders of parents and guardians?

As mentioned in the preface to this book, the distribution and appearance of media content has changed dramatically over the years. As mediated images become more realistic through computer enhancement or computer generation, studies of perception will undoubtedly change too. And, as individuals continue to use interactive media, we can expect to see more sophistication in future studies about the effects of media content on audiences of different ages, and in different circumstances.

If you would like to focus on additional studies of understanding how to evaluate important questions such as these, you may consider Brad J. Bushman and Craig A. Anderson's, "Media Violence and the American Public: Scientific Facts Versus Media Misinformation," in *American Psychologist* (June/July, 2001, pp. 477–489). (Note, one of the authors of this study is also the author of the first selection in this issue). A more traditional approach toward understanding the relationship among violent/aggressive media content and individuals' use of media may be found in *The Case for Television Violence* (Sage, 2001), by Jib Fowles.

If you are concerned about the way the entertainment industry targets young audiences, you may want to read an article by Thomas A. Hemphill, "The Entertainment Industry, Marketing Practices, and Violent

Content: Who's Minding the Children?" in *Business and Society Review* (2003, vol. 108, pp. 263–277).

Finally, as more researchers apply new methods to studying the impact of video games, you might find an interesting approach toward balancing older research with newer media use (among other topics) in the popular book by Steven Johnson, *Everything Bad Is Good For You* (London: Penguin Press, 2005).

ISSUE 5

Do Copyright Laws Protect Ownership of Intellectual Property?

YES: Siva Vaidhyanathan, from "Copyright Jungle," *Columbia Journalism Review* (September–October 2006)

NO: Stephanie C. Ardito, from "MySpace and YouTube Meet the Copyright Cops,"*Searcher* (May 2007)

ISSUE SUMMARY

YES: In this article, Professor Siva Vaidhyanathan discusses how applications of copyright to music, film, publishing, and software companies all result in a complex system of trying to protect original ownership of intellectual property. The author gives several examples, including Google's efforts to digitize entire libraries, but reminds us that copyright also gives owners the right to say no.

NO: Independent researcher Stephanie C. Ardito examines how social networking sites have created problems for protecting copyright, because laws and enforcement of copyright law are so difficult. She believes big media companies and social networking sites will ultimately give up trying to enforce copyright, because it is too expensive and time consuming.

Copyright, or the legal protection of ownership of original materials in a tangible, fixed medium, has a long history. U.S. copyright law was established in 1790, and was based on the British Licensing Act of 1662, created not long after the invention of the printing press, and the distribution of printed materials to the masses. In 1886, the Berne Convention resulted in copyright principles for most nations of the globe, and established principles for fair and equitable treatment for original authors of artifacts resulting from scientific and creative endeavors.

Once digital technology began to make it easy and cheap to duplicate media content with virtually no signal degradation, the foundation of the old copyright law began to crumble. Now, when it is possible for someone to record, edit, and rearrange material into a new form, like that often posted on MySpace or YouTube, it becomes increasingly difficult to police the ownership of the original material.

The authors of these selections provide a number of examples to show how copyright law is being challenged in a number of ways. Siva Vaidhyanathan focuses on the adaptation of traditional print media to electronic form, discusses how copyright, filesharing, plagiarism, and fair use have all become muddled in the world of digital forms of media. Stephanie C. Ardito focuses more on social networking sites on which anyone can post creative works of their own—often using material from other sources. She discusses how various companies have attempted to create service agreements that place the responsibility for copyright clearance on the person posting information, not the company distributing the message—but how the legal agreements are complicated, difficult to enforce, and probably doomed to extinction. She also discusses digital rights management and attempts to protect copyright, which have not served their purpose as well as one might hope.

The positions taken for this issue raise many more questions as well. If it does become increasingly difficult to protect one's creative products, will there be a chilling effect on innovation, or will different structures of payment or control of the product have to be considered? Who does copyright violation actually hurt? Can the definition of fair use be extended to a greater number of media forms, or uses of content?

At this time in history, newer technologies, like digital forms, are challenging older laws and practices that had been created to protect earlier forms of media. How might industries change in the future, if the economic base of copyright is eroded? What other laws, regulations, and practices could also be challenged by the growth of user-friendly, low-cost digital technologies? The answers to these questions are put into perspective by Professor Vaidhyanathan who reminds us that "the copyright system will help determine the richness and strength of democracy in the twenty-first century."

YES

Siva Vaidhyanathan

Copyright Jungle

Last May [2005], Kevin Kelly, *Wired* magazine's "senior maverick," published in *The New York Times Magazine* his predictive account of flux within the book-publishing world. Kelly outlined what he claimed will happen (not might or could—*will*) to the practices of writing and reading under a new regime fostered by Google's plan to scan millions of books and offer searchable texts to Internet users.

"So what happens when all the books in the world become a single liquid fabric of interconnected words and ideas?" Kelly wrote. "First, works on the margins of popularity will find a small audience larger than the near-zero audience they usually have now. . . . Second, the universal library will deepen our grasp of history, as every original document in the course of civilization is scanned and cross-linked. Third, the universal library of all books will cultivate a new sense of authority. . . ."

Kelly saw the linkage of text to text, book to book, as the answer to the information gaps that have made the progress of knowledge such a hard climb. "If you can truly incorporate all texts—past and present, multilingual—on a particular subject," Kelly wrote, "then you can have a clearer sense of what we as a civilization, a species, do know and don't know. The white spaces of our collective ignorance are highlighted, while the golden peaks of our knowledge are drawn with completeness. This degree of authority is only rarely achieved in scholarship today, but it will become routine."

Such heady predictions of technological revolution have become so common, so accepted in our techno-fundamentalist culture, that even when John Updike criticized Kelly's vision in an essay published a month later in *The New York Times Book Review*, he did not so much doubt Kelly's vision of a universal digital library as lament it.

As it turns out, the move toward universal knowledge is not so easy. Google's project, if it survives court challenges, would probably have modest effects on writing, reading, and publishing. For one thing, Kelly's predictions depend on a part of the system he slights in his article: the copyright system. Copyright is not Kelly's friend. He mentions it as a nuisance on the edge of his dream. To acknowledge that a lawyer-built system might trump an engineer-built system would have run counter to Kelly's sermon.

Much of the press coverage of the Google project has missed some key facts: most libraries that are allowing Google to scan books are, so far, providing only books published before 1923 and thus already in the public domain, essentially missing most of the relevant and important books that scholars and researchers—not to mention casual readers—might want. Meanwhile, the current American copyright system will probably kill Google's plan to scan the collections of the University of Michigan and the University of California system—the only libraries willing to offer Google works currently covered by copyright. In his article, Kelly breezed past the fact that the copyrighted works will be presented in a useless format—"snippets" that allow readers only glimpses into how a term is used in the text. Google users will not be able to read, copy, or print copyrighted works via Google. Google accepted that arrangement to limit its copyright liability. But the more "copyright friendly" the Google system is, the less user-friendly, and useful, it is. And even so it still may not fly in court.

Google is exploiting the instability of the copyright system in a digital age. The company's struggle with publishers over its legal ability to pursue its project is the most interesting and perhaps most transformative conflict in the copyright wars. But there are many other battles—and many other significant stories—out in the copyright jungle. Yet reporters seem lost.

Copyright in recent years has certainly become too strong for its own good. It protects more content and outlaws more acts than ever before. It stifles individual creativity and hampers the discovery and sharing of culture and knowledge. To convey all this to readers, journalists need to understand the principles, paradoxes, licenses, and limits of the increasingly troubled copyright system. Copyright is not just an interesting story. As the most pervasive regulation of speech and culture, the copyright system will help determine the richness and strength of democracy in the twenty-first century.

The Copyright Wars

It's not that the press has ignored copyright. Recent fights have generated a remarkable amount of press. Since Napster broke into the news in 2000, journalists have been scrambling to keep up with the fast-moving and complicated stories of content protection, distribution, and revision that make up the wide array of copyright conflicts.

During this time of rapid change it's been all too easy for reporters to fall into the trap of false dichotomies: hackers versus movie studios; kids versus music companies; librarians versus publishers. The peer-to-peer and music-file-sharing story, for instance, has consistently been covered as a business story with the tone of the sports page: winners and losers, scores and stats. In fact, peer-to-peer file sharing was more about technological innovation and the ways we use music in our lives than any sort of threat to the commercial music industry. As it stands today, after dozens of court cases and congressional hearings, peer-to-peer file-sharing remains strong. So does the music industry. The sky did not fall, our expectations did.

The most recent headline-grabbing copyright battle involved *The Da Vinci Code*. Did Dan Brown recycle elements of a 1982 nonfiction book for his bestselling novel? The authors of the earlier book sued Brown's publisher,

Random House U.K., in a London court in the spring of 2006 in an effort to prove that Brown lifted protected elements of their book, what they called "the architecture" of a speculative conspiracy theory about the life of Jesus. In the coverage of the trial, some reporters—even in publications like *The New York Times*, *The Washington Post*, and *The San Diego Union-Tribune*—used the word "plagiarism" as if it were a legal concept or cause of action. It isn't. Copyright infringement and plagiarism are different acts with some potential overlap. One may infringe upon a copyright without plagiarizing and one may plagiarize—use ideas without attribution—without breaking the law. Plagiarism is an ethical concept. Copyright is a legal one.

Perhaps most troubling, though, was the way in which the *Da Vinci Code* story was so often covered without a clear statement of the operative principle of copyright: one cannot protect facts and ideas, only specific expressions of ideas. Dan Brown and Random House U.K. prevailed in the London court because the judge clearly saw that the earlier authors were trying to protect ideas. Most people don't understand that important distinction. So it's no surprise that most reporters don't either.

Reporters often fail to see the big picture in copyright stories: that what is at stake is the long-term health of our culture. If the copyright system fails, huge industries could crumble. If it gets too strong, it could strangle future creativity and research. It is complex, and complexity can be a hard thing to render in journalistic prose.

The work situation of most reporters may also impede a thorough understanding of how copyright affects us all. Reporters labor for content companies, after all, and tend to view their role in the copyright system as one-dimensional. They are creators who get paid by copyright holders. So it's understandable for journalists to express a certain amount of anxiety about the ways digital technologies have allowed expensive content to flow around the world cheaply.

Yet reporters can't gather the raw material for their craft without a rich library of information in accessible form. When I was a reporter in the 1980s and 1990s, I could not write a good story without scouring the library and newspaper archives for other stories that added context. And like every reporter, I was constantly aware that my work was just one element in a cacophony of texts seeking readers and contributing to the aggregate understanding of our world. I was as much a copyright user as I was a copyright producer. Now that I write books, I am even more aware of my role as a taker and a giver. It takes a library, after all, to write a book.

The Right to Say No

We are constantly reminded that copyright law, as the Supreme Court once declared, is an "engine of free expression." But more often these days, it's instead an engine of corporate censorship.

Copyright is the right to say no. Copyright holders get to tell the rest of us that we can't build on, revise, copy, or distribute their work. That's a fair bargain most of the time. Copyright provides the incentive to bring work to market. It's impossible to imagine anyone anteing up $300 million for *Spider-Man 3* if we did not have a reasonable belief that copyright laws would limit its distribution to mostly legitimate and moneymaking channels.

Yet copyright has the potential of locking up knowledge, insight, information, and wisdom from the rest of the world. So it is also fundamentally a *conditional* restriction on speech and print. Copyright and the First Amendment are in constant and necessary tension. The law has for most of American history limited copyright—allowing it to fill its role as an incentive-maker for new creators yet curbing its censorious powers. For most of its 300-year history, the system has served us well, protecting the integrity of creative work while allowing the next generation of creators to build on the cultural foundations around them. These rights have helped fill our libraries with books, our walls with art, and our lives with song.

But something has gone terribly wrong. In recent years, large multinational media companies have captured the global copyright system and twisted it toward their own short-term interests. The people who are supposed to benefit most from a system that makes ideas available—readers, students, and citizens—have been excluded. No one in Congress wants to hear from college students or librarians.

More than ever, the law restricts what individuals can do with elements of their own culture. Generally the exercise of copyright protection is so extreme these days that even the most innocent use of images or song lyrics in scholarly work can generate a legal threat. Last year one of the brightest students in my department got an article accepted in the leading journal in the field. It was about advertising in the 1930s. The journal's lawyers and editors refused to let her use images from the ads in question without permission, even though it is impossible to find out who owns the ads or if they were ever covered by copyright in the first place. The chilling effect trumped any claim of scholarly "fair use" or even common sense.

What has Changed

For most of the history of copyright in Europe and the United States, copying was hard and expensive, and the law punished those who made whole copies of others' material for profit. The principle was simple: legitimate publishers would make no money after investing so much in authors, editors, and printing presses if the same products were available on the street. The price in such a hypercompetitive market would drop to close to zero. So copyright created artificial scarcity.

But we live in an age of abundance. Millions of people have in their homes and offices powerful copying machines and communication devices: their personal computers. It's almost impossible to keep digital materials scarce once they are released to the public.

The industries that live by copyright—music, film, publishing, and software companies—continue to try. They encrypt video discs and compact discs so that consumers can't play them on computers or make personal copies. They monitor and sue consumers who allow others to share digital materials over the Internet. But none of these tactics seem to be working. In fact, they have been counterproductive. The bullying attitude has alienated consumers. That does not mean that copyright has failed or that it has no future. It just has a more complicated and nuanced existence.

Here is the fundamental paradox: media companies keep expanding across the globe. They produce more software, books, music, video games, and films every year. They charge more for those products every year. And those industries repeatedly tell us that they are in crisis. If we do not radically alter our laws, technologies, and habits, the media companies argue, the industries that copyright protects will wither and die.

Yet they are not dying. Strangely, the global copyright industries are still rich and powerful. Many of them are adapting, changing their containers and their content, but they keep growing, expanding across the globe. Revenues in the music business did drop steadily from 2000 to 2003—some years by up to 6.8 percent. Millions of people in Europe and North America use their high-speed Internet connections to download music files free. From Moscow to Mexico City to Manila, film and video piracy is rampant. For much of the world, teeming pirate bazaars serve as the chief (often only) source of those products. Yet the music industry has recovered from its early-decade lull rather well. Revenues for the major commercial labels in 2004 Were 3.3 percent above 2003. Unit sales were up 4.4 percent. Revenues in 2004 were higher than in 1997 and comparable to those of 1998—then considered very healthy years for the recording industry. This while illegal downloading continued all over the world.

Yet despite their ability to thrive in a new global/digital environment, the companies push for ever more restrictive laws—laws that fail to recognize the realities of the global flows of people, culture, and technology.

Recent changes to copyright in North America, Europe, and Australia threaten to chill creativity at the ground level—among noncorporate, individual, and communal artists. As a result, the risk and price of reusing elements of copyrighted culture are higher than ever before. If you wanted to make a scholarly documentary film about the history of country music, for example, you might end up with one that slights the contribution of Hank Williams and Elvis Presley because their estates would deny you permission to use the archival material. Other archives and estates would charge you prohibitive fees. We are losing much of the history of the twentieth century because the copyright industries are more litigious than ever.

Yet copyright, like culture itself, is not zero-sum. In its first weekend of theatrical release, *Star Wars Episode III. Revenge of the Sith* made a record $158.5 million at the box office. At the same time, thousands of people downloaded high-quality pirated digital copies from the Internet. Just days after the blockbuster release of the movie, attorneys for 20th Century Fox sent thousands of "cease-and-desist" letters to those sharing copies of the film over the Internet. The practice continued unabated.

How could a film make so much money when it was competing against its free version? The key to understanding that seeming paradox—less control, more revenue—is to realize that every download does not equal a lost sale. As the Stanford law professor Lawrence Lessig has argued, during the time when music downloads were 2.6 times those of legitimate music sales, revenues dropped less than 7 percent. If every download replaced a sale, there would be no commercial music industry left. The relationship between the free version and the legitimate version is rather complex, like the relationship between a public library and a book publisher. Sometimes free stuff sells stuff.

Checks And Unbalances

Here's a primer for reporters who find themselves lost in the copyright jungle: American copyright law offers four basic democratic safeguards to the censorious power of copyright, a sort of bargain with the people. Each of these safeguards is currently at risk:

1. First and foremost, copyrights eventually expire, thus placing works into the public domain for all to buy cheaply and use freely. That is the most important part of the copyright bargain: We the people grant copyright as a temporary monopoly over the reproduction and distribution of specific works, and eventually we get the material back for the sake of our common heritage and collective knowledge. The works of Melville and Twain once benefited their authors exclusively. Now they belong to all of us. But as Congress continues to extend the term of copyright protection for works created decades ago (as it did in 1998 by adding twenty years to all active copyrights) it robs the people of their legacy.
2. Second, copyright restricts what consumers can do with the text of a book, but not the book itself; it governs the content, not the container. Thus people may sell and buy used books, and libraries may lend books freely, without permission from publishers. In the digital realm, however, copyright holders may install digital-rights-management schemes that limit the transportation of both the container and the content. So libraries may not lend out major portions of their materials if they are in digital form. As more works are digitized, libraries are shifting to the lighter, space-saving formats. As a result, libraries of the future could be less useful to citizens.
3. Third, as we have seen, copyright governs specific expressions, but not the facts or ideas upon which the expressions are based. Copyright does not protect ideas. But that is one of the most widely misunderstood aspects of copyright. And even that basic principle is under attack in the new digital environment. In 1997, the National Basketball Association tried to get pager and Internet companies to refrain from distributing game scores without permission. And more recently, Major League Baseball has tried, but so far has failed, to license the use of player statistics to limit "free riding" firms that make money facilitating fantasy baseball leagues. Every Congressional session, database companies try to create a new form of intellectual property that protects facts and data, thus evading the basic democratic right that lets facts flow freely.
4. Fourth, and not least, the copyright system has built into it an exception to the power of copyright: fair use. This significant loophole, too, is widely misunderstood, and deserves further discussion.

Generally, one may copy portions of another's copyrighted work (and sometimes the entire work) for private, noncommercial uses, for education, criticism, journalism, or parody. Fair use operates as a defense against an accusation of infringement and grants confidence to users that they most likely will not be sued for using works in a reasonable way.

On paper, fair use seems pretty healthy. In recent years, for example, courts have definitively stated that making a parody of a copyrighted work is considered "transformative" and thus fair. Another example: a major ruling in 2002 enabled image search engines such as Google to thrive and expand beyond simple Web text searching into images and video because "thumbnails" of digital photographs are considered to be fair uses. Thumbnails, the court ruled, do not replace the original in the marketplace.

But two factors have put fair use beyond the reach of many users, especially artists and authors. First and foremost, fair use does not help you if your publisher or distributor does not believe in it. Many publishers demand that every quote—no matter how short or for what purpose—be cleared with specific permission, which is extremely cumbersome and often costly.

And fair use is somewhat confusing. There is widespread misunderstanding about it. In public forums I have heard claims such as "you can take 20 percent" of a work before the use becomes unfair, or, "there is a forty-word rule" for long quotes of text. Neither rule exists. Fair use is intentionally vague. It is meant for judges to apply, case by case. Meanwhile, copyright holders are more aggressive than ever and publishers and distributors are more concerned about suits. So in the real world, fair use is less fair and less useful.

The Biggest Copy Machine

Fair use is designed for small ball. It's supposed to create some breathing room for individual critics or creators to do what they do. Under current law it's not appropriate for large-scale endeavors—like the Google library project. Fair use may be too rickety a structure to support both free speech and the vast dreams of Google.

Reporters need to understand the company's copyright ambitions. Google announced in December 2004 that it would begin scanning in millions of copyrighted books from the University of Michigan library, and in August 2006 the University of California system signed on. Predictably, some prominent publishers and authors have filed suit against the search-engine company.

The company's plan was to include those works in its "Google Book Search" service. Books from the library would supplement both the copyrighted books that Google has contracted to offer via its "partner" program with publishers and the uncopyrighted works scanned from other libraries, including libraries of Harvard, Oxford, and New York City. While it would offer readers full-text access to older works out of copyright, it would provide only "snippets" of the copyrighted works that it scans without the authors' permission from Michigan and California.

Google says that because users will only experience "snippets" of copyrighted text, their use of such material should be considered a fair use. That argument will be tested in court. But whether those snippets constitute fair use is just one part of the issue. To generate the "snippets," Google is scanning the entire works and storing them on its servers. The plaintiffs argue that the initial scanning of the books itself-done to create the snippets from a vast database—constitutes copyright infringement, the very core of copyright. Courts will have to weigh whether the public is better served by a strict and clear conception of copyright law—that only the copyright holder has the right to give permission for any copy, regardless of the ultimate use or effect on the market—or a more flexible and pragmatic one in which the user experience matters more.

One of the least understood concepts of Google's business is that it copies everything. When we post our words and images on the Web, we are implicitly licensing Google, Yahoo, and other search engines to make copies of our content to store in their huge farms of servers. Without such "cache" copies, search engines could not read and link to Web pages. In the Web world, massive copying is just business as usual.

But through the library project, Google is imposing the norms of the Web on authors and publishers who have not willingly digitized their works and thus have not licensed search engines to make cache copies. Publishers, at first, worried that the Google project would threaten book sales, but it soon became clear that project offers no risk to publishers' core markets and projects. If anything, it could serve as a marketing boon. Now publishers are most offended by the prospect of a wealthy upstart corporation's "free-riding" on their content to offer a commercial and potentially lucrative service without any regard for compensation or quality control. The publishers, in short, would like a piece of the revenue, and some say about the manner of display and search results.

Copyright has rarely been used as leverage to govern ancillary markets for goods that enhance the value or utility of the copyrighted works. Publishers have never, for instance, sued the makers of library catalogs, eyeglasses, or bookcases. But these are extreme times.

The mood of U.S. courts in recent years, especially the Supreme Court, has been to side with the copyright holder in this time of great technological flux. Google is an upstart facing off against some of the most powerful media companies in the world, including Viacom, News Corporation, and Disney—all of which have publishing wings. Courts will probably see this case as the existential showdown over the nature and future of copyright and rule to defend the status quo. Journalists should follow the case closely. The footnotes of any court decision could shape the future of journalism, publishing, libraries, and democracy.

Out Of The Jungle

Google aside, in recent years—thanks to the ferocious mania to protect everything and the astounding political power of media companies—the basic, democratic checks and balances that ensured that copyright would not operate as an instrument of private censorship have been seriously eroded. The most endangered principle is fair use: the right to use others' copyrighted works in a reasonable way to promote important public functions such as criticism or education. And if fair use is in danger then good journalism is also threatened. Every journalist relies on fair use every day. So journalists have a self-interest in the copyright story.

And so does our society. Copyright was designed, as the Constitution declares, to "promote the progress" of knowledge and creativity. In the last thirty years we have seen this brilliant system corrupted and captured by the very industries that the old laws fostered. Yet the complexity and nuanced nature of copyright battles make it hard for nonexperts to grasp what's at stake.

So it's up to journalists to push deeper into stories in which copyright plays a part. Then the real challenge begins: explaining this messy system in clear language to a curious but confused audience.

Stephanie C. Ardito

 **NO**

MySpace and YouTube Meet the Copyright Cops

Since the dawn of the Internet, many of us have marveled at the ground-breaking novelty of Internet sites that seem to appear from nowhere, gain rapid popularity, and become staples on everyone's set of bookmarks. The founders of these sites do not usually come from traditional content providers, so the phenomenon of Web-based services such as Yahoo!, Amazon, Travelocity, MapQuest, and Google continue to amaze us.

And just when we think there can't possibly be any more innovation, along come social networking and video-sharing sites such as MySpace and YouTube and their hundreds of imitators.

As these companies take off and continue to soar, inevitably, it seems, the copyright infringement lawsuits begin, often initiated by the traditional media powerhouses which feel threatened by the upstarts' popularity. The truly groundbreaking Internet companies manage to survive. Negotiations and settlements are worked out, conglomerates with bottomless financial pockets come to the rescue, or deep-rooted media companies finally accept the need to change their business paradigms or lose their considerable customer base.

The latest round of battles is occurring within the music and movie industries. The background and conflicts are no different than what we've seen before. Ten years ago, the scientific, technical, and medical (STM) publishers resisted placing full-text articles on the Internet. These publishers worried about losing expensive annual subscriptions if individual articles were easily accessible for purchase, as well as about how to collect royalties on multiple copies of articles circulating on the Web. Although struggling with customer demand for replication of Web services inspired by Internet technology, publishers finally figured out how to make their content widely and instantly available. Now publishers struggle with open access and end users (both authors and readers) going directly to the Web. The music and movie industries are bound to do the same.

The New Reality

A former employee of mine will graduate from music school this year. His dream is to earn a living as a jazz drummer. Recently, he created a MySpace page, listing upcoming band engagements, announcing his availability as a private instructor, and providing videos and audio clips of his live performances. There are no copyright notices on the page, but Matt shared his opinion that the original purpose of MySpace was to make budding artists known. If his videos and music show up somewhere else on the Internet or if users download the clips, Matt doesn't care. Copyright won't become an issue for him until he's famous. His major concern now is to get his name known.

As for school policies and educational efforts informing kids about copyright, teachers at my nephews' and niece's high schools and colleges do not discuss the ramifications of downloading content from the Internet. English and computer science teachers who require electronic copies of papers talk to their students about plagiarism and warn students that their compositions are being run against the Turnitin . . . to verify originality.

However, colleges and universities may soon intensify instructional efforts to enlighten students about copyright, including possible litigation initiated around the illegal downloading and storing of videos and music. On Feb. 28, 2007, the Recording Industry Association of America (RIAA) announced another round of lawsuits against college students for copyright infringements. . . .

Regarding my own personal experience with the social networking sites, I will admit that I'm a frequent user of YouTube. A while back, I saw a VH1 documentary on Meat Loaf, in which the television show played clips from Meat Loaf's *Bat Out of Hell* video. Being a fan, after the program ended, I immediately went to YouTube and looked for the full videos of a couple of songs from the album—"You Took the Words Right Out of My Mouth" and "Paradise by the Dashboard Light" (a particular favorite of mine). I was tempted to down-load the videos to my computer so I could view them whenever the mood struck, but my niece told me that the videos remain on YouTube "forever," so I wouldn't have a problem finding them whenever I wanted. Since I still worry that someday the copyright police will knock on my door, take my computer, and lock me up in copyright jail, I listened to my niece's advice and did not download the videos.

However, my niece's assertion that videos stay on YouTube into infinity isn't true. I'm also a celebrity news junkie. Earlier this year, I was intrigued about the scuttlebutt surrounding the Justin Timberlake/Scarlett Johannsson video, "What Goes Around ... Comes Around." I had seen clips of a steamy swimming pool scene from the video and immediately went to YouTube to find it. And there it was. In fact, there were several uploads of the video from a number of the site's users. I watched the entire video to see what the fuss was about and told my neighbor about it. Of course she asked me for the URL, but when I went back to look for the video on YouTube, it had vanished. Since Sony, the legal distributor, allows "sharing" of the video directly from its Musicbox Web site, I emailed the URL to my neighbor. . . . I suspect that Sony must have warned YouTube to take the illegal copies off its site.

So, what prompts my nephews, niece, colleagues, and me to go to MySpace and YouTube to view grainy, unprofessional, uploaded videos and audios recorded on camera phones and camcorders versus searching the music label or movie studio Web sites for the originals? The answer lies in the ease and convenience of MySpace and YouTube. Without much fuss and no required registration, you can quickly identify videos of interest, see which ones are the most popular with others (both sites rank videos by the number of hits received, similar to Amazon's "Top Sellers"), click on the videos you want to watch, and, within a matter of seconds, have them appear on your screen. In comparison, the traditional media companies often require users to download special software to view videos and click through several pages of terms and conditions before gaining access. Even when that access is finally granted, you may sit for several minutes waiting for the videos to download to your screen. Since consumers want instant gratification, the established players need to learn some lessons from MySpace and YouTube. So, let's review the genesis and appeal of these two Web sites.

YouTube

Founded in February 2005, YouTube is typical of many startup Internet companies. It originated in a garage, followed quickly by significant funding from a venture capital company, in this case, Sequoia Capital. At first, users shared personal videos, but as the Web site's popularity grew rapidly, YouTube contracted with traditional content providers (television and movie studios and record labels) to load commercial clips. In less than a year, the video and user statistics were staggering. The company claims that 65,000 videos are uploaded daily, with consumers watching more than 100 million videos a day. Twenty million unique users, mainly in the 18–49 age range, view the Web site monthly.

In October 2006, Google, also initially funded by Sequoia Capital, bought YouTube for $1.65 billion. YouTube has struggled to find advertising revenue, so it should benefit from Google's ownership and experience in generating revenue. Although YouTube faced some copyright legal challenges from the music industry prior to Google's purchase, lawsuits seemed to have multiplied since the takeover. Some industry analysts speculate this litigiousness stems from the arrival of Google's deep financial pockets. For now, Google doesn't seem deterred by the legal wrangling.

YouTube's Boilerplate

Let's take a look at YouTube's copyright notices. Within the Terms of Use document . . . section 4 deals with Intellectual Property Rights. The section's statements are typical of the notices we see on the Web sites of publishers, database producers, and other content providers:

The content on the YouTube Website, except all User Submissions (as defined below), including without limitation, the text, software, scripts, graphics, photos, sounds, music, videos, interactive features and the like ("Content") and the trademarks, service marks and logos contained therein ("Marks"), are owned by or licensed to YouTube, subject to copyright and other intellectual property rights under United States and foreign laws and international conventions. Content on the Website is provided to you AS IS for your information and personal use only and may not be used, copied, reproduced, distributed, transmitted, broadcast, displayed, sold, licensed, or otherwise exploited for any other purposes whatsoever without the prior written consent of the respective owners. YouTube reserves all rights not expressly granted in and to the Website and the Content. You agree to not engage in the use, copying, or distribution of any of the Content other than expressly permitted herein, including any use, copying, or distribution of User Submissions of third parties obtained through the Website for any commercial purposes. If you download or print a copy of the Content for personal use, you must retain all copyright and other proprietary notices contained therein. You agree not to circumvent, disable or otherwise interfere with security related features of the YouTube Website or features that prevent or restrict use or copying of any Content or enforce limitations on use of the YouTube Website or the Content therein.

As with traditional content providers who negotiate author contracts, those who upload original videos "grant YouTube a worldwide, non-exclusive, royalty-free, sublicenseable and transferable license to use, reproduce, distribute, prepare derivative works of, display, and perform the User Submissions in connection with the YouTube Web site and YouTube's (and its successor's) business, including without limitation for promoting and redistributing part or all of the YouTube Web site (and derivative works thereof) in any media formats and through any media channels."

But YouTube goes one step further than traditional publishers and database producers by granting "each user of the YouTube Website a non-exclusive license to access your User Submissions through the Website, and to use, reproduce, distribute, prepare derivative works of, display and perform such User Submissions as permitted through the functionality of the Website and under these Terms of Service." In other words, as I interpret this clause, those who upload videos they have created own the rights to their works. In the publishing world of newspapers, journals, and books, authors generally turn over their rights to the publishers, who then own the authors' works into perpetuity.

By clicking on the Terms of Use, YouTube's registered users also agree they will not submit any copyrighted material, with YouTube reserving the right to remove content if it detects infringement. YouTube cites the Digital Millennium Copyright Act (DMCA) of 1998 as the company's guideline for dealing with potential copyright violations, requiring written communication if copyright holders find their intellectual property has been illegally uploaded to the YouTube Web site. . . . DMCA seems to protect YouTube and Google from lawsuits if the infringing works are removed when copyright holders notify them, but actual litigation that would give us precedent has yet to be established.

In a separate document, "Copyright Tips,". . . . YouTube admits: "The most common reason we take down videos for copyright infringement is that they are direct copies of copyrighted content and the owners of the copyrighted content have alerted us that their content is being used without their permission." YouTube mentions "fair use," providing links to four Web sites that outline the factors considered to establish fair use status: U.S. Copyright Office; . . . Stanford University Libraries and Academic Information Resources; . . . Copyright Web site LLC; . . . and the Chilling Effects Clearinghouse. . . .

MySpace

MySpace . . . was founded in 2003 as a social networking Web site. In 2005, Rupert Murdoch's News Corporation acquired MySpace as part of a $580 million acquisition, with the "lifestyle portal" now a unit of Fox Interactive Media Inc. Users must be at least 14 to join MySpace (one must be 13 to access YouTube), but I'm not sure how this is enforced on either site.

The MySpace Terms of Use Agreement is similar to YouTube's and applies to users who are Visitors (those who browse the Web site) or Members (those who register). . . . Under the section titled Proprietary Rights in Content on MySpace.com, when members display, publish, or post any content on the Web site, MySpace acknowledges that ownership rights belong to members, but members grant MySpace "a limited license to use, modify, publicly perform, publicly display, reproduce, and distribute such Content solely on and through the MySpace Services." The license is "non-exclusive ... fully-paid and royalty-free (meaning that MySpace.com is not required to pay you for the use on the MySpace Services of the Content that you post), sublicenseable (so that MySpace.com is able to use its affiliates and subcontractors such as Internet content delivery networks to provide the MySpace Services), and worldwide (because the Internet and the MySpace Services are global in reach)." Members must "warrant" that the posted content "does not violate the privacy rights, publicity rights, copyrights, contract rights or any other rights of any person" and agree "to pay for all royalties, fees, and any other monies owing any person by reason of any Content posted ... through the MySpace Services."

The Agreement includes a "partial" list of 27 prohibitive content activities. Illicit activities include promoting an "illegal or unauthorized copy of another person's copyrighted work, such as providing pirated computer programs or links to them, providing information to circumvent manufacture-installed copy-protect devices, or providing pirated music or links to pirated music files." Advertising and paid commercial activity is also prohibited. As with YouTube, MySpace includes several paragraphs on liabilities and disclaimers.

The Agreement is dated Oct. 25, 2006, coinciding with MySpace's announcement that the company had implemented a filtering system to identify copyrighted materials posted by its users. The audio fingerprinting technology came from Gracenote . . . , a California-based company specializing in the organization of digital music. Music files uploaded by MySpace users are run against Gracenote's MusicID software and Global Media Database to detect copyright infringements.

In February 2007, MySpace announced the implementation of a second program to block videos containing copyrighted content posted by its users.

In this case, digital fingerprinting technology licensed from Audible Magic . . . is used to screen and block videos.

YouTube seems to lag behind MySpace in applying filtering technology. The company hoped to introduce a new mechanism to filter out unauthorized videos by the end of 2006. On Feb. 22, 2007, the Mercury News reported that Google had signed a deal with Audible Magic to provide its filtering technology on the YouTube Web site. However, YouTube and Audible Magic had not directly issued an "official" statement about such a deal as of that date, nor would either company comment.

Storms of Litigation

On Oct. 11, 2006, *The Wall Street Journal* interviewed two copyright experts about the Google purchase of YouTube: John Palfrey, a Harvard University law professor and director of the Berkman Center for Internet & Society . . . , and Stan Liebowitz, an economics professor at the University of Texas at Dallas and director of the Center for the Analysis of Property Rights and Innovation. . . . Mr. Palfrey said, "Google is no stranger to copyright risk. Much to their credit, Google has not let a lack of precision in the copyright context stop them from taking on major projects. The YouTube deal is no exception. As with Google News and the Libraries Project, the YouTube technology and service is going to make some people—competitors and people elsewhere in the value chain alike—somewhat unhappy."

Mr. Liebowitz agreed with Palfrey: "Google is no stranger to these issues. Its attempt (the library project) to copy all the books in existence without getting copyright permission in advance has led to a lawsuit against it by copyright owners. Perhaps there are economies of scale in fighting such lawsuits. I also agree that YouTube is no Napster. Nevertheless, whether there will be copyright litigation depends on several issues. Although the purpose of YouTube might be to encourage home-grown creative endeavors, some portion of YouTube files have been pure copyrighted files with no home-grown component, although it appears that YouTube has taken them down when requested."

Palfrey expressed his opinion that if users agree to YouTube's Terms of Service agreement—"not to post anything that violates anyone else's copyright," and YouTube removes copyrighted works immediately that come to the company's attention—then YouTube and Google should be protected by the DMCA if lawsuits are filed. If the companies ignore or don't respond to claims of infringement, he considered litigation inevitable.

In fairness to YouTube, the company has quickly responded when notified about copyrighted materials, not only from media conglomerates, but also from individual directors and writers. For example, in July 2006, journalist Robert Tur sued YouTube for posting a video he had shot of a white truck driver named Reginald Denny being dragged out of his truck and beaten during the Los Angeles riots in 1992. When YouTube learned of the lawsuit, the video was immediately removed. Shortly before Google's purchase of YouTube, the Japanese Society for Rights of Authors, Composers and Publishers notified the company of nearly 30,000 illegal clips floating around the YouTube Web site. Again, when alerted, YouTube removed the offending clips.

Preceding the sale of YouTube to Google, a flurry of announcements appeared regarding potential content deals with Sony, Bertelsmann, Universal Music, and CBS. While the CBS talks ultimately broke down, YouTube brokered a deal with the British Broadcasting Company to load selective BBC news and entertainment content on the company Web site. Analysts forecast that Google's significant financial resources would prompt an immediate upsurge in copyright litigation after the company's takeover of YouTube. In fact, as this issue of Searcher went to press, lawsuits were being announced on a daily basis, so many, that it was difficult for me to keep up. For example, on Jan. 18, 2007, competitor News Corp. subpoenaed YouTube for the identity of users who uploaded full episodes of Fox's TV show 24 before the episodes debuted. Apparently, YouTube gave in to Fox's pressure and identified the users.

In addition, Viacom Inc.—which owns MTV, Nickelodeon, Comedy Central, and Paramount, not to mention, the immortal I Love Lucy and Perry Mason TV series—ordered YouTube to remove more than 100,000 video clips. Viacom had been in discussions with YouTube to keep the videos on the Web site. Some critics speculated that Viacom may have demanded the removal of the videos to force YouTube into a quicker royalty arrangement, rather than let negotiations drag on indefinitely. Since Comedy Central's The Daily Show with Jon Stewart is among the most heavily viewed videos on the YouTube Web site, industry analysts thought Viacom's strategy would compel YouTube to immediately agree on terms favorable to Viacom. As of this writing, YouTube and Google had not budged.

Shortly after the breakdown in talks, on March 13, 2007, Viacom filed a lawsuit against Google and YouTube, seeking more than $1 billion in damages for "160,000 unauthorized clips of Viacom's programming . . . viewed more than 1.5 billion times" on the YouTube Web site. Some critics commented that Viacom not only wants control over its media programs, but doesn't like its materials displayed along side the work of amateurs on YouTube, mainly because the unprofessional videos turn off advertisers. However, the real truth may lie in the threat Viacom is experiencing over YouTube's popularity and the significant Google resources supporting the Web site. Interestingly, in the month prior to the lawsuit announcement, Viacom signed a licensing deal with Joost . . . , a company whose technology will be used to load videos from Viacom's television networks onto the Internet. One has to wonder if Viacom entered into the Joost deal knowing that the lawsuit against Google and YouTube would follow. The Viacom lawsuit will be the one to watch, as the company will argue that YouTube had direct knowledge of the illegal videos and profited from the postings (i.e., most likely citing Section 512 from the DMCA safe harbor clause).

In an ironic twist, on March 22, 2007, the Electronic Frontier Foundation (EFF) sued Viacom on behalf of MoveOn.org and Brave New Films. In August 2006, the two companies had created and uploaded a video, Stop the Falsiness, to YouTube. The video parodied The Colbert Report, another popular Comedy Central program owned by Viacom, and included clips from the show as well as original interviews. EFF argues that Viacom unlawfully asked YouTube to remove the video parody, which EFF claims was protected by free speech and fair use. Google and YouTube are not named in the lawsuit.

Another conglomerate, Vivendi (and its subsidiary, Universal Music Group), has received frequent press coverage for its aggressive tactics in filing copyright infringement lawsuits against social networking and video Web sites. The company continues to pressure MySpace and YouTube to pay royalties, either by forcing users to "pay-per-play" or by sharing ad revenues. These tactics are being blasted by critics, who write that customers are alienated when media companies fail to adopt to new technology.

As an aside, in early February 2007, a privately held video-sharing company called Veoh Networks, Inc. was formed by media giants Time Warner and Michael Eisner (former Disney Chairman and CEO) and various investment firms. In a bit of irony, considering the corporate backgrounds of the founders, Veoh found itself facing copyright infringement lawsuits less than a week after its video Web site debuted.

Watching and Waiting

Some media giants are choosing to stay out of the copyright fray but continue to cautiously watch legal developments at their competitors. For example, late in 2006, Warner Music chose not to sue YouTube for uploading songs and videos, but rather, negotiated a deal to share revenue from ads placed next to Warner material. Warner's strategy differed sharply from the approach employed against Napster nearly 6 years ago. In that case, a class action suit from a number of music companies shut down Napster.

Commenting on the Viacom lawsuit against YouTube, Paul Cappuccio, Time Warner's general counsel, expressed his opinion that "companies should reach a compromise ... We are still of the opinion that we can negotiate a business solution with YouTube that will efficiently identify and filter out unauthorized copyrighted works while also allowing us to license copyright works to them for a share of revenue."

Some conglomerates decide to sit back because they have found themselves between a rock and a hard place. Illegal videos and music give them exposure and may help to generate sales. Sound familiar? Years ago, information professionals pleaded with traditional publishers to allow access to individual articles and to consider alternative forms of electronic advertising to generate revenue, foreseeing that money (and profits) could be made without paying for annual subscriptions. Back then, we called the publishers dinosaurs. Now, the media conglomerates are being labeled with the same term.

Personally, I think the media giants will eventually calm down and learn to work with social networking and video Web sites. Otherwise, these outlets risk losing their substantial customer base, not to mention access to revolutionary marketing strategies and technologies that only upstart Internet companies can seem to initiate. For example, YouTube is piloting some innovative advertising programs that may allay the fears of the conglomerates, while at the same time, rewarding them with revenue. One program, called "participatory video ads," is being embraced by companies such as General Motors, Adidas, and Coca-Cola. These firms have purchased YouTube video space to spotlight their brands. As with personal videos placed on the Web site, users can rate and comment on the commercially made videos.

In a separate marketing development, on Feb. 22, 2007, Fox Interactive Media (owner of MySpace) announced that it had acquired Strategic Data Corporation. Like DoubleClick . . . Strategic Data is a digital advertising company. Fox hopes to use Strategic Data's systems to persuade more users to click on ads placed on the MySpace Web site.

Until the media giants simmer down, however, MySpace and YouTube will face legal battles over copyrighted music and movie clips for some time to come. The confrontations will be fierce, but Google and News Corp. have significant financial resources and large legal staffs to handle the lawsuits. In fact, after its takeover of YouTube, Google set aside more than $200 million (funded through stock held in escrow) to cover future litigation costs.

As we went to press, News Corp. and NBC Universal announced plans to launch a legally pure, video distribution network some view as a potential competitor to YouTube. Scheduled to launch this summer, the new service will stock an online video site with masses of TV shows and videos, plus clips that users will be allowed to modify and share. Partners in the project already include the usual Google competitors—AOL, MSN, and Yahoo!. Television library content will be advertiser-supported and free to users. Some outlets will support mashups and online communities. Downloading movies will require user payments.

Digital Rights Management and the Steve Jobs Controversy

Like the digital object identifier (DOI) technology developed by publishers to tag and track electronic copyrighted works, media companies have created features in digital rights management (DRM) technology to make it difficult for users to copy or transfer audio and video files. Generally, technologies to thwart file sharing have failed, with media companies relying on their own personnel to scan the Internet for unauthorized copies. Even after threatening the offending parties, content providers continue to struggle in tracking down the same illegal copies likely to appear elsewhere on the Web.

On Feb. 6, 2007, Apple's Steve Jobs posted an essay on his company's Web site . . . entitled "Thoughts on Music." Jobs proposed that digital rights management (DRM) software preventing music reproduction and piracy be eliminated, so that songs could be played on any device. Apple licenses music rights from the "big four" music companies: Universal, Sony BMG, Warner, and EMI. According to Jobs, these companies "control the distribution of over 70% of the world's music." When Apple started its iTunes service, the company "was able to negotiate landmark usage rights at the time, which include allowing users to play their DRM protected music on up to 5 computers and on an unlimited number of iPods. Obtaining such rights from the music companies was unprecedented at the time, and even today is unmatched by most other digital music services. However, a key provision of our agreements with the music companies is that if our DRM system is compromised and their music becomes playable on unauthorized devices, we have only a small number of weeks to fix the problem or they can withdraw their entire music catalog from our iTunes store.... So far we have met our commitments to the music companies to protect their music, and we have given users the most liberal usage rights available in the industry for legally downloaded music."

The controversy with Jobs' posting comes with his proposal to completely abolish blocking DRM protections. He wrote: "Imagine a world where every online store sells DRM-free music encoded in open licensable formats. In such a world, any player can play music purchased from any store, and any store can sell music which is playable on all players." Jobs justifies such an open source solution because he believes that DRM systems have never worked to prevent music piracy. He claims that music CDs are completely unprotected, so that "all the music distributed on CDs can be easily uploaded to the Internet, then (illegally) downloaded and played on any computer or player. In 2006, under 2 billion DRM-protected songs were sold worldwide by online stores, while over 20 billion songs were sold completely DRM-free and unprotected on CDs by the music companies themselves. The music companies sell the vast majority of their music DRM-free, and show no signs of changing this behavior, since the over-whelming majority of their revenues depend on selling CDs which must play in CD players that support no DRM system. ... Convincing [the big four] to license their music to Apple and others DRM-free will create a truly interoperable music marketplace."

Many music industry analysts agree with Jobs—that nothing will prevent piracy. Those who buy iPods are not purchasing many DRM-protected recordings. Rather, consumers purchase music on CDs and down-load individual tracks into the format of their choice on the iPods. Jobs justified his position on DRMs by providing statistics on what the iTunes store sells: "Today's most popular iPod holds 1000 songs, and research tells us that the average iPod is nearly full. This means that only 22 out of 1000 songs, or under 3% of the music on the average iPod, is purchased from the iTunes store and protected with a DRM. The remaining 97% of the music is unprotected and playable on any player that can play the open formats. It's hard to believe that just 3% of the music on the average iPod is enough to lock users into buying only iPods in the future. And since 97% of the music on the average iPod was not purchased from the iTunes store, iPod users are clearly not locked into the iTunes store to acquire their music."

On the flip side, those opposed to Jobs' proposal to eliminate DRM protections point out the pressure Jobs faces from European fair trade laws that will soon mandate making iTunes music available to non-Apple devices. If an unrestricted MP3 format is adopted across the music industry, any digital device could download music from any source. Looking to the future, Jobs may envision expanding the iTunes concept to movies, TV programs, electronic books, and other media. With DRM blocking eliminated, content from a wide range of formats could be downloaded to any digital device.

On Feb. 15, 2007, Rob Pegoraro, a reporter with *The Washington Post*, succinctly summarized all the fuss whirling in the entertainment industry:

The [DRM] technology can still serve a role in online music or movie rental services, which have drawn far fewer customers than stores like iTunes, but for purchases it does too little to justify its costs. In practice, it only stops copying by the unmotivated, the over-scheduled or the inexperienced—the people most likely to buy a song or movie online as long as they can do so quickly, easily and cheaply. In the music industry, a growing number of outlets beyond the big-name companies, from tiny indie-rock operations to the Philadelphia Orchestra and the Smithsonian Institution's Folkways label, have realized the futility of copy-restriction software and now sell digital downloads in open, unrestricted formats. At this point, this all amounts to little more than expensive psychotherapy for Hollywood executives. It's the height of arrogance for them to keep sending us the bill.

My thoughts exactly! . . .

POSTSCRIPT

Do Copyright Laws Protect Ownership of Intellectual Property?

One of the most difficult aspects about copyright is that depending on how the law is enforced, the result can be a form of censorship. The challenge, then, is to find the balance of protecting original work that truly belongs to an author who justifiably can claim credit for the work it took to produce something, versus creating an atmosphere that either does not recompense an author, or shifts all work into public domain.

As courts have tried to sort out problems with traditional copyright legislation and newer technologies, several attempts have been made to narrow the focus of the application of the law. The court case that resulted in a consumer's right to record film and television programs off of the television came from *Universal City Studios, Inc. v. Sony Corp. of America, 659 F.2d 963* (9th Cir. 1981), but stipulated that the copy was to be for personal use only. The current Copyright Act allows consumers to duplicate CDs and computer software for backup purposes, and to modify them as necessary, but all of these court cases favored the consumer with clear stipulation that duplicated material cannot and should not be sold to anyone else.

Problems with copyright become much more difficult when people post things on the Internet, digitally manipulate images, or link to other Web sites. Does the content copied from one form take on a new identity as "creative, original work" when an artist (or home consumer) manipulates images and puts them into a new form—such as taking still pictures and animating them, then posting them on the Web? How might a wiki, like wikipedia, inadvertently violate copyright? It may come as no surprise that copyright law is one of the fastest growing topics and areas of specializations in law schools around the country.

In addition to the way a home consumer might harmlessly use someone else's copyrighted work, organizations that deal with fairness legal issues are concerned about their involvement in abuses of copyright, and their liability. James G. Neal writes in "Copyright Is Dead . . . Long Live Copyright," *American Libraries* (December 2002, pp. 48–51) of the problems public institutions have with trying to police the Internet and duplication technologies in their organizations. Heather Green's article, "Whose Video Is It, Anyway? YouTube's Runaway Success Has Opened a Pandora's Box of Copyright Issues," *BusinessWeek* (August 7, 2006, p. 38), explains how businesses should be aware of copyright violations. Rob Pegorano, the technology writer for the *Washington Post*, has written a series of articles on copyright infringements, including "Time to Face the Music on File Sharing" (February 15, 2007, p. D1).

As you consider the many sides of the debate on copyright and digital technology, it might be useful to think of how different persons might respond to the issues. For example, how might a screenwriter think about file sharing of his or her film, downloaded from the Internet? How would the author of a book feel about electronic distribution of the book she or he wrote, if no royalties, or lesser royalties were paid for the copies of the work? How do those people who work in the important—yet often less visible fields—such as CD package design, feel about digital duplication? And of course, what would the position of an independent retailer be, on the elimination of copyrighted works for sale? How would you feel if a paper you wrote over a long period of time, were posted to the Internet and other people used your work without attributing credit to you?

ISSUE 6

Is Advertising Good for Society?

YES: John E. Calfee, from "How Advertising Informs to Our Benefit," *Consumers' Research* (April 1998)

NO: Dinyar Godrej, from "How the Ad Industry Pins Us Down," *New Internationalist* (September 2006)

ISSUE SUMMARY

YES: John E. Calfee, a former U.S. Trade Commission economist, takes the position that advertising is very useful to people and that the information that advertising imparts helps consumers make better decisions. He maintains that the benefits of advertising far outweigh the negative criticisms.

NO: Author Dinyar Godrej makes the claim that advertising doesn't really tell us anything new about products, but instead, it acts upon our emotions to create anxiety if we don't buy products. The result then, is a culture in which we consume more than we need to, and still feel badly about ourselves. This type of consumer culture then permeates our lifestyles.

Professor Dallas Smythe first described commercial media as a system for delivering audiences to advertisers. This perception of the viewing public as a "market" for products as well as an audience for advertising—a main source of media revenue—reflects the economic orientation of the current media system in America. The unplanned side effects of advertising, however, concern many critics. The creation of a consumer society, materialism, and high expectations are one set of concerns, but these issues also conflict with many cultural expectations, histories, and social systems in many countries where advertising is considered a Western, capitalist construct.

John E. Calfee addresses many of these issues, but also focuses on how the information in ads benefits consumers. He takes the position that advertising functions in the public's interest, and that even the controversies about ads can be beneficial because they can result in competitive pricing for consumers. Citing some specific cases, he states that individuals can learn about important issues (such as health) through ads. He even considers what he calls "less bad" ads, which give consumers important negative information that can be useful to their well-being.

In the second selection, Dinyar Godrej takes the perspective that advertising creates an assault on our senses, that advertising can act as a "compulsive liar," and that the clutter that advertising creates bombards us with images, and ideas that result in a subtle cultural shift that creates desires that only the wealthy can actually attain. This author takes the point of view that there is really nothing positive that advertising contributes to a society, and that just about everything about advertising is negative.

These views illustrate the extreme polarities in positions that people often take when it comes to the topic of advertising. There are also other, more neutral views, such as those held by people who don't mind advertising, and see it as an economic engine to deliver "free" programs to people, or the idea that advertising is an art form in itself, that, if viewed critically, can make a social comment on the styles, consumer culture, and artifacts of different social groups. Yet others focus on the creative aspects of advertising and revere the way it can stimulate, motivate, or resonate with viewers. Whatever the perspective, one thing is true: advertising can have both manifest and latent impact. It can be defended on solid ground, and criticized on solid ground.

Many students today don't seem to mind advertising. A typical comment is that they just don't let the messages "get" to them, but it is important to think about one's own critical faculties, and those of others. Do you think of advertising as one of today's most persuasive forms of communication, or just a by-product of something else? It might be interesting to try to think about how a person's environment would be different if there were no ads.

A thorough understanding of how advertising functions in society, and as an industry that is responsible for billions of dollars annually, helps form a person's views on the impact of advertising in their lives, and in the lives of others. It also helps to think about what products are advertised and to whom: Should tobacco and alcohol ads be targeted to children and teens? Do advertising costs actually raise the price of goods, rather than stimulate the circulation of goods in society? Is advertising the engine that runs a consumer society, or does capitalism create industries, like advertising, to continue to support its operation within a society? Furthermore, as Godrej points out, what impact does advertising (particularly from Western societies) have on traditional cultures?

It should also be noted that there are many forms of advertising. We often first think of product advertising, but what of corporate sponsorship, or indirect advertising through product placement (referred to in the industry as "product enhancement")? Dinyar Godrej does an excellent job of reminding us that there are many subtle styles of influence that go beyond the initial knee-jerk reaction to advertising as a harmless by-product of industry in the twenty-first century.

YES

John E. Calfee

How Advertising Informs
to Our Benefit

A great truth about advertising is that it is a tool for communicating infor-mation and shaping markets. It is one of the forces that compel sellers to cater to the desires of consumers. Almost everyone knows this because consumers use advertising every day, and they miss advertising when they cannot get it. This fact does not keep politicians and opinion leaders from routinely dis-missing the value of advertising. But the truth is that people find advertising very useful indeed.

Of course, advertising primarily seeks to persuade and everyone knows this, too. The typical ad tries to induce a consumer to do one particular thing—usually, buy a product—instead of a thousand other things. There is nothing obscure about this purpose or what it means for buyers. Decades of data and centuries of intuition reveal that all consumers everywhere are deeply suspicious of what advertisers say and why they say it. This skepticism is in fact the driving force that makes advertising so effective. The persuasive purpose of advertising and the skepticism with which it is met are two sides of a single process. Persuasion and skepticism work in tandem so advertising can do its job in competitive markets. Hence, ads represent the seller's self interest, consumers know this, and sellers know that consumers know it.

By understanding this process more fully, we can sort out much of the popular confusion surrounding advertising and how it benefits consumers.

How useful is advertising? Just how useful is the connection between advertising and information? At first blush, the process sounds rather limited. Volvo ads tell consumers that Volvos have side-impact air bags, people learn a little about the importance of air bags, and Volvo sells a few more cars. This seems to help hardly anyone except Volvo and its customers.

But advertising does much more. It routinely provides immense amounts of information that benefits primarily parties other than the advertiser. This may sound odd, but it is a logical result of market forces and the nature of infor-mation itself.

The ability to use information to sell products is an incentive to create new information through research. Whether the topic is nutrition, safety, or more mundane matters like how to measure amplifier power, the necessity of achieving credibility with consumers and critics requires much of this research to be placed in the public domain, and that it rest upon some academic credentials. That kind of research typically produces results that apply to more than just the brands sold by the firm sponsoring the research. The lack of property rights to such "pure" information ensures that this extra information is available at no charge. Both consumers and competitors may borrow the new information for their own purposes.

Advertising also elicits additional information from other sources. Claims that are striking, original, forceful or even merely obnoxious will generate news stories about the claims, the controversies they cause, the reactions of competitors (A price war? A splurge of comparison ads?), the reactions of consumers and the remarks of governments and independent authorities.

Probably the most concrete, pervasive, and persistent example of competitive advertising that works for the public good is price advertising. Its effect is invariably to heighten competition and reduce prices, even the prices of firms that assiduously avoid mentioning prices in their own advertising.

There is another area where the public benefits of advertising are less obvious but equally important. The unremitting nature of consumer interest in health, and the eagerness of sellers to cater to consumer desires, guarantee that advertising related to health will provide a storehouse of telling observations on the ways in which the benefits of advertising extend beyond the interests of advertisers to include the interests of the public at large.

A cascade of information   Here is probably the best documented example of why advertising is necessary for consumer welfare. In the 1970s, public health experts described compelling evidence that people who eat more fiber are less likely to get cancer, especially cancer of the colon, which happens to be the second leading cause of deaths from cancer in the United States. By 1979, the U.S. Surgeon General was recommending that people eat more fiber in order to prevent cancer.

Consumers appeared to take little notice of these recommendations, however. The National Cancer Institute decided that more action was needed. NCI's cancer prevention division undertook to communicate the new information about fiber and cancer to the general public. Their goal was to change consumer diets and reduce the risk of cancer, but they had little hope of success given the tiny advertising budgets of federal agencies like NCI.

Their prospects unexpectedly brightened in 1984. NCI received a call from the Kellogg Corporation, whose All-Bran cereal held a commanding market share of the high-fiber segment. Kellogg proposed to use All-Bran advertising as a vehicle for NCI's public service messages. NCI thought that was an excellent idea. Soon, an agreement was reached in which NCI would review Kellogg's ads and labels for accuracy and value before Kellogg began running their fiber-cancer ads.

The new Kellogg All-Bran campaign opened in October 1984. A typical ad began with the headline, "At last some news about cancer you can live with." The ad continued: "The National Cancer Institute believes a high fiber, low fat diet may reduce your risk of some kinds of cancer. The National Cancer

Institute reports some very good health news. There is growing evidence that may link a high fiber, low fat diet to lower incidence of some kinds of cancer. That's why one of their strongest recommendations is to eat high-fiber foods. If you compare, you'll find Kellogg's All-Bran has nine grams of fiber per serving. No other cereal has more. So start your day with a bowl of Kellogg's All-Bran or mix it with your regular cereal."

The campaign quickly achieved two things. One was to create a regulatory crisis between two agencies. The Food and Drug Administration thought that if a food was advertised as a way to prevent cancer, it was being marketed as a drug. Then the FDA's regulations for drug labeling would kick in. The food would be reclassified as a drug and would be removed from the market until the seller either stopped making the health claims or put the product through the clinical testing necessary to obtain formal approval as a drug.

But food advertising is regulated by the Federal Trade Commission, not the FDA. The FTC thought Kellogg's ads were non-deceptive and were therefore perfectly legal. In fact, it thought the ads should be encouraged. The Director of the FTC's Bureau of Consumer Protection declared that "the [Kellogg] ad has presented important public health recommendations in an accurate, useful, and substantiated way. It informs the members of the public that there is a body of data suggesting certain relationships between cancer and diet that they may find important." The FTC won this political battle, and the ads continued.

The second instant effect of the All-Bran campaign was to unleash a flood of health claims. Vegetable oil manufacturers advertised that cholesterol was associated with coronary heart disease, and that vegetable oil does not contain cholesterol. Margarine ads did the same, and added that vitamin A is essential for good vision. Ads for calcium products (such as certain antacids) provided vivid demonstrations of the effects of osteoporosis (which weakens bones in old age), and recounted the advice of experts to increase dietary calcium as a way to prevent osteoporosis. Kellogg's competitors joined in citing the National Cancer Institute dietary recommendations.

Nor did things stop there. In the face of consumer demand for better and fuller information, health claims quickly evolved from a blunt tool to a surprisingly refined mechanism. Cereals were advertised as high in fiber and low in sugar or fat or sodium. Ads for an upscale brand of bread noted: "Well, most high-fiber bran cereals may be high in fiber, but often only one kind: insoluble. It's this kind of fiber that helps promote regularity. But there's also a kind of fiber known as soluble, which most high-fiber bran cereals have in very small amounts, if at all. Yet diets high in this kind of fiber may actually lower your serum cholesterol, a risk factor for some heart diseases." Cereal boxes became convenient sources for a summary of what made for a good diet.

Increased independent information   The ads also brought powerful secondary effects. These may have been even more useful than the information that actually appeared in the ads themselves.

One effect was an increase in media coverage of diet and health. *Consumer Reports*, a venerable and hugely influential magazine that carries no advertising, revamped its reports on cereals to emphasize fiber and other ingredients (rather than testing the foods to see how well they did at providing a complete diet for laboratory rats). The health-claims phenomenon generated its own press coverage, with articles like "What Has All-Bran Wrought?" and "The Fiber Furor." These stories recounted the ads and scientific information that prompted the ads; and articles on food and health proliferated. Anyone who lived through these years in the United States can probably remember the unending media attention to health claims and to diet and health generally.

Much of the information on diet and health was new. This was no coincidence. Firms were sponsoring research on their products in the hope of finding results that could provide a basis for persuasive advertising claims. Oat bran manufacturers, for example, funded research on the impact of soluble fiber on blood cholesterol. When the results came out "wrong," as they did in a 1990 study published with great fanfare in *The New England Journal of Medicine*, the headline in *Advertising Age* was "Oat Bran Popularity Hitting the Skids," and it did indeed tumble. The manufacturers kept at the research, however, and eventually the best research supported the efficacy of oat bran in reducing cholesterol (even to the satisfaction of the FDA). Thus did pure advertising claims spill over to benefit the information environment at large.

The shift to higher fiber cereals encompassed brands that had never undertaken the effort necessary to construct believable ads about fiber and disease. Two consumer researchers at the FDA reviewed these data and concluded they were "consistent with the successful educational impact of the Kellogg diet and health campaign: consumers seemed to be making an apparently thoughtful discrimination between high- and low-fiber cereals," and that the increased market shares for high-fiber non-advertised products represented "the clearest evidence of a successful consumer education campaign."

Perhaps most dramatic were the changes in consumer awareness of diet and health. An FTC analysis of government surveys showed that when consumers were asked about how they could prevent cancer through their diet, the percentage who mentioned fiber increased from 4% before the 1979 Surgeon General's report to 8.5% in 1984 (after the report but before the All-Bran campaign) to 32% in 1986 after a year and a half or so of health claims (the figure in 1988 was 28%). By far the greatest increases in awareness were among women (who do most of the grocery shopping) and the less educated: up from 0% for women without a high school education in 1984 to 31% for the same group in 1986. For women with incomes of less than $15,000, the increase was from 6% to 28%.

The health-claims advertising phenomenon achieved what years of effort by government agencies had failed to achieve. With its mastery of the art of brevity, its ability to command attention, and its use of television, brand advertising touched precisely the people the public health community was most desperate to reach. The health claims expanded consumer information along a broad front. The benefits clearly extended far beyond the interests of the relatively few manufacturers who made vigorous use of health claims in advertising.

A pervasive phenomenon   Health claims for foods are only one example, however, of a pervasive phenomenon—the use of advertising to provide essential health information with benefits extending beyond the interests of the advertisers themselves.

Advertising for soap and detergents, for example, once improved private hygiene and therefore, public health (hygiene being one of the underappreciated triumphs in twentieth century public health). Toothpaste advertising helped to do the same for teeth. When mass advertising for toothpaste and tooth powder began early in this century, tooth brushing was rare. It was common by the 1930s, after which toothpaste sales leveled off even though the advertising, of course, continued. When fluoride toothpastes became available, advertising generated interest in better teeth and professional dental care. Later, a "plaque reduction war" (which first involved mouthwashes, and later toothpastes) brought a new awareness of gum disease and how to prevent it. The financial gains to the toothpaste industry were surely dwarfed by the benefits to consumers in the form of fewer cavities and fewer lost teeth.

Health claims induced changes in foods, in non-foods such as toothpaste, in publications ranging from university health letters to mainstream newspapers and magazines, and of course, consumer knowledge of diet and health.

These rippling effects from health claims in ads demonstrated the most basic propositions in the economics of information. Useful information initially failed to reach people who needed it because information producers could not charge a price to cover the costs of creating and disseminating pure information. And this problem was alleviated by advertising, sometimes in a most vivid manner.

Other examples of spillover benefits from advertising are far more common than most people realize. Even the much-maligned promotion of expensive new drugs can bring profound health benefits to patients and families, far exceeding what is actually charged for the products themselves.

The market processes that produce these benefits bear all the classic features of competitive advertising. We are not analyzing public service announcements here, but old-fashioned profit-seeking brand advertising. Sellers focused on the information that favored their own products. They advertised it in ways that provided a close link with their own brand. It was a purely competitive enterprise, and the benefits to consumers arose from the imperatives of the competitive process.

One might see all this as simply an extended example of the economics of information and greed. And indeed it is, if by greed one means the effort to earn a profit by providing what people are willing to pay for, even if what they want most is information rather than a tangible product. The point is that there is overwhelming evidence that unregulated economic forces dictate that much useful information will be provided by brand advertising, and *only* by brand advertising.

Of course, there is much more to the story. There is the question of how competition does the good I have described without doing even more harm elsewhere. After all, firms want to tell people only what is good about their brands, and people often want to know what is wrong with the brands. It turns out that competition takes care of this problem, too.

Advertising and context   It is often said that most advertising does not contain very much information. In a way, this is true. Research on the contents of advertising typically finds just a few pieces of concrete information per ad. That's an average, of course. Some ads obviously contain a great deal of information. Still, a lot of ads are mainly images and pleasant talk, with little in the way of what most people would consider hard information. On the whole, information in advertising comes in tiny bits and pieces.

Cost is only one reason. To be sure, cramming more information into ads is expensive. But more to the point is the fact that advertising plays off the information available from outside sources. Hardly anything about advertising is more important than the interplay between what the ad contains and what surrounds it. Sometimes this interplay is a burden for the advertiser because it is beyond his control. But the interchange between advertising and environment is also an invaluable tool for sellers. Ads that work in collaboration with outside information can communicate far more than they ever could on their own.

The upshot is advertising's astonishing ability to communicate a great deal of information in a few words. Economy and vividness of expression almost always rely upon what is in the information environment. The famously concise "Think Small" and "Lemon" ads for the VW "Beetle" in the 1960s and 1970s were highly effective with buyers concerned about fuel economy, repair costs, and extravagant styling in American cars. This was a case where the less said, the better. The ads were more powerful when consumers were free to bring their own ideas about the issues to bear.

The same process is repeated over again for all sorts of products. Ads for computer modems once explained what they could be used for. Now a simple reference to the Internet is sufficient to conjure an elaborate mix of equipment and applications. These matters are better left vague so each potential customer can bring to the ad his own idea of what the Internet is really for.

Leaning on information from other sources is also a way to enhance credibility, without which advertising must fail. Much of the most important information in advertising—think of cholesterol and heart disease, antilock brakes and automobile safety—acquires its force from highly credible sources *other* than the advertiser. To build up this kind of credibility through material actually contained in ads would be cumbersome and inefficient. Far more effective, and far more economical, is the technique of making challenges, raising questions and otherwise making it perfectly clear to the audience that the seller invites comparisons and welcomes the tough questions. Hence the classic slogan, "If you can find a better whisky, buy it."

Finally, there is the most important point of all. Informational sparseness facilitates competition. It is easier to challenge a competitor through pungent slogans—"Where's the beef?", "Where's the big saving?"—than through a step-by-step recapitulation of what has gone on before. The bits-and-pieces approach makes for quick, unerring attacks and equally quick responses, all under the watchful eye of the consumer over whom the battle is being fought. This is an ideal recipe for competition.

It also brings the competitive market's fabled self-correcting forces into play. Sellers are less likely to stretch the truth, whether it involves prices or subtleties about safety and performance, when they know they may arouse a merciless response from injured competitors. That is one reason the FTC once worked to get comparative ads on television, and has sought for decades to dismantle government or voluntary bans on comparative ads.

'Less-bad' advertising   There is a troubling possibility, however. Is it not possible that in their selective and carefully calculated use of outside information, advertisers have the power to focus consumer attention exclusively on the positive, i.e., on what is good about the brand or even the entire product class? Won't automobile ads talk up style, comfort, and extra safety, while food ads do taste and convenience, cigarette ads do flavor and lifestyle, and airlines do comfort and frequency of departure, all the while leaving consumers to search through other sources to find all the things that are wrong with products?

In fact, this is not at all what happens. Here is why: Everything for sale has something wrong with it, if only the fact that you have to pay for it. Some products, of course, are notable for their faults. The most obvious examples involve tobacco and health, but there are also food and heart disease, drugs and side effects, vacations and bad weather, automobiles and accidents, airlines and delay, among others.

Products and their problems bring into play one of the most important ways in which the competitive market induces sellers to serve the interests of buyers. No matter what the product, there are usually a few brands that are "less bad" than the others. The natural impulse is to advertise that advantage— "less cholesterol," "less fat," "less dangerous," and so on. Such provocative claims tend to have an immediate impact. The targets often retaliate; maybe their brands are less bad in a different respect (less salt?). The ensuing struggle brings better information, more informed choices, and improved products.

Perhaps the most riveting episode of "less-bad" advertising ever seen occurred, amazingly enough, in the industry that most people assume is the master of avoiding saying anything bad about its product.

Less-bad cigarette ads   Cigarette advertising was once very different from what it is today. Cigarettes first became popular around the time of World War I, and they came to dominate the tobacco market in the 1920s. Steady and often dramatic sales increases continued into the 1950s, always with vigorous support from advertising. Tobacco advertising was duly celebrated as an outstanding example of the power and creativity of advertising. Yet amazingly, much of the advertising focused on what was wrong with smoking, rather than what people liked about smoking.

The very first ad for the very first mass-marketed American cigarette brand (Camel, the same brand recently under attack for its use of a cartoon character) said, "Camel Cigarettes will not sting the tongue and will not parch the throat." When Old Gold broke into the market in the mid-1920s, it did so with an ad campaign about coughs and throats and harsh cigarette smoke. It settled on the slogan, "Not a cough in a carload."

Competitors responded in kind. Soon, advertising left no doubt about what was wrong with smoking. Lucky Strike ads said, "No Throat Irritation—No Cough . . . we . . . removed . . . harmful corrosive acids," and later on, "Do you inhale? What's there to be afraid of? . . . famous purifying process removes certain impurities." Camel's famous tag line, "more doctors smoke Camels than any other brand," carried a punch precisely because many authorities thought smoking was unhealthy (cigarettes were called "coffin nails" back then), and smokers were eager for reassurance in the form of smoking by doctors themselves. This particular ad, which was based on surveys of physicians, ran in one form or another from 1933 to 1955. It achieved prominence partly because physicians practically never endorsed non-therapeutic products.

Things really got interesting in the early 1950s, when the first persuasive medical reports on smoking and lung cancer reached the public. These reports created a phenomenal stir among smokers and the public generally. People who do not understand how advertising works would probably assume that cigarette manufacturers used advertising to divert attention away from the cancer reports. In fact, they did the opposite.

Small brands could not resist the temptation to use advertising to scare smokers into switching brands. They inaugurated several spectacular years of "fear advertising" that sought to gain competitive advantage by exploiting smokers' new fear of cancer. Lorillard, the beleaguered seller of Old Gold, introduced Kent, a new filter brand supported by ad claims like these: "Sensitive smokers get real health protection with new Kent," "Do you love a good smoke but not what the smoke does to you?" and "Takes out more nicotine and tars than any other leading cigarette—*the difference in protection is priceless,*" illustrated by television ads showing the black tar trapped by Kent's filters.

Other manufacturers came out with their own filter brands, and raised the stakes with claims like, "Nose, throat, and accessory organs not adversely affected by smoking Chesterfields. First such report ever published about any cigarette," "Takes the fear out of smoking," and "Stop worrying . . . Philip Morris and only Philip Morris is entirely free of irritation used [sic] in all other leading cigarettes."

These ads threatened to demolish the industry. Cigarette sales plummeted by 3% in 1953 and a remarkable 6% in 1954. Never again, not even in the face of the most impassioned anti-smoking publicity by the Surgeon General or the FDA, would cigarette consumption decline as rapidly as it did during these years of entirely market-driven anti-smoking ad claims by the cigarette industry itself.

Thus advertising traveled full circle. Devised to bolster brands, it denigrated the product so much that overall market demand actually declined. Everyone understood what was happening, but the fear ads continued because they helped the brands that used them. The new filter brands (all from smaller manufacturers) gained a foothold even as their ads amplified the medical reports on the dangers of smoking. It was only after the FTC stopped the fear ads in 1955 (on the grounds that the implied health claims had no proof) that sales resumed their customary annual increases.

Fear advertising has never quite left the tobacco market despite the regulatory straight jacket that governs cigarette advertising. In 1957, when leading cancer experts advised smokers to ingest less tar, the industry responded by cutting tar and citing tar content figures compiled by independent sources. A stunning "tar derby" reduced the tar and nicotine content of cigarettes by 40% in four years, a far more rapid decline than would be achieved by years of government urging in later decades. This episode, too, was halted by the FTC. In February 1960 the FTC engineered a "voluntary" ban on tar and nicotine claims.

Further episodes continue to this day. In 1993, for example, Liggett planned an advertising campaign to emphasize that its Chesterfield brand did not use the stems and less desirable parts of the tobacco plant. This continuing saga, extending through eight decades, is perhaps the best documented case of how "less-bad" advertising completely offsets any desires by sellers to accentuate the positive while ignoring the negative. *Consumer Reports* magazine's 1955 assessment of the new fear of smoking still rings true:

> ". . . companies themselves are largely to blame. Long before the current medical attacks, the companies were building up suspicion in the consumer by the discredited 'health claims' in their ads.... Such medicine-show claims may have given the smoker temporary confidence in one brand, but they also implied that cigarettes in general were distasteful, probably harmful, and certainly a 'problem.' When the scientists came along with their charges against cigarettes, the smoker was ready to accept them."

And that is how information works in competitive advertising.

Less-bad can be found wherever competitive advertising is allowed. I already described the health-claims-for-foods saga, which featured fat and cholesterol and the dangers of cancer and heart disease. Price advertising is another example. Prices are the most stubbornly negative product feature of all, because they represent the simple fact that the buyer must give up something else. There is no riper target for comparative advertising. When sellers advertise lower prices, competitors reduce their prices and advertise that, and soon a price war is in the works. This process so strongly favors consumers over the industry that one of the first things competitors do when they form a trade group is to propose an agreement to restrict or ban price advertising (if not ban all advertising). When that fails, they try to get advertising regulators to stop price ads, an attempt that unfortunately often succeeds.

Someone is always trying to scare customers into switching brands out of fear of the product itself. The usual effect is to impress upon consumers what they do not like about the product. In 1991, when Americans were worried about insurance companies going broke, a few insurance firms advertised that they were more solvent than their competitors. In May 1997, United Airlines began a new ad campaign that started out by reminding fliers of all the inconveniences that seem to crop up during air travel.

Health information is a fixture in "less-bad" advertising. Ads for sleeping aids sometimes focus on the issue of whether they are habit-forming. In March 1996, a medical journal reported that the pain reliever acetaminophen, the active ingredient in Tylenol, can cause liver damage in heavy drinkers. This fact immediately became the focus of ads for Advil, a competing product. A public debate ensued, conducted through advertising, talk shows, news reports and pronouncements from medical authorities. The result: consumers learned a lot more than they had known before about the fact that all drugs have side effects. The press noted that this dispute may have helped consumers, but it hurt the pain reliever industry. Similar examples abound.

We have, then, a general rule: sellers will use comparative advertising when permitted to do so, even if it means spreading bad information about a product instead of favorable information. The mechanism usually takes the form of less-bad claims. One can hardly imagine a strategy more likely to give consumers the upper hand in the give and take of the marketplace. Less-bad claims are a primary means by which advertising serves markets and consumers rather than sellers. They completely refute the naive idea that competitive advertising will emphasize only the sellers' virtues while obscuring their problems.

How the Ad Industry Pins Us Down

Buddhism and Hinduism recommend it. A retreat from clamour, a wondrous detachment that allows the material world to float up, like a sloughed-off skin, for one's dispassionate consideration. Whether they offer useful advice on re-engaging after this revelation, I don't know. The first astronauts saw a floating world, too. It provoked suitably joined-up thoughts about its (and our) fragility and essential unity.

But there are other worlds. And the one that elbows itself to the front of our attention's queue painstakingly creates surface and whips up froth. It's the one that the 125 residents of Clark, Texas, signed up to in 2005 when they changed the name of their township to Dish in return for a decade's free cable TV from the DISH Network. Hey, what's in a name except a wacky corporate PR opportunity, right?

The bubbly, dazzling world of which Dish has become an emblem shows little sign of floating up for our inspection. If we inspect it nonetheless, it reveals itself to be firmly riveted down by that old culprit—disproportionate corporate power.

Advertising is a bit of a compulsive liar. In the early days it was quite bare-faced—the beverage giant, Dewar's, claiming in the 1930s that their Scotch whiskey repelled colds and flu; cigarette brands claiming that they soothed the throat and helped asthma. Some of this still goes on. Quack cures are advertised in numerous Majority World countries. The half of all Mexican citizens who are overweight are pummelled daily on TV by products that promise to melt 10 centimetres off the waistline in two hours.

Repeat After Me

Nowadays, regulatory bodies will see off many of the more obviously fraudulent claims.

But advertising is involved in soul fraud instead. If that sounds a bit deep, just stay with me a while.

Advertising today has little to do with introducing a new product or describing an existing one's virtues. It has everything to do with images, dreams and emotions; stuff we are evolutionarily programmed to engage with but which is, almost without exception in the ad biz, fake. Imagine how much attention you would pay if there were just text and no images. When ads for Sprite (owned by Coca-Cola) proclaimed: 'Image is nothing, thirst is everything', they were reassuring people that they were right to be distrustful, while building up images of honesty and straight talk, using professional basketball players to push the product: Sprite jumped several notches up the soft-drink rankings; moolah was minted. Image was everything, even if it was purporting to be an anti-image.

Amid the visual clutter, advertising—the chief agent of the mess—has to jump out at us. It must trigger off associations, however tangential, that will keep our attention. Endless repetition through media channels should build up a handy cloud of associations. According to one industry executive: 'In the context of most advertising, particularly passively consumed media like television and cinema, learning is incidental, not deliberate. This is why people tell you they are not influenced by advertising. They are not actively trying to take anything away from the experience, and therefore are not influenced at that time; but the effects will show up later, long after a particular viewing experience is forgotten.

Much effort is expended upon trying to sink boreholes into the vast iceberg of the subconscious mind, probably because the products being flogged are in reality just variations on the same old same old. A recent buzzword is 'neuromarketing'. Neuroscientists and psychiatrists are searching for the buy-button in the brain. This involves putting subjects into brain-scanning machinery and pitching concepts and images at them to see which ones make the lights flash. In one experiment, subjects were made to blind-taste Pepsi and Coke. Pepsi scored higher in terms of response in the ventral putamen, the part of the brain associated with feelings of reward—ie, most thought Pepsi tasted better. But when the subjects were informed which drink was Coke before they tried it, their medial prefrontal cortexes lit up. This is an area of the brain believed to control cognition. Most now said they preferred Coke. So just the name had prompted memories and brand nostalgia which influenced the taste of the stuff. One might question the validity of using expensive hospital equipment and highly trained medical professionals to explain choices of fizzy drinks with no nutritional value whatsoever—but that would be to get a bit real.

The good news is that all this dubious effort is just as likely to fail as it is to succeed. If an ad can latch on to the emotion of a winning goal in a football match or the tears and triumphs of Pop Idol, then there's a good chance it will do the trick. Much else is trial and error. Focus groups assembled to pretest the vibe are notoriously unreliable as they can be suggestible and become dominated by loudmouths.

Anxieties of Influence

One might well ask: so what? So what if silly money . . . pushes the usual goods/junk, if I can still make an informed choice about what I buy?

Well, maybe . . . But how would you react if all this were seeping into the very pores of the culture you're part of—and changing it? Mass advertising is about brands with the most money behind them pushing to the top. Smaller companies with less of this fluff-muscle don't always survive.

More perniciously, corporate giants try every trick in the book to control our media channels. Much of the mainstream media exists to sell audiences to advertisers. Newspapers aren't profitable based on sales alone. The missing factor is ad money. It's their lifeblood. Teen magazines (especially those aimed at girls) are little more than catalogues for products—and that's the content. The profile of the chubby hero who saved a life is usually tucked away at the end.

Here's what an agency representing Coca-Cola demanded in a letter to magazines: 'We believe that positive and upbeat editorial provides a compatible environment in which to communicate the brand's message . . . We consider the following subjects to be inappropriate and require that our ads are not placed adjacent to articles discussing the following issues: Hard News; Sex related issues; Drugs (Prescription or Illegal); Medicine (eg chronic illnesses such as cancer, diabetes, AIDS, etc); Health (eg mental or physical conditions); Negative Diet Information (eg bulimia, anorexia, quick weight loss, etc); Food; Political issues; Environmental issues; Articles containing vulgar language; Religion. So, not much chance of a mention of the intimidation of union workers in Coke's Colombian plant, or of the charges of water pollution in India, then (read more at www.killercoke.org).

If anyone still thought they were watching 'the news' on CNN, anchor Jack Cafferty's on-air views might disabuse them: 'We are not here as a public service. We're here to make money. We sell advertising, and we do it on the premise that people are going to watch. If you don't cover the miners because you want to do a story about a debt crisis in Brazil at the time everybody else is covering the miners, then Citibank calls up and says, "You know what? We're not renewing the commercial contract." I mean, it's a business. In the US, one study found that 40 per cent of the 'news' content of a typical newspaper originated in press releases, story memos and suggestions from PR companies.

Hungry for Cool

More subtle is the cultural shift wrought in the media—light, non-political television programming that contributes to a 'buying mood'; magazines filled with little nuggets of 'instant gratification'; serious newspapers that insert lengthy travel and fashion sections for no obvious reason. So much happiness, so unbearable.

Advertising consistently portrays 'lifestyles' that are beyond the reach of all but the wealthy. This is somehow viewed as 'apolitical'. Yet charities' ads calling for dropping Southern debt or opposing cruelty to animals often fall foul of regulators or media ad-sales teams for being 'too political'.

As a child I loved the ads before the movie. They were zippy and bright. I found the varied angles they took before the 'Ta-dahhh!' moment when the product was plugged ingenious. I still find the creative energy that goes into them intriguing, but feel tired by their consistently conservative values and know better about the social, economic and environmental issues behind the products they push. I also feel fed up by the sheer volume of the glitzy deluge. Corporate advertisers know this fed up feeling all too well and have responded with marketing moves that look less like traditional advertising but seep more than ever into our lives. The upshot is that everything gets branded, logoed or sponsored. Supermarkets that shaft farmers sponsor children's play areas and school computers. Children are employed to hand out freebies to other kids and talk them up ('peer marketing'). Conspicuous charity abounds, trying to make the brand look more benign—for example, Ronald McDonald House offers accommodation to families with sick children. Product placement sneaks into movies, TV shows, computer games and even novels. Our email and cell phones are bombarded. Most websites would collapse without revenue from ads that get ever more lively and mysterious.

With traditional advertising showing diminishing returns, corporations get into all sorts of contortions. The apparel company Diesel ran a multimillion-dollar campaign contrasting clothing ads with scenes of hardship in North Korea; Benetton notoriously used the image of a man dying of AIDS to push its duds. Wow, just feel that edge!

A certain amount of advertising is probably unavoidable—indeed, countries that curb it often flood mental spaces with political propaganda instead. But the worldview the ad biz pushes is so out of touch with real life that it can mess up our heads. Ever wondered where that urge to shop when you're feeling a bit down comes from? Or how our desire for social change or rebellion gets transformed into speed, sex, indulgence and living for the moment? Why is so much of our culture about dictating taste (the tyrannies of 'cool') and transforming it into want? Why are disadvantaged groups (be they dark-skinned, sexual minorities, people with disabilities, you name it) so absent from this trendy world, unless they are being fetishized by niche marketing?

With the deluge comes avoidance. Ungrateful wretches that we are, we try to block out as much as we can. TV advertising is in crisis. Ad guru Lord Saatchi thinks young people nowadays have 'continual partial attention—the kind of brain that's constantly sifting but records little. His answer is for companies to strive for 'one-word equity' to fit this goldfish attention span—Be™, Live™, Buy™, anyone?

This dizziness is reflected in the philosophical musings of Maurice Levy, top honcho of advertising giant Publicis: 'Consumers do not want only to be given an astonishingly wide-ranging choice. They want that choice to be renewed at intervals that are always shorter. This is the reason why we have to redefine our very notion of time. What we have to deal with is not only change, but an accèleration of change itself. Not only transformations, but the transformation of transformations: it will be a real challenge to make fidelity out of inconstancy.'

He doesn't stop to ponder how his work is all about creating this blur of inconstancy. Advertising's influence is being implicated in eating, compulsive and attention-deficit disorders. In the Majority World the big brand steamroller is intent on creating Westernized aspirational cultures often at odds with local cultures.

If we are to free identity from consumerism, reality checks are our strongest weapon. If struck by an ad, it's useful to measure how much of it is actually telling you something about the product and how much is image.

Brands are eager that you identify with them, make them a part of your lives—deny them that privilege. Independent media (like the NI and, yes, this is a shameless plug) can give us all the dirt we need to chuck at corporate ad lies. Thinking before we buy, and buying nothing—especially when irrational urges prompt us to do otherwise—are bound to punch a few holes. The idea of our world and its public spaces as shared commons is becoming increasingly visible. Streets are being reclaimed by 'citizen artists' redrawing ads to reveal their subterfuges, and by social movements gathering to protest government by corporations.

There's quite a bit of ad-industry nervousness as brands come under attack and marketing tactics backfire. Could the industry one day start to tell us things we actually want to know? The distorting mirror will need to shatter first before a floating world comes into view.

POSTSCRIPT

Is Advertising Good for Society?

Since the development of the advertising industry, the question of advertising ethics has periodically resurfaced. Advertising was once considered a way to keep the cost of newspapers down, to help deliver "free" TV and radio to the public, and to help consumers understand what issues were important in society. Many defenses of advertising relied on helping consumers make more informed decisions about how to spend their money. But over the years, the real impact of advertising has been more critically considered. Today, issues of corporate power, mind-control, deceptive advertising, and cultivating desires in children and people who can't afford to buy products are considered to be more pressing social problems.

The ad industry has responded to criticism in many ways. Traditional defenses of tobacco and alcohol advertising have resulted in the creation of industry-supported projects to "prevent" misuse, but the purpose of these projects must also be carefully considered. Do industries attempt to fight regulation by doing "something" about a problem—like establishing programs to prevent underage drinking, or placing warning labels on cigarettes—or do they exercise "good neighbor" practices because they feel that they have a moral obligation to do so? In most cases, the real reason is that the industries would prefer to demonstrate that they can police their own industries, rather than accept regulation from outside.

Since the growth of technologies that are more individually used, like the Internet, the advertising industry has responded with a far more complicated structure to attract attention, and a far more complicated system of appealing to audiences they consider are most easily persuaded. Use of pop-up ads, banners, and promises of easy consumption permeate Internet sites. Advertisers don't seem to mind spam, or links that lead to new products or services, or cookies that unobtrusively collect consumer data about computer users.

Digital video recorders have the technological capability of screening out commercials, but advertisers have created ways to insert ads into programs so that the eye catches them, even if the conscious brain does not. Even some television programming has become a substitute for ads, when products used in shows like *Extreme Make-Over* and *Queer Eye for the Straight Guy*, are mentioned and highlighted.

Ultimately, as the authors of these two selections indicate, advertising does infiltrate society on a number of levels. Fortunately, we have many wonderful sources to consider to help us understand advertising's social impact. Jean Kilbourne's *Can't Buy My Love* (Touchstone, 1999), provides a social critique of what advertising does to our feelings. Arthur Asa Berger's *Ads, Fads, and Consumer Culture: Advertising's Impact on American Character and Society*, now in its third edition (Rowman and Littlefield, 2007), has a number of contemporary examples, and covers critical analysis methods, sexuality in advertising, global advertising, and neuromarketing. Finally, Alissa Quart's *Branded: The Buying and Selling of Teenagers* (Basic Books, 2003) reflects on the impact advertising has had on today's typical college student.

Students are also encouraged to examine some of the academic journals that deal with issues of advertising in a number of venues, such as *The Journal of Advertising Ethics, Ethics and Society,* and the *Journal of Mass Media Ethics,* and to become familiar with Web sites that call attention to examples of blurring ads and ethical practices. The *Center for Media and Democracy* (http://www.prwatch.org/) regularly posts interesting items on the interface between politics and advertising, and Project Censored (http://www.projectcensored.org/) often reports on attempts by the ad industry to control information.

Internet References . . .

Center for Media and Public Affairs

This site offers information about ongoing debates concerning media fairness and impact, with particular attention to political campaigns and political journalism.

http://www.cmpa.com

Poynter Online: Research Center

The Poynter Institute for Media Studies provides extensive links to information and resources on all aspects of media, including political journalism.

http://www.poynter.org/resource_center

Pew Research Center for People and the Press

The purpose of the Pew Research Center for People and the Press is to serve as a forum for ideas on the media and public policy through public opinion research.

http://people-press.org

Society of Professional Journalists

The Web site for *The Electronic Journalist*, the online service for the Society of Professional Journalists (SPJ), will lead you to a number of articles on media ethics, accuracy, media leaders, and other topics.

http://www.spj.org

NewsSources

The *American Journalism Review*'s NewsSources section of their Web site provides links to newspapers around the country. Links to organizations that are concerned with the ethics and quality of media coverage may be found on this site, as well.

http://www.ajr.org

The Project for Excellence in Journalism

The Project for Excellence in Journalism is a research organization that studies the performance of the press. Their goal is to help both journalists and citizens understand what the press is delivering.

http://www.journalism.org

The Annenberg Public Policy Center

FactCheck.org within the political communication research section aims to reduce the level of deception and confusion in U.S. politics. Fact Check monitors the accuracy of what is said by major U.S. political players in the form of TV ads, debates, speeches, interviews, and news.

http://www.annenbergpublicpolicycenter.org

News and Politics

*A*t one time, one of the most hotly debated questions about media
was whether media content demonstrated a liberal or conservative
bias. In recent years, this question has receded, while other, more
important issues have risen to the fore. Since the FCC began to revise
ownership restrictions for media outlets, and since the Bush administration's attention to information control has grown throughout the
Iraq War, news and politics have begun to be viewed through a slightly
different social lens. Issues about news control are now far more complicated than the days when Walter Lippman wrote about the ideal of
objectivity. While many cities and regions once had many newspapers,
now, they may have one. Broadcast news dominated the airwaves by
powerful networks. Today, a person is as likely to start the day with
checking the news on the Internet as they are to pick up a newspaper or
watch TV sometime through the day. One of the most popular "news"
programs for college-aged students is on Comedy Central. The issues in
this section address three important, contemporary topics, and lead us
toward discussions of how much, and what type of information we
actually use.

- Are Political/Military Leaders to Blame for Misinformation in Time of
  War?
- Is Negative Campaigning Bad for the American Political Process?
- Is Fake News Journalism?

ISSUE 7

Are Political/Military Leaders to Blame for Misinformation in Time of War?

YES: Daniel Schulman, from "Mind Games," *Columbia Journalism Review* (May/June 2006)

NO: Michael Ryan, from "Mainstream News Media, an Objective Approach, and the March to War in Iraq," *Journal of Mass Media Ethics* (vol. 21, no. 1, 2006)

ISSUE SUMMARY

YES: Information has always been a weapon in the battle to frame reality. Schulman traces the efforts of military information operations (IO) to wage psychological warfare against the enemy, and outlines some ways in which this has blurred the line between providing truthful information to the public and press and conducting propaganda campaigns.

NO: Mainstream media failed in their responsibility to provide sound news and commentary for Americans to base their critical decisions about invading Iraq, according to Ryan. One reason is that journalists did not use an objective approach to executive and military information and assertions. This abdication of responsibility allowed the government and media to frame reality unchallenged.

Following the attacks of September 11, 2001, the United States decided to launch a war in Afghanistan to capture the architect of these attacks, Osama bin Laden. In March 2003, the United States launched an invasion of Iraq with the explicit goal of toppling the regime of Saddam Hussein. The interplay of public opinion, governmental objectives, and press reporting about these events are the subjects of the articles in this issue.

From the vantage point of 2006, both of these authors are troubled by what has occurred since 9/11. Both argue that a disservice has been done to the American public, but they locate that disservice differently. Schulman argues that the government, particularly the executive branch and the military, conducted a "war of perceptions" in the run-up to the war and in the time since the invasion. As Schulman notes, "It is not the use of information as a weapon that is new, but rather the scale of the strategy and the nature of the targets" (p. 40). New technology complicates the once-easy distinction between the use of disinformation within a war zone as a military tactic, and the transmission of news to the press and the American public. With Internet distribution of news globally, accurate and balanced information dissemination can be threatened by a desire to frame stories for international consumers.

Domestically, issues concerning the legitimacy of information that led to the Iraq war strained press—White House relations. Geoffrey Stone, author of *Perilous Times: Free Speech in Wartime from the Sedition Act of 1798 to the War on Terrorism* (2004), asserts that the government "has been obsessively and unduly secretive" since 9/11. Journalists fear that the inaccessibility of Bush's administration may become the pattern of the future.

Ryan places the disservice to the American public at the feet of the media. Examining media content during the run-up to the war in Iraq, he finds few and feeble attempts to critically examine the information and the framing by then–President Bush and other government sources. Ryan lays out the communicative strategy of dichotomous language used by the administration, and shows how these were replicated in the content of print and electronic media. This occurred, he argues, because the practices of journalism were changed by the attacks on the concept of objectivity. Attempts to be objective in journalistic writing encouraged certain practices such as trying to achieve balance by finding sources on both sides of an issue, seeking accuracy, looking for multiple confirmation of information by various sources, and a commitment to being impartial. With the concept of objectivity weakened, the culture of journalism has changed with advocacy journalism being at least one of the emerging approaches.

Ryan's analysis threatens an important perception of the press. The press is sometimes called the "fourth estate," a concept that envisions the press as the guardians of the public interest and watchdogs of the executive, legislative, and judicial activities of the state. Media are seen from this perspective as providing a space for democratic debate on important issues of the day. Media are also seen as responsible for revealing abuses by the state and protecting the rights of citizens. Such premises underlie the logic of the First Amendment that grants freedom of the press. Observers worry that modern-day concentration and consolidation of media corporations may stifle that function of media by privileging commercial over editorial decisions. This concern is explored in more detail in Issue 17. Technology also threatens traditional balances. Schulman shows how the globalization of information confuses traditional divisions between public affairs and information operations. How do you communicate accurate information to the homefront, while not compromising your information strategies within the war zone? Will it be the American public who loses in this compromise? And, a subtext of Ryan's article is how the Internet has accelerated changes in press practices as the speed and weight of public comment on issues force journalistic response. Press and government ideas and practices are changing; "we the people" need to weigh the consequences.

YES

Daniel Schulman

Mind Games

When the United States launched Operation Iraqi Freedom in March 2003, Sam Gardiner, a sixty-four-year-old retired Air Force colonel, was a regular on *The NewsHour with Jim Lehrer* on PBS, where it was his job to place the day's events in context. As the campaign wore on, and he monitored the press coverage and parsed the public statements of military and administration officials, he at first became uneasy, then deeply concerned.

A longtime Defense Department consultant who has taught strategy at three of the military's top war colleges, Gardiner had participated throughout the 1990s in a series of war games that simulated attacks on Iraq. He was familiar with Iraq's military and was therefore surprised to hear officials, such as the Army Brigadier General Vincent Brooks, the deputy director of operations of Central Command's headquarters in Qatar, tell the press of ongoing operations to eliminate "terrorist death squads." The allegation struck Gardiner as odd. Matter-of-fact and precise in their speech, military officers would not typically refer to irregulars as "death squads." More important, as far as Gardiner knew, in 2003, when the invasion began, Iraq had no "terrorist death squads."

Gardiner believes that this formulation, which first entered the official vernacular a week after the invasion began, was a skillful execution of a classic propaganda technique known as the "excluded middle." The excluded middle is premised on the idea that people, provided with incomplete but suggestive information, will draw false assumptions—in this case that Saddam Hussein had ties to terrorism and therefore to Al Qaeda (a connection that administration officials actively pushed during the run-up to the war).

As Gardiner further analyzed the coverage in the early days of the invasion, he saw what he believed was a pattern of misinformation being fed to the press. There was the report, carried by The Associated Press, CNN, and *The New York Times*, among many other news outlets, that Iraq was seeking uniforms worn by U.S. and British troops ("identical down to the last detail") so that atrocities carried out on Iraqis by Saddam's Fedayeen could be blamed on the coalition. There was the claim that prisoners of war had been executed by their Iraqi captors, and there was the announced surrender of Iraq's entire Fifty-first Division. Government officials eventually eased off the POW assertion, and the story of the uniforms was never corroborated and soon disappeared. As for the Fifty-first Division, on March 21 a cascade of news stories, citing

Reprinted from *Columbia Journalism Review*, May/June 2006, pp. 39–49. Copyright © 2006 by Columbia Journalism Review, Columbia University.

anonymous British and American military officials, reported its mass surrender. "Hordes of Iraqi soldiers, underfed and overwhelmed, surrendered Friday in the face of a state-of-the-art allied assault," the AP reported. "An entire division gave itself up to the advancing allied forces, U.S. military officials said." Unnamed "officials in Washington" told *The Washington Post* that the division had been taken "out of the fight for Basra." Days later, however, coalition troops were still clashing with units of the Fifty-first there. And two days after it was reported that General Khaled Saleh al-Hashimi and the 8,000 men under his command had surrendered, the general was interviewed in Basra by Al Jazeera. "I am with my men. . . . We continue to defend the people and riches" of this city, he told the network. Was this the fog of war or was something else at play?

Gardiner believes that the story of the Fifty-first's mass capitulation may have been part of a psychological operation, its goal to "broadcast to the other units in Iraq that troops were giving up en masse and very quickly, so there was no reason to resist," he said. "That's a valid psychological operation. But it was directly entered into a press briefing." Gardiner eventually concluded that the flow of misinformation to the press was no accident. It was a well-coordinated campaign, intended not only to confound Iraqi combatants but to shape perceptions of the war back home. . . .

The weaponization of information is not original to the war in Iraq, nor is it unique to any military engagement during what has come to be known as the information age. Journalists have always encountered wartime spin, they have been the targets of propaganda and selective leaks, and, on occasion, have been used for purposes of deception (which has resulted, in certain cases, in saving the lives of American soldiers). In *The Art of War*, which remains an influential text among military strategists though it was written during the sixth century B.C., the Chinese general Sun Tzu writes: "All warfare is based on deception. Hence, when able to attack, we must seem unable; when using our forces, we must seem inactive; when we are near, we must make the enemy believe that we are far away; when far away, we must make him believe we are near."

In Iraq then, and indeed in the broader war on terror, it is not the use of information as a weapon that is new, but rather the scale of the strategy and the nature of the targets. Increasingly, the information environment has become the battlefield in a war that knows no boundaries, its offensives directed not just at the insurgents in Iraq and the Taliban in Afghanistan, or at regimes that take an adversarial posture to U.S. policy, but at the world at large. Technological advances, meanwhile, have made access to information instantaneous and ubiquitous, erasing longstanding barriers, legal and otherwise, that in the past have protected the American public and press from collateral damage in propaganda campaigns.

In addition, the aggressive manner in which this administration has pursued its information campaigns has in some cases blurred the bright line between two distinct military missions—providing truthful information about the war to the press and public, and waging psychological warfare. . . .

More than ever, information warfare is a military imperative. The problem is that in the government's haste to sow democratic seeds in the Muslim world, it has at times forsaken the very principles it has sought to proliferate. "They are screwing with democracy," Sam Gardiner told me.

Indeed, after the Lincoln Group's Pentagon-funded propaganda campaign, in which Iraqi media outlets were paid to run stories written by military information operations troops, was uncovered in late November, the Defense Department announced that it would consider whether it must amend its current guidelines on communications and information warfare. In many ways, this could be a turning point.

Early this year, military and administration officials began to reframe the vague and fluid concept that has come to be known as the war on terror. Though it had always been fought in the informational realm, more and more the conflict was becoming one of values and ideologies, not bullets and bombs. Struggles of this sort are measured not in years but in decades, so officials took to calling it, simply, "the long war."

They also began conceding setbacks. In mid-February, Secretary of Defense Donald Rumsfeld addressed the Council on Foreign Relations at its Park Avenue mansion in New York, telling its members that the U.S. was losing the war of ideas. Now, he said, "some of the most critical battles may not be in the mountains of Afghanistan or the streets of Iraq, but in newsrooms—in places like New York, London, Cairo, and elsewhere. Consider this statement: 'More than half of this battle is taking place in the battlefield of the media. . . . We are in a media battle in a race for the hearts and minds of [Muslims].' The speaker was not some modern-day image consultant in a public relations firm in New York City," Rumsfeld continued. "It was Osama bin Laden's chief lieutenant, Ayman al-Zawahiri."

The lines that Rumsfeld quoted come from a letter, dated July 9, 2005, said to be from Zawahiri to Abu Musab al-Zarqawi. Intercepted by the U.S. military, the thirteen-page document makes it clear that Al Qaeda understands that the battlefield has shifted. It must be conscious of its image, for it, too, is in a battle for world opinion. Admonishing Zarqawi for the scenes of brutality that had become his signature, Zawahiri wrote that "among the things which the feelings of the Muslim populace who love and support you will never find palatable . . . are the scenes of slaughtering the hostages." (Zarqawi has publicly declared the letter a fake.)

Two days before Rumsfeld's speech, the International Crisis Group, a nonprofit that focuses on preventing and resolving international conflicts, released a report that detailed just how sophisticated the insurgents in Iraq have become at disseminating their propaganda. The major players, which include Zarqawi's group and three others, all have published magazines and operated Web sites. Most have a spokesman who deals with the press. Seeking coverage, insurgent groups have delivered videos depicting their military exploits to hotels that are frequented by foreign journalists and often strike locations that will ensure maximum exposure. At points, the report's description of their propaganda network begins to sound remarkably like America's own. ("Websites are used to announce new policy positions, alliances, or strategic shifts, react to breaking news, or comment on how the Western media is addressing the struggle." . . .)

As Americans struggled to make sense of the attacks of September 11, 2001, Rumsfeld and others within the Bush administration quickly realized that the nation had entered a new variety of conflict that would necessitate more than military muscle. Particularly in the Muslim world, where the motivations of the U.S. were regarded with suspicion.

In November 2001, a secretive Pentagon directorate took shape within the Office of the Assistant Secretary of Defense for Special Operations and Low Intensity Conflict, known as SOLIC, whose purview includes aspects of military information operations. Headed by an Air Force brigadier general, Simon "Pete" Worden, an astrophysicist and the former deputy director of operations for the U.S. Space Command, its role was to harness a variety of informational activities to sway public opinion in the Middle East in favor of the administration's war on terror. It was called the Office of Strategic Influence.

Budgeted at $100 million for its first year of operations, OSI's staff of twenty consisted of experts in psychological and cyber warfare, authorities on the Middle East and Islamic studies, and contractors from Science Applications International Corporation (SAIC), the Fortune 500 research and engineering firm that considers itself a specialist in "information dominance." OSI envisioned itself as an incubator for the development of novel information-warfare strategies and a focal point for the coordination of interagency influence operations, Worden, who is now retired from the military, told me. Its staff members had big ideas, but even before they could fully formulate their strategy, let alone carry it out, the office had become the focus of controversy within the Pentagon. Members of the Pentagon's public affairs staff, in particular, were concerned that the methods OSI might use to carry out its mission, specifically those related to the development and dissemination of propaganda, could undermine the Pentagon's credibility. Several people I spoke with, including Worden and another former Pentagon official, are convinced that, in the end, OSI was sabotaged from within the Pentagon when word of its reported mission was leaked to *The New York Times* in February 2002. The *Times* and other news outlets reported that OSI had entertained plans to dabble in the darkest arts of persuasion, including planting false news stories in the foreign press. "It goes from the blackest of black programs to the whitest of white," a senior Pentagon official told the *Times*.

Worden, however, contends that OSI was not the Orwellian enterprise that reporters and their Pentagon sources believed it to be. He denies that the office had any plans to misinform or otherwise manipulate the media, which he said was confirmed by a review of OSI documents, computer files, and proposals by the Pentagon's general counsel that was completed in the spring of 2002. In March, Worden provided me with a seventy-page document he co-wrote, along with two former OSI staff members, Air Force Colonel Martin E.B. France and retired Air Force Major Randall R. Correll, following OSI's demise. Worden has not sought to publish the paper, titled "Information War: Strategic Influence and the Global War on Terrorism," believing that bringing up the controversial office will not endear him to the Bush administration as he seeks a federal job. It contains, however, what is to date the most detailed account of OSI's rise and fall.

As the office formulated its influence plan, Worden and his staff came to see OSI's mission as threefold. First, it would use the informational tools at its disposal to stanch the flow of young Muslims to extremist causes. It would also seek, according to Worden's paper, to "undermine anti-United States regimes through providing unfettered access to global information," possibly directing satellite-fed radio transmissions at repressive nations. Finally, it would combat "negative perceptions of the United States and its goals" wherever they existed—"throughout the world, not just the Islamic world."

Worden saw the Internet as a powerful tool that could be used to divert Muslims from fundamentalist ideology. With tactics pioneered by Internet marketers—such as offering a free music download, or some other lure—young Muslims might be steered to Web sites carrying pro-U.S. messages. Worden reasoned that satellite uplinks and downlinks could circumvent government censors and provide exposure to Western influences. In "Information War," Worden and his colleagues note that young men often use the Internet to connect with the opposite sex, "sometimes pornographically!" "A focus on the charms of Western women in the here-and-now might divert would-be terrorists from contemplating the purported charms of virgins in the afterlife as a reward for Martyrdom."

Discrediting extremist groups among foreign populations, Worden realized, would take "respected authorities such as journalists, clerics, and artists within that group to denounce" them. But "simply paying them to do so is likely to boomerang," he believed: "Even if some can be so induced, the likely exposure of such tactics will do more to discredit our objectives than any gain achieved." Therefore, "a subtle mesh of inducements and disincentives must be developed. At the outset, we may offer free or increased access to the increasingly high technology means of communications . . . to moderate voices."

A large-scale information offensive using cyber warfare tactics and forms of propaganda, Worden understood, would probably make the press, the public, and even some government officials uneasy, but he made no apologies for it.

> Within the United States we must come to a consensus within our society that we will conduct an energetic information war to defeat global terrorism. . . . The American public will need to accept that certain information warfare tactics may not seem, on the surface, to be consistent with a global free press. Clearly, this debate will identify some things that will generally be considered "off-limits," such as deliberate disinformation distributed through open press sources.

While Worden believed that the best informational weapon the U.S. could employ was "the truth and unlimited access to it," he also saw a place, under rare circumstances, for deception. "There is little doubt that disinformation and lies can be initially effective, and that outright lies can be effective, particularly when the promulgator has a long history of apparent 'truth telling.' This suggests that outright disinformation in the case of the United States is somewhat like an information warfare analog to using nuclear weapons."

Though OSI was disbanded, it's likely that it disappeared in name alone, its duties delegated elsewhere within the Pentagon. Donald Rumsfeld said as much when, referring to OSI in November 2002, he told reporters that "you can have the name, but I'm gonna keep doing every single thing that needs to be done, and I have."

Whether or not OSI continued to operate under different auspices, many other organizations, inside and outside the Pentagon, were simultaneously or subsequently created to focus on the information effort overseas.

The Defense Department's Information Operations Task Force, created shortly after September 11, was to focus on "developing, coordinating, deconflicting, and monitoring the delivery of timely, relevant, and effective messages to targeted international audiences."

The Office of Global Communications, under Tucker Eskew, a deputy assistant to the president and a longtime Republican communications consultant, touted a similar mission. A government organizational chart, dated July 2003, places this office at the nexus of the government's strategic communications apparatus. But Daniel Kuehl, a retired Air Force lieutenant colonel who directs the Information Strategies Concentration Program at the National Defense University, believes the global communications office never lived up to its mandate.

Nor, perhaps, did it ever intend to. "In my opinion, the global issue wasn't the reason why they were created," he told me. "They clearly had a completely domestic focus. They were part of the effort to re-elect the president. . . . I'm going to be real pejorative here: Their goal was psychological operations on the American voting public. That was part of the political arm doing that." He added, "You'll notice that not long after the election, the Office of Global Communications no longer existed." (Technically, it still exists, though it has been without a director for more than a year. No new content has been posted on its Web site, once updated regularly, since March 2005.)

The government also outsourced part of the war of perceptions to private-sector firms, including John Rendon's strategic communications consultancy, the Rendon Group, whose services have been retained during "nearly every shooting conflict in the past two decades," as James Bamford, an investigative reporter, wrote in *Rolling Stone* last fall. Hired by the CIA after the first gulf war to pave the way for regime change in Iraq, John Rendon helped to organize the Iraqi National Congress, Ahmed Chalabi's dissident group (which was later responsible for feeding bogus stories about Iraq's weapons of mass destruction to the press). More recently, though, as Bamford has reported, Rendon's firm received a Pentagon contract to mount "a worldwide propaganda campaign deploying teams of information warriors to allied nations to assist them 'in developing and delivering specific messages to the local population, combatants, front-line states, the media and the international community.'" . . .

When Lieutenant Colonel Pamela Keeton of the Army arrived in Afghanistan in August 2004 to take over the coalition's public affairs operation, Effects, as it was known, had been in place for several months. The command structure had shifted to accommodate the new organization and

Keeton found she would no longer report directly to the commanding general, as is typically the case. "Traditionally public affairs officers are special staff to the commander, just like his lawyer and his surgeon," Keeton told me. "Now I was reporting to a colonel"—who headed Effects—"that had no experience in public affairs, psyops, or information operations. He was being advised by me; he was being advised by his IO guy and by his psyops guy. He was trying to figure out who was right, what we should do." She felt she was in competition to get her point of view across, and, to an extent, kept out of the loop. "They were going to the director of IO for advice on messages," she said.

Shortly before Keeton's arrival, other, more dramatic changes had taken place. The officer in charge of information operations, Major Scott Nelson, had taken over as the command's chief spokesman. "He ran the press conferences," Keeton, who is now retired from the military, said. Nelson's dual roles would seem to be in conflict. . . .

A Marine public affairs officer who served in Iraq until last fall, primarily in the Sunni Triangle, told me of being asked in a number of cases to draft news stories that the officer believed would be translated and placed, perhaps covertly, in local newspapers. The officer was also asked to write stories that omitted the role of U.S. troops, in one case to obscure their involvement in spearheading an infrastructure project, making it seem as if it were solely a product of Iraqi initiative. (The officer refused to participate in the propaganda efforts.) Particularly when it comes to slanting news stories or press releases to emphasize the self-sufficiency of the Iraqis, that practice appears fairly widespread. Last summer, *Jane's Defence Weekly* reported that the technique has been used to make the Iraqi military appear more competent than it is, primarily by playing up the role of Iraqi troops in military operations. "We say what we want people to believe even if it's not fully grounded in facts or the truth, and that is becoming a very disturbing trend in the military," a Pentagon public affairs officer told the reporter, Joshua Kucera. . . .

The State Department's Future of Iraq Project, which convened a series of working groups between the spring of 2002 and the spring of 2003 to focus on planning for post-Saddam Iraq, warned specifically against using the Iraqi press as a propaganda platform. "New forms of propaganda are totally out of the question, even with the best of intentions," the project's Free Media working group recommended in a December 2002 paper. "The help the media can give in keeping the social peace (which is actually their natural role in a democracy) . . . is too important to be spoiled by a continued lack of trust from the public." The document also discourages the idea that regional or Western governments should directly fund Iraqi news outlets, suggesting instead that governments "should be allowed only to contribute to a general fund." These, like most of the other recommendations made by this State Department initiative, were apparently ignored by the Pentagon. Rather, under the purview of IO, the Lincoln Group was designated to operate a government-funded propaganda franchise in Iraq that would ultimately be discovered.

Before the Lincoln Group's covert campaign began sometime in early 2005, the firm (then operating as Iraqex) had been chosen to carry out a p.r. contract, worth more than $5 million, that was overseen by the coalition's public affairs staff in Baghdad. An army officer, who was involved in selecting the Lincoln Group for the contract and who worked extensively with its employees when they arrived in Iraq in November 2004, told me it had initially been hired to provide basic communications support, such as polling and media analysis, not for the clandestine placement of news stories or paying off the Iraqi press.

"In terms of their proposal, they were head and shoulders above everybody," the officer said. "The problem was they couldn't do a third of what they said they were going to do." He continued, "They were my little Frankensteins. They were sending guys over there that had absolutely no knowledge of Iraqis whatsoever. It was like the Young Republican fucking group—some guy who was working for the governor-elect in Michigan, a guy from the Beltway who was part of some Republicans for Democracy group—not a fucking clue. It was a scheme written up on a cocktail napkin in D.C. They were just completely inept." The public affairs staff became increasingly frustrated with the contractor. Some officers, including two brigadier generals, refused even to work with them. "That's when they moved under IO," the officer said. Eventually, the Lincoln Group was responsible for planting hundreds of stories in Iraqi newspapers. . . .

Michael Ryan

 **NO**

Mainstream News Media, an Objective Approach, and the March to War in Iraq

Journalists in a democracy have a moral covenant with their readers and viewers to provide complete, balanced, fair, and accurate information and commentary. It has seldom been more important for journalists to honor that covenant than it was from September 12, 2001 (the day following the 9/11 attacks) until March 20, 2003 (the day the United States invaded Iraq).

Americans responded to the 9/11 attacks within a context of intense anger, confusion, shock, and awe. It was during this period and within this context that Americans decided to launch a war against Afghanistan, and ultimately to invade Iraq. The international community may not know for years the impact on international terrorism (and on economies, cultures, societies, and political systems) of the wars against Afghanistan and Iraq, but the performance of the media during the critical period can be evaluated now. This article examines that performance. An objective approach is briefly summarized, followed by discussions of war and dichotomous language, media, and the prelude to war in Iraq.

An Objective Approach

Journalists began using "objectivity" to describe their work in the 1920s. Objectivity "was viewed not as something simple-minded and pallidly neutral, but as a demanding, intellectually rigorous procedure holding the best hope for social change," said Streckfuss (1990, p. 973). Many journalists viewed an objective approach as a way to compensate for the human inability to be objective and not simply as a way to ensure neutrality; "the objective method was seen as an antidote to the emotionalism and jingoism of the conservative American press" (p. 973).

Some current writers reject the view that one can be objective, but they do argue, as writers in the 1920s did, that one can use an "objective approach" (Gauthier, 1993). This means they report information that is complete, precise, balanced, and accurate; view powerful authorities and institutions with skepticism; consider new evidence and alternative interpretations; serve no religious, economic, social, or political agenda; attend to the views of the marginalized;

From *Journal of Mass Media Ethics*, Vol. 21, No. 1, 2006, pp. 4–29. Copyright © 2006 by Lawrence Erlbaum Associates. Reprinted by permission of Lawrence Erlbaum Associates via the Copyright Clearance Center.

try to be fair, disinterested, and impartial; recognize their own predispositions and not allow those predispositions to determine outcomes; use creativity in the search for facts and opinions that do not conform to the dominant narrative; and share all information freely (Ryan, 2001).

Strategic decisions (e.g., selecting sources), critical analyses, and interpretations are based on professional norms and not on personal values or emotion. "Objectivity in journalism or science does not mean that all decisions do not have underlying values, only that within the 'rules of the game' a systematic attempt is made to achieve an impartial report" (Dennis, 1984, p. 118). . . .

Many critics have expressed the common view that objectivity is a myth because individuals—who reflect their cultures, educational systems, religious teachings, economic circumstances, and many other facets of life—can never be objective (e.g., Merrill, 1984; Rosen, 1993). Smith (1980) argued that, "The structure of the news story [is] a value-loaded device structuring reality according to preconceptions, not a device for exploring reality according to a professional canon of neutrality" (p. 62).

Other critics have suggested that an objective approach ensures (a) that writers are mere spectators in the economic, cultural, political, and social stories they cover—that they are not responsible for what they write (T. L. Glasser, 1984); (b) that writers who use an objective approach help the powerful maintain order, build support for policies that advance their own self-interests, and avoid change (Koch, 1990); and (c) that writers use the objective approach simply to protect themselves from criticism and legal actions (Tuchman, 1972).

Some critics of an objective approach recommended different approaches to journalism, five of which are "new journalism" (Wolfe & Johnson, 1973), advocacy journalism (Lazarus, 2001), standpoint epistemology (Durham, 1998), existential journalism (Merrill, 1996; Stoker, 1995), and public or civic journalism (Charity, 1995; Merritt, 1995).

These approaches are complex and all obviously have a place in journalism. However, each one essentially rejects an objective approach . . . and each requires a writer to take a position—to make a personal, subjective decision. . . .

Objectivity had been attacked on many grounds at the turn of the 21st century. Regardless of the reasons for the attacks, an objective approach was so discredited and misunderstood, it was not widely practiced, at least not as originally intended. Critics had managed to change the culture of journalism—so that it obscured and devalued, or even rejected, an objective approach—at the very time that approach was needed most.

War and Dichotomous Language

Governments, individuals, and groups who want to generate support for the causes or ideologies they champion typically use dichotomous language to assign meanings to visual and oral signs (Tewksbury, Jones, Peske, Raymond, & Vig, 2000). The Bush administration and other war advocates used the "good" versus "evil" dichotomy to assign meanings to the words they used to market their war against Iraq.[1] . . .

Two Overarching Themes

War advocates, led by Bush, stressed two overarching themes as they struggled to ensure that the United States would invade Iraq . . . (a) There were only two options in dealing with Iraq—"do nothing" or "use military force," and (b) anyone who was not "with us" was "with the terrorists." The sale of these themes was crucial to those who were marketing war in Iraq, and it was critical that the semantic space between these polar opposites not be explored.[2] If that space were carefully examined, the narrative would be less effective as a tool for war. This is precisely the space that journalists who use an objective approach *do* explore.

Do nothing or use military force.   The war advocates needed to paint Iraq as evil as they tried to discredit the do nothing option, which they defined as anything less than military intervention. If Iraq was indeed evil, the do nothing option was unacceptable. This view clearly stops debate, said Tony Lang of the Carnegie Council on Ethics and International Affairs (Cabrejas, 2003): "[T]he very concept of evil is problematic. When it becomes used as part of political rhetoric it silences conversation. . . . Once you've defined something that way, the only policy option is to destroy the evil" (p. 22). To "destroy the evil" was defined, in this instance, as invading Iraq.

President Bush and others frequently asserted that the embargo against Iraq failed to neutralize Saddam Hussein as a threat to the United States, and that the evidence for a preemptive strike was unassailable. It was not necessary to the success of this narrative that they prove their assertions beyond doubt; it was necessary only that they convince people that both assertions might be true. . . .

Stand with us or with the terrorists.   War advocates typically manipulate language to define, or to create, an "enemy" who can be used as the focal point to rally support for war. War proponents frequently use the good versus evil dichotomy to gain widespread acceptance for their definitions. Proponents of the invasion of Iraq moved quickly to assign *their* values to a number of words that had no intrinsic meaning, but that could—defined "properly"— polarize rhetoric and help categorize people as "us" or "them." One of the most important words in the pro-war lexicon was *terrorist,* which is one of the more difficult terms to define, as Nacos (2002) suggested:

> [T]he definitional difficulty is rooted in the evaluation of one and the same terrorist act as either a despicable or a justifiable means to political ends, as either the evil deed of ruthless terrorists or the justifiable act of freedom fighters and/or warriors of god. The slogan that "one person's terrorist is another person's freedom fighter" captures these contrasting value judgments. (p. 16)

War advocates successfully assigned the worst and broadest possible meanings to the term terrorist and then used the word effectively to inflame a general hatred against the "other side."[3] The narrative never allowed for the possibility that terrorists had a story to tell—that they had legitimate grievances against the United States and other Western powers, that they felt they had exhausted their options and turned to violence as their only recourse, or that they felt they had nothing left to lose. It also never allowed for the possibility that the United States and its allies had no moral or legal right to put at risk the populations in which terrorists were embedded. Bush and others successfully discouraged any exploration of that semantic space.

The words used to describe the good people were at the other pole of the dichotomous scale. President Bush, attack victims, rescue workers, and allies, for example, were described by such words as brave, beloved, and heroic, particularly in the early months of the buildup to invasion.

War advocates tried to marginalize war critics by binding them directly or indirectly to the evil ones. Former White House spokesman Ari Fleischer's attack against comedian–commentator Bill Maher is a good example of the attempt to silence dissent. Maher commented that cowards launch missiles from thousands of miles away, but that those who die when they crash airplanes into buildings are not cowards. "Americans need to watch what they say, what they do, and this is not the time for remarks like that; there never is," Fleischer said (Debatin, 2002, p. 174). . . .

Media and the Buildup to War

The period studied here is September 12, 2001 to March 20, 2003. Two periods within that overarching time frame are important: September 12 through October 8, 2001 (the day the war against Afghanistan was launched), and February 20, 2003 (1 month before the invasion of Iraq began) through March 20, 2003. The focus here is on news coverage and commentary primarily during these two periods. . . .

September 12–October 8, 2001

Network television coverage during the 8 hours following the 9/11 attacks focused mainly on fact finding and reporting (Mogensen, Lindsay, Li, Perkins, & Beardsley, 2002). The U.S. intelligence community was so surprised by the 9/11 attacks, everyone from the president on down learned initial details from broadcast news (Bamford, 2004, pp. 33–37). . . .

ABC, CBS, CNN, Fox News, and NBC aired 1,117 stories, of which 29% focused on the World Trade Center; 18% focused on the president and government; 10% focused on criminal activity and terrorism; 10% focused on providing an overview; 8% focused on the Pentagon; and 27% focused on other topics. "[T]he journalists did not focus their attention on democratic values or patriotism during the first 8 hours of coverage" (Mogensen et al., 2002, p. 120).

U.S. news magazines, in the first week following the attacks, covered the aftermath as a funeral ritual (Kitch, 2003). The covers of *Newsweek* and *Time* featured black rather than red borders, and they and *U.S. News & World Report* used black backgrounds on their pages. The news magazines expressed disbelief and shock, they quoted those who could bear witness to and give testimony about the tragic events, and they published photographs to record the suffering and the heroism.

Photographs published in the weeks following 9/11 by *Time, U.S. News & World Report,* and *Newsweek* followed the typical four-stage formula for disaster coverage. First, pictures focused on the explosions, fires, and suffering; second, on rescue efforts and the heroism of the rescuers; third, on aid efforts; and fourth, on families, victims, and the disruption of the economy (Griffin, 2004, p. 388).

Media coverage and rhetoric dramatically shifted after the first several days, and much of it supported the two main war themes.

Do nothing or use military force.   Television frequently invoked the war metaphor with such banners as "America's New War" and "War Against Terrorism." Nacos (2002) reported that "ABC News broadcast eighty-six stories that contained the terms 'war' and 'terrorism,' CBS News aired ninety-six such segments, NBC News broadcast 133, CNN televised 316, and National Public Radio aired 166" (p. 146). American newspapers archived in Lexis–Nexis published 5,814 articles that mentioned these words. . . .

The war metaphor frequently was reinforced visually. Tom Brokaw of NBC was surrounded by flags as he presented the news each evening, and his network included a flag in its onscreen logo (Kellner, 2003). CNN had by November "developed an introductory news collage of patriotic images that identify the U.S., war, Bush, and CNN in a harmonious unity of patriotism and goodness" (Kellner, 2003, p. 105). . . .

The official voices of America's 10 largest newspapers also supported the war narrative (Ryan, 2004). All of the 104 editorials published between September 12 and October 8, 2001 assumed military intervention. Seventy-nine editorials invoked the war metaphor by referring to World War II, to Pearl Harbor, to the Gulf War, or to the Cold War. None suggested alternatives to military strikes (doing nothing was not an option), and 15 said military strikes would help stop terrorism. . . .

A study of 20 newspapers' editorials across the 18-month period examined here suggests editorials published within 2 days following Bush's addresses about an invasion echoed the binary language the president used to justify war (Coe, Domke, Graham, John, & Pickard, 2004). After the 9/11 attacks, 7.7% of the president's statements reflected the good versus evil dichotomy, and 28.6% of newspaper editorials reflected that dichotomy. Five percent of the president's statements reflected a "security" versus "peril" dichotomy after 9/11; that dichotomy was present in 14.3% of editorials. The language reflected the president's discourse so closely, "citizens and other political leaders . . . could not help but interpret these editorials as a message of support for the president and his (and his party's) agenda" (p. 248).

Stand with us or with the terrorists.   Television and radio journalists were particularly dedicated to reinforcing the us versus them dichotomy. The CNN collage, for example, showed a photograph of bin Laden "followed by two pictures of American soldiers with the flag as a background and the slogan 'Trust' scrolling across the screen" (Kellner, 2003, p. 105). ABC, NBC, CBS, and CNN all aired more news stories mentioning bin Laden than Bush following 9/11, thus creating a "celebrity terrorist" to personify "them" (Nacos, 2002, p. 149).[4] . . .

Demons and heroes also were created in the editorials of America's largest newspapers. Osama bin Laden was demonized in 71 of 104 editorials as corrupt, hated, murderous, cowardly, and ruthless. The Taliban were declared "the enemy" in 62 editorials (Ryan, 2004). In a sign of things to come, three editorials in Ryan's (2004) study said the United States should depose Saddam Hussein. According to *The Washington Post*, "It is impossible to imagine the United States 'winning' this war in any meaningful sense while Saddam Hussein remains in power in Iraq ("Afghanistan," 2001, p. A26).

Some newspapers were prepared to support indiscriminant mayhem to punish the evil-doers and to protect Americans. *Newsday* urged the president to lift the 25-year-old ban against the assassination of foreign citizens ("Change the Rules," 2001); and New York *Daily News* columnist Zev Chafets (2001) called for the immediate invasion of Iran, Iraq, Syria, Libya, Sudan, and Afghanistan. . . . Such assertions were not atypical in newspapers and other media.

The media also marginalized the antiwar movement by ignoring, downplaying, or attacking it. ABC News aired only one story that mentioned domestic antiwar activists from September 15 until December 15, 2001. CBS News broadcast three, CNN aired two, and NBC News broadcast one (Nacos, 2002, p. 159). . . .

The media even policed their own ranks against those who would criticize the march to war. Dan Gutherie, a Grants Pass, Oregon *Daily Courier* columnist, and Tom Gutting, editor of the *Texas City Sun,* both were fired for criticizing Bush's behavior on 9/11. Peter Werbe, a radio host, lost his job for criticizing Bush's failure to protect the nation against a terrorist attack (Kellner, 2003, p. 68).

The heroes, of course, were "us"; everyone who was not "with the terrorists.". . . Writers reached across the semantic space to find heroic words to contrast with the words used to describe bin Laden and Saddam Hussein. Bush was called able, strong, wise, and resolute.

February 20–March 20, 2003

The Bush administration and other war advocates struggled during the 18 months following 9/11 to convince the world that an invasion of Iraq was practical, necessary, legal, and moral.

Circumstances had changed, however, since September and October 2001. Osama bin Laden was free; Saddam Hussein was allowing United Nations inspectors into Iraq; and casualties were mounting, innocent people were dying, and support for war in Afghanistan was fading. A public opinion poll conducted several months after the war in Afghanistan started, for example, showed that only 15% of Americans thought the war against terror in Afghanistan was a success (Madigan, 2002).

Important elites were questioning whether the use of violence in the war against terrorism made sense. Many religious leaders, for example, argued that a preemptive strike would not meet the moral standard for a just war (Gibson, 2002). . . . This was the context in which the media reported the buildup to the invasion.

Do nothing or use military force.   Television support for war remained strong during this period. An enthusiastic war advocate on television was Fox News (Getlin, 2003). "Fox News' coverage was noticeably pro-war and pro-military, using unexpectedly bold and provocative statements and providing politically entertaining rather than objective and balanced reporting" (Fleming & Thorson, 2004, p. 9). Coverage by network television and CNN was . . . somewhat more skeptical about U.S. military involvement in Iraq (Deggans, 2003).[5] Still, few alternatives to military violence were explored on television.

Radio continued to support the war message strongly. Clear Channel Communications, for example, organized pro-war rallies around the country. Conservative radio host Glenn Beck promoted demonstrations under the banner, "Rally for America." . . .

Newspapers' editorial support for the pro-war message was still strong, but it had eroded somewhat. Editorial writers supported Bush's war rhetoric by asserting that the United States wanted to bring "freedom" and "liberty" to Iraq and beyond. "'Freedom' and 'liberty' language and emphasis on these values as universal norms significantly increased in analyzed newspaper editorials after September 11; these shifts over time paralleled the patterns of the president's communications" (Domke et al., 2004, p. 23).[6] Approximately 30% of the editorials mentioned freedom and liberty after 9/11, and 50% of these portrayed freedom and liberty as universal norms.[7] . . .

Newspapers frequently supported the war narrative in their news columns as well. In fact, some news coverage was so bad, [that] newspapers [in retrospect] took the extraordinary step of acknowledging the poor coverage in print. *The New York Times,* for example, launched an internal analysis of its war coverage. Editors "found a number of instances of coverage that was not as rigorous as it should have been. . . . Looking back, we wish we had been more aggressive in re-examining the claims as new evidence emerged—or failed to emerge" ("From the Editors," 2004, p. A10).[8]

A major problem with *The Times'* coverage was its reliance on self-interested sources who were committed to regime change in Iraq. "Complicating matters for journalists, the accounts of these exiles were often eagerly confirmed by United States officials convinced of the need to intervene in Iraq" ("From the Editors," 2004. p. A10). *The Times* acknowledged that stories about dire claims got prominent display, "while follow-up articles that called the original ones into question were sometimes buried. In some cases, there was no follow-up at all" ("From the Editors," 2004, p. A10). . . .

The Washington Post also acknowledged serious problems with its war coverage. Howard Kurtz (2004), who analyzed the coverage and interviewed editors and reporters, reported that *The Post* seldom published on the front page stories that challenged the Bush administration. . . .

Kurtz (2004) quoted assistant managing editor Bob Woodward as saying, "We should have warned readers we had information that the basis for [the war] was shakier" (p. A1) than some thought. "Those are exactly the kind of statements that should be published on the front page" (p. A1). He quoted Pentagon correspondent Thomas Ricks as saying, "There was an attitude among editors: Look, we're going to war, why do we even worry about all this contrary stuff?" (p. A20).

Stand with us or with the terrorists.   Fox News once again took the lead in reinforcing the us versus them dichotomy. Anchor Neil Cavuto asserted, for instance, that there is nothing amiss in taking sides during a war (Deggans, 2003), and Fox personalities typically referred to U.S. military units as "our," "we," and "us" (Farhi, 2003). Fox's E.D. Hill said, "But a lot of these protesters now are International Workers Party members and socialists. . . . If you don't support the decision to go to war, once that decision has been made, you're not being patriotic" (Farhi, 2003, p. C7).

The editorials Ryan and Switzer (in press) analyzed, particularly those of the pro-war newspapers, supported the administration's effort to demonize the "other." Almost every editorial mentioned Saddam Hussein. The neutral newspapers usually said he was a leader or a dictator, although he was called a tyrant, murderer, global menace, despot, and repressive. The pro-war newspapers more closely mirrored the language of the war advocates. Hussein was cited as a dictator, but he was also defined by such words as murderer, bully, thug, cruel, despot, dirty, deceptive, dastardly, tyrant, and monster. . . .

Pro-war newspapers embraced the war proponents' effort to demonize and marginalize potential dissidents both in the United States and abroad. France was the main international target, followed by Russia, Germany, the U.N., and weapons inspectors. . . .

Newspaper commentary also supported the war advocates' attack against dissent at home. The New York *Daily News* said, for example, that "too many [war protesters] are determinedly blind to the facts. Or sadly ignorant of them" ("Peaceniks Couldn't," 2003, p. 34). Boot (2003) wrote in *Newsday* that dissidents are "making war more—not less—likely" (p. A39).

Conclusions

The evidence is compelling that media covering the prelude to the war in Iraq failed in their primary responsibility: to provide sound news and commentary on which Americans could base critical decisions about war and peace. This was not because objectivity failed, but because too few journalists in 2001 through 2003 understood and were committed to an objective approach.

Journalism failed because writers and editors were not skeptical of authority or institutions (at least skepticism was not reflected in their writing); they did not challenge questionable assertions by authorities each time they made them; they did not consider new evidence and alternative interpretations; they served (or at least reflected) narrow religious and political agendas; they did not seek and report the views of the marginalized; they were not creative in seeking information and opinion that did not support the dominant narrative; and they allowed their own predispositions to dictate outcomes.

There are many reasons for this failure. Some journalists apparently believed . . . that Saddam Hussein should be removed. . . . Had they examined [this] predisposition, journalists—at least those committed to an objective approach—would have worked hard to ensure their personal views did not affect their news coverage and commentary.

Some journalists might have skewed their war coverage to protect their jobs. After all, some journalists were fired or ostracized for being critical of the war message. Some news media may have boarded the war wagon to increase circulation or audience share. . . . Some news media may have been reluctant to criticize the war message because they feared readers or viewers would desert them for other media.

Most important, journalists avoided an objective approach because it is difficult and because they could. Objectivity was so thoroughly marginalized, criticized, and misunderstood at the time of the 9/11 attacks, they did not feel obligated to use it. Critics—some of whom had the best of intentions—obscured the real nature of an objective approach and they made it acceptable for writers to avoid it.

Journalists who were committed to and able to use an objective approach would have . . . explored the semantic space between the war advocates' polar positions. They would have questioned, for example, (a) whether there were really only two options regarding Iraq (do nothing or use military force) and (b) whether such actions as tightening the embargo or giving weapons inspectors more time actually constituted doing nothing. . . . Their failure to do that allowed the war advocates to nurture the polarizing narrative that precluded exploration of other options.

They would have been skeptical of sources and every story and commentary would have reflected that skepticism. *The New York Times* was not skeptical enough of the exiled Iraqi engineer who said Saddam Hussein had hidden throughout Iraq hundreds of bunkers for unconventional weapons research (Bamford, 2004, p. 295). . . .

Journalists committed to an objective approach also would have been skeptical of U.S. government leaders. Before the war, Massing (2004) wrote:

> [T]he coverage was highly deferential to the White House. This was especially apparent on the issue of Iraq's weapons of mass destruction—the heart of the President's case for war. Despite abundant evidence of the administration's brazen misuse of intelligence in this matter, the press repeatedly let officials get away with it. (p. 43)

. . . Journalists committed to an objective approach would have referred often to these and other "errors" or "lies" told by the administration and others. . . . They would have tapped sources in the scientific or scholarly community who could have helped answer many of the questions Americans asked about the administration's response to the 9/11 attacks. They also would have interviewed the marginalized who were being ignored by the war advocates.

They would have interviewed ordinary Iraqis to discover how they would react to an invasion and Arabs and Muslims who thought the terrorists' ideas were just even if their tactics were wrong. Journalists using an objective approach would have given more space and attention to those who criticized the march to war. Critics who suggested options that occupied the space between the poles—such as giving aggressive diplomacy and weapons inspections more time and tightening the embargo that would have made it impossible for Hussein to ship or use unconventional weapons even if he had them—were largely ignored or downplayed. . . .

Criticism of U.S. foreign policy or corporate behavior was dismissed as "caving in to terrorists," and the news media put any such discussion off limits. *The Wall Street Journal* ("A Terrorist," 2001), for example, said that terrorism "is intended to intimidate America into standing aside humiliated while the Arab despots and fanatics destroy Israel and thereby prove that freedom and democracy are not after all the wave of the future" (p. A18). It would be difficult to write a statement that is more polarizing or inhibiting. . . .

This is not to suggest that an objective approach is easy to use. Indeed, it is more difficult and more stressful than the approaches that currently pass for journalism. Editorial writers and other commentators who believe in an objective approach would not have presented as "fact" much of the . . . unsupported information the Bush administration disseminated during the 18 months before the invasion. . . .

It would not have been easy for news reporters to use an objective approach, but some did, with commendable results. Strobel, Landay, and Walcott (2002) of Knight-Ridder, for example, questioned the administration's claim that Iraq had purchased special aluminum tubes for centrifuges that would be used to enrich uranium. They interviewed several knowledgeable sources who said the administration's claims were false.[9] They reported that, "While President Bush marshals congressional and international support for invading Iraq, a growing number of military officers, intelligence professionals, and diplomats in his own government privately have deep misgivings about the administration's double-time march toward war" (p. 1).

Many newspapers also published stories . . . about religious opposition to the potential war, and some editorial pages—such as those of *The New York Times,* the *Houston Chronicle,* and the *Los Angeles Times*—expressed skepticism about the administration's rush to war during the month before the invasion (Ryan & Switzer, in press). Finally, many newspapers published opinion pieces like Carter's (2003), which questioned the morality of a preemptive war against a nonthreatening country.

The sound journalism (news and commentary), however, was simply overwhelmed by the bad journalism.

Journalists will not have learned much if they subscribe to the view of executive editor Leonard Downie, Jr. of *The Washington Post,* who said:

> People who were opposed to the war from the beginning and have been critical of the media's coverage in the period before the war have this belief that somehow the media should have crusaded against the war. They

have the mistaken impression that somehow if the media's coverage had been different, there wouldn't have been a war. (Kurtz, 2004, p. A20)

Downie and others who subscribe to his view miss (or dodge) several points completely. First, journalists are not forced to choose one of two dichotomous approaches: bad journalism or a crusade. Second, critics did not argue for a crusade. Third, the occurrence of war (or not) is irrelevant; it is the media's job to provide solid information that can be the basis for informed decisions, whatever they may be. . . .

Journalists . . . should help create a journalism culture in which an objective approach can flourish—and become the standard. If they do not, journalism performance in all areas (e.g., science, politics, religion, the environment, and economics) is unlikely to improve. . . .

Notes

1. President Bush apparently had a war to sell almost from the beginning since, he has claimed, he decided in that second-grade classroom in Florida that America was at war (Bamford, 2004, p. 37). His administration was seriously considering an invasion of Iraq within days of the 9/11 attacks (Weisman, 2001).

2. For interesting discussions of the application of marketing strategy to the sale of war, see Hiebert (2003); Miller, Stauber, and Rampton (2004); and Rutherford (2004).

3. It is interesting to note that signals from the Bush administration suggested in early 2005 that it wanted to shift the focus from "a global war on terrorism" to a "strategy against violent extremism" that would emphasize nonmilitary options (diplomacy, economic and legal sanctions, cooperation with allies). This "repackaging," had it come much earlier, might have had important consequences for the national march to war.

4. The preoccupation with bin Laden "seemed to attribute the terror problem to one star terrorist and his group, fostering a false perception as to the scope of the threat and the prospect for its removal" (Nacos, 2002, p. 153).

5. Viewers apparently coped with the mixed messages by changing their attitudes so they were consistent with those of the medium they viewed most, or they watched news shows that reflected their views (Fleming & Thorson, 2004).

6. Universal norms cross geographical, cultural, historical, and social boundaries and are shared with all peoples and nations. If norms are universal, then they may be imposed legitimately (by the United States) on those to whom they are denied (Iraqis).

7. Bush, in essence, was saying that "to question the pre-emptive doctrine and Iraq war meant not only to disagree with the providential design, but also the nation's founders, FDR, Truman and Reagan. Such an overt convergence of religion and politics is indicative of the heights of self-assuredness that had emerged for the president and his advisors by spring 2003" (Domke, Coe, & Tynes, 2004, p. 23).

8. Mainstream media writers, for a variety of reasons, tend to rush into print or onto the air with stories and then to correct inaccurate or misleading information in follow-up stories. This practice may not have worked well for coverage of the invasion of Iraq, however, because research suggests that U.S. readers were not sensitive to corrected information (Lewandowsky, Stritzke, Oberauer, & Morales, 2005).

9. *The New York Times,* on the other hand, published a story by Gordon and Miller (2002) suggesting that Hussein's attempt to purchase aluminum tubes was evidence that the dictator was pursuing a nuclear weapons program.

References

Afghanistan. (2001, September 15). *The Washington Post,* p. A26.

Bamford, J. (2004). *A pretext for war: 9/11, Iraq, and the abuse of America's intelligence agencies.* New York: Doubleday.

Boot, M. (2003, February 28). Anti-war protests make it worse. *Newsday,* p. A39.

Cabrejas, J. (2003, November/December). Behind Bush's drive to war. *The Humanist, 63*(6), 20–24.

Carter, J. (2003, March 9). Just war—Or a just war? *The New York Times,* p.13 Week in Review.

Chafets, Z. (2001, September 17). It's really war against the Islamic axis. New York *Daily News,* p. 18.

Change the rules. (2001, September 18). *Newsday,* p. A16.

Charity, A. (1995). *Doing public journalism.* New York: Guilford.

Coe, K., Domke, D., Graham, E. S., John, S. L., & Pickard, V. W. (2004). No shades of gray: The binary discourse of George W. Bush and an echoing press. *Journal of Communication, 54,* 234–252.

Debatin, B. (2002). "Plane wreck with spectators": Terrorism and media attention. In B. S. Greenberg (Ed.), *Communication and terrorism: Public and media responses to 9/11* (pp. 163–174). Cresskill, NJ: Hampton.

Deggans, E. (2003, April 14). In TV war news, the hits and misses. *St. Petersburg Times,* pp. D1, D2.

Dennis, E. E. (1984). Journalistic objectivity *is* possible. In E. E. Dennis & J. C. Merrill (Eds.), *Basic issues in mass communication: A debate* (pp. 111–118). New York: Macmillan.

Domke, D., Coe, K., & Tynes, R. (2004, August). *The gospel of freedom and liberty: George W. Bush, the "war on terror," and an echoing press.* Paper presented to the Religion and Media Interest Group, Association for Education in Journalism and Mass Communication annual convention, Toronto, Ontario, Canada.

Durham, M. G. (1998). On the relevance of standpoint epistemology to the practice of journalism: The case for "strong objectivity." *Communication Theory, 8,* 117–140.

Farhi, P. (2003, April 4). The gung-ho morning gang: Cable's "Fox & Friends" prides itself on patriotic patter. *The Washington Post,* pp. C1, C7.

Fleming, K., & Thorson, E. (2004, August). *Effects of positive media images, media use, and information-processing strategies on attitudes and international knowledge during wartime.* Paper presented to the Communication Theory and Methodology Division, Association for Education in Journalism and Mass Communication annual convention, Toronto, Ontario, Canada.

From the editors: The Times and Iraq. (2004, May 26). *The New York Times,* p. A10.

Gauthier, G. (1993). In defence of a supposedly outdated notion: The range of application of journalistic objectivity. *Canadian Journal of Communication, 18,* 497–505.

Getlin, J. (2003, April 11). Fox News' patriotic fervor sets it apart in ratings race. *Los Angeles Times,* p. A16.

Gibson, D. (2002, October 13). A just war? Religious leaders have no faith in an offensive against Iraq. Newark, N.J. *Sunday Star-Ledger,* pp. 10–1, 10–16.

Glasser, T. L. (1984, February). The puzzle of objectivity I: Objectivity precludes responsibility. *The Quill, 72*(2), 12–16.

Gordon, M. R., & Miller, J. (2002, September 8). U.S. says Hussein intensifies quest for A-bomb parts. *The New York Times,* pp. A1, A25.

Griffin, M. (2004). Picturing America's "War on Terrorism" in Afghanistan and Iraq: Photographic motifs as news frames. *Journalism, 5,* 381–402.

Hiebert, R. E. (2003). Public relations and propaganda in framing the Iraq war: A preliminary review. *Public Relations Review, 29,* 243–255.

Kellner, D. (2002). September 11, the media, and war fever. *Television & New Media, 3,* 143–151.

Kellner, D. (2003). *From 9/11 to terror war: The dangers of the Bush legacy.* Lanham, MD: Rowman & Littlefield.

Kitch, C. (2003). "Mourning in America": Ritual, redemption, and recovery in news narrative after September 11. *Journalism Studies, 4,* 213–224.

Koch, T. (1990). *The news as myth: Fact and context in journalism.* New York: Greenwood.

Kurtz, H. (2004, August 12). The Post on WMDs: An inside story. *The Washington Post,* pp. A1, A20.

Lazarus, M. (2001, Fall). Documenting social ills with an eye toward advocacy. *Nieman Reports, 55*(3), 57–58.

Lewandowsky, S., Stritzke, W. G. K., Oberauer, K., & Morales, M. (2005). Memory for fact, fiction, and misinformation: The Iraq war 2003. *Psychological Science, 16*(3), 190–195.

Madigan, C. M. (2002, September 5). Poll: Public leery of war on Iraq. *Chicago Tribune,* p. 10.

Massing, M. (2004, February 26). Now they tell us. *The New York Review of Books,* pp. 43–49.

Merrill, J. C. (1984). Journalistic objectivity is *not* possible. In E. E. Dennis & J. C. Merrill (Eds.), *Basic issues in mass communication: A debate* (pp. 104–110). New York: Macmillan.

Merrill, J. C. (1996). *Existential journalism.* Ames: Iowa State University Press.

Merritt, D. (1995). *Public journalism and public life: Why telling the news is not enough.* Hillsdale, NJ: Lawrence Erlbaum Associates, Inc.

Miller, L., Stauber, J., & Rampton, S. (2004). War is sell. In D. Miller (Ed.), *Tell me lies: Propaganda and media distortion in the attack on Iraq* (pp. 41–51). London: Pluto.

Mogensen, K., Lindsay, L., Li, X., Perkins, J., & Beardsley, M. (2002). How TV news covered the crisis: The content of CNN, CBS, ABC, NBC and Fox. In B. S. Greenberg (Ed.), *Communication and terrorism: Public and media responses to 9/11* (pp. 101–120). Cresskill, NJ: Hampton.

Nacos, B. L. (2002). *Mass-mediated terrorism: The central role of the media in terrorism and counterterrorism.* Lanham, MD.: Rowman & Littlefield.

Peaceniks couldn't be more wrong. (2003, March 14). New York *Daily News,* p. 34.

Rosen, J. (1993, Winter). Beyond objectivity: It is a myth, an important one, but often crippling and it needs to be replaced with a more inspiring concept. *Nieman Reports, 47*(4), 48–53.

Rutherford, P. (2004). *Weapons of mass persuasion: Marketing the war against Iraq.* Toronto, Ontario, Canada: University of Toronto Press.

Ryan, M. (2001). Journalistic ethics, objectivity, existential journalism, standpoint epistemology, and public journalism. *Journal of Mass Media Ethics, 16,* 3–22.

Ryan, M. (2004). Framing the war against terrorism: US newspaper editorials and military action in Afghanistan. *Gazette, 66,* 363–382.

Ryan, M., & Switzer, L. (2005). Using binary language to sell the war in Afghanistan. In D. O'Hair, R. Heath, & G. Ledlow (Eds.), *Community preparedness and response to terrorism: Communication and the media* (pp. 97–124). New York: Praeger.

Ryan, M., & Switzer, L. (in press). Mirror on a war agenda: Conservative Christian activists and media coverage of the invasion of Iraq. In D. O'Hair, R. Heath, K. J. Ayotte, & G. Ledlow (Eds.), *Terrorism: Communication and rhetorical perspectives.* Cresskill, NJ: Hampton.

Smith, A. (1980, May/June). Is objectivity obsolete? Journalists lost their innocence in the seventies—And gained new voices for the eighties. *Columbia Journalism Review, 19*(1), 61–65.

Streckfuss, R. (1990). Objectivity in journalism: A search and a reassessment. *Journalism Quarterly, 67,* 973–983.

Strobel, W. P., Landay, J. S., & Walcott, J. (2002, October 8). Dissent over going to war grows among U.S. government officials. *Miami Herald,* p. 1.

A terrorist Pearl Harbor. (2001, September 12). *The Wall Street Journal,* p. A18.

Tewksbury, D., Jones, J., Peske, M. W., Raymond, A., & Vig, W. (2000). The interaction of news and advocate frames: Manipulating audience perceptions of a local public policy issue. *Journalism & Mass Communication Quarterly, 77,* 804–829.

Tuchman, G. (1972). Objectivity as strategic ritual: An examination of newsmen's notions of objectivity. *American Journal of Sociology, 77,* 660–679.

Weisman, J. (2001, September 20). Administration splits over whether to attack Iraq. *USA Today,* p. A6.

Wolfe, T., & Johnson, E. W. (Eds). (1973). *The new journalism.* New York: Harper & Row.

POSTSCRIPT

Are Political/Military Leaders to Blame for Misinformation in Time of War?

Schulman describes the complex informational activities of the government, particularly the military as they weigh the multiple uses and consequences of messages for both the American and Iraqi publics. The strategic use of information and the press to achieve governmental objectives is a theme of this work, and threatens any simple belief in the "transparency" of news information. Ryan shows how the dichotomous language of the Bush administration was replicated in the media, and attributes the failure of the press to be skeptical to the failure of the journalistic tenet of objectivity.

Other causes of the failure of the American press to be more skeptical in those crucial months can be posited. First, it is historically important to note that the press often reflects in pre-war times support for the impending action. This can be seen as a social consensus, wherein the press reflects a commitment of both government and the public to that action. Both Schulman and Ryan would agree that the appearance of such a consensus emerged, but for different reasons. Schulman would attribute it to the powerful information campaign of the administration, and Ryan to the failure of the press. A communciation theory may give us another insight into what happened. The "spiral of silence" theory of Noelle-Neumann suggests that individuals are less likely to express their opinion if they feel themselves to be in the minority. Media are important in this process as mass media coverage of opinion becomes the status quo, and those who perceive themselves as the minority become less likely to speak out due to fear of reprisal or isolation. Certainly, Ryan provides examples of how minority views were attacked.

Who gets to frame reality? The agenda-setting theory of the press suggests that media tell the public what to think about. Studies of media sources reveal that "official" or "powerful" sources account for much of media content. In an overly simplistic formulation, media make selections of stories to cover, based in large part on what official sources put on the agenda. This formulation ignores journalistic practices designed to investigate issues that are not on the official agenda, but we should not underestimate the importance of official and powerful sources on setting the agenda for the news. The classic watchdog function of the press with a duty to operate with autonomy, represent the interests of the public, and challenge dominant groups is not accomplished when powerful sources are not questioned. If truth and propaganda are intermixed, if journalists are not skeptical and analytic, how is the public to know?

It is easy to conclude that both government and press are to blame, but the heart of this issue asks us to establish our public standards for press, in its increasing multiplicity of forms, and government dissemination of information in the support of democratic decision making.

These issues have generated a lot of debate. Some books that may provide additional information for you include *The Media and the War on Terrorism,* edited by Stephen Hess and Marvin Kalb (2003). This book offers conversations with distinguished journalists concerning the difficulties of reporting during a crisis, with particular emphasis on the tensions between the government and the press.

ISSUE 8

Is Negative Campaigning Bad for the American Political Process?

YES: Bruce E. Pinkleton, Nam-Hyun Um, and Erica Weintraub Austin, from "An Exploration of the Effects of Negative Political Advertising on Political Decision Making," *Journal of Advertising* (Spring 2002)

NO: Ruth Ann Weaver Lariscy and Spencer F. Tinkham, from "Accentuating the Negative," *USA TODAY Magazine* (May 2004)

ISSUE SUMMARY

YES: Mass communication scholars examine the truth behind the assumption that negative campaigning has a negative impact on voters. Their experimental research study found that participants deemed negative ads fairly worthless and that such ads increased negativity about campaigns. Other potential consequences such as cynicism, efficacy, and apathy were not found.

NO: Political advertising scholars report on the lessons of their studies of negative campaign advertising. Negative ads, they argue, are more memorable. They help voters make distinctions between candidates; they influence voters. But not all negative ads are useful, and the authors help us make the distinction. Despite the revulsion that pervades public opinion toward negative ads, these authors argue that they are helpful to voters.

Nothing has transformed the American political process as much as the emergence of television as a force in elections. Today, many more people see candidates on television than hear them in person. Candidates appear in a variety of media formats—newspapers, television and radio interview shows, late-night talk shows, magazine covers, online, and even MTV. Never before have candidates used the power of media to such a comprehensive extent to reach potential voters.

But much of the public is fed up with political campaigns. Voters are disgusted with candidates and with politics in general. Viable candidates choose not to run rather than subject themselves and their families to the scrutiny of the press and the negativity of their opponent. Many in the public point the finger of blame at a relentless negativism governing the coverage and conduct of political campaigns that favors a horse-race mentality, leaps at opportunities to "go negative," and gleefully breaks stories of private failures.

Pinkleton, Um and Austin set out to prove what most already believe: that attack ads foster negative perceptions of politics, and ultimately voter apathy and cynicism. Their experimental study of college student reactions to a variety of campaign messages lends support to the fear that current campaign messages contribute to public disdain of politics and politicians. Extensive public discourse certainly lays the blame for these woes on the negativity of contemporary campaigning. *Peepshow: Media and Politics in an Age of Scandal* by Larry Sabato, Mark Stencel and Robert Lichter argues that scandal coverage has degraded politics, and blames journalists, politicians, and the public. In *The Nightly News Nightmare: Network Television's Coverage of U. S. Presidential Elections, 1988-2000*, Stephen Farnsworth and Robert Lichter (2002) look at campaign coverage over the past four presidential elections and track its changing nature in terms of objectivity, negativity, quantity, and overall quality.

Lariscy and Tinkham argue that negative campaigning persists because it works. The spin doctors have it right: negative campaigns can have a positive effect for their candidates. More importantly, from the perspective of Lariscy and Tinkham, it can be beneficial to voters. They find negative campaigning allows individuals to distinguish between candidates. They join with the others in decrying some forms of negative campaigning, but instead of calling for its abolition, they call for its appropriate use. Lariscy and Tinkham challenge the common perception that all negativity is bad. Rather than a bland campaign where each candidate speaks in favor of broad generalities, let record and behavior be revealed and debated. There must be a way for people to judge the character and record of those they select, otherwise the information needed to discriminate among candidates will never emerge.

The careful reader will notice that a number of issues are implicated in this discussion. Beyond negative campaigning, issues such as attack journalism, dirty politics, and general incivility are referenced in public discourse. Politicians seeking votes and journalists seeking stories have created election politics that disappoint and alienate voters. Attempts at reform are many. In the 2004 Democratic primaries, John Edwards refused to "go negative." According to Lariscy and Tinkham, that may have cost him the nomination. The media are much better at policing false assertions. Journalists routinely engage in "ad watches" where the validity of claims made in ads is evaluated.

What should be the rules for politicians and journalists in an era of media preoccupation with private lives and political scandal? Despite the incivility of present campaigns, do we want to return to an era in which private lives are never considered appropriate for public discussion? Does it matter if candidates have experimented with drugs, joined subversive organizations as college students, made mediocre grades, evaded war service, or had affairs? What changes would make political campaigns and their coverage more substantive?

Bruce E. Pinkleton, Nam-Hyun Um,
and Erica Weintraub Austin

An Exploration of the Effects of Negative Political Advertising on Political Decision Making

A total of 236 students participated in an experiment testing the effects of positive, negative, and negative comparative political advertising on key variables in the political decision-making process. Participants exposed to negative advertising found it less useful for political decision making and were more negative toward political campaigns than were participants exposed to positive advertising. Negative political advertising had no effect on participants' cynicism, efficacy, or apathy. The findings suggest that, though negative advertising contributes to citizens' disgust with campaigns, this strategy does not automatically increase citizens' cynicism or apathy.

Negative campaign tactics and questionable media election coverage continue to attract the attention of citizens, journalists, and researchers. Citizens commonly complain about the negative tenor of campaigns, especially about negative political advertising. Researchers, political observers, and others, meanwhile, suggest that negative campaign tactics result in negativism toward the political process, ultimately producing cynicism and apathy among voters (Crotty and Jacobson 1980; Grove 1989; Taylor 1989). Scholars' concerns about negative political advertising seem particularly disconcerting when considered alongside complaints that media coverage of the political process lacks both depth and context. Political observers and others have singled out broadcast media in particular for providing "horserace"-oriented campaign coverage that focuses on who leads or trails in the polls rather than identifying and discussing candidates' issue stands and policy proposals relevant to voters.

Nevertheless, the impact of repeated citizen exposure to negative political advertising and poor public affairs media coverage is difficult to determine with specificity. Scholars express concern that the ultimate outcome may be citizens high in cynicism and apathy, unwilling to engage in the most basic forms of public affairs participation, such as voting (Ansolabehere and Iyengar 1995; Cappella and Jamieson 1997; Crotty and Jacobson 1980). Despite this plethora of arguments connecting exposure to negative political advertising and mediated campaign coverage to political disaffection and apathy, it is difficult to verify and measure the nature of these relationships on the basis of existing research.

From *Journal of Advertising*, Spring 2002, pp. 13–25. Copyright © 2002 by M.E. Sharpe, Inc. Reprinted by permission.

Although general agreement exists that citizens' faith in government and related institutions has been declining along with voter turnout (e.g., Dennis and Webster 1975; Dionne 1991), less agreement exists regarding the reasons for this decline, and many questions remain unanswered pertaining to the links among media use, exposure to negative political advertising, and citizens' political malaise. Research makes it clear, for example, that voters dislike and distrust negative political advertisements (Garramone 1984). In fact, research results indicate that negative political advertising sometimes works against a sponsoring candidate by engendering more support for a targeted candidate (Faber, Tims, and Schmitt 1990; Garramone 1984; Roddy and Garramone 1988), typically referred to as a backlash effect. It is equally as clear, however, that candidates use negative political ads because they often contribute to campaign success (Doak 1995; Johnson-Cartee and Copeland 1991a; Nugent 1987; Pinkleton 1997, 1998). An examination of the role of negative political advertising in citizens' development of negativism, cynicism, and apathy provides the opportunity to reconcile these seemingly contradictory findings. Therefore, this study tests the effects of negative political advertising strategies on key aspects of voter decision making, including perceptions of the credibility and utility of advertising, negativism toward political campaigns, cynicism toward the political system, efficacy toward political participation, and voting apathy. This makes it possible to explore the potential for short-term, situationally based effects as well as longer term, more systemic-level effects.

Negative Political Advertising and Political Decision Making

Negative political advertising typically contains a one-sided attack on a targeted candidate designed to draw attention to the target's weaknesses, such as character flaws, voting record, public misstatements, broken promises, and the like (Johnson-Cartee and Copeland 1991a; Merritt 1984; Surlin and Gordon 1977). The contents of such advertising, sometimes called "mudslinging" or "attack advertising," impugn the character, record, or positions of the targeted candidate, creating doubt in voters' minds about the ability of the target to govern successfully. Negative campaign tactics are an often-used part of a candidate's campaign arsenal, despite the risk of creating sympathy for the target of the advertising, as already noted. Research results indicate that evaluations of both the sponsor and target of negative advertising worsen when campaigns use negative campaign tactics (Kaid and Boydston 1987; Merritt 1984; Pinkleton 1997), and study participants have rated the sponsor of negative advertising as more mean-spirited than the target (Pinkleton 1998). Nevertheless, when carefully constructed and used, negative campaign tactics reduce targeted candidate evaluations and voting intention to a much greater extent than they do sponsoring candidate evaluations (e.g., Johnson-Cartee and Copeland 1989, 1991a; Perloff and Kinsey 1992; Pinkleton 1997, 1998; Roddy and Garramone 1988), even among members of the targeted candidate's political party (Kaid and Boydston 1987).

Scholars generally attribute the reason for the greater effectiveness of negative advertising over positive advertising to the impact of negative information on information processing and judgmental decision making. Research regarding the role of negative information in individual impression formation, person perception, and various other information-processing tasks indicates that people tend to weight negative information more heavily than they do positive information when forming evaluations of social stimuli, including assessments of individual likability (Anderson 1965; Hamilton and Huffman 1971; Hamilton and Zanna 1972; Hodges 1974; Jordan 1965; Kellermann 1989). Research by Lau (1982, 1985) and Kernell (1977) has provided evidence supportive of negativity effects in political perception and behavior, including increased voter turnout due to negative candidate performance evaluations.

Not surprisingly, voters quickly tire of negative campaign tactics and commonly complain about the negative tenor of campaigns. Citizens consistently say negative advertising is unfair, uninformative, unethical, and deceptive (Garramone 1984; Merritt 1984; Steward 1975; Surlin and Gordon 1977). As a result, campaign consultants have increased the sophistication of campaigns by turning to a mix of strategies and tactics that includes the use of comparative advertising (Pfau et al. 1990; Salmore and Salmore 1989). Such advertising communicates negative information about a targeted candidate to voters while helping reduce the potential for backlash voting associated with the use of more obvious forms of attack advertising. The results of an analysis of the political advertising used in three national elections indicates that nearly half the advertising mentioned both candidates and almost a quarter contained direct candidate comparisons (Boiney and Paletz 1991).

Even though research results indicate that comparative advertising can be as effective as standard negative advertising in reducing targeted candidate evaluations and voting preferences, such advertising continues to suffer from perceptions of poor credibility (Johnson-Cartee and Copeland 1991a; Pinkleton 1997, 1998). Given voters' intense dislike of negative campaign tactics, study participants are likely to provide a low utility rating for negative political advertising.

H1: Participants will rate negative advertisements lower in utility than positive advertisements.

Negativism

Voter disgust with negative campaign tactics also should result in greater negativism toward political campaigns more broadly. Scholars and journalists regularly express concerns about the detrimental impact of negative campaign tactics on citizens' attitudes toward politics. If negativism decreases citizens' interest in campaigns and attention to public affairs information, the result is potentially disastrous for democracies, because they rely on citizens to make informed decisions and vote accordingly. Research confirms that heightened citizen interest and involvement in public affairs is associated with increased use of information sources and greater public affairs knowledge (Chaffee and

Schleuder 1986; McLeod and McDonald 1985; Pinkleton et al. 1997; Reagan 1996). If the public dislikes and distrusts negative campaign tactics, however, it seems more likely that its feelings of negativity will be directed toward the campaigns more than toward the media. Previous research shows that negativism toward the media is associated with decreased media use, but negativism toward campaigns is not (Pinkleton, Austin, and Fortman 1998). As a result, it is reasonable to expect that negativity increases resulting from exposure to negative political advertising will be directed toward political campaigns, as hypothesized.

H2: Participants' negativism toward political campaigns will increase as advertisement negativity increases.

Cynicism

Cynicism, perhaps the most frequently explored aspect of political disaffection, commonly refers to a lack of confidence in and a feeling of distrust toward the political system (Dennis and Webster 1975; Dionne 1991; Lau and Erber 1985; Perloff and Kinsey 1992). This represents a more broadbased aspect of disaffection than negativism toward campaigns, which is likely more situation based. Crotty and Jacobson (1980) suggest that cynical citizens have essentially given up on the political process, viewing it as irrelevant to their lives. Scholars and others frequently express concern that increased cynicism—most commonly blamed on negative campaign tactics—contributes to low interest in public affairs and reduced voter turnout (Ansolabehere, Behr, and Iyengar 1993; Cappella and Jamieson 1997; Crotty and Jacobson 1980; Dennis and Webster 1975). Negative political advertising, these authors argue, turns off voters and contributes to an electorate that is ill informed and uninvolved (Cappella and Jamieson 1997; Diamond and Bates 1988; Salmore and Salmore 1989).

Some authors have argued that some negativism toward political messages may represent healthy skepticism rather than cynicism, which is characterized by an openness to additional information (e.g., Austin and Pinkleton 1995; Cappella and Jamieson 1997; Pinkleton, Austin, and Fortman 1998; Wilkins 2000). Skeptical citizens may seek information to confirm or disconfirm the veracity of previously received messages. Cynicism, however, represents a cognitive state essentially closed to new information (Cappella and Jamieson 1997). As a result, cynical persons may respond more to messages that further confirm their distrustful beliefs and less to positive messages.

Voters have expressed strong disengagement from gubernatorial and senatorial elections based on the negative tenor of the election campaigns and the lack of substantive discussion pertaining to issues of interest to voters (Ansolabehere and Iyengar 1995). Ultimately, previous studies suggest that negative election environments increase voter cynicism, particularly for voters who already feel alienated or disenfranchised. Some scholars have suggested that voters—especially young voters—get trapped in a downward cycle in which cynicism breeds low efficacy, which in turn increases cynicism and apathy (Chaffee and Becker 1975; Jennings and Niemi 1978; Lau and Erber 1985). Other experimental studies have found that negative political advertising tends to increase cynicism, whereas positive advertising tends to decrease cynicism (Ansolabehere and Iyengar 1995). According to this research evidence, candidates' negative messages may further clutter and reinforce a negative campaign environment, contributing to an increase in voters' cynicism, as hypothesized.

H3: Participants' cynicism will increase as advertisement negativity increases.

Efficacy

Scholars frequently define self efficacy as a person's belief that, through his or her efforts, he or she can influence political and social events (Bandura 1986, 1997). Political decision-making studies often use the term "internal efficacy" to reflect people's beliefs about their own competence to understand and participate effectively in politics. According to Craig, Niemi, and Silver (1990), internal efficacy differs from distrust/cynicism, which refers to whether or not the government meets expectations and operates fairly. Internal efficacy also differs from external efficacy, which political scientists use to refer to beliefs about the responsiveness of governmental authorities and institutions. External efficacy parallels distrust/cynicism, which Craig, Niemi, and Silver (1990) have treated separately. Other studies have treated distrust/cynicism as a single construct on the basis of factor loadings (e.g., Austin and Pinkleton 1995; Pinkleton, Austin, and Fortman 1998). Scholars believe that cynical citizens' distrust of the government decreases their internal efficacy, the belief that they can exert any influence over systems of governance. This then leads them essentially to opt out of the political process.

Some researchers have found that voters may participate, despite their cynicism, if they are high in efficacy (Horn and Conway 1996). Others have found that negative advertising can both increase cynicism and decrease efficacy (Ansolabehere and Iyengar 1995). These scholars, however, have not separated measures of efficacy from measures of cynicism. Efficacy appears to have a direct, negative relationship with cynicism (Austin and Pinkleton 1995), and some scholars have combined measures of efficacy and cynicism as opposites of the same construct (Ansolabehere and Iyengar 1995). Others, however, have found them to be separate, if related, constructs (e.g., Austin and Pinkleton 1995; Bowen, Stamm, and Clark 2000; Chen 1992; Pinkleton et al. 1998). As a result, it is useful to test the effects of negative advertising on cynicism and efficacy separately. According to Bandura (1986, 1997), efficacy develops through successful experiences that cultivate confidence and expertise. Unsuccessful or frustrating experiences, however, can decrease efficacy. Thus, to the extent voters find negative advertising frustrating or lacking in usefulness, negative advertising should decrease individuals' efficacy, as hypothesized.

H4: Participants' self efficacy will decrease as advertising negativity increases.

Apathy

In studies of the electorate, apathy reflects a failure to engage in even the most basic forms of public affairs participation, usually including voting. Research findings regarding self efficacy indicate that political disaffection may actually lead to greater action among citizens who posses higher levels of self efficacy (Bandura 1997). When typical methods of achieving social change appear ineffective, citizens with higher self efficacy may intensify their efforts rather than abandoning them. The likelihood of action is highest among those with high levels of self efficacy combined with cynicism toward the political system (Bandura 1986, 1997).

This reasoning, however, runs counter to the opinions of many other scholars, who suggest that the ultimate outcome of a political election process corrupted by negative political advertising is an apathetic citizenry (Ansolabehere, Behr, and Iyengar 1993; Cappella and Jamieson 1997; Crotty and Jacobson 1980; Dennis and Webster 1975). These scholars suggest that negative campaign tactics contribute to high levels of citizen cynicism and negativism and low levels of citizen efficacy. Ultimately, these authors argue, negative campaign tactics turn citizens off to such an extent that they simply refuse to participate in a political system they view as corrupt and largely unresponsive to their needs. Although scholars can make a reasonable argument connecting both cynicism and apathy to negative campaign tactics, researchers have not determined the basis for this relationship with empirical specificity. The problem may be that, whereas critics link cynicism with apathy, some scholars have found them to be separate and unrelated constructs (Austin and Pinkleton 1995; Chen 1992). Without scientific evidence, it is difficult to blame apathy on the existence of negative campaign messages in the media or even on the frequency of people's exposure to the media in general or public affairs information specifically (Pinkleton and Austin 1998). A research question regarding the effect of negative political advertising on apathy is in order, given the competing opinions about negative campaign tactics and voter apathy.

> RQ1: What is the effect of negative political advertising on participants' apathy?

In summary, existing research and criticisms suggest that negative political advertising can produce both deleterious and beneficial effects. To improve scholars' understanding of the effects of negative political advertising, this study tests hypotheses on variables that suggest the potential for short-term, situationally based effects as well as longer term, more systemic-level effects.

Method

Undergraduate students participated in a 1×4 pretest-posttest (between groups) experiment to test the hypotheses and answer the research question. . . . Female and male participants participated nearly equally. Participants' ages ranged from 18 to 37 years; just over 85% of participants were between the ages of 19 and 22 years. More than 60% of participants had voted in a previous election.

A total of 246 participants received one of three randomly assigned treatments or a control activity. A total of 236 usable cases remained after the elimination of 10 incomplete instruments . . . Participants in the treatment conditions received different messages about fictional candidates for a state senate seat in Georgia. The campaign ostensibly occurred far away from participants' home state to increase its realism and decrease the potential for students' knowledge of local election issues.

Procedures

The experiment employed a double-exposure design. Initially, participants read each candidate's biographic profile and completed a series of pretest scales. Following the completion of the pretest scales, participants read a stimulus advertisement or control essay. Participants listed the thoughts they had about each candidate following initial stimulus exposure. This free-recall protocol ensured that participants thought about the candidates and stimuli, with the results not analyzed for the purpose of this study. Following the thought-listing exercise, participants again read the advertising stimuli or control essay and filled out posttest scales. Debriefing followed the completion of the post-test scales.

Stimuli

The experiment employed three types of stimuli, including biographic candidate profiles, political advertisements, and a control group essay. Biographic profiles contained information about each candidates' education, employment background, political accomplishments, family, and related information. Pretesting of the stimuli, along with manipulation checks, confirmed that both of the profiles were approximately equal in communicating information about candidates' qualifications, intelligence, credibility, and related characteristics.

Three advertisements constituted the treatments and were based on real-world examples of direct mail political advertising. The stimuli contained two different candidate names for both the sponsoring and targeted candidates to avoid name-specific effects. To determine the specific issue positions used in the stimuli, pretest participants rated the importance of issues using seven-point, semantic differential scales. Instrument pretesting procedures served to identify five issues for inclusion in the stimuli. The issues pertained to the environment, crime and community safety, higher education funding, development of employment opportunities, and increased support for elementary and secondary education.

Each stimulus contained a similar execution of a different creative strategy. The most negative stimulus contained a direct attack on the targeted candidate. The headline encouraged readers to vote for the sponsoring candidate and contained biographic highlights of the ad's sponsor. The remaining copy in this stimulus directly attacked the targeted candidate on the key issue positions identified through pretesting. A comparative version of this ad received somewhat less negative ratings from participants in pretests. The headline and sponsoring candidate biographic information were the same. The candidates were directly compared in this ad; however, the sponsoring candidate was portrayed as supporting the desired position on the key pretest issues, and the targeted candidate was assailed as supporting the opposite position. The final stimulus received a positive evaluation from pretest participants. This ad contained the same headline and biographic information as the other ads but did not mention the target ed candidate. Only the desired positions of the sponsoring candidate were mentioned in this stimulus.

Control group participants read an essay. The essay contained geographic and historical information about Georgia and did not mention either the sponsoring or the targeted candidate. . . .

Variable Measurement

[Items used to measure each variable are shown in Table 1.] . . .

As predicted by Hypothesis 1 and shown in Table 2, participants gave the negative ads a lower utility rating. There was no significant difference between the control group and the positive advertising strategy condition. There also were no significant differences between the comparative ad and the negative ad strategies, with both reported as less useful than the positive ad strategy, as shown in Figure 1.

As predicted by Hypothesis 2 and shown . . . in Figure 2, the more negative the advertisement, the more negativism subjects reported toward political campaigns. There was no significant difference between the control group condition and the positive advertising condition. . . .

Discussion

Despite widespread concern about the effects of negative campaign techniques, the effects of negative advertising strategies on voter decision making are poorly understood. Campaigns use them because they seem to work, and critics decry them because they appear to depress political participation. Therefore, this study tested the effects of negative political advertising on key variables in the political decision-making process to help explain how negative advertising affects political participation. Study results indicate that participants found negative advertising less useful than positive advertising. Whereas negative advertising produced greater contempt for campaigns, however, it had no effects on apathy.

As expected, the more negative the advertising, the less useful participants found it. This supports the findings of others who have suggested that negative ads provide little information that is helpful to voters (Ansolabehere and Iyengar 1995; Cappella and Jamieson 1997). Voters frequently say they dislike and distrust negative political advertising. These results appear to confirm that such feelings of dislike translate into more cognitively based assessments of information benefit. Nevertheless, political campaign consultants find negative political campaign advertising useful, because, when carefully created

Table 1

Descriptive Statistics for Variables Used in the Analyses

Variable	m	alpha
Variables at Pretest		
Negativism toward campaigns	17.79	.76
Pol. campaigns too mean-spirited	4.38	
In general, pol. campaigns too negative	4.34	
Seems pol. ads are *against* something more often than they are *for* something	4.61	
Pol. advertising is too negative	4.46	
Cynicism	23.38	.84
Pol.s lose touch with people quickly	4.71	
Cand.s only interested in people's votes, not their opinions	4.51	
Too many pol.s only serve themselves or special interests	4.82	
Seems gov't run by a few big interests just out for themselves	4.50	
Pol.s lie to media & public	4.85	
Efficacy	11.82	.77
I have a real say in what the government does	3.11	
My vote makes a difference	3.82	
Voting an effective way to influence what government does	4.91	
Apathy (reverse coded)	15.44	.93
Voting in each election a high priority for me	3.68	
Voting in elections is important to me	4.10	
Would feel guilty if I didn't vote	3.41	
I like to vote	4.24	
Variables at Posttest		
Advertising utility	17.51	.81
Believable–unbelievable	4.40	
Unfair–fair	3.99	
Informative–uninformative	4.72	
Interesting–uninteresting	4.36	
Negativism re campaigns	18.68	.88
Pol. campaigns too mean-spirited	4.55	
In general, pol. campaigns too negative	4.66	
Seems like pol. ads *against* something more than they are *for* something	4.73	
Pol. advertising is too negative	4.73	
Cynicism	23.38	.88
Pol.s lose touch with people quickly	4.64	
Cand.s only interested in people's votes, not in their opinions	4.60	
Too many pol.s only serve themselves or special interests	4.68	
Seems our gov't run by a few big interests just out for themselves	4.63	
Pol.s lie to media & public	4.85	
Efficacy	11.46	.86
I have a real say in what the government does	3.47	
My vote makes a difference	3.81	
Voting is an effective way to influence what government does	4.19	
Apathy (reverse coded)	15.39	.94
Voting in each election a high priority for me	3.75	
Voting in elections important to me	4.03	
Would feel guilty if I didn't vote	3.50	
I like to vote	4.13	

Note: All items measured on seven-point scales. Except for semantic differential items, a high score indicates stronger agreement, and a low score indicates stronger disagreement. Reverse-coded items recoded for consistent directionality before inclusion in the appropriate index.

Figure 1

Effects of Experimental Manipulation on Advertising Utility Ratings

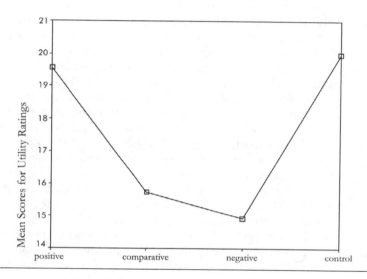

Figure 2

Effects of Experimental Manipulation on Participants' Negativity Toward Campaigns

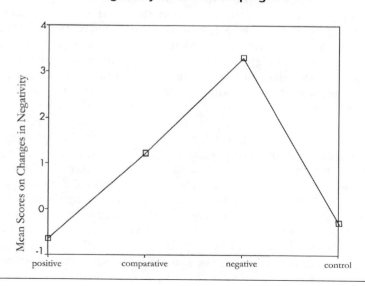

and executed, it successfully denigrates targeted candidate evaluations and voting intentions (Johnson-Cartee and Copeland 1991a; Kaid and Boydston 1987; Perloff and Kinsey 1992; Pinkleton 1997, 1998). This indicates that voter assessments of usefulness do not necessarily indicate effects or effectiveness.

Participants' assessments of usefulness were consistent with their perceptions of negativism toward political campaigns, indicating that the advertisements had some effects, despite their perceived uselessness among message recipients. Those exposed to the most negative stimuli reported the most negativity toward campaigns. In fact, the fully negative advertising condition produced perceptions nearly three times as negative (m = 3.31) as the comparative advertising condition (m = 1.23). The positive advertising condition (m = −.66) was no different than the control condition in terms of negativity. This finding is not surprising because of voters' stated disgust with negative political advertising. The bigger issue is whether increased negative advertising effects translate into long-term, systemic cynicism or whether they merely reflect a short-term response to the campaign at hand. Scholars suggest that some aspects of disaffection can be motivating to potential voters, in which case the heightened negativity effects could be viewed as a successful outcome for the promotion of political participation. When citizens engage in backlash voting, for example, this represents a form of political participation motivated by negativism (e.g., Faber, Tims, and Schmitt 1990; Garramone 1984; Roddy and Garramone 1988). One study found that negativism predicted a greater intention for voting through its effect on third-person perceptions, or the belief that others would be more gullible to the advertising (Austin and Pinkleton 1995). Others have noted that negative advertising tends to depress voting among less involved or less partisan citizens, tending to polarize more involved voters (e.g., Ansolabehere and Iyengar 1995).

The investigation of negative political advertising's effects on cynicism produced a result less consistent with common criticisms of political advertising, seeming to confirm that, at least in the short term, campaign-related negativism and cynicism, though related, have different causes and different outcomes. Campaign-related negativism appears to be a direct response to a specific, ongoing campaign or campaigns, representing a more transient state than cynicism. Cynicism, at least in this experimental manipulation, was not affected by negative political campaign techniques, in support of the position that it is more global and stable.

Scholars have only recently begun to delineate the differences between campaign-related negativism, which appears to be affected by negative political advertising, and more enduring cynicism, which does not change as easily. As a result, these findings suggest that what scholars and critics often say about cynicism may be true of negativism rather than cynicism. For example, though cynicism often is blamed for a lack of participation among citizens, it does not always associate directly with behavior (Pinkleton, Austin, and Fortman 1998). In contrast, researchers have found that negativism can be associated with public affairs behavior, in some cases motivating participation rather than discouraging it (Austin and Pinkleton 1995; Lau 1982). In addition, cynicism in some previous research has had sizable negative associations with efficacy, whereas negativism toward campaigns appears to affect efficacy less directly (Austin and Pinkleton 1995). Nevertheless, negativism—particularly toward the media rather than toward campaigns—and cynicism are clearly associated (Pinkleton, Austin, and Fortman 1998). As a result, critics' concerns that negativism may evolve into more global cynicism may be well placed, but short-term effects such as those demonstrated in this study should not be assumed to have long-term significance. More research would be helpful on this point.

Study results suggest that a drop in efficacy may occur as the negativity of political advertising increases, but our findings only bordered on statistical significance. This suggests that negative advertising may have the potential to damage political participation by virtue of its influences on efficacy, but it also suggests that efficacy may be somewhat resilient to short-term negative campaign cycles. Scholars have found that efficacy develops through continuing experiences (Bandura 1986, 1997), with some scholars suggesting that more novice participants tend to be more affected by negative events and news coverage (Chaffee and Becker 1975) and have less stable political orientations (Jennings and Niemi 1978; Lau and Erber 1985). It could be that a stronger manipulation in a more realistic campaign setting might produce significant changes in voter efficacy. As a result, concerns about the effects of negative campaign tactics cannot be dismissed on the basis of these results.

The findings regarding voting apathy, which associates with efficacy (Austin and Pinkleton 1995), were unambiguous, with the negative advertising executions having no effect on judgments of apathy. This could suggest that apathetic citizens are less affected by the negativism in advertising as a result of their lack of involvement in or attention to the political process. As a result, citizens who blame negative campaign tactics for their own lack of participation could be making excuses after the fact rather than reporting accurately on the roots of their own disinterest. It also could indicate that negative advertising's effects on apathy and efficacy, as well as on cynicism, are cumulative and difficult to detect in a short-term manipulation. It would be useful to replicate this study with more experienced voters and over a longer time period to determine whether the results would differ and to get a clearer understanding of the cause-and-effect relationship among variables. In particular, a study incorporating multiple messages and multiple exposures could provide more measurement opportunities and, thus, more powerful evidence of changes that may occur. . . .

In summary, this study has demonstrated the complexities of political decision making, indicating that more studies need to address intermediary variables in political decision making. Despite scholars' concerns about the deleterious effects of negative campaign tactics on political participation, this study found little evidence of systemic-level damaging effects. Over the course of a campaign, however, people will likely see a barrage of both negative and comparative advertising. If this crush of advertising and media coverage has effects on negativity but none on efficacy, apathy, or cynicism, then the results of negative advertising may be what campaign strategists desire: A short-term increase in negativity that damages targeted candidate evaluations but leaves no long-term, damaging effects on the electorate. These results, however, do not rule out the possibility that, ultimately, negative advertising reduces public affairs participation. Although this study further confirms that negative advertising is perceived as negative and contributes to short-term disgust with campaigns, the findings suggest that this strategy does not automatically increase cynicism or citizen apathy.

References

Anderson, Norman H. (1965), "Averaging vs. Adding as a Stimulus-Combination Rule in Impression Formation," *Journal of Experimental Psychology, 70* (4), 394–400.

Ansolabehere, Stephen, Roy Behr, and Shanto Iyengar (1993), *The Media Game*, New York: Macmillan.

——— and Shanto Iyengar (1995), Going Negative: *How Political Advertisements Shrink & Polarize the Electorate*, New York: The Free Press.

Austin, Erica W. and Bruce E. Pinkleton (1995), "Positive and Negative Effects of Political Disaffection on the Less Experienced Voter," *Journal of Broadcasting and Electronic Media*, 39 (2), 215–235.

Bandura, Albert (1986), *Social Foundations of Thought and Action: A Social Cognitive Theory*, Englewood Cliffs, NJ: Prentice-Hall

——— (1997), *Self Efficacy: The Exercise of Control*, New York: W. H. Freeman and Company.

Boiney, John and David L. Paletz (1991), "In Search of the Model Model: Political Science Versus Political Advertising Perspectives on Voter Decision Making," in *Television and Political Advertising, Volume 1: Psychological* Processes, Frank Biocca, ed., Hillsdale, NJ: Lawrence Eribaum Associates, 3–26.

Bowen, Lawrence, Keith Stamm, and Fiona Clark (2000), "Television Reliance and Political Malaise: A Contingency Analysis," *Journal of Broadcasting & Electronic Media*, 44 (1), 1–15.

Cappella, Joseph N. and Kathleen Hall Jamieson (1997), *Spiral of Cynicism: The Press and the Public Good*, New York: Oxford University Press.

Chaffee, Steven H. and Lee B. Becker (1975), "Young Voters' Reactions to Early Watergate Issues," American Politics Quarterly, 3 (4), 360–385.

——— and Joan Schleuder (1986), "Measurement and Effects of Attention to Media News," *Human Communication Research*, 13 (1), 76–107.

Chen, Kevin (1992), *Political Alienation and Voting Turnout in the United States 1960-1988*, San Francisco: Mellen Research University Press.

Craig, Stephen C., Richard G. Niemi, and Glenn E. Silver (1990), "Political Efficacy and Trust: A Report on the NES Pilot Study Items," *Political Behavior*, 12 (3), 289–313.

Crotty, William J. and Gary C. Jacobson (1980), *American Parties in Decline*, Boston: Little, Brown, and Company.

Dennis, Jack and Carol Webster (1975), "Childrens' Images of the President and of Government in 1962 and 1974," *American Politics Quarterly*, 3 (4), 386–405.

Diamond, Edwin and Stephen Bates (1988), *The Spot: The Rise of Political Advertising on Television*, Cambridge, MA: MIT Press.

Dionne, E.J., Jr. (1991), *Why Americans Hate Politics*, New York: Simon and Schuster.

Doak, David (1995), "Attack Ads: Rethinking the Rules," *Campaigns & Elections*, 16 (July), 20–21.

Faber, Ronald J., Albert R. Tims, and Kay G Schmitt (1990), "Accentuate the Negative?: The Impact of Negative Political Appeals on Voting Intent," in *Proceedings of the American Academy of Advertising*, Patricia Stout, ed., Austin, TX: American Academy of Advertising, 10–16.

Garramone, Gina M. (1984), "Voter Responses to Negative Political Ads," *Journalism Quarterly*, 61 (2), 250–259.

——— (1985), "Effects of Negative Political Advertising: The Roles of Sponsor and Rebuttal," *Journal of Broadcasting and Electronic Media*, 29 (2), 147–159.

—— and Sandra J. Smith (1984), "Reactions to Political Advertising: Clarifying Sponsor Effects," *Journalism Quarterly*, 61 (4), 771–775.

Grove, Lloyd (1989), "How Experts Fueled a Race with Vitriol," *The Washington Post*, (January 18), A1 and A14.

Hamilton, David L. and Leroy J. Huffman (1971), "Generality of Impression-Formation Processes for Evaluative and Nonevaluative Judgments," *Journal of Personality and Social Psychology*, 20 (2), 200–207.

—— and Mark P. Zanna (1972), "Differential Weighting of Favorable and Unfavorable Attributes in Impression Formation," *Journal of Experimental Research in Personality*, 6(2–3), 204–212.

Hodges, Bert H. (1974), "Effect of Valence on Relative Weighting in Impression Formation," *Journal of Personality and Social Psychology*, 30 (3), 378–381.

Horn, Randolph C. and M. Margaret Conway (1996), "Public Judgment and Political Engagement in the 1992 Election," in *Broken Contract? Changing Relationships Between Americans and Their Government*, Stephen C. Craig, ed., Boulder, CO: Westview Press, 110–126.

Jennings, Kent M. and Richard G. Niemi (1978), "The Persistence of Political Orientations: An Over-Time Analysis of Two Generations," British Journal of Political Science, 8, 333–363.

Johnson-Cartee, Karen S. and Gary A. Copeland (1989), "Southern Voters' Reaction to Negative Political Ads in 1986," *Journalism Quarterly*, 66 (4), 888–893, 986.

—— and —— (1991a), "Candidate-Sponsored Negative Political Advertising Effects Reconsidered," paper presented to Association for Education in Journalism and Mass Communication Convention, (August), Boston.

—— and —— (1991b), *Negative Political Advertising: Coming of Age*, Hillsdale, NJ: Lawrence Eribaum Associates.

Jordan, Nehemiah (1965), "The 'Asymmetry' of 'Liking' and 'Disliking': A Phenomenon Meriting Further Replication and Research," *Public Opinion Quarterly*, 29 (2), 315–322.

Kaid, Lynda L. and John Boydston (1987), "An Experimental Study of the Effectiveness of Negative Political Advertisements," *Communication Quarterly*, 35 (2), 193–201.

Kellermann, Kathy (1989), "The Negativity Effect in Interaction: It's All in Your Point of View," *Human Communication Research*, 16 (2), 147–183.

Kernell, S. (1977), "Presidential Popularity and Negative Voting: An Alternative Explanation of the Mid-Term Congressional Decline of the President's Party," *American Political Science Review*, 71, 44–66.

Lau, Richard R. (1982), "Negativity in Political Perception," *Political Behavior*, 4 (4), 353–377.

—— (1985), "Two Explanations for Negativity Effects in Political Behavior," *American Journal of Political Science*, 29 (1), 119–138.

—— and Ralph Erber (1985), "Political Sophistication: An Information-Processing Perspective," in *Mass Media & Political Thought*, Sidney Kraus and Richard M. Perloff, eds., Beverly Hills, CA: Sage Publications, 37–64.

McLeod, Jack M. and Daniel G. McDonald (1985), "Beyond Simple Exposure: Media Orientations and Their Impact on Political Processes," *Communication Research*, 12 (1), 3–33.

Merritt, Sharyne (1984), "Negative Political Advertising: Some Empirical Findings," *Journal of Advertising*, 13 (3), 27–38.

Nugent, John F. (1987), "Positively Negative," *Campaigns and Elections*, 7 (March/April), 47–49.

Perloff, Richard M. and Dennis Kinsey (1992), "Political Advertising as Seen by Consultants and Journalists," Journal of Advertising Research, 36 (May/June), 53–60.

Pfau, Michael, Henry C. Kenski, Michael Nitz, and John Sorenson (1990), "Efficacy of Inoculation Strategies in Promoting Resistance to Political Attack Messages: Application to Direct Mail," *Communication Monographs*, 57 (1), 25–43.

Pinkleton, Bruce E. (1997), "The Effects of Negative Comparative Political Advertising on Candidate Evaluations and Advertising Evaluations: An Exploration," *Journal of Advertising*, 26 (1), 19–29.

——— (1998), "Effects of Print Comparative Political Advertising on Political Decision-Making and Participation," *Journal of Communication*, 48 (4), 24–36.

——— and Erica W. Austin (1998), "Media and Participation: Breaking the Spiral of Disaffection," in *Engaging the Public: How Government and the Media Can Reinvigorate American Democracy*, Thomas J. Johnson, Carol E. Hays and Scott P. Hays, eds., Lanham, MD: Rowman & Littlefield Publishers, 75–86.

———, ———, and Kristine K. J. Fortman (1998), "Relationships of Media Use and Political Disaffection to Political Efficacy and Voting Behavior," *Journal of Broadcasting & Electronic Media*, 42 (1), 34–49.

———, Joey Reagan, Dustin Aaronson, and Chien-Fei Chen (1997), "The Role of Individual Motivations in Information Source Use and Knowledge Concerning Divergent Topics," *Communication Research Reports*, 14 (3), 291–301.

Reagan, Joey (1996), "The 'Repertoire' of Information Sources," *Journal of Broadcasting & Electronic Media*, 40 (1), 112–121.

Roddy, Brian L. and Gina M. Garramone (1988), "Appeals and Strategies of Negative Political Advertising," *Journal of Broadcasting & Electronic Media*, 32 (4), 415–427.

Salmore, Barbara G. and Stephen A. Salmore (1989), *Candidates, Parties, and Campaigns*, Washington, DC: Congressional Quarterly Press.

Steward, Charles J. (1975), "Voter Perception of Mudslinging in Political Communication," *Central States Speech Journal*, 26 (4), 279, 286.

Surlin, Stuart H. and Thomas F. Gordon (1977), "How Values Affect Attitudes Toward Direct Reference Political Advertising," *Journalism Quarterly*, 54 (1), 89–95.

Taylor, Paul (1989), "Consultants Rise Via the Low Road," *The Washington Post*, (January 17), A1, A14.

Wilkins, Karin Gwinn (2000), "The Role of Media in Public Disengagement from Public Life," *Journal of Broadcasting & Electronic Media*, 44 (4), 569–580.

Ruth Ann Weaver Lariscy and
Spencer F. Tinkham

 **NO**

Accentuating the Negative

"...**S**tudies demonstrate that, as time passes, the source of a negative [political advertisement] decays, but its content remains and becomes even more powerful."

BEWARE, Mr. and Ms. American Voter, highly skilled spinmeisters are coming after you—more precisely, your vote—with unprecedented negative attack advertising. Despite legislation designed to limit campaign mudslinging, negative advertising began earlier in this presidential race than any other in modern political history. To understand how the marketing consultants are working on you, keep in mind three important items: an ad does not have to be liked to be effective; negative ads help voters make distinctions among candidates; and not all negative ads are created equal.

Voters have a hard time with this first concept. Think for a few minutes about an ad slogan you find really annoying. If you are like most of us, you remember the ad, slogan, and product clearly, even if you disliked the ad intensely when it came on the radio or television. One reason why this type of negative ad works is because it is more complex than a positive one.

A positive ad ("Joe Smith is a war veteran, a patriot, and has true American values.") presents no overt conflict, elicits less rebuttal, and is absorbed easily. While "feel good" commercials can be enjoyable to viewers, they are not particularly informative, educational, or memorable. A positive message glides through the brain in much the same way that water from a garden hose washes easily over a smooth patio—nothing gets in its way, slows it down, or "sticks" very long.

A negative ad, however, sticks in the memory. ("Joe Smith never has served his country, used personal influence to avoid military service, and his commitment to true American values should be questioned.") Negative ads cause voters to think, make comparisons, sort through meanings, and assess the validity of claims. The brain expends more time and energy processing the negative message because of its complexity. A negative message is not smooth. It is like water from a garden hose running through a rocky ravine full of crags and cracks that make the journey more difficult. The water has to traverse slowly, navigating around obstacles, and sometimes getting stuck in little pools.

Negative information carries an inherent memory bias that the positive variety does not. Consider the following illustration: You walk into a room wearing a new suit and receive 15 compliments. It feels great. Then, one person says, "That is an okay look for last year's style." The good feelings stop. Regardless of the number of compliments received and how much you want to remember them, it is the one snide remark that sticks. Negative ads are more memorable than positive ones, even when you do not want them to be.

Not only does negative information stick, it sticks longer. In a series of experimental studies a couple of years ago with groups of registered voters from northeast Georgia, we produced professional quality political commercials for a fictitious candidate and his fictitious opponent in, of course, a fictitious congressional campaign. Using all the appropriate experimental protocol and controls, the participants were asked to evaluate a series of commercials, then answer the question, "If the election for Congress was held today between Candidate X and Candidate Y, who would you vote for?"

We were not surprised that the negative ad we created was especially effective immediately after it was shown, when there was no chance for response or rebuttal. In fact, a majority of those who saw only the attack ad voted for the attacker. When a specific rebuttal ad sponsored by the victim of the attack was viewed, the vote went to the victim. This, too, is not intuitively surprising.

The findings from the next stage of these studies were an eye-opener, however. In a period covering six weeks from the day of his or her vote for the fictitious candidate, each study participant was called back on the telephone. After reacquainting each with some basic information, we repeated the question we had asked the day of the study. The numbers shifted rather dramatically. The attacker overwhelmingly won the election. There even were a couple of instances when a participant would say, "You know, I'm not clear on the name, but I definitely would not vote for that one who lied." Of course, "being a liar" was at the heart of the attack ad.

In these experiments, we tested what psychologists call "the sleeper effect" and generated some intriguing results. The studies demonstrate that, as time passes, the source of a negative attack decays, but its content remains and becomes even more powerful. Simply put, you may forget where or when you learned something, but the negative information stays with you.

During the last two decades, political advertising has become (to the distress of many journalists and political observers) an increasingly important source of information for voters. Some scholars estimate that as many as half of the electorate make voting decisions based upon information from advertising. You may lament the rise of "instantaneous information" in the 30-second commercial spot, but it is a vital feature of the election campaign landscape, particularly aimed at less involved (but responsible) voters. This group needs to receive easily understood, straightforward information in a simple format.

However, not all negative ads are created equal. Up to this point, we have used a general umbrella term to cover a wide range of negative messages. Yet, not all negative attack ads work effectively. A poor ad can blow up in the face of the candidate who sponsored it. There are in fact "good" negative ads and "bad" ones, but you may be surprised at what constitutes each.

Good negative ads create all the desirable effects discussed earlier. Bad negative ads, however, produce something different—a backlash or boomerang.

When a boomerang does occur, viewers have a strong, immediate reaction against the attacker and lots of empathy for the victim of the attack. It is fairly easy to recognize when an ad is attacking a candidate's stand on an issue versus when one is attacking a personal characteristic, such as likening someone to terrorist Osama bin Laden or dictator Adolf Hitler. Issues-based negative advertisements are more likely to elicit an instantaneous acceptance and less revulsion. Similarly, an ad that is considered below the belt or in poor taste (implied character assassination of a candidate's family member, for example) most likely will be condemned on the spot.

Good and Bad Negative Ads

A negative ad is not good or bad based exclusively on content, nor whether it is funny, entertaining, or well produced. The most important element is how useful the information is judged to be. For instance, conventional wisdom suggests an ad that alludes to the sexual exploits of a married candidate outside of marriage is inappropriate. If the criterion simply was "below the belt," the ad, based on this view, would be rejected and likely produce a backlash. In reality, though, the ad, which the attacker's campaign organization had predicted would have powerful effects, has virtually no impact since the extramarital activities of the attacked candidate were widely known. The information was old news and therefore judged not useful.

A second judgment enters voters' evaluation process of ads here as well: The attack must strike them as at least plausible. When viewing an attack ad, individuals certainly do not know if the information is true. Beyond the accuracy or perceived truthfulness, it seems to be quite important—if a message is going to work—that listeners would find the content within the realm of possibility.

Meanwhile, one component (Sec. 311) of the McCain-Feingold Campaign Finance Reform Law is popularly called the "stand by your ad" provision. As seen in the first negative attack ad that Pres. Bush's campaign levied against Sen. John Kerry (D.-Mass.), the President introduces the ad personally, saying, "I'm George W. Bush and I approved this message." Clearly, the logic behind the provision is that candidates and the independent organizations that sponsor ads for them will be less likely to "go negative" or to levy particularly vicious attacks if the candidates personally are tied to the message for fear of backlash or boomerang. Additionally, the provision does not allow soft money organizations to air any negative ads in the six weeks immediately preceding Election Day. Although it is too early to conclude that the provision is not working, there has been an early onslaught of attacks from both sides. As to the "softening" of attack ads, that, too, is difficult to assess, as it is impossible to know what ads might have been aired if the new regulations did not exist.

Moreover, the legislation may have an unintended effect. Since many of the attack ads will be restricted in the six weeks immediately prior to Election Day, the harshest will occur early on. By doing so, they are most likely to benefit from the sleeper effect, and, by November, many voters will forget where they heard it, but will remember the content of the attacks.

As protected political speech, negative campaign ads, regardless of any legislation, are here to stay. They can be informative, entertaining, interesting, and motivating. The best ones are. They also can be trashy, boring, and create a backlash. The worst ones do. Yet, an armed, informed audience—even one that claims "We can't stand all that mudslinging!"—is able to recognize that these messages have their place.

POSTSCRIPT

Is Negative Campaigning Bad for the American Political Process?

A 1996 Freedom Forum poll found that three-quarters of American voters believe that the press has a negative impact on U.S. presidential campaigns, detracts from a discussion of the issues, gives undue advantage to front-running candidates, is often confusing and unclear, and even discourages good people from running for president. Despite the criticism, these same voters rely heavily on journalists to provide the information needed to make informed voter decisions. They turn to journalists for information about the candidates, particularly their issue positions, and for information about how election outcomes will affect voters.

The implications of these findings for judgments about negativity in political campaigns are important. It seems clear that people are unhappy with current political coverage. People want more information, and they want it tailored to their questions and their needs. Political internet sites are perhaps one answer. They are proliferating; yet, even these suffer from the familiar problem of too much trivia and too little debate. It remains to be seen whether or not the advent of new technology will be able to fulfill its promise of creating a more positive dialogue between candidate and voter.

Lest a reader begin to feel too self-righteous about these issues, let us remember the complicity of the viewing public. Candidate debates attract a small number of viewers; political scandal sells. Just as in television entertainment, what the public gets is influenced by what the public selects from the available options. Certainly with the advent of cable niche programming, the public can select much more informative and less scandal-oriented programming than ever before. Thus, the critique that implicates the press and the politician also implicates the viewer.

A number of books try to analyze the consequences of negativity. One book that has specifically tackled the history and problem of campaign advertising is *Going Negative: How Attack Ads Shrink and Polarize the Electorate*, by Stephen Ansolabehere and Shano Iyengar (Free Press, 1997). Examining the consequences for the voter are Joseph Capella and Kathleen Hall Jamieson in *Spiral of Cynicism* (Oxford University Press, 1997). For an insight into the campaign planning process of the 2000 election, see *Electing the President, 2000: The Insiders' View* by Kathleen Jamieson and Paul Waldman (Editors) (University of Pennsylvania Press, 2001). For a journalistic take on the issue, see Mike McCurry, "Getting Past the Spin," *The Washington Monthly* (July/August 1999).

ISSUE 9

Is Fake News Journalism?

YES: Julia R. Fox, Glory Koloen, and Volkan Sahin, from "No Joke: A Comparison of Substance in *The Daily Show with Jon Stewart* and Broadcast Network Television Coverage of the 2004 Presidential Election Campaign," *Journal of Broadcasting & Electronic Media* (June 2007)

NO: Barry A. Hollander, from "Late-Night Learning: Do Entertainment Programs Increase Political Campaign Knowledge for Young Viewers?" *Journal of Broadcasting & Electronic Media* (December 2005)

ISSUE SUMMARY

YES: This study examined political coverage of the first presidential debate and the political convention on *The Daily Show* and on network nightly newscasts. The study found the network coverage to be more hype than substance, and *The Daily Show* to be more humor than substance. The amount of substantive information between the two newscasts was about the same for both the story and for the entire half-hour program.

NO: Hollander examined learning from comedy and late-night programs. National survey data were used to examine whether exposure to comedy and late-night programs actually inform viewers, focusing on recall and recognition. Some support is found for the prediction that the consumption of such programs is more associated with recognition of information than with actual recall.

T raditionally journalism has been defined as what appears in newspapers, newsmagazines, and electronic media news programming. In the age of the Internet, simple "medium-based" descriptions of news are no longer accurate. Shifting trends in media usage see young voters turning to comedic sources for information, rather than traditional media. Programs such as *The Daily Show with Jon Stewart* are cited by youth as among the most important sources of political information.

If an enlightened citizenry is one of the foundations of a successful democracy, what are the consequences of this shift for an informed electorate? In *Tuned Out: Why Americans Under 40 Don't Follow the News*, David Mindich notes that fewer than 20 per cent of youth read a newspaper daily. While tele-vision news has an average viewer age near 60, the Pew Center for the People and the Press report on the fragmented political universe of 2004, noting that television is still the public's—including youth's—main source of campaign news. Nontraditional and Internet sources are on the rise, but are still not the major news source for youth. Within the age group 18–29, 27 per cent reported that they got *no* news yesterday.

This generational shift in declining audience is matched with a decline in average political awareness according to Mindich. Younger citizens have lower rates of news and current affairs awareness. In addition to knowing less, this group cares less, votes less, and follows the news less than their elders. Additionally, youth are less likely to trust political systems, or believe that they can have an influence. If it is true as believed by many in the media industries, that in their adult years individuals will follow the media patterns of their youth, the decline in newspapers and traditional television newscasts will certainly continue. The 2004 Pew Report finds, however, that the most knowledgeable Americans were those who use the Internet (primarily using Web-based versions of traditional media sites), listeners of National Public Radio, and readers of newsmagazines. By comparison, the least knowledge-able Americans got their news from comedy and late-night TV shows, more often viewed by youth. The effects of advocacy journalism on television are being felt in that about 40 per cent of the public believe that news is biased in favor of one of the two parties. This is matched by the 40 per cent who say there is no bias.

These confusing trends should not obscure the improved youth voter turnout of 2004. In "No Joke," Fox, Koloen, and Sahin compare the substan-tive information in network newscasts with substantive information in *The Daily Show with Jon Stewart*. Their surprising conclusion is that level of sub-stance is remarkably similar across the shows. Perhaps the shift to comedic news will begin to engage viewers who would not be involved without the humor and skepticism of fake news.

Hollander wonders what we learn from fake news. His question is simple: Does late-night and comedic news exposure actually inform viewers? He distinguishes between recall and recognition memory. Recognition memory is the less demanding measure, asking to recognize some fact or person from a list. Recall would ask the respondent to simply know the answer. Hollander found the consumption of comedic viewers to be more related to recognition than to recall.

Journalism functions to maintain the level of knowledge and involve-ment necessary for a democracy. In this increasingly diverse world of media forms, what is the implication of fake news for journalism and for democracy?

YES

Julia R. Fox, Glory Koloen and Volkan Sahin

No Joke

The 2004 elections saw the highest turnout among voters under 30 in more than a decade ("Election Turnout," 2005). As this age group becomes more important in the political process it has also shifted trends in media usage. In particular, young voters are turning to comedic sources for campaign information, rather than more traditional news formats (Pew Research Center, 2004a). What are the implications of this new trend in information seeking, given the presumption that a successful democracy depends on an informed electorate (Williams & Edy, 1999)? Can a humorous political news source possibly be as informative as traditional political news sources? To answer such questions requires multiple studies addressing a wide range of related concerns. Yet, to date there has been little scholarly attention to and no systematic examination of how comedic television messages compare to more traditional television news messages as sources of substantive political information. This study begins to address the questions raised by this new trend by systematically comparing *The Daily Show with Jon Stewart* and broadcast television network newscasts as sources of political campaign information, using content analysis to compare the quality and quantity of 2004 presidential campaign information provided by *The Daily Show with Jon Stewart* and television networks.

Media Dependency Theory

Communication scholars have long considered providing information about the world to be a central function of media (Fox, 2003; Lasswell, 1948; Lippmann, 1921; Price & Roberts, 1987; Wright, 1974). Among the classic writings in this area, Lippmann (1921) noted that the pictures in one's head of the world outside are based on information provided by the press, particularly for the world beyond one's direct experience. Media theorists DeFleur and Ball-Rokeach (1989) define this relationship with media as one of dependency based on goals and resources. According to their media dependency theory, media control information resources that are important for individual goals, such as goals of social understanding (Ball-Rokeach, 1998; DeFleur & Ball-Rokeach, 1989). For issues and events outside of direct experience, people lack information needed to create social meaning, which creates ambiguity (Ball-Rokeach, 1998).

Media can fill those voids with second-hand information that is central to constructions of social reality (Ball-Rokeach, 1998). Such media effects on knowledge and beliefs, as well as behaviors, are more likely when media serve a central information function (Ball-Rokeach, 1998; DeFleur & Ball-Rokeach, 1989). "If, out of habit or necessity, we incorporate the media system as a major vehicle for understanding, then the media system takes on a certain power to influence how we think, feel, and act" (DeFleur & Ball-Rokeach, 1989, p. 316).

For political information, in particular, most people have very little direct contact with politicians and get most of their political information from the media. Media dependency theory suggests, then, that it is critically important to examine the content of mediated political communication as such information may well be used as the basis for political knowledge, attitudes, and behaviors. Such examinations should, of course, include traditional sources of news on which people have relied for decades for political information, such as the broadcast television networks' nightly newscasts. But media dependency theory suggests it is also critical to examine emerging and increasingly important mediated sources of political information, as media dependencies are considered to be a function of expectations about the potential utility of the media content (DeFleur & Ball-Rokeach, 1989). Given the growing number of young voters who say they expect *The Daily Show with Jon Stewart* to fulfill their political information needs, it begs the question as to whether those needs can be satisfied with that show as well as they can be with more traditional television news coverage of political information.

The Daily Show with Jon Stewart as a Source of Campaign Information

More than 20 million under-30 voters cast their ballots in the 2004 presidential election, marking the highest voter turnout for that age group in more than 12 years (Fleischer, 2004; "Under-30," 2004). As voter turnout among this age group increased, news sources of political information for these voters shifted away from the broadcast television networks and toward comedy programs such as *The Daily Show with Jon Stewart*. Specifically, a Pew Research Center (2004a) nationwide survey found the percentage of under-30 respondents (21%) who said they relied regularly upon comedy shows such as *The Daily Show with Jon Stewart* for campaign information was the same as the percentage of under-30 respondents (23%) who said they regularly relied upon the television networks' evening news for campaign information. The percentage of under-30 respondents who said they relied on comedy shows for campaign information is more than double the percentage found in a similar Pew study in 2000 (9%), while the percentage of under-30 voters who regularly relied on broadcast network news declined to almost half of what was found in 2000 (39%) (Pew Research Center, 2004a). Furthermore, television ratings during the Iowa Caucus, New Hampshire primary, and State of the Union address found more male viewers in the 18- to

34-year-old demographic watched *The Daily Show with Jon Stewart* than network news ("Young America's," 2004).

Despite the growing reliance in recent years among young voters on comedy programs for campaign information, there has been precious little systematic examination of this information source, and no published systematic comparison of substantive political coverage in *The Daily Show with Jon Stewart* with traditional television newscasts. In discussing whether or not *The Daily Show with Jon Stewart* should be considered real "news," McKain (2005) describes how the format and formal structural features (e.g. "live" reports) of *The Daily Show with Jon Stewart* mimic those of traditional television newscasts. He also discusses how much of *The Daily Show with Jon Stewart* focuses on skewering broadcast and cable network television news coverage of politics as well as politicians' efforts to spin that coverage. McKain goes so far as to consider whether those who only get their news from *The Daily Show with Jon Stewart* will "get" the jokes without benefit of learning factual information first from traditional news sources. And, he points out that, occasionally, content first presented on *The Daily Show with Jon Stewart*, notably John Edwards announcing his candidacy on the show, is later covered as legitimate news by traditional news outlets. But McKain never makes a direct comparison between the substantive political content presented on *The Daily Show with Jon Stewart* and on more traditional television newscasts.

What would such a comparison find? First, the sources must be considered separately in terms of their substantive political content. Concerning the relative amount of substantive political information presented on *The Daily Show with Jon Stewart*, it seems somewhat obvious that a systematic analysis is likely to find considerably more humorous content than substantive political information on the show. While *The Daily Show with Jon Stewart* was nominated for a Television Critics Association award for "Outstanding Achievement in News and Information" in 2003 and in 2005 and won the award in 2004 ("Comedy Central's," 2003; "The Daily Show's," 2005), Stewart insists that he is a comedian, not a journalist, and that his program is a comedy show, not a newscast (Armour, 2005; Davies, 2005; Gilbert, 2004; "The Jon Stewart," 2004). Thus, this study predicts:

H_1: Both the video and audio emphasis in *The Daily Show with Jon Stewart* will be on humor rather than substance.

The question remains, however, as to how this new source of political information will stack up to more traditional sources of television news as far as substantive political information is concerned.

Broadcast Television Network News as a Source of Campaign Information

Broadcast television networks were American's primary source of news and information about presidential elections for much of the second half of the 20th century (Baker & Dessart, 1998; "Despite Uncertain," 2000; Fox,

Angelini, & Goble, 2005; Graber, 1993; Pew Research Center, 2002). In 2000, cable television news sources surpassed the broadcast television networks' as the primary source of political campaign information ("Despite Uncertain," 2000). Still, there are a number of compelling reasons to compare coverage of the most recent presidential election presented on the broadcast television networks and on *The Daily Show with Jon Stewart*.

First, the trend found in the Pew (2004a) study findings suggests that broadcast network news is being supplanted by comedy programs as a regular source of campaign information for young adults. Furthermore, the broadcast network newscasts still have millions more viewers than cable and still draw the largest audience for a news program at a particular time (Johnson, 2004; Lazaroff, 2004). Finally, given the passing of Peter Jennings and the retirements of Tom Brokaw and Dan Rather, all within 9 months of the 2004 presidential election, this particular election campaign marks a significant historic moment in broadcast journalism, as it was the last presidential election campaign that the three long-time broadcast television network news anchors covered.

A robust finding from previous studies since the 1970s has been the emphasis on hype rather than on more substantive matters, often described in terms of issue versus image, in the broadcast television networks' coverage of presidential election campaigns (Broh, 1980, 1983; Clancey & Robinson, 1985; Farnsworth & Lichter, 2003; Fox et al., 2005; Graber, 1976, 1980; Hofstetter, 1981; Lichter, Amundson, & Noyes, 1988; Lichter & Lichter, 1996; Patterson, 1977, 1980; Patterson & McClure, 1976). For example, an examination of the final 2 weeks of network coverage of the 1988, 1992, 1996, and 2000 election campaigns found the emphasis to be on horse race and hoopla rather than on campaign issues and candidate qualifications (Fox et al., 2005). While that study specifically examined the final 2 weeks of campaign coverage, other studies examining a longer period, for example from the traditional start of the general campaign after Labor Day, have found a similar emphasis on horse race over more substantive coverage during those years (Farnsworth & Lichter, 2003; Lichter & Lichter, 1996).

Given the lack of substantive coverage found in previous studies, this study is expected to replicate those findings. Specifically:

H_2: The video and audio emphasis in the broadcast network newscasts will be on hype rather than substance.

The bigger question posed here is whether there will be more substance in the broadcast television networks' coverage or in *The Daily Show with Jon Stewart's* coverage. Given the long-established emphasis on hype rather than substance in television network campaign coverage, it is not at all clear whether a carefully conducted content analysis would find broadcast television network coverage to be more substantive than coverage on *The Daily Show with Jon Stewart*. While Stewart is the first to say that his program is a comedy show and not a news show (Davies, 2005; "The Jon Stewart," 2004), instances such as his telling the hosts of CNN's *Crossfire* that their show was hurting America and telling the host of NPR's *Fresh Air* that, in asking probing questions, he's doing what journalists often don't do clearly show his interest in substantive reporting (Cook, 2004; Davies, 2005; Ryan, 2005). Thus, this study poses the following research question:

> RQ_1: Will there be more substance in the video and audio of the broadcast television networks' coverage than in the video and audio of *The Daily Show with Jon Stewart*'s coverage of the 2004 presidential election?

Method

This study compares the emphasis on hype versus substance in the broadcast television networks' coverage of the first presidential debate and the Democratic and Republican conventions in 2004, the emphasis on humor versus substance in the same debate and convention coverage on *The Daily Show with Jon Stewart*, and the substantive coverage presented on *The Daily Show with Jon Stewart* and in the broadcast television networks' coverage of the first debate and the party conventions.

Debate and Convention Coverage

As noted, other studies have sampled content from the final weeks of a campaign or from the general campaign time frame to examine political news coverage (Farnsworth & Lichter, 2003; Fox et al., 2005; Lichter & Lichter, 1996). However, there is also good reason to specifically examine coverage of debates and conventions. Conventions offer the candidates a chance to present their views on what they consider to be the important issues facing the nation (Scheele, 1984; Sesno, 2001; Trent & Friedenberg, 2004) and are critically important for shoring up political bases and reaching out to independent voters (Dearin, 1997). Political conventions increase voter attention to the campaign, often through news media coverage of the conventions rather than first-hand viewing of the convention proceedings (Jamieson, Johnston, Hagen, Waldman, & Kenski, 2000). As the election draws nearer, the candidates square off in the presidential debates, giving voters an opportunity to compare the candidates and their stands on issues (Just, Crigler, & Wallach, 1990). Although much of the information presented in the debates may have been presented earlier in the campaign, many voters are just beginning to pay attention to campaign messages during late September and October, when the debates are usually held (Jamieson & Adasiewica, 2000). While debates tend to reinforce preexisting candidate preferences, they are particularly important for activating supporters and can sway undecided voters (Kraus, 1979; Lang & Lang, 1961; Lowery & DeFleur, 1983; Middleton, 1962; Ranney, 1979; Salant, 1962; Willis, 1962).

Concept Operationalization

Following a coding scheme developed in previous research (Fox et al., 2005), substantive coverage, as a meta-concept, is categorized by the concepts of campaign issues and candidate qualifications while hype, as a meta-concept, is categorized by the concepts of horse race and hoopla. Indicators of campaign issues are references to or images of issues included in the party platforms such as defense and security, the economy, the environment, education, health care, and crime. Indicators of candidate qualifications are references to or images of the candidates' experience, such as political accomplishments and political positions held. Indicators of horse race are references to or images of the campaign contest, such as who's ahead and behind in the polls, campaign strategies and tactics, and political endorsements. Indicators of hoopla are references to or images of activities and items related to campaign events and their trappings, such as photo opportunities, rallies, flag-waving, handshaking, baby kissing, ball throwing, crowds, balloons, and celebrities.

This study also includes categories for humor, a meta-concept categorized by the concepts of joking and laughing. Joking is indicated by funny music, silly and untrue statements, silly voices, tone of voice (sarcastic or mocking or a sudden change in pitch or volume), silly faces (raised eyebrows or a skewed, wide-open or pinched mouth), mocking faces, silly or exaggerated gestures, and obviously altered images. Laughter is indicated by sounds of laughing or chuckling, smiling, and eye crinkling.

Sampling

For the convention coverage, this study used a saturation sample by examining all newscasts from ABC's *World News Tonight with Peter Jennings*, CBS's *Evening News with Dan Rather*, and NBC's *The Nightly News with Tom Brokaw* and all *The Daily Show with Jon Stewart* programs that covered the conventions; specifically, the study examined the broadcast television networks' nightly news programs on July 26–30, August 30 and 31, and September 1–3, and *The Daily Show with Jon Stewart* on July 27–30, August 31, and September 1–3.

Only the first presidential debate is examined in this study as the second debate, a town hall-style debate held on a Friday night, was not covered by ABC's *World News Tonight with Peter Jennings*, CBS's *Evening News with Dan Rather*, and NBC's *The Nightly News with Tom Brokaw* or *The Daily Show with Jon Stewart*, nor was the third debate covered by *The Daily Show with Jon Stewart*.

Coding

Because the audio and video channels in television news stories carry separate and sometimes conflicting messages (Fox et al., 2005), this study examines the coverage in the audio and video channels separately. The coding instrument was modified from one developed in a previous study (Fox et al., 2005) to include the additional categories of joking and laughing. Nominal codings were made for network, date, study coder, and whether the story was about the presidential election. Stories coded were read by the newscast anchors or were packaged by reporters, including the anchor lead-ins to reporters' stories. Story length (in seconds) was recorded for each story in each program in the study sample. In addition, the amount of time (in seconds) in the audio and video messages devoted to horse race, hoopla, campaign issues, candidate qualifications, joking, and laughter was also coded for stories about the presidential election. Coding directions, category definitions, examples, and sample coding sheets were provided to study coders during coder training.

Reliability

When coding interval or ratio-level data, such as the number of seconds of network evening news coverage devoted to a topic, Pearson's correlation coefficient (r) is used to measure the degree to which coders vary together in their observations (Riffe, Lacy, & Fico, 1998). This study uses Pearson correlation coefficients from distances correlations, which measure similarities or dissimilarities between pairs of cases based on particular variables of interest (Fox et al., 2005; Fox & Park, 2006). Here, pairs of coders were compared for similarities in their codings of the study categories—audio horse race, audio hoopla, audio issue, audio qualifications, audio joking, audio laughing, video horse race, video hoopla, video issue, video qualifications, video joking, and video laughing. The Pearson correlation for interval data is parsimonious in that it indicates how similar two coders are on all of these variables by rendering one statistic (Fox et al., 2005; Fox & Park, 2006). But this same statistic also provides a more complete picture of coder reliability compared to other measures as it provides detailed information about where reliability problems might be occurring among the particular study coders, unlike other measures of coder reliability for multiple coders that only render one statistic for the entire group of coders (Fox et al., 2005; Fox & Park, 2006). Study coders each coded a network newscast and one program of *The Daily Show with Jon Stewart* to test coder reliability. Pearson correlation coefficients from the distances correlations indicated that the data coders had both high intercoder reliability (Pearson correlation coefficients $r = .988$ or higher) and intracoder reliability (Pearson correlation coefficients $r = .975$ or higher).

Results

An analysis of variance was run prior to analyzing the data, using network as the independent variable, to examine whether the three broadcast television networks varied significantly in their coverage of the coding categories. No significant differences were found. In addition, separate analyses for each political convention found similar emphases on hype versus substance for the broadcast networks and similar emphases on humor versus substance for *The Daily Show with Jon Stewart* for both the Democratic and the Republican conventions.

Not surprisingly, the average amounts of video [60.27] and audio [114.73] humor were significantly more than the average amounts of video

[2.16] and audio [19.78] substance in *The Daily Show with Jon Stewart* stories about the presidential election.

Also as predicted, the average amounts of video [58.18] and audio [80.69] hype were significantly more than the average amounts of video [2.2] and audio [26.13] substance in the broadcast network news stories about the presidential election.

Interestingly, the average amounts of video and audio substance in the broadcast network news stories were not significantly different than the average amounts of visual and audio substance in *The Daily Show with Jon Stewart* stories about the presidential election (see Table 1).

It should be noted that the broadcast network news stories about the presidential election were significantly shorter, on average, than were *The Daily Show with Jon Stewart* stories about the presidential election. Thus, the argument could be made that while the amount of substance per story was not significantly different, the proportion of each story devoted to substance was greater in the network news stories than in stories from *The Daily Show with Jon Stewart*. On the other hand, the proportion of stories per half hour program devoted to the election campaign was greater in *The Daily Show with Jon Stewart* than in the broadcast network newscasts. Thus, the analysis was run again using the half-hour program, rather than the story, as the unit of analysis. The results showed that there was still no significant difference in the average amounts of video and audio substance per program on *The Daily Show with Jon Stewart* and on the broadcast network newscasts (see Table 2).

Table 1

Substance in the Network News and *The Daily Show with Jon Stewart* Stories

RQ 1: Audio/Video Substance	Network News		The Daily Show		Significance Test		
	M	SD	M	SD	t	d	p (two-tailed)
Video substance	2.29	5.37	2.16	8.95	−0.11	165	p = .91
Audio substance	26.13	33.38	19.78	36.05	1.00	165	p = .32

Table 2

Substance in the Network News and *The Daily Show with Jon Stewart* Programs

RQ 1: Audio/Video Substance	Network News		The Daily Show		Significance Test		
	M	SD	M	SD	t	d	p (two- tailed)
Story length	135.40	60.20	233.16	80.00	−8.07	165	p < .001
Video substance	9.03	9.33	8.89	17.13	−0.3	40	p = .97
Audio substance	102.94	75.59	81.33	92.63	.73	40	p = .47

Discussion

At first blush, the increasing reliance among young voters on comedic sources of political information appears to turn the long-held assumption of rational citizens making informed, thoughtful decisions (Noelle-Neumann, 1995; Schudson, 1995) on its ear. Not surprisingly here, in keeping with Stewart's insistence that he is a comedian not a journalist, this study found considerably more humor than substance in *The Daily Show with Jon Stewart*'s political coverage. Yet, this study also found Stewart's program to be just as substantive as the broadcast networks' campaign coverage, regardless of whether the story or the program was used as the unit of analysis. As we've known for years that the broadcast networks place substantial emphasis on insubstantial information in their political coverage, this finding is perhaps not altogether surprising, either.

Although the two sources were found here to be equally substantive, are they equally informative? There is debate among scholars as to how well soft news shows, in which *The Daily Show with Jon Stewart* is categorized by some (Baumgartner & Morris, 2006), can inform their viewers. Baum (2002, 2003) concludes from survey research that soft news may help inform an otherwise inattentive public, although Hollander's (1995) survey data found viewing late-night programs was unrelated to general knowledge about the campaign. However, Hollander's study did not specifically examine viewing of *The Daily Show with Jon Stewart*. To the contrary, the University of Pennsylvania's National Annenberg Election survey found younger viewers of *The Daily Show with Jon Stewart* answered more political questions correctly than respondents who did not watch that show ("Stewart's 'stoned slackers,'" 2004).

Experimental research may well substantiate this correlational survey data suggestion that viewers may actually process and remember substantive information presented on *The Daily Show with Jon Stewart* better than when it is presented on more serious sources of political information. When viewers see positive messages they are appetitively activated (in an approach mode toward the message) and tend to encode more information than when they are aversively activated while viewing a negative message (Fox, Park, & Lang, 2006; Lang, 2006a, 2006b; Lang, Sparks, Bradley, Lee, & Wang, 2004). Previous studies have found that political coverage is often negative. For example, media coverage of presidential debates tends to include a greater proportion of attacks and a smaller proportion of acclaims compared to the actual candidate utterances during the debates (Benoit & Currie, 2001; Reber & Benoit, 2001). Thus, traditional television news campaign stories may activate the aversive motivational system. While such coverage is clearly different than, say, gory and graphic war coverage, which would clearly activate the aversive system, studies have found physiological indications of aversive system activation for socially as well as biologically threatening information (Blanchette, 2006; Lethbridge, Simmons, & Allen, 2002; McRae, Taitano, Kaszniak, & Lane), and in some cases the contemporary social threats elicited stronger responses than their biological counterparts (Blanchette, 2006). In contrast, although *The Daily Show with Jon Stewart* may also be negative in tone, the appetitive system is likely to be activated by the humor on *The Daily Show with Jon Stewart* and by the audience's laughter, which may elicit emotional contagion (McDonald & Fredin, 2001). Additionally, the audience laughter may elicit automatic attentional responses called orienting responses that bring additional processing resources to the viewing task (Lang, 2000).

For that matter, onset of visual information on screen also elicits orienting responses (Lang, 2000). Yet, in one of the limitations of this study, only the total time during which visuals were present on screen was coded here and not the frequency of visual onsets.

Clearly, there is much more to be examined in considering the phenomenon that *The Daily Show with Jon Stewart* has become, particularly experimental research to examine differences in the ways in which viewers process and remember political information presented on that show compared to more traditional, serious television newscasts. Also, other content analyses might examine differences in tone between *The Daily Show with Jon Stewart* and more traditional news sources, for example examining whether one source is more negative or more biased toward a particular political party. Other experiments might examine the impact of that emphasis on viewer attitudes, perhaps similar to Baumgartner and Morris's (2006) examination of effects on candidate evaluations and voter efficacy, but using a broader efficacy scale than used by those authors. Studies could also examine whether younger voters may be particularly susceptible to media dependency effects from *The Daily Show with Jon Stewart*. As Sears (1986) points out, this age group, particularly at the lower end of the age range, tends to have less "crystallized" social and political attitudes than older adults (p. 521). Previous studies have found that voters who are less partisan tend to be more influenced by media than those who are more set in their views (Chaffee, 2001; Chaffee & Choe, 1980; Lazarsfeld, Berelson, & Gaudet, 1944; Mendelsohn & O'Keefe, 1975). Thus, these younger voters, with more fluid social and political attitudes, may be even more susceptible to media dependency effects than their older counterparts. Indeed, a recent analysis (Baumgartner & Morris, 2006) of Pew Center (2004b) data found viewing *The Daily Show with Jon Stewart*, which regularly skewers traditional news media coverage (McKain, 2005), was significantly related to respondents 18–25 saying they were less likely to trust what news organizations say, but the same was not true for older viewers of the show.

In the meantime, the data reported here offer the first systematic comparison of substantive information presented in campaign coverage on *The Daily Show with Jon Stewart* and more conventional television news sources of political information. The results provide valuable information on the substantive quality of this increasingly important source of campaign information for young voters. The findings should allay at least some of the concerns about the growing reliance on this nontraditional source of political information, as it is just as substantive as the source that Americans have relied upon for decades for political news and information. However, while this is true in a comparative sense, in an absolute sense neither of the sources examined here was particularly substantive, which should give pause to broadcast news executives in particular, and more generally to all politicians, citizens, and scholars concerned with the important informative function that mass media, particularly television news sources, serve in this democracy.

References

Armour, T. (2005, April 24). It's a dirty job . . . *Chicago Tribune*, sec. 7, p. 18.

Baker, W., & Dessart, G. (1998). *Down the tube: An inside account of the failure of American television*. New York: Basic Books.

Ball-Rokeach, S. (1998). A theory of media power and a theory of media use: Different stories, questions, and ways of thinking. *Mass Communication and Society*, 1(1/2), 5–40.

Baum, M. (2002). Sex, lies, and war: How soft news brings foreign policy to the inattentive public. *American Political Science Review*, *96*(1), 91–109.

Baum, M. (2003). Soft news and political knowledge: Evidence of absence or absence of evidence? *Political Communication*, *20*, 173–190.

Baumgartner, J., & Morris, J. (2006). "The Daily Show" effect: Candidate evaluations, efficacy, and American youth. *American Politics Research*, *34*(3), 341–367.

Benoit, W. L., & Currie, H. (2001). Inaccuracies in media coverage of the 1996 and 2000 presidential debates. *Argumentation and Advocacy*, *38*(1), 28–39.

Blanchette, I. (2006). Snakes, spiders, guns, and syringes: How specific are evolutionary constraints on the detection of threatening stimuli? *The Quarterly Journal of Experimental Psychology*, *59*(8), 1394–1414.

Broh, C. A. (1980). Horse-race journalism: Reporting the polls in the 1976 presidential election. *Public Opinion Quarterly*, *44*, 515–549.

Broh, C. A. (1983). Presidential preference polls and network news. In W. C. Adams (Ed.), *Television coverage of the 1980 presidential campaign* (pp. 29–48). Norwood: Ablex Publishing Corporation.

Chaffee, S. (2001). Studying the new communication of politics. *Political Communication*, *18*, 237–244.

Chaffee, S., & Cho, S. (1980). Time of decision and media use during the Ford-Carter campaign. *Public Opinion Quarterly*, *44*, 53–69.

Clancey, M., & Robinson, M. J. (1985). General election coverage: Part I. In M. Robinson & A. Ranney (Eds.), *The mass media in campaign 84: Articles from Public Opinion magazine* (pp. 27–33). Washington, DC: American Enterprise Institute for Public Policy Research.

Comedy Central's *"The Daily Show with Jon Stewart" honored with four TCA awards nominations*. (2003, June 5). . . .

Cook, J. (2004, November 24). CBS' Rather to sign off as news anchor. *Chicago Tribune*, sec. 1, pp. 1, 14.

"The Daily Show's" Jon Stewart wins prestigious TCA award. (2005, July 25). . . .

Davies, D. (Host). (2005, July 22). *Fresh Air* [Radio broadcast]. Philadelphia, PA: WHYY.

Dearin, R. D. (1997). The American dream as depicted in Robert J. Dole's 1996 presidential nomination acceptance speech. *Presidential Studies Quarterly*, *27*(1), 698–711.

DeFleur, M., & Ball-Rokeach, S. (1989). *Theories of mass communication* (5th ed.). White Plains, NY: Longman, Inc.

Despite uncertain outcome campaign 2000 highly rated. (2000). Washington, DC. Retrieved July 30, 2001, from Election turnout in 2004 was highest since 1968. (2005, January 16). *Hoosier Times*, p. A6.

Farnsworth, S. J., & Lichter, S. R. (2003). *The nightly news nightmare: Network television's coverage of U.S. presidential elections, 1988-2000*. Lanham, MD: Rowman & Littlefield Publishers, Inc.

Fleischer, M. (2004, November 3). *Youth turnout up sharply in 2004* [Press release]. Washington, DC: The Center for Information & Research on Civic Learning & Engagement.

Fox, J. R. (2003). The alarm function of mass media: A critical study of "The plot against America," a special edition of NBC Nightly News with Tom Brokaw. In N. Chitty, R. Rush, & M. Semati (Eds.), *Studies in terrorism: Media scholarship and the enigma of terror* (pp. 55–71). Penang, Malaysia: Southbound (in association with the *Journal of International Communication*).

Fox, J. R., Angelini, J. R., & Goble, C. (2005). Hype versus substance in network television coverage of presidential election campaigns. *Journalism and Mass Communication Quarterly, 82*(1), 97–109.

Fox, J. R., & Park, B. (2006). The "I" of embedded reporting: An analysis of CNN coverage of the "Shock and Awe" campaign. *Journal of Broadcasting & Electronic Media, 50*, 36–51.

Fox, J. R., Park, B., & Lang, A. (2006, June). *Complicated emotional messages produce liberal bias: Effects of valence and complexity on sensitivity and criterion.* Top paper presented to the Information Systems Division at the International Communication Association annual conference, Dresden, Germany.

Gilbert, M. (2004, December 30). Pop culture swung wildly left, right in election year. *Chicago Tribune*, sec. 2, p. 2.

Graber, D. A. (1976). Press and TV as opinion resources in presidential campaigns. *Public Opinion Quarterly, 40*, 285–303.

Graber, D. A. (1980). *Mass media and American politics*. Washington, DC: Congressional Quarterly Press.

Graber, D. A. (1993). *Mass media and American politics* (4th ed.). Washington, DC: Congressional Quarterly Press.

Hofstetter, C. R. (1981). Content analysis. In D. D. Nimmo & K. R. Sanders (Eds.), *Handbook of political communication* (pp. 529–560). Beverly Hills, CA: Sage Publications.

Hollander, B. (1995). The new news and the 1992 presidential campaign: Perceived vs. actual political knowledge. *Journalism and Mass Communication Quarterly, 72*(4), 786–798.

Jamieson, K. H., & Adasiewicz, C. (2000). What can voters learn from election debates? In S. Coleman (Ed.), *Televised election debates: International perspectives* (pp. 25– 42). New York: St. Martin's Press, Inc.

Jamieson, K. H., Johnston, R., Hagen, M. G., Waldman, P., & Kenski, K. (2000). *The public learned about Bush and Gore from conventions; half ready to make an informed choice.* Philadelphia: Annenberg Pubic Policy Center.

Johnson, S. (2004, November 28). The future of network news: Follow the money. *Chicago Tribune*, sec. 7, pp. 1,8–9.

The Jon Stewart and undecided voter connection. (2004, September 20). New York: Fox News Network. . . .

Just, M., Crigler, A., & Wallach, L. (1990). Thirty seconds or thirty minutes: What viewers learn from spot advertisements and candidate debates. *Journal of Communication, 40*(3), 120–133.

Kraus, S. (Ed.). (1979). *The great debates: Carter v. Ford, 1976*. Bloomington: Indiana University Press.

Lang, A. (2000). The limited capacity model of mediated message processing. *Journal of Communication, 50*(1), 46–70.

Lang, A. (2006a). Motivated cognition (LC4MP): The influence of appetitive and aversive activation on the processing of video games. In P. Messarsis & L. Humphries (Eds.), *Digital Media: Transformation in human communication* (pp. 237–254). New York: Peter Lang Publishing.

Lang, A. (2006b). Using the limited capacity model of motivated mediated message processing to design effective cancer communication messages. *Journal of Communication, 56*(Suppl.), S57–S81.

Lang, A., Sparks, J. V., Bradley, S. D., Lee, S., & Wang, Z. (2004). Processing arousing information: Psychophysiological predictors of motivated attention. *Psychophysiology, 41*(Suppl. 1), S61.

Lang, K., & Lang, G. E. (1961). Ordeal by debate: Viewer reactions. *Public Opinion Quarterly, 25,* 277–288.

Lasswell, H. (1948). The structure and function of communication in society. In L. Bryson (Ed.), *The communication of ideas* (pp. 37–51). New York: Harper and Row.

Lazaroff, L. (2004, November 24). Audience decline an old story. *Chicago Tribune,* sec. 3, pp. 1, 8.

Lazarsfeld, P., Berelson, B., & Gaudet, H. (1944). *The People's Choice.* New York: Columbia University Press.

Lethbridge, R., Simmons, J., & Allen, N. (2002). All things unpleasant are not equal: Startle reflex modification while processing social and physical threat. *Psychophysiology, 39*(Suppl. 1), S51.

Lichter, S. R., Amundson, D., & Noyes, R. (1988). *The video campaign: Network coverage of the 1988 primaries.* Washington, DC: American Enterprise Institute and the Center for Media and Public Affairs.

Lichter, S. R., & Lichter, L. S. (1996). Campaign '96 final: How TV news covered the general election. *Media Monitor.* Washington, DC: Center for Media and Public Affairs.

Lippmann, W. (1921). *Public opinion.* New York: Macmillan Company.

Lowery, S. A., & DeFleur, M. L. (1983). *Milestones in mass communication research.* New York: Longman.

McDonald, D., & Fredin, E. (2001, May). *Primitive emotional contagion in coviewing.* Paper presented to the Information Systems Division at the International Communication Association 51st annual conference, Washington, DC.

McKain, A. (2005). Not necessarily not the news: Gatekeeping, remediation, and *The Daily Show. The Journal of American Culture, 28*(4), 415–430.

McRae, K., Taitano, E., Kaszniak, A., & Lane, R. (2004). Differential skin conductance response to biologically and non-biologically relevant IAPS stimuli at brief exposure durations before a backward mask. *Psychophysiology, 41*(Suppl. 1), S60.

Mendelsohn, H., & O'Keefe, G. (1975). *The people choose a president: Influences on voter decision making.* New York: Praeger Publishers.

Middleton, R. (1962). National TV debates and presidential voting decisions. *Public Opinion Quarterly, 26,* 426–429.

Noelle-Neumann, E. (1995). Public opinion and rationality. In T. Glasser & C. Salmon (Eds.), *Public opinion and the communication of consent* (pp. 33–54). New York: The Guilford Press.

Patterson, T. E. (1977). The 1976 horserace. *The Wilson Quarterly, 1,* 73–79.

Patterson, T. E. (1980). *The mass media election: How Americans choose their president.* New York: Praeger Publishers.

Patterson, T. E., & McClure, R. D. (1976). *The unseeing eye: The myth of television power in national politics.* New York: Paragon Books.

Pew Research Center for the People & the Press. (2002, June 9). *Public's news habits little changed by September 11.* Washington, DC: Author. Retrieved August 15, 2002, from http://people-press.org

Pew Research Center for the People & the Press. (2004a, January 11). *Cable and Internet loom large in fragmented political universe: Perceptions of partisan bias seen as growing.* Washington, DC: Author. . . .

Pew Research Center for the People & the Press. (2004b, June 8). *Online news audience larger, more diverse.* Washington, DC: Author. . . .

Price, V., & Roberts, D. (1987). Public opinion processes. In C. Berger & S. Chaffee (Eds.), *Handbook of communication science* (pp. 781–816). Newbury Park, CA: Sage.

Ranney, A. (Ed.). (1979). *The past and future of presidential debates.* Washington, DC: American Enterprise Institute for Public Policy Research.

Reber, B. H., & Benoit, W. L. (2001). Presidential debate stories accentuate the negative. *Newspaper Research Journal, 22*(3), 30–43.

Rifle, D., Lacy, S., & Fico, F. (1998). *Analyzing media messages: Using quantitative content analysis in research*. Mahwah, NJ: Lawrence Erlbaum Associates, Inc.

Ryan, M. (2005, April 8). Good decision: Putting "Indecision" on DVD. *Chicago Tribune*, sec. 2, p. 2.

Salant, R. S., (1962). The television debates: A revolution that deserves a future. *Public Opinion Quarterly, 26*, 335–350.

Scheele, H. Z. (1984). Ronald Reagan's 1980 Acceptance Address: A focus on American values. *Western Journal of Speech Communication, 48*(1), 51–61.

Schudson, M. (1995). *The power of news*. Cambridge, MA: Harvard University Press.

Sears, D. (1986). College sophomores in the laboratory: Influences of a narrow data base on social psychology's view of human nature. *Journal of Personality and Social Psychology, 51*(3), 515–530.

Sesno, F. (2001). Let's cover the conventions. *The Harvard International Journal of Press/Politics, 6*(1), 11–15.

Stewart's "stoned slackers"? Not quite. (2004, September 28). Atlanta, GA: CNN.com. . . .

Trent, J. S., & Friedenberg, R. V. (2004). *Political campaign communication: Principles and practices* (5th ed.). Lanham, MD: Rowman & Littlefield.

Under-30 voters top 20 million. (2004, November 6). *The Herald-Times*, p. A5.

Williams, B., & Edy, J. (1999). Basic beliefs, democratic theory, and public opinion. In C. Glynn, S. Herbst, G. O'Keefe, & R. Shapiro (Eds.), *Public Opinion* (pp. 212–245). Boulder, CO: Westview Press.

Willis, E. F. (1962). Little TV debates in Michigan. *Quarterly Journal of Speech, 48*, 15–23.

Wright, C. (1974). The nature and functions of mass communication. In J. Civikly (Ed.), *Messages: A reader on human communication* (pp. 241–250). New York: Random House. (Reprinted from *Mass communication: A sociological perspective*, pp. 11–23, by C. Wright, Ed., 1959, New York: Random House).

Young America's news source: Jon Stewart. (2004, March 2). CNN.com. . . .

Barry A. Hollander

 **NO**

Late-Night Learning

The fragmenting mass media environment has created a host of new ways people say they learn about public affairs. In the early 1990s, researchers explored the role of the "new news" in U.S. politics, particularly the influence of talk radio (Hollander, 1994, 1995). An emerging body of scholarly work has expanded this analysis to entertainment-based television and how it affects political perceptions and knowledge. The scope ranges widely to include television talk shows (Prior, 2003), dramas such as *The West Wing* (Holbert, Pillion, et al., 2003; Parry-Giles & Parry-Giles, 2002; Rollins & O'Connor, 2003), situation comedies (Holbert, Shah, & Kwak, 2003), police dramas (Holbert, Shah, & Kwak, 2004), and the political content of late-night comedy shows (Moy, Xenos, & Hess, 2004; Niven, Lichter, & Amundson, 2003; Parkin, Bos, & van Doom, 2003).

Among the concerns is whether entertainment programs actually inform viewers, specifically younger people who may get their news from late-night television hosts such as Jay Leno or comedy programs like *The Daily Show*. Anecdotal evidence and surveys suggest that for many young people, such programs and their hosts are perceived as vital sources of political information and news (Pew Research Center, 2000, 2002, 2004). Not everyone is convinced, especially Stewart, the host of *The Daily Show*. "I still think that's a fallacy that they get most of their news from us," Stewart told television critics (McFarland, 2004, ¶ 14).

Not all knowledge is the same. Whether viewers of entertainment-based programs learn about public affairs is reminiscent of earlier concerns about the informative power of television news as compared to print sources, most often newspapers. Shoemaker, Schooler, and Danielson (1989) argued that medium differences and their subsequent effects were best addressed through understanding the differences between recall versus recognition of political information. This position is echoed by those who examined the differential effects of intentional and incidental exposure to information (Eagle & Leiter, 1964; Stapel, 1998). In brief, what viewers glean from such programs may be a function of many factors: the cognitive effort expended, political interest and sophistication, and exactly what kind of knowledge is tapped in surveys or questionnaires. This study presents two tests of knowledge—recall and recognition—and argues that entertainment-based programs are better suited for the latter in terms of understanding what they contribute to a viewer's public affairs knowledge, particularly for younger viewers.

Political Knowledge

An enlightened citizenry remains one of the foundations of a successful and thriving democracy, and yet the U.S. public is relatively uninformed about their political world (Bennett, 1996). Despite advances in education and an exploding number of available news sources, scholars have discovered no corresponding increase in political knowledge (Neuman, 1986; Smith, 1989). As Delli Carpini and Keeter (1992) noted: "To say that much of the public is uninformed about much of the substance of politics and public policy is to say nothing new" (p. 19).

Measures of newspaper use are often associated with political knowledge (Becker & Dunwoody, 1982; Chaffee & Tims, 1982; Chaffee, Zhao, & Leshner, 1994; Pettey, 1988; but see also Weaver & Drew, 1995). Exposure to or reliance on television news has not fared as well (Becker & Whitney, 1980; Patterson & McClure, 1976), although a few studies have uncovered a positive relationship (e.g., Zhao & Chaffee, 1995). To make sense of these findings, some have suggested that how people orient toward a medium (McLeod & McDonald, 1985), attend to a medium (Chaffee & Schleuder, 1986), or involve themselves with a medium (Shoemaker et al., 1989) can mask the existence of positive effects on knowledge. These approaches are similar to that of Salomon's (1983) position that people assess the amount of cognitive effort necessary for a particular medium and expend only that amount, with television perceived as requiring the least amount of effort and therefore leading to reduced learning as compared to print, which is perceived to require greater mental effort. The result is a self-fulfilling prophecy, with print information generating superior learning as compared to television or video presentations.

Taken together, these studies suggest that measures of recall alone may not be sensitive enough to uncover the effects of televised entertainment-based programming. Intention to learn or attention to a message is often associated with superior recall, whereas incidental exposure to a message leads to greater recognition of information (Beals, Mazis, Salop, & Staelin, 1981; Eagle & Leiter, 1964; Stapel, 1998). When involvement is high, measures of recall perform best, but in situations in which only marginal interest exists, recognition is often the best measurement strategy (Singh & Rothschild, 1983). Thus, television is ill suited for measures of recall as compared to print. Some argue the differences lie in left-brain versus right-brain processing, in which print learning is best tapped by asking recall questions and television learning is best tapped by recognition questions (Krugman, 1977, but see du Plessis, 1994, for an alternate view).

Entertainment Media and Politics

This discussion is particularly apt when considering the emergence of entertainment-based media as a form of political communication. Indeed, interpersonal conversations now rely on the fictional television content in addition to news as people make sense of their social and political world (Delli Carpini & Williams, 1996). Popular late-night and comedy programs have taken an increasingly political bent, with the number of political jokes on late-night TV steadily rising from 1989 to 2000 (Parkin et al., 2003). Thus, the audience is exposed to campaign politics and public affairs as part of the entertainment whole, but the quality of the information remains in doubt. Late-night humor's focus on the presidency and presidential candidates, for example, rarely includes issue content and instead highlights the miscues of political actors (Niven et al., 2003). The audience of such entertainment-oriented talk shows and comedy programs is often less educated and interested in politics than the mainstream news audience (Davis & Owen, 1998; Hamilton, 2003), suggesting viewers less capable of making sense of the political content. Indeed, in an examination of talk radio, Hollander (1995) found that among less educated listeners, exposure to such programs led to a sense of feeling informed but was unrelated to actual campaign knowledge. Among listeners of greater education, talk radio exposure was related to both the feeling of being informed and campaign information holding, suggesting that greater cognitive ability and motivation brought about by education increases the ability to glean useful information from such programs.

Most studies find no relationship between entertainment-based or "soft" news and political knowledge (Chaffee et al., 1994; Hollander, 1995; McLeod et al., 1996; Pfau, Cho, & Chong, 2001; Prior, 2003), and an analysis by Parkin et al. (2003) reports a negative relationship. This is not to say watching entertainment programs is unrelated to how people make sense of the political world. Such programs can influence perceptions of political actors or how people process political information (Moy et al., 2004; Pfau et al., 2001).

The question of how much is actually learned from entertainment television remains open to debate, and some argue that passive learning or awareness of issues does occur from casual television viewing (see Baum, 2003, for a discussion). As Shoemaker et al. (1989) noted in their examination of differences among newspaper-reliant and television-news-reliant respondents, the kind of knowledge one measures can help explain many of the confusing and contradictory findings from previous studies. In addition, the gratifications sought from such viewing can also play a role (Becker & Whitney, 1980), and thus, we need to consider more than mere exposure to a medium in order to understand how it may influence the ways in which people process public affairs information. Therefore, the following hypothesis was posited:

H_1: Viewing comedy and late-night programs for political information will be associated with recognition of campaign knowledge but not with recall of campaign knowledge.

A number of other factors can also influence processing strategies and information processing, such as political sophistication, cognitive ability, and motivation. The self-reported reliance of younger viewers on entertainment-based fare has drawn both popular and academic attention, making age a normative factor of interest and one often associated with political sophistication and motivation. Shoemaker et al. (1989) found age to be a significant factor in their recall and recognition study in terms of reliance on either newspapers or television news. Younger respondents recalled more election facts only if they relied on newspapers for their campaign information, suggesting that their peers who relied on television news were either unable or unmotivated to process information from that medium. In a similar vein, Young (2004) found people with greater political knowledge to be largely unaffected by late-night programming, but those with less knowledge were more volatile in their candidate evaluations depending on how much they watched such programming. Baum (2005) also found that politically unengaged voters who watch entertainment TV were more influenced by such heuristics in their perceptions of candidates. Given that age and political knowledge are often negatively correlated (Delli Carpini & Keeter, 1996) and that younger persons might be expected to rely on television-based fare for information, this suggests that younger respondents may be less successful at tests of recall as compared to recognition. Therefore, the following hypotheses were posited:

H_2: Younger viewers of entertainment programs will be more likely than older viewers to identify such programs as a method of learning about political campaigns.

H_3: Watching such programs for campaign information will be associated with recognition of campaign events for younger viewers but not with recall of campaign events.

Method

Data were drawn from the January 2004 Political Communications Study conducted by the Pew Research Center for the People and the Press. This national telephone survey of 3,188 adults includes a battery of questions tapping the use of various media sources, from print to television, and a small set of items asking for recall and recognition of events in the campaign for the Democratic Party nomination. In addition, the availability of a large number of demographic and political variables allows for stringent multivariate controls in subsequent analyses.

Entertainment Media Measures

Rather than focus on mere exposure to a medium or category of programs, the analysis here examines those who say they use various programs specifically for the purpose of keeping up with the election campaign. Survey respondents were asked a battery of possible sources of such information and whether they use them to "learn something about the presidential campaign or the candidates."[1] Responses could range from 1 (*never*) to 4 (*regularly*), creating a 4-point scale for each category of programming or specific program. The 15 possible sources include 2 of most interest here: late-night TV shows such as *Letterman* and *Leno* and comedy shows such as *Saturday Night Live* and *The Daily Show*. In addition, respondents answered questions about religious radio shows, talk radio, the Internet, local TV news, national network broadcast news, cable news networks, C-SPAN, TV magazine shows, NPR, public broadcasting news, morning TV news shows, political talk shows such as CNN's *Crossfire* and CNBC's *Hardball*, and Sunday morning network talk shows.

Political Knowledge

The survey provides a small set of questions that tap both recall and recognition of events tied to the Democratic Party as candidates vied for its nomination to face incumbent President George W. Bush. Recall is measured by two questions: one asking if a respondent can correctly identify which Democratic presidential candidate served as an Army general (Wesley Clark) and which served as majority leader in the House of Representatives (Richard Gephardt). Correct responses were coded as 1, and all other responses were coded as 0, with the responses summed to create an index that ranged from 0 (*none of the questions answered correctly*) to 2 (*both items answered correctly*). There is a strong relationship between answering these two questions correctly ($\chi^2 = 921.3$, $p < .001$, Kendall's τ_b ordinal-by-ordinal correlation = .54, $p < .001$, Cronbach's $\alpha = .70$). Recognition is measured by asking respondents if they had heard of Al Gore's endorsement of Howard Dean and of Dean's comment about wanting to win the votes of "guys with Confederate flags in their pickup trucks." Respondents were presented a 3-point scale ranging from 1 (*never heard of it*) to 3 (*heard a lot*). These responses were summed into a index with a range from 0 (*never heard of either incident*) to 6 (*heard a lot about both incidents*). The two items are highly correlated ($r = .46$, $p < .001$, Cronbach's $\alpha = .63$).

Analytic Strategy

The first step is to establish who uses the various media to learn about political campaigns through bivariate analysis in tandem with demographic and political variables, specifically whether younger respondents are more likely to identify late-night and comedy programs as sources of information. The true test of these relationships will follow with multivariate analysis in which the "usual suspects" of political knowledge research are used as either statistical controls or as interaction terms to address the three hypotheses. These controls are age, education, gender, income, race, campaign interest, newspaper exposure, political participation, strength of ideology, and strength of partisanship.[2] Newspaper exposure was included because among all media variables, it is the one that in the literature consistently predicts political knowledge. Interaction terms with age are also included to test the third hypothesis.

Results

Patterns of Media Use

Respondents who said they used late-night and comedy television programs to learn about the political campaign also tended to use other media for the same information.[3] Age was significantly associated with these two kinds of programming, with the younger the respondent, the more likely he or she was to name late-night and comedy programs as an information source, supporting the hypothesized relationships.[4] The audience of these two types of programming—at least those who identify it as an important source of campaign news—tended to be younger rather than older, minority, more male than female, leaning toward the Democratic Party, politically liberal rather than conservative, and somewhat more interested in political campaigns. Indeed, few significant differences exist between the audience of these two kinds of programming, although age has a greater association with comedy viewing ($r = -.32$, $p < .01$) than with late-night television viewing ($r = -.19$, $p < .01$).[5]

Overall, most respondents did not score well on the test of recall, with 62% unable to answer either of the two questions in the survey. The index created from these two items had a mean of 0.6 ($SD = 0.8$), whereas the recognition index had a mean of 3.6 ($SD = 1.3$). . . . Recall knowledge was negatively correlated with watching late-night programs ($r = -.09$, ns) and comedy programs ($r = -.05$, $p < .01$), whereas recognition was unrelated to either media variable ($r = .02$, ns, and $r = -.00$, ns, respectively). The lack of a relationship with recognition is at odds with other studies, which suggest that such a measure might be the best method for tapping the kinds of knowledge gleaned from such programs. It is also important to note that using the other media for campaign news was often positively associated with both recall and recognition. Given the high correlation between late-night and comedy viewing and the correlation patterns with the key dependent variables among the various media, these two sources appear to have more in common with each other than with other communication channels.

Multivariate Analyses

A more stringent test is provided by . . . regression, which statistically controls for the effects of demographic and political factors. . . . The predictive power demonstrated by the demographic factors [of age, education, income, sex, and race] is particularly revealing, with all five achieving statistical significance. The political factors perform less well, although campaign interest and reading newspapers do contribute significantly to the model. The final step [enters] the two entertainment-based media. . . . Despite the large number of statistical controls, watching late-night programming to learn about the news was significantly associated with recall and recognition, but in opposite directions as predicted by Hypothesis 1. Watching late-night programs was negatively associated with recall ($\beta = -.06$, $p < .01$) and positively associated with recognition ($\beta = .05$, $p < .01$). The results for comedy television use do not support the hypothesis, with use of these programs for campaign information being unrelated to both recall ($\beta = -.03$, ns) and recognition ($\beta = .01$, ns).

Hypothesis 2 predicted that age would be significantly associated with program viewing. By regressing the demographic and political factors listed previously on use of both programs, age was the most powerful predictor, far outstripping the predictive power of other variables.[6] This hypothesis was supported.

To answer Hypothesis 3 on whether age and viewing act together to explain campaign knowledge, interaction terms were created. The interaction of age and watching late-night programs for campaign news was negatively related to recall ($\beta = -.04$, $p < .05$) but not significantly associated with recognition ($\beta = -.02$, ns). . . . That is, for young people at the lowest and highest levels of viewing late-night programs, the recall of campaign information is relatively low as compared to more moderate viewing of such programs. Older respondents demonstrate more of a linear relationship. This suggests a function of diminishing returns for younger viewers in how much they actually learn from late-night programs. The interaction term of age with comedy television viewing created a similar result on recall ($\beta = -.05$, $p < .01$) but also achieved statistical significance on recognition as well ($\beta = -.04$, $p < .05$). Although comedy viewing alone was not associated with either knowledge measure, when combined with age the results suggest that young people do receive a modest benefit from viewing comedy programs in terms of both recall and recognition.

Summary

As predicted in the hypothesis, younger viewers identified comedy and late-night television programs as a source of political campaign news. In addition, there was some support for the prediction that the consumption of such programming, particularly late-night television shows, was more associated with recognition than recall. Little support was found, however, for the hypothesized interaction between age and media use in predicting recognition but not recall. For example, watching comedy programs for news improved both recognition and recall for younger viewers, but age made no difference in the relationship between watching late-night programs and recognition of political information. However, age did interact with late-night viewing and recall but not in the expected direction, with younger respondents contradicting the general tendency of a negative relationship between viewing such programs and recall of campaign information.

Conclusion

This study began with a basic question: Do young people learn about a political campaign from such entertainment fare as late-night and comedy television programs? That a younger audience is drawn to such content is without doubt, and in surveys and anecdotal accounts, they often identify *The Daily Show* and similar programs as the source of their political information. The research here supports the idea that younger people seek out entertainment-based programs to keep up with a political campaign and that watching such programs is more likely to be associated with recognition of campaign information than it is with recall of actual information. This is an important difference. Previous research has identified two key methods of measuring political knowledge—recall and recognition. Successful recall of factual information is often associated with use of the print media, particularly newspapers, and scholars suggest that lower motivation and differences in how information is processed makes tests of recognition the preferred method of measuring the effects of television news—and by extension such entertainment-based programming as comedy and late-night shows. In addition, some have found that age can play an important role in the ability to answer public affairs questions.

Overall, younger viewers do appear to get more out of such programs as compared to older viewers, although in some cases it is a matter of diminishing returns. Beyond moderate levels of viewing late-night programs, the improvement in recall disappears while the improvement in recognition increases. Or to put it another way, late-night television viewing increases what young people think they know about a political campaign but provides at best modest improvements to actual recall of events associated with the campaign.

Does political knowledge truly matter? As Rousseau (1762/1968) wrote: "The very right to vote imposes on me the duty to instruct myself in public affairs, however little influence my voice may have in them" (p. 49). Democratic theory rests on the assumption of an informed electorate, and there is some fear that viewers face a diet of empty calories and may "fill up" on programming that does little to actually improve their knowledge about public affairs and political campaigns, a finding reminiscent of Hollander's (1995) results concerning education and listening to talk radio and the effects on actual versus perceived knowledge.

Some 20 years ago, Postman (1985) warned that a reliance on perpetual entertainment and trivia will harm public conversation, placing the nation and its culture at risk. A demand that all content be entertaining, even the most serious questions of politics and public affairs, appears a trend that has captured the attention of the youngest in society. As the political content of comedy and late-night television programs continues to rise, as does an audience turned off by mainstream news sources, then the significance of this exposure increases to the point where, for many, they become the lone source of news. Such a possibility seems to stun host Jon Stewart, who says the possibility either "says something terrible about news organizations, or something terrible about the comedy we're doing, or terrible about teenagers" (McFarland, 2004, ¶ 9). There is some good news here, that young people are capable of gleaning at least modest amounts of campaign information from such content, but how competent it leaves them to participate in a meaningful manner remains an open question.

Notes

1. The items were randomized to control for the influence of question order. For some items, a spit-method was used, meaning half of the respondents were randomly assigned to receive one of two program questions. The split variables are religious radio shows such as *Focus on The Family*, talk radio shows, local TV news about your viewing area, TV news magazine shows such as *60 Minutes, 20/20*, and *Dateline*, and morning television shows such as *The Today Show* and *Good Morning America*. In these cases, half of the 3,188 respondents received these items, and half did not.

2. The strength of partisanship and ideology measures are the typical folded scales in which extremes on party identification and political ideology are

scored as high, and scores in the middle of both measures are scored as low. These measures then set aside the direction of a respondent's ideological or partisan leanings and instead focus on how strongly they feel about either political factor.

3. Indeed there is some suggestion here of a response bias, given the positive correlations found between late-night and comedy viewing and all of the other media save one, a hardly surprising nonsignificant relationship between watching comedy programs and listening to religious radio programming. The most powerful correlation in the analysis, however, is between both late-night and comedy TV for information ($r = .50$, $p < .001$), suggesting a significant overlap in the viewing of these two genres to learn about campaign information.

4. However, age also is associated with using other channels for campaign information. Younger users are more likely to also report getting information from the Internet, C-SPAN, talk radio, NPR, and cable news channels such as CNN. Older respondents favor TV news magazines, religious radio, public broadcasting, Sunday morning political talk shows, local television news, and national television news broadcasts.

5. Minor differences can be found, although most are of little substantive difference. Newspaper exposure, for example, is negatively correlated with late-night viewing ($r = -.06$, $p < .01$) but is unrelated to watching comedy shows ($r = -.03$, ns). In addition, education is weakly but positively associated with comedy viewing ($r = .07$, $p < .01$) but not with late-night viewing ($r = .01$, ns). Overall, a weak trend in correlations suggests that late-night viewing, as compared to comedy viewing, is somewhat more tied to less use of regular news and less education. However, no differences can be seen in partisan or ideological strength, ties to a specific party or ideology, or in campaign interest, making any suggestion of audience differences here more speculative than likely.

6. No table provided. The top predictors of late-night television viewing were age ($\beta = -.20$, $p < .01$), income ($\beta = -.07$, $p < .01$), and campaign interest ($\beta = .07$, $p < .01$). The top predictors of comedy show viewing were age ($\beta = -.31$, $p < .01$), campaign interest ($\beta = .09$, $p < .01$), and race ($\beta = -.08$, $p < .01$). The only difference other than the relative predictive power of age between the two variables is the role of newspaper reading ($\beta = -.05$, $p < .01$, for late-night television, and $\beta = -.00$, ns, for comedy shows).

References

Baum, M. A. (2003). Soft news and political knowledge: Evidence of absence or absence of evidence? *Political Communication, 20*, 173–190.

Baum, M. A. (2005). Talking the vote: Why presidential candidates hit the talk show circuit. *American Journal of Political Science, 49*, 213–234.

Beals, H., Mazis, M. B., Salop, S. C., & Staelin, S. (1981). Consumer search and public policy. *Journal of Consumer Research, 8*, 11–22.

Becker, L. B., & Dunwoody, S. (1982). Media use, public affairs knowledge and voting in a local election. *Journalism Quarterly, 59*, 212–218.

Becker, L. B., & Whitney, D. C. (1980). Effects of media dependencies: Audience assessment of government. *Communication Research, 7*, 95–120.

Bennett, S. E. (1996). "Know-nothings" revisited again. *Political Behavior, 18*, 219–233.

Chaffee, S. H., & Schleuder, J. (1986). Measurement and effects of attention to media news. *Human Communication Research, 13*, 76–107.

Chaffee, S. H., & Tims, A. R. (1982). News media use in adolescence: Implications for political cognitions. In M. Burgoon (Ed.), *Communication yearbook 6* (pp. 736–758). Beverly Hills, CA: Sage.

Chaffee, S. H., Zhao, X., & Leshner, G. (1994). Political knowledge and the campaign media of 1992. *Communication Research, 21*, 305–324.

Davis, R., & Owen, D. (1998). *New media and American politics.* New York: Oxford University Press.

Delli Carpini, M. X., & Keeter, S. (1992). The public's knowledge of politics. In J. D. Kennamer (Ed.), *Public opinion, the press, and public policy* (pp. 19–40). Westport, CT: Praeger.

Delli Carpini, M. X., & Keeter, S. (1996). *What Americans know about politics and why it matters.* New Haven, CT: Yale University Press.

Delli Carpini, M. X., & Williams, B. A. (1996). Constructing public opinion: The uses of fictional and nonfictional television in conversations about the environment. In A. N. Crigler (Ed.), *The psychology of political communication* (pp. 149–175). Ann Arbor: University of Michigan Press.

du Plessis, E. (1994). Recognition versus recall. *Journal of Advertising Research, 34*, 75–91.

Eagle, M., & Leiter, E. (1964). Recall and recognition in intentional and incidental learning. *Journal of Experimental Psychology, 68*, 58–63.

Hamilton, J. T. (2003). *All the news that's fit to sell: How the market transforms information into news.* Princeton, NJ: Princeton University Press.

Holbert, R. L., Pillion, O., Tschida, D. A., Armfield, G. G., Kinder, K., Cherry, K., et al. (2003). The *West Wing* as endorsement of the American presidency: Expanding the domain of priming in political communication. *Journal of Communication, 53*, 427–443.

Holbert, R. L., Shah, D. V., & Kwak, N. (2003). Political implications of prime-time drama and sitcom use: Genres of representation and opinions concerning women's rights. *Journal of Communication, 53*, 45–60.

Holbert, R. L., Shah, D. V., & Kwak, N. (2004). Fear, authority, and justice: The influence of TV news, police reality, and crime drama viewing on endorsements of capital punishment and gun ownership. *Journalism and Mass Communication Quarterly, 81*, 343–363.

Hollander, B. A. (1994). Patterns in the exposure and influence of the Old News and the New News. *Mass Comm Review, 21*, 144–155.

Hollander, B. A. (1995). The new news and the 1992 presidential campaign: Perceived versus actual campaign knowledge. *Journalism and Mass Communication Quarterly, 72*, 786–798.

Krugman, H. E. (1977). Memory without recall, exposure without perception. *Journal of Advertising Research, 17*, 7–12.

McFarland, M. (2004). Young people turning comedy shows into serious news source. *Seattle Post-Intelligencer.* . . .

McLeod, J. M., Guo, Z., Daily, K., Steele, C. A., Horowitz, E., & Chen, H. (1996). The impact of traditional and nontraditional media forms in the 1992 presidential election. *Journalism and Mass Communication Quarterly, 73*, 401–416.

McLeod, J. M., & McDonald, D. G. (1985). Beyond simple exposure: Media orientations and their impact on political processes. *Communication Research, 12*, 3–33.

Moy, P., Xenos, M. A., & Hess, V. K. (2004, May). *Priming effects of late-night comedy.* Paper presented at the annual meeting of the International Communication Association, New Orleans, LA.

Neuman, W. R. (1986). *The paradox of mass politics: Knowledge and opinion in the American electorate.* Cambridge, MA: Harvard University Press.

Niven, D., Lichter, S. R., & Amundson, D. (2003). The political content of late night comedy. *Press/Politics, 8*, 118–133.

Parkin, M., Bos, A., & van Doom, B. (2003, November). *Laughing, learning and liking: The effects of entertainment-based media on American politics.* Paper presented at the annual meeting of the Midwest Political Science Association, Chicago.

Parry-Giles, T., & Parry-Giles, S. J. (2002). The *West Wing's* prime time presidentality: Mimesis and catharsis in a postmodern romance. *Quarterly Journal of Speech, 88,* 209–227.

Patterson, T. E., & McClure, R. (1976). *The unseeing eye: The myth of television power in national elections.* New York: Putman's.

Pettey, G. R. (1988). The interaction of the individual's social environment, attention and interest, and public affairs media use on political knowledge holding. *Communication Research, 15,* 265–281.

Pew Research Center for the People and the Press. (2000, February 5). *The tough job of communicating with voters. . . .*

Pew Research Center for the People and the Press. (2002, June 9). *Public's news habits little changed since September 11. . . .*

Pew Research Center for the People and the Press. (2004, January 11). *Cable and Internet loom large in fragmented political news universe. . . .*

Pfau, M., Cho, J., & Chong, K. (2001). Communication forms in U.S. presidential campaigns: Influences on candidate perceptions and the democratic process. *Press/Politics, 6,* 88–105.

Postman, N. (1985). *Amusing ourselves to death: Public discourse in the age of show business.* New York: Viking.

Prior, M. (2003). Any good news in soft news? The impact of soft news preference on political knowledge. *Political Communication, 20,* 149–171.

Rollins, P. C., & O'Connor, J. E. (2003). *The West Wing: The American presidency as television drama.* Syracuse, NY: Syracuse University Press.

Rousseau, J.-J. (1968). *The social contract* (M. Cranston, Trans.). Harmondworth, England: Penguin. (Original work published 1762)

Salomon, G. (1983). Television watching and mental effort: A social psychological view. In J. Bryant & D. R. Anderson (Eds.), *Children's understanding of television: Research on attention and comprehension* (pp. 181–198). New York: Academic.

Shoemaker, P. J., Schooler, C., & Danielson, W. A. (1989). Involvement with the media: Recall versus recognition of election information. *Communication Research, 16,* 78–103.

Singh, S. N., & Rothschild, M. L. (1983). Recognition as a measure of learning from television commercials. *Journal of Marketing Research, 20,* 235–248.

Smith, E. R. A. N. (1989). *The unchanging American voter.* Berkeley: University of California Press.

Stapel, J. (1998). Recall and recognition: A very close relationship. *Journal of Advertising Research, 38,* 41–45.

Weaver, D., & Drew, D. (1995). Voter learning in the 1992 presidential election: Did the "nontraditional" media and debates matter? *Journalism and Mass Communication Quarterly, 72,* 7–17.

Young, D. G. (2004). Late-night comedy in election 2000: Its influence on candidate trait ratings and the moderating effects of political knowledge and partisanship. *Journal of Broadcasting & Electronic Media, 48,* 1–22.

Zhao, X., & Chaffee, S. H. (1995). Campaign advertisements versus television news as sources of political issue information. *Public Opinion Quarterly, 59,* 41–65.

POSTSCRIPT

Is Fake News Journalism?

Comedic news has captured the public imagination. The August 2007 *Critical Studies in Mass Communication* journal featured a humorous debate concerning Jon Stewart. Hart and Hartelius accuse Stewart of the sin of "unbridled political cynicism," luring youth into abandoning conventional society and attempting to foster social change, or shunning involvement in civic and political issues. Continuing with the lighthearted tone, but serious issues, Bennett defends the importance of comedy in an age of cynicism, and argues that it breeds instead an independence of perspective.

Robert Love in "Before Jon Stewart" (*Columbia Journalism Review*, March/April 2007) outlines the history of fake news, ranging from Hearst to the "yellow press" to video news releases. He reveals a long and undistinguished history of journalistic fakes. John Pavlik in "Fake News" (*Television Quarterly*, 2005) details his experience as a interviewee for *The Daily Show*. His careful retelling of his experience, from the point of view of an established department head in a major mass communication program, is both humorous and troubling.

An interesting feature of Pew Research Center Online at http://www.pewresearch.org is the News IQ quiz that allows you to assess your level of political knowledge, and compares your results to a national sample. The Pew Internet and American Life Project at http://www.pewinternet.org offers many reports on uses and consequences of Internet and online activities for American life, including political concerns.

There are two issues entangled in these readings; the first has to do with the worth of fake news in contemporary society. Does it function to invite knowledge and debate within society, or is it mere entertainment? The lines between news and entertainment have long been blurred. Consider, just as one example, the frequent insertion of celebrity news into front pages of newspapers and packages on national newscasts. The line between journalists and the public are now blurring even more. Consider news and political bloggers, who have had major influence when they have upon occasion broken news stories before the mainstream media. Do we define journalism by where it appears or by how it functions in society?

The second has to do with the chief audience of the currently popular fake news: youth. Are they disadvantaged as citizens by their reliance on this form of news? Is it somehow less substantive than "real" news? Fox and colleagues think not. Does its presentation style inhibit learning? Hollander fears so. These are among the few works that have seriously studied this phenomenon, so additional research is needed. What are the questions that you think researchers need to ask? Part of what is implied by this concern for the youth audience is the fear that participation in the political life of our democracy will be harmed by nontraditional news sources. Is it information that threatens the political involvement of youth? What other factors influence youth engagement in political and civic issues? And most importantly, what can be done to enhance that engagement and participation?

Internet References . . .

American Civil Liberties Union

This official site of the ACLU provides a general introduction of issues involving individual rights.

http://aclu.org

Fairness and Accuracy in Reporting (FAIR)

FAIR is a national media watch group that offers criticism of media bias and censorship. FAIR advocates for greater diversity in the press and scrutinizes media practices that marginalize public interest, minority and dissenting viewpoints.

http://www.fair.org

The Federal Communications Commission (FCC)

This official cite of the FCC provides comprehensive information about the rules and guidelines, official inquiries, and other operations of this complex agency.

http://www.fcc.gov

Freedom Forum

Freedom Forum is a non-partisan international foundation dedicated to free press and free speech, and to helping media and the public understand one another. The Web site includes extensive resources and excellent discussion of issues of free speech and press, as well as religion, technology, and international issues. The Press Watch area is intriguing.

http://www.freedomforum.org

PR Watch

The Center for Media and Democracy's PR watch program investigates public relations spin through their PR Watch journal, Spin of the Day, Congresspedia, and SourceWatch.

http://www.prwatch.org

Regulation

*F*or the media, the First Amendment entails both rights and responsibilities. How to ensure that these responsibilities will be met is the subject of much of communications law and legislative action. What are the valid limits of the rights of free speech and the press? How should society respond when First Amendment rights are in conflict with other individual rights? What changes will new technology force upon our operation of these rights? The issues in this section deal with who should be responsible for media content and with the rights of groups who find that content inappropriate.

- Should the Public Support Freedom of the Press?
- Should Freedom of Speech Ever Be Restricted?
- Has Industry Regulation Controlled Indecent Media Content?
- Is the use of Video News Releases Bad Journalism?

ISSUE 10

Should the Public Support Freedom of the Press?

YES: Jeffrey J. Maciejewski and David T. Ozar, from "Natural Law and the Right to Know in a Democracy," *Journal of Mass Media Ethics* (vol. 21, no. 1, 2006)

NO: First Amendment Center, from *State of the First Amendment: 2004* (Freedom Forum, 2004)

ISSUE SUMMARY

YES: Citizens' "right to know" in a democratic society is a foundation of freedom of the press. Maciejewski and Ozar examine multiple meanings of the concept of right to know, asking what this implies about conduct at the personal and institutional level. Maciejewski and Ozar then situate the concept in natural law and applies that understanding to journalistic decisions.

NO: In contrast, the *State of the First Amendment: 2004* report reveals lackluster support for the First Amendment in general and its application to controversial cases in particular. Few know the freedoms guaranteed or care passionately about them—almost one-third feel the freedom granted under the First Amendment "goes too far." Moreover, Americans seem less supportive of freedom of the press than of any other freedoms guaranteed in our Bill of Rights.

The First Amendment to the U.S. Constitution states:

> Congress shall make no law respecting an establishment of religion, or prohibiting the free exercise thereof; or abridging the freedom of speech, or of the press; or the right of the people peaceably to assemble, and to petition the government for a redress of grievances.

Thomas Jefferson said, "Were it left to me to decide whether we should have government without newspapers, or newspapers without government, I should not hesitate a moment to prefer the latter." Yet freedoms are never absolute. Justice Holmes was writing for the Supreme Court in 1919 when he said: "The most stringent protection of free speech would not protect a man in falsely shouting fire in a theater and causing a panic. . . . The question in every case is whether the words are used in such circumstances and are of such a nature as to create a clear and present danger that they will bring about the substantive evils that Congress has a right to prevent." Yet Benjamin Franklin cautioned, "Those who give up essential liberty for a little safety deserve neither."

In the United States, we have been loath to create systems to control or restrict these freedoms. The First Amendment guarantees freedom of speech and of the press, as well as of religion, the right to assemble and the right to petition the government. This discussion will focus on the rights of speech and press. In general, attempts to regulate communication always generate questions about the First Amendment, but words such as "regulation" or "restriction" bring to mind the guarantee of free press and speech that is at the heart of so many of our communication laws.

Maciejewski and Ozar argue that the basis of First Amendment rights is in the concept of the public's right to know. Rarely will you read an article that is so explicit in outlining its underlying premises. Outline what these authors are putting forward, in order to understand the important distinctions they make. But, ask your own questions. Do you agree with their fundamental presuppositions? Is the right to know both clear and valid? Can you derive other possible dimensions of analysis than those given? And, would you select the same possibilities to define the concept? This article outlines the importance of the right to know, locates it in natural law, and establishes, for the authors, the important parameters of the law. So why do we find so many, in the following article, willing to give up these rights when we move from the abstract concept to its operationalization in contemporary society?

The First Amendment Center report describes a population grappling with practical issues and generally unimpressed with current media practices. Potential harm to vulnerable populations, such as children, is one area where much of the public is willing to accept some restrictions. Offensiveness is another area of confusion: what can you say or write, and when does it cross over into something that should not be allowed? Long ago when I was in college, a local woman tried to prevent our university from bringing to campus a speaker on socialist and communist ideas. Students protested this attempt, and the university supported the students against the community outcry. A speech that would have attracted about 20 students brought out hundreds in protest—and I got my first lesson in appreciating something only when it could be taken away.

YES

**Jeffrey J. Maciejewski and
David T. Ozar**

Natural Law and the Right to Know in a Democracy

Journalists frequently accept burdens and defend actions risking harm or ill-will from others on the basis of "the public's right to know." The Code of Ethics of the Society of Professional Journalists, which many American journalists take very seriously, refers twice to this right (Society of Professional Journalists, 1996). . . . This article asks what "the public's right to know" might mean (i.e., what its moral implications are and also whether there is a sound basis for thinking there is such a right).

The first part of the article will use a simple philosophical interpretive tool to explore 12 possible meanings of "the public's right to know." This will bring to light a set of core questions that anyone referring to this right ought to be asking. . . . Part 2 focuses on . . . particular interpretation of this right . . . in an effort to identify an appropriate moral foundation for this right. [The] article examines in more detail . . . the moral implications of this right and a reason for thinking there is such a right (i.e., a reason for thinking that, in the sense specified, the public does have a "right to know"). Part 3 of the article discusses implications and offers a number of applications based on our interpretation.

Part 1

Some Preliminaries

Ethical and social policy issues can be parochial when formulated as rights issues, adopting uncritically a particular understanding of rights or of their foundations. . . .

A truly complete account of "the public's right to know" would need to be sensitive to the many ways in which rights and their foundations have been understood; that enterprise is well beyond the scope of this article. In the interests of transparency and clarity, however, it is important to state several presuppositions of the questions this article has posed for itself, although it is beyond its scope to defend them.

First, this article will be examining "the public's right to know" from the point of view of a democratic polity in which there is a widely shared conviction that extensive freedom in the open sharing of information and

From *Journal of Mass Media Ethics*, Vol. 20, Nos. 2 & 3, 2005, pp. 121–138. Copyright © 2005 by Lawrence Erlbaum Associates. Reprinted by permission of Lawrence Erlbaum Associates via the Copyright Clearance Center.

opinion by the populace, both by individual persons and by groups and organizations, is a valuable feature of society and is important to the workings of democratic government. This does not imply a presumption that the United States is an ideal democracy. However it does mean that an image of a well functioning democracy is at work in the background of this article's reflections. Those for whom the ideal polity has a significantly different character might reject the article's conclusions on this basis, or they might find that the article's conclusions translate more or less effectively into another system of political organization.

Second, this article presupposes that, at least in the long run when the human community has engaged fully in respectful dialogue on how to live together, a shared set of ethical and social standards for individuals and for organizations is possible and that natural law is worth exploring as such a moral framework. The article therefore formulates its questions as part of just such a search and offers its conclusions as hypotheses for consideration by others engaged in the same search.

Thinkers not willing to presume affirmatively that such a set standards might ever be grasped, but still willing to say that the possibility of this remains an open question, should read the reflections offered here as hypothetical in two ways. First, the article formulates an hypothesis about how to understand "the public's right to know" and about whether there is any basis for affirming such a right. Second, the article itself is an effort to explore the very possibility of current social and ethical reflection and dialogue making genuine progress, albeit on a small, carefully circumscribed issue.

With these as framing comments, the next task is to explore 12 possible meanings of "the public's right to know" and thereby to identify a set of core questions about such a right.

Rights Talk

Rights talk is powerful talk. To say something is a right is to say that it is the most important moral consideration in the matter at hand. That is why a person who can assert a right so often acts as if the moral debate is now over. Political philosopher Dworkin (1978) expressed this point by describing rights as "moral trump." When you can play a trump in a card game, you expect to win the trick because the trump suit is the most powerful suit. However, it is important to remember that you cannot play a trump in cards whenever you wish, just to assert your power. The same is true of rights talk (Ozar, 1986).

A rights claim must be appropriate in two distinguishable ways to have moral power. First, the rights claim must be clear in what it implies about conduct. Second, the rights claim must be valid, true, resting on a sound basis. As an example, consider the legal right to free speech in the United States. We all know that a person having this right means that everyone is legally obligated not to interfere in the person expressing his or her mind, at least within certain limits. However, the meaning of this right does not include anyone having a legal obligation to assist a hesitant or ill-trained speaker in stating his or her views. The meaning of this right is quite clear in this regard. Rights' scholars will note that the analysis here is in terms of what Hohfeld (1923) called "rights in the strict and narrow sense," or claim rights. This form of analysis has been deemed sufficient for these purposes.

Second, we all know the basis of this legal right in our society, in the language of the Constitution, in statutes, judicial opinions, executive orders, and so on. Moreover, if this right is asserted in a particular case, we have well understood procedures for determining if there is a basis in law for that particular application of it. Precisely because it is a legal right, its basis is to be found in the law.

However, the meaning and the basis of "the public's right to know" are not so clear. What does this right imply about conduct? What is the basis of this right? Why should we think there is such a right, within whatever limits we have identified for its scope? To explore these questions, the next section offers a test to unpack possible meanings of "the public's right to know." The test works like this: Whenever anyone makes a rights claim, he or she is implying that someone else, either an individual or a group, has an obligation to either act or refrain from acting in some way. Therefore the question is "If the public has 'a right to know,' then who has obligations to act or refrain how?"

Twelve Possible Meanings

There is not one clear answer. There are at least 12 possible interpretations of "the public's right to know" in terms of who has obligations to act or refrain how, all of which make some sense. It will be useful to examine and compare these 12 interpretations.

Possibility 1.   If the public has a right to know, then everyone is obligated not to interfere at all with a person's taking action to learn something that the person values learning.

Possibility 2.   If the public has a right to know, then everyone is obligated not to interfere with a person's taking action to learn something that the person values learning, provided that the actions being taken by the person are not themselves harmful (by some appropriate standard) to other persons or institutions.

Comment.   Notice the question that differentiates Possibility 1 from 2. Is the right we are referring to unconditional? Or is this right conditional, dependent on the actions undertaken in the name of the right being harmless (by some appropriate standard) to other persons and institutions? This is a question anyone referring to "the public's right to know" needs to think about.

Possibility 3.   If the public has a right to know, then all persons are obligated to actively share with the public any information they control that the public (or a significant portion of the public) values knowing.

Possibility 4.   If the public has a right to know, then everyone is obligated to actively share with the public any information he or she controls on which the well-being (or the basic needs) of the public (or a significant portion of the public) is significantly dependent.

Comment.   Possibilities 3 and 4 differ from 1 and 2. . . . The first two possibilities focused on not interfering; the second pair propose the people have an obligation to actively assist in other people's obtaining of knowledge. Anyone who talks about "the public's right to know" needs to think about this difference between an obligation to refrain from interfering and an obligation to actively assist in the acquisition of information.

In addition, Possibility 4 introduces a possibility not mentioned in 1, 2, or 3; namely, that what "the public's right to know" is about knowledge on which the well-being (or the basic needs) of the public (or a significant portion of the public) is significantly dependent. Those who talk about "the public's right to know" need to think about this distinction as well.

Possibility 5.   If the public has a right to know, then everyone is obligated not to interfere at all with the community's efforts to establish institutions to communicate to the public anything that the public happens to value learning.

Possibility 6.   If the public has a right to know, then everyone is obligated not to interfere at all with the community's efforts to establish institutions to communicate to the public information on which the well-being (or basic needs) of the public (or a significant portion of the public) is significantly dependent.

Comment.   Possibilities 5 and 6 introduce the theme of institutions whose social role is to provide the public with information. Is the public's right to know that journalists talk about really more about a society's journalistic institutions than it is about any particular individual's acquisition of information? Note also the difference between 5 and 6. It is again the distinction between the social value of whatever information people happen to value and the social value of information on which the well-being or basic needs of the public depends. In addition, Possibilities 5 and 6 focus on the establishment of such institutions rather than on their daily activities. The daily activities of such institutions are the focus of the six possibilities that follow.

Possibility 7A.   If the public has a right to know, then everyone is obligated to not interfere at all with the efforts of institutions (and those who carry out their mission) established to communicate to the public anything that the public happens to value learning.

Possibility 7B.   If the public has a right to know, then everyone is obligated to not interfere with the efforts of institutions (and those who carry out their mission) established to communicate to the public anything that the public happens to value learning, provided that the actions being taken by the institution (or its representatives) are not themselves harmful (by some appropriate standard) to other persons or institutions.

Possibility 7C.   If the public has a right to know, then everyone is obligated to actively assist community-established institutions (and those who carry out their mission) that have been established to communicate to the public anything that the public happens to value learning.

Possibility 8A.   If the public has a right to know, then everyone is obligated to not interfere at all with the efforts of institutions (and those who carry out their mission) established to communicate to the public information on which the well-being (or basic needs) of the public (or a significant portion of the public) is significantly dependent.

Possibility 8B.   If the public has a right to know, then everyone is obligated to not interfere with the efforts of institutions (and those who carry out their mission) established to communicate to the public information on which the well-being (or basic needs) of the public (or a significant portion of the public) is significantly dependent, provided that the actions being taken by the institution (or its representatives) are not themselves harmful (by some appropriate standard) to other persons or institutions.

Possibility 8C.   If the public has a right to know, then everyone is obligated to actively assist community-established institutions (and those who carry out their mission) that have been established to communicate to the public information on which the well-being (or basic needs) of the public (or a significant portion of the public) is significantly dependent.

Comment.   What distinguishes Possibilities 7A through 7C from Possibilities 8A through 8C is again the difference between the social value of whatever information people happen to value and the social value of information on which the well-being or basic needs of the public depends. Then, within each of these sets, three different interpretations of the implied obligation are considered: (a) an unconditional obligation to refrain from interfering, (b) a conditional obligation to refrain from interfering (i.e., unless the action undertaken in the name of the right is, by some appropriate standard, harmful), and (c) an obligation to actively assist in the process of providing information. References to "the public's right to know" need to be clear about which of these kinds of conduct is implied by this right when it is invoked.

Five Crucial Questions

From this comparison of possible interpretations, five crucial questions have come to light that all who speak of the public's right to know will need to address if their words are to be clear enough to guide conduct. These questions are as follows:

1. Does the proposed right imply an obligation that someone act positively toward the right holder or only refrain from acting in certain ways?

2. Is the proposed right unconditional or does its implied obligation to act or refrain apply only under certain conditions? If the latter, what are the conditions (e.g., the proviso that the actions being taken by the person acted for or not interfered with are not themselves harmful, by some appropriate standard, to other persons or institutions)?

3. Does the "knowing" that the proposed right fosters or protects include whatever the right holder happens to value knowledge of, or does the knowing that is protected or fostered include only certain classes of knowledge? If the latter, which classes of knowledge (e.g., knowledge on which the well-being or the basic needs of the public or of a significant portion of the public is significantly dependent)?

4. Is the proposed right directly a right of journalists (so the rights specifically obligate others to act positively toward or to refrain from interfering with journalists), or are journalists involved more indirectly because the right is understood literally as a right of "the public," whose access to truth depends on certain kinds of institutions whose proper functioning depends in turn on the actions of journalists?

5. If the proposed right is about the public's access to truth through appropriate institutions, then is its focus on the establishment and general maintenance of such institutions, or is its focus on the daily operations of such institutions where journalists obviously play a direct role, or is its focus some combination of these two?

Selecting a Focus: An Interpretation Worth Examining

Some who examine the public's right to know might well conclude that this idea is hopelessly vague and that we should speak of our moral concerns about journalistic practice and the public's desire or need for information in other moral terms than these. Others are confident that there is a deep moral basis for this right and that careful social and ethical reflection can uncover it even if, in most ordinary usage, it is often difficult to know what the expression is intended to mean.

The position taken in this article is that there is one particular focus among the 12—or rather a combination of two of them—that offers a clear set of moral implications and articulates some very important moral content about human society, journalistic institutions, and the role of journalists in society. The proposed interpretation is a combination of what were labeled Possibility 6 and Possibility 8B. Both of these rights refer to "institutions to communicate to the public information on which the well-being (or basic needs) of the public (or a significant portion of the public) is significantly dependent."

Possibility 6 could be labeled the "establishment right" for such institutions. It held "If the public has a right to know, then everyone is obligated not to interfere at all with the community's efforts to establish institutions to communicate to the public information on which the well-being (or basic needs) of the public (or a significant portion of the public) is significantly dependent."

Possibility 8B could be labeled the "limited practice right" for such institutions. It held "If the public has a right to know, then everyone is obligated to not interfere with the efforts of institutions (and those who carry out their mission) established to communicate to the public information on which the well-being (or basic needs) of the public (or a significant portion of the public) is significantly dependent, provided that the actions being taken by the institution (or its representatives) are not themselves harmful (by some appropriate standard) to other persons or institutions."

The establishment right emphasizes the importance for a society of institutions whose social role is to communicate to the society information on which the public's well-being, especially its ability to fulfill its most basic needs, depends. Included in such information is surely information about the conduct of government, the kinds of information on which the functioning of democracy depends and in terms of which most First Amendment debates are conducted. . . .

In terms of the establishment right, when people refer to the public's right to know, one thing they should be referring to is the social value of institutions that fill this kind of need in society. It is surely impossible for members of the public to fill this need without the aid of institutions and therefore this right posits obligations on individuals and institutions (including and perhaps especially the institutions of government) to at least not interfere in the establishment of such institutions.

The implications of the "limited practice right" concern the daily practice of these institutions; they cannot fulfill their role day-in and day-out if they and those who represent them are interfered with. So the focus is on an obligation of not interfering. However, an unconditional obligation of noninterference would be excessive because we know that these institutions have the potential to cause harm, deliberately or inadvertently, to other persons and institutions. Therefore the limited practice right implies that the daily efforts of these institutions, and of those who represent them, are not to be interfered with unless they are harmful (by some appropriate standard) to other persons or institutions. . . .

Thus the interpretation of the public's right to know that will be the subject of the remainder of this article (the combination of Possibility 6, the establishment right and Possibility 8B, the limited practice right) is the following:

> If the public has a right to know, then (a) everyone is obligated not to interfere at all with the community's efforts to establish institutions to communicate to the public information on which the well-being (or basic needs) of the public (or a significant portion of the public) is significantly dependent, and (b) everyone is obligated to not interfere with the efforts of institutions (and those who carry out their mission) established to communicate to the public information on which the well-being (or basic needs) of the public (or a significant portion of the public) is significantly dependent, provided that the actions being taken by the institution (or its representatives) are not themselves harmful (by some appropriate standard) to other persons or institutions.

Part 2

Some Preliminaries on Natural law

We now turn to the task of explicating a moral foundation for the right to know as we have proposed it. We maintain that any moral foundation for the right to know must not only lend itself to the general moral convictions espoused by democracy, but it must be congruent with the very notion of rights (and the moral "trump" implied by them) to begin with. We propose that one such moral paradigm that fits these two criteria is natural-law theory.

We must, however, make one important caveat: Our task here will not be to suggest that the right to know may be universalized as some "natural right," a claim that might apply to all individuals. Rather, we will suggest that the moral principles that support the right to know are congruent with the moral foundations of democracy and offer moral justification for the right to know.

Natural Law and Democracy

Natural law theory has been positively associated with American conceptions of democracy through much of the latter's history. Its association with a representative form of government has stemmed primarily from what has been seen as a natural tendency of humans to associate and a concomitant need for a mechanism by which liberty may be assured when such associations occur and are formalized. By exploring the link between natural law and democracy, it is possible to see with greater clarity a strong moral justification for the right to know.

Although "it is well known that the Declaration of Independence was based on the natural rights philosophy of John Locke" (Sigmund, 1982, p. 98), the framers of democracy in the United States also looked to writers in the natural law tradition such as Grotius and Pufendorf for justification for their actions. By reason of our fundamental tendency to associate with one another, Pufendorf (1994) held that democracy is "the most ancient [form of government] among most nations" (p. 226).

At the forefront of such thoughts is the concept of liberty. The doctrine that the natural benefits of association need to be joined with the protection of liberty was extracted, in major part, from the Lockean (Loke, 1966) discussion of "state of nature," a state that

> all men are naturally in, and that is a state of perfect freedom to order their actions and dispose of their possessions and persons as they think fit, within the bounds of the law of nature, without asking leave, or depending upon the will of any other man. (p. 287).

The philosophical purpose of this state of nature was to highlight the essential role of natural liberty in social thinking. In the Lockean state of nature, liberty and freedom were inexorably linked. Freedom was viewed as "natural and therefore inalienable" (Murray, 1991, p. 191), derived from a single law, the law of nature, which was based on a single precept: self preservation or the preservation of one's own life, liberty, and property. Such was the Lockean influence on early American democratic thought . . . expressed eloquently in the Declaration of Independence.

Inasmuch as freedom necessitated the preservation of liberty in the midst of association, it paradoxically required that individuals, in accordance with the principle of self-preservation, sacrifice a portion of their natural liberty to civil government. Hamburger (1993) wrote that this in turn made necessary a written Constitution to keep a proper balance.

Among the freedoms not to be given up were freedom of speech and freedom of the press, and it is important for the purpose of this article to ask why this is so. Indeed, freedom of speech and press were themselves broadly thought of as natural rights, freedoms that individuals could enjoy as humans in the absence of government. However, in describing what portions of natural liberty would have protection, American constitutionalists appear to have referred to a limited form of the freedom of speech and press, not every aspect of these liberties that might have been possible in the state of nature. "For example, as historians have pointed out, Americans frequently said or assumed that certain types of speech and press—including blasphemous, obscene, fraudulent, or defamatory words—lacked or should lack protection" (Hamburger, 1993, p. 935). Such limitations were deemed necessary, according to Jefferson, to prevent the publishing of "false facts affecting injuriously the life, liberty, property or reputation of others or affecting the peace of the confederacy with foreign nations" (Hamburger, 1993, note 83, p. 936).

Natural Law and the Right to Know

Despite the limitations placed on freedom of speech and freedom of the press, "evidence suggests that some of the framers intended to embody a 'right to know' in the first amendment" (Olsen, 1979, p. 507). For if natural law prescribed that democracy was arguably the form of government most conducive to the preservation of the natural liberties, if freedom of speech and freedom of the press constituted one such liberty (its constitutional limitations notwithstanding), then by implication it would follow that individuals ought to be at liberty (i.e., not interfered with) to receive information.

This "new" element of freedom actually has two parts: The first is that information itself is a necessary constituent of the exercise of liberty; receiving information is viewed as being necessary to preserve it . . .

Bollan and Alexander, appealing to free expression, believed in "the necessity and right of the people to be informed of the conduct of their governors so as to shape their own judgments on 'Publik Matters' and be qualified to choose their representatives wisely" (Levy, 1960, p. 137).

Second, information has been seen as being not only necessary to choose democratic officers and representatives and to evaluate their conduct in office, but also in order for human beings in association to function properly in the first place (Messner, 1949, p. 565). Therefore, a right to know (or, more accurately, a right to receive information) is consistent with a form of government derived from natural rights and liberties and related freedoms.

Within the context of representative government, a right to receive information, particularly concerning the functioning of government, was clearly deemed necessary to assure the liberty the framers sought.

However, what of a right to create institutions that are responsible for delivering information? Although freedom of the press was conceived to protect the "marketplace of ideas" . . . in and to protect the dialectic that is the hallmark of participatory government, one might assert that if indeed freedom of the press was a natural right, it was so by virtue of its communicative function. Here, as Hamburger (1993) suggested, the freedoms of speech and press are very much related to one another. The former was intended to put "the decision as to what views shall be voiced largely into the hands of each of us, in the hope that use of such freedom will ultimately produce a more capable citizenry and more perfect polity" (Olsen, 1979, note 3, p. 506). Whereas, in tandem with free speech, freedom of the press was intended to produce a more capable citizenry by virtue of being informed and thus expression the people's will. According to Madison . . .

> The liberty of the press is expressly declared to be beyond the reach of this Government; the people may therefore publicly address their representatives, may privately advise them, or declare their sentiments by petition to the whole body; in all these ways they may communicate their will. (note 4, p. 506)

So although the framers were likely not aware that they were articulating a right to create the institutions of information (i.e., the press), the freedoms of speech and press nevertheless refer to both aspects of the interpretation of "the people's right to know" formulated previously. This right, so interpreted, aims to secure, in the context of the values and attendant risks of association, several key liberties that are at the basis of the practice of democracy and that are in turn manifestations of the sort of natural-law inspired rights that serve as the moral foundation for our form of representative government.

Part 3

Some Implications

Two things have been argued for in Part 2 that are relevant as bases of the specific right proposed at the conclusion of Part 1. First, it has been argued that certain characteristics of democratic polity either are themselves aspects of human experience valuable in themselves or have extremely important instrumental value in humans' pursuit of the activities. . . . Furthermore, it has been argued that these elements of democratic society are impossible to achieve and secure without the proper functioning of those social institutions by which truth is disseminated. Therefore there are strong moral reasons not to interfere with the creation and functioning of such institutions. . . .

Second, it has been argued that for anyone who considers the activity of pursuing truth to be valuable in itself, those social institutions by which truth is disseminated and on which the members of society are therefore dependent have extremely important instrumental value. Thus there will be strong moral reasons not to interfere with the creation and functioning of such institutions, in the interest of humans' fulfillment of their efforts to pursue truth. Similarly, these moral reasons may not overrule all other moral considerations. However only other moral reasons of high social and human importance will weigh favorably in comparison.

What are some of the implications of this right, assuming that it has a sound moral basis? Although detailed implications of this right for particular concrete situations cannot be described in advance, some important characteristics of conduct conforming to and respectful of this right can still be identified.

Example and Variations

Suppose a meteor or comet was threatening life on earth. What would the proposed interpretation of the public's right to know imply about conduct in such a situation? That is, if there is such a right, who has an obligation to act or refrain how?

If the object hit earth without anyone's prior knowledge, it would be difficult for anyone to claim that rights to knowledge had been violated. However, suppose someone did know in advance about the event. Suppose, for example, that scientists at NASA knew about the inbound object. Almost certainly, if the NASA scientists were going to inform the public of the risk, they would use—and indeed would almost have to use—social institutions specifically designed for the dissemination of information. Suppose that, by reason of the actions of powerful persons or organizations in the society, there were no such institutions for the NASA scientists to use. Or suppose that the efforts of persons or groups to create such institutions were so regularly hindered by powerful individuals or groups in the society that the institutions of information that did exist were unable to function with any efficiency, and suppose that, as a consequence, the efforts of the NASA scientists to inform the public of the risk were ineffective.

On either of these scenarios, the public's right to know as interpreted in Part 1 (i.e., the combination of the establishment right and the limited practice right) would be violated. The value of knowledge, especially knowledge essential for life, means that the institutions that a complex society needs to have access to that knowledge have extremely high moral value and that parties who would use their power to prevent such institutions from coming into being or from performing their social function effectively (provided these institutions are not doing other forms of harm, for this is a conditional right) are violating that value for the public.

Or suppose that the institutions were in place, but that, for personal reasons of some sort, a NASA scientist charged with communicating the risk to the media refrained from doing so. Or suppose a journalist who received the information did not report it responsibly for some reason. Here too the proposed right would be violated.

Now consider some variations on this scenario. Suppose the reason that government officials were hindering the institutions that would disseminate the NASA information is that the nation was then under direct military attack from an enemy and publishing the information about the meteor would inform the enemy of the existence of NASA's satellite systems so as to severely compromise our nation's defensive abilities. Now, even though the same values of public knowledge are at risk as in the previous scenario, other extremely important public values are also at risk. . . . In such a situation, even though the public's right to know as interpreted here is certainly at stake, it may be that this particular right does not trump all the other moral considerations in the case. In a similar way, suppose the journalist who is given the information about the meteor by NASA is briefed by the mentioned military strategists and warned of the serious dangers of informing the enemy of NASA's satellite network. Again the right being considered here would be relevant, but would not necessarily be the determining factor for ethically appropriate conduct by the journalist.

The point of discussing these variations is that, even when a soundly based right with a clear general meaning is at risk, there may well be other moral considerations of sufficient moral weight that alternative courses of action have to be carefully weighed to determine the morally best course of action. This is particularly true when complex institutions with multiple stakeholders are involved. The moral "overriding-ness" of rights does not change the moral complexity of human life, even if it does sometimes provide a clear answer about conduct in a simple case.

Implications for Professional Journalists

The single most important source of guidance for journalists and journalistic organizations trying to determine how to act in a morally complex situation remains the standards of ethical conduct for the profession of journalism. Neither the existence of a sound basis for the proposed right nor the meaningfulness and moral significance of any other possible interpretations of the public's right to know changes this reality for journalistic practice.

That is, if a journalist or an organization wants to know whether a particular action is morally or ethically appropriate in a given situation, the first question to ask is whether it is in accord with the standards of professional practice. The Code of Ethics of the Society of Professional Journalists (Society of Professional Journalists, 1996) is a useful summary statement of these standards for journalists in the United States. However, it is important to remember that no such summary is exhaustive, and concrete situations often need careful examination from the point of view of many stakeholders and the multiple core values of professional journalistic practice to be properly judged. In any case, questions about whether the issues at hand violate the public's right to know should always come second to a careful examination of the situation from the perspective of the professional obligations of journalistic practice.

Unfortunately, not a few journalists employ the notion of the public's right to know as if it was their personal right and a mandate for them to conduct the business of journalism as they see fit. Some news organizations defend their actions in similar terms. However, this is clearly a mistake if the meaning of the public's right to know is interpreted as proposed in this article. In other words, the right whose moral basis has been argued for in Part 2 is not a right of journalists as such. It is a right, in the first line of argument, of the members of a democratic polity (or, if certain elements of democratic polity are held to be valuable in themselves, then of all persons in their pursuit of these aspects of social life) and, in the second line of argument, of humans as pursuers of truth in a complex society. However, when this right implies an obligation not to interfere with journalists' professional efforts, it is not because the journalists involved have such a right in their role as journalists. They do have a right to know, and the implications of proposed right apply to them in that respect, but they have this right only and precisely as members of a democratic polity. In neither case may a journalist or organization properly assert this right as if it were a right of journalists or journalistic organizations as such.

Conclusions

There are therefore good reasons to be skeptical about the moral or ethical weight of claims that journalists or journalistic organizations make in terms of the public's right to know. . . . Careful moral argument is needed to demonstrate that a proposed right has a sound moral basis, and such argument depends in turn on complicated claims of what is of value in human life and what institutions or other means are necessary for its achievement. Journalists and organizations who employ appeals to the public's right to know need to assure their audiences that their appeal to this moral standard . . . is made only after the situation has been fully and carefully examined from the perspective of the professional standards of journalistic practice.

. . . There is an interpretation of the public's right to know that is clear in its meaning and general implications and that rests on a defensible foundation of moral reflection. Therefore, when journalists and journalistic organizations—who have already done the careful ethical reflection on professional standards that is their first recourse in ethically complex situations—appeal to the public's right to know, so interpreted, that appeal is something of great moral importance and should be taken very seriously.

References

Corbin, A. L. (1919). Legal analysis and terminology. *Yale Law Journal, 29*, 163–173.
Dworkin, R. (1978). *Taking rights seriously.* Cambridge, MA: Harvard University Press.
Hamburger, P. A. (1993). Natural rights, natural law, and American constitutions. *Yale Law Journal, 102*, 907–960.
Hohfeld, W. (1923). *Fundamental legal conceptions.* New Haven, CT: Yale University Press.
Levy, L. (1960). Legacy of suppression: Freedom of speech and press in early American history. Cambridge, MA: Harvard University Press.

Locke, J. (1966). *Two treatises of civil government.* Cambridge, England: Cambridge University Press.

Madison, J. (1910). Letter from James Madison to W.T. Barry (Aug. 4, 1822). In G. Hunt (Ed.), *Writings of James Madison* (Vol. 9, p. 103). New York: Putnam.

Messner, J. (1949). *Social ethics: Natural law in the modern world.* St. Louis, MO: Herder.

Murray, J. C. (1991). The doctrine lives: The eternal return of natural law. In C. E. Curran & R. A. McCormick, S. J. (Eds.), *Natural law and theology* (pp. 184–220). New York: Paulist.

Olsen, E. G. (1979). Note, the right to know in First Amendment analysis. *Texas Law Review, 57,* 505–521.

Ozar, D.T. (1986). Rights: What they are and where they come from. In P. Werhane, A. R. Gini, & D. Ozar (Eds.), *Philosophical issues in human rights: Theories and application* (pp. 3–25). New York: Random House.

Pufendorf, S. (1994). On the law of nature and of nations in eight books. In C. Carr (Ed.), *The political writings of Samuel Pufendorf* (pp. 95–269). New York: Oxford University Press.

Sigmund, P. E. (1982). *Natural law in political thought.* Washington, DC: University Press of America.

Society of Professional Journalists. (1996). *Code of ethics.* Available at www.spj.org/ethics_code.asp

United Nations. (1948). *Declaration of human rights.* Available at www.un.org/overview/rights.html

State of the First Amendment: 2004

The First Amendment to the U.S. Constitution has long been considered a fundamental pillar in the American scheme of ordered liberties, and a guiding influence in American life. Those on all sides of the political spectrum hail its guarantees of protection for the individual from government censorship and official efforts to curb reasonable and fair dissent. Of course at various times in our nation's history, some of the amendment's provisions have come into conflict with what many perceive to be national security interests. In the minds of some, the terrorist attack of Sept. 11, 2001, led some federal government officials to subordinate civil liberties in the name of fighting a heightened war on terrorism. The broadcast media's inundation of the airwaves with material that may be inappropriate to children also has been the subject of recent controversy. Devices such as the v-chip allow parents to monitor materials viewed at home.

How cherished are our First Amendment guarantees? To date, only a handful of detailed and comprehensive surveys on issues pertaining to the First Amendment have ever been conducted. Few, if any, of those surveys follow the state of the First Amendment over an extended period of time. While some civil libertarians contend that First Amendment freedoms are being threatened on a daily basis, others believe the First Amendment enjoys unprecedented strength in the American constitutional system.

Since 1997, the First Amendment Center has sought to discover American attitudes toward the First Amendment by asking a series of questions designed to evaluate both general and specific First Amendment issues. For the third consecutive year, the First Amendment Center has been joined by *American Journalism Review* in this effort. Together, they commissioned the Center for Survey Research & Analysis at the University of Connecticut to conduct this year's survey. Along with asking a number of important new questions, the 2004 survey sought to trace trends in public attitudes over time by repeating some of the more important questions asked in previous surveys.

This report presents the findings from the 2004 survey and includes noteworthy comparisons from seven earlier polls. . . . Although the First Amendment itself encompasses numerous specific rights (including the right of people to peaceably assemble and to petition the government), we targeted for intensive study the freedoms of speech and press. . . .

Recent revelations that reporters in *The New York Times* and other newspapers falsified stories have gotten considerable attention. The 2004 survey considered the degree to which those problems have influenced perceptions of local media. Has the falsifying or making up of stories become a widespread problem?

The v-chip and other forms of technology now make it possible for parents to regulate media to their children. Should it be their responsibility? Are government regulations of the media justified when applied to broadcast media in the daytime and early evening, when children are most likely to be tuning in? The 2004 survey paid special attention to these as well other issues concerning the status of the First Amendment.

Specifically, the 2004 survey addressed the following issues:

- Do Americans know the freedoms guaranteed to them by the First Amendment? Does the American educational system do a good enough job teaching students about these freedoms?
- Are Americans generally satisfied with current levels of First Amendment freedom afforded to individuals in society, or is there a sense that there is overall too much or too little of these freedoms in America?
- Should people be allowed to say offensive things in public? Should musicians be allowed to sing offensive songs? Should flag burning as a means of political dissent be protected under the Constitution?
- Is it important that the news media act as a watchdog on government? Have recent revelations about the falsification of news stories in *The New York Times* and elsewhere undermined the people's trust in their own local media? Is such falsification of stories considered a widespread problem? Overall, do the media enjoy too much freedom to publish?
- Should government officials have the power to regulate basic television, cable television, and radio programming that contain references to sexual activity? At what times of the day should such regulations be allowed? Who should be responsible for keeping inappropriate print or broadcasted materials away from children? Is the v-chip being used? . . .

The First Amendment Center/*American Journalism Review* poll on the First Amendment was conducted under the supervision of the Center for Survey Research & Analysis at the University of Connecticut. A random sample of 1,002 national adults age 18 and over were interviewed between May 6 and June 6, 2004. Sampling error is ±3.1% at the 95% confidence level. For smaller groups, the sampling error is slightly higher. Weights were assigned to reflect the characteristics of the adult U.S. population. . . .

General Orientations toward the First Amendment

Highlights:

- 30% of those surveyed in 2004 indicated that the First Amendment goes too far in the rights it guarantees. That's slightly less than the

34% who responded that way in 2003, and a significant drop from the 49% in the 2002 survey. Meanwhile, 65% disagreed that the First Amendment goes too far, the highest percentage recorded since 2000, and an 18-point jump from two years ago.

- Education is a key factor in determining levels of public satisfaction with the First Amendment. Those respondents who graduated from college are significantly more likely (77%) to disagree with the premise that the First Amendment goes too far than those who never advanced beyond high school (57%). Young adults aged 18–30 (74%) are also more likely to disagree that the First Amendment goes too far than do senior citizens (47%).
- Just 58% of those surveyed were able to name freedom of speech as one of the specific rights guaranteed by the First Amendment. Still, no other right was named by even one in five respondents, and freedom of the press was identified by just 15% of those surveyed.
- Americans expressed greater satisfaction with current levels of free speech and religion than with current levels of press freedom. While less than half (46%) indicated the nation currently has the right amount of press freedom, 60% said we have the right amount of free speech and 64% said we have the right amount of religious freedom. Interestingly, 28% said Americans have too little freedom to speak freely, the highest percentage in the last seven surveys.
- Dissatisfaction with First Amendment education practices rose: 35% rated the American educational system as "poor" in teaching students about First Amendment freedoms, compared with less than 30% who rated it that low in 2002 and 2003, and 24% who rated it as poor in 2001.

In every survey conducted since 1999, the First Amendment Center has investigated the public's overall perceptions of the First Amendment. Do Americans respond positively or negatively to its words? More specifically, do Americans think the First Amendment "goes too far in the rights it guarantees"?

In the 2004 survey, 65% of those surveyed disagreed with the premise that the First Amendment goes too far, more than twice the percentage (30%) that agreed with that premise. This represents the highest level of general satisfaction registered with the First Amendment since 2000, when 74% disagreed with the statement that the First Amendment goes too far. Even more stark, the 65% figure represents an 18-point jump in disagreement from 2002, when 47% said the First Amendment goes too far in the rights it guarantees.

"The First Amendment became part of the U.S. Constitution more than 200 years ago. This is what it says: 'Congress shall make no law respecting an establishment of religion or prohibiting the free exercise thereof, or abridging the freedom of speech or of the press, or the right of the people peaceably to assemble, and to petition the government for a redress of grievances.' Based on your own feelings about the First Amendment, please tell me whether you agree or disagree with the following statement: The First Amendment goes too far in the rights it guarantees."

Education is a key determinant of satisfaction with the First Amendment: 77% of those who attended college or beyond disagreed with the premise that the First Amendment goes too far in the rights it guarantees, as compared to 57% among those who never advanced beyond high school. Meanwhile, fundamentalist/evangelicals (41%) and senior citizens (44%) were far more likely than the general public to agree that the First Amendment goes too far.

Recognition for First Amendment rights other than freedom of speech was low. While 58% were able to identify freedom of speech as a specific right guaranteed by the First Amendment, not even one in five respondents could name any other right, including freedom of the press (15%), freedom of religion (17%) and the right of free assembly (10%). And 35% could not name even one right afforded to them under the First Amendment to the U.S. Constitution.

Among the various freedoms contained within the First Amendment, the public generally registers far greater satisfaction with freedom of speech and freedom of religion than it does with freedom of the press. The majority of respondents (64%) said the religious freedom afforded to Americans under the Constitution is "about right," and six in 10 were similarly satisfied with their current amount of freedom to speak freely. If anything, Americans would prefer even more freedom in this regard. Almost four times as many people said Americans have too little religious freedom (27%) as think they have too much religious freedom (7%). Meanwhile, 28% indicated Americans have too little freedom to speak freely, compared to 11% who said they receive too much of such freedom.

Not surprisingly, greater amounts of religious freedom are especially favored by fundamentalist/evangelicals, 37% of whom said there is too little such freedom. (By contrast, 16% of Catholics felt that way).

As for freedom of the press, less than half of those surveyed (46%) said Americans have the right amount of that freedom, and 36% said Americans have too much press freedom—more than twice the percentage indicating that there is too little of such freedom. When phrased as a freedom that belongs to the press (as opposed to Americans), dissatisfaction increases even further: 42% of respondents said that the press has too much freedom to do what it wants. Of those with a college education, 28% felt the press has too much freedom.

Additionally, respondents exhibited increased levels of frustration with the overall quality of First Amendment education. Specifically, 35% rated the educational system as "poor" in teaching students about First Amendment freedoms. By contrast, less than 30% rated it as poor in the previous three years of the survey, with not even a quarter (24%) of respondents ranking it as poor in 2001.

Freedom of Speech

Highlights:

- Not all forms of controversial speech draw significant levels of support from Americans. A majority (54%) agreed that people should be allowed to say things in public that might be offensive to religious groups. By contrast, 35% said people should be allowed to say things that might be offensive to racial groups.

- Nearly six in 10 agreed that musicians should be allowed to sing songs with lyrics that others might find offensive; 38% disagreed with that right.
- 53% opposed amending the U.S. Constitution to prohibit flag burning, as compared to 45% who said they favor such an amendment. Three years ago, before the events of Sept. 11, 59% opposed a flagburning amendment, significantly more than the 39% who favored an amendment at that time. Of the various subgroups surveyed, fundamentalist/evangelicals (36%) were least likely to oppose such an amendment.
- Nearly twice as many people (29%) said students in public high schools have too little freedom to express themselves as said that students have too much freedom (15%). 51% said the amount of freedom they have to express themselves is about right.
- A substantial majority (72%) opposed allowing public school students to wear a T-shirt with a potentially offensive message or picture, with a majority saying they strongly disagree with that right.

Although Americans continue to exhibit strong support for the freedom of speech in the abstract, a significance percentage of the public still exhibits a reluctance to extend protection to some forms of controversial speech, including those which offend various groups. For example, while nearly six in 10 said they support the right of musicians to sings songs that may have offensive lyrics, 38% disagreed with that right, and more than a quarter (26%) strongly disagreed with that right.

The public is more split on whether people should be allowed to say things in public that might be offensive to religious groups. While 54% said they favored such a right, 44% of Americans disagreed, led by those with incomes under $40,000 per year (53% of that subgroup disagreed with the right) and fundamentalist/evangelicals (52% said they would not support such a right).

Meanwhile, when it comes to speech that might be offensive to racial groups, there is no split in public opinion. The public overwhelmingly opposed such speech by a margin of 63% to 35%, with nearly half (49%) strongly disagreeing with that right. Here too, education plays a significant role in explaining levels of tolerance. Almost three in four (74%) of those surveyed who never advanced beyond high school disagreed with the right to say things that may be offensive to racial groups, while less than half (46%) of those who graduated college were opposed to that right. Thus while the less educated lead the way in opposition, the more educated are almost split on whether such free speech rights should be allowed.

For the fifth consecutive year, a majority of those surveyed (in 2004 it was 53%) opposed amending the Constitution to specifically prohibit flag burning or desecration. Opposition to such an amendment reached a zenith in the last survey conducted before the Sept. 11 terrorist attacks, as 59% opposed such an amendment in the spring of 2001. In recent years this percentage has dipped slightly, though never below a majority.

Among the various subgroups surveyed, fundamentalist/evangelicals are most likely to support an amendment to prohibit flag burning: While 36% said they opposed such an amendment, 58% said they favored it. Additionally, those who completed a college education (66%) are far more likely to oppose that constitutional amendment than those who never went beyond high school (48%). And Midwesterners (60%) are far more resistant to such an amendment than those who hail from any other region; Northeasterners actually support the amendment by a margin of 51% to 47%.

A slim majority (51%) also said that students in public high schools have "the right amount" of freedom to express themselves. Meanwhile, for the second year in a row, those who believe students have "too little freedom" (29%) outnumber those who think they have "too much freedom" (15%) by an approximately 2-1 margin.

Finally, for the third time in the history of the survey, the First Amendment Center inquired as to whether public school students should be allowed to wear a T-shirt with a message or picture that others might offensive. As was indicated in the 1997 and 1999 surveys, the public overwhelmingly opposes granting public students such a right. In all, 72% said they did not think students should be allowed to wear such controversial T-shirts, and a majority (51%) strongly disagreed with that right. Not surprisingly, 57% of those aged 18–30 (the subgroup that most recently attended high school) opposed the wearing of T-shirts under those circumstances, while 83% of the senior citizens surveyed expressed similar opposition.

Freedom of the Press

Highlights:

- Nearly half of those surveyed (49%) said the media have too much freedom to publish whatever they want; 15 points greater than the percentage (34%) that indicated there is too much government censorship. Republicans (64%) are far more likely than Democrats (43%) and Independents (43%) to indicate the media has too much freedom to publish.
- 77% said it is important for our democracy that the news media act as a watchdog on government. Still, 39% said the news media try to report the news without bias.
- 70% said journalists should be allowed to keep a news source confidential. That is a slight drop from 2000, when 77% agreed with this policy.
- 56% said that newspapers should be allowed to freely criticize the U.S. military about its strategy and performance.
- Meanwhile, Americans remain split over issues of access to information about the war on terrorism: Half said they have too little access to such information, as compared with 46% who said we have "too much" or "just about the right amount" of access.

- 52% followed reports concerning the falsifying of news stories in 2004. Among those, 30% said such incidents have decreased the level of trust they have in their local newspaper. Meanwhile, 59% believed the falsifying of stories in the news media has become a widespread problem.

As was noted earlier, Americans are generally less supportive of press freedoms in the abstract than they are of other First Amendment freedoms. Distrust of the media is one source of the problem. When forced to choose between competing problems, more respondents tend to think there is "too much media freedom" (49%) than think there is "too much government censorship" (34%). A partisan divide on this issue is evident. While 64% of Republicans said there is too much media freedom, 43% of those identifying themselves as Democrats and Independents felt that way.

Still, citizens continue to express support both for a principle justification that underlies press rights in this country, and to a lesser degree, for the rights of the press to engage in specific activities that may appear controversial to some.

More than three in four respondents (77%) agreed that it is important for our democracy that the news media act as a watchdog on government, with 49% indicating that they strongly adhered to that principle. Although support for this premise was widespread across the populace, it was especially well-pronounced among Democrats (84%) and non-whites (83%). Perhaps some of that intense support arises out of those groups' distaste for the Republican administration and the current Congress.

With regard to more specific press functions, public support for First Amendment rights is once again evident, although not to the degree detected in past surveys. Exactly seven in 10 agreed that journalists should be allowed to keep a news source confidential, a slight drop from the 77% who felt that way in 2000 and a substantial drop from the 1997 survey, when 85% supported that right. Additionally, while 42% said they strongly agreed with the right to keep sources confidential, that's quite a bit less than in 2000, when more than half (52%) indicated that they strongly supported the right to maintain the secrecy of sources.

The war on terrorism has heightened tensions between freedom of press and the need for the military to control information. Since Sept. 11, 2001, Americans have only narrowly supported the right of newspapers to freely criticize the U.S. military about its strategy and performance—in this year's survey 56% supported the right, while 41% opposed it. Support for the newspapers in this context is especially weak among those who never attended college (46% of that subgroup support the press's right to criticize the military) and among Republicans (42% support the right).

Americans are also split on whether there is too little access to information about the war on terrorism. Exactly half said there is too little access; 46% said that there is either "too much" access or that the current amount of access is "about right." By contrast, in 2002, four in 10 thought there was "too little access" to such information.

Concerns about media bias also have received considerable attention in recent years. Not even four in 10 (39%) said the media tries to report the news without bias. One finds a partisan divide on this question, as 28% of Republicans said the news media is free of such biased motives (48% of Democrats felt that way). More interesting, however, is the income divide revealed on this issue: those with higher incomes ($75,000 or more) are even less trusting of media motives, as just 27% of that subgroup said the media try to report the news without bias.

What about the recent newspaper scandals implicating Jayson Blair of *The New York Times* and others? More than half (52%) of those surveyed said they've heard or read about reports concerning the falsifying of facts and columns in newspapers. Of that number, three in 10 said those incidents have decreased the level of trust they maintain in their local newspapers. As for the population as a whole, 59% of those surveyed indicated that the falsifying or making up of stories in the American news media is now a "widespread problem." These suspicions are especially rampant among those who never advanced beyond high school, as 68% of that less educated group believes falsification is a widespread problem.

Government Regulation of the Media

Highlights:

- Nearly six in 10 said they are satisfied with the current amount of regulation of entertainment programming on both television and radio.
- With regard to programming that contains references to sexual activity, respondents favor government regulation of broadcast television (65%) and radio programming (63%) during the morning, afternoon and early evening hours. By contrast, 55% favor government regulation of such sexual material on basic cable television programs during those same hours.
- Respondents favor expanding the reach of the "do not call" registry, as 62% said they favor adding charities and other nonprofit organizations to the current lists, as compared to 36% who opposed such expansion.
- A vast majority of those surveyed said parents should be primarily responsible for keeping all forms of inappropriate material away from children. The public places tremendous responsibility on parents in monitoring inappropriate printed materials in particular: 87% said parents should be primarily responsible for keeping those materials away, as compared to 10% who said it should be the primary responsibility of publishers.
- 35% of respondents said that their television is equipped with a v-chip. Of those, less than a quarter (24%) indicated that they are currently using the v-chip to monitor programs in their household.

Apparently there exists no public groundswell to overthrow the current system of regulating entertainment television and radio. Nearly six in 10 (58%) said the current amount of government regulation of entertainment television is "about right," nearly three times the percentage (21%) who said there is too little of such regulation. Similarly, 59% are satisfied with the current amount of government regulation of entertainment programming on the radio.

But what about more controversial content that is published or broadcast on the air? In an age where the public as a whole has unprecedented access to materials featuring explicit references to sexual activity, some have started to look to the government for assistance in monitoring and filtering such materials before they reach the hands of consumers, especially children. Is this an appropriate function for government? Do government efforts to impose restrictions on such materials run up against public concerns that free speech rights not be violated?

Explicit references to sexual activity have become a staple of many prime time shows. Still, the public draws critical distinctions between the time of day and the type of medium in which such references should be allowed. Not even half of those surveyed (49%) said government officials should have the power to regulate such programming by over-the-air television networks (ABC, CBS, etc) during the late evening and overnight hours, and even fewer (45%) would tolerate similar regulations of basic cable television programming during late hours.

Meanwhile popular support for regulation of programs that contain references to sexual activity increases substantially when it applies to programming during the morning, afternoon and early evening: 65% would afford the power to regulate over-the-air network broadcasts during those earlier hours, and a majority (55%) would even favor regulation of basic cable television networks such as CNN, ESPN, etc., that air sexual references during the morning, afternoon and early evening.

The public also distinguishes between regulations of radio programs that contain references to sexual activity at different times of the day. Sixty-three percent approved of such regulations during the morning, afternoon and early evening, while only half favored regulations of radio programming during the late evening and overnight hours.

One of the more popular laws passed in recent years created a "do not call" registry, which allows individuals to block many telemarketers from making calls. A majority (62%) favored adding charities and other non-profit organizations to the list of those who must defer to the registry, with 42% indicating that they strongly favor such an expansion. Only 36% opposed any such expansion.

Who should be responsible for keeping inappropriate content away from children? Americans overwhelmingly favor placing such responsibility with parents themselves. A vast majority (87%) indicated parents should be responsible for keeping inappropriate printed materials away from children, almost nine times the number that would prefer publishers to be primarily responsible. Among subgroups, whites (90%) are more likely to identify parents for this task than non-whites (78%). And parents of children under age 6 (94%) are especially likely to think that parents in general should primarily assume that role.

The public is nearly as adamant that parents maintain the primary responsibility for keeping away from children inappropriate television programming (81%), inappropriate radio programming (77%), and even inappropriate movies shown in theaters (71%). In the latter category, 19% would make theater owners and operators responsible for keeping inappropriate movies away from children, and 3% would place that responsibility with government officials.

How can parents keep track of their children's television viewing habits? In recent years the v-chip has gotten considerable attention. Yet just 35% of those surveyed said their television sets are equipped with a v-chip, and of those, only 24% admitted to using the v-chip to monitor programs being viewed in their household. If parents are truly assuming the responsibility for monitoring their children's viewing habits, it is largely happening without the benefits of this new technology. . . .

POSTSCRIPT

Should the Public Support Freedom of the Press?

Maciejewski and Ozar remind us of the philosophy behind the public right to know. What are the obligations of individuals and institutions to not interfere with the individuals or institutions that fulfill that need? The First Amendment Report pulls us into the practical applications of these principles to complex issues. Beyond the thorny philosophical questions of, "What constitutes freedom?" and "What constitutes protection?," lurk some surprisingly practical issues. Does pretrial publicity bias juries? Should journalistic sources be protected? Offensive jokes, pornography in an office setting, ethnic slurs, online discussions, and even public meetings can pose problems about restriction on freedom of speech. Can speech be sexual harassment? Should libraries restrict Internet sites available to children? If so, should they do the same thing with the sensitive books on their shelves? When do the rights of the individual take precedence over the general rights guaranteed by the First Amendment?

These are important questions for debate. Decisions can be difficult when you have a constitutionally guaranteed right that becomes very complicated in the specific context, and in which rights may conflict with each other. Sometimes it is easy to support the First Amendment in general, until you are personally made uncomfortable or offended by the exercise of these unrestricted rights. Just as sometimes it is easy to ignore rights until they are taken away.

Those who argue that freedom must be absolute often invoke the concept of the "slippery slope." Any defection from absolute adherence to total freedom of expressions is attacked. It is too easy a move from credentialing reporters, to licensing newspapers, to yanking the credentials and licenses of those who are troublesome. Is it a short step from limiting Internet access of children, to removing similarly troublesome materials from the library bookshelves, or making them only available by special request? Once you start, the argument goes, each step is easier and soon freedom slips away. What restrictions or regulations on absolute freedom of speech and press would you support, and why?

Issues of speech and press freedom are global. The Committee to Protect Journalists maintains a chilling website, www.cpj.org. Type "Attacks on the Press in 2006" into the search box for a report on who is killing and incarcerating journalists and why. Throughout the globe, journalists face oppression, incarceration, and even death to report on issues of importance. In many cases governments and their policies fail to protect journalists. Think about what is needed to have a free and independent press: decriminalization of media output, so that you can't legally be jailed for writing something that others disagree with; rule of law, so that these laws are followed; perhaps some form of private ownership; professionally trained journalists; a business model that works. What would you think to be essential? *Freedom of the Press 2006* by Freedom House (available at `http://www.freedomhouse.org` under publications) talks about the development of media independence, and the many legal, business, and social areas that must converge to allow that development.

So the simple question: Do we really need the First Amendment? How much should we bother about its application to complex issues in our society? Do you count yourself among those who really care?

ISSUE 11

Should Freedom of Speech Ever Be Restricted?

YES: Eugene Volokh, from "Freedom of Speech, Cyberspace, Harassment Law and the Clinton Administration," *Law and Contemporary Problems* (2000)

NO: Edison and Jacobs Media Research, from "Indecency Survey," www.edisonresearch.com (March 2004)

ISSUE SUMMARY

YES: Law professor Eugene Volokh examines several situations in which absolute freedom of speech would very likely conflict with the precedents that have been set in the realm of creating "hostile environment law." For example, if any offensive speech or images were transmitted in a public arena, the law would side with the more conservative approach toward restricting speech or images that would offend certain people, or that would create an uncomfortable atmosphere.

NO: Two media consulting firms collaborated on a survey of rock radio listeners to discover what might be offensive to them. The results, taken from the perspective of the audience who listens to rock, create an argument for restricting government involvement in censoring content, and a clear preference for allowing individuals to choose what they hear, or requiring parental involvement in the cases of radio content and audiences of children.

While there are many legal views about how inclusive our First Amendment "freedom of speech" should be, this issue examines content that often falls into the category of "offensive" content. One of the authors (Volokh) examines the perspective specifically from the use of the Internet (cyberspace) and how messages may offend, or create hostile environments for people who are using a linked "system" for communication. In the opposing view, two research companies that have undertaken a survey of rock radio listeners come up with a different approach for whom should make the decision of whether to listen to content that may be offensive.

Lawyer and law professor Eugene Volokh examines how offensive jokes, mocking racial or ethnic speech patterns, pornography in an office environment, on-line campus bulletin boards and public libraries may all pose problems that could or should see restrictions on freedom of speech. In particular, he looks at how creating hostile environments through the allowing of an atmosphere that demeans individuals has been upheld in recent harassment cases. While he agrees that restricting some speech in certain environments could have a chilling effect on free exchange of ideas, he argues that the rights of the individuals should take precedence over the general right of free speech. Among his most persuasive examples is the issue of hate speech, and whether that type of expression should be allowed to exist in settings where individuals must interact.

Edison Media Research and Jacobs Media surveyed 13,798 individuals who listen to rock radio to learn what, and when, those listeners might be offended by what they hear. Overwhelmingly, the respondents who chose to listen to rock were not offended by the content. While there was greater agreement that shock radio disc jockeys have gone too far these days, there was also an agreement that shock jocks should also have freedom of speech.

Also of importance was the Super Bowl 2004 event in which singer Janet Jackson's "costume malfunction" resulted in her baring a breast on national television at a time in which children could be watching. While most of the respondents were not personally offended by the action, they did express views that it was inappropriate, though most felt that the government should not be involved in restricting content. Rather, parents should exercise more control over what their children hear and watch.

This is an important issue because each of the authors focus on different examples that show how difficult it is to have one constitutionally guaranteed "right" (to free speech) that does not become complicated within specific situations. There may be times when rights and privileges have to be viewed within specific contexts. As you read these selections, please consider other situations in which the clarity of the law becomes more difficult to discern.

Eugene Volokh

Freedom of Speech, Cyberspace, Harassment Law, and the Clinton Administration

During the height of the Clinton-Lewinsky scandal, many lawyer pundits talked about impeachment. Some talked about independent counsels and separation of powers. Some talked about the criminal law of perjury, or the rules of evidence, or whether indecent exposure constituted sexual harassment.

A few experts, though, focused on a more practical issue: Saying certain things about the scandal, they advised people, might be legally punishable. "Be careful what you say," one headline warned, when you discuss "the Starr report and Clinton/Lewinsky matter" in certain ways. "Talking about Clinton? Tread carefully," says another, pointing out the risk of "a lawsuit from an offended co-worker." Such discussions "ought to be avoided" because of the risk of legal liability. "[I]t's best to choose carefully who you share your remarks, your jokes, with. . . . 'Attorneys warn us about [legal liability]. . . .' Office humor in particular 'is always quicksand'. . . ." "There's no right [to make certain statements about the Clinton/Lewinsky affair] just because it's a public issue." "We had quite a few clients calling us when Lewinsky jokes . . . were making the rounds." "People think that if they hear something on TV or the radio they can say it at work [without fear of legal liability]. But that of course is not the case."

What body of law, one might ask, would suppress jokes about the President or discussion of the Starr Report? Not the most publicized free speech restriction of the Clinton years, the Communications Decency Act of 1996, (CDA) which was struck down 9–0 by the Supreme Court.

Rather, this remarkable speech restriction is hostile environment harassment law. Under this doctrine, speech can lead to massive liability if it is "severe or pervasive" enough to create a "hostile, abusive, or offensive work environment" for the plaintiff and for a reasonable person based on the person's race, religion, sex, national origin, disability, age, veteran status, and in some jurisdictions a variety of other attributes. And this rather vague and broad test has long been interpreted to cover not just face-to-face slurs or repeated indecent propositions, but also sexually themed jokes and discussions, even ones that aren't about co-workers or directed at particular co-workers. The prudent employer is wise to restrict speech like this, whether it is about President Clinton, Monica Lewinsky, Kenneth Starr, or anyone else—not just because of professionalism concerns (which some employers might care more about and others less), but because of the risk that this speech will be found to be legally punishable. . . .

The words "in cyberspace" in the phrase "restrictions on free speech in cyberspace" are generally, in my view, not terribly significant; the medium by and large does not and should not affect the protection—or lack of protection—given to the content. The CDA and the Child Online Protection Act do pose some interesting cyberspace-specific questions, but even with these laws, most of the important issues are broader free speech questions: May speech be restricted if the restriction is in fact necessary to effectively serve a compelling government interest? What burdens may be placed on adults in order to shield children? . . .

The Hidden Communications Decency Act

In 1997, the Equal Employment Opportunity Commission filed a workplace harassment lawsuit, which is still pending, against the Federal Home Loan Mortgage Corporation, also known as Freddie Mac. The lawsuit alleged various misconduct by Freddie Mac employees, including the following item: Some employees allegedly sent to a department-wide distribution list "derogatory electronic messages regarding 'ebonics'"—a list of jokes mocking the black dialect, seemingly a response to the then-current Oakland School Board proposal to treat "ebonics" as a separate language. This, the EEOC claimed, contributed to a racially hostile work environment, and it was thus illegal for Freddie Mac to tolerate such speech; Freddie Mac had a duty to "take prompt and effective remedial action to eradicate" it.

Nor was this an isolated incident. In 1997, for instance, R. R. Donnelly, Morgan Stanley, and Citibank were all sued based in part on offensive jokes sent through e-mail. Newspaper articles reporting on these lawsuits featured headlines such as "Defusing the E-Mail Time Bomb . . . Establish Firm Workplace Rules to Prevent Discrimination Suits," "E-Mail Humor: Punch Lines Can Carry Price; Jokes Open Employers To Discrimination Suits," and "Firms Get Sobering Message; E-mail Abuses May Leave Them Liable." In a less widely reported case, the New Jersey Office of Administrative Law recently found a single incident of a long joke list being forwarded by e-mail to the whole department to be "sexual harassment," creating an "offensive work environment." The judge "f[ou]nd [that] the 'jokes' degrade, shame, humiliate, defame and dishonor men and women based upon their gender, sexual preference, religion, skin pigmentation and national and ethnic origin" and are thus illegal. Similarly, in *Trout v. City of Akron*, a jury awarded a plaintiff $265,000 based in part on coworkers viewing pornographic material on their computers. . . .

Imagine how a cautious employer would react to a decision imposing liability in the Freddie Mac harassment case or even to the EEOC's decision to sue Freddie Mac. Though in theory individual offensive political statements are not actionable under harassment law unless they are aggregated with at least some other speech or conduct, in practice the employer can't just tell its employees, "It's fine for you to e-mail political statements that some may find racially, religiously, or sexually offensive, *unless* there have been other incidents in which other people have also been mistreating the offended worker in other ways—incidents of which you, the employee, might not even be aware." So long as constitutionally protected speech can be part of a hostile environment claim, the cautious employer must restrict each individual instance of such speech: After all, this particular statement might make the difference between a legally permissible, nonhostile environment, and an illegal hostile environment. The employer must say, "Do not circulate *any* material, even isolated items, that anyone might find racially, religiously, or sexually offensive, since put together such material may lead to liability."

This is exactly what employment experts are counseling employers to do. For instance, according to an article called *Employers Need to Establish Internet Policies*, "avoiding potential sex-harassment liability is a major incentive for companies to establish Internet policies." To prevent "incurring liability under state and federal discrimination laws," businesses should have written policies that bar, among other things, "download[ing] pornographic picture[s]"—not just distributing them but even simply downloading them—and sending "messages with derogatory or inflammatory remarks about an individual or group's race, religion, national origin, physical attributes, or sexual preference." The advice is, of course, not to "bar downloading pornographic pictures and sending messages with derogatory remarks when they are severe or pervasive enough to create a hostile, abusive, or offensive work environment"; rather, the advice is to bar any such downloading and any such messages.

The government, through threat of massive legal liability, is pressuring people to block access to material that it finds offensive. Obviously, private employers may, on their own, choose to restrict speech on their computers—just like private publishers may choose (and routinely do choose) not to publish profane, insulting, or politically offensive material, and just as Internet service providers may choose to restrict the material that they carry and to which they allow access. But when the law uses the threat of legal liability to pressure publishers or service providers into restricting speech on their property, the First Amendment is implicated. This is exactly what happens with harassment law.

True, the law isn't demanding a total ban: People whose Web access is blocked and whose e-mail is restricted because of the legal pressure can still read and write from home, though even from home they should not send e-mail to co-workers who might be offended, since a hostile environment at work may be created by speech sent from one employee's home e-mail address to another's. But the Communications Decency Act didn't impose a total ban, either—it would have still let people read and post what they wanted, so long as the material was difficult for minors to access, which probably meant that the sites would have had to charge for access using a credit card. The Supreme Court correctly concluded that this burden, even though it wasn't a total ban, violated the First Amendment; the same should go for the burden imposed on speech by harassment law.

What's more, harassment law is in many ways broader than the CDA; the CDA, at least, didn't purport to cover allegedly racist, sexist, or religiously insulting statements. The CDA would not have imposed liability for ebonics jokes (unless they contained highly explicit sexual or excretory references), or for most Clinton-Lewinsky jokes. And the one other body of law that refers to "indecent speech"—the regime governing television and radio broadcasting—tolerates such jokes, as long as they aren't extraordinarily graphic.

But harassment law is not limited to indecency; it operates to generally suppress speech, whether or not sexually explicit or highly profane, that is potentially offensive based on race, religion, sex, and so on. And the evidence of harassment law's chilling effect on protected speech is much more concrete than the speculative (though plausible) evidence on which the Court relied in *Reno v. ACLU*. Harassment law goes where the CDA was forbidden to tread—and so far it hasn't been stopped. . . .

The Hidden Campus Speech Code

In late 1994, the Santa Rosa Junior College newspaper ran an advertisement containing a picture of the rear end of a woman in a bikini. A student, Lois Arata, thought the advertisement was sexist; when the newspaper refused to let her discuss this concern at a staff meeting, she organized a boycott of the newspaper and wrote to the College Trustees to express her objections.

This led to a hot debate in a chat room on SOLO, a college-run online bulletin board for students, and some of the debate contained personal attacks on Arata and on Jennifer Branham, a female newspaper staffer. Some of the messages referred to Arata and Branham using "anatomically explicit and sexually derogatory" terms. Arata and Branham quickly learned of the messages (the two weren't chat room members themselves) and complained to the college, which put the journalism professor who had set up the bulletin board on administrative leave pending an investigation.

This suspension naturally intensified the controversy. Some of the new SOLO posts insulted Arata's personal appearance and said that she was protesting the ad because she was jealous. Others called Arata a "fascist" and a "feminazi fundamentalist." Branham, the newspaper staffer, was especially criticized. At two newspaper staff meetings, many of her fellow staffers "directed angry remarks at [her] and blamed her for the journalism professor's absence." Another staff member produced a parody "lampoon[ing] the newspaper's coverage of Branham's complaint, implying that the complaint was trivial."

I have no doubt that Arata and Branham were genuinely upset by this speech; but, especially on a college campus, such speech, warts and all, seems to be the sort of "uninhibited, robust, and wide-open" debate that we must expect when people debate issues that are important to them. Likewise, I had thought people were free to criticize classmates who organize boycotts or file complaints against a newspaper, bulletin board, or a respected community figure, even if the criticisms are unfair, personal, and intemperate.

The U.S. Department of Education Office for Civil Rights, however, took a different view. The students' speech, the OCR concluded, created a "hostile educational environment" for Branham based on her sex, and for Branham and Arata based on their actions in complaining about the original posts. What about the First Amendment? Well, the OCR reasoned,

> [s]tatutes prohibiting sexual harassment have been upheld against First Amendment challenges because speech in such cases has been considered indistinguishable from other illegal speech such as threats of violence or blackmail. . . . The Supreme Court has repeatedly asserted that the First Amendment does not protect expression that is invidious private discrimination. Thus, the First Amendment is not a bar to determining whether the messages . . . created a sexually hostile educational environment.

Moreover, the OCR had a plan to prevent such "illegal speech" in the future. "A new paragraph," the plan said, "shall be added to the [Santa Rosa Junior College] 'Administrative Computing Procedures,'" which shall bar (among other things) online speech that "harass[es], denigrates or shows hostility or aversion toward an individual or group based on that person's gender, race, color, national origin or disability, and . . . has the purpose or effect of creating a hostile, intimidating or offensive educational environment." And this prohibition shall cover "epithets, slurs, negative stereotyping, or threatening, intimidating or hostile acts . . . that relate to race, color, national origin, gender, or disability," including "acts that purport to be 'jokes' or 'pranks,' but that are hostile or demeaning." This is of course at least as broad as many of the campus speech codes that were struck down in the late 1980s and early 1990s—again, harassment law goes where the government has before been told it may not tread. Rather cryptically, the proposed speech code ends with "Nothing contained herein shall be construed as violating any person's rights of expression set forth in the Equal Access Act or the First Amendment of the United States Constitution."

The College settled the case by paying the complainants $15,000 each, and by adopting the OCR's policy. At a college run by the state government, and under pressure from the federal government, cyberspace communications containing "negative stereotyping," "denigrat[ion]," and "hostility or aversion" based on race or sex are now "illegal speech." And other administrators and legal experts agree; in the words of a New Jersey Law Journal article co-written by a computer science professor and a state court judge,

> [a]lthough a school [in context, referring to colleges and universities] by its very nature must provide for the guarantees of free speech as to classroom expression and assignment, the use of computers, [and] access to the Internet in open computer labs, should be appropriately regulated to avoid a hostile environment for offended students. Not to take such preventive actions at the . . . school is to place the . . . school at risk.

. . . First, the free speech issue here has little to do with the speech being in cyberspace. The Santa Rosa incidents started with online posts, but then went on to include a printed parody and oral comments at a newspaper staff meeting; the OCR correctly treated them similarly, because there was no real reason to treat them differently. And the hostile educational environment theory is already being used elsewhere to justify general speech codes that likewise apply equally to cyberspace speech and to other speech: Consider, for instance, a 1996 Kansas Attorney General Opinion, which argues that campus speech codes are constitutionally permissible, so long as they are written by analogy to hostile work environment law, or the Central Michigan University speech code, which prohibited any behavior creating a "hostile or offensive" educational environment and was struck down in *Dambrot v. Central Michigan University*.

Second, the Clinton Administration was mostly just tagging along for the ride. True, the Department of Education is pushing for speech restrictions. Besides the SOLO case, consider the Department of Education's *Sexual Harassment in Higher Education—From Conflict to Community*, which lists "sexist statements and behavior that convey insulting, degrading, or sexist attitudes" as examples of "sexually harassing behavior." Likewise, consider the OCR publication *Sexual Harassment: It's Not Academic*, which states that even in universities, "displaying or distributing sexually explicit drawings, pictures and written materials" may constitute harassment if it is unwelcome and "severe, persistent, or pervasive" enough.

Still, the OCR is only doing what the Kansas Attorney General, Central Michigan University, and others are doing. Maybe a more ideological Administration might have tried to lead some sort of anti-"hate-speech" crusade, but that's not what happened under Clinton. Rather, we have a specialist agency quietly trying to implement its own goal (protecting people against racist or sexist behavior) and seeing the First Amendment as largely an incidental barrier to be overcome if it's easy to do so.

Third, we see here how narrow speech restrictions beget broader ones. The OCR's argument starts with the uncontroversial assertion that threats and blackmail are punishable as "illegal speech." Then comes the assertion, which the OCR treats as uncontroversial, that harassing speech in workplaces (the subject of the statutes to which the OCR must have been referring) is likewise illegal speech. Then it follows that such speech in colleges is illegal speech.

Similarly, consider the OCR's argument that "The Supreme Court has repeatedly asserted that the First Amendment does not protect expression that is invidious private discrimination." It's true that the Court held that the First Amendment does not protect discriminatory acts, such as refusals to admit people into a school, university, or club, refusals to promote people, or the selection of a victim for a physical assault. It's also true that in *R.A.V. v. City of St. Paul*, the Court said in dictum that a "content-based subcategory of a *proscribable* class of speech" such as "sexually derogatory 'fighting words,' among other words" might be punishable by harassment law, without discussing whether harassment law may constitutionally punish otherwise nonproscribable, constitutionally protected speech. But from here the OCR makes an analogical jump, inferring from cases discussing bans on conduct and on constitutionally unprotected speech (such as fighting words) that the government may punish as "illegal speech" any expression that may create a "hostile, abusive, or offensive" environment and that thus supposedly constitutes "invidious private discrimination."

Analogy is a powerful force in our legal system. Supporters of workplace harassment law regularly use existing restrictions—such as obscenity law and bans on fighting words—as justification. It's hardly surprising that workplace harassment law would then itself be used as an analogy to justify educational harassment law. . . .

Harassment by Library Internet Access

In 1997, the Loudoun County Public Library made the news by installing filters on all library computers. Such policies are usually justified by the desire to block children from accessing sexually explicit material, but here the stated rationale—reflected in the policy's title, *Policy on Internet Sexual Harassment*—was quite different:

> 1. Title VII of the Civil Rights Act prohibits sex discrimination. Library pornography can create a sexually-hostile environment for patrons or staff. . . . Permitting pornographic displays may constitute unlawful sex discrimination in violation of Title VII of the Civil Rights Act. This policy seeks to prevent internet sexual harassment [by installing software that blocks sexually explicit material, including "soft core pornography"]

The policy's author, library trustee (and lawyer) Dick Black, echoed this:

> The courts have said, for example, that someone can have materials—racist materials dealing with the Ku Klux Klan—in their home. However, the courts have upheld very strict limitations on having that in the workplace because of the racially discriminatory environment.
>
> Same thing applies here. People can do certain things in the privacy of their own homes that they cannot do in the workplace.
>
> Now this is not limited strictly to libraries. But the courts have said that whether it's a public state facility or whether it's a manufacturing plant, people cannot deprive women of their equal access to those facilities and their equal rights to employment through sexual harassment.

Nor is this an isolated incident; other libraries throughout the country have been doing the same thing, and offering the same justification. In the words of one article,

> [b]lue movie night in the computer lab [where users accessed sexually explicit material online] was not the end of the world as we know it. Left unaddressed, however, it could have become a problem of sexual harassment, with charges that such usage created an uncomfortable situation for many library users—not to mention library staff. Linked to other instances of insensitive, arguably sexist behavior, it could contribute to charges that a hostile environment existed—and could become evidence in a lawsuit.

> . . . Playboy pinups in work areas invite sexual harassment suits.
> Why should the Internet be any different?

Again we see how some speech restrictions are used as analogies to support other ones, though here the analogy is not from workplaces to colleges or to service providers but the much more direct analogy from "normal" workplaces to libraries as workplaces. "Racist materials dealing with the Ku Klux Klan" are limited in workplaces generally; "same thing applies here" in libraries. Sexually suggestive materials are illegal in "a manufacturing plant"; same goes for libraries. "Playboy pinups in work areas invite sexual harassment suits. Why should the Internet be any different?"

The library case is different in an important way from the other three areas described above. Here, a government agency is acting as proprietor to restrict what is done with its own property, and thus may have far more authority than it would if it were acting as sovereign. It might be legitimate for the library board members as managers to try to shield library users or employees from involuntary exposure to offensive material, or even to entirely refuse to participate in disseminating material that they think offensive and harmful. Whether a government-owned library may install filters, quite apart from the harassment issues, remains an unsettled matter.

But the harassment question is nonetheless significant, because if libraries must filter to prevent harassment claims, then this rationale extends equally to private libraries and other private Internet access centers. A publicly accessible library at Duke University, for instance, would be obligated by state and federal law to install filters to prevent workplace harassment complaints by librarians and public accommodation harassment complaints by patrons; likewise for an Internet cafe. Here, the government would indeed be acting as sovereign controlling what private institutions do: Even if a private library wanted to provide unlimited access, it would face legal liability for doing so.

Judge Leonie Brinkema's decision in *Mainstream Loudoun v. Board of Trustees of the Loudoun County Library* struck an early blow against library Internet filtering. Such filtering, the decision held, violated the First Amendment (at least when it wasn't limited to child-only computers), notwithstanding the potential risk of harassment liability.

One of Judge Brinkema's rationales—that the defendants could point to very few harassment complaints that were brought as a result of patrons accessing sexually explicit materials—isn't promising for the long term, because such complaints are now piling in. For instance, seven librarians recently filed an EEOC complaint based on what they say is "repeated exposure to sexually explicit materials," and an environment "which is increasingly permeated by [pornographic] images on computer screens, [and] is also barraged by hard copies of the same, created on Library provided printers." Forty-seven of the 140 or so library employees signed a letter saying, in response to a library patron's complaint about other patrons accessing sexually explicit material, that "Every day we, too, are subjected to pornography left (sometimes intentionally) on the screens and in the printers. We do not like it either. We feel harassed and intimidated by having to work in a public environment where we might, at any moment, be exposed to degrading or pornographic pictures."

In response the library enacted a new policy that, among other things, bars even adult patrons from accessing material that is "harmful to minors"—a category of speech that includes material that's constitutionally protected as to adults—and also from otherwise "[e]ngag[ing] in any activity that . . . creates an intimidating or hostile environment." "The Library," the policy says, "is committed to providing its employees and patrons with an environment that is free from all forms of harassment, including sexual harassment, and prohibiting the display of obscene material, child pornography, and material that is harmful to minors."

Nor is the Minneapolis incident an isolated one; librarians in other places have likewise complained about patrons accessing material that they feel is sexually harassing. Judge Brinkema's argument that "[s]ignificantly, defendant has not pointed to a single incident in which a library employee or patron has complained that material being accessed on the Internet was harassing or created a hostile environment" thus seems to be no longer available. If that were the only argument in support of her decision, we would face the specter of harassment law being used to punish private and public libraries and Internet cafes that allow unfiltered access.

The judge's second justification—that the library could avoid harassment liability by placing computers in places where passers-by couldn't routinely see them, or installing privacy screens that make the screen visible only from the place where the user is sitting—seems, however, to be more robust. Such alternative solutions would not be perfect; a library patron may sit down to use a terminal and find that a pornographic site had been left on the screen by a previous patron, someone who's accessing a pornographic site might have technical trouble and ask a librarian for help, privacy screens may be imperfect, and patrons or librarians may see offensive material in a printer output bin. But courts might conclude that these situations are rare enough that when the proper measures are taken, technology does let libraries largely avoid the risk of harassment liability and at the same time provide unfiltered access.

Here, then, might be a case where the speech being in cyberspace does make a difference. To begin with, in the pre-cyberspace world, libraries generally did not stock illustrated pornography. Because buying and shelving books cost money, library decisions not to get a certain book were practically and perhaps even doctrinally immune from review, and to my knowledge few libraries decided to spend their funds on *Hustler*. They may have stocked a few "legitimate" books that included sexually explicit pictures, and it was possible that a patron might leave such a book open on the table, but I suspect this happened quite rarely.

On the other side of the ledger, computer technology makes it easier to decrease the risk that offended patrons or librarians will inadvertently see offensive material. Privacy screens on computers generally ensure that casual passers-by won't see what's going on. Any attempts to control offensive print materials (once the library had bought them) would probably be much less effective.

Conclusion

Forty years after the end of the Eisenhower Administration, what can we say about how it affected the freedom of speech? Not that much, probably, except of course for the way the Eisenhower appointees to the Supreme Court (and perhaps to lower courts) affected Free Speech Clause case law. Free speech concepts may have changed during the Eisenhower years, but little of that change comes from the legislative or executive agenda of the Eisenhower White House. This is true of many presidencies, and it will probably be true of the Clinton Administration.

Likewise, what can we say now about freedom of speech in movies, on telephones, via faxes, on television, in cyberspace, and in other media? By and large, the answer is that free speech jurisprudence has evolved to be comparatively medium-independent. Early holdings that movies are constitutionally unprotected have been reversed. In its very first cyberspace case, the Court refused to create a medium-specific test. While broadcast television and radio are still subject to different rules than other media, even this traditional distinction is now somewhat precarious. Medium does matter with regard to content-neutral distinctions that are justified by noncommunicative concerns, because different media raise different noncommunicative concerns—soundtrucks are loud, billboards block the view, cable television systems are often monopolies. As to content-based distinctions, though, medium is not terribly relevant.

But the basic concepts underlying the free speech exceptions remain important for decades. For instance, incitement, bad tendency, commercial speech, obscenity, libel, and now speech that creates a hostile environment are powerful concepts that can mold free speech thinking over a wide range of cases. Some of these free speech exceptions are eventually discarded (for instance, bad tendency). Others are changed (commercial speech, obscenity, libel), though many of the principles underlying them remain. Still others, such as "speech that creates a hostile environment," spread from their roots in narrow situations where they seem proper and even morally imperative into considerably broader areas, and can provide indirect precedential support for even broader restrictions.

Free speech law certainly must recognize exceptions to the core First Amendment principle that the government acting as sovereign generally may not restrict speech because of its content. But before endorsing any such exception, we should consider it carefully, and try to come up with principles that can limit its scope. The risk of speech restrictions growing by analogy in a legal system built on analogy is very real. And so far, the harassing speech exception has not gotten the judicial and academic scrutiny that it deserves, and that is needed to properly cabin the exception and to prevent its unchecked growth. . . .

Indecency Survey

Background

On February 1st, 2004, the singer Janet Jackson, in what she termed a "wardrobe malfunction" exposed her right breast during the television broadcast of the halftime of the Super Bowl. This incredibly high-profile event unleashed a firestorm of publicity and recriminations.

The backlash from the Jackson affair has been particularly strong in the world of radio. Politicians, eager to "clean up the airwaves" and to respond to various groups targeting "edgy" or "shocking" programming, have called radio executives in front of their committees and have chastised the FCC for not responding to public complaints and for not levying enough fines. Also, and perhaps most importantly, Congress has rushed through a variety of new laws that massively increase potential fines to broadcasters, as well as to threaten license revocations for repeat offenders.

Our two companies, Edison Media Research and Jacobs Media, have investigated the issues of "indecency" in the past, most notably in a survey performed in the fall of 2002 for Rock radio stations around the country. With the current level of interest in these issues, we felt it was time to talk to Rock radio listeners again, and to see if their feelings have changed. This survey furthers our inquiries into the topics and issues of indecency and adult material with regard to Rock radio listeners around the country.

Methodology

Jacobs Media and Edison Media Research collectively designed and administered this survey. We collected interviews via the Internet from a total of 13,798 respondents. In total, 40 Rock Radio stations around the United States invited their listeners to participate in the survey. The number of respondents who could come from any individual radio station was capped at 6% of the total sample. The interviews were conducted between March 12th and March 19th 2004.

As with all Internet-based research projects of this kind, the results reflect only those who choose to participate in the survey and do not necessarily represent the views of all Rock radio listeners in the country. Still, the 40 radio stations that invited their listeners are a broad cross-section of rock stations, with large and small markets, large and small stations, some stations with very edgy morning shows and some with very mild ones, and those that play the newest Rock music and those that play only Classic Rock.

According to audience estimates from Arbitron, just over 50 million people listen to Rock radio stations every week.

Sample Demographics

In total, there were 13,798 Rock radio listeners who completed our survey; these people were distributed as follows:

Men	61%
Women	39%
Under 18	5%
18–24	19%
25–34	28%
35–44	29%
45–54	17%
Over 54	2%
Democrat	26%
Republican	27%
Independent	34%
Attend Church Regularly	27%
Attend Church Few Times/Yr	19%
Rarely or Never Attend Church	54%
Listen to station with "Very Edgy" Morning Show	49%
Listen to station with "Moderately Edgy" Morning Show	24%
Listen to station with "Not Edgy" Morning Show	27%
Listen to "Alternative Rock" Station	24%
Listen to "Active Rock" Station	36%
Listen to "Classic Rock" Station	40%

Key Findings

- **Few Rock radio listeners are offended by what they hear on the radio.** We asked respondents: "Think about the radio station you listen to most often in the morning. How often does it offend you in some way?" More than half (55%) of respondents said "Never"; only 11% of respondents said more than "Rarely."

  Significantly, the answers are nearly identical among those who listen to stations with all kinds of shows, from the most "edgy" to the least. This implies that people choose a show that is unlikely to offend them.

  Women were only slightly more likely than men to be offended by what they hear (Women: 47% "Never Offended"; Men: 60%). Parents with children under 13 are no more likely to be offended than the group as a whole. Republican and Democrat Rock listeners have no significant difference between them with regard to this question.

As one respondent pointed out, "I am the parent of a 13-year-old boy. If I hear something potentially offensive, I have the right to change the station with my own hand. I am disturbed that the government will 'parent' me by choosing what I can and cannot choose to listen to.

One interesting twist—there was a sizeable minority of respondents who said, "Shock Jock radio personalities have gone too far." More than one-quarter of respondents (28%) agreed with this statement. Certain subgroups, such as women (32%), parents (32%), frequent church-goers (40%), Republicans (35%) and Classic Rock listeners (43%) agreed with this statement in larger numbers. Among those who listen to the mildest morning radio shows, 43% agreed with this statement.

- **While not personally offended by it, a majority finds the Janet Jackson/Super Bowl incident a "major issue."** Our respondents had interesting views on the Janet Jackson kerfuffle. Only 14% of respondents said that they were personally offended by it. Yet, just over half said it is an "important issue." We see the implication that our respondents can separate what is offensive to them and what is appropriate in different contexts.

  This is summarized by one of the web poll's participants who opines, "I believe in freedom of speech, and I believe that even shock jocks are entitled to this right. However, I think that programmers should be cognizant of what the expected audience will be. Without a doubt, the 'expected audience' for the Super Bowl halftime show included children. That act was totally inappropriate, and anyone who was privy to the planned exposure should be held responsible for abusing the broadcast."

  Perhaps not surprisingly, men were much less likely to be offended by Ms. Jackson's "costume reveal" than women. But only 17% of our female respondents said they were personally offended by the stunt. Frequent church-goers (24%) and Republicans (20%) were slightly more likely than the group as a whole to have been personally offended—but clearly overwhelming majorities of these groups were also not offended.

  Those who listen to the edgiest morning shows, as might be expected, were the most likely to say it was not an important issue (56%); among those who listen to the mildest morning shows only 39% thought the incident was "not important."

  Well over half of all respondents, including many who thought the issue "not important," feel that someone should be punished or sanctioned for the Super Bowl incident. The entity most felt should be held accountable is Ms. Jackson herself (59%), followed by Justin Timberlake (50%), and MTV (21%). Only 34% of our respondents felt no one should be punished for what transpired.

- **Rock listeners overwhelmingly support Howard Stern.** Howard Stern is the rare radio personality who, because of his exposure across many media, is well known even in markets where his show doesn't run. Fully 98% of respondents (from a mix of markets where Howard is and isn't aired) said that they have heard of Howard Stern. More than 90% of those respondents were aware that Howard Stern's show had recently been taken off the air in a handful of radio markets because of indecency concerns.

Those who knew of Howard Stern's removal in these markets overwhelmingly believe that this was an unfair decision. When given the choice between two statements about Howard Stern's elimination, they answered as follows:

- They were right to take Howard Stern off the air   20%
- People who want to listen to Howard Stern
  should be allowed to do so   80%

In every subgroup a strong majority said that people who want to listen to Howard Stern should be allowed to do so. The groups most likely to say, "They were right to take Howard Stern off the air" were listeners to stations with mild morning shows (30%) and frequent church-goers (32%).

- **Rock listeners are extraordinarily sensitive to government involvement in programming.** We asked a series of questions to evaluate respondents' feelings about the government's role in overseeing programming on the radio. In pretty much every case, the group overwhelmingly felt negatively towards government involvement in programming. Even those who felt that the Janet Jackson incident was an "important issue" felt that the government should not overly restrict radio talent. Here are some example responses:

  o "The FCC should take programs that it considers indecent off the air"

* Agree	12%
* Disagree	71%
* Neutral	17%

  o "It angers you that the government is attempting to regulate the radio shows that you can listen to"

* Agree	72%
* Disagree	12%
* Neutral	15%

  o "Radio personalities should be able to say whatever they please; if people don't want to listen they can change the station"

* Agree	58%
* Disagree	26%
* Neutral	16%

These findings were consistent among subgroups.

- **Respondents overwhelmingly feel that it is parents' responsibility to keep adult material away from children.** We asked respondents which of these statements best describes who is responsible when it comes to radio programming and listening:

  - It's the parents responsibility to keep material they find indecent away from their children   87%
  - It's the broadcasters' responsibility to eliminate indecent material from the airwaves so children can't hear it   13%

Every subgroup we looked at gave similar answers. Parents broke 86%/14% to parents' responsibility. Frequent church-goers were 81%/19%. Both Democrats and Republicans, who one might think would have differing opinions about the role of government, agreed with the first statement in similar numbers.

- **Rock radio listeners are suspicious of what's behind the current environment.** A strong majority of respondents says, "The investigation of some radio shows is an overreaction to the Janet Jackson/Super Bowl incident." Just under seven-in-ten agreed with this statement, and this held among all subgroups.

    Further, a strong percentage were suspicious of the role of politicians in this situation:

  o "The crackdown on radio personalities is clearly an election year ploy by politicians"

      * Agree   49%
      * Disagree   23%
      * Neutral   28%

Interestingly, this is the one place where we saw a large difference between Democrats and Republicans. A full 56% of Democrats thought that this is an election year ploy; only 38% of Republicans think so.

- **There is concern of a new "tyranny of the minority."** We asked if "small groups of people are having too much influence over whether radio programs should be fined or punished." Fully three-in-four (75%) agreed with this statement. Here, all subgroups gave responses within a similar range. One of our participants states, "I feel the vocal minority is the only groups that are ever heard from."

    What's more, our Rock radio listening respondents don't approve of the new standard that seems to exist—where if anyone is offended then the show should be fined. The statement that received the most uniform response in our entire survey was to the following:

  o "If even a small group of listeners is offended by a radio show's content, the FCC should take action against it."

        * Agree   5%
        * Disagree   81%
        * Neutral   14%

When one reads the comments that our respondents sent us, this stands out as one of the clear findings: Rock radio listeners feel that by dint of the size of the audience, they prove that these shows are meeting "community standards." The Rock radio listeners are saying, essentially, "50 Million Elvis Fans Can't Be Wrong."

- **It's shocking what Rock listeners want.** One cannot look at these results without coming to one easy conclusion: the people who are consuming shows that the government is investigating as being "indecent" or "offensive" are seldom offended by what they hear.

     The relentless findings that these listeners are not offended by what they hear implies that those who are offended are *not listening.*

Conclusions and Recommendations

Based on this research, the following areas should be considered for further thought and discussion:

1. **"Shock" is often a matter of expectation.** This might explain why half the respondents believe the Janet Jackson incident is an important issue. When they sat down to watch the Super Bowl—an American tradition and a family television experience—they were expecting to see a good football game, and the typical music-oriented halftime show. Instead, they saw something altogether different—a violation of their expectations.

     This might also explain why the drumbeats weren't all that loud when Madonna and Britney Spears liplocked on the MTV Video Music Awards. That event almost always provides a controversial moment or two.

     Had the Janet Jackson/Justin Timberlake "costume malfunction" occurred on "Saturday Night Live," the reactions would have likely been muted. Why? SNL is a show that is famous for over-the-top behavior, and celebrities displaying out-of-character performance.

     When listeners listen to a show like Howard Stern's, however, most know what they're going to hear. The show's content and emphasis are not secret or surprising. There is an implicit "R" rating. Many morning radio shows have a reputation for shaking the tree, generating controversy, and making noise. This is why most of these shows rarely field listener complaints. Listeners are there not despite the controversial content, but *because* of it. On the other hand, those who are likely to be offended by "Shock Jock" antics typically don't listen. It is important also to point out that few teenagers are regular listeners to shows like Stern's.

2. **While there are listeners who feel that some morning radio shows have indeed gone "too far," they overwhelmingly are against the idea of government regulation of their content.** As the analysis

clearly pointed out, an overwhelming majority feels that government control of radio content is not the way to address content issues. They also feel strongly that it is *their* responsibility to ensure their children's media safety when it comes to radio content. Perhaps this is an outgrowth from years of more controversial content on television, be it on cable or broadcast network programs. Whether it's sex, violence, or other adult-oriented programming, parents of young children (who comprise nearly 40% of our respondents) told us they don't feel it is the job of broadcasters to censor programming. This says a great deal about how consumers have been able to handle the many media options that enter their lives. Most have a firm understanding of where there are "danger signs," and act accordingly. Again, this is probably why the Janet Jackson incident was so shocking—it was unexpected for something like it to occur during the Super Bowl.

It is interesting to see that while many people think some radio shows have gone too far—so few people say they are ever offended by what they themselves hear. This implies that in a radio market with so many options, most people are regulating themselves. This might explain why so many people who feel "Shock Jock radio personalities have gone too far" still say that the FCC should not regulate these shows nor do they personally get offended.

3. **Rockers are people, too.** One should not discount this survey as representative of a small faction. As noted in the analysis, 50 million listeners tune in Rock stations every week. In our sample, nearly half were over the age of 35, while over half are either married or living with a partner. Also 38% have children. These listeners are more likely to be exposed to controversial morning programming—and that's precisely the point. Because so much noise on this issue is coming from people and groups that *don't* listen to these shows, it is important to listen to the opinions of those who regularly consume them.

These facts also beg the question about community standards, and how to identify them. If indeed, the "community" for morning shows, or for radio programming in general, is comprised of those who actually listen, this study indicates that most are not surprised by what they hear. And an overwhelming majority tells us emphatically that they know what to do when they hear something that runs afoul of their tastes. This speaks to the issues the FCC is grappling with—defining community standards and acting accordingly.

4. **Research among fans of other formats should be conducted.** To get a full spectrum of how other radio listeners perceive some of the issues discussed in this study, follow-up projects should be conducted among partisans to other radio formats. Again, if the FCC and Congress hope to reflect the will of the people in decisions that have been or will be made, understanding how "end users"—in this case, radio listeners—feel is essential.

5. **Radio should consider adopting a ratings system.** With the superimposed letters that accompany every TV show from "SpongeBob SquarePants" to "N.Y.P.D. Blue," television viewers are given information to help them decide whether to watch, and whether to let

their children watch. If radio broadcasters were willing, airing the audio version of this type of rating system at every commercial break might provide the same type of information—or warning. If, for example, Howard Stern's listeners were clearly notified that the show is "intended for mature audiences," that might go a long way in dissuading listeners for whom his show is not targeted to go elsewhere.

6. **Small groups do not necessarily represent the larger population.** And listeners are very skeptical of the power and influence of certain small interest groups in the current radio regulatory controversy. Three-quarters are concerned about these groups and their potential to affect and impact radio programming. And as we clearly saw when given a choice, 97% of our sample would not contact the FCC if they heard something objectionable. Most understand they have the power to do the one thing that may hurt radio companies and so-called "shock jocks" the most—change stations.

We are hopeful that this unique view of a large number of radio listeners—including many of those who tune in some of these controversial morning shows—will stimulate discussion in both the radio, legislative, and regulatory communities.

POSTSCRIPT

Should Freedom of Speech Ever Be Restricted?

Sometimes it is easy to argue for a specific interpretation of the First Amendment until you personally become offended, or are made to feel uncomfortable by the unrestricted speech of others. Has this ever happened to you? This issue asks us to think not only about what we see and hear, but also what we do. Just as we are led to think about specific contexts for questionable content, we could also think of our own speech in professional, personal, and social environments, and how we might have different personal standards for what we might say at certain times, in specific places.

Considering whether the "audience" has any choice about attending to content is often one of the most critical issues in free speech cases. It may be true that we do often have choices of whether to listen to certain stations, personalities, or content, but sometimes technologies have programs associated with transmission that we don't willingly accept. If you've ever had the experience of computer pop-ups, spam, or unwanted adverting when you use Internet services, you've probably dealt very specifically with the question of unwanted content.

There are many specific legal cases addressing the topics in this issue, such as *Reno v. the American Civil Liberties Union*, 521 U.S. 866 (1997) on the issues behind the short-lived Communications Decency Act; *Trout v. City of Akron*, No. CV-97-115879 (filed Nov. 17, 1997), on Internet pornography and harassment.

Newspapers have also treated these topics seriously over the years, and the titles of these articles give you a good sense of what contexts are addressed. See for example, "Online Jokes Can Lead to Serious Problems; Offensive Messages Might become Basis of Lawsuits," *Cincinnati Enquirer* (Sept. 14, 1998, B15); Michael Stetz, "E-Mail Humor in Eye of Beholder," *South Dakota Union-Tribune* (Nov. 29, 1998, A1); and Rick Anderson, "No Blonde Jokes," *Seattle Weekly* (June 3–9, 1999, 7).

ISSUE 12

Has Industry Regulation Controlled Indecent Media Content?

YES: Rhoda Rabkin, from "Children, Entertainment, and Marketing," *Consumer Research* (June 2002)

NO: James Poniewozik, from "The Decency Police," *Time* (March 28, 2005)

ISSUE SUMMARY

YES: Author Rhoda Rabkin strongly defends the industry system of self-censorship, and feels that any government intervention toward monitoring media content is doomed to failure. She examines a number of media forms and claims that any time there has been a question about content, the industry generally re-packages the products for different audiences and age groups. She advocates for voluntary codes of conduct over federal censorship of entertainment.

NO: James Poniewozik profiles the Parents Television Council's Entertainment Tracking System and discusses parents' complaints about contemporary television content. He discusses the FCC's present position, and some of the steps the television industry has taken to encourage parents to exercise more control over what their children watch (like the V-chip), but finds that the issues of morality and indecency have been addressed inconsistently, resulting in a wider array of viewpoints concerning indecent material.

Since the early days of the Hays Commission in Hollywood film, the controversy over what type of content should be available to different consumers has plagued the relationship of between media industries and the FCC. As Rhoda Rabkin writes, the history of ratings systems were attempts by various industries to self-regulate, and keep the government from exercising what would probably be even stronger controls or issuing penalties concerning questionable media.

While the FCC is structurally the "regulator" of the media, the Commission has never been comfortable in the role of an arbiter of consumer taste.

Ever since the now infamous Janet Jackson/Justin Timberlake "wardrobe malfunction" occurred during the international broadcast of the Super Bowl in 2004, the topic of indecent programming has skyrocketed to a near national obsession. The result of the event was that the FCC began to fine "indecent" episodes on radio and television more than in the past—but at the same time, the definition of "indecency" has remained clouded and problematic.

James Poniewozik focuses specifically on one group of people who monitor media content, and see themselves as judges of culture. When they create a database that proves their point, they complain loudly, and, get the attention of authorities. But at the same time—he questions whether these individuals overstep the boundaries of their mission and assume the role of censors of programs—which may be in conflict with issues related to freedom of expression. He questions whether television has gone too far—or whether the critics of television content have gone too far. And still, it is clear that he agrees that there is more questionable content today than in the past, and therefore, the self-regulation of the industry hasn't worked.

There is no doubt that values change over time, and that different applications of speech styles, fashion, and attitudes toward sexual intimacy or sexual activity have changed throughout history. It might also be fair to say that children are more sophisticated today than they were in earlier years when they might have been more sheltered from media content that could be considered "indecent." At the same time, it is also true that the media have changed. While most of television is no longer "broadcast," the distinctions of what once clarified the difference between "broadcast standards" and "cable standards" have changed. Each assumed a different approach toward audiences, and toward audience choice of content. Similarly, films, radio content, games—all are delivered through more personal media (like the Internet or subscription services) and no longer are viewed as unique forms for mass audiences.

But the changes in social interpretations and the proliferating distribution forms for media actually do make some issues more complicated—like considering who should have access to "indecent" content, and whether the FCC should assume more responsibility, or if groups like the PTC should have a bigger influence over media providers. Exactly who, or what group, should have the authority to dictate cultural trends and media content?

YES

Rhoda Rabkin

Children, Entertainment, and Marketing

Most American parents want to restrict children's access to entertainment glamorizing violence, sex, drug use, or vulgar language. Ideally, purveyors of "mature" entertainment would voluntarily adhere to a code of advertising ethics. Self-regulation would obviate the need for burdensome government regulation. In practice, threats of legal restriction have always played an important role in persuading "morally hazardous" industries to observe codes of conduct and to avoid aggressive marketing to young people. Specifically, self-regulation on the part of makers of entertainment products (for example, movies and comic books) has allowed Americans to shield children and adolescents from "mature" content with minimal recourse to government censorship.

This tradition may, however, be about to change. In April 2001, Sen. Joseph Lieberman (D-Conn.) introduced the Media Marketing Accountability Act (MMAA)—a bill to prohibit the marketing of "adult-rated media," i.e., movies, music, and computer games containing violent or sexual material, to young people under the age of 17. The MMAA would empower the Federal Trade Commission to regulate the advertising of entertainment products to young people. The proposed legislation, if enacted, would inject a federal agency into decisions about the marketing of movies, music, and electronic games—and thereby potentially into decisions about what sorts of movies, music, and games are produced. Lieberman's hearings, well publicized at the time, provided a valuable forum for exposing entertainmentindustry practices to public scrutiny. Even so, the expansion of the federal government's regulatory powers in the area of entertainment and culture is undesirable compared to the traditional, and still-workable, system of industry self-censorship. It is worth noting that the FTC itself, in its testimony before the House Commerce Subcommittee on Telecommunications in July 2001, did not seek regulatory authority over the marketing of entertainment products, and in fact argued, in view of the First Amendment protections enjoyed by these products, that industry self-regulation was the best approach.

Why voluntary ratings?   Even in the 1930s, when America was a much more conservative country (at least in terms of popular culture) than it is today, public outrage over the emphasis on sex and crime in the movies led not to

From *Consumer Research*, June 2002, pp. 14–18, 29. Copyright © 2002 by Rhoda Rabkin. Reprinted by permission.

censorship by the federal government but to a system wherein Hollywood regulated itself. The movie moguls created their own Production Code Administration (PCA) in 1930, supervised first by William Hays and later, in 1934, with more seriousness, by Joseph Breen.

The so-called Hays Code presumed that movies were far more influential than books and that standards of cinematic morality consequently needed to be much stricter than those governing novels and other literature. The code forbade any mention at all of certain controversial topics, such as "illegal drug traffic," "sex perversion," "white slavery," and "miscegenation." The code did allow for the depiction of some crime and some immorality (such as adultery), but stipulated that no presentation should encourage sympathy for illegal or immoral acts.

The American film industry has a long history of self-censorship for the simple reason that offending audiences has never been in its self-interest. Business concern for the bottom line, not moral sensitivity, dictated the willingness of the film industry to regulate itself. For example, during the 1920s and 1930s, Hollywood seldom produced mass market movies with dignified portrayals of black Americans. Scenes of racial mixing on terms of social equality were avoided because they were known to offend white Southern audiences. By the 1940s, however, tentative efforts at more dignified portrayals could be seen, and soon the industry was censoring itself to avoid offending black Americans. The National Association for the Advancement of Colored People's threat of a boycott caused Walt Disney to withdraw *Son of the South* (1946), a partly animated musical based on the Uncle Remus stories. The NAACP found the film's depiction of happy slaves demeaning. For a long time, this feature was available only on a Japanese laserdisc, and even today one can obtain a video version only from Britain or Germany.

The Hays Code assumed that adults and children would and should share the same entertainment at the movie theater. But the code applied only to American-made films, and in the 1950s and '60s, Hollywood found itself losing box office share to "sophisticated" European imports. In 1968, the movie industry abandoned its code of conduct approach and replaced it with a system of age-based ratings devised by Jack Valenti, then (as now) president of the Motion Picture Association of America.

The history of the comic book industry also illustrates the effectiveness of industry self-regulation in shielding the young from "mature" content. Public concern about crime and horror comics in the 1950s led to congressional hearings sponsored by Sen. Estes Kefauver (D-Tenn.) The hearings did not come close to proving that lurid comics caused juvenile delinquency, but in the face of negative publicity, an embarrassed comic book industry opted for self-regulation. The system was voluntary, but the fact that most retailers chose not to display or sell comics without the industry seal of approval meant that objectionable comics soon languished, unable to reach their intended market.

Television greatly reduced the popularity of comic books among children, but the comic book medium did not die. Instead, a new reading audience for "adult" comics came into being. In the 1970s and '80s, as graphic violence became more acceptable in movies and on television, the industry rewrote its code to be more permissive. In September 2001, the largest comic book company, Marvel, released several new lines (Fury, Alias, and U.S. War Machine) completely without code approval. The new titles, which allowed for profanity, sexual situations, and violence, were big sellers. But they are not sold at newsstands, airports, or convenience stores; they are distributed through specialized comic book stores which tend to be patronized by older purchasers (average age: 25).

An age-based classification system has also been employed since 1994 by the video and computer games industry, which has an Entertainment Software Rating Board. The board classifies products as EC (everyone including young children), E (everyone), T (teen), M (mature—may not be suitable for persons under 17), and AO (adults only).

The oppositional music industry   Of all branches of entertainment, the music recording industry has been least responsive to parental concerns and most resistant to self-regulation. The best explanation is that "oppositional" teenage music, although far from the whole of youth-oriented recordings, accounts for a significant proportion of sales. Many music performers who cater to the adolescent audience view themselves as anti-establishment rebels, and this self-image is inseparable from their marketing strategies. Irreverence and defiance seem grown-up and sophisticated to many teenagers.

What comic books were to young people in the 1930s and '40s, popular music is to today's generation of adolescents. Many adults focus on television as a baleful influence on the younger generation, but this is just a sign of how out of touch with teenagers they are. Survey evidence indicates that, in terms of both hours logged and overall meaningfulness, music listening has an importance in the lives of many adolescents far beyond what most parents understand. Parents can easily monitor what their children watch on television, but most adults find it impossible to listen to teenage "noise" on the radio or CD, let alone distinguish among the many varieties, such as album rock, alternative, grunge, world beat, progressive rock, salsa, house, technopop, etc. Yet involvement in a particular subgenre of music is often an important aspect of adolescent social identity. Conversance with popular culture seems to enhance a teenager's social contacts and status, and contrariwise, the young person who remains aloof from pop music is likely to be excluded from many teen peer groups.

One should not assume that music with lyrics featuring profanity, violence, casual sex, drug use, and so on is itself the cause of negative behaviors. Adolescence is a time of life when young people must adjust to startling discoveries about sex, violence, and other potentially troubling aspects of the real world. Just as many adults enjoy watching movies about gangsters, with no inclination toward becoming gangsters themselves, many teenagers find in their music a safe way to satisfy curiosity about the darker aspects of life. The key to understanding this segment of the entertainment industry is that "mature" content actually signifies the opposite, a puerile interest in everything so taboo that parents will not discuss it with their children. The good news is that the teenager who does not die first (or become pregnant or addicted to drugs) almost always grows out of it. On the other hand, undoubtedly some troubled teenagers focus on music with morbid, aggressive, profane, or vulgar lyrics because it seems to legitimize their impulses—in which case the music may indeed reinforce their predispositions. Many different forms of music are popular with teenagers, so preoccupation with "oppositional" music should draw parental attention—which does not mean that underlying problems are addressed by simply prohibiting a form of music.

Movies were controversial from their inception. Comic books were born innocent, but aroused parental concern when they began to exploit themes of violence and sex. Scantily clad women and heads dripping blood came as a shock to adults who had thought comics were about funny talking animals. Similarly, coarse, violent, misogynistic lyrics (to say nothing of offensive references to race, religion, and sexual orientation) prevalent in some youth-oriented music came as a shock to many parents raised on the "outrageous" music of their day, 1950s rock and roll.

Back in 1985, when Tipper Gore, together with several other Washington wives of politicians, founded the Parents Music Resource Center (PMRC), their new organization successfully drew public attention to the problematic content of rock lyrics, particularly those of heavy metal groups with names like Twisted Sister, Black Sabbath, Judas Priest, etc. In the view of the PMRC, it was a straightforward issue of consumers' rights that parents know about references to sex, drugs, alcohol, suicide, violence, and the occult in their children's music. The PMRC proposed that music companies affix warning labels to their products to alert parents about questionable content (for example, V for violence, X for sexually explicit lyrics, O for occult).

Defenders of the music industry predictably accused the PMRC of advocating censorship. The charge was unfair, but the music industry was right that there were real problems with the PMRC approach, which viewed any reference to a topic, regardless of how the topic was treated, as cause for a warning label. Thus, an anti-drug song would call for a warning sticker the same as a song that promoted drug use. This was one of the problems with the Hays Code and the comics code as well. For years, movie executives shied away from *The Man with the Golden Arm,* until Otto Preminger made this powerful anti-drug drama and successfully released it without PCA approval. In 1970, after receiving a letter from the Department of Health, Education, and Welfare, Marvel Comics incorporated an antidrug story into its popular Spider-Man series, but had to release the titles without code office approval.

Another difficulty that arises with attempts at age-classification of music lyrics is the problem of double meanings, which have a long tradition in songwriting. John Denver testified to good effect at the 1985 hearings that his song "Rocky Mountain High" about the beauty of nature had been unfairly banned by some radio stations out of misplaced zeal against drug references. But those responsible for age-ratings will have to face such issues as what Marilyn Manson means when he sings about someone who "powders his nose." Most parents will not have a problem with children hearing Bessie Smith sing: "Nobody in town can bake a sweet jelly-roll like mine"—but of course she meant something by that, too. The enterprise of routing out double-entendres can quickly turn ridiculous, seeming to prove the truth of Lenny Bruce's observation: "There are no dirty words; there are just dirty minds."

In response to the 1985 Commerce Committee hearings, and because of a wave of local prosecutions (utilizing charges of obscenity) against retailers, in 1990, the Recording Industry Association of America (RIAA) announced that it had designed a "Parental Advisory/Explicit Lyrics" label, with a distinctive logo. But whereas the movie industry's trade association, the MPAA, rates individual movies, the RIAA created no guidelines or recommendations and left the use of the labels to the discretion of the individual recording companies. "This consistent reference to parents is offensive. We are all parents," said RIAA president Hilary Rosen. "I don't want to tell parents whether Chuck Berry is singing about his ding-a-ling."

The PMRC was disturbed by the lyrics of heavy metal rock groups, but many parents soon would be concerned by the violence and sexual vulgarity in a new form of teenage music: hiphop, or as it is sometimes (though not accurately) called, rap music. And with this new form of music, the question of morality in music became entwined in questions about racism and double standards.

Sen. Lieberman did not invite Russell Simmons, a longtime hip-hop entrepreneur and chairman of the Hip-Hop Summit Action Network, to testify at his hearings. But Simmons attended anyway and managed to speak. Simmons complained that Lieberman had unfairly targeted hip-hop as objectionable. In the *New York Times,* he wrote: "hip-hop is an important art form, really the first new genre of music to emerge since rock and roll. . . . To deny its power and artistic merit in an attempt to silence it is downright dangerous." Criticism of violent, profane, and vulgar music lyrics, Simmons implied, betrays unconscious racism because black performers are the main creators of "gangsta rap" and hip-hop.

Simmons was wrong to equate Lieberman's proposed legislation with censorship but still had a point worth considering: Many parents upset by hip-hop would not be similarly disturbed by traditional songs, such as "Whiskey in the Jar," an Irish song that celebrates drinking or "Tom Dooley," a Civil War-era song (which became a popular hit for the Kingston Trio in the early 1960s) that recounts a murder. Of course, some parents would be equally disturbed by these songs (just as some are offended by the "occult" in a children's classic such as *The Wizard of Oz*). Many parents believe that evil has enormous inherent attractiveness, so that any depiction of wicked conduct is morally dangerous. But should the law require the makers of all such recordings and videos to affix a warning sticker and submit their advertising plans to federal supervision?

There is some basis for optimism that the value of voluntary labeling has become apparent even to the music industry. A hiphop summit held in July 2001 brought recording company executives together with established black organizations, such as the NAACP. The three-day conference (at which Minister Louis Farrakhan spoke and urged the musicians to display more "responsibility") led to considerable reflection within the hiphop community. Industry representatives at the summit agreed on a uniform standard for the "Parental Advisory" label, which should be one size, plainly displayed, and not removable, on the cover art of the recordings and visible on all advertising as well. The RIAA continues to insist, however (as noted critically in the FTC's December 2001 report), on its right to market labeled music aggressively to young people.

The tobacco model   As it turns out, the music industry was right to argue that any concession to parental interest in labeling would stimulate additional demands for regulation of entertainment. One of the most well-respected citizen groups concerned with media, the National Institute on Media and the Family (NIMF), has paid considerable attention to media ratings and is dissatisfied with the current system. The NIMF, along with other children's health advocates, has argued for an independent ratings oversight committee and a unified media ratings system to cover movies, television programs, music, and games.

Some politicians and children's "advocates" seem entranced by the prospect of identifying the entertainment industry in the public mind as the successor to Big Tobacco as a threat to the health of young people. In the late 1990s, Sen. Sam Brownback (R-Kan.) helped persuade the American Medical Association to assert a causal connection between violent entertainment and individual acts of aggressiveness and violence. In fact, an impressive list of highly respectable organizations, such as the National Institute of Mental Health, the National Academy of Sciences, the American Psychological Association, and the American Academy of Pediatrics, are on record agreeing that exposure to media violence presents a risk of harmful effects on children. These claims in turn help support litigation that seeks tort damages from the producers of violent entertainment. For example, families of victims of the Paducah, Ky. school shooting filed lawsuits against entertainment companies on the grounds that their products created a mindset that led to murder. Thus far, lawsuits of this nature have been dismissed in court, but then, so were tobacco suits—until they weren't.

Many essentially moral concerns tend to be packaged and presented in terms of concern for danger to "children's health." And there is no shortage of experts whose research alleges that violence (and sometimes sex) in entertainment presents proven health hazards analogous to cigarette smoking. According to Harvard researcher, Dr. Michael Rich: "The findings of hundreds of studies, analyzed as a whole, showed that the strength of the relationship between television exposure and aggressive behavior is greater than that of calcium intake and bone mass, lead ingestion and lower IQ, condom nonuse and sexually acquired HIV, or environmental tobacco smoke and lung cancer, all associations that clinicians accept and on which preventive medicine is based." Of course, some experts have come to the opposite conclusion about the effects of media on behavior. The September 2000 FTC report acknowledged that there are abundant studies on both sides of the issue.

It is possible that, even if passed, the Media Marketing Accountability Act would be found unconstitutional in the first federal court to hear a challenge to it. In one recent case, *Lorillard v. Reilly* (2001), which involved efforts by Massachusetts to restrict the advertising of tobacco products, the Supreme Court stated that retailers and manufacturers have a strong First Amendment interest in "conveying truthful information about their products to adults." Supreme Court decisions in recent years have tended to expand protection for commercial speech, even when the advertising in question is for products recognized as presenting moral hazards.

"Marketing to children" is not a clear, unambiguous concept. Many adults watch children's programming, such as "The Wonderful World of Disney," and more than two-thirds of the audience for MTV consists of viewers aged 18 or older. The FTC objected to the industry practice of showing movie trailers for R-rated movies before G- and PG-rated movies. But as Valenti testified, "the R rating does not mean 'Adult-Rated'—that is the province of the NC-17 rating. Children are admitted to R-rated movies if accompanied by a parent or adult guardian. The rating system believes that only parents can make final decisions about what they want their children to see or not to see." A Pennsylvania statute banning the practice of showing previews for R-rated features at G- and PG-rated movies was ruled unconstitutional by a federal court. Some industry executives responded to complaints about movie trailers for R-rated movies by asking where the regulation of advertising would stop: Should R-rated movies be removed from newspaper ads? But Jack Valenti eventually responded to congressional criticism by promulgating new MPAA guidelines, including: "Each company will request theater owners not to show trailers advertising films rated R for violence in connection with the exhibition of its G-rated films. In addition, each company will not attach trailers for films rated R for violence on G-rated movies on videocassettes or DVDs containing G-rated movies." This suggests that parent groups have enough clout to persuade the entertainment industry that it should voluntarily refrain from advertising R-rated movies in certain venues.

Valenti, representing the movie industry at the Senate hearings on the Media Marketing Accountability Act, argued convincingly that the proposed legislation would likely jeopardize the voluntary ratings system on which the FTC regulatory regime is supposed to be based. As Valenti noted, "the bill immunizes those producers who do not rate their films." "Why," he asked, "would sane producers continue to submit their films for voluntary ratings when they could be subjected to fines of $11,000 per day per violation?" A good question. What seems likely is that Lieberman's approach requires the creation of a different, compulsory ratings system staffed not by unaccountable, anonymous industry insiders but by "members of the entertainment industry, child development and public health professionals, social scientists and parents," as one witness recommended.

If children's "health" is the primary concern, there is no reason to expect such an independent board to stop with rating entertainment for violent content when there are so many other "threats" to the health of young people and so many pressure groups concerned with such health. What would certainly follow would be calls for adding a ratings category to restrict the depiction of tobacco and alcohol products. There would also be pressure to address other social problems as well, such as eating disorders among teenage girls allegedly promoted by unrealistically slender actresses. Health-oriented raters might consider "safe sex" scenes with condoms more youth-appropriate than sexual depictions without them. Racial, religious, and sexual stereotyping also present a threat to the health of children, to be dealt with accordingly.

In Britain and Canada, where age rating has legal force, all kinds of issues, such as cruelty to animals, racial slurs, and even "presentation of controversial lifestyles" can be grounds for restriction. At least in those countries, local authorities have the final say, an important check on the system lacking in Lieberman's plan to give the FTC regulatory authority.

The bull in the (video) shop   Representatives of the entertainment industry have deployed two serious arguments against the MMAA: first, that violence in entertainment does not cause young people to behave violently; and second, that the proposed legislation excessively empowers government to control speech and art through control over the marketing of entertainment.

Entertainment executives are right that media messages have a complex, indirect relationship to behavior. Consequently, our society wisely vests control over the entertainment choices of young people in their parents using common sense, not in a clumsy, heavy-handed government bureaucracy relying on the latest, and soon to be controverted, social science research. A sense of proportion is needed if we are to reinforce parental authority without attempting to supplant it. Self-regulation is a system in which all citizens assume civic responsibility. The MMAA, by contrast, assumes that young people are helpless victims of the advertising and media to which they are exposed. Much of the rhetoric supporting the legislation is uncomfortably reminiscent of the campaigns directed at tobacco products, junk foods, and guns. One collateral result is likely to be encouragement for lawyers to sue entertainment companies.

What cannot be achieved by the heavy hand of the law can be achieved by industry self-regulation—but this requires the cooperation of the regulated. Lieberman's bill does not seem well thought out. It would punish companies that rate their material, but no law can compel the companies to rate their material satisfactorily in the first place. What is involved here obviously calls for much more complex judgments than, for example, listing the alcohol content of a beverage or the nicotine content of a cigarette. If the music or movie industry resists rating because it leads to punitive fines, the next step would have to be rating by quasi-official "independent" boards whose judgments would then be utilized by FTC regulators. Self-censorship would give way to federal regulation. Congress will have performed its usual sorry trick—enact a vague regulatory regime and then settle back as lobbying interest groups funnel money to Washington politicians in hope of gaining favorable treatment.

The MMAA empowers the FTC only to regulate advertising to young people, so the legislation would not truly establish a system of federal censorship over entertainment. But it would bring us much closer to such a system than we have ever come in our history. Averting this outcome is in everyone's interest, but the entertainment industries themselves have the greatest responsibility to do so—through voluntary observance of codes of conduct acceptable to American parents.

The Decency Police

The parents television council believes that too much prime-time TV is indecent. So indecent that it never misses a show. In the group's Alexandria, Va., offices, five analysts sit at desks with a VCR, a TV and a computer. They tape every hour of prime-time network TV, and a lot of cable. CSI. The Apprentice. God help them, even Reba. And they watch. Every filthy second.

This afternoon, PTC analyst Kristine Looney is sitting in her cubicle, whose bookshelf holds volumes by Ann Coulter and G. Gordon Liddy. Headphones over her ears, hand on the remote, she is watching the March 13 episode of Crossing Jordan. Suddenly, she hits the pause button. Why? "'Damn,'" she says. "And also they were talking about drugs." Looney, 25, transcribes the quote-" Damn. The second suitcase is still out there"—and it goes into the Entertainment Tracking System (ETS), the PTC's database on more than 100,000 hours of programming. "We track even those minor swears," says Looney's supervisor, Melissa Caldwell, "because it's a way of tracking trends." The ETS, in the words of PTC executive director Tim Winter, logs "every incident of sexual content, violence, profanity, disrespect for authority and other negative content." The ETS analysts don't monitor premium channels, which is just as well, because an episode of *Deadwood* would presumably crash the system. The ETS is thoroughly indexed by theme— "Threesome," "Masturbation," "Obscene Gesture." With it, the group can detect patterns of sleaze and curses and spotlight advertisers who buy on naughty shows. It is a meticulously compiled, cross-referenced, multimegabyte Alexandria Library of smut.

The Entertainment Tracking System—it sounds like something the Pentagon would have if we had fought a war to depose Viacom's Sumner Redstone instead of Saddam Hussein. And in a way, the ETS is the nerve center of a war: the War on Indecency. It is a war that had a shot seen round the world—Janet Jackson at the 2004 Super Bowl—but had been simmering much longer. It is a war with strange allies and enemies: it pits free-market conservatives against family-values conservatives, free-speech liberals against Big Government liberals, and a normally pro-business Congress and White House against megacorporations. (Among them is TIME's parent company, Time Warner, which owns a major cable business, the WB broadcast network and several cable channels, including HBO and TNT.) A war that has TV programmers scrambling for cover—or at least pixelation—and has led

Howard Stern to decamp from his broadcast-radio shock show for a satellite-radio gig in January.

And that war is only getting hotter. Over the past year, a reawakened Federal Communications Commission (FCC), prodded by values activists, has rebuked or fined broadcast networks including CBS, Fox and NBC for flesh and *F* bombs. Now Congress is gearing up to give the FCC stronger weapons: far steeper fines and possibly the power to regulate decency on cable and satellite radio. (That means you, Howard.) George W. Bush last week named a new FCC chairman, Kevin Martin, who talks even tougher on decency than the departed chair, Michael Powell. To emboldened decency monitors, this is a chance to tame an out-of-control pop culture in which drunk *Real World* housemates have three-ways in hot tubs and shock jocks broadcast live sex acts on air. To broadcasters—and many viewers—it's the censorial hysteria that's out of control, as when Fox, in a rerun of *Family Guy,* chose to remove the bare bottom of the character Stewie, who is 1) a baby and 2) a cartoon. From Washington to Hollywood to your living room, the air war is in full effect.

On the Front Lines

It is a heady time to be the man who commands the ETS, and a busy one. L. Brent Bozell spun off the Parents Television Council in 1995 from his Media Research Center, a watchdog group that monitors media bias. The cop drama *NYPD Blue* had recently debuted to controversy (and huge ratings), and, as Bozell puts it, "suddenly it became artistic to see Dennis Franz's rear end." In 1998 the PTC launched a membership drive that Bozell says netted 500,000 members. (The group now claims a million.) "We awoke a sleeping giant," he says.

The Jackson incident gave the giant a hotfoot. Before that—despite Powell's reputation as Howard Stern's Inspector Javert—the group found the former chair unresponsive to its concerns. ("I don't want the government as my nanny," Powell said in 2001.) Winter, a lifelong Democrat who heads the PTC's Los Angeles and Alexandria offices (to Hollywood, he's the good cop to Bozell's bad cop), says, "We embarrass the FCC. We prove that they're not doing their job, and they are embarrassed."

Almost single-handedly, the PTC has become a national clearinghouse for, and arbiter of, decency (though other groups, like the Rev. Donald Wildmon's American Family Association, remain active in the cause as well). It has focused heavily on advertisers; for instance, it claims to have driven away 50 sponsors from FX's edgy *Nip/Tuck* and *The Shield*. It offers program-content reviews and other tools for parents, who, Bozell stresses, have the chief responsibility for their kids. "It's not as simple as 'It's all Hollywood's fault,'" he says. And the PTC has harnessed technology: besides the ETS, it says it has an e-mail list of 125,000 "online members," and its website offers complaint form letters and streaming video clips of TV episodes so that visitors can watch, be offended and click to zap off a letter.

There's plenty out there to offend. TV's mores have become looser in just a few years. In 1999 it was shocking for Fox's sitcom *Action* to use obscenities that were bleeped out. Now the same words are bleeped routinely (often barely) all over network TV—and go unbleeped on basic-cable networks like FX and ESPN, let alone Showtime and HBO. In an episode of Fox's since-canceled *Keen Eddie,* three men enlist a hooker to arouse a horse to extract semen from him. The PTC recently protested an episode of NBC's *Medium* in which the police burst into a bedroom to find a suspect in bed—with a two-week-old corpse.

As that recent example shows, it sometimes seems as if the Janet Jackson aftermath changed very little. It has—but in scattershot and inconsistent ways. In November, 65 ABC affiliates refused to air the uncut war movie *Saving Private Ryan* because of its profanity—although it had run without incident twice before. "It's a shame people couldn't see this patriotic film," said former Democratic presidential candidate General Wesley Clark, criticizing the FCC for waiting until February to rule that the film was not indecent. "They deserve an opportunity to see as much of the unvarnished truth as possible." (Even the PTC, incidentally, didn't object to *Ryan's* airing.) In February PBS advised member stations to air a bowdlerized version of a *Frontline* documentary about the war in Iraq because the uncut version also had soldiers swearing.

In the March 7 episode of the sitcom *Two and a Half Men,* creator Chuck Lorre inserted a statement, which flashed onscreen for a second, protesting that CBS had made him trim a scene that showed the naked back of a young woman—a common enough sight on crime dramas and, say, shampoo commercials. "My problem," he wrote, "is knowing that I work in an industry, or perhaps I should say a culture, that is more comfortable showing a dead naked body than a live one." Says David Nevins, president of Imagine Entertainment Television, which produces *24* and *Arrested Development:* "The climate has definitely changed in a significant way, and the networks are under enormous pressure."

But though the PTC has a loud voice, just whom they speak for is debatable. Last year, in response to viewer complaints, the FCC levied its largest TV fine ever, $1.2 million, against Fox for an episode of the reality show *Married by America,* which featured strippers covered in whipped cream. The commission said the broadcast had generated 159 letters of complaint. Jeff Jarvis, a former TV critic who writes the blog BuzzMachine.com, filed a Freedom of Information Act request to see the letters. Because of multiple mailings, the letters actually came from just 23 people, 21 of whom used a form.

In other words, three people composing letters of complaint precipitated a seven-digit fine. "The problem," argues Jarvis, "is that the media swallows [the data] whole, and it takes on a life of its own. There was no flood of letters. It was a trickle." The PTC strongly denies trying to create an illusory mass of outraged citizens. Of the 1.1 million complaints filed with the FCC last year, Winter says, only about 230,000 came from the PTC.

The larger question is, Do the PTC and other decency campaigners simply want the freedom to find safe zones for their kids? Or do they want to bring you into the safe zone too—if necessary, by cleaning up shows that you have chosen to watch? The slogan that greets visitors to the PTC's website is "Because our children are watching." But for some decency advocates, the problem is also that *someone else's* children are watching—it's the problem, which both liberal and conservative parents experience, of being exposed to "secondhand smut." Jack Thompson is a Coral Gables, Fla., attorney who filed a series of complaints against Stern that resulted in a $495,000 fine against Clear Channel Communications. A decency hard-liner—he thinks shock jock Stern should be in jail—Thompson doesn't buy the argument that parents should just turn off the TV or radio. "It isn't necessarily what we keep our kids from," he says, "but our inability to keep other kids from certain material, who then share it with our kids in school and elsewhere. It's like dumping toxic waste in a playground."

Bringing in the Law

There is no shortage of volunteers to legislate decency. A bill that overwhelmingly passed in the House would increase indecency fines to $500,000 (from $32,500 for stations and $11,000 for individual performers). A Senate bill introduced last week by John D. Rockefeller, Democrat of West Virginia, and Kay Bailey Hutchison, Republican of Texas, also ups the ante to $500,000, plus would bring cable and satellite under FCC purview, though vaguely. Yet most frightening to media executives are the warnings of Senator Ted Stevens, Republican of Alaska and the powerful chairman of the Commerce Committee, that he may push his own legislation to curb cable. "Eighty-five percent of the people watching televisions today are watching through cable, but they think they're watching local TV," he says. "They have to have some protection."

If the laws pass, the FCC's Martin is likely to be aggressive with them. In the past, he criticized some decisions during Powell's tenure as too lenient— such as not fining Fox for the horse prostitute liaison on *Keen Eddie*—and called for fines not only to be stiffer but also to be assessed "per utterance," not per incident (one unbleeped Dave Chappelle routine, and you're in the poorhouse). He also wants to restore the "family hour" to prime time. Decency advocates are big fans. "He can send the signal that the agency has to get serious," says Bozell. And—*Nip/Tuck* viewers, take heed—he has spoken favorably about regulating cable and satellite to "level the playing field."

Is that possible? The reason the government can regulate broadcast TV and radio at all is that it owns the air. The FCC licenses frequencies on the airwaves, a public resource. In return, broadcasters must meet public-service requirements and obey decency rules, which ban "language or material that, in context, depicts or describes, in terms patently offensive as measured by contemporary community standards for the broadcast medium, sexual or excretory activities or organs." That's why the FCC can police four-letter words on NBC but not in a movie or this magazine. (Pornography is different, because the law distinguishes "obscenity" from "indecency.")

Cable TV doesn't use those airwaves. It transmits over cables laid and paid for by private industry. So it's questionable whether any extension of the FCC's powers to cable would be constitutional. Likewise, many legal experts think the fact that satellite radio requires a subscription fee would make it tough for regulations there to stand up in court. "I'd love to see cable and satellite covered," says conservative Senator Sam Brownback, Republican of Kansas. "But I just think you have limitations."

Yet the mere threat of legislation can create a chill. Law professor Robert O'Neil, director of the Thomas Jefferson Center for the Protection of Free Expression, calls this "regulation by raised eyebrow. If it goes too far, it gets out of hand. Then the government is at risk of acting beyond its constitutional powers." And that chill can have effects far beyond what the FCC is empowered to do directly. Says *Shield* creator Shawn Ryan: "There will be things that we will never see, that are victims of this mind-set. Nobody is really brave enough to take away the shows that people love. But it will have an effect on shows that the networks look at and decide aren't even worth producing."

Even more daunting to broadcasters is uncertainty. They say they have no idea what is acceptable now, and the FCC won't spell it out. Contrary to popular belief—and George Carlin's seven-words-you-can't-say-on-TV routine—there are no stone tablets to clarify that thou shalt never utter this word or show that body part. The FCC will rule on indecency after the fact—sometimes twice. At the 2003 Golden Globes, singer Bono of U2 called his band's winning Best Original Song from a Film "f__ing brilliant." In October 2003, the FCC ruled that the expletive was not indecent, because Bono was not describing a sex act. The following March, the commission reversed itself, though it did not fine NBC. After the ABC affiliates passed on *Saving Private Ryan*—which uses the same expletive in the same nonliteral way—the commission said the film was not indecent because of its critical praise and wartime context.

"You don't know where the line is," says John Ridley, a novelist and a TV and film writer who has written for cable and broadcast, "and that's what's scaring people." To better draw the line, industry sources tell TIME, broadcasters are considering a court test case—possibly even trying to overturn the 1978 ruling that defined the FCC's indecency standard, on the grounds of inconsistency. "There are two difficulties" that the FCC faces, says a broadcast executive. "One is that extreme [regulatory] positions are going to run into constitutional problems. The second is inconsistent and vague rulings are going to run into constitutional problems." Another strategy for networks is to argue that the existence of the V chip—a device, mandated on all television sets 13 in. or larger manufactured since 2000, that allows parents to block content considered suspect—demonstrates that there are less intrusive means of controlling content. The PTC counters that the V chip is not ubiquitous or widely used enough and that the voluntary ratings system it draws on is faulty.

The FCC also has the power to make regulatory decisions—from mergers to ownership rules—worth billions to media companies. That alone can be powerful incentive to self-censor. One proposal by Senator Stevens—and a longtime goal of the PTC's—is to make cable companies offer subscribers a bundle of channels rated according to their content. They could either buy channels separately or choose only a family-friendly "tier" of channels. That would be a boon for viewers who don't want to subsidize MTV's spring-break parties, but media companies claim it would raise prices and drive smaller channels out of business.

In any event, it would roil a very profitable business. And so last week Disney broke ranks with its media brethren and backed FCC regulation of cable—as an alternative to Congress imposing à la carte offerings. (Disney's cable holdings include tamer channels like ABC Family and The Disney Channel, but its ESPN often lets profanities fly.) Some broadcast executives, meanwhile, have called for decency control over cable so that they could better compete with cable channels. The greatest hope for those who want to extend the state's power over media may be in the fact that most executives would rather lose freedom than money.

So What's Filth?

Given the postelection focus on "moral values," indecency has been even more oversimplified as a red-state vs.-blue-state issue. But it doesn't break neatly along Republican and Democrat lines. It is one of the few issues capable of uniting, on one side, Rush Limbaugh and Howard Stern, and on the other, New York Senator Hillary Rodham Clinton and Pennsylvania Senator Rick Santorum. If the FCC is strengthened, Limbaugh has argued, what happens when a future Democratic Administration decides that conservative talk radio is violence-inciting "hate speech"? Meanwhile, earlier this month, Clinton took the stage with Santorum and Brownback to decry indecency in pop culture and call for a federal study of its effect on children. The issue is even thorny for Bush, who knows his debt to social conservatives but told C-SPAN in January that parents are "the first line of responsibility. They put an off button [on] the TV for a reason."

Granted, conservatives and liberals tend to be offended by different things. Conservatives tend to see a culture glorifying promiscuity and drug use. Liberals get more concerned about violence and degradation of women. The right sees the machinations of amoral Hollywood. The left sees soulless megabusinesses dropping their standards to court the coveted 18- to 34-year-old male demographic. "Obviously, you have an incentive to program material that will appeal directly to that market," says Michael Copps, a Democratic FCC commissioner, who argues that the rise of indecency and megamergers are related. "This whole issue of media consolidation goes not only to the quality of entertainment that we get but the very core of civic dialogue and the collective decisions we make as a democracy." But members of both camps are concerned about a media market in which whatever sells goes.

James Steyer, a law professor at Stanford University, describes himself as "a progressive parent who lives in San Francisco." That didn't stop him from founding in 2003 Common Sense Media, which runs a website that rates TV shows, video games, music, books and websites for age appropriateness. "I'm no right-winger or religious ideologue," he says. "This is a nonpartisan issue." Kathleen Richardson of Des Moines, Iowa, is executive secretary of the Iowa Freedom of Information Council and the mother of three kids, 12, 16 and 18. "Here I'm promoting free speech and the values of the First Amendment professionally," she says, "and yet it drives me crazy that my kids are swimming around in this pop culture that is becoming a sort of sewer."

But it's not only politicians and activists who experience cognitive dissonance on indecency—so do everyday citizens. They want protection from smut yet don't use the V chip. They talk about competing with pop culture to parent their children yet give kids TVs and computers in their bedrooms. They rail against sex and violence in entertainment, yet—as a group, anyway—reward it and punish the alternatives. The most wholesome new network show of last fall was CBS's *Clubhouse,* a sweet drama about a teenage bat boy for a baseball team, executive-produced by Mel (*The Passion of the Christ*) Gibson. It was canceled by November. *Desperate Housewives* is still going strong.

In an exclusive TIME poll, more than half the respondents say there's too much violence, profanity and sex on TV, but most say they aren't personally offended by it and don't want that content banned. Slightly more than half believe the FCC should be stricter, but 66% say it overreacted to Janet Jackson. Yet what may seem like confusion—or just hypocrisy—may also be something too often missing from the indecency debate: subtlety.

When you talk to people about what bothers them in pop culture—if anything does—they tend not to talk about discrete, FCC-finable offenses. They talk about video games, ads, innuendos, magazine covers—things that the FCC doesn't police or that are so nebulous and environmental as to be unpoliceable in a free society. They don't want absolute rules. They want boundaries: they just want to know where the cultural deep end and the kiddie pool are.

In the classic definition, a conservative is a liberal who has been mugged. Today some people feel mugged by pop culture. It's not just watching a football game and getting flashed by a singer's breast. It's the unwanted porn e-mail or the hamburger commercial with a woman lasciviously riding a mechanical bull. It's watching a sports program with your young child and hearing the host blurt, "A_____!" Tim Tutt, a single, third-grade teacher in Des Moines, calls himself "a liberal, anticensorship person." But he was furious when he visited a website for his students and up popped an ad with a sexy blond. "Boy, did I lose control of the class for a moment," he says. "Then I felt this conservative rage within me—'Why was that necessary?'" People care, in other words, about context as well as content.

Who Sets the Standard?

In indecency then, context is king. The PTC and the FCC say it was not indecent to air *Saving Private Ryan* on network TV—even though children might be watching during prime time—because of the context: soldiers swear in war. But of course, mobsters swear too. So could *The Sopranos,* just as critically praised, air on NBC? Can only good guys drop the *F* bomb? Indecency activists often cite the dictum of Supreme Court Justice Potter Stewart on obscenity: "I know it when I see it." But who knows indecency, and what do they see?

Consider the Feb. 17 episode of *CSI.* A form complaint letter available at the PTC website describes the episode, and it's icky stuff. The plot is about infantilism, a sexual fetish that involves adults wearing diapers and suckling at women's breasts. But the letter includes a curious argument: "complainant urges the Commission to take notice of the high ratings for this episode of *CSI* ratings [sic]—reportedly viewed in 30.72 million households. Given its relatively early broadcast time [9 p.m. E.T.], it was without question viewed by millions of children."

That's one way of interpreting the number. Here's another: more than 30 million people watched the Feb. 17 episode of *CSI,* a show that has been on the air since 2000. It is probably the most gruesome, explicit drama on broadcast TV—and it is the single most popular. Did all those people tune in by accident? When the greatest plurality of viewers choose to watch a show they know to be graphic, can that show be beyond the pale? Or does *complainant* simply not like where the pale is nowadays? Robert Acosta, a police officer from Florida who worries about protecting his 6-year-old son from dirty TV, expresses that sentiment plaintively: "We have to go back to the '50s. The world is going crazy. The '50s was a great time." Perhaps decency advocates mourn not only the moral standards of the '50s but also the social consensus. Opinion about today's balkanized media is as fragmented as their audience. So who should set the standard? Parents of kids under 18? (They make up only 36% of U.S. households.) Senior citizens? That gay guy with the nipple ring?

In reality, they each do, in their own home. And it's likely to stay that way, however the current skirmishes play out, as media evolve and technology advances beyond attempts to corral it. Digital video recorders like TiVo, for instance, may make the concept of family hour moot, since their users can watch programs whenever they want. In the meantime, it wouldn't hurt for decency proponents to recognize that different people define "values" differently, for media companies to take more seriously the genuine concerns of their customers who feel ambushed by their products and for all of us to recognize that making choices is a right for others and a responsibility for ourselves. There's a word for that kind of attitude, right? Oh, yeah: decent.

POSTSCRIPT

Has Industry Regulation Controlled Indecent Media Content?

The history of questionable media content and the desire of some groups to exercise control over content is a long, bumpy history. Even different constituents in the FCC have trouble finding one answer to the myriad problems of questionable content. While extreme cases of content are easier to deal with, many of the subjects discussed in these selections show that even word choice or suggestion might be problematic in some contexts. And, while more media industries have attempted to use ratings systems to attempt to control access to material that may be inappropriate for some audiences, the number of problems seem to grow.

Perhaps the "poster boy" for questionable content is Howard Stern, who had a very successful radio show and television show, until after the Super Bowl incident of 2004, when the FCC began issuing more fines for indecent content than ever before. Stern ultimately decided to leave broadcast radio and opt for a satellite service, which is unregulated by the FCC, and where he would have greater control over the content of his programs. Whether Stern's popularity and the power of satellite broadcasting is successful, still remains to be seen.

Once again, the issues become even more complicated when we consider how often children have access to media content that may not be supervised. Probably the best answer might be to have the parents control what their children see and hear, and discuss the content with them. Unfortunately, that easy answer is often very difficult to ensure.

If you are interested in how the controversy over "appropriate" children's programming has fared, you might want to read *The Faces of Television Media: Teaching Violence, Selling to Children*, by Edward L. Palmer and Brian M. Young (Mahwah, NJ: Erlbaum, 2003), or *Saturday Morning Censors: Television Regulation Before the V-Chip*, by Heather Hendershot (Durham, NC: Duke University Press, 1998).

Another interesting approach toward understanding the role of outside groups and the way they influence media content through their own actions can be found in John A. Fortunato's book, *Making Media Content: The Influence of Consitutency Groups on Mass Media,* (Mahwah, NJ: Erlbaum, 2005).

ISSUE 13

Is the Use of Video News Releases Bad Journalism?

YES: Trudy Lieberman, from "Epidemic," *Columbia Journalism Review (*March/April 2007*)*

NO: Public Relations Society of America, from "Video News Releases: Comment of Public Relations Society of America to FCC," *Response to Request for Comment, Federal Communications Commission* (June 24, 2005)

ISSUE SUMMARY

Trudy Lieberman investigates the use of video news releases (VNRs) in newscasts that are really marketing endeavors by hospitals and health companies. Who is in control of health news? Lieberman worries that newsrooms substitute "feel good" VNRs for in-depth reporting. Can reliance on the slickly produced packages and profitable relationships formed threaten journalistic independence? In their Comment to the Federal Communications Commission, the Public Relations Society of America (PRSA) defends the production of VNRs and argues against imposing additional restrictions on their use. PRSA argues that their current code of ethics is sufficient, and that PR professionals strongly object to the use of VNRs when sponsors or financial interests are not fully disclosed.

You've seen them, although you may not have recognized them. Video news releases (VNRs) are produced by public relations professionals for government, corporations, and public interest groups. Public relations professionals prepare a taped news story, which is made available to local stations for use on the air. Usually the piece resembles a typical broadcast news package. Sometimes a national congressperson will prepare a VNR on an important issue, often designed to look like a press conference or interview. Sometimes a medical firm may produce a story on a recent breakthrough medicine or treatment. Lieberman finds the potential for hidden relationships and poor journalism troublesome.

Should such stories ever be used? One point of view says no: News prepared to promote a certain point of view does not belong in newscasts, which should be operating under standards of fairness and accuracy. VNRs are persuasive documents, advocating a certain point of view, and thus are not true journalism. Thus, these critics ague, VNRs are deceptive. Others would argue that VNRs are appropriate as long as there is complete disclosure; they see them as analogous to the press release long used in print newsrooms. This is the position of PRSA, the professional association of public relations practioners. Yet many broadcasts do not provide full disclosure. The Center for Media and Democracy (CMD) in April 2006, followed newsrooms' use of 36 VNRs. They found 98 separate instances where these were "actively disguised" (i.e., the source was not attributed) by 77 stations. In September 2007, the FCC fined Comcast $16,000 for violation of FCC rules that require sponsorship identification when presenting matter in return for money, service, or other valuable consideration in the case of four VNRs that they aired.

In pursuing an answer to these issues, Lieberman investigates the relationship between newsrooms and hospitals. They are trying to attract patients, particularly for elective procedures that are profitable for the hospital. Local news is receiving money or other considerations for these "product placements," and thus is unwilling to harm this profitable relationship. Does this profit-centered news relationship put journalistic standards in danger? Lieberman certainly says yes.

The PRSA document defends the VNR as useful information, controversial only when they are used inappropriately by the media. Ironically, it was production of VNRs by government agencies that focused public attention on the issue. The promotion of new prescription drug laws for the elderly and the contract with columnist and talk show host Armstrong Williams to produce ads and to promote Bush's No Child Left Behind (NCLB) law in his TV and radio shows and newspaper column came under public scrutiny. Called by the Government Accountability Office "covert propaganda," this scandal prompted congressional and FCC examination of current regulation concerning VNRs. Williams ultimately was fined by the Justice Department and lost his newspaper column. This is the context in which the PRSA Comment was made to the FCC.

Is this simply a problem of media behavior, or are there ethical obligations beyond those called for by the PRSA that we might wish to impose on the production and use of such material? Public relations professionals must guide the accuracy of their VNRs, thus providing information that could be useful to the public. Their behavior should be in line with the PRSA Member Code of Ethics. Media organizations must disclose the source of the package to their audiences. Media organizations should adopt a similar code of ethics concerning the ethical use of VNRs. These organizations, therefore, can self regulate. Lieberman challenges us to take the question to a second, institutional level. Does the use of prepackaged information undercut journalistic standards? Should stations be willing to use on their air material that they have not investigated and created themselves? Should those companies with money to produce exciting news packages be allowed special access to the airwaves? Does the access granted to commercial VNRs displace other more important news stories? Most importantly, will such relationships influence the tone of future journalistic stories about that organization, particularly when a profitable relationship has been developed?

Epidemic

When 19 thousand viewers tuned in to the 7 a.m. news on KTBC-TV, the local Fox channel in Austin, Texas, in mid-January, they heard the anchor, Joe Bickett, introduce a story about a new electronic rehabilitation system for injured kids. "Sharon Dennis has more on that," Bickett said. Dennis then described how a lively fifteen-year-old named Merrill, who had sprained her ankle, was getting better thanks to the computer-guided rehab program that Cleveland Clinic researchers are calling "the world's first virtual-only gym."

The professional-looking story had that gee-whiz feel so typical of TV health news, explaining how the technology was making it easier for patients to get back to normal. It ended with "Sharon Dennis reporting."

Viewers could be forgiven if they thought they were seeing real news reported by one of the station's reporters. But Sharon Dennis does not work for KTBC. The story had been fed to the station by the Cleveland Clinic, the health care behemoth. Dennis, who earned her broadcasting bona fides at ABC News and at KOMO-TV in Seattle, works in Cleveland as the executive producer of the Cleveland Clinic News Service, in a windowless office on the fourth floor of the Intercontinental Hotel on the clinic's sprawling 140-acre campus. There the clinic has constructed broadcast facilities for Dennis and her four-person staff, complete with three cameras, a background set, and an ON AIR sign purchased at Target. Every day, Dennis sends out prepackaged stories to, among others, Fox News Edge, a service for Fox affiliates that in turn distributes the pieces to 140 Fox stations. What Texas viewers heard that January morning was a script written at the Intercontinental Hotel.

In essence, the story was a hybrid of news and marketing, the likes of which has spread to local TV newsrooms all across the country in a variety of forms, almost like an epidemic. It's the product of a marriage of the hospitals' desperate need to compete for lucrative lines of business in our current health system and of TV's hunger for cheap and easy stories. In some cases the hospitals pay for airtime, a sponsorship, and in others, they don't but still provide expertise and story ideas. Either way, the result is that too often the hospitals control the story. Viewers who think they are getting news are really getting a form of advertising. And critical stories—hospital infection rates, for example, or medical mistakes or poor care—tend not to be covered in such a cozy atmosphere. The public, which could use real health reporting these days, gets something far less than quality, arms-length journalism.

The story about the virtual gym—which ran on twenty-one other stations, too—ended with Bickett saying that its developers hope to have the technology available in hospitals around the U.S. by the end of the year. Though he didn't mention which hospitals, viewers could easily conclude that the Cleveland Clinic was one of them. Indeed that is what the clinic hopes, Cleveland Clinic News Service stories almost always feature Cleveland Clinic doctors and patients touting some new surgical technique or medical breakthrough, like antiaging proteins or a new sensor to measure spinal disc damage, or sometimes offering basic health tips, like flu shots or exercise. Stories occasionally mention research from another institution or a medical journal, but never a doctor from a rival hospital in Cleveland. That would hardly further the underlying goal of the news service: public awareness of the Cleveland Clinic brand.

The Cleveland Clinic News Service is just one variation on the new alliance between hospitals and local TV news. Most of these arrangements are between a single health institution and a single TV station. They take different forms in different cities, but the deals all too frequently slide across the ad-edit wall. The partnerships may involve traditional commercials, but they often include a promise of some kind of "news" stories, too, involving reporters or news anchors. These can take the form of "ask the expert" programs, quick helpings of medical advice, short stories inserted into the newscasts, or longer, news-like specials that may be hosted by a news anchor or health reporter. In the worst cases, hospitals create the storyline, supplying both the experts and the patients. Some partnerships include a Web component; viewers are sent to the TV station Web site, where they find links to hospital Web sites that provide referrals to doctors or hospital services, and it becomes nearly impossible to separate news and marketing.

Rick Wade, senior vice president for strategic communications at the American Hospital Association, says that the TV/hospital partnerships are an unwelcome result of fierce marketplace competition in health care. "There's a lot of it going on," says Wade. "It happens in major media markets where TV stations are starving and hospitals are under competitive pressure." In response to cost-cutting by managed-care firms over the last decade, hospitals have glued themselves into large systems to fight back. Branding and marketing have become the weapons of choice. Ultimately the goal is to attract patients.

The hospitals don't want just any patient, though—only those with good insurance to pay for the big-ticket procedures that bring in the big bucks. One result of the epidemic is that the health stories that dominate local TV news tend to push expensive specialties and procedures—like bariatric surgery for obesity, which can cost upwards of $20,000, or expensive gamma knife surgery for brain cancer, with a price tag of $10,000 or more. Stories about less profitable diagnoses, like AIDS or pneumonia, are rare, let alone pieces about care for the uninsured. The bland stories almost always discuss non-controversial topics, such as new technology, a hospital's special services, or health and nutrition tips.

Worse, since TV news operations are finding that they can get this kind of health "news" supplied to them—and might even make money on the deal—they are tempted not to invest in a legitimate health reporter who would ask harder questions and look at the larger picture in health care. "I don't feel we need a full-time health reporter," says Regent Ducas, news director at KCTV in Kansas City, which had a lucrative partnership with the HCA hospital system until the end of 2006. When it lost the HCA partnership, KCTV moved quickly to look for a new one. Not all TV stations, of course, strike such deals. Sam Rosenwasser, president and general manager of WTSP-TV in St. Petersburg, Florida, says his station just hasn't pursued one, but said he would "entertain anything if it makes sense." It would make sense, he said, "as long as you let people know you have some partnership." But too often the full nature of the arrangements is not disclosed, or inadequately disclosed, leaving the viewer without any understanding of what it means when the hospital gets involved in the content of news.

Good reporters are often afraid to talk on the record about the partnerships, but it's clear that they don't like them. "How are you as a journalist supposed to impart a sense of trust if the story is essentially directed and produced by a company not related to your news department?" asks one TV health reporter whose news director would not let her speak for attribution.

"I have to do these. I'm not given a choice," said another reporter who asked for anonymity. "I kick, scream, and fight, and make them as journalistically ethical as possible. It makes me sick."

The Cleveland Clinic started its news service nearly four years ago with a pilot sent to NBC affiliates that signed up and a handshake agreement with Fox News. The service acts as "a customer service arm for reporters," says the Cleveland Clinic's media relations specialist, Raquel Santiago.

At one end of the customer-service spectrum, NBC seems to use the Cleveland Clinic material as a kind of story-idea service. Helen Chickering, a medical reporter for NBC News Channel, which sends stories to NBC affiliates, says the network cannot use prepackaged Video News Releases, known as VNRS, in stories, but will make its own interview requests based on them. "The only way we can connect is with an interview request," she says of the rules about dealing with VNR providers. One story in a special series called Modern Medical Miracles, which aired on NBC'S *Today* at the end of November, demonstrates how the network uses the clinic's material. In October, the Cleveland Clinic sent out a story called "Racing Hearts," which showed how race-car drivers are testing a new heart-monitoring device, and featured a Cleveland Clinic doctor. *Today* then created its own story featuring the Cleveland Clinic doctor; the medical affairs director for the Champ Car World Series, an international car race; and NBC'S chief medical editor, Dr. Nancy Snyderman, who called the device a "very cool breakthrough." The segment discussed other kinds of heart devices and did note that the one tested on race-car drivers was not yet on the market.

Toward the other end of the spectrum is Fox. As Cleveland Clinic's Sharon Dennis sees it, "We act as a news bureau for Fox." A CJR analysis shows just how true that is. We traced the use of eight stories the clinic sent out last fall and found that twenty-six stations—all Fox except three—used them almost verbatim. Dave Winstrom, the director of Fox News Edge, says Fox approves the scripts before the packages are sent to the stations, and adds that the stations may choose how to use them. "Some may use them verbatim, or cut them down, or not use them at all." What's sent to the stations, he says, is identified as being from the Cleveland Clinic, but "it's up to them how they present the story." (The piece about the virtual gym that ran in Austin did not tell viewers the source of the story.)

Marketing like that can produce a big return on a hospital's investment. The Mayo Clinic, which started its own news service in 2000, sends its weekly Medical Edge stories to 130 TV stations in the U.S. and Canada. No other station in those markets can use Mayo's Medical Edge offerings. Stations using the material must agree to say that the featured physician belongs to the Mayo Clinic and provide a link from the station Web site to Mayo's.

How well does that work? CJR obtained a PowerPoint presentation given in 2004 to hospital marketers by the Mayo Clinic's media relations manager, Lee Aase. It showed that brand preference for Mayo for serious medical conditions had increased 59 percent three years after the service began, and brought in new patients to boot. One story, called "Same-Day Teeth," which told of a quicker way of doing lower-jaw dental implants, generated more than 175 calls, Aase's report said. It resulted in twenty-three scheduled appointments and downstream revenue—money from patients who eventually had the procedure—estimated at $345,000. The presentation noted that 8.6 million people had seen the December 2001 Medical Edge stories. The value, said Mayo, was greater than ten times the cost of producing the shows.

Sharon O'Brien, the marketing director for University Health System in San Antonio, says she is moving away from paid advertising in favor of such media partnerships. "The hallmark of these packages is that they don't look like paid advertising," she says.

Marketing like this is so powerful, in fact, that some TV stations have found that they can charge serious money for "news." Their sales departments aggressively pitch business proposals to health institutions, laid out in thick spiral binders that look like a prospectus, according to L. G. Blanchard, media relations manager for the University of Alabama Health System, who has seen many of them. Most hospital officials that CJR interviewed would not talk about their financial arrangements with TV stations, but the few who did offered a glimpse into how profitable the deals can be to those stations willing to charge for them.

Leni Kirkman, the executive director of corporate communications at University Health System in San Antonio, said her hospital paid about $90,000 in 2002 to KENS-TV for a year-long sponsorship that involved thirty-second promotions, prominent placement of the hospital's logo—and a monthly feature called "Family First" that was narrated by the station's news anchor but written by the hospital's p.r. staff. Kirkman says the hospital has also had a deal with Univision, in which no money changed hands. In that partnership, she says, the hospital provides a tape with B-roll footage and interviews for a show called "A Su Salud (To Your Health)," which features the hospital's experts and patients. "We get to have our experts interviewed, so we get the PR value." But there's a bonus: "When we want them to cover something else," Kirkman adds, "they are extremely receptive."

Rob Dyer, a vice president for marketing and public relations at HCA hospitals in Kansas City, said his organization paid KCTV $1.5 million over the three years of their partnership, which ended in December. That deal involved advertising spots, promotion on the station's Web site, four Doctor on Call specials each year with the station's morning anchor and hospital medical personnel.

In 2002, the Radio-Television News Directors Association (RTNDA) established voluntary guidelines for balancing business pressures and journalism values. One RTNDA standard says advertisers should have no influence over news content. Yet in many of these TV partnerships, hospital p.r. people decide the story and may even write or edit the script.

Another standard says that a news operation's online product should clearly separate commercial and editorial content. But such clarity is often lacking. For example, WIS-TV in Columbia, South Carolina, featured one of its former reporters in a Web story as she had her risk for heart disease assessed by a local hospital heart center; the story blended so smoothly on the site with the hospital's ads it was difficult to tell the difference.

For the most part, TV stations and hospitals see little wrong with their partnerships. Hospital p.r. officials often believe it is simply another way to inform consumers about health care. Chad Dillard, a former hospital marketing vice president for Good Samaritan Hospital in Baltimore, said he didn't think the partnerships crossed the line. "I never honestly thought it was anything more than getting a good story out to the consumer." For his part, Regent Ducas of Kansas City's KCTV concedes that his station's Doctor on Call programs are not news, but are more like "a Billy Graham special." But, says Barbara Cochran, the president of the RTNDA: "If your viewers and listeners start to think your news content is for sale, you'll lose credibility and the value that advertisers want will be damaged."

TV anchors and health reporters lend credibility to stories resulting from partnerships. In Seattle, the popular KING-TV anchor Jean Enersen starred in a package on lung cancer that ran last October and was promoted as a "KING 5 Cancer Free Washington Special." Although the program reported on patients in lung cancer support groups and smokers trying to kick the habit, it was also unquestionably a plug for the work of three hospitals that formed the Seattle Cancer Care Alliance, which partners with KING. Enersen has hosted eight hour-long shows on cancer over the last two years, as well as shorter "health link" pieces that run during the primetime news once a week. Sometimes anchors also appear in commercials for the hospitals, giving the ads the patina of news. Wayne Dawson, a news anchor at Cleveland's Fox station WJW, for example, does spots promoting MetroHealth's help line. The spots run during WJW's news and entertainment programming, earmarked as commercials.

In its 2003 annual report, Meredith Corporation, which owns fourteen TV stations, noted, "Now everyone at each station, including news anchors and other on-air personalities, is playing a role in generating advertising revenues or supporting sales operations." Thus it was only natural that Meredith's station in Kansas City, KCTV, would agree that, as part of its deal with HCA, one of the station's anchors would host the Doctor on Call specials that featured HCA doctors and nurses answering viewer questions. HCA'S Dyer says the station wanted a representative to host the shows and "we didn't mind that."

The larger problem with TV-hospital partnerships is that in many of them the hospitals effectively co-opt the station's journalistic duties. How much control the hospitals get varies from partnership to partnership, but they often select the topics, choose the patients and doctors, and sometimes write or edit the script. Shawnee Mission Medical Center just outside Kansas City, Kansas, for example, has a sponsorship deal with an ABC affiliate, KMBC, owned by Hearst-Arygle, to air stories called Health Watch for Women, which airs every Wednesday and Sunday, featuring only the health system's medical experts. Shannon Cates, a hospital media relations specialist, says the stories, which discuss such subjects as osteoperosis, progesterone, and bladder control, are "definitely" news. "I develop the story ideas and arrange for the physicians and patients to speak on the air," she says. "Channel 9 comes to do the interview for the segment. It's like any other news story they would do." The partnership goes deeper. "Working on a regular basis we've come to trust each other. They feel comfortable with me developing story ideas, and I trust them to put the story together that represents the hospital well."

Thomas McCormally, a public information officer at rival Children's Mercy Hospitals, based in Kansas City, Missouri, says this about the women's health stories: "As a consumer you wouldn't know they are advertising."

He should know. His hospital has its own unpaid arrangement with KMBC and with the same reporter, Kelly Eckerman, who also anchors the evening news. Every other Wednesday between 12 p.m. and 2 p.m., Eckerman and a camera crew arrive at the hospital, where McCormally has lined up doctors, a family, and a child for interviews and B-roll shots on a topic the hospital has suggested. McCormally describes the hospital as a "quasi producer," though it doesn't write the script. At each session the station gets two packages—four in total for the month—which run on Thursday's 5 p.m. broadcast. "Kelly gets a ready-made story. We're getting what we want," McCormally says. What he wants is visibility, in order to recruit physicians and to "plant seeds in the minds of donors we're working hard to take care of children." The easier you make things for a TV news operation, he says, the easier it is to get your message out.

Another seed that gets planted is that the doctor or hospital featured on TV is the best around, whether true or not. KOCO-TV in Oklahoma City devotes airtime to health care providers—a Lasik eye specialist, plastic surgeons affiliated with a hospital that is one of the program sponsors, and a dentist specializing in cosmetic procedures—to perform what the station brands "Oklahoma's Ultimate Makeover." Two people are chosen from the community to have a complete make-over with some aspects of their transformation woven into a one-hour TV special. Dominique Homsey Gross, the station's sales marketing manager, says the makeover is a source of "nontraditional revenue." Viewers might easily assume that because the doctors were picked to "perform" on camera, they must be top-notch. But the actual requirement seems to be that, as Gross put it, "these people partner with the TV station to show what they do."

Such branding partnerships can even obscure problems at a hospital. The CBS station KYW-TV in Philadelphia has a partnership with Temple University Hospital. Stories resulting from the partnership, called Temple LifeLines specials, won two mid-Atlantic regional Emmys—one in 2004 for a story about the hospital's heart transplant program and one last September for a story on bone marrow transplants. According to a hospital press release, the transplant program profiled "some of the wonderful patients who have benefited from their quality-care experiences at Temple." The hospital pays for the airtime and, although the station's medical reporter, Stephanie Stahl, hosts the half-hour show, hospital officials are very much a part of the creative process. Charles Soltoff, associate vice president for marketing at Temple, says the hospital presents ideas to the station—what's interesting, where the hospital has opportunities for new business development, advances in treatment options. "We tell them what's valuable," Soltoff says. The decision on topics is "shared," he says, but a hospital official who talked to CJR on the condition of anonymity said: "Ultimately it's Temple's decision about what to feature," further explaining that "the writer does the script and submits a draft to us. We edit the script." Soltoff says, "We edit it down from various perspectives."

But there have been problems with Temple's transplant services. In a 2006 series on organ transplants, the *Los Angeles Times* reported that Temple had found a way to move prospective heart recipients ahead in the queue by saying they were sicker than they actually were, a practice that's unfair to those lower on the list, but one that might boost volume and thus revenue—and, of course, help Temple's own patients. The *Times* also reported that Temple's story has "never been publicly disclosed." The public did not know that the United Network for Organ Sharing (UNOS), a private, nonprofit group that has a federal contract to ensure safety and equity in the nation's transplant system, had disciplined the hospital. In 2002, UNOS found more evidence that the hospital was inflating its patients' conditions, and in November of that year placed the hospital on "confidential probation." The probation ended in January 2006, which means that it spanned the time that Temple and KYW were producing and airing their award-winning specials promoting the hospital's transplant services.

Another example: the Alta Bates Summit Medical Center, with campuses in Oakland and Berkeley, California, part of the Sutter Health Network, got into trouble in early 2005. The Joint Commission on the Accreditation of Health Care Organizations (JCAHO) gave a preliminary accreditation denial to Alta Bates. In 2004 JCAHO had issued only twelve preliminary denials out of about 1,500 hospitals it surveyed. Later JCAHO changed its rating to a conditional accreditation, indicating the hospital still had to prove it had corrected deficiencies that inspectors had found. The *San Francisco Chronicle* and the *Contra Costa Times* both covered the problems at Alta Bates. But a search of the video library of KPIX-TV, which partners with Sutter Health, turned up no stories about Alta Bates and JCAHO. The station's communications director, Akilah Monifa, confirmed that no such stories had run on the newscast. As part of its advertising deal with Sutter Health, KPIX receives a fully produced program called "Your Health," which it runs twice a month. The annual cost of the program, according to Tracy Murphy, a marketing vice president at Sutter Health, is about $350,000.

The clever packaging and convergent marketing that come with TV-hospital partnerships fly in the face or a consumer empowerment movement for transparency in health care, pushed by some academics, employers, and patient advocacy groups, that is beginning to take root in the U.S. The movement envisions that educated patients will take responsibility for choosing the best care by using scientific and objective data—if data are available. But when patients get the impression through branding activities with local news stations that hospital A is superior, data that show hospital B is really better may have little meaning. In fact, such data may be overlooked entirely by TV news departments as well as patients. The tremendous investment being made to devise fair and useful health care metrics may well be wasted because television's complicity in hospital branding activities will ultimately overwhelm those efforts.

The partnerships also contribute to the dysfunction of the U.S. health care system. Hospitals understandably want high revenue from high-cost services to help subsidize the uncompensated care they provide to the uninsured who can't pay on their own, a practice that might be eliminated with a more rational payment system. But stories about profitable, high-tech, yet often unproven procedures stimulate demand for them, fueling ever-rising health care costs.

Local TV health journalism doesn't often discuss those big issues, or even often take on the smaller stories that together weave a tale of a health care system in trouble. And marketing partnerships with local hospitals almost mandate that it will be so, substituting lazy journalism and gee-whiz technology stories for the real thing.

It's hard to see that the TV-hospital partnerships do much for the public interest. Citizens groups have challenged the licenses of stations in Illinois, Wisconsin, and Oregon for offering scant local election coverage. Perhaps fake health news should be their next target.

Last October at a reunion of fellows from the Joan Shorenstein Center on the Press, Politics, and Public Policy, Vartan Gregorian, president of the Carnegie Corporation, spoke of a problem with choice in America. "Choice can be manipulated," Gregorian said. "Choice without knowledge is no choice at all." That's what local TV news is in danger of giving us when it comes to health care.

Video News Releases

The Federal Communications Commission seeks public comment on its recent reiteration of commission rules governing prepackaged news, like Video News Releases (VNRs) and whether those rules are sufficient to insure that the public is well informed concerning all sources and financial sponsorship of materials broadcast by licensees and cable TV outlets.

The Public Relations Society of America has standing to provide comment on that issue because many of its more than 20,000 members are actively engaged in the production of VNRs and other prepackaged materials distributed to the media. Furthermore, PRSA, and the Public Relations Student Society of America with its more than 8,000 members, have a longstanding commitment to preserving and improving ethical practices in all aspects of the public relations profession. . . .

In the mix of important tools for communication in an open society, PRSA stands for nothing short of excellent practice in the use of video news releases and other prepackaged news. PRSA'S definition of excellence includes complete disclosure and transparency in the production and distribution of these materials to leave no doubt with anyone who should view them as to the sources of information and financial sponsorship of those materials. We believe that most of those involved in the production and distribution of VNRs adhere to that standard.

Prepackaged news releases are an essential part of the open and free flow of information throughout our society. Their proper use can facilitate communications between government and non-government organizations and their publics. Video and print news releases package and distribute information in a way that is most easily used by broadcast and print media.

In the government sector, for example, VNRs have been effective components of government sponsored public service campaigns. They have informed the public about new labeling requirements for over-the-counter drug supplements, promoted seat belt usage, introduced new currency, informed taxpayers about online filing, and encouraged individual actions for cancer detection and prevention. These campaigns have served the good of society and the American people.

VNRs also help advance communication between corporations, nonprofit organizations and other entities in communicating vital and important information. The *Journal of the American Medical Association* (JAMA) produces weekly

From *Response to Request for Comment, Federal Communications Commission*, The Public Relations Society of America. Reprinted by permission.

VNRs that include interviews with top medical authorities from around the world on topics related to health and wellness of Americans. *JAMA* is able to film interviews with the leading expert on a particular topic, no matter where that expert is located—New York City or Salt Lake City. Via the VNR, *JAMA* is able to make those interviews available to local TV news organizations in cities across the United States that would never be able to obtain such interviews on their own because of time, travel and budgetary constraints.

A foreign aircraft manufacturer, for example, recently conducted a test flight in France of its newest commercial airliner—an event of interest to news organizations around the world. There is no way that all those organizations could have all had cameras in the cockpit of that aircraft during the flight, so the manufacturers' prepackaged video from that flight helped bring that story to people around the globe.

And some VNRs and prepackaged broadcast news and feature material, while promoting brand awareness or new products, are important purely for their creativity and entertainment value. Numerous television stations around the United States, for example, ran VNRs and other prepackaged material associated with the 100th anniversary of the Harley-Davidson motorcycle while local television weather reports found amusing on the hottest day of the year to use prepackaged video from an ice cream manufacturer from a staged event in Death Valley, Calif., that involved tons of snow trucked in from the Sierra Mountains.

PRSA has stated clearly and emphatically that the use of such important and effective communication tools carries with it some significant responsibility. The organization's current code of ethics and the code that preceded it both advise members to reveal the sponsors for causes and interests they represent and to avoid deceptive practices. In early 2004, when the current controversy over prepackaged news emerged in the media, PRSA issued a statement to its members and the media stating that organizations that produce VNRs should clearly identify the VNR as prepackaged news and fully disclose who produced and paid for it at the time the VNR is provided to TV stations. In addition, the statement recommended that organizations that prepare VNRs should not use the word "reporting" If the narrator is not a reporter. The statement also recommended to broadcasters who used such materials that they should identify the source when any of the material is aired. On May 12, 2005, testifying before the U.S. Senate Committee on Commerce, PRSA President and CEO Judith T. Phair supported legislation to "require full disclosure of the sources of government VNRs." Although Phair stated that disclosure to the public of the sources of such materials could come in many forms and should ultimately be the responsibility of each broadcaster as to how that disclosure occurs, she added:

> We believe public relations professionals involved in producing video news releases should provide broadcasters with all the information they need in order to decide the best way to use the information contained in the releases.

On a direct question by U.S. Sen. Ted Stevens of Alaska, Phair stated that PRSA would have no objection to the Byrd amendment's being enacted into permanent law.

In January 2005, PRSA issued to the media and its members a statement prompted by news reports of allegations of impropriety in government-sponsored dissemination of news. Quoting Ms. Phair, the statement said:

> PRSA strongly objects to any paid endorsement that is presented as objective news coverage and is not fully disclosed. Such practices are clearly contrary to the PRSA Member Code of Ethics, which requires that public relations professionals engage in open, honest communications, and fully disclose sponsors or financial interests involved in any paid communications activities. We encourage all public relations professionals to follow the responsible and ethical practice of public relations, as outlined by our Code of Ethics.

PRSA's position on VNRs and prepackaged news, however, goes well beyond those prepared by, and on behalf of, agencies of the U.S. government. PRSA insists that *any* VNR or prepackaged broadcast material should be produced and disseminated with the highest levels of transparency, candor and honesty. To provide open communication that fosters informed decision, we must do more than simply funnel information to the public through the media. We must reveal the sponsors for the causes and interests represented and disclose all financial interests related to the VNR.

The PRSA Code of Ethics, professional development initiatives and even the PRSA awards presented for best practices in production of VNRs and other prepackaged broadcast materials emphasize honesty and accuracy in all communications and that all public relations practitioners involved in the production and dissemination of these materials must always reveal the sponsors for, causes addressed and interests represented by these materials and disclose all financial interests related to the materials to the broadcast entities receiving the materials.

Although there have been a few well-publicized departures from those guidelines, PRSA believes, based on experience of its leaders and members, that most public relations professionals and the firms they work with to produce and disseminate VNRs are consistently practicing full disclosure of sources and sponsors to the broadcast media.

PRSA believes that all of those involved at any point in the chain of production and distribution of prepackaged material for broadcast media should voluntarily and painstakingly disclose original sources and sponsorship of the material to broadcasters so the broadcasters themselves will have the information they need to:

1. Make informed decisions about whether to use the materials and how to use the materials.
2. Make better decisions on how to disclose sources of information to their viewers within the confines of their own production values and news-gathering and reporting standards.

PRSA also discourages and condemns use of any technique in the production and dissemination of a VNR that could mislead the public or broadcasters as to the true source and sponsorship of the material. As an example, PRSA does not condone the use of individuals who are hired to pose as news reporters and news anchors to convey the impression that the material was produced by an independent news-gathering organization or by a freelance reporter/producer who gathers news objectively and independently and packages it for sale to broadcast news outlets. In another example, PRSA would discourage production of a VNR by a "front group" or an organization that masks the true source of information and sponsorship or the point of view expressed in the prepackaged material from the public or broadcasters. PRSA's concern about some of the proposed congressional initiative and about the broader application of existing FCC regulations is that they could exceed the initial intent of the initiatives, which was to ensure full disclosure to the public of all information they receive through broadcast media. PRSA believes, for example, that the establishment of a specific format for disclosure of sources and sponsorship within the prepackaged material or VNR would actually discourage broadcasters from using the material and deprive the public of the kinds of information it needs and wants.

Additionally there is a concern that some of the initiatives—and those involved with them—equate prepackaged news and feature material with "propaganda." Although some of the elements associated with propaganda—using half-truths and one-sided arguments, manufactured "evidence" and dubious statistics, broad statements, emotion-laden terms, guilt by association and "bandwagon" appeals—certainly could be fomented in a VNR or prepackaged news story, the issue should not be with the cosmetic configuration of the "tool" but with the people or organizations who would use that tool improperly and unethically.

Furthermore, an industry-imposed 'self-regulation" that would fully and accurately identify sources and sponsorship would also counteract some of the vagaries that exist in current regulations. For example, a broadcaster might more easily determine that a VNR addresses a potentially "controversial" subject, or an issue related to a "political" initiative, if sources and sponsorship of prepackaged materials were apparent.

For self-regulation to be effective, PRSA suggests that this disclosure should be proactive, rather than merely a passive attempt to comply with standards or regulations. For example, source and sponsorship information should be clearly stated on the VNR package itself. In addition, the public relations practitioner who may call or e-mail a broadcast news director as an alert to the VNR, or to pitch it for use in a specific broadcast program, should also state clearly the source of the material.

Here are some of the steps PRSA takes to keep its members informed about the ethical standards that come into play in the day-to-day course of their business activities and the importance of proactive approaches to building public trust and credibility:

- PRSA routinely publishes ethics and standards advisories to its members, as it did in mid-2004 when some of the first news reports about questionable VNRs surfaced. The organization states its positions in opinion pieces and provides interviews to both trade media and general consumer media at every opportunity.

- PRSA annually bestows awards for best practices in audio and video news release production and part of the criteria for selecting recipients—reinforced with the latest panel of judges who selected the best practices of the art—is the disclosure.
- PRSA routinely offers professional development courses on specific tactics, such as production of VNRs and in those the disclosure requirements are also reinforced.
- In PRSA's Accreditation in Public Relations, individuals who go through the APR Accreditation process must be well versed in such ethical practices of the profession as proper disclosure of the sources and sponsorship of materials sent to the media.

PRSA is the largest professional organization serving the public relations profession, but it is not the only one. In the past year, due to action influenced in large measure by the controversy surrounding VNRs, PRSA has reached out not only to other public relations organizations, but also to organizations representing corporate ethics officers, investor relations personnel and the media, to enhance uniform understanding and application of the ethical standards all the organizations embrace.

One result was the first "ethics summit," which occurred in March 2005 in New York and involved a number of organizations, including PRSA. As result of that meeting, PRSA and the Society of Professional Journalists have taken the initiative to create cross-discipline panels for sessions at each of our national conferences later this year that will discuss, among other things, the ethical, transparent use of prepackaged news materials. Subsequently, PRSA and the Radio and Television News Directors Association initiated preliminary discussions about working together on cross-industry education and informational programs on this subject.

FCC Regulation of Prepackaged News

VNRs, even those used by government agencies, are not new. And as the Federal Communication Commission demonstrated in its April 13, 2005 call for comment on the use of VNRs by broadcasting entities, neither are VNRs new to controversy and confusion.

One example of this is the very definition of prepackaged news for broadcast media. In its call for comment on this issue, the FCC defined VNRs as VNRs are essentially prepackaged news stories that may use actors to play reporters and include suggested scripts to introduce the stories. These practices allow such externally prepackaged news stories to be aired, without alteration, as broadcast or cable news.

The GAO in its definition said that:

> Prepackaged news stories are complete, audio-video presentations that may be included in video news releases or VNRs. (footnote: Among other things, typical VNRs may also contain "B-roll" video clips, advertisements, and public service announcements.) They are intended to be indistinguishable from news segments broadcast to the public by independent television news

organizations. To help accomplish this goal, these stories include actors or others hired to portray "reporters" and may be accompanied by suggested scripts that television news anchors can use to introduce the story during the broadcast. These practices allow prepackaged news stories to be broadcast, without alteration, as television news.

The various definitions tend to combine a variety of materials and techniques and cross some demarcations lines between unrelated disciplines (i.e., public relations and advertising). For example, advertising professional generally deal with "paid" media. In other words, advertising professionals buy space in a newspaper or magazine, on a Web site, or commercial time from a television or radio station, that guarantee broadcast or dissemination of their "unedited" messages. Public relations professionals, on the other hand, routinely work with "unpaid" media. They provide material, free of charge, to news organizations. There are no guarantees that the material will not be edited or discarded entirely. Whereas advertising—even broadly disseminated advertising—involves some kind of individual contract with each media organization that displays the material, the kinds of prepackaged media associated with public relations is almost always distributed broadly without any sort of prearranged agreement about its use.

The commission, in its call for comment, focused on two types of material furnished to broadcasters:

1. Prepackaged material that involves some financial or promotional agreement between the provider and the broadcaster.
2. Prepackaged material that involves political or controversial materials.

Although PRSA would contend that prepackaged material that involves some financial or promotional agreement between the provider and the broadcaster falls under the definition of advertising, and is subject to FCC sponsorship rules already in place, to the extent that public relations professionals are involved in arrangements that include financial or promotional considerations, the same rules should apply.

The commission notes that there currently is no specific disclosure requirement on broadcasters for materials provided to the broadcasters free—unless the materials are deemed to be of a controversial or political nature, PRSA maintains, however, that those who provide any VNRs or prepackaged materials to broadcasters, even if they are not deemed to be political or controversial in nature, should fully disclose the exact source and sponsorship of those materials.

The Sponsorship Identification Rules

According to the FCC call for comment, the sponsorship identification rules contained in sections 317 and 507 of the Communications Act of 1934 and in the Commission's rules generally require that, when payment has been received or promised to a broadcast licensee or cable operator for the airing of program material, the station or cable system must disclose at the time of the airing that fact and identify who paid or promised to provide the consideration.

There are also provisions in section 507 of the law and for reporting such financial or promotional considerations by those who engage in such arrangements with broadcasters in exchange for airing prepackaged materials.

PRSA unequivocally and enthusiastically supports both the spirit and the letter of the law and regulations in this manner. There should be full disclosure by all parties involved.

Political and Controversial Issue Programming

PRSA contends that the FCC rules for disclosure by broadcasters of materials that are controversial or political materials are inherently vague. Similar to provisions in the regulations governing broadcast of materials that could be deemed objectionable or obscene, broadcasters must at the time of broadcast make the determination for themselves as to whether material is political or controversial in nature. But the fact is that in this day and time in a free society almost any subject matter could be deemed controversial or political in nature by some individual or special interest organization. And that "after the fact" determination of the nature of the material could pose a threat to broadcasters.

The Commission notes that "Congress has acknowledged the danger that groups advocating ideas or promoting candidates, rather than consumer goods, might be particularly inclined to attempt to mask their sponsorship in order to increase the apparent credibility of their messages," which further exacerbates the problem for broadcasters.

PRSA, however, believes that application and self-enforcement of full disclosure standards on ALL prepackaged materials that are distributed to broadcasters will provide broadcasters with enough information for them to make better, more informed decisions about the nature of the materials and reduce prospects that they will inadvertently broadcast as "news" materials that could later prove to be controversial or political in nature. Self-regulation, based on existing standards for disclosure and transparency within the industry, should alleviate concerns of the Commission in this respect. . . .

POSTSCRIPT

Is the Use of Video News Releases Bad Journalism?

Most of us are unaware of the public relations content that appears in media. Media relations is a basic component of public relations that focuses on working with mass media in seeking publicity, and responding to requests for information about the organization or cause. Newspapers and magazines depend extensively on press releases. Some research suggests that nearly 50 percent of news articles are generated from these releases. Events are sometimes created to attract media coverage. The appearance of reclusive stars on morning or late-night talk shows is to promote their new movie or book. Activist organizations have had some success in promoting television story lines that revolve around their issue, such as a breast cancer story line in a soap opera. VNRs are sometimes used in crisis situations. When some customers claimed they had found syringes in Pepsi cans, the company produced a VNR of its high-speed bottling process showing that introducing these objects into the product was basically impossible. The claim was found to be a hoax. Producers would like VNRs to be used as received, but they are often used instead as B-roll, where selected footage is used in stories produced by the stations. Many VNRs now include extensive B-roll footage, recognizing that stations will often use that footage instead of the prepared package.

The PRSA has a code of ethics that all members must sign. It stresses core values of the profession and are designed to set high ethical standards for profesional practice. These include acting as reponsible advocates, adhering to high standards of accuracy and truth in advancing these interests, independent counsel and accountability.

The issues are complex. If Habitat for Humanity drops off a press release at a local paper about a project in that community, no one would raise questions. What about if it drops off a VNR at the local television station? What about press releases or VNRs from local officials? National pharmacy or medical companies? What is the potential for harm? Can the lines be drawn by relying on self-regulation by the public relations and media companies involved? If not, what kinds of regulations should be in place? Should they apply only to electronic media, or also to print?

Much has been written on both sides of the argument, for some the failure of regulation allows abuse. See Janel Alania, "The "News" from the Feed Looks Like News Indeed: On Video News Releases, the FCC, and the Shortage of Truth in the Truth in Broadcasting Act of 2005," *Cardozo Arts & Entertainment Law Journal* (2006). Alternatively, David Meerman, in *The New Rules of Marketing and PR: How to Use News Releases, Blogs, Podcasting, Viral Marketing and Online Media to Reach Buyers Directly* (2007) speaks to the many ways in which messages can be used to reach the public. It shows that VNRs are only one of many ways in which companies are using PR to reach us, sometimes without our conscious awareness.

Internet References . . .

National Association of Broadcasters (NAB)

The NAB is an organization dedicated to promoting the interests of broadcasters. Some of the pages include information such as TV parental guidelines, laws and regulation, research, and current issues.

http://www.nab.org

National Cable TV Association (NCTA)

The NCTA is an organization dedicated to promoting the interests of the cable industry. See their Web page for discussion of current issues, and updates on issues of importance to cable.

http://www.ncta.com

Television Bureau of Advertising

The Television Bureau of Advertising is a non-profit trade association of the broadcast television industry. This Web site provides a diverse variety of resources to help advertisers make the best use of local television. Go to "television facts" for useful information.

http://www.tvb.org

Yahoo Finance

From the site below, click through investing to industries to the industry center where you can access information on individual companies, industry rivals, strategies and value, and stock prices. This is an invaluable resource for learning more about specific firms and their markets.

http://www.finance.yahoo.com

Investopedia

Investopedia is a Forbes Media Company financial education site. The URL below will take you through a tutorial on mergers and acquisitions. The concentration of media industries is accomplished primarily through these business activities.

http://www.investopedia.com/university/mergers

Cynopsis

*Cyn*opsis is a free daily trade publication for the television industry. There are four daily early morning editions—*Cyn*opsis, *Cyn*opsis: Kids, *Cyn*opsis: International, and *Cyn*opsis: Digital—that can be read on the Web or sent via email.

http://www.cynopsis.com

Media Business

*I*t is important to remember that media industries are businesses and that they must be profitable in order to thrive. Changes in ownership rules have resulted in a new group of media companies and corporations, but at the same time, very few traditional media systems have failed. Most have retooled and have focused on smaller, targeted audiences. In this section we discuss what has changed in traditional media outlets, and how new special-interest groups and new technologies are changing the type of media that is available to the public. Are changes to traditional industries inevitable? What aspects of law, regulation, and business practices have come together to change the nature of the media "playing field?" How likely are new services to survive? Is the era of mass media now over?

- Can the Independent Musical Artist Thrive in Today's Music Business?
- Can Present Technology Support Internet Growth?
- Does Big Media Control the FCC?
- Will Print Newspapers Survive in the Current Business Environment?

ISSUE 14

Can the Independent Musical Artist Thrive in Today's Music Business?

YES: Chuck Salter, from "Way Behind the Music," *Fast Company* (February 2007)

NO: Eric Boehlert, from "Pay for Play," *Salon.com* (March 14, 2001)

ISSUE SUMMARY

YES: Chuck Salter looks at the way musical artists have had to become business people to control the branding of their "products." He examines the business model established by John Legend, and describes how today's musical artists must retain control of their brand to survive in the music industry today.

NO: Eric Boehlert describes why radio has become so bad, with regard to diversity of music, and how little opportunity there is for new artists to get their music on the air. He describes what has happened to the traditional music industry/radio alliance, and how independent record promoters have influenced both businesses.

For many years, the Recording Industry Association of America (RIAA) has vigorously fought the use of the Internet to distribute music. Though the RIAA could not prohibit the use of MP3 technology and file sharing, they did mount an attack on individuals who apparently downloaded large files of music. One of the RIAA's chief claims was that free downloading of music punished the musical artist, who would no longer make any royalties in his or her work. As you read these selections, you'll see that the legality of downloading music is not really a concern of these writers. Instead, each focuses on the Internet's impact in one way or another on consumption practices and music, and how new business models have emerged that influence what we hear.

What the RIAA was really concerned about was how the Internet would influence the sale of records and CDs, thus affecting the entire structure of the RIAA. But the Internet alone was not to blame for changes to the recording industry. New business models, like those in these selections, have emerged to shift power away from the traditional RIAA structure, and put the power into other hands. The selections in this issue focus on how that power has shifted, for whom, and with what effect.

Chuck Salter describes how entrepreneurs in the music business have had to learn how to conduct the business that corporations and the RIAA once controlled. Many artists now control every aspect of their enterprises, from recording their music to selling products with their logos, tour merchandise, and controlling their brand. While this model helps established artists, it also gives new hope to emerging artists and allows them to market themselves in a way that gives them a greater opportunity to succeed. The Internet then, becomes a distribution agency for music, products, publicity, fan clubs, and more.

Eric Boehlert examines the music industry from a different perspective. As large corporations bought smaller record labels, the role of the independent record promoter shifted enormous power to people who would pay to have records played on certain radio stations. The indie promoter then earned money on how many plays he could arrange, and fewer new groups could get to be heard on radio. Boehlert describes what happened to the disc jockey's choices about music, and traces the money trail to see what happened to the recording industry in the process.

Probably the most common defense for downloading music for free is that "I'm a student, and I don't have any money." But at the same time, changes in industries are created because purchasing patterns change. Both of these authors show how the recording industry has undergone shifts in recent years, in part, because of the Internet, but also, because of corporate greed that has given us music that is packaged for consumption by the greatest number of individuals, at the lowest cost to producers. It's important for us to realize that whenever there is one shift to an industry, it doesn't take much to search for other seismic encounters.

As you consider the positions taken by these authors, remember that the recording industry and the radio industry are always changing. What may be true today can also change again tomorrow. This is particularly important for anyone who wishes to work in these ever-changing industries, and understanding how and why industries change is important for understanding the impact the industries have on our culture, but also, to understand the dynamics that are in play in the world of media, popular culture, and business.

YES

Chuck Salter

Way Behind the Music

If there's any musician who can make sense of the tectonic upheaval in the industry, it's John Legend. Before teaming with Kanye West and Snoop Dogg on his major-label debut, *Get Lifted*, the ultrasmooth R&B singer-songwriter worked as an associate consultant for the Boston Consulting Group (under his given name, John Stephens). When the recording sold north of 3 million copies worldwide—and snagged a trio of 2006 Grammys, including best new artist—John Stephens the consultant had some cautionary words for John Legend the musician: Protect your brand. It was some of the best advice he'd ever gotten.

Legend, who's 28, knew people would be lining up to take a piece of every dollar he could pull down, and that if he went the traditional route, there wasn't much he could do to stop them. After all, it was the label, retailers, and ticket companies in the sweet spot at the center of every transaction with his fans. "I can't let someone else have more control over the relationship people have with my music than I do," he says.

So Legend took control in a way that would have been unthinkable for a new artist just 10 years ago. He still releases music through a major label, Sony BMG, but last fall he formed John Legend Ventures with two friends and began researching how other bands were creating their own businesses and increasing their leverage in the market.

They found that the Internet has become not only a channel for distributing music but one for insinuating bands into the lives of their most enraptured fans. They found that the efficiencies of the Web are such that for very little cost, an artist can build his own online operation and outsource everything, from peddling "merch" to boosting the fan club to ticketing and marketing. And they found a full-service company that had built an infrastructure so vast and so efficient that no one could rival it.

Legend's new partner is a virtual unknown outside the industry. The machine, by design, remains invisible. It's called Musictoday.

Founded by Coran Capshaw, the storied but reticent manager of the Dave Matthews Band, Musictoday works behind the scenes to fashion an online identity for artists, then connects them with fans—and drives commerce. It feeds the sort of passion, or obsession, that turns a $20 teddy bear in a Dylan shirt or a $45 Red Hot Chili Peppers messenger bag into a necessity. It fulfills fantasies: owning Carlos Santana's black fedora, say, or playing blackjack and softball with the Backstreet Boys, or sitting in on a soundcheck with John Mayer. Musictoday can even help fans become part of the music itself, as when Christina Aguilera incorporated their voice-mail messages into "Thank You," a song on *Back to Basics*, her most recent release. "This is all about taking your fans behind the velvet rope," says Matt Blum, Musictoday's fan-club manager.

While the big money is still in touring, Musictoday rechannels revenue streams—merchandise margins and ticket fees that traditionally padded someone else's pocket—in the talent's direction. For new or lesser-known bands, that money could mean the difference between touring and trading in that Stratocaster for a busboy tray. "Somebody you've never heard of will sell $10 million in merchandise in two years," says Jim Kingdon, executive vice president. And for megabands like Dave Matthews, which has more than 80,000 fans paying $35 a year for fan-club membership alone, the money can snowball.

"We're heading to a do-it-yourself world where artists will be taking more control of their careers," says Michael McDonald, John Mayer's manager. Or as Legend puts it: "In the not-too-distant future, this could mean you won't need a label anymore. That's the pot of gold at the end of the rainbow."

In The Foothills of the Blue Ridge Mountains, in an unmarked former chicken-pot-pie plant outside Charlottesville, Virginia, the music revolution is humming along nicely. Here in Musictoday's 350,000-square-foot headquarters, that revolution is most visible in the plastic bins filled with stuff: shower slippers, coasters, and leather coats plastered with the Rolling Stones' wagging-tongue logo. Eminem bobbleheads. Phish onesies. Snoop Dogg rubber wrist bands. Carole King yoga pants. As harmless, even useless, as these tchotchkes may seem, they are upending the industry for one simple reason: Traditional retailers aren't selling them—the artists themselves are. "That direct interaction is unique," says Capshaw. "It's a bonding experience."

Of course, this direct interaction involves some sleight of hand. Behind any given band's online store, it's Musictoday that actually performs the "unfun, unsexy part of the business," says Bruce Flohr, an executive with Red Light Management, one of Capshaw's many ventures. Musictoday's 200 employees are responsible for emailing fans, processing orders, printing tickets, mailing merchandise, fielding complaints, monitoring message boards—all of it. "When you stand in that warehouse, you realize the industry is healthy," says Flohr, who also manages several bands. "It no longer hinges on a silver disc."

But there's a compelling lesson here for any company that makes a product: If you control a piece of the transaction, you understand more about your customers. By aggregating fan data that artists haven't usually been privy to, Musictoday can help shape decisions such as where to tour, advertise, or deploy superfans to evangelize. Considering that an estimated 60% of concert tickets typically go unsold every year, that kind of targeting is no small contribution. "We're able to say to artists, 'We know more about your fans than you do,'" says Nathan Hubbard, 31, who runs Musictoday as Capshaw's chief of staff. "Let's put our heads together and figure out how to monetize this relationship."

Monetize it they have. Musictoday's roster now counts more than 700 clients using some combination of its services. ("We're a little embarrassed by our scale," says Hubbard, "but it helps.") That list includes newcomers like Legend, legacy bands like the Doors, and everyone in between—Kenny Chesney, Justin Timberlake, Taylor Hicks, Janet Jackson, Britney Spears. The company has also begun expanding beyond music, nabbing Tiger Woods, the Miami Heat's Dwyane Wade, Maria Sharapova, the New York Knicks, comedian Dane Cook, and CNN chatterbox Glenn Beck. "We're genre agnostic," says Hubbard. Fans are fans.

And revenue is revenue. By the end of 2006, Musictoday was on pace to sell more than $200 million worth of concert tickets, CDs, merchandise, and fan-club memberships, roughly twice what it sold the previous year. In keeping with its low profile, the seven-year-old company remains tight-lipped about earnings and its cut of online purchases, other than to say it has been profitable for several years and expects to keep growing. That seems a safe bet given that in September, Live Nation, the industry's largest concert promoter, acquired a majority stake in Musictoday (it won't disclose the purchase price). Live Nation, which does about $3 billion in annual sales and produces more than 33,000 shows a year, is eager to keep moving into Live recordings and other concert-related goods. "There's a lot of fragmentation right now, a lot of new products," says Michael Rapino, CEO of Live Nation. "Artists are looking for partners who can deliver these products to their fan base. It's what the labels did for so long. Musictoday is a mile ahead of anyone else."

Capshaw's long, strange journey from fan to mogul began years earlier with the Grateful Dead. "I went to a lot of their shows," he says, "and was exposed to the do-it-yourself model." Jerry Garcia and the boys, whose instrumental jams shot the bird at the radio-hit formula, were touring tour de force. But behind the reefer haze was a larger, iconoclastic strategy. Deadheads were encouraged to tape shows, which fostered a tribe of bootleggers. The Dead shrugged at the lost record revenue and cashed in by selling its tickets and merchandise directly to fans.

Capshaw didn't consider managing until the early 1990s, when the Dave Matthews Band became a Tuesday night fixture at Trax, one of his two clubs in Charlottesville. He'd gotten into the business as a student at the University of Virginia back in the late 1970s, booking bands for fraternity parties. Eventually, he became a nightclub owner, one with an innate sense of how to take care of the talent: Ann Jones Donohue, now director of sales at Musictoday, started out by researching the artists' favorite foods and preparing home-cooked meals. Grilled seafood for the Neville Brothers. Barbecue for Jane's Addiction's Perry Farrell. "They came to town expecting a deli tray," she says.

Dave Matthews's crew reminded Capshaw of the Dead. How they thrived onstage, improvising, giving a different performance each night. How the crowds grew, attracting fans from around the state. How they taped shows, which Capshaw and the band encouraged to gin up word of mouth. It was a prototypical social network. "I remember talking to Coran once, and he held his phone outside his office for me to hear them," says Donohue. "He said they were going to be huge."

The first time he met Capshaw, Flohr recalls, "I was scared s—tless." It was 1993. Flohr was then vice president of A&R (artists and repertoire) at RCA and had come to Charlottesville hoping to sign Matthews. Capshaw had deliberately avoided a recording contract; the band was playing 200 or so gigs a year across the Southeast, building a rabid, mostly collegiate audience. "We needed them more than they needed us," Flohr admits. At dinner, Capshaw wavered, but eventually the two hammered out a deal largely influenced by the Dead's philosophy. "Rather than the label's saying, 'Here's what we're going to do with you,' they called the shots," Flohr recalls. "They said, 'We'll take some of your money, we'll put out an independent record, and we'll tour—boom, boom, boom.'" Boom is right: *Under the Table and Dreaming*, the group's first album for RCA, has sold nearly 7 million copies to date, and the band has become one of the industry's top-grossing concert acts.

The incident revealed what has become a recurring theme in Capshaw's career: a tenacity and talent for challenging the status quo, finding a soft spot in the industry's armor, and ultimately exploiting it to secure power for the artist. RCA got recording rights, but Dave Matthews retained merchandise and online rights. Later, the band negotiated the ability to release its own live recordings. Piece by piece, Capshaw was crafting a highly profitable and largely independent operation. Within a few years of teaming up with RCA, Matthews had produced three multimillion-selling albums and was filling football stadiums (and selling half of those tickets). Along the way, Capshaw built the mechanism for recording live shows (ATO Records, which now boasts more than a dozen acts, including David Gray and My Morning Jacket) and selling shirts, CDs, and tickets (Red Light Management).

Those early CDs contained the seed of what Musictoday would eventually become, in the form of a mail-order insert for merchandise. Capshaw and the band were designing and selling their own goods and pocketing "the retail spread." As that business expanded, it outgrew the spare room at Trax. Then, in the late 1990s, they began offering items online—and the bigger picture revealed itself. The infrastructure had fallen into place for a much bigger operation. "I realized that we could do it with more than just Dave Matthews," says Capshaw. "We had the potential to help other bands."

It wasn't just the artists' interests he was thinking of; Capshaw's a fan himself and wanted to change an industry that all too often took people like him for granted. His "pre-sale," for example, was a reward for a band's most loyal fans, a way of giving them the first shot at great seats for a few bucks less (typically, half the usual surcharge) before the public sale. By winning over more bands to the concept, Capshaw was in position to propel broader changes in the industry. But not before encountering big-time resistance. In 2002, Ticketmaster—the Microsoft in that space—sensed a potentially lethal threat and deployed its lawyers. "They tried to shut down the artist-to-fan concept," Capshaw says matter-of-factly. "There was a series of letters they sent to promoters and venues, some back and forth there." Pause. "But we worked it out."

Ulysses S. Grant couldn't have said it better. As part of an exclusive agreement, Ticketmaster would allow Musictoday to sell 10% of tickets for its clients' shows. That sounds modest, but it represented a seismic power shift, as even Ticketmaster will tell you: "Musictoday went up against a big entrenched company and got it done," rays David Marcus, Ticketmaster's vice president of music. "That requires a serious amount of fighting and skirmishing. You have to give them credit for shining a light on the path to the future. Coran's an aggressive, smart entrepreneur. Sometimes it takes small innovators to get mature companies back to innovating again."

Capshaw doesn't come across as the skirmishing type. Sitting in the top-floor conference room of Red Light Management, in downtown Charlottesville, he seems every bit the 48-year-old Deadhead, as laid-back as his black Lab Emmy (as in singer Emmylou Harris). He has thick, bushy gray hair, a reflective manner, and a deep voice softened by a slight drawl. *C-Ville Weekly*, a local paper, once called Capshaw the Donald of Charlottesville because of his many real estate projects, which include this very office building, an amphitheater, various apartments, several restaurants, a club, and a microbrewery. ("We joke that Coran pays you on Friday, and you give it back to him over the weekend," says Donohue.)

In fact, Capshaw, Pollstar's manager of the year in 2004, is notoriously media shy. It took more than a year to arrange this interview, which proceeds with all the brio of a Quaker meeting. However detached he may seem, Capshaw is intimately familiar with every gear in the machine. "He gets the same reports every day that I do," Hubbard says. Capshaw will weigh in on the wording of a fan email, the timing of a promotion. "He'll ask, 'What was Robert Randolph's ticket count Saturday night in DC?'" says Flohr. "'What was Trey Anastasio's pre-sale?'"

Flohr's so confident in Capshaw's model that he switched sides. Four years ago, he left RCA and came to work for him.

What the Musictoday machine does particularly well is tame the chaos inherent in the unfun, unsexy part of the business. In early November, once again it's fans of the Dave Matthews Band triggering a frenzy in the warehouse, this time with pre-orders for its latest live compilation, *The Best of What's Around, Volume 1*. Tens of thousands of orders pile in, many to be delivered on the exact release date. (In the past, as many as 70,000 of the 470,000 or so CDs sold in the first week were purchased through the band's site.)

This massive facility, with white-tile walls from its days as a frozen-food factory, is the clincher for visiting band managers, agents, and artists—the part of the tour that seals the deal. Often, bands have come after trying to run their own stores and getting overwhelmed. "Sometimes we're competing against somebody's uncle who makes the band's T-shirts in his garage," says Hubbard. "In many ways, this is still an unsophisticated business."

Musictoday couldn't possibly coordinate orders of this scale, complexity, and precision without state-of-the-art warehouse-management software and equipment, such as handheld scanners and a $200,000 automated packing machine. The logistics are made even gnarlier by the special offers that bundle in exclusive knick-knacks and routinely turn the sale of a single CD into a shopping spree. It's a fine example of Capshaw's vision of the symbiotic artist-fan relationship—fans get special items, the artist gets the profits. But that kind of customization creates a fulfillment nightmare that would challenge any retailer—and bring a hungover band to its knees. All the more amazing that Musictoday boasts "a 98.4% to 99.8% accuracy rate," according to Chief Operations Officer (COO) Del Wood.

The other side of the warehouse is like the stash of some obsessive-compulsive collector: 30,000 items from about 400 clients. The shelves, lined with different-colored bins, keep going and going. Ramones flip-flops. Cans of Arnold Palmer iced tea. AC/DC boxer shorts. And behind a locked door, pricier items, like a $5,000 lithograph signed by the Stones. The inventory, too, is organized for maximum efficiency, with the fastest-moving items on the front racks, within easy reach—"nose to knees," as Hubbard says.

Logistically, selling tickets is equally complex, with even less room for error. Just ask U2, not a Musictoday client. In 2005, it had to issue an apology when fans were left in the lurch by scalpers who'd infiltrated its site. "When we screw up, fans don't blame Musictoday," says Hubbard. "They blame the artist." So the company's system is built to handle near-instantaneous sell-outs as well as several hundred simultaneous events. It sells tickets for its clients as well as handling all the ticketing for certain arenas. The arena business is sure to grow since Live Nation owns, operates, or has booking rights at 170 venues worldwide, and its Ticketmaster contract expires next year. "Our system runs like a Ferrari," says Wood. For an Eric Clapton concert in October, it allocated 15,000 seats in 15 seconds.

Before acquiring Musictoday, Rapino, Live Nation's CEO, visited Charlottesville. "I was blown away," he says. "This is not a business you can dabble in. You have to invest in the infrastructure or you can't execute, and they have." The company's remote location has built-in cost advantages, namely affordable space and a top-flight young talent pool at UVA. In that sense, says Rapino, Musictoday "is impossible to replicate."

A few years ago, Nikki Vinci heard a song by a little-known rock band called the Damnwells and "fell in love." She went to the group's site and bought a T-shirt. "I felt like I was supporting them," she says. Without knowing it, though, Vinci had become a Musictoday customer. Now she manages dozens of Musictoday online stores—for Tiger Woods, Led Zeppelin, the Bonnaroo Music & Arts Festival . . . , even her beloved Damnwells. "I never forget what it feels like to he a fan," she says.

That sort of empathy is another key ingredient in the Musictoday formula. Employees are focused on being "artist friendly" and "fan friendly," the bedrock of Capshaw's philosophy. They're expected to be kindred spirits as well as music experts. Each band, after all, has its own subculture, with certain rules and tastes. ("Incense, rolling papers, and shot glasses won't work with Christina Aguilera," says Dave Kostelnik in client services, "but they will for the Black Crowes.") Dozens of employees play in bands of their own, including Hubbard, who's half of the acoustic duo Rockwell Church and a Musictoday client (its CDs, alas, don't qualify for "knees to nose"). They even get two "concert days" apiece every year. And they, like their boss, are discreet, refusing to dish on clients. "We're an invisible service provider," says Hubbard.

Although the music business traditionally revolves around product cycles, Musictoday takes a longer view, developing what Donohue calls "a fan for life." Staying on the radar. Creating products in between CDs and tours. Vinci follows her clients and their fans like a dogged reporter. She checks in with artist management, sometimes several times a day, to learn what the talent is up to. She reviews dozens of Google alerts on her clients. Most nights and weekends, she pores through magazines online and off (the usual suspects, plus *Filter, Relix,* and *Paste*), industry trade journals (*Billboard, Pollstar*), message boards, and a couple of dozen blogs (An Aquarium Drunkard, Coolfer, Stereogum). "That's why they're partners with us," she says. "They know I'll find out what's going on and call."

With the right touch, says Hubbard, this sort of micromanaged online presence can prolong a musician's career. And he's not kidding: Frank Zappa—dead since 1993—is a client. The challenge, then, is not to taint the relationship by coming on too strong. So Musictoday tries to be more like a church that happens to sell communion wafers. "It sounds schlocky," says Kingdon in corporate strategy, "but we're trying to maximize that fan relationship, not maximize sales. If you do the first part, the rest will take care of itself. But if it smacks of commerce, you risk diluting the brand."

To fend off the competition spawned by its own success, Musictoday is always looking for ways to deepen its relationship with artists. The latest is by being a "strategic consultant," says Hubbard. The company's data mining could provide customer insight to drive decisions beyond ticketing or merchandise. "There's always been a real shoot-from-the-hip mentality in this business," he says. "Gut, not data." By mapping merch or ticket sales by geography, for instance, Musictoday can identify where marketing dollars are needed or where an artist should tour. "If you know you're drawing fans from Utah to drive to shows out of state," says Hubbard, "you need to add that 43rd tour date in Salt Lake City."

The Live Nation acquisition should crank up Musictoday's volume even further, like plugging an acoustic guitar into an amp. Live Nation gives it "a broader reach," says Capshaw. Yeah, broader by about 30 million potential customers. According to Live Nation, more than half of its fans visited an artist's Web site last year. "What was it five years ago, zero?" says Rapino. "This channel is as big as you can make it."

That's music to John Legend's ears. His Musictoday paid membership site . . . was slated to launch in December. In November, he posted a preview. Riding his tour bus through a snowstorm in Wisconsin, he filmed a video clip, singing a few bars of a Christmas carol and signing off: "God bless y'all, I love y'all, I appreciate y'all—Peace." Musictoday allows him to add messages himself—immediate, unfiltered access to his supporters. The idea, he says, "is to let them get to know me better."

And vice versa. *Get Lifted* may have sold 3 million copies, but Legend didn't own those sales data, so he had no way of contacting those fans. When people join his new club, they provide demographic information, which he hopes to build a business around. "You need to know who those people are, where they're from," Legend says. "What if you could find out what other products they like to buy? You might use that information to approach other brands—clothing and car companies that want to cater to the same market."

Legend pauses, reins in his inner consultant. "But if I don't make good music, none of this stuff is going to work. I never forget that."

Eric Boehlert

NO

Pay for Play

Does radio seem bad these days? Do all the hits sound the same, all the stars seem like cookie cutouts of one another?

It's because they do, and they are.

Why? Listeners may not realize it, but radio today is largely bought by the record companies. Most rock and Top 40 stations get paid to play the songs they spin by the companies that manufacture the records.

But it's not payola—exactly. Here's how it works.

Standing between the record companies and the radio stations is a legendary team of industry players called independent record promoters, or "indies."

The indies are the shadowy middlemen record companies will pay hundreds of millions of dollars to this year to get songs played on the radio. Indies align themselves with certain radio stations by promising the stations "promotional payments" in the six figures. Then, every time the radio station adds a Shaggy or Madonna or Janet Jackson song to its playlist, the indie gets paid by the record label.

Indies are not the guys U2 or Destiny's Child thanked on Grammys night, but everyone in the business, artists included, understands that the indies make or break careers.

"It's a big f---ing mudball," complains one radio veteran. At first glance, the indies are just the people who grease the gears in a typical mechanism connecting wholesaler with retailer. After all, Pepsi distributors, for example, pay for placement in grocery stores, right?

Except that radio isn't really retail—that's what the record stores are. Radio is an entity unique to the music industry. It's an independent force that, much to the industry's chagrin, represents the one tried-and-true way record companies know to sell their product.

Small wonder that the industry for decades has used money in various ways to influence what radio stations play. The days are long gone when a DJ made an impulse decision about what song to spin. The music industry is a $12 billion-a-year business; today, nearly every commercial music station in the country has an indie guarding its playlist. And for that right, the indie shells out hundreds of thousands of dollars a year to individual stations—and collects a lot more from the major record labels.

Indeed, say many industry observers, very little of what we hear on today's radio stations isn't bought, one way or another.

The indie promoter was once a tireless hustler, the lobbyist who worked the phones on behalf of record companies, cajoling station jocks and program directors, or P.D.s, to add a new song to their playlists. Sure, once in a while the indies showed their appreciation by sending some cocaine or hookers to station employees, but the colorful crew of fix-it men were basically providing a service: forging relationships with the gatekeepers in the complex world of radio, and turning that service into a deceptively simple and lucrative business. If record companies wanted access to radio, they had to pay.

In the 1990s, however, Washington moved steadily to deregulate the radio industry. Among other things, it removed most of America's decades-old restrictions on ownership. Today, the top three broadcasters control at least 60 percent of the stations in the top 100 markets in the U.S.

As that happened, indie promoters became big business.

Drugs and hookers are out; detailed invoices are in. Where indies were once scattered across the country, claiming a few dozen stations within a geographic territory, today's big firms stretch coast to coast, with hundreds of exclusive stations in every major format.

In effect, they've become an extraordinarily expensive phalanx of toll collectors who bill the record company every time a new song is added to a station's playlist.

And the indies do not come cheap.

There are 10,000 commercial radio stations in the United States; record companies rely on approximately 1,000 of the largest to create hits and sell records. Each of those 1,000 stations adds roughly three new songs to its playlist each week. The indies get paid for every one: $1,000 on average for an "add" at a Top 40 or rock station, but as high as $6,000 or $8,000 under certain circumstances.

That's a minimum $3 million worth of indie invoices sent out each week.

Now there's a new and more ominous development. There are rampant industry rumors that Clear Channel Communications, the country's largest radio station owner, is on the verge of formalizing a strategic alliance with one of the biggest indie promotion firms, Tri State Promotions & Marketing. The Cincinnati indie company has been closely aligned with the radio chain for years; now, sources suggest, Clear Channel will be using Tri State exclusively for the company's hundreds of music stations.

If the talk proves to be true, the move would dramatically alter radio's landscape in several ways—and raise new questions about the effect of the nation's payola laws at a time when the Federal Communications Commission has seemingly given up on regulating radio.

According to the FCC, there's nothing wrong with a radio station's accepting money in exchange for playing a song. The payment only becomes payola—and illegal—if the station fails to inform listeners about the cash changing hands.

But stations, of course, are reluctant to pepper their programming with announcements like "The previous Ricky Martin single was paid for by Sony Records." Besides that, stations want to maintain the illusion that they sift through stacks of records and pick out only the best ones for their listeners.

The secretive, and at times unseemly, indie system has been in place for decades. Rock radio pioneer Alan Freed was convicted in 1960 for accepting bribes in exchange for playing records. (What became known as the payola laws were passed as a response soon afterward.) More recently, legendary indie heavyweight Joe Isgro battled prosecutors for nearly a decade over payola-related charges before they were dismissed in 1996.

Isgro's tale of money, drugs and the mob was told in "Hit Men," Fredric Dannen's revealing 1991 book about the world of independent promoters and the extraordinary power they wielded over record companies.

Amazingly, says one radio veteran, "nothing's changed since 'Hit Men.' The cast of characters is different, but nothing's really changed."

One major-label V.P. agrees: "It's only changed color and form, but in essence it's the same. It's nothing but bullshit and operators and wasted money. But it's very intricate, and the system has been laid down for years."

Some in the increasingly sophisticated and global music business wonder if the time has finally come to break free from the costly chains of independent promotion. After all, no other entertainment industry vests so much power and pays so much money to outside sources who do so little work. Yet just-released figures indicate music sales were soft last year. Will record companies have the power, or the nerve, to walk away?

"Labels claim they're trying to cut back on indies, but everybody just laughs," says one radio veteran, who has both programmed stations and done indie promotion work. (He, like most of the people interviewed for this story, asked that his name not be used.) Adds another veteran: "Labels are pissed off and want to cut back, but they're powerless to do anything about it."

"The labels have created a monster," agrees longtime artist manager Ron Stone. Nevertheless, Stone views indies as an important insurance policy for his clients. "I never want to find out after the fact that we should've hired this indie or that indie. I want to cover all the bases.

"Because you only get 12 weeks for your record to get any traction at radio. After 12 weeks the next wave of record company singles come over the breach and if you don't have any traction you get washed away. But now it's become even more complicated and expensive because of consolidation. It's a high-stakes poker game."

Playing off record industry insecurities, indies have been winning this poker game for decades.

The Clear Channel/Tri State move would be a watershed. Arguably the most powerful force in the music business, Clear Channel's multibillion-dollar assets include 60 percent of the United States' rock-radio business and the leading Top 40 stations in major markets across the country, including KIIS Los Angeles, WHTZ New York, WJMN Boston, WKSC-FM Chicago, KHKS-FM Dallas and WHYI Miami. The company also has extensive holdings in concert venues, concert production firms and outdoor advertising companies, stemming from its merger with the SFX conglomerate last year.

In that arena, Tri State would appear to be a minor player. But by maintaining a close relationship with Clear Channel as the conglomerate mushroomed and bought hundreds of new radio stations in recent years, Tri State has become synonymous with Clear Channel in the industry.

That relationship has translated into power and wealth. "Tri State's billings are probably up more than 1,000 percent since deregulation, considering how many more stations they have influence over," says one indie promoter.

Tri State's chiefs, Lenny Lyons and Bill Scull, did not return phone calls seeking comment.

Clear Channel stations not already using Tri State exclusively are likely to have to terminate their contracts with indie competitors, such as longtime powerhouse Jeff McClusky & Associates. That already may be happening. "They're clearing the decks," says one person who works at a major-label radio promotion department. (McClusky declined to comment.)

The move could mean higher indie fees for record companies. Tri State was charging labels $1,000 an add at some stations, but sources say those rates could jump considerably if Clear Channel and Tri State join forces.

Indeed, particularly in this deregulatory era, Clear Channel can basically charge whatever it wants. Why? Because record companies realize they can't create a hit without help from the conglomerate.

With that kind of clout, Clear Channel, through Tri State, could institute national buys for new singles. "Labels would pay $100,000 or $200,000 to get a single added to all the Clear Channel format stations one week," suggests one radio source. "And if they don't pay, there is no chance in hell they're getting that song on the radio without Tri State. If it's not on the list, it's not on stations."

And if the song isn't played on the radio, chances are it's not going to make the record company any money.

That raises real red flags at the record companies. "Tolls go up if there's only one road into town. And today you cannot have a hit record without Clear Channel or Tri State," says one record company president whose label recently scored a top-five hit on pop radio with the help of indie promoters. "That allows for an abusive type of toll collections. It seems to be getting out of hand. It's creating burdensome costs and it's screwing with the economics of the music business."

And perhaps most important, any long-term deal between Clear Channel and Tri State would essentially eliminate the all-important middleman. Record companies would instead be paying Tri State for airplay on Clear Channel stations. "That would put it into the realm of payola," says one record company promotion exec.

Clear Channel CEO Randy Michaels recently told the *Los Angeles Times* that the company does want a piece of the promotional pie, but only through an odd new twist: It plans to sell promotional packages to record companies that would identify the artist after each song is played.

But in a business swimming in money, some doubt things could become that cut and dried. For instance, what Clear Channel is proposing is something stations usually do for free; it's called "back-announcing," letting listeners know which artist they just heard. Will Clear Channel stations now only I.D. songs if the labels pay for the service?

"It sounds like extortion to me," says a former programmer. (Clear Channel executives were not available for comment.)

If the practice takes hold, look for competing groups, like Viacom's Infinity Broadcasting, to start hitting up labels for similar commercial buys. "It will throw the whole system into chaos," fears one indie.

⋅᠊◉᠊⋅

The indies' power illustrates just how crucial radio, especially Top 40, is in generating CD sales. (U.S. consumers bought more than 700 million CDs last year.) Steady touring, an Internet presence, glowing press and MTV help, of course, but mainstream radio play is still the engine that drives the music business.

Yet radio has traditionally been a brood of literally thousands of sometimes spatting siblings, each typically run by a P.D. with high self-regard.

The problem for record companies has always been that there are too many radio stations—and too many egos—nationwide for label staffers to keep close tabs on. So they need to hire indies, people with close business relationships in different markets. (Third-party indies have traditionally insulated labels from direct involvement in any payola activity as well.)

Here's how the game is played today:

The reality is, disc jockeys were cut out of music-making decisions at stations many years ago. Virtually all commercial radio airplay is determined by program directors, who typically construct elaborate schedules directing the DJs what to play and when.

Today, thanks to consolidation, even station program directors often get their playlist cues from above—from general managers, station owners or, in this age of consolidation, regional program directors.

So many indies no longer bother to target the P.D.s. Instead, they go straight to the general managers or owners and cut deals, typically guaranteeing a station in a medium-sized market roughly $75,000 to $100,000 annually in what is termed "promotional support." The station claims that the money goes to buying new station vans, T-shirts or giveaway prizes; in reality, the station spends the cash any way it wants.

That payment makes the indie the station's exclusive point man, the only one (or at least the first one) its programmers will talk to about adding new singles. Once that indie has "claimed" a station, he (there are very few shes in the business) sends out a notice to record companies, letting them know he will invoice them every time the station adds a song to its playlist.

"The truth is, you could [be] making a handsome living, and have a gigantic house in Greenville, S.C., for instance, if you have just six exclusive stations there," explains one industry veteran. (Arbitron ranks Greenville as the 61st largest radio market, with a metro population of 750,000.) "You could gross between half a million and 1 million dollars each year. That's with no staff—just a couple of phones and a fax machine. Because somebody is going to pay you

$1,000 every time one of those Greenville stations adds a song. And that $1,000 is just the average. Columbia records may be dying to get a single on, so they say, 'We'll pay you $2,500 for this add.'"

Do the math: six stations in a market like Greenville adding three songs a week, 50 weeks of the year. That represents about $900,000 worth of invoiced adds. If the indie is paying each station $75,000 a year in "promotional support," that leaves him with $450,000.

But that's just the beginning. There are additional sources of indie income, including retainers, "bill-backs" and "spin maintenance." Along with being paid on a per-add basis, some indies earn a retainer (roughly $800 a week) just to call stations on behalf of a song. Bill-backs are essentially second invoices—to cover "promotional purposes"—that indies send to record companies on top of the one for the add. If the add cost $2,000, the indie often sends a $1,000 bill-back invoice as well.

Meanwhile, the cost of the add covers just that: getting the song added to the playlist. If labels want to increase the spins (or number of times a song is played each week), that costs money, too. "There are spin programs you can buy," explains one record company source, such as "$4,000 to make the song top 15 at the station."

In the past, if indies wanted to increase their billings by getting stations to add more songs, they could employ "paper adds." Stations would notify labels that a song was on the playlist so the indie got paid, but in reality the single never got spun. Today, however, all key radio stations are monitored electronically by a company called Broadcast Data Service, which gives labels a detailed readout of actual airplay. Paper adds no longer pass the test.

The solution? A so-called lunar rotation.

"I've got one station that during crunch time in September and October, when every label is desperate for fourth-quarter adds, will do eight adds a week for four weeks in a row at $2,000 a pop," says one label source. That's 32 added songs—and $64,000 in indie invoices—for just one month. But the station's playlist could never support that many new songs. (With today's tightly controlled playlists, any new song is a risk that can cause listeners to switch to a channel with an older and more comforting hit.) Most of these new "adds" are played only in the early-morning hours, or in the "lunar rotation." They are detected by BDS, but don't really affect the station's playlist or ratings.

For record companies, indie costs can be staggering. Just to launch a single at rock radio over several weeks can cost between $100,000 and $250,000 in indie fees. What exactly do labels get in return? "I'll be damned if I know," says artist manager Stone. "It's bizarre." (Labels can sometimes get artists to pay the indie promotion costs, but not always.)

Regardless, the No. 1 rule of radio promotion is that the indie always gets paid. Even if rock programmers discover a good song by a new band on their own, and add it to their playlists because they like it, the station's indie gets paid for it.

Even if someone at Universal Records persuades a pop station to play Nelly's new single "Ride Wit Me," the indie gets paid. Even if the song is a sure hit that needs almost no promotion, like Aerosmith's latest, "Jaded," the indie gets paid. "Either way the invoices arrive and you pay, in the interest of keeping everybody happy," says one former programmer.

The fear is that if a label tangles with an indie over billing, he could torpedo the label's next project by bad-mouthing a new single or keeping it off the air until his previous invoice is paid. As messy as the relationship can be, the third-party arrangement between labels, indies and stations is crucial for appearance' sake. Today, indies pay stations for "access," not airplay. At least in theory.

"Everyone says indies don't force stations to add records. That's ridiculous," says one rock programmer who has worked in a Top 10 market. "Because [if there is friction] the indie will get on the phone with the station G.M. and say, 'Look, your P.D. has not been cooperative over the last few months on adds I need.' The G.M. either says to the indie, 'Our relationship is about access, not influence,' or he caves. Most G.M.s cave and have a word with the P.D.: 'Look, we have $100,000 a year riding on this relationship with our indie.' Then suddenly—bam—a song you know the P.D. hates shows up on the air."

"Record companies say, 'We're not doing anything illegal; we're just paying indies to promote the records," says another programmer. "And indies say we're not doing anything wrong; we're just helping market a radio station. Everybody toes the company line on this.

"But indies are like money launderers; they make sure record company money gets to radio stations, but in a different form."

POSTSCRIPT

Can the Independent Musical Artist Thrive in Today's Music Business?

Both of the authors speaking to this issue focus on a different aspect of how the music industry is changing. One looks at the entrepreneurial activity that new artists can avail themselves of, and the other looks at the role of the indie record promoter and that person's influence on what does, or does not, get played on the radio. Obviously, the recording industry has undergone many changes since the development of the Internet, and these examples represent only two of the many business models that are emerging at this time in history. Since Eric Boehlert's article, the FCC has attempted to crack down on the practice of justified payola—which is the term given to the way indie record promoters work. But despite a short flurry of activity with threats of penalties and greater regulation, little has been effective to curb the "pay for play" model.

The digital technologies used for recording today have drastically changed the way the recording industry operates. Not only does downloading digital information result in high-quality copies, but the number of musical artists who have access to low-cost recording devices is growing. There is probably no other media industry that has changed as rapidly as the recording industry, but others are not far behind.

One matter that will still be debated is the ownership of digital material. The Digital Millennium Copyright Act (DMCA) has attempted to clarify who controls what in the recording and re-recording of material, but the act is still vague and subject to many revisions in the future. Encryption technologies and dissolving digital signals may be short-term solutions for the industry to control content, but even these methods can be easily overwritten by a knowledgeable consumer.

Some good sources address the changing music business. Steve Gordon has written *The Future of the Music Business: How to Succeed with the New Digital Technologies* (Backbeat Books, 2005), which specifically says that "copyright is the basis of virtually every music business transaction." In a little more progressive vein, Dave Kusek and Gerd Leonhard have written *The Future of Music: Manifesto for the Digital Music Revolution* (Berlee Press, 2005) in which they envision "a future in which music will be like water: ubiquitous and free-flowing." A DVD featuring Russell Simmons and Lyor Cohen called *The Industry* (Kwame Amoaku, director, 2005) portrays the executive side of the music industry and the stresses of working in that industry today.

Students should also become familiar with some of the trade magazines in the industries they hope to pursue. If you are interested in the recording industry or radio, you should familiarize yourself with *Record World* and *Billboard*. Both are required reading for people who work in these industries (and also have job listings in the classified sections).

ISSUE 15

Can Present Technology Support Internet Growth?

YES: Spencer E. Ante, from "Back from the Dead," *Business Week* (June 25, 2007)

NO: David Talbot, from "The Internet Is Broken," *Technology Review* (December 2005/January 2006)

ISSUE SUMMARY

YES: Computer expert Spencer E. Ante claims that recent growth in new start-up firms that have learned how to compress information for the Internet, and increase options for message delivery, have created business opportunities for firms to compete in video and data delivery, resulting in a new telecom boom.

NO: *Technology Review* correspondent David Talbot claims that the problems that were originally in the Internet's architecture have only worsened, and that we need to reconceptualize a whole new structure for online communication before users get frustrated with the fragile Internet we now have.

$\mathbf{A}$s recently as 5 years ago, it looked as though major telecommunications firms would be given government approval to control the Internet. Users (particularly business users) complained of slow speed, lack of security, and too much spam. Individual users also started to find using the Internet for a greater number of personal interactions more problematic, since additional passwords, firewalls, viruses, worms, and other problems all had to be dealt with, often at expense to the user, or at least, a greater amount of time was required to overcome these problems.

The two selections in this issue think of the problems of using the Internet in different ways. Spencer E. Ante sees the business opportunities that arise when different companies find ways to deal with the problems, and sees online video as the engine that has begun to change the Internet's architecture. David Talbot warns that there are already so many problems associated with the current Internet, we should probably just start over and redesign a better network from scratch. He cites the efforts of many research projects that are trying to improve on the present Internet.

For many of us, using the Internet has become a daily event. We seldom think of the many problems associated with transmitting and receiving electronic information until we are hit with a problem we have to fix, like a worm or virus that infects our computers, causing it to lose files, or our computer hard drives to "fry." But as we begin to rely on the Internet more, for daily activities, business operations, the transmission of personal information, and receiving large data files of television programs, films, or even books, we need to think about security, privacy, and control, even more than we now do. Even though we might tend to think of our computers and using the Internet as a convenience, we would be incensed if we found that the government's data banks of our personal information, our school's data bank, or our doctor's medical files, were breached, causing personal information to get into the wrong hands.

Any history of the Internet discusses how the architecture was originally thought of as a platform built on trust. The idea of hackers attempting to disrupt the system, either for profit or for fun, just seemed too farfetched to bother about. Today though, online crime has skyrocketed, and there is an enormous market for personal information about individuals. Personal data mining has become a very lucrative business. Many of us find that we have to increasingly pay for services to run security checks, clean up fragmented hard drives, and help us control the technologies we use. When we do this, we have to question how "free" the Internet is for users.

The scenarios these authors portray show how more reliance on the Internet for a greater number of purposes results in controversial positions regarding security and privacy, and at the same time, fosters new markets for the solution of Internet-use problems. Clearly, traditional media industries have viewed the Internet as a new distribution medium for old technologies, like print, television, radio, and film, which require much more bandwidth than afforded by earlier infrastructures, but what will the end cost be? Will we have to sacrifice privacy and security to use the Internet for a greater number of purposes? What happens to critical industries that rely on the Internet if the Internet crashes? As we increasingly see more use of the Internet for communication purposes, might we end up communicating more, or less?

Back From The Dead

Peals of laughter rippled through the ether in April [2007] when hundreds of thousands of people clicked on YouTube.com to watch comedian Will Ferrell's short video, *The Landlord*. It's pretty hilarious, after all, to see a tiny 2-year-old girl in a party dress playing the part of an irate landlord, squeaking, "I am tired of this crap. . . . I want my money!" at Ferrell, her distraught, bushy-haired tenant.

What chuckling viewers couldn't see was the sprawling framework that companies have cobbled together to zap millions of clips like this one around the Internet every day. After a student, say, at Rutgers University in New Brunswick, N.J., clicked on *The Landlord*, one of hundreds of thousands of computer servers in Google's numerous California data centers pushed the video through Web networking gear from Cisco Systems and Juniper Networks. Last year, Google, YouTube's parent company, spent $1.9 billion, or 18% of its sales, on technology systems and other capital expenditures to serve videos speedily and process search-engine queries.

From Google's facility, the video shot across the U.S. on Level 3 Communications Inc.'s fiber-optic network, which encompasses 47,000 miles of cable. Reaching New Jersey, the clip was then handed off to a new fiber loop run by Verizon Communications Inc. Milliseconds later, Verizon served up the video to an apartment in New Brunswick through a broadband connection wired directly into the building.

In those taken-for-granted wires, cables, and computers lies a remarkable tale of resurrection. Seven years ago the communications business, made up of companies providing everything from phones to computer networks to routers and switches, was laid low by the worst collapse to hit a U.S. industry since the Great Depression. With breathtaking speed and little advance warning, high-flying companies like Global Crossing Ltd. and WorldCom Inc., which had loaded up on debt to build out fiber-optic networks and buy up companies in anticipation of a never-ending e-commerce boom, collapsed into bankruptcy. Giants such as AT&T were ripped apart as they scrambled to recover from free-falling sales and profits. Hundreds of thousands of workers lost their jobs. Prices of some inflated stocks—boasting price-to-earnings ratios that topped 400 in the most extreme cases—tumbled 95% or more.

Investors saw some $2 trillion of market value vanish in a little more than two years—twice the damage caused by the parallel bursting of the Internet bubble. Amid the wreckage, some predicted it could take a decade or more before the industry would climb back and fill all those empty pipes that starry-eyed executives had buried beneath the earth and oceans.

Over the past year, however, the telecom industry has roared back to life. Credit a steady rise in appetite for broadband Internet connections, which enable easy consumption of watch-my-cat video clips, iPod music files, and such Web-inspired services as free Internet phoning. Indeed, this year broadband adoption among U.S. adults is expected to cross the important threshold of 50%. Capital spending is on the rise as companies invest to build high-speed networks. Private equity players are placing enormous bets on the industry, such as the $8.2 billion that Silver Lake Partners and the Texas Pacific Group agreed to pay for networking gearmaker Avaya on June 5. And the glut in broadband communications capacity is all but gone.

About half of the Internet's transmission capacity was going unused in 2002. Today that pipeline has almost doubled in size, and yet the unused portion is down to about 30%. As a result, the price that companies pay for bandwidth in some parts of the U.S. is on the rise after six years of declines. "All of us are planning expansions of our backbones in order to support growth in Internet applications and video," says Dan Yost, executive vice-president for product at Denver-based communications provider Qwest Communications International Inc.

Perhaps the best indicator of the telecom revival is this startling data point: Profits for the industry this year are expected to reach an all-time high of $72 billion, topping for the first time the high-water mark of $65 billion in 1998.

You don't have to tell investors that telecom is back. It has been one of the hottest sectors in the stock market over the past 18 months. In 2006 big phone company and other stocks represented in the Telecom HOLDRS exchange-traded fund rose 34%, after a nearly 10% decline in 2005. And the fund is up 14.8% so far in 2007, compared with a 7.7% gain for the Dow Jones industrial average.

But telecom's revival has implications way beyond Wall Street. A dollar spent on telecom infrastructure produces an outsize impact on the U.S. economy as a whole. Indeed, a growing body of research has found that telecom investment plays a vital role in stimulating economic growth and productivity—more so than money spent on roads, electricity, or even education. Communication assets generate massive benefits by slashing the cost of doing business across the economy. A high-speed data network suddenly makes it easier and cheaper for all kinds of workers to place orders, service customers, and drum up new business.

A 2001 paper in the *American Economic Review*, written by Lars-Hendrik Röller of Berlin's Social Science Research Center and Leonard Waverman of the London Business School, concluded that the spread of land-based telecommunications networks in 21 developed nations accounted for one-third of the increase in economic output between 1970 and 1990. Other studies suggest fiber-optic and wireless networks provide their own special jolt to the economies of rich and poor nations alike. "Out of the ashes of the tech crisis we got a world-class, spanking-new communications network," says Mark Zandi, chief economist for Moody Corp.'s Economy.com Inc. "That has been key to outsized productivity gains ever since."

The $900 billion industry looks far different than it did in 2000. The balance of power has shifted toward Web upstarts such as YouTube and MySpace that barely registered seven years ago. The Bell phone companies, meanwhile, have consolidated and are furiously developing services they hope will let them capitalize on the billions they're investing to build speedy new networks.

It's not clear, though, how much of the value flowing from those networks will be captured by the Bell companies themselves. The big phone companies don't have a history of developing game-changing technologies in a competitive arena. "They've got a high hill to climb," says William E. Kennard, a former Federal Communications Commission chairman who is now managing director of Carlyle Group, a large private equity firm that has purchased some telecom assets. Meanwhile, Web companies such as Google are making a push to introduce more competition into the wireless industry and loosen the Bells' control over the Internet's distribution. . . .

The long-awaited arrival of Apple Inc.'s iPhone, which surfs the Web, takes pictures, plays music—and oh, yeah makes phone calls—may herald a new round of disruption for the big telcos. By allowing software developers to write applications for a better mobile Web device, Apple is attempting to shatter the so-called walled-garden model of wireless companies in which they control the wireless Internet gateway and the content that is featured on the handset screen. If the iPhone's Web browser performs as hyped, customers could start demanding a full range of Internet service on their phones and new freedom in their service plans. That, in turn, could create ever more demand for servers and routers, video services, and upgraded wireless networks.

Within the broad industry comeback are some remarkable turnarounds. Few companies got whipsawed harder by the bust than Level 3 Communications. Founder and Chief Executive James Q. Crowe started Level 3 in 1998 with a dream of building the world's largest, most advanced fiber-optic network—and with $3 billion raised from investors that included Walter Scott Jr., an Omaha construction magnate and friend of Warren Buffett. Before long, the company was digging up earth in 20 time zones with 250 crews installing fiber at a blistering pace of 19 miles a day. In March, 2000, Level 3's stock peaked at $130 a share. But with money flowing like water, by the end of the year at least 50 other companies jumped in to offer Internet backbone services. When it became apparent that Crowe's network was attracting more competitors than customers, the stock tumbled off a cliff, nearly killing the company. By October, 2001, it had bottomed out at $1.98 a share, sticking investors with tens of billions in losses.

Today, Level 3 is alive and growing again. Over the past three years a strong bond market enabled the company to refinance its massive debt at lower rates and pull off 10 acquisitions worth more than $4 billion. Level 3 says more than half of its network traffic today is from Web video, vs. no such traffic in 2000. High debt levels are keeping its business in the red; analysts don't expect Level 3 to generate positive cash flow until the end of this year. But over the past nine months, Level 3's stock has jumped 60%, to about 5½, as it reaps a kind of survivor's premium. "For a long time they were on death watch, but now they are the last guy standing in the U.S. wholesale [bandwidth] business," says Stephan Beckert, an analyst with Washington-based TeleGeography Research.

Now even some initial public offerings are drawing interest on Wall Street. Shares in Dallas-based wireless service provider MetroPCS Communications Inc. have jumped nearly 50% since the company went public on Apr. 22 at $23 a share. The stock price of communications gearmaker Riverbed Technology Inc. has more than quadrupled, to 40, since a September, 2006, IPO. "There's a huge amount of startup innovation" in the communications industry, says Morgan Jones, a partner with Battery Ventures, a venture-capital firm in Waltham, Mass., that invested in MetroPCS.

Of course, that's how it felt back in 2000—in spades. Then, it seemed as if demand for optical routers, "pump lasers," and other whiz-bang broadband technologies would grow forever. But when dot-coms started flopping in the spring of 2000, the absurdity of projections calling for Internet traffic to double every three months was revealed. The capital spigot, which had been gushing with cash for upstart phone companies and established carriers alike, shut off. With too many bandwidth providers chasing falling demand, wholesale Internet connection prices began falling by 50% a year.

The first big dominos fell in 2001, when broadband providers Winstar Communications and 360Networks filed for bankruptcy. Over the next three years 655 telecom companies, with a combined $749 billion in assets, filed for bankruptcy, according to BankruptcyData.com. On July 21, 2001, after an accounting scandal revealed billions of dollars of overstated profits, World-Com Inc., the giant that embodied the boom era's promise, filed the largest bankruptcy claim ever.

The scope of the wipeout was breathtaking, conjuring comparisons with the savings-and-loan crisis of the 1980s. But this time it was private investors who ate the losses, not the government. And the speed of creative destruction had one advantage: By early 2004, recovery was already under way. In a key deal in February of that year, Cingular Wireless agreed to buy AT&T Wireless Services for about $41 billion. Soon the consolidation shifted into overdrive. In December, Sprint announced a deal to buy Nextel Communications for $35 billion; a month later, SBC Communications said it would buy AT&T for $16 billion; a month after that, Verizon struck a deal to acquire MCI, the former WorldCom, for $8.4 billion.

But while the phone and cable companies tightened their grips on the transmission pipes, an army of upstarts went to work filling them. It's no accident that the explosion of online video and the rebirth of telecom happened around the same time. A typical video consumes 1,000 times as much bandwidth as a sound file. (Likewise, high-definition video, which consumes 7 to 10 times as much bandwidth as normal video, could trigger the next surge in network growth.)

Online video barely existed in 2000. Today, fully one-third of all Internet traffic comes from Web videos, *The Landlord* included. Thanks to bandwidth-hungry services such as YouTube, global Internet traffic from 2003 to 2006 grew at a compounded annual rate of 75% a year, according to TeleGeography. "When you compound those numbers, I don't care how much inventory you have, it's going to disappear off the shelf," says Level 3 CEO Crowe.

To understand the velocity at which video is taking over the Web, consider the experience of VideoEgg Inc. While not nearly as well known as YouTube, VideoEgg in less than two years has grown to become the largest video service for social-networking Web sites. Instead of building their own Web video services, big online communities such as Bebo and hi5 use VideoEgg technology to let members broadcast videos on their sites.

Today, VideoEgg serves up about 15 million videos a day across 70 Web sites. To deliver them, the company works with giants such as AT&T and Verizon as well as Web content-delivery service Akamai Technologies. By year end, VideoEgg CEO and co-founder Matt Sanchez believes the company could more than triple its current traffic.

Mainstream organizations also have knit broadband networks into the fabric of their daily operations. Take something as simple as mail delivery. Since 2005 the U.S. Postal Service has been using wireless scanners so mail handlers can keep tabs on the location of every one of the 200 billion pieces of mail it delivers in a year. And it is now testing a wireless system that will keep track of thousands of mail trailers parked in its 22 bulk mail centers. Since 2001 the Postal Service has boosted its network capacity tenfold to support these systems. As a result, the service has become a major buyer of telecom infrastructure, spending hundreds of millions of dollars a year on communications services provided by Verizon and AT&T.

Indeed, while companies remain tightfisted in their spending on computers and other information technology, many of them believe new networks provide a big bang for their bucks. Global spending on communications equipment for corporations is forecast to grow 20% over the next three years, according to Infonetics Research of Campbell, Calif. Consider the experience of clothing maker Liz Claiborne Inc.: In late 2005 employees were becoming increasingly frustrated when it was taking up to half an hour just to open up a 40-megabyte spreadsheet. After the company installed new gear from Riverbed Technology that compresses the files and stores the most popular data closer to the users, documents popped open in a few minutes. "People were like, Wow, I can't believe how fast this is,'" says Rakesh Patel, Liz Claiborne's technical architect.

If the old telecom world was dominated by bloated regional monopolies, the new world is a competitive mosh pit stocked with sinewy players. That's reflected in how much more productive the industry has become. While telecom revenues are now 19% higher than they were in 2000, that money supports just 1.1 million workers, down nearly 30% from boom-era levels. "It has gotten unrelentingly competitive in every area: broadband, land line, and wireless," says AT&T's new CEO, Randall Stephenson.

For the big carriers such as AT&T, Verizon, and Qwest, the main challenge is to slow defections of traditional land-line customers while producing faster revenue growth in new markets such as wireless, Internet service, pay TV, and advertising. The carriers must overcome their reputation for being "dumb pipes" and prove they can fill their networks with innovative bundles of products and services that strike a chord with customers—all while battling cable operators, which are poaching millions of phone customers, and fending off or making peace with aggressive new entrants such as Google and Apple.

There is reason to believe the phone companies are reinventing themselves. Verizon, for example, will soon offer services that allow consumers to personalize and share photos, videos, and other media among their cell phones, PCs, and TVs. Five years ago, Verizon employed about 100 software developers who were mostly focused on installing products developed outside the company. Today, Chief Technology Officer Shaygan Kheradpir oversees more than 1,000 developers. In July the company will launch an interactive media guide for Verizon's FiOSTV service; by clicking on it, couch potatoes can access all of the photos, music, and videos they have stored on a PC. Further down the road, Verizon says it will steal a page from YouTube and allow TV customers to create their own personalized video channels. "We don't have to own every service," says Verizon CEO Ivan G. Seidenberg. "We just have to package a lot of them and help the customer find the things they like."

It doesn't help that American phone companies can no longer rely on the wireless business for growth as much as they have in the past. Mobile telephony is a maturing market. For the first time, this year the growth rate for new wireless subscribers in the U.S. is expected to decline. To continue generating double-digit revenue growth, wireless carriers must steal customers from one another or persuade more consumers to buy next-generation phones and purchase so-called 3G services such as games, music, and videos. Every major wireless service provider is upgrading its networks to provide faster speeds for uploading and downloading wireless content. But only 15% of the wireless handsets in the U.S. are capable of handling 3G services.

That raises a troubling question: Could another unpleasant surprise await investors who have bought into this shiny image of telecom transformation? Maybe. Some of the projections for new mobile-phone businesses, especially video downloads, seem over-the-top in a late-'90s kind of way. But there's nowhere near the sense of limitless expectations that drove telecom investors off the cliff last time. Despite strong performances of late, stocks such as AT&T, Verizon, and Cisco Systems are trading today at 15 to 20 times 2007 earnings. Cisco's price-earnings ratio in 2000 hit 145.

Perhaps Cisco, the No. 1 seller of network gear, is emblematic. In what seemed at the time like a milestone in the Net's ascendency, Cisco briefly passed Microsoft Corp. in March, 2000, to become the most valuable company on the planet. Soon after, Cisco had to write down $2 billion of unsellable routers and other equipment. By July, 2002, its stock price had tumbled from 77 to 12. Cisco cut costs, laid off workers for the first time, and weathered the storm. Today, it is flowering again, selling equipment to cable and phone companies that are expanding their services, and branching out into new business and consumer markets. In the most recent quarter, the company reported profits of $1.9 billion, up 34%, on strong sales of $8.9 billion. On June 12, the stock was trading around 26.

CEO John Chambers tells a post-bust story that sums up how quickly things have turned around. Back in 2004, he recalls, critics laughed when

Cisco rolled out an audacious new router, the CRS-1, capable of transmitting the entire contents of the Library of Congress in a few seconds. Analysts predicted only a handful would sell. This year, thanks to the video bandwidth hogs, sales of the CRS-1 are expected to hit $1 billion, more than double the figure for 2006. Says Chambers, who has never lacked for confidence throughout the boom, bust, and boom again: "The market is going exactly where we thought."

David Talbot

The Internet Is Broken

In his office within the gleaming-stainless-steel and orange-brick jumble of MIT's Stata Center, Internet elder statesman and onetime chief protocol architect David D. Clark prints out an old PowerPoint talk. Dated July 1992, it ranges over technical issues like domain naming and scalability. But in one slide, Clark points to the Internet's dark side: its lack of built-in security. In others, he observes that sometimes the worst disasters are caused not by sudden events but by slow, incremental processes—and that humans are good at ignoring problems. "Things get worse slowly. People adjust," Clark noted in his presentation. "The problem is assigning the correct degree of fear to distant elephants."

Today, Clark believes the elephants are upon us. Yes, the Internet has wrought wonders: e-commerce has flourished, and e-mail has become a ubiquitous means of communication. Almost one billion people now use the Internet, and critical industries like banking increasingly rely on it. At the same time, the Internet's shortcomings have resulted in plunging security and a decreased ability to accommodate new technologies. "We are at an inflection point, a revolution point," Clark now argues. And he delivers a strikingly pessimistic assessment of where the Internet will end up without dramatic intervention. "We might just be at the point where the utility of the Internet stalls—and perhaps turns downward."

Indeed, for the average user, the Internet these days all too often resembles New York's Times Square in the 1980s. It was exciting and vibrant, but you made sure to keep your head down, lest you be offered drugs, robbed, or harangued by the insane. Times Square has been cleaned up, but the Internet keeps getting worse, both at the user's level, and—in the view of Clark and others—deep within its architecture. Over the years, as Internet applications proliferated—wireless devices, peer-to-peer file-sharing, telephony—companies and network engineers came up with ingenious and expedient patches, plugs, and workarounds. The result is that the originally simple communications technology has become a complex and convoluted affair. For all of the Internet's wonders, it is also difficult to manage and more fragile with each passing day.

That's why Clark argues that it's time to rethink the Internet's basic architecture, to potentially start over with a fresh design—and equally important, with a plausible strategy for proving the design's viability, so that it stands a chance of implementation. "It's not as if there is some killer technology at the protocol or network level that we somehow failed to include," says Clark. "We need to take

From *Technology Review*, December 2005/January 2006, pp. 63–69. Copyright © 2006 by Technology Review. Reprinted by permission of Technology Review via the Copyright Clearance Center.

all the technologies we already know and fit them together so that we get a different overall system. This is not about building a technology innovation that changes the world but about architecture—pulling the pieces together in a different way to achieve high-level objectives."

Just such an approach is now gaining momentum, spurred on by the National Science Foundation. NSF managers are working to forge a five-to-seven-year plan estimated to cost $200 million to $300 million in research funding to develop clean-slate architectures that provide security, accommodate new technologies, and are easier to manage. They also hope to develop an infrastructure that can be used to prove that the new system is really better than the current one. "If we succeed in what we are trying to do, this is bigger than anything we, as a research community, have done in computer science so far," says Guru Parulkar, an NSF program manager involved with the effort. "In terms of its mission and vision, it is a very big deal. But now we are just at the beginning. It has the potential to change the game. It could take it to the next level in realizing what the Internet could be that has not been possible because of the challenges and problems."

Firewall Nation

When AOL updates its software, the new version bears a number: 7.0, 8.0, 9.0. The most recent version is called AOL 9.0 Security Edition. These days, improving the utility of the Internet is not so much about delivering the latest cool application; it's about survival. In August, IBM released a study reporting that "virus-laden e-mails and criminal driven security attacks" leapt by 50 percent in the first half of 2005, with government and the financial-services, manufacturing, and healthcare industries in the crosshairs. In July, the Pew Internet and American Life Project reported that 43 percent of U.S. Internet users—59 million adults—reported having spyware or adware on their computers, thanks merely to visiting websites. (In many cases, they learned this from the sudden proliferation of error messages or freeze-ups.) Fully 91 percent had adopted some defensive behavior—avoiding certain kinds of websites, say, or not downloading software. "Go to a neighborhood bar, and people are talking about firewalls. That was just not true three years ago," says Susannah Fox, associate director of the Pew project.

Then there is spam. One leading online security company, Symantec, says that between July 1 and December 31, 2004, spam surged 77 percent at companies that Symantec monitored. The raw numbers are staggering: weekly spam totals on average rose from 800 million to more than 1.2 billion messages, and 60 percent of all e-mail was spam, according to Symantec. But perhaps most menacing of all are "botnets"—collections of computers hijacked by hackers to do remote-control tasks like sending spam or attacking websites. This kind of wholesale hijacking—made more potent by wide adoption of always-on broadband connections—has spawned hard-core crime: digital extortion. Hackers are threatening destructive attacks against companies that don't meet their financial demands. According to a study by a Carnegie Mellon University researcher, 17 of 100 companies surveyed had been threatened with such attacks.

Simply put, the Internet has no inherent security architecture—nothing to stop viruses or spam or anything else. Protections like firewalls and antispam software are addons, security patches in a digital arms race. The President's Information Technology Advisory Committee, a group stocked with a who's who of infotech CEOs and academic researchers, says the situation is bad and getting worse. "Today, the threat clearly is growing," the council wrote in a report issued in early 2005. "Most indicators and studies of the frequency, impact, scope, and cost of cyber security incidents—among both organizations and individuals—point to continuously increasing levels and varieties of attacks." And we haven't even seen a real act of cyberterror, the "digital Pearl Harbor" memorably predicted by former White House counterterrorism czar Richard Clarke in 2000. Consider the nation's electrical grid: it relies on continuous network-based communications between power plants and grid managers to maintain a balance between production and demand. A well-placed attack could trigger a costly blackout that would cripple part of the country. The conclusion of the advisory council's report could not have been starker: "The IT infrastructure is highly vulnerable to premeditated attacks with potentially catastrophic effects."

The system functions as well as it does only because of "the forbearance of the virus authors themselves," says Jonathan Zittrain, who cofounded the Berkman Center for Internet and Society at Harvard Law School and holds the Chair in Internet Governance and Regulation at the University of Oxford. "With one or two additional lines of code . . . the viruses could wipe their hosts' hard drives clean or quietly insinuate false data into spreadsheets or documents. Take any of the top ten viruses and add a bit of poison to them, and most of the world wakes up on a Tuesday morning unable to surf the Net— or finding much less there if it can."

Patchwork Problem

The Internet's original protocols, forged in the late 1960s, were designed to do one thing very well: facilitate communication between a few hundred academic and government users. The protocols efficiently break digital data into simple units called packets and send the packets to their destinations through a series of network routers. Both the routers and PCs, also called nodes, have unique digital addresses known as Internet Protocol or IP addresses. That's basically it. The system assumed that all users on the network could be trusted and that the computers linked by the Internet were mostly fixed objects.

The Internet's design was indifferent to whether the information packets added up to a malicious virus or a love letter; it had no provisions for doing much besides getting the data to its destination. Nor did it accommodate nodes that moved—such as PDAs that could connect to the Internet at any of myriad locations. Over the years, a slew of patches arose: firewalls, antivirus software, spam filters, and the like. One patch assigns each mobile node a new IP address every time it moves to a new point in the network.

Clearly, security patches aren't keeping pace. That's partly because different people use different patches and not everyone updates them religiously;

some people don't have any installed. And the most common mobility patch—the IP addresses that constantly change as you move around—has downsides. When your mobile computer has a new identity every time it connects to the Internet, the websites you deal with regularly won't know it's you. This means, for example, that your favorite airline's Web page might not cough up a reservation form with your name and frequent-flyer number already filled out. The constantly changing address also means you can expect breaks in service if you are using the Internet to, say, listen to a streaming radio broadcast on your PDA. It also means that someone who commits a crime online using a mobile device will be harder to track down.

In the view of many experts in the field, there are even more fundamental reasons to be concerned. Patches create an ever more complicated system, one that becomes harder to manage, understand, and improve upon. "We've been on a track for 30 years of incrementally making improvements to the Internet and fixing problems that we see," says Larry Peterson, a computer scientist at Princeton University. "We see vulnerability, we try to patch it. That approach is one that has worked for 30 years. But there is reason to be concerned. Without a long-term plan, if you are just patching the next problem you see, you end up with an increasingly complex and brittle system. It makes new services difficult to employ. It makes it much harder to manage because of the added complexity of all these point solutions that have been added. At the same time, there is concern that we will hit a dead end at some point. There will be problems we can't sufficiently patch."

The patchwork approach draws complaints even from the founder of a business that is essentially an elaborate and ingenious patch for some of the Internet's shortcomings. Tom Leighton is cofounder and chief scientist of Akamai, a company that ensures that its clients' Web pages and applications are always available, even if huge numbers of customers try to log on to them or a key fiber-optic cable is severed. Akamai closely monitors network problems, strategically stores copies of a client's website at servers around the world, and accesses those servers as needed. But while his company makes its money from patching the Net, Leighton says the whole system needs fundamental architectural change. "We are in the mode of trying to plug holes in the dike," says Leighton, an MIT mathematician who is also a member of the President's Information Technology Advisory Committee and chair of its Cyber Security Subcommittee. "There are more and more holes, and more resources are going to plugging the holes, and there are less resources being devoted to fundamentally changing the game, to changing the Internet."

When Leighton says "resources," he's talking about billions of dollars. Take Microsoft, for example. Its software mediates between the Internet and the PC. These days, of the $6 billion that Microsoft spends annually on research and development, approximately one-third, or $2 billion, is directly spent on security efforts. "The evolution of the Internet, the development of threats from the Internet that could attempt to intrude on systems—whether Web servers, Web browsers, or e-mail-based threats—really changed the equation," says Steve Lipner, Microsoft's director of security strategy and engineering strategy. "Ten years ago, I think people here in the industry were designing software for new features, new performance, ease of use, what have you. Today, we train everybody for security." Not only does this focus on security siphon resources from other research, but it can even hamper research that does get funded. Some innovations have been kept in the lab, Lipner says, because Microsoft couldn't be sure they met security standards.

Of course, some would argue that Microsoft is now scrambling to make up for years of selling insecure products. But the Microsoft example has parallels elsewhere. Eric Brewer, director of Intel's Berkeley, CA, research lab, notes that expenditures on security are like a "tax" and are "costing the nation billions and billions of dollars." This tax shows up as increased product prices, as companies' expenditures on security services and damage repair, as the portion of processor speed and storage devoted to running defensive programs, as the network capacity consumed by spam, and as the costs to the average person trying to dodge the online minefield of buying the latest firewalls. "We absolutely can leave things alone. But it has this continuous 30 percent tax, and the tax might go up," Brewer says. "The penalty for not [fixing] it isn't immediately fatal. But things will slowly get worse and might get so bad that people won't use the Internet as much as they might like."

The existing Internet architecture also stands in the way of new technologies. Networks of intelligent sensors that collectively monitor and interpret things like factory conditions, the weather, or video images could change computing as much as cheap PCs did 20 years ago. But they have entirely different communication requirements. "Future networks aren't going to be PCs docking to mainframes. It's going to be about some car contacting the car next to it. All of this is happening in an embedded context. Everything is machine to machine rather than people to people," says Dipankar Raychaudhuri, director of the Wireless Information Network Laboratory (Winlab) at Rutgers University. With today's architecture, making such a vision reality would require more and more patches.

Architectural Digest

When Clark talks about creating a new architecture, he says the job must start with the setting of goals. First, give the medium a basic security architecture—the ability to authenticate whom you are communicating with and prevent things like spam and viruses from ever reaching your PC. Better security is "the most important motivation for this redesign," Clark says. Second, make the new architecture practical by devising protocols that allow Internet service providers to better route traffic and collaborate to offer advanced services without compromising their businesses. Third, allow future computing devices of any size to connect to the Internet—not just PCs but sensors and embedded processors. Fourth, add technology that makes the network easier to manage and more resilient. For example, a new design should allow all pieces of the network to detect and report emerging problems—whether technical breakdowns, traffic jams, or replicating worms—to network administrators.

The good news is that some of these goals are not so far off. NSF has, over the past few years, spent more than $30 million supporting and planning such research. Academic and corporate research labs have generated a number of promising technologies: ways to authenticate who's online; ways to identify criminals while protecting the privacy of others; ways to add wireless devices and sensors. While nobody is saying that any single one of these technologies will be included in a new architecture, they provide a starting point for understanding what a "new" Internet might actually look like and how it would differ from the old one.

Some promising technologies that might figure into this new architecture are coming from PlanetLab, which Princeton's Peterson has been nurturing in recent years *(see "The Internet Reborn," October 2003)*. In this still-growing project, researchers throughout the world have been developing software that can be grafted onto today's dumb Internet routers. One example is software that "sniffs" passing Internet traffic for worms. The software looks for telltale packets sent out by worm-infected machines searching for new hosts and can warn system administrators of infections. Other software prototypes detect the emergence of data traffic jams and come up with more efficient ways to reroute traffic around them. These kinds of algorithms could become part of a fundamental new infrastructure, Peterson says.

A second set of technologies could help authenticate Internet communications. It would be a huge boon to Internet security if you could be sure an e-mail from your bank is really from your bank and not a scam artist, and if the bank could be sure that when someone logs in to your account, that person is really you and not someone who stole your account number.

Today, the onus of authentication is on the Internet user, who is constantly asked to present information of various kinds: passwords, social-security numbers, employee ID numbers, credit card numbers, frequent-flyer numbers, PIN numbers, and so on. But when millions of users are constantly entering these gate-opening numbers, it makes it that much easier for spyware, or a thief sniffing wireless Internet traffic, to steal, commit fraud, and do damage.

One evolving solution, developed by Internet2—a research consortium based in Ann Arbor, MI, that develops advanced Internet technologies for use by research laboratories and universities—effectively creates a middleman who does the job. Called Shibboleth, the software mediates between a sender and a recipient; it transmits the appropriate ID numbers, passwords, and other identifying information to the right recipients for you, securely, through the centralized exchange of digital certificates and other means. In addition to making the dispersal of information more secure, it helps protect privacy. That's because it discloses only the "attributes" of a person pertinent to a particular transaction, rather than the person's full "identity."

Right now, Shibboleth is used by universities to mediate access to online libraries and other resources; when you log on, the university knows your "attribute"—you are an enrolled student—and not your name or other personal information. This basic concept can be expanded: your employment status could open the gates to your company's servers; your birth date could allow you to buy wine online. A similar scheme could give a bank confidence that online account access is legitimate and conversely give a bank customer confidence that banking communications are really from the bank.

Shibboleth and similar technologies in development can, and do, work as patches. But some of their basic elements could also be built into a replacement Internet architecture. "Most people look at the Internet as such a dominant force, they only think how they can make it a little better," Clark says. "I'm saying, 'Hey, think about the future differently. What should our communications environment of 10 to 15 years from now look like? What is your goal?'"

The Devil We Know

It's worth remembering that despite all of its flaws, all of its architectural kluginess and insecurity and the costs associated with patching it, the Internet still gets the job done. Any effort to implement a better version faces enormous practical problems: all Internet service providers would have to agree to change all their routers and software, and someone would have to foot the bill, which will likely come to many billions of dollars. But NSF isn't proposing to abandon the old network or to forcibly impose something new on the world. Rather, it essentially wants to build a better mousetrap, show that it's better, and allow a changeover to take place in response to user demand.

To that end, the NSF effort envisions the construction of a sprawling infrastructure that could cost approximately $300 million. It would include research labs across the United States and perhaps link with research efforts abroad, where new architectures can be given a full work-out. With a high-speed optical backbone and smart routers, this test bed would be far more elaborate and representative than the smaller, more limited test beds in use today. The idea is that new architectures would be battle tested with real-world Internet traffic. "You hope that provides enough value added that people are slowly and selectively willing to switch, and maybe it gets enough traction that people will switch over," Parulkar says. But he acknowledges, "Ten years from now, how things play out is anyone's guess. It could be a parallel infrastructure that people could use for selective applications."

Still, skeptics claim that a smarter network could be even more complicated and thus failure-prone than the original bare-bones Internet. Conventional wisdom holds that the network should remain dumb, but that the smart devices at its ends should become smarter. "I'm not happy with the current state of affairs. I'm not happy with spam; I'm not happy with the amount of vulnerability to various forms of attack," says Vinton Cerf, one of the inventors of the Internet's basic protocols, who recently joined Google with a job title created just for him: chief Internet evangelist. "I do want to distinguish that the primary vectors causing a lot of trouble are penetrating holes in operating systems. It's more like the operating systems don't protect themselves very well. An argument could be made, 'Why does the network have to do that?'"

According to Cerf, the more you ask the network to examine data—to authenticate a person's identity, say, or search for viruses—the less efficiently it will move the data around. "It's really hard to have a network-level thing do this stuff, which means you have to assemble the packets into something bigger and thus violate all the protocols," Cerf says. "That takes a heck of a lot of resources." Still, Cerf sees value in the new NSF initiative. "If Dave Clark . . . sees some notions and ideas that would be dramatically better than what we have, I think that's important and healthy," Cerf says. "I sort of wonder about something, though. The collapse of the Net, or a major security disaster, has been predicted for a decade now." And of course no such disaster has occurred—at least not by the time this issue of *Technology Review* went to press.

The NSF effort to make the medium smarter also runs up against the libertarian culture of the Internet, says Harvard's Zittrain. "The NSF program is a worthy one in the first instance because it begins with the premise that the current Net has outgrown some of its initial foundations and associated tenets," Zittrain says. "But there is a risk, too, that any attempt to rewrite the Net's technical constitution will be so much more fraught, so much more self-conscious of the nontechnical matters at stake, that the cure could be worse than the problem."

Still, Zittrain sees hazards ahead if some sensible action isn't taken. He posits that the Internet's security problems, and the theft of intellectual property, could produce a counterreaction that would amount to a clamp-down on the medium—everything from the tightening of software makers' control over their operating systems to security lockdowns by businesses. And of course, if a "digital Pearl Harbor" does occur, the federal government is liable to respond reflexively with heavy-handed reforms and controls. If such tightenings happen, Zittrain believes we're bound to get an Internet that is, in his words, "more secure—and less interesting."

But what all sides agree on is that the Internet's perennial problems are getting worse, at the same time that society's dependence on it is deepening. Just a few years ago, the work of researchers like Peterson didn't garner wide interest outside the networking community. But these days, Clark and Peterson are giving briefings to Washington policymakers. "There is recognition that some of these problems are potentially quite serious. You could argue that they have always been there," Peterson says. "But there is a wider recognition in the highest level of the government that this is true. We are getting to the point where we are briefing people in the president's Office of Science and Technology Policy. I specifically did, and other people are doing that as well. As far as I know, that's pretty new."

Outside the door to Clark's office at MIT, a nametag placed by a prankster colleague announces it to be the office of Albus Dumbledore—the wise headmaster of the Hog-warts School of Witchcraft and Wizardry, a central figure in the Harry Potter books. But while Clark in earlier years may have wrought some magic, helping transform the original Internet protocols into a robust communications technology that changed the world, he no longer has much control over what happens next.

But "because we don't have power, there is a greater chance that we will be left alone to try," he says. And so Clark, like Dumbledore, clucks over new generations of technical wizards. "My goal in calling for a fresh design is to free our minds from the current constraints, so we can envision a different future," he says. "The reason I stress this is that the Internet is so big, and so successful, that it seems like a fool's errand to send someone off to invent a different one." Whether the end result is a whole new architecture—or just an effective set of changes to the existing one—may not matter in the end. Given how entrenched the Internet is, the effort will have succeeded, he says, if it at least gets the research community working toward common goals, and helps "impose creep in the right direction."

POSTSCRIPT

Can Present Technology Support Internet Growth?

Threats to the Internet come in many forms. Hackers sometimes choose to disrupt communications just to show they can; technologies and systems do sometimes fail; electrical energy collapses in storms when batteries aren't charged or when you forget to pay a bill. Some of these problems are human-made; others are not. But if we are going to rely more on the Internet, we should do so thoughtfully and sensibly.

While we all would like to know that the technologies we use on a daily basis are reliable, there have been many examples of how fragile our information infrastructure can be. When Hurricane Katrina destroyed all communications in and around New Orleans and the Gulf region in 2005, we saw how devastating lack of communication became to effectively trying to help those who were stranded in the storm. In 2003, power outages in the Midwestern region of the United States affected 800,000 people who could not use any electrical technologies. Even the most optimistic of Internet prophets acknowledge that it wouldn't take much to wipe out personal records or affect communications for every Internet user in the world, and that we will eventually have to deal with the problem of an Internet crash of some sort.

It may be true that there are many people working on trying to prevent such a crash from occurring, but their efforts are only as good as the systems available. Do you think that added patches, programs, and services can protect the Internet, or do you agree that while the Internet is still young, effective measures should be taken to redesign and improve the entire structure? Do you take the position that the Internet should be regulated and controlled so tightly by businesses, the government, or service providers that problems could be more easily traced?

There are many suggestions for how we can improve our communication networks, and the Internet in particular. We think some good sources of information are already available to us in a number of forms. Robert D. Oberst has an optimistic view of what the future will be like in *2020 Web Vision: How the Internet Will Revolutionize Future Homes, Business & Society* (Universal Publishers, 2001), and one of the editors of this volume, Jarice Hanson, has a more critical examination of how increased reliance on the Internet affects our social interactions and our sense of self in society in *24/7: How Cell Phones and the Internet Change the Way We Live, Work and Play* (Praeger, 2007).

Attempting to come to terms with some of the problems of the Internet, if left unchecked, are described in Sebastian Rupley's 2005 article in *PC Magazine*, called "The Net's Next Ten Years," and an article in *Wired* magazine by Joshua Davis describes what recently happened in Estonia, the most wired country in Europe, when bots invaded the Internet and shut down communications throughout the country in "Web War I" (September 2007). Whatever your position on this issue, remember to back up your files, online, and off!

ISSUE 16

Does Big Media Control the FCC?

YES: Ted Turner, from "My Beef with Big Media: How Government Protects Big Media—and Shuts Out Upstarts Like Me," *Washington Monthly* (July/August 2004)

NO: Michael K. Powell, from "Yes, The FCC Should Relax Its Ownership Rules," *Congressional Digest* (October 2003)

ISSUE SUMMARY

YES: Ted Turner, founder of CNN, argues that government protects big media, and shuts out upstarts like him. Throughout his career he has seen regulations emerge that transfer power to larger corporations, making it impossible to survive as an independent. Important people, ideas, and innovations are lost with this model.

NO: Federal Communications Commission (FCC) ex-Chairman Michael Powell, in testimony before the Senate Committee on Commercial, Science and Transportation, outlined the FCC proposal to relax ownership rules. He cites changes in the marketplace and argues that these changes will benefit the public interest through protecting viewpoint diversity, enhancing competition, and fostering localism.

Since the 1980s, the U.S. media industries have undergone a shift in a) the economy within which the media industry functioned, b) the technology through which media are distributed, and c) the regulatory philosophy through which media are viewed by government and the public. At the same time, changing national and global economies offered other challenges. Even while media corporations were subject to extreme pressures for financial performance, they were experiencing a decline in viewer loyalty and an increase in sources of media that led to market fragmentation. Pressure to create larger corporate entities and changes in the ownership rules made by the Telecommunications Act of 1996 opened the market for substantial restructuring, in which acquisitions, mergers, and takeovers abounded. Although the restructuring of the U.S. media industry is still very much underway, the effects are clear: the U.S. media is much more consolidated. It is easy to expect that the industry will continue to respond to financial performance demands with ongoing efforts to consolidate, cluster properties, gain market power within local and regional operational areas, and capture synergies through vertical and horizontal integration.

As part of the 1996 Telecommunications Act, Congress mandated that the FCC review its broadcast ownership rule to determine "whether any of such rules are necessary in the public interest as a result of competition." In 2003 the FCC voted to loosen ownership regulations. See these original ownership rules outlined at `http://www.fcc.gov/cgb/consumerfacts/reviewrules.html`. Proposed changes included allowing a company to own both a newspaper and TV or radio station in the same market. It also proposed allowing a company to own 2 or 3 stations in a market, depending on market size. Another decision allowed a single company to own enough local stations to reach 45% of U.S. households, up from 35% previously. Congress scaled this back to 39%.

There was a storm of protest over these changes, so much so that Congress stepped in and created regulation concerning television ownership, and the FCC withdrew some of its other suggestions. These protests focused on the problems of a media system defined by commercial and corporate concerns, and the implications for diversity, localism, and quality. Ted Turner makes these claims, but his main argument is that big business is bad for media businesses. Turner argues that small, emerging corporations have to innovate to succeed. They are quicker with new technologies and new ideas. They take risks that larger conglomerates won't touch. If these independents are squeezed out, the industry suffers. If the publicly traded conglomerates shape what we see, both the economy and the quality of public life will suffer.

Ex-FCC Chairman Michael Powell argues that current media systems give us more media, more diversity, more choices and more control than ever before. Moreover, these conglomerates can protect viewpoint diversity, enhance competition, and foster localism. He argues that we have very little evidence that the proposed rule changes would have negative consequences and that corporations are responsive to social needs. Even though the public has repudiated this plan, it very clearly outlines the perspective of big business, which continues its pattern of consolidation.

YES

Ted Turner

My Beef with Big Media: How Government Protects Big Media—and Shuts Out Upstarts Like Me

In the late 1960s, when Turner Communications was a business of billboards and radio stations and I was spending much of my energy ocean racing, a UHF-TV station came up for sale in Atlanta. It was losing $50,000 a month and its programs were viewed by fewer than 5 percent of the market.

I acquired it.

When I moved to buy a second station in Charlotte—this one worse than the first—my accountant quit in protest, and the company's board vetoed the deal. So I mortgaged my house and bought it myself. The Atlanta purchase turned into the Superstation; the Charlotte purchase—when I sold it 10 years later—gave me the capital to launch CNN.

Both purchases played a role in revolutionizing television. Both required a streak of independence and a taste for risk. And neither could happen today. In the current climate of consolidation, independent broadcasters simply don't survive for long. That's why we haven't seen a new generation of people like me or even Rupert Murdoch—independent television upstarts who challenge the big boys and force the whole industry to compete and change.

It's not that there aren't entrepreneurs eager to make their names and fortunes in broadcasting if given the chance. If nothing else, the 1990s dot-com boom showed that the spirit of entrepreneurship is alive and well in America, with plenty of investors willing to put real money into new media ventures. The difference is that Washington has changed the rules of the game. When I was getting into the television business, lawmakers and the Federal Communications Commission (FCC) took seriously the commission's mandate to promote diversity, localism, and competition in the media marketplace. They wanted to make sure that the big, established networks—CBS, ABC, NBC—wouldn't forever dominate what the American public could watch on TV. They wanted independent producers to thrive. They wanted more people to be able to own TV stations. They believed in the value of competition.

So when the FCC received a glut of applications for new television stations after World War II, the agency set aside dozens of channels on the

From *The Washington Monthly*, July/August 2004. Copyright © 2004 by Washington Monthly Publishing, LLC, 1319 F St. NW, Suite 710, Washington, DC 20004. 202-393-5155. Reprinted by permission. www.washingtonmonthly.com

344

new UHF spectrum so independents could get a foothold in television. That helped me get my start 35 years ago. Congress also passed a law in 1962 requiring that TVs be equipped to receive both UHF and VHF channels. That's how I was able to compete as a UHF station, although it was never easy. (I used to tell potential advertisers that our UHF viewers were smarter than the rest, because you had to be a genius just to figure out how to tune us in.) And in 1972, the FCC ruled that cable TV operators could import distant signals. That's how we were able to beam our Atlanta station to homes throughout the South. Five years later, with the help of an RCA satellite, we were sending our signal across the nation, and the Superstation was born.

That was then.

Today, media companies are more concentrated than at any time over the past 40 years, thanks to a continual loosening of ownership rules by Washington. The media giants now own not only broadcast networks and local stations; they also own the cable companies that pipe in the signals of their competitors and the studios that produce most of the programming. To get a flavor of how consolidated the industry has become, consider this: In 1990, the major broadcast networks—ABC, CBS, NBC, and Fox—fully or partially owned just 12.5 percent of the new series they aired. By 2000, it was 56.3 percent. Just two years later, it had surged to 77.5 percent.

In this environment, most independent media firms either get gobbled up by one of the big companies or driven out of business altogether. Yet instead of balancing the rules to give independent broadcasters a fair chance in the market, Washington continues to tilt the playing field to favor the biggest players. Last summer, the FCC passed another round of sweeping pro-consolidation rules that, among other things, further raised the cap on the number of TV stations a company can own.

In the media, as in any industry, big corporations play a vital role, but so do small, emerging ones. When you lose small businesses, you lose big ideas. People who own their own businesses are their own bosses. They are independent thinkers. They know they can't compete by imitating the big guys—they have to innovate, so they're less obsessed with earnings than they are with ideas. They are quicker to seize on new technologies and new product ideas. They steal market share from the big companies, spurring them to adopt new approaches. This process promotes competition, which leads to higher product and service quality, more jobs, and greater wealth. It's called capitalism.

But without the proper rules, healthy capitalist markets turn into sluggish oligopolies, and that is what's happening in media today. Large corporations are more profit-focused and risk-averse. They often kill local programming because it's expensive, and they push national programming because it's cheap—even if their decisions run counter to local interests and community values. Their managers are more averse to innovation because they're afraid of being fired for an idea that fails. They prefer to sit on the sidelines, waiting to buy the businesses of the risk-takers who succeed.

Unless we have a climate that will allow more independent media companies to survive, a dangerously high percentage of what we see—and what we don't see—will be shaped by the profit motives and political interests of large, publicly traded conglomerates. The economy will suffer, and so will the quality of our public life. Let me be clear: As a business proposition, consolidation makes sense. The moguls behind the mergers are acting in their corporate interests and playing by the rules. We just shouldn't have those rules. They make sense for a corporation. But for a society, it's like over-fishing the oceans. When the independent businesses are gone, where will the new ideas come from? We have to do more than keep media giants from growing larger; they're already too big. We need a new set of rules that will break these huge companies to pieces.

The Big Squeeze

In the 1970s, I became convinced that a 24-hour all-news network could make money, and perhaps even change the world. But when I invited two large media corporations to invest in the launch of CNN, they turned me down. I couldn't believe it. Together we could have launched the network for a fraction of what it would have taken me alone; they had all the infrastructure, contacts, experience, knowledge. When no one would go in with me, I risked my personal wealth to start CNN. Soon after our launch in 1980, our expenses were twice what we had expected and revenues half what we had projected. Our losses were so high that our loans were called in. I refinanced at 18 percent interest, up from 9, and stayed just a step ahead of the bankers. Eventually, we not only became profitable, but also changed the nature of news—from watching something that happened to watching it as it happened.

But even as CNN was getting its start, the climate for independent broadcasting was turning hostile. This trend began in 1984, when the FCC raised the number of stations a single entity could own from seven—where it had been capped since the 1950s—to 12. A year later, it revised its rule again, adding a national audience-reach cap of 25 percent to the 12 station limit—meaning media companies were prohibited from owning TV stations that together reached more than 25 percent of the national audience. In 1996, the FCC did away with numerical caps altogether and raised the audience-reach cap to 35 percent. This wasn't necessarily bad for Turner Broadcasting; we had already achieved scale. But seeing these rules changed was like watching someone knock down the ladder I had already climbed.

Meanwhile, the forces of consolidation focused their attention on another rule, one that restricted ownership of content. Throughout the 1980s, network lobbyists worked to overturn the so-called Financial Interest and Syndication Rules, or fin-syn, which had been put in place in 1970, after federal officials became alarmed at the networks' growing control over programming. As the FCC wrote in the fin-syn decision: "The power to determine form and content rests only in the three networks and is exercised extensively and exclusively by them, hourly and daily." In 1957, the commission pointed out, independent companies had produced a third of all network shows; by 1968, that number had dropped to 4 percent. The rules essentially forbade networks from profiting from reselling programs that they had already aired.

This had the result of forcing networks to sell off their syndication arms, as CBS did with Viacom in 1973. Once networks no longer produced their own content, new competition was launched, creating fresh opportunities for independents.

For a time, Hollywood and its production studios were politically strong enough to keep the fin-syn rules in place. But by the early 1990s, the networks began arguing that their dominance had been undercut by the rise of independent broadcasters, cable networks, and even videocassettes, which they claimed gave viewers enough choice to make fin-syn unnecessary. The FCC ultimately agreed—and suddenly the broadcast networks could tell independent production studios, "We won't air it unless we own it." The networks then bought up the weakened studios or were bought out by their own syndication arms, the way Viacom turned the tables on CBS, buying the network in 2000. This silenced the major political opponents of consolidation.

Even before the repeal of fin-syn, I could see that the trend toward consolidation spelled trouble for independents like me. In a climate of consolidation, there would be only one sure way to win: bring a broadcast network, production studios, and cable and satellite systems under one roof. If you didn't have it inside, you'd have to get it outside—and that meant, increasingly, from a large corporation that was competing with you. It's difficult to survive when your suppliers are owned by your competitors. I had tried and failed to buy a major broadcast network, but the repeal of fin-syn turned up the pressure. Since I couldn't buy a network, I bought MGM to bring more content in-house, and I kept looking for other ways to gain scale. In the end, I found the only way to stay competitive was to merge with Time Warner and relinquish control of my companies.

Today, the only way for media companies to survive is to own everything up and down the media chain—from broadcast and cable networks to the sitcoms, movies, and news broadcasts you see on those stations; to the production studios that make them; to the cable, satellite, and broadcast systems that bring the programs to your television set; to the Web sites you visit to read about those programs; to the way you log on to the Internet to view those pages. Big media today wants to own the faucet, pipeline, water, and the reservoir. The rain clouds come next.

Supersizing Networks

Throughout the 1990s, media mergers were celebrated in the press and otherwise seemingly ignored by the American public. So, it was easy to assume that media consolidation was neither controversial nor problematic. But then a funny thing happened.

In the summer of 2003, the FCC raised the national audience-reach cap from 35 percent to 45 percent. The FCC also allowed corporations to own a newspaper and a TV station in the same market and permitted corporations to own three TV stations in the largest markets, up from two, and two stations in medium-sized markets, up from one. Unexpectedly, the public rebelled. Hundreds of thousands of citizens complained to the FCC. Groups from the

National Organization for Women to the National Rifle Association demanded that Congress reverse the ruling. And like-minded lawmakers, including many long-time opponents of media consolidation, took action, pushing the cap back down to 35, until—under strong White House pressure—it was revised back up to 39 percent. This June, the U.S. Court of Appeals for the Third Circuit threw out the rules that would have allowed corporations to own more television and radio stations in a single market, let stand the higher 39 percent cap, and also upheld the rule permitting a corporation to own a TV station and a newspaper in the same market; then, it sent the issues back to the same FCC that had pushed through the pro-consolidation rules in the first place.

In reaching its 2003 decision, the FCC did not argue that its policies would advance its core objectives of diversity, competition, and localism. Instead, it justified its decision by saying that there was already a lot of diversity, competition, and localism in the media—so it wouldn't hurt if the rules were changed to allow more consolidation. Their decision reads: "Our current rules inadequately account for the competitive presence of cable, ignore the diversity-enhancing value of the Internet, and lack any sound bases for a national audience reach cap." Let's pick that assertion apart.

First, the "competitive presence of cable" is a mirage. Broadcast networks have for years pointed to their loss of prime-time viewers to cable networks—but they are losing viewers to cable networks that they themselves own. Ninety percent of the top 50 cable TV stations are owned by the same parent companies that own the broadcast networks. Yes, Disney's ABC network has lost viewers to cable networks. But it's losing viewers to cable networks like Disney's ESPN, Disney's ESPN2, and Disney's Disney Channel. The media giants are getting a deal from Congress and the FCC because their broadcast networks are losing share to their own cable networks. It's a scam.

Second, the decision cites the "diversity-enhancing value of the Internet." The FCC is confusing diversity with variety. The top 20 Internet news sites are owned by the same media conglomerates that control the broadcast and cable networks. Sure, a hundred-person choir gives you a choice of voices, but they're all singing the same song.

The FCC says that we have more media choices than ever before. But only a few corporations decide what we can choose. That is not choice. That's like a dictator deciding what candidates are allowed to stand for parliamentary elections, and then claiming that the people choose their leaders. Different voices do not mean different viewpoints, and these huge corporations all have the same viewpoint—they want to shape government policy in a way that helps them maximize profits, drive out competition, and keep getting bigger.

Because the new technologies have not fundamentally changed the market, it's wrong for the FCC to say that there are no "sound bases for a national audience-reach cap." The rationale for such a cap is the same as it has always been. If there is a limit to the number of TV stations a corporation can own, then the chance exists that after all the corporations have reached this limit, there may still be some stations left over to be bought and run by independents. A lower limit would encourage the entry of independents and promote competition. A higher limit does the opposite.

Triple Blight

The loss of independent operators hurts both the media business and its citizen-customers. When the ownership of these firms passes to people under pressure to show quick financial results in order to justify the purchase, the corporate emphasis instantly shifts from taking risks to taking profits. When that happens, quality suffers, localism suffers, and democracy itself suffers.

Loss of Quality

The *Forbes* list of the 400 richest Americans exerts a negative influence on society, because it discourages people who want to climb up the list from giving more money to charity. The Nielsen ratings are dangerous in a similar way— because they scare companies away from good shows that don't produce immediate blockbuster ratings. The producer Norman Lear once asked, "You know what ruined television?" His answer: when *The New York Times* began publishing the Nielsen ratings. "That list every week became all anyone cared about."

When all companies are quarterly earnings-obsessed, the market starts punishing companies that aren't yielding an instant return. This not only creates a big incentive for bogus accounting, but also it inhibits the kind of investment that builds economic value. America used to know this. We used to be a nation of farmers. You can't plant something today and harvest tomorrow. Had Turner Communications been required to show earnings growth every quarter, we never would have purchased those first two TV stations.

When CNN reported to me, if we needed more money for Kosovo or Baghdad, we'd find it. If we had to bust the budget, we busted the budget. We put journalism first, and that's how we built CNN into something the world wanted to watch. I had the power to make these budget decisions because they were my companies. I was an independent entrepreneur who controlled the majority of the votes and could run my company for the long term. Top managers in these huge media conglomerates run their companies for the short term. After we sold Turner Broadcasting to Time Warner, we came under such earnings pressure that we had to cut our promotion budget every year at CNN to make our numbers. Media mega-mergers inevitably lead to an overemphasis on short-term earnings.

You can see this overemphasis in the spread of reality television. Shows like "Fear Factor" cost little to produce—there are no actors to pay and no sets to maintain—and they get big ratings. Thus, American television has moved away from expensive sitcoms and on to cheap thrills. We've gone from "Father Knows Best" to "Who Wants to Marry My Dad?", and from "My Three Sons" to "My Big Fat Obnoxious Fiance."

The story of Grant Tinker and Mary Tyler Moore's production studio, MTM, helps illustrate the point. When the company was founded in 1969, Tinker and Moore hired the best writers they could find and then left them alone—and were rewarded with some of the best shows of the 1970s. But eventually, MTM was bought by a company that imposed budget ceilings and laid off employees. That company was later purchased by Rev. Pat Robertson; then, he was bought out by Fox. Exit "The Mary Tyler Moore Show." Enter "The Littlest Groom."

Loss of Localism

Consolidation has also meant a decline in the local focus of both news and programming. After analyzing 23,000 stories on 172 news programs over five years, the Project for Excellence in Journalism found that big media news organizations relied more on syndicated feeds and were more likely to air national stories with no local connection.

That's not surprising. Local coverage is expensive, and thus will tend be a casualty in the quest for short-term earnings. In 2002, Fox Television bought Chicago's Channel 50 and eliminated all of the station's locally produced shows. One of the cancelled programs (which targeted pre-teens) had scored a perfect rating for educational content in a 1999 University of Pennsylvania study, according to *The Chicago Tribune*. That accolade wasn't enough to save the program. Once the station's ownership changed, so did its mission and programming.

Loss of localism also undercuts the public-service mission of the media, and this can have dangerous consequences. In early 2002, when a freight train derailed near Minot, N.D., releasing a cloud of anhydrous ammonia over the town, police tried to call local radio stations, six of which are owned by radio mammoth Clear Channel Communications. According to news reports, it took them over an hour to reach anyone—no one was answering the Clear Channel phone. By the next day, 300 people had been hospitalized, many partially blinded by the ammonia. Pets and livestock died. And Clear Channel continued beaming its signal from headquarters in San Antonio, Texas—some 1,600 miles away.

Loss of Democratic Debate

When media companies dominate their markets, it undercuts our democracy. Justice Hugo Black, in a landmark media-ownership case in 1945, wrote: "The First Amendment rests on the assumption that the widest possible dissemination of information from diverse and antagonistic sources is essential to the welfare of the public."

These big companies are not antagonistic; they do billions of dollars in business with each other. They don't compete; they cooperate to inhibit competition. You and I have both felt the impact. I felt it in 1981, when CBS, NBC, and ABC all came together to try to keep CNN from covering the White House. You've felt the impact over the past two years, as you saw little news from ABC, CBS, NBC, MSNBC, Fox, or CNN on the FCC's actions. In early 2003, the Pew Research Center found that 72 percent of Americans had heard "nothing at all" about the proposed FCC rule changes. Why? One never knows for sure, but it must have been clear to news directors that the more they covered this issue, the harder it would be for their corporate bosses to get the policy result they wanted.

A few media conglomerates now exercise a near-monopoly over television news. There is always a risk that news organizations can emphasize or ignore stories to serve their corporate purpose. But the risk is far greater when there are no independent competitors to air the side of the story the corporation wants to ignore. More consolidation has often meant more news-sharing. But closing bureaus and downsizing staff have more than economic consequences. A smaller press is less capable of holding our leaders accountable. When Viacom merged two news stations it owned in Los Angeles, reports *The American Journalism Review*, "field reporters began carrying microphones labeled KCBS on one side and KCAL on the other." This was no accident. As the Viacom executive in charge told *The Los Angeles Business Journal*: "In this duopoly, we should be able to control the news in the marketplace."

This ability to control the news is especially worrisome when a large media organization is itself the subject of a news story. Disney's boss, after buying ABC in 1995, was quoted in *LA Weekly* as saying, "I would prefer ABC not cover Disney." A few days later, ABC killed a "20/20" story critical of the parent company.

But networks have also been compromised when it comes to non-news programs which involve their corporate parent's business interests. General Electric subsidiary NBC Sports raised eyebrows by apologizing to the Chinese government for Bob Costas's reference to China's "problems with human rights" during a telecast of the Atlanta Olympic Games. China, of course, is a huge market for GE products.

Consolidation has given big media companies new power over what is said not just on the air, but off it as well. Cumulus Media banned the Dixie Chicks on its 42 country music stations for 30 days after lead singer Natalie Maines criticized President Bush for the war in Iraq. It's hard to imagine Cumulus would have been so bold if its listeners had more of a choice in country music stations. And Disney recently provoked an uproar when it prevented its subsidiary Miramax from distributing Michael Moore's film *Fahrenheit 9/11*. As a senior Disney executive told *The New York Times*: "It's not in the interest of any major corporation to be dragged into a highly charged partisan political battle." Follow the logic, and you can see what lies ahead: If the only media companies are major corporations, controversial and dissenting views may not be aired at all.

Naturally, corporations say they would never suppress speech. But it's not their intentions that matter; it's their capabilities. Consolidation gives them more power to tilt the news and cut important ideas out of the public debate. And it's precisely that power that the rules should prevent.

Independents' Day

This is a fight about freedom—the freedom of independent entrepreneurs to start and run a media business, and the freedom of citizens to get news, information, and entertainment from a wide variety of sources, at least some of which are truly independent and not run by people facing the pressure of quarterly earnings reports. No one should underestimate the danger. Big media companies want to eliminate all ownership limits. With the removal of these limits, immense media power will pass into the hands of a very few corporations and individuals.

What will programming be like when it's produced for no other purpose than profit? What will news be like when there are no independent news organizations to go after stories the big corporations avoid? Who really wants to find out? Safeguarding the welfare of the public cannot be the first concern of a large publicly traded media company. Its job is to seek profits. But if the government writes the rules in a way that encourages the entry into the market of entrepreneurs—men and women with big dreams, new ideas, and a willingness to take long-term risks—the economy will be stronger, and the country will be better off.

I freely admit: When I was in the media business, especially after the federal government changed the rules to favor large companies, I tried to sweep the board, and I came within one move of owning every link up and down the media chain. Yet I felt then, as I do now, that the government was not doing its job. The role of the government ought to be like the role of a referee in boxing, keeping the big guys from killing the little guys. If the little guy gets knocked down, the referee should send the big guy to his corner, count the little guy out, and then help him back up. But today the government has cast down its duty, and media competition is less like boxing and more like professional wrestling: The wrestler and the referee are both kicking the guy on the canvas.

At this late stage, media companies have grown so large and powerful, and their dominance has become so detrimental to the survival of small, emerging companies, that there remains only one alternative: bust up the big conglomerates. We've done this before: to the railroad trusts in the first part of the 20th century, to Ma Bell more recently. Indeed, big media itself was cut down to size in the 1970s, and a period of staggering innovation and growth followed. Breaking up the reconstituted media conglomerates may seem like an impossible task when their grip on the policy-making process in Washington seems so sure. But the public's broad and bipartisan rebellion against the FCC's pro-consolidation decisions suggests something different. Politically, big media may again be on the wrong side of history—and up against a country unwilling to lose its independents.

Michael K. Powell

 **NO**

Should the FCC Relax Its Ownership Rules?

I am proud that this Commission and its staff can say that we conducted the most exhaustive and comprehensive review of our broadcast ownership rules ever undertaken. We have done so, obligated by our statutory duty to review the rules biennially and prove those rules are "necessary in the public interest." The Court of Appeals has interpreted this standard as placing a high hurdle before the Commission for maintaining a given regulation, and made clear that failure to surmount that hurdle, based on a thorough record, must result in the rule's modification or elimination.

Over the past 20 months we have been working tirelessly towards achieving three critically important goals in this proceeding: (1) reinstating legally enforceable broadcast ownership limits that promote diversity, localism, and competition (replacing those that have been struck down by the courts); (2) building modern rules that take proper account of the explosion of new media outlets for news, information, and entertainment, rather than perpetuate the graying rules of a bygone black and white era; and (3) striking a careful balance that does not unduly limit transactions that promote the public interest, while ensuring that no company can monopolize the medium.

To achieve these goals, however, the Commission needed to come face to face with reality. So, we faced the reality of the law and our responsibility to implement Congress's will, as interpreted by the courts. We faced the reality of having to compile and analyze a record unlike any other in our history. We faced the reality of the modern media marketplace. And by doing so, the Commission was able to craft a balanced package of enforceable and sustainable broadcast ownership limits.

Statutory Mandate and Court Decisions

In the Telecommunications Act of 1996, Congress established the biennial review mandate. In relevant part, Section 202(h) requires that the Commission review all of its broadcast ownership rules every two years and determine "whether any of such rules are necessary in the public interest as a result of competition." The Commission, as a consequence, is required to repeal or modify any regulation it cannot prove is necessary in the public interest. Congress gave the Commission a sacred responsibility, one that I do not take lightly.

From *Congressional Digest*, October 2003, pp. 234, 236, 238, 240, 242. Published by Congressional Digest Corporation. Reprinted by permission.

Recent court decisions have established a high hurdle for the Commission to maintain a given broadcast ownership regulation. As interpreted by the U.S. Court of Appeals for the District of Columbia Circuit in the 2002 *Fox* [*Television Stations v. FCC* (2001)] and *Sinclair* [*Broadcast Group v. FCC* (2002)] cases, Section 202(h) requires the Commission to study and report on the current status of competition. Both decisions provide that the survival of any prospective broadcast ownership rules depends on this Commission's ability to justify those rules adequately with record evidence on the need for each ownership rule, and ensure that the rules are analytically consistent with each other. The implications of the court decisions were clear—fail to justify the necessity of each of our broadcast ownership regulations at the rules' and our sacred goals' peril.

The Modern Marketplace

Our fact-gathering effort demonstrated that today's media marketplace is marked by abundance. Since 1960, there has been an explosion of media outlets throughout the country. Even in small towns like Burlington, Vermont, the number of voices—including cable, satellite, radio, TV stations, and newspapers— has increased over 250 percent during the last 40 years. Independent ownership of those outlets is far more diverse, with 140 percent more owners today than in 1960.

What does this abundance mean for the American people? It means more programming, more choice, and more control in the hands of citizens. At any given moment, our citizens have access to scores of TV networks devoted to movies, dramatic series, sports, news, and educational programming, both for adults and children; in short, niche programming to satisfy almost any of our citizens' diverse tastes.

In 1960—the "Golden Age of Television"—if you missed the half-hour evening newscast, you were out of luck. In 1980, it was no different. But today, news and public affairs programming—the fuel of our democratic society—is overflowing. There used to be three broadcast networks, each with 30 minutes of news daily. Today, there are three 24-hour all-news networks, seven broadcast networks, and over 300 cable networks. Local networks are bringing the American public more local news than at any point in history.

The Internet is also having a profound impact on the ever-increasing desire of our citizenry to inform themselves and to do so using a wide variety of sources. Google news service brings information from 4,500 news sources to one's fingertips from around the world, all with the touch of a button. As demonstrated by this proceeding, diverse and antagonistic voices use the Internet daily to reach the American people. Whether it is the *The New York Times* editorial page, or Joe Citizen using email to let his views be known to the Commission, or the use by organizations such as MoveOn.org to perform outreach to citizens, the Internet is putting the tools of democracy in the hands of speakers and listeners more and more each day.

I have not cited cable television and the Internet by accident. Their contribution to the marketplace of ideas is not linear, it is exponential.

Cable and the Internet explode the model for viewpoint diversity in the media. Diversity-by-appointment has vanished. Now, the media makes itself available on our schedule, as much or as little as we want, when we want. In sum, citizens have more choice and more control over what they see, hear, or read than at any other time in history. This is a powerful paradigm shift in the American media system, and is having a tremendous impact on our democracy.

Public Interest Benefits

The marketplace changes mentioned above were only the beginning, not the end of our inquiry. The balanced set of national and local broadcast ownership rules we adopted preserve and protect our core policy goals of diversity, competition, and localism. Certain public interest benefits have clearly been documented in the record and the rules we adopted embrace and advance those benefits for the American public.

As an initial matter, the public interest is served by having enforceable rules that are based on a solid, factual record. For the last year, several of the Commission's broadcast ownership regulations have been rendered unenforceable—vacated or remanded by the courts.

Protecting Viewpoint Diversity

In addition, the Commission, recognizing that "the widest possible dissemination of information from diverse and antagonistic sources is essential to the welfare of the public," introduced broadcast ownership limits that will protect viewpoint diversity. The Commission concluded that neither the newspaper-broadcast prohibition nor the TV-radio cross-ownership prohibition could be justified in larger markets in light of the abundance of diverse sources available to citizens to rely on for their news consumption.

By implementing our cross-media limits, however, the Commission will protect viewpoint diversity by ensuring that no company, or group of companies, can control an inordinate share of media outlets in a local market. We developed a Diversity Index to measure the availability of key media outlets in markets of various sizes.

By breaking out markets into tiers, the Commission was able to better tailor our rules to reflect different levels of media availability in different sized markets. For the first time ever, the Commission built its data in implementing this rule directly from input received from the public on how they actually use the media to obtain news and public affairs information.

Furthermore, by instituting our local television multiple ownership rule (especially by banning mergers among the top-four stations, which the record demonstrated typically produce an independent local newscast) and our local radio ownership limit, the Commission will foster multiple independently owned media outlets in both broadcast television and radio—advancing the goal of promoting the widest dissemination of viewpoints.

Enhancing Competition

Moreover, our new broadcast ownership regulations promote competition in the media marketplace. The Commission determined that our prior local television multiple ownership limits could not be justified as necessary to promote competition because it failed to reflect the significant competition now faced by local broadcasters from cable and satellite TV services. Our revised local television limit is the first TV ownership rule to acknowledge that competition.

This new rule will enhance competition in local markets by allowing broadcast television stations to compete more effectively not only against other broadcast stations, but also against cable and/or satellite channels in that local market. In addition, the record demonstrates that these same market combinations yield efficiencies that will serve the public interest through improved or expanded services such as local news and public affairs programming and facilitating the transition to digital television through economic efficiencies.

The Commission found that our current limits on local radio ownership continue to be necessary to promote competition among local radio stations and we reaffirmed the caps set forth by Congress in the 1996 Telecommunications Act. The Order tightens the radio rules in one important respect—we concluded that the current method for defining radio markets was not in the public interest and thus needed to be modified. We found that the current market definition for radio markets, which relies on the signal contour of the commonly owned stations, is unsound and produces anomalous and irrational results, undermining the purpose of the rule.

We therefore adopted geographic-based market definitions, which are a more rational means for protecting competition in local markets. For example, we fixed the case of Minot, North Dakota, which under our former rules produced a market with 45 radio stations. Under our reformed market definition, Minot would have only 10 radio stations included in the relevant geographic market.

By promoting competition through the local television and radio rules, the Commission recognized that the rules may result in a number of situations where current ownership arrangements exceed ownership limits. In such cases the Commission made a limited exception to permit sales of grandfathered station combinations to small businesses. In so doing, the Commission sought to respect the reasonable expectations of parties that lawfully purchased groups of local radio stations that today, through redefined markets, now exceed the applicable caps. We promote competition by permitting station owners to retain any above-cap local radio clusters but not transfer them intact unless such a transfer avoids undue hardships to cluster owners that are small businesses or promote the entry into broadcasting by small businesses—many of which are minority- or female-owned.

Finally, by retaining our ban on mergers among any of the top four national broadcast networks, the Commission continues to promote competition in the national television advertising and program acquisition markets.

Fostering Localism

Recognizing that localism remains a bedrock public interest benefit, the Commission took a series of actions designed to foster localism by aligning our ownership limits with the local stations' incentives to serve the needs and interests of their local communities.

For instance, by retaining the dual network prohibition and increasing the national television ownership limit to 45 percent, the Commission promoted localism by preserving the balance of negotiating power between networks and affiliates. The national cap will allow a body of network affiliates to negotiate collectively with the broadcast networks on network programming decisions to best serve the needs of their local community, while at the same time allowing the networks to gain critical mass to prevent the flight of quality programs, such as sports and movies, to cable or satellite.

The record further demonstrated that by both raising the national cap to 45 percent and allowing for cross-ownership combinations in certain markets the Commission would promote localism. Indeed, the record showed that broadcast network owned-and-operated stations served their local communities better with respect to local news production airing more local news programming than did affiliates. Furthermore, the record demonstrated that where newspaper-broadcast television combinations were allowed, those televisions stations have produced dramatically better news coverage in terms of quantity (over 50 percent more news) and quality (outpacing non-newspaper-owned television stations in news awards).

The Commission crafted a balanced set of broadcast ownership restrictions to preserve and promote the public interest goals of diversity, competition, and localism.

Conclusion

This critical review has been an exhaustive one. The Commission has struggled with a difficult conundrum: building an adequate record, satisfying the administrative burden of the Section 202(h) mandate, and ultimately justifying its rules before the courts that have expressed growing impatience with irrational and indefensible ownership rules.

Four years ago, in the last completed biennial review, I concluded "[I]t is indeed time to take a sober and realistic look at our broadcast ownership rules in light of the current competitive communications environment." With a full record in hand, it was appropriate to fulfill Congress's mandate of completing our broadcast ownership review. The extraordinary coverage of the issue and the comments and evidence on the record have allowed the Commission to make an informed judgment, and hopefully to resist claims of being both "arbitrary and capricious" before the courts.

POSTSCRIPT

Does Big Media Control the FCC?

What are the consequences of consolidation for the role and responsibility of media in society? Unfortunately, there is little research on the effects of media restructuring. Is media concentration a problem? We may not think so if economies of scale reduce the prices we pay for media products. We may, however, have problems if most of the media outlets in our community are owned by the same corporation. For example, is a chain owner more likely to impose a one-size-fits-all perspective on its coverage of local events, thus reducing diversity?

The tension between the historical public interest paradigm of media in the United States and the current focus on the industry's economics and financial performance may well be the fundamental question to be answered about the future of the U.S. media industry. How American policymakers and the public address that issue will have significant impact on the direction in which the industry develops in the next few decades. If media companies are viewed as private enterprises whose primary responsibility is to attract consumers and generate profits for stockholders, deregulation and consolidation will continue and media markets will be controlled by an ever-smaller number of players generating whatever type of content sells best. If, however, the pendulum of regulatory philosophy and public pressure begins swinging back toward the view that the media have a responsibility to serve the public interest commensurate with the special legal protections accorded media corporations, a return to more regulation on industry structure and behavior is likely to follow.

What *is* certain is that the media industry in the United States is still in the midst of a period of rapid, transformational change, the outcome of which has significant implications for civic society and the global media economy. The realization of synergy from consolidation is elusive, which is why, in general, across all industries, approximately half of all mergers are undone within a decade.

The issues of corporate restructuring are being played out daily in the pages of the business press and media trade publications. See for example the *Wall Street Journal* and *Broadcasting/Cable Magazine* for discussions of the successes and failures in this realm. *The Business of Media: Corporate Media and the Public Interest* (2nd ed.) by David Croteau and Williams Hoynes (Pine Forge Press, 2005) is an excellent exploration of the tensions between corporate ownership and traditional obligations of the press. For an overview of the issues of media and the economy, see *Media Economics: Theory and Practice* (Erlbaum, 2004). For more discussion of issues and the effects of conglomerates, see *The Problem of the Media: U.S. Communication Politics in the Twenty-First Century,* by Robert W. McChesney (Monthly Review Press, 2004) and *The New Media Monopoly* by Ben Bagdikian (Beacon Press, 2004). Robert McChesney was a leader in the grassroots protests that prevented the liberalization of ownership rules. He and many public interest groups say that the attempted change goes too far in giving big media corporations control over all the souces of information.

ISSUE 17

Will Print Newspapers Survive in the Current Business Environment?

YES: Robert Kuttner, from "The Race," *Columbia Journalism Review* (March/April 2007)

NO: Eric Klinenberg, from "Breaking the News," *Mother Jones* (March/April 2007)

ISSUE SUMMARY

Robert Kuttner discusses the future of traditional newspapers in the age of the Internet. Newspapers can make it, he argues, but only if they partner with the Internet to provide the quality journalism that is the hallmark of print, and the immediacy, comprehensiveness, and innovativeness of the best of the Internet. This requires a commitment to the process of developing a dual product that is expensive, but cannot be achieved at the expense of quality journalism. One study found that local news diminished under corporate ownership. Increasingly cross-ownerships are proposed to allow local television and newspaper outlets in a single market to be owned by a single company. As concentration increases, news departments are slashed, ultimately threatening the ability to produce quality reporting.

You've heard it before: Circulation is down, newspapers are losing readers, young people only use the Internet, paper and distribution costs are rising. Newspapers, or so the conclusion goes, are an old technology that will not survive in the age of the Internet. The Project for Excellence in Journalism 2007 report on news media notes that circulation is declining and advertising is flat. Big metro papers had deep newsroom cuts that have made a difference in the content of the papers. On the positive side, there is growth in online revenue and readership.

Newspapers are often seen as facing disruptive technology, defined as technology that transforms the business, changing it forever. Think buggy whips as cars began production, or typewriters as computer word-processing software and keyboards entered the workplace. Are newspapers the next victim of disruptive technology? This issue examines how older media forms are

360

responding to newer distribution forms, how economics and technology force change, and how industries may be maintained in the future of digital media.

Kuttner argues that newspapers can break through into a brave new world of cooperation, where print and digital media support one another. Newspapers become a hybrid of part print and part Web. This is, he asserts, the way for newspapers to survive as a viable business model. Yet, even he suggests that newspapers will probably survive in their current state for another decade. Rising costs of paper and distribution will give way to the lesser costs of Internet distribution. James Smith, vice president of market research for Morris Communications, agrees that traditional daily newspapers are threatened, and predicts that we will see some major metropolitan dailies vanishing within the next decade.

One industry initiative is the Newspaper Next Project, which suggests that publishers rethink their product. Steve Gray, managing director of the Newspaper Next project, argues newspaper companies must rethink the notion of a monolithic newspaper product and instead focus on delivering a portfolio of products. That means creating new niche publications for target audiences, expanding online and appealing to small businesses and online advertisers. Currently several newspapers are trying to implement this plan. Again, James Smith sees hope in the strong recent development of what are called hyperlocal community papers. These show promise for survival within local areas, providing content that is necessary for daily life, and that helps create a sense of community in a way that national media content alone cannot.

Klinenberg doubts that newspapers can thrive in the current business environment, but he attributes their potential demise to the search for "outsize profits" that will kill the newspaper business. Newspapers have traditionally been a profitable enterprise. At a time when technology changes call for more reinvestment in the company (e.g., expanding Internet capability), funds to do so are scarcer. This is aggravated by recent mergers and divestitures that have changed paper ownership, often leaving the new owners with debt to pay off from the purchase of the paper, with stockholders to increase, and perhaps with less willingness to re-invest in an already expensive firm.

Similarly, optimistic interpretation of rising Internet revenue may not translate into Internet-only "newspapers." Currently the cost of the newsroom (i.e., reporters, editors, copyeditors, facilities, etc) is "charged off" on the newspaper side. In an Internet-only operation, all these costs would have to be borne by the Internet revenue, and that seems unlikely at this time.

It is difficult to make predictions about how long the present media environment will last, and what the "drivers" of change will lead us to. For students of media, the many possible scenarios of the future mean that individuals will have to be flexible about career plans and training. Traditional systems have lasted many decades, but those very businesses seem to be changing at an accelerated rate. We can assume that in 20 years, there will be far more complex media industries, more opportunities, and more content geared to specialized audiences. At the same time, we will probably have many more complicated issues to debate about the role of media, the forms of media, and the understanding of how media will be used in our lives.

YES

Robert Kuttner

The Race

By the usual indicators, daily newspapers are in a deepening downward spiral. The new year brought reports of more newsroom layoffs, dwindling print circulation, flat or declining ad sales, increasing defections of readers and advertisers to the Internet, and sullen investors. Wall Street so undervalues traditional publishing that McClatchy's stock price briefly rose when it sold off the Minneapolis *Star Tribune* at a fire-sale price, mainly for the $160 million tax benefit. As succeeding generations grow up with the Web and lose the habit of reading print, it seems improbable that newspapers can survive with a cost structure at least 50 percent higher than their nimbler and cheaper Internet competitors. ("No trucks, no trees," says the former *Boston Globe publisher* Ben Taylor). . . .

Yet a far more hopeful picture is emerging. In this scenario the mainstream press, though late to the party, figures out how to make serious money from the Internet, uses the Web to enrich traditional journalistic forms, and retains its professionalism—along with a readership that is part print, part Web. Newspapers stay alive as hybrids. The culture and civic mission of daily print journalism endure.

Can that happen? Given the financial squeeze and the shortsightedness of many publishers and investors, will dailies be able to navigate such a transition without sacrificing standards of journalism? Or will cost-cutting owners so thoroughly gut the nation's newsrooms that they collapse the distinction between the rest of the Internet and everything that makes newspapers uniquely valuable?

Which newspapers are most likely to survive? And, while we are at it, why does the survival of newspapers matter? In an era when the Web explodes the monopoly of the print newspaper as authoritative assembler of the day's news and invites readers to be both aggregators and originators of content, what remains distinctive about newspapers?

Defenders of print insist that nothing on the Web can match the assemblage of reportorial talent, professionalism, and public mission of a serious print daily. The 2006 State of the News Media Report by the Project for Excellence in Journalism found that just 5 percent of blog postings included "what would be considered journalistic reporting." Nicholas Lemann, dean of Columbia's Graduate School of Journalism, wrote a skeptical piece about Web journalism in *The New Yorker* last July, concluding that not much of the

Reprinted from *Columbia Journalism Review*, March/April 2007, pp. 24–32. Copyright © 2007 by Columbia Journalism Review, Columbia University.

blogosphere "yet rises to the level of a journalistic culture rich enough to compete in a serious way with the old media—to function as a replacement rather than an addendum." John Carroll, the former editor of the *Los Angeles Times*, says, "Take any story in a blog and trace its origins, about eighty-five percent of it can be traceable to newspapers. They break nearly all of the important stories. Who's going to do the reporting if these institutions fade away?"

By contrast, celebrants of the Web contend that the Internet is freer, more democratic, deliberative, interactive, and civic than the self-interested elites of old media dare admit. "The priesthood of gatekeepers is being disbanded. It's over," says Christopher Lydon, a one-time *New York Times* reporter, now hosting *Open Source* on Public Radio International.

In exploring whether newspapers as we know them are likely to endure, and why we should care, I sought out Wall Street analysts, press critics, journalism professors, business consultants, publishers, editors, reporters, and the search-engine companies and multifarious originators of Web content that are challenging newspapers. The Internet has famously turned the authority structure upside down; so perhaps not surprisingly, one of my most informative interviews was with a colleague, a twenty-two-year-old prodigy we can call Ezra. Before we defenders of newspapers become too smug about what makes us special, he's worth listening to.

I opened the conversation by inviting us to compare how we get our daily ration of information. I begin my day, I immodestly confessed, by reading four newspapers. What do you do?

Ezra suppressed a smirk. I use about 150 or 200 RSS feeds and bookmarks, he explained. Ezra scans four newspapers online. He checks sites of research organizations such as the Center on Budget and Policy Priorities. He indulges his taste for gossipy pop culture with a few favorites such as defamer.com. Ezra surfs a few political blogs, too, but he particularly relies on expert sites that are not exactly blogs and not exactly journalism; rather they are a very important category often left out by old media critics who divide the world into amateur bloggers versus trained reporters. Many such sites are operated by academics or think-tank researchers who have developed a taste for a popular audience, mixing blog-style comment on breaking news with original analysis, and serious research. . . .

Ezra wagered that his hour of Web culling gave him more and better news and analysis than my hour of newspaper reading. He guessed—correctly—that 90 percent of the three pounds of newsprint that I skim every day gets thrown away, unread. (Indeed, at *The Boston Globe*, surveys show that two of the top reasons nonrenewing newspaper readers give for their lapsed subscriptions are "not enough time" and "green guilt." In an age of environmental consciousness and scarce time, people feel bad that so many pounds of newsprint go virginally into the trash.)

So I started playing my few trump cards. Even for casual readers, scanning a newspaper contributes to civic democracy through what sociologists call "incidental learning." You pick up the paper for the sports or the crossword puzzle, and you find yourself reading about the school board election or the international diamond trade. What about incidental learning? I asked.

Don't newspapers do that better? Nope, Ezra replied. You'd be surprised how much interesting serendipity you pick up from skimming a lot of blogs. For instance, the Berkeley economics professor Brad DeLong, who operates an excellent blog on economics topics, also peppers his blog with *Star Trek* trivia.

But, I persisted, you are hardly typical. As diligent self-improvers go, Ezra is to the average Web user as the NFL is to Oberlin football. Maybe, countered Ezra, but search technology is making it easier all the time for citizens to be their own aggregators. Isn't that just what we want?

By now I was feeling very last century. And then Ezra, perhaps taking pity, handed *me* a trump. You have one thing right, he volunteered. The best material on the Internet consistently comes from Web sites run by print organizations.

So journalism reigns after all. But can this supremacy continue? Here we encounter a paradox on top of an irony. The paradox is that new forms of media, while challenging the very survival of newspapers, are quickly becoming their savior—both as a journalistic and a business proposition.

Newspapers are embracing the Web with the manic enthusiasm of a convert. The Internet revenue of newspaper Web sites is increasing at 20 percent to 30 percent a year, and publishers are doing everything they can to boost Web traffic. Publishers know they are in a race against time, they are suddenly doing many things that their Internet competitors do, and often better.

The irony is that in their haste both to cut newsroom costs and ramp up Web operations, some newspapers are slashing newsroom staff and running the survivors ragged. At many dailies, today's reporter is often pressed into Web service: writing frequent updates on breaking stories, wire-service fashion; posting blog items; and conducting interviews with a video camera. If journalism is degraded into mere bloggery, newspapers will lose their competitive advantage, not to mention their journalistic calling.

That is a deeper problem at papers with the deepest cost-cutting and lay-offs. At the quality dailies, which are adding Web staff, most reporters, after initial hesitancy, have embraced the new hybrid news model. "This is our salvation," says Steve Pearlstein, a longtime business reporter at *The Washington Post*. "Most people around here say, 'Bring it on.'" In my interviews, I expected mixed reviews of the hybrid life, but found nothing but enthusiasm.

And if most reporters are taking happily to the Web, the several editors I interviewed are positively euphoric. Five years ago, editors were haltingly and grudgingly adding a few bloggers and chat features, because the Web was something that had to be lived with. "It wasn't very long ago that I and a lot of other people in the newsroom were worried about the competition from the Web, and its effect on the journalism," says Leonard Downie, executive editor of *The Washington Post*. "We were wrong. The Web is not the distraction we feared it would be, and all the feedback improves the journalism." For example, for several months last year, the *Post* ran a highly praised series called "Being a Black Man." The Web allowed a vivid extension of what could be done in print, including narratives, photo galleries, videos, and extensive reader involvement. . . .

Where print and Web are integrated at the *Times*, the *Post* still has its separate Internet operation across the Potomac in Arlington, Virginia. This was set up over a decade ago, partly so that the *Post* could pay young Webbies non-union wages in a right-to-work state. However, as New York University's Jay Rosen observes, allowing a separate Web culture to emerge outside the *Post*'s print culture turns out to have been shrewd. "Today, most of us would like to see one newsroom," says the *Post*'s Pearlstein. "But if we had been in charge of the Web back then, we would have screwed it up."

By most accounts, the *Post* leads the nation's print papers in its use of the Web's interactive potential with readers. . . . reporters . . . found that readers who linked to talkback features had at least read the story, and the Web generally produced higher-quality feedback than reader mail.

For publishers and business strategists, the Web is about nothing less than financial survival. Donald Graham, the *Post*'s CEO, was an early Web enthusiast. . . . The paper's much-admired Web journalism turns a healthy profit now. Online revenue at the *Post* was $72.7 million, in the first nine months of 2006, up 31 percent. . . . Caroline Little, CEO of Washingtonpost. Newsweek Interactive, says online income has vast potential. "The ratio of the huge amount of time people spend using the net to the relatively low ad revenue realized from the net is way out of whack," she explains. Internet ad income should grow rapidly at the expense of both print ads and TV ads. "The question," Little adds, "is how can we contribute enough to the bottom line to keep the core journalism alive?"

The Internet now accounts for about 5 to 6 percent of newspaper advertising income. With Web income soaring and print revenue basically flat, analysts expect the lines to cross within fifteen years. By about 2020, if current trends persist, half of a newspaper's income and most of its readership will be via the Internet.

Despite the seeming anachronism of paper in a digital age, however, the economics of the business require newspapers to persist as partly print media for at least another generation. Some Americans still want to pick up a daily paper rather than read content on a screen. And as a business proposition, the average monetary value of a visitor to a newspaper's Web site is only 20 to 30 percent of a newspaper's print reader; Web ads command lower rates because of the greater competition among Web sites. So even if a newspaper shut down its print operation, published only on the Internet, and somehow managed to keep its entire circulation, the revenue loss would exceed the cost savings.

A key to the transition to a hybrid world is investment. *The New York Times* is currently spending several million dollars a year on a new R&D unit, Web staff, and new products. Depending on how you count, the *Times* has over 100 people in the newsroom whose duties are more Web than print, including producers, software developers, and reporters and editors. . . . The *Times* is rolling out a nifty digital device called Times Reader, developed in partnership with Microsoft. . . .With Times Reader, the on-screen page offers stories in the same fonts, look, and print-like appearance of the familiar print *Times*, but allows a variety of search, page-flip, and rearrange options. . . .

For its digital revenue, the *Times* has bet heavily on a mainly ad-driven business model. Both print and Web content are mostly free, though users have to register, which helps the *Times* maximize advertising revenue by pinpointing demographic characteristics of its readers. Only about 2 percent to 3 percent of the material in the paper or the online edition—most notably the columnists—is "behind the wall" and requires an annual premium subscription. . . . The Times Company last year earned about $273 million in digital income, out of total revenues of around $3.3 billion. Of that, about two-thirds came from the *Times* itself. Only about $10 million of that Web revenue is from premium content, the rest is ad income. . . .

The more highly diversified Dow Jones Company, meanwhile, enjoyed increased earnings last year. Its *Wall Street Journal* [Now famously sold to RupertMurdock] uses a business model that gives far greater emphasis than the *Times* to paid Internet content. Dow Jones executives believe their material is so specialized and valuable to its affluent, Web-savvy readers that the potential audience is in the millions. A great deal of Web effort goes into online updates to provide investors with breaking business news, according to Web managing editor Bill Grueskin. At the end of 2006, the *Journal* reported about 811,000 premium online-only subscribers who paid $99 a year each. An undisclosed number of print subscribers paid $49 for the additional Web content. With its paid-subscription model, the Journal has far less Web traffic than the *Times*, despite its larger print circulation. But the *Journal* can charge more to advertisers for its premium audience, according to Grueskin. The *Journal* projects 2007 growth in online revenue of 20 percent, somewhat below the industry average. Some in the industry think the *Journal* is mistaken in its strategy of forgoing more Web visitors in exchange for premium subscription income. On the other hand, as Grueskin puts it, "The marginal cost of servicing an additional Web subscriber is basically free." . . .

The *Times*, *Post*, and *Journal*, already well on their way to becoming print-digital hybrids, will surely navigate this transition. At the other end of the spectrum, small-town and suburban weeklies, community tabloids, and papers targeted to ethnic groups are much better defended against Internet incursions. Readership of print weeklies continues to grow, using a model that is part paid and part "controlled," meaning free to readers but guaranteed to advertisers, thus aping the free content of the Internet. Free community papers clearly have momentum; subscription and single-copy income is down, but ad income, and overall income, is up. The advertising base of local weeklies was never as reliant on large national advertisers, and their intensely local franchise is retaining both a readership and local advertising bond that the Web is challenging at a far slower rate than it assaults regional dailies.

At greatest risk are newspapers in between—the mid-sized regional metropolitan dailies, like *The Philadelphia Inquirer* and the Minneapolis *Star Tribune*. For example, when McClatchy bought the hugely profitable *Star Tribune* from the Cowles family in 1998, the paper was one of the Internet pioneers. The family had invested heavily in *startribune.com*. But when the dot-com bubble burst, and profit margins fell from over 30 percent to under 20 percent, McClatchy began disinvesting. To make matters worse, the innovative *startribune.com* was ordered to convert to the technology of McClatchy Interactive, which was based on the successful site of another McClatchy paper, the Raleigh *News & Observer*. "We lost at least a year," says one reporter. And not long after the technical overhaul was complete, the paper was sold again; the Web staff is now scrambling to disengage from an alien technology that it never liked. Sources at the paper say that Web traffic and Web advertising revenue were close to flat in 2006, while they rose sharply at most newspapers.

In January, *The Philadelphia Inquirer* laid off sixty-eight people from the newsroom—and then turned around and hired five of them back for its Web site. That doesn't sound like much, but the move increased the Web staff from eight to thirteen. "What happened here was a disaster, but they managed to salvage something good out of it," says the reporter Daniel Rubin. . . .

Rubin, fifty, epitomizes the old-school print reporter who has found the leap to Web journalism intoxicating. A nineteen-year veteran of the *Inquirer*, he writes a very popular, link-rich, and witty blog called *Blinq.com* and also covers the business of entertainment for print and Web—everything from auto shows to sports and popular culture. Rubin's home page says, "It was a wise man who said news is a conversation. Let's talk." He says Web journalism is "a shot of adrenaline. It makes me superproductive. The feedback is immediate. I know almost instantly what's working. It's like I'm back in my father's hardware store, deciding what to put in the front window to bring in customers."

The *Inquirer*'s editor, Bill Marimow, a two-time Pulitzer Prize winner, sees Web journalism as a lifeline. On the afternoon that we talked, the big breaking local story was the indictment of State Senator Vincent J. Fumo, a longtime South Philadelphia powerbroker. Within a couple of hours the *Inquirer* had posted many multimedia items—among them a PDF of the full text of the indictment, dueling press releases, Fumo's floor speech, audio of the U.S. Attorney's press conference, a special blog from Harrisburg, archives of related stories, photos, comments by other officials, and five features on other facets of the story. It was the perfect vindication of the idea that old media can use the tools of the new to do journalism better than anyone else. . . .

There are some encouraging exceptions to this picture of the squeezed midsize daily. Several strategists are promoting a blend of the civic journalism movement with a business strategy that builds on the local paper's brand awareness to create the most comprehensive and interactive Web site in town. In principle, this strategy invigorates the journalism, engages the community in new ways, and increases Web traffic that can bring in ad revenue. . . .

Some of the most creative service journalism on the Web comes from small papers. At the *Naples Daily News* in Florida, readers can get podcasts, videocasts, and photo galleries; check hurricane damage or local high school sports, or dig into an ingenious database of 80,000 recent local housing transactions—and more. The designer of this hyper-local site, a thirty-five-year-old self-described Internet nerd named Rob Curley, became a Web legend for his award-winning Web work at the *Lawrence Journal-World* and the *Topeka Capital-Journal*, in Kansas, and the *Hannibal Courier-Post* in Missouri. Last October, Donald Graham of *The Washington Post* hired him away from Florida to be vice president for new product development at *Washington Post*. Newsweek Interactive. "We have learned a great deal from the Web operations of small papers," Graham says.

"They hired me to do the same cool stuff, only with more resources," says Curley. "The only difference is that they don't wake me at home at 3 a.m. when the classifieds go down. And don't tell me that what I do isn't journalism."

A slicker, more explicitly business-oriented project called Newspaper Next, launched by the American Press Institute in late 2005 in collaboration with a team of Harvard Business School professors, is promoting a similar model. Harvard's Clayton Christensen, who advises the project, counsels newspapers to "engage, enrich, empower, and entertain" members of their larger communities, taking advantage of their branding and the Web's interactive potential.

Newspaper Next is trying out variants of its model, working with seven newspaper companies. At *The Dallas Morning News*, the target audience is 700,000 busy mothers who are online every day, but only 15 percent of whom currently read the Morning News or its Web site. The idea is to build the ultimate site for moms, called GuideFamily.com, and match the traffic with prospective advertisers.

Other major chains have their own variations on this community approach. E. W. Scripps' version is called YourHub, described as "a network of community-based Web sites featuring stories, photos, blogs, events, and classified ads posted by community residents and supported by local advertisers." It's a little ironic that a model of community journalism that was created before there was an Internet is now being seized on by the business side as a road to profitability.

Can it also enrich the journalism? At their best, these experiments promise to revive community connections and revenue opportunities, as well as local journalism, and to lift newspapers out of their revenue and morale funk. But absent serious investment and commitment from publishers to devote adequate staff, such Web sites can deteriorate into a stew of bratwurst recipes, police blotter, high school reunions, and inane comment.

Jay Rosen observes that a dramatic change in the newspaper culture occurred only in late 2004, when newspaper people finally grasped that, as he says, "the tools of content production had been distributed to people formerly known as the audience." For a decade, Rosen adds, most publishers and editors had misunderstood the Web, seeing it mainly as a new way of delivering print content. By no small coincidence, 2004 marked the beginning of the current financial downturn in newspaper profitability and share prices, and a mood of crisis and even desperation stimulated a new openness and creativity. "Once you let go emotionally, you realize that as journalism, online is infinitely superior to print," says Tom Rosenstiel of The Project for Excellence in Journalism, "in its ability to offer links to other material, original documents, full texts of interviews, video, and as much statistical backup as the reader can stand."

If newspapers are now finding their digital footing faster than observers feared, will Wall Street allow this promising transition to maximize its potential? In 2006, supposedly a disastrous year for newspapers, the average profit margins for the newspaper divisions of publicly traded publishing companies was 17.8 percent, according to the Merrill Lynch media analyst Lauren Rich Fine. That's well above the average for all industries. Yet newspaper stocks lagged the S&P 500 last year by 21 percent, after another disastrously down year in 2005. Is there something fatally wrong with newspapers that their profit margins conceal? Or is there something amiss with the way Wall Street values newspapers?

As recently as 2002, newspapers and their mostly institutional shareholders were enjoying profit margins in excess of 22 percent, margins that beat even the fabulously lucrative pharmaceutical industry. Newspapers had been local monopolies, and they got used to charging monopoly prices for their most reliable moneymaker, the classifieds. Given Craigslist and Cars.com and Monster.com, those days are never coming back.

Analyst Fine says some newspapers should just level with investors about the need to plow money back into the Internet: "Just put up a sign, work in progress, come back and see us in two years," she advises. "You're going to have to judge us differently." But, as Fine quickly adds, that's not the way Wall Street works. Further depressions in stock prices invite hostile takeovers and shareholder demands of the sort that killed Knight Ridder. The media analyst John Morton says, "I worry that some publishers will look on their Internet operations as found money, without appreciating that the print is what supports the journalism that attracts the traffic. I worry that they won't sufficiently invest in people to do it well."

Even if newspaper publishers do everything right, however, in the Internet age they will have a smaller share of the total advertising pie than they enjoyed in the print era. Newspapers' share of the $424 billion spent globally last year on advertising, according to ZenithOptimedia, was still a considerable 29.1 percent—but shrinking. The Internet share was just 5.8 percent—but growing. And most Web dollars will not go to newspapers. The Internet competition to monetize traffic is fierce, with most sites designed as pure revenue plays unencumbered by news or civic mission. For example, Barry Diller's IAC/Interactive Corp. is thriving with Web service businesses, such as Match.com, Ask.com, the invitation service Evite, and local city search sites. As newspapers complement their traditional news content with local consumer services and ingenious interactive features, they face competitors who enjoyed earlier market entry and who have high brand awareness. . . .

Meanwhile, Google, Yahoo, and Microsoft are investing massively in ever more sophisticated search technology. Along with other non-newspaper sites like Wikipedia, Amazon, and eBay, such pure Internet entrepreneurs capture the lion's share of traffic that can bring in ad money. And none of them has expensive newsrooms to feed. *The New York Times* and its affiliated papers get visits from 13 million distinct individuals a month. But the nation's top thirty newspaper Web sites together have under 100 million such monthly visits, while Microsoft, Google, and Yahoo have well over 100 million each, according to Nielsen Net Ratings. The search engines do share some of this ad revenue with newspapers through a variety of ad partnership models—Google wrote checks of $780 million to its ad "content partners" in the last quarter of 2006—but the other large Web entrepreneurs are pure rivals.

On the other hand, newspaper companies themselves are increasingly investing in the purchase of Web income-generators, such as the *Times*'s 2005 acquisition of About.com, and Dow Jones's decision to sell six of its fifteen Ottaway dailies in late 2006 and use the proceeds to purchase Factiva.com, a subscription-only search company. In 2000, the Tribune Company and Knight Ridder bought Career-Builder.com, later joined by Gannett; it's now the most popular online recruiting site. Here again, independent newspapers with shallower pockets do not have this capacity. They have to invent their own Internet services, and hope that if they build the traffic, ad revenue will come. . . .

Are there other economic models, either of ownership or of revenue, that might provide some relief from Wall Street pressure and Internet competition, and allow newspapers to invest adequately in a hybrid future? Tycoons once ran newspapers not just for the income, but for the influence and prestige. Sometimes, family-owned papers have been willing to ride out business cycles and to invest more in the newsroom and in far-flung correspondents than a pure market calculation of optimized revenue would otherwise dictate.

New forms of ownership might include a new generation of civic-minded local owners, or more nonprofit foundations, modeled on the Poynter Institute's ownership of the *St. Petersburg Times* or the *British Guardian*, which has been owned by a nonprofit trust on behalf of the employees since 1933, when the young paper's editor, Edward Scott, was killed in a boating accident and the Scott family set up the trust. Far from causing the *Guardian* to rest on its laurels, the trust has enabled the paper to be one of the great innovators. It has one of the most imaginative and interactive Web sites around, with 13 million monthly users, roughly matching *The New York Times* and its affiliates. The *Guardian* editor, Alan Rusbridger, speaking at Harvard's Shorenstein Center, recently observed that the Scott trustees do not demand "the sort of returns many big American media organizations are used to. . . . Trustees understand that serious public service journalism isn't always compatible with enormous circulations or huge profits."

In Minneapolis, after the sale of the *Star Tribune* to Avista Capital Partners was announced, the new private-equity owners paid a call on the newsroom, swore fealty to the sacred profession of journalism, and insisted that they were in it for the long haul, and not for a quick turnaround and sale. If so, however, they will be playing very much against type. Absent some dramatic sales to community owners, such as a hoped-for breakup of the Tribune chain, the dream of nonprofit foundations or benign billionaires seems remote.

The more likely economic salvation of newspapers will come from Web ingenuity, married to new business strategies and revenue sources. In this respect, the immensely lucrative search engine companies that now provide newspapers with both digital readers and online revenue are something of a mixed blessing. "Some day," says Tom Rosenstiel of the Project for Excellence, "the lawyers for *The New York Times* and for Google are just going to fight it out." . . .

As both a source and a diversion of ad revenues and readers alike, Google is both competitor and partner to publishing companies. One executive I interviewed termed Google a "frenemy." Another called the process "co-opetition." Looking down the road, there are other "frenemies." Mochila.com is a fast-growing Web syndicator of content to newspapers. The idea is that with newspapers squeezed and laying off producers of news room content, Mochila can license high-quality content from freelancers and offer it to newspapers, and perhaps eventually to consumers. The content also comes bundled with ads sold by Mochila, and the revenue is split with newspapers. This is also a delicate balancing act. The cheaper content and new revenues are found money. But if newspapers increasingly become purveyors of freelance content, they lose their distinctive franchise. And all those intermediaries are more claimants on the ad revenue pot. . . .

So neither of the deus ex machina solutions to the newspapers' (somewhat exaggerated) financial plight—different ownership structures, or more favorable revenue sharing with search engines—seems likely. Rather, publishers need to work with what they have, investing in people and technology to get through this transition to the promised land of hybrid print-Web publishing.

Given that America's newspapers collectively employ far fewer R&D people than Microsoft, Google, Yahoo et al., it is remarkable that newspapers have emerged as formidable Web innovators. And so far nobody has succeeded in replicating the range, depth, and quality of a newspaper in a Web-only daily (or hourly). You can click on Google News for a quick snapshot of breaking stuff, but most of that content originates in newspapers. "The cliché used to be, 'Call me anything you want as long you spell my name right,'" says the *Post*'s James Brady. "Today, it's call me whatever you like as long as you link to me." Far more bloggers are linking to newspapers than vice-versa.

Web-only journalism has been surprisingly slow to challenge newspapers on their home court. When *Slate* launched the first online magazine in 1996, it appeared to signal a whole trend. But journalism turns out to be expensive. *Slate* briefly tried a $19.95 paid-subscription model in 1998, but lost far more readers than it gained income, and abandoned the approach. Even though it is now owned by *The Washington Post*, *Slate* was in many ways a higher quality journalistic product when Michael Kinsley began it. Today *Slate*, *Salon*, *Huffington Post*, and the rest, offer far more comment than news, since talk is cheap and reportage isn't.

Four years after *Slate*, in November 2000, Josh Marshall launched his superb *Talking Points Memo*. As the Internet's first I.F. Stone, Marshall looked to be the harbinger of independent, branded, Web-only investigative reporting, using his own diligence combined with tips forwarded by his tens of thousands of fans, and breaking a lot of news, sometimes scooping the dailies. Today Marshall presides over a small conglomerate of interconnected sites and colleagues, one of which is the excellent *TPM Muckraker*, with two regular employees who practice Marshall's brand of investigation. As a whole, however, the much-expanded *TPM* now has a far higher ratio of comment and interpretation (some of it first-rate) to enterprise reporting.

In their modern classic, *The Elements of Journalism*, Bill Kovach and Tom Rosenstiel write that, "In the end, the discipline of verification is what separates journalism from entertainment, propaganda, fiction, or art." Robert Putnam's *Bowling Alone*, recounting a half-century's decline of civic engagement (a decline that began long before the Internet), reports that newspaper readers are more likely than nonreaders to participate in politics and local public life.

Cities and towns with newspapers have a more transparent civic and public life than those without them.

In effect, we deputize editors to be our proxies, delegating to them the task of assigning reporters and deciding what news we need to know on a given day and to certify its pertinence and accuracy. We trust them to do a more reliable job than even our own Web-surfing. (As Chico Marx famously put it in *Duck Soup*, "Who are you going to believe, me or your own eyes?"). But as readers, we no longer have to make that either/or choice between newspapers and the wild Web. We can have both the authoritative daily newspaper to aggregate and certify, *and* the infinite medley of the Web—all of which puts the traditional press under salutary pressure to innovate and to excel.

As Generation Y grows up, and Generation Z finds the idea of getting news on paper even quainter, more people like Ezra (and his children) will become their own editor-aggregators. But if the dailies do their jobs, the next generation will still read newspapers—online.

My reporting suggests that many big dailies have turned the corner, though only barely and just in time, that newspapers have started down a financially and journalistically viable path of becoming hybrids, without losing the professional culture that makes them uniquely valuable.

Assuming that most dailies survive the transition, my guess is that in twenty-five years they will be mostly digital; that even people like me of the pre-Internet generation will be largely won over by ingenious devices like Times Reader, supplemented by news alerts, RSS feeds, and God knows what else. But whether newspapers are print or Web matters far less than whether they maintain their historic calling.

Eric Klinenberg

Breaking the News

Senate reconfirmation hearings tend to be predictable affairs, marked by polite give-and-take and senatorial grandstanding, but generally free of surprise plot twists. And so it was supposed to go last September 12, when Federal Communications Commission (FCC) chairman Kevin Martin appeared before the Commerce Committee. In March 2005, following the departure of Michael Powell (Colin's son), President Bush had named the young Republican lawyer to head the extraordinarily powerful five-person panel that oversees the nation's media and telecommunications policies. Martin, a boyish-looking 40-year-old who'd been on the FCC since 2001, planned to carry on much of his predecessor's unfinished business, particularly stiffening penalties for on-air indecency and the sweeping deregulation of media ownership rules. But unlike Powell, who was confrontational and contemptuous of his critics, the bland and soft-spoken Martin seemed unlikely to attract controversy.

But controversy caught up with him when Senator Barbara Boxer (D-Calif.) strayed from the script at his reconfirmation hearing. Boxer began by asking Martin about an FCC study, commissioned by Powell, on the impact of media ownership on local news. Unsuspecting, Martin said that it had never been completed. Then, as he watched glumly, Boxer brandished a draft of the study, which had, in fact, been written more than two years earlier, only to be buried by the FCC. The report found that locally owned television stations, on average, presented 5½ minutes more local news per broadcast than stations owned by out-of-town conglomerates. The findings squarely contradicted the claims made by Martin, Powell, and big media companies, who have argued that lifting limits on ownership would improve local news coverage.

"Now, this isn't national security, for God's sakes," Boxer continued, unable to resist making Martin squirm. "I mean, this is important information. So I don't understand who deep-sixed this thing." Martin meekly said he had no idea, and promised he'd look into it. Within a week, a former FCC lawyer claimed that "every last piece" of the report had been ordered destroyed before it was leaked, and a second unreleased study came to light, prompting Boxer to refer the matter to the FCC's inspector general.

The discovery of the missing studies wasn't just bad for Martin's image, it was a blow to his pet project—trying to repeal what's known as the cross-ownership ban, a 31-year-old FCC rule that prohibits a single company from owning a newspaper and a TV station in the same regional market. Powell had repealed the rule in 2003 amid public outcry, only to have a federal court reinstate it the following year. Last April, Martin told the members of the Newspaper Association of America that he would renew the effort to end this regulatory relic from "the days of disco and leisure suits." Lifting the ban, he said, "may help to forestall the erosion in local news coverage." But now, the FCC's own internal findings confirmed what its critics had been saying for years—that letting one company dominate a city's news business actually undermines the quality of the local media that most Americans rely on for their news.

The renewed push to consolidate even more of the nation's newsprint and airwaves comes as the media are in profound transition. Although we are bombarded with a seemingly endless supply of media options—from cable television to blogs to satellite radio—more and more of the actual news and information we consume comes from a handful of giant media companies. (See "And Then There Were Eight," page 48.) Meanwhile, locally owned outlets are being squeezed out of business or absorbed at an ever faster clip. In the past three decades, two-thirds of newspaper owners and one-third of television owners have shut down. Newspapers are particularly feeling the pinch: Fewer than 300 of the nation's 1,500 daily papers are still independently owned, and more than half of all markets are dominated by a single paper. The number of newspaper employees has dropped nearly 20 percent since 1990. Hardly a week goes by without another pundit lamenting the demise of the great American newspaper.

The eulogies are also coming from the newspaper executives and investors whose pursuit of phenomenal profits has turned many dailies into shadows of their former selves. They claim that ending the cross-ownership ban will throw a lifeline to foundering papers by allowing them to merge with TV stations and compete with the Internet. In reality, such a move would only fuel the "cut-and-gut" strategies that generate short-term value at the expense of the kind of journalism that exposed Watergate, NSA eavesdropping, and countless corrupt politicians. To see how disastrous this could be for the future of news, just take a look at the cities where the FCC has already allowed cross-ownership to get a toehold.

Three weeks after Martin's embarrassing Senate appearance, the FCC held a rare public hearing in Los Angeles, the first of six that Martin had promised before his planned proposal of new ownership rules later this year. He had hoped the event would be a chance to win over skeptics. But it would be a tough sell: The ban on cross-ownership has bipartisan support from a loose-knit coalition that includes religious conservatives, centrist Democrats, and an array of progressive groups. "The failure to implement these rule changes is not our fault alone," Martin had told a meeting of newspaper publishers last spring. "The public is not convinced of the need to change these rules, and if you can't convince the public, our chances to do that are dim."

Martin assured the more than 500 people who had packed into an auditorium at the University of Southern California that "public input is critical to this process." Yet once the microphone was opened to the floor, it was obvious that he didn't like what he heard. "There were about 100 people who spoke," recalled Jonathan Adelstein, one of two Democrats on the FCC, "and I'd say 99 of them spoke out against media consolidation while one spoke out in favor of it. And I thought that was great, because that's just about the breakdown of how Americans feel about this issue." As speaker after speaker pounded the FCC's cozy relationship with the companies it's supposed to regulate, Martin slumped in his seat, head in hands. By the time his staff rescued him to attend another event, he looked like a man who wished he'd never gotten out of bed.

Martin had made the mistake of kicking off his final deregulatory push in Los Angeles. Having witnessed the havoc the Chicago-based Tribune Co. had wreaked upon the *Los Angeles Times* during the past six years, Angelenos were familiar with what can happen when an out-of-town company tries to control the local media.

Tribune Co. is the nation's second-largest newspaper owner (behind Gannett)—and is, more importantly, the only corporation to own both a newspaper and a television station in the three largest markets in the United States—Chicago, New York City, and Los Angeles. (The Chicago arrangement is grandfathered; the FCC has granted Tribune temporary waivers to cross-own properties in the other cities.) The company acquired the *Los Angeles Times*, along with New York's *Newsday*, the *Baltimore Sun*, and the *Hartford Courant*, when it purchased Times Mirror Co. for $8.3 billion in 2000. Its executives proclaimed that the deal would make Tribune "the premier multimedia company in America." They marched into Los Angeles prepared to merge news production at the *Times* and the WB network affiliate KTLA, folding another city into their "convergence media" model, in which journalistic and corporate "synergies" between newspapers, TV stations, and websites reduce inefficiency and maximize profits.

The paper's employees and readers soon discovered that this jargon was code for old-fashioned downsizing. The *Los Angeles Times* had long been known for its extensive local coverage as well as national and international reporting on a par with the *New York Times* and the *Washington Post*. Indeed, it won six Pulitzers in 2004, before Tribune started slashing its domestic and international bureaus—just as world events and Southern California's booming immigrant population made their reporting more necessary than ever. By 2006, Tribune had eliminated one-fourth of the editorial staff, trimmed the news section, and canned two popular editors-in-chief after disputes over cutbacks, losing 335,000 subscribers in the process. (See "Reckless Disregard," page 46.)

The *Times'* critics also charge that the leaner publication lost touch with local issues and its civic mission. "A succession of publishers and editors who don't know an Amber Alert from a SigAlert"—warnings to look for kidnapped children and massive tie-ups on L.A. freeways, respectively—"have been parachuted in to run the *Times*," wrote Harry B. Chandler, a former *Times* executive whose family owned the paper for nearly 120 years, in an oped last November. "The paper needs executives who understand the area. Providing great editorial coverage and civic leadership for this, the largest, most complicated urban space in the world, are tasks unsuited to outsiders whose tour of duty in the Southland may not outlast the Santa Anas."

When convergence failed to produce a windfall, and Tribune Co. stock dropped almost 35 percent in three years, shareholders—including many members of the Chandler clan-revolted. Last fall, Tribune put its entire business on the block. The decision fed hopes that David Geffen or another benevolent mogul would acquire the *Times* (at press time, sharks including Rupert Murdoch were also circling). The auction also added to suspicions that Tribune had been, as one *Hartford Courant* writer put it, "bleeding its local properties to keep the corporate mother ship in Chicago above water."

If Tribune's record in Los Angeles should give pause to advocates of consolidation, so too should its stranglehold on its hometown media market, where its holdings include the *Chicago Tribune*; "superstation" CW affiliate WGN-TV; WGN, the region's top AM radio station; CLTV, the only local cable news station; *Chicago* magazine; the top online entertainment guide; the most popular Spanish-language daily; a tabloid aimed at readers 18 to 34; and the Chicago Cubs.

Tribune Co.'s presence is so powerful that locals refer to Chicago as "Trib Town"; the *Wall Street Journal* observed that the company has become "synonymous with the part of the world in which its audience lives." When a story piques the interest of Tribune's managers and editors, it echoes through the company's news outlets, giving it extraordinary influence in setting the local political and cultural agenda. Independent and locally owned news outlets often take their cues from Tribune. As Steve Edwards, host of a popular local affairs program on public radio station WBEZ, told me: "If the *Tribune* decides something was a major story and runs front-page coverage and repeated editorials on it, you would hear that story topping many local newscasts; you would hear other reporters doing more coverage of that issue. . . . There's no question there would be a ripple effect." Or, as a Chicago media critic puts it, "Tribune is the 800-pound gorilla."

The company also has the power to relegate a story to obscurity merely by ignoring it. Mayor Richard M. Daley, who has himself enjoyed nearly unchecked power in the city for almost two decades, acknowledged this when Tribune Co. all but ignored his favorite team, the Chicago White Sox, during its march to the 2005 World Series. "How can you compete-with Tribune?" he asked. "I mean, give me a break. They own the Cubs, they own WGN Radio [and] TV and CLTV. Come on. You think you are going to get any publicity for the White Sox? You can't. Let's be realistic."

And Tribune's ability to decide what becomes news goes far beyond baseball. In 2000, for instance, the Chicago Housing Authority announced the city's largest planning initiative since the urban renewal programs of the 1950s, proposing a 10-year, $1.6 billion scheme to demolish 18,000 units of public housing, forcing thousands of families into the private market. Local and federal agencies implemented the massive, controversial plan without significant public input, not even from public housing residents. The project was ripe for investigation, yet Tribune's management didn't take issue with it, and the *Chicago Tribune* and its media siblings barely took notice. Almost 50 "special reports" are listed on the newspaper's website, yet not one concerns public housing. This oversight was consistent with the paper's larger blind spot concerning issues affecting black Chicagoans, says local author and activist Jamie Kalven. "What about coverage of segregation? Or poverty?" he asks. "You can't make up for that with a special report."

But is it truly possible for a company—no matter how large—to dominate a local market in the digital age? According to Tribune Co. executives, the company's editorial decisions have limited impact in Chicago because consumers there have an infinite number of additional news sources. "In an environment where people's choices for obtaining information have radically multiplied, there is no risk of one voice dominating the marketplace of ideas," Jack Fuller, then-president of Tribune's publishing division, told the Senate Commerce Committee in 2001. "Today in clamorous cities such as Los Angeles, Chicago, and New York, it is frankly a challenge for any voice—no matter how booming—to get itself heard." Yet Tribune has told a different story to investors. Speaking to shareholders in 2005, President and CEO Dennis Fitz Simons boasted that the company's "varied media choices" for Chicagoans reached 6.4 million people, or more than 90 percent of the market.

This is exactly the kind of imbalance the FCC had sought to prevent when it passed the 1975 newspaper-broadcast cross-ownership ban, and it's why Tribune Co. has long sought to roll back the rule. The company spent billions acquiring properties that are only temporarily exempt from being found in violation of the ban—unless the FCC changes the rules first. Between 1998 and 2005, it spent $1.1 million on lobbying and more than $380,000 on political contributions, trying to convince lawmakers that its business model proved the rule unnecessary.

This strategy seemed brilliant when President Bush put Michael Powell in charge of the FCC in 2001, giving him a mandate to clear away the agency's regulatory underbrush. Powell, after all, had famously quipped that he did not know what "the public interest" meant. "The night after I was sworn in, I waited for a visit from the angel of the public interest," he told a crowd of executives in 1998, after President Clinton appointed him to the commission. "1 waited all night, but she did not come. And, in fact, five months into this job, I still have had no divine awakening and no one has issued me my public interest crystal ball."

Breaking with precedent, Powell announced that the burden of proof no longer rested on the opponents of ownership limits, suggesting that most regulations were unnecessary unless it was otherwise demonstrated. In June 2003, he led a 3-2 party-line vote to relax cross-ownership restrictions. (The commission also voted to significantly loosen television ownership caps.) The decision was made in spite of the 3 million public comments that had flooded into the FCC, the overwhelming majority of them opposing deregulation. "Seldom have I seen a regulatory agency cave in so completely to the big economic interests," said Senator Byron Dorgan (D-N.D.). Trent Lott, his Republican colleague from Mississippi, stated simply, "This is a mistake."

Powell may have been deaf to the public interest, but the courts were not. A year later, the 3rd U.S. Circuit Court of Appeals blocked his order, finding that although the FCC had the right to ease cross-ownership laws, it had not shown sufficient justification to do so. It was a stunning blow to Powell, who announced his resignation nine months later, walking through the revolving door into a job at a media and telecommunications investment firm.

But repealing the ban still remains a holy grail for media companies, and the newspaper industry's bumpy entrance into the digital age has provided them with a new rationale. Consolidation, they claim, is necessary to save newspapers, which otherwise can't compete in the new economy.

In fact, falling circulation numbers and sinking stock prices notwithstanding, corporate executives' cries of impending poverty are exaggerated. Newspaper chains routinely generate profit levels that most companies would kill for. ExxonMobil topped the Fortune 500 list for 2005, reporting 11 percent profit margins, while the average profit for the entire list was 5.9 percent. That year, the top 13 publicly traded newspaper companies enjoyed average profit margins of 20 percent; the 3 most financially successful chains, Gannett, McClatchy, and E.W. Scripps, earned around 25 percent margins. The Tribune Co.'s newspaper division earned 20 percent, as did the beleaguered *Los Angeles Times*. And this during a year that analysts lamented as "the industry's worst" since the 2001 recession.

What newspaper executives do not exaggerate is the pressure they get from investment analysts and large shareholders, who demand extraordinary, constantly growing profit margins and punish companies that fail to achieve them. But the newspaper chains themselves are partly responsible for setting unrealistic expectations. During the '70s and '80s, Gannett developed what would become a popular formula for making papers more profitable: Buy up a local newspaper, crush the competition, jack up ad rates, downsize the editorial staff (and, if required, break the union), then watch earnings soar.

The cut-and-gut approach does not treat newspaper ownership as a public service, but rather as an investment in a commodity like any other. This can make dumping papers an attractive option when profits sag or shareholders get antsy. Last spring, the Knight Ridder chain succumbed to pressure from its largest private investor and sold off its entire lineup of 32 papers to the McClatchy Co. for more than $4 billion. McClatchy then made a healthy profit flipping 12 of its new titles, including the well-respected *Philadelphia Inquirer* and *San Jose Mercury News*. Then, in December, McClatchy reaped a $160 million tax write-off by selling its "underperforming" marquee paper, the *Minneapolis Star-Tribune*. The buyer, a private equity firm, had no experience running a newspaper. "They're buying cash flow and tax benefits," an analyst told the *New York Times*. "It's not the sort of religious commitment that you hope to get from newspaper owners."

Obviously, the newspaper business is changing. The Internet has made it harder to sustain high profit margins, not because readers are abandoning news but because publishers have not yet figured out how to make more money from their websites. Until now, papers sustained themselves by selling a physical product and the ad space in it. With online readers refusing to pay for what they read and web ads generating pennies on the dollar, the old model is collapsing. As Jay R. Smith, president of Cox Newspapers, told *Editor & Publisher*, newspapers are "finding whole new pockets of audiences for which they get no credit," clocking record-breaking readership figures if online traffic is included. But online advertising will account for just 6 percent of newspapers' $50 billion in ad revenues in 2007, the Newspaper Association of America predicts.

What's really at risk here is not the future of newspapers but of the news itself. While our democratic culture could survive the loss of the daily paper as we know it, it would be endangered without the kinds of reporting that it provides. It's the journalism, not the newsprint, that matters.

Even in the online era, more than 60 percent of Americans say they read a local newspaper daily or several times a week. And with good reason: Few of the cable channels and websites that newspaper chains claim as competitors actually provide original news and information. Cable networks do virtually no local reporting of their own, and while bloggers do a good job exposing journalistic lapses, they generally aren't doing the muckraking, beat reporting, and pavement pounding that generate news. (See "A Blogger Says: Save the MSM!" page 50.) As the 3rd Circuit Court stated in its opinion upholding the cross-ownership ban, the Internet "may be useful for finding restaurant reviews and concert schedules," but it does not offer "the type of 'news and public affairs programming'" that public policies should promote.

FCC head kevin martin has suggested that "newspaper-owned [television] stations provide more news and public affairs programming and also appear to provide higher quality programming," echoing the findings of a 2003 study by the Project for Excellence in Journalism. However, the study did not examine what happens to the quality of newspapers after they merge with television stations. From what I've seen of these hybrid operations, the results are discouraging.

In the late 1990s, I spent two weeks inside Tribune Co.'s famous Chicago office tower interviewing reporters and editors for a book about a local heat wave, but found that everyone wanted to talk instead about "corporate synergies" and "cross-platform production." The company had just started to require its newspaper staff to report breaking stories on its cable news station, CLTV. Many reporters were anxious about the new arrangement, which meant more work without more pay, and less time to do their regular jobs. They weren't comforted when managers announced that they were remodeling the newsroom to put a television studio directly outside the editor-in-chief's door. These reporters recognized that technology was changing their industry, and most were eager to learn new digital skills and make the occasional TV appearance. Their main concern was that as "content providers," they were losing time for reporting, thinking, and writing—the essential ingredients of their craft—forcing them to churn out increasingly dumbed-down articles.

It didn't help that their bosses had abandoned even a rhetorical commitment to newspaper journalism and the values it represents. "I am not the editor of a newspaper," Editor-in-Chief Howard Tyner told the *American Journalism Review* in 1998, "I am the manager of a content company." Tyner's predecessor, James Squires, had already observed this shift. "Journalism, particularly newspaper journalism, has no real place in the company's future," he wrote after leaving the paper. "No one ever uses the word. The company bills itself as an 'information and entertainment' conglomerate and hopes that newspapers will become a smaller factor in its total business."

Media General, a newspaper and television chain in the Southeast, became a leader in convergence journalism due to its long-standing ownership of the Tampa Tribune and NBC affiliate WFLA. In 2002, I spent a week at its Tampa *News* Center, a cutting-edge facility where the newspaper, television, and web departments shared an editorial "Superdesk" that looked like the bridge of the starship Enterprise. Although the Tampa market is considerably smaller than Chicago's or Los Angeles', the *News* Center is one of the world's most technologically sophisticated and innovative convergence complexes, drawing visits from media executives eager to see the future of 21st-century *News* production.

Editors and reporters at the *News* Center were trained to constantly look for ways to make stories overlap in as many outlets as possible. Every day, print, TV, and online editors held a 15-minute "convergence meeting" to discuss shared projects. And every month, the company's multimedia manager compiled a report that listed successful overlap and praised "overt acts of convergence."

While the Superdesk enabled editors to do more with less, some Tampa. Tribune reporters were finding themselves juggling competing demands. I shadowed several print journalists who were pulled away from their desks to do short spots and longer stories for television. While one was waiting to tape a shot, I asked her how she felt about the added work. "Well," she began, "the good part is that it's fun, it's different, it's difficult, and it's interesting for me. It's a break from my regular routine. But a few weeks ago I did TV every day for two weeks. And every day—when you spend 40 minutes writing the script, 20 minutes putting on makeup, 20 to 30 minutes taping, and then taking the makeup off-it takes, like, two hours to do the job. That's two hours—a quarter of my day—and that doesn't help my reporting." As their job descriptions required them to be more telegenic, some reporters feared that the norms of TV *News* production—short stories, soft features, celebrity journalism—were creeping into the print side.

These concerns reveal the vicious cycle that drives the newspaper business today: Slashing editorial content and standards may be a recipe for quick revenue, but it doesn't retain readers. However, doing the meaningful, quality reporting that print and online readers expect is expensive. And so each new round of convergence, downsizing, or outsourcing further erodes the product, paving the way for yet another round. As *Los Angeles Times* columnist Tim Rutten commented last fall, "A newspaper that is indifferent to its bottom line goes out of business; a newspaper that thinks only of its bottom line has a business that isn't worth saving." He knew what he was writing about: In October 2005, as its circulation plummeted, the *Times* announced that it would attempt to regain readers by running shorter articles and more celebrity stories.

This is the choice that Kevin Martin, the Tribune Co., and other advocates of continued media deregulation seem to be offering: We must destroy our newspapers in order to save them.

It doesn't have to be this way. Citizens, communities, and even a few media executives are beginning to make intriguing suggestions about how to reverse the course of radical deregulation and replenish the nation's supply of local media outlets. Frank Blethen, whose family has owned and published the *Seattle Times* since 1896, has been advocating newspaper ownership caps that would discourage chain journalism and create new opportunities for locally controlled dailies. Grassroots organizations in several states, including California and Illinois, are calling for the FCC to put teeth back into the broadcast license-renewal process. And radio enthusiasts, recalling the '60s boom of free-spirited FM radio, are asking why radio and TV stations should not be required to air original programming on the 1,000-plus new channels they will get on the digital spectrum.

Meanwhile, the FCC says it will continue to hold public hearings on the future of America's media. The question is how closely Martin will be listening. Last November, he quietly commissioned his staff and a few select contractors to complete new studies on media ownership, which will presumably bolster the rule changes he unveils. Whatever happens next, the stakes couldn't be higher. As Michael Copps, the other Democrat on the FCC, observed at October's hearing in Los Angeles, "We're back at square one. It's all up for grabs."

At risk isn't the future of newspapers but the *News* itself. It's the journalism, not the newsprint, that matters.

Despite their cries of poverty, newspaper chains earn profits that most Fortune 500 companies would kill for.

POSTSCRIPT

Will Print Newspapers Survive in the Current Business Environment?

Forecasts of the future are often exciting to contemplate, though they may often give us nothing more than utopian or dystopian visions of what to expect. Although these articles focus on changes in the newspaper business, it is inevitable that change will occur in many of our existing media systems. What changes would you predict? If we were to make predictions today about what the media environment of the future holds, we would probably say that most of the technologies will be wireless (including the Internet) and portable. Media may become much more localized and reliant on consumer-generated content. Yet, there may be benefits to existing systems that we should not overlook. In Marc Fisher's "Essential Again" article in *American Journalism Review* (Oct/Nov 2005), he considers what happened during Hurricane Katrina. In this case, the Internet was useless in the key areas; the systems were down and there was no electricity to get communication to and from residents. At the same time, traditional media did what they have always done best—they united the nation in a common story that had a devastating impact on so many citizens.

For a couple of sources that address changes in traditional news media, consider Philip Meyer's *The Vanishing Newspaper: Saving Journalism in the Information Age* (2004). He looks at how the Internet and other new information technologies have fragmented the audience, threatening the business models of newspapers, but he provides a model to make it work again. Dan Gillmor sees a bright future for citizen journalism. In *We the Media: Grassroots Journalism by the People, for the People* (2006), he reflects on how the online media will change journalism for the better as grassroots journalists take over the production of news. Finally, in *Knightfall: Knight Ridder and How the Erosion of Newspaper Journalism Is Putting Democracy at Risk* (2005), Davis Merrit argues that corporate balance sheets now dictate what we read, and that freedom of speech is endangered. He outlines the struggle to reconcile the role of the press in a democracy with the pressure to produce profits. For a look at potential changes in the entertainment media, see the special edition of *The Annals of the American Academy of Political and Social Sciences*, vol. 597, edited by Eric Klinenberg (January 2005). In this publication, you will find a variety of articles dealing with the future changes in gambling, marketing, children's media, and more.

On a final note, it might be important to consider what other social and cultural institutions may have to change to keep pace with new technology and changing media forms and use. Do you think your current college or university will still operate as it does now? Will the FCC ever be able to keep up with new communications challenges? Might some of our constitutional rights be re-evaluated? Could the content of online media papers be regulated, as electronic media now is, but newspapers have never been? Will freedom of the press still be a fundamental tenet of our society in such a system?

Internet References . . .

Center for the Digital Future

Maintained by the University of Southern California, the Center for the Digital Future is a research and policy institute seeking to maximize the positive potential of the mass media and our rapidly evolving communication technologies.

http://www.digitalcenter.org

Electronic Frontier Foundation

Electronic Frontier Foundation is a non-profit civil liberties organization working to protect free expression and access to public resources and information online and to promote responsibility in the new media.

http://www.eff.org

Yahoo International

The Yahoo service can access a number of countries, provide information about the media systems, and list media programming.

http://www.yahoo.com/Regional/Countries/

The Media Lab

MIT's Media Lab allows you to glimpse the many ways that researchers are thinking about the digital media future. Look at the research groups listed in the research section of the Web site, and then visit the group Web sites of the ones that interest you.

http://www.media.mit.edu

Life in the Digital Age

*P*redictions of a world that is increasingly reliant upon media and communication technologies have generally provided either utopian or dystopian visions about what our lives will be like in the future. New media distribution technologies present new options for traditional ways of doing things. Not too many years ago, people were talking about the possibility of an information superhighway. Today, surfing the World Wide Web is common. Although we are still learning how electronic communication may change our lives and the ways we work and communicate, many questions have not changed. Will new ways of communication change the way individuals interact? Will the decision making of citizens change? Will everyone have access to the services and technologies that enable more immediate information exchange? What will new technologies mean to us as individuals as we live in the information age?

- Can Privacy Be Protected in the Information Age?
- Are People Better Informed in the Information Society?

ISSUE 18

Can Privacy Be Protected in the Information Age?

YES: Simson Garfinkel, from "Privacy and the New Technology," *The Nation* (February 28, 2000)

NO: Adam L. Penenberg, from "The End of Privacy," *Forbes* (November 29, 1999)

ISSUE SUMMARY

YES: Journalist Simson Garfinkel discusses how today's technology has the potential to destroy our privacy. He makes the case that the government and individuals could take steps to protect themselves against privacy abuse, particularly by returning to the groundwork set by the government in the 1970s and by educating people on how to avoid privacy traps.

NO: *Forbes* reporter Adam L. Penenberg discusses his own experiences with an Internet detective agency, and he explains how easy it is for companies to get unauthorized access to personal information. He specifically describes how much, and where, personal information is kept and the lack of safeguards in our current system.

Privacy, or the legal right "to be left alone," is something we often take for granted until we feel that our privacy has been violated. In the following selections, Simson Garfinkel and Adam L. Penenberg discuss the range of privacy issues with which we now are faced, due to the computer's ability to store and match records for virtually any transaction we make using a computer. Data companies are emerging that have various standards about seeking the permission to save and sell personal information. While Garfinkel discusses how we could protect our privacy by drawing from already existing laws and statutes, Penenberg explains that many companies have avoided any prior legislation or standards to become information brokers.

This issue brings up questions of what privacy is, and what it means to us, but it also reminds us that as we use newer technologies, there are often unavoidable problems caused by and related to their use. The "transparency," or lack of obvious technological control, is apparent in uses of the Internet and in the ability of high-speed computers to match check numbers, driver's license numbers, and other identifying bits of information. For those who wonder why their names appear on certain mailings, why they are contacted by telemarketers, or how secure their personal information is, this issue will bring up questions and uncover some of the answers.

Survey research reveals that many people feel that their privacy has been invaded at some time and that concerns about privacy are growing. But there are also some disturbing studies to indicate that young people are far less concerned about privacy issues than their parents. Could it be that younger people have not yet experienced the potential situations for privacy invasion, or, are we seeing a social value, in this case the right to privacy, in some type of transition?

Garfinkel advocates a position on privacy protection that would return us to a time in history when government was much more proactive in protecting the rights of citizens and residents. If his theory is correct, many agree that it would not be very expensive for the government to ensure safeguards about this basic right. However, trends in government involvement in businesses seem to be leading away from government oversight and toward giving greater control to businesses to monitor their own actions. Many of the companies discussed by Penenberg operate with few standards or guidelines at all. When the government itself is one of the primary repositories for personal information, could it, or should it, take the lead in defining certain standards and criteria for the protection of the innocent? Furthermore, if control should be exercised, would it be best left to the federal government, state, or local legislators?

Perhaps one of the key issues behind the privacy dilemma is the question of how and what people can do if they find that their privacy is invaded. With so many laws and statutes on the books, the legal wrangling over questions of privacy can be expensive and difficult to challenge. Many times people do not know how much information has been gathered about them until they find that the information is wrong, and it causes a problem. Consider the person who knows that he or she always pays bills on time, but for some reason, a credit reporting agency finds him or her negligent. Consequently, his or her new car loan or credit card application is denied because of the incorrect records. What recourse should that person have, and how long would it take to correct any misinformation? How could that person find out what other records might be inaccurate?

One of the growing areas of privacy concern is the collection and appropriate distribution of medical information about a person. Is it right to let others know the status of someone's confidential medical records? Should the results of voluntary or required drug testing, pregnancy tests, or AIDS tests be available to employers or anyone else without written authorization of the person being tested? Can those confidential records be used to prevent someone from buying insurance, getting a job, or getting a driver's license?

There are many questions related to issues of privacy, and we will undoubtedly see the courts debating exact parameters of privacy and information control in the near future. For now, we all need to think of the related issues of privacy and keep searching for answers to these important questions.

YES

Simson Garfinkel

Privacy and the New Technology

You wake to the sound of a ringing telephone—but how could that happen? Several months ago, you reprogrammed your home telephone system so it would never ring before the civilized hour of 8 AM. But it's barely 6:45. Who was able to bypass your phone's programming?

You pick up the receiver, then slam it down a moment later. It's one of those marketing machines playing a recorded message. What's troubling you now is how this call got past the filters you set up. Later on you'll discover how: The company that sold you the phone created an undocumented "back door"; last week, the phone codes were sold in an online auction.

Now that you're awake, you decide to go through yesterday's mail. There's a letter from the neighborhood hospital you visited last month. "We're pleased that our emergency room could serve you in your time of need," the letter begins. "As you know, our fees (based on our agreement with your HMO) do not cover the cost of treatment. To make up the difference, a number of hospitals have started selling patient records to medical researchers and consumer-marketing firms. Rather than mimic this distasteful behavior, we have decided to ask you to help us make up the difference. We are recommending a tax-deductible contribution of $275 to help defray the cost of your visit."

The veiled threat isn't empty, but you decide you don't really care who finds out about your sprained wrist. You fold the letter in half and drop it into your shredder. Also into the shredder goes a trio of low-interest credit-card offers. Why a shredder? A few years ago you would never have thought of shredding your junk mail—until a friend in your apartment complex had his identity "stolen" by the building's superintendent. As best as anybody can figure out, the super picked one of those preapproved credit-card applications out of the trash; called the toll-free number and picked up the card when it was delivered. He's in Mexico now, with a lot of expensive clothing and electronics, all at your friend's expense.

On that cheery note, you grab your bag and head out the door, which automatically locks behind you.

This is the future—not a far-off future but one that's just around the corner. It's a future in which what little privacy we now have will be gone. Some people call this loss of privacy "Orwellian," harking back to *1984*, George Orwell's classic work on privacy and autonomy. In that book, Orwell imagined a future in which a totalitarian state used spies, video surveillance, historical revision-ism and control over the media to maintain its power. But the age of mono-lithic state control is over. The future we're rushing toward isn't one in which our every move is watched and recorded by some all-knowing Big Brother. It is instead a future of a hundred kid brothers who constantly watch and interrupt our daily lives. Orwell thought the Communist system represented the ulti-mate threat to individual liberty. Over the next fifty years, we will see new kinds of threats to privacy that find their roots not in Communism but in cap-italism, the free market, advanced technology and the unbridled exchange of electronic information.

The problem with this word "privacy" is that it falls short of conveying the really big picture. Privacy isn't just about hiding things. It's about self-possession, autonomy and integrity. As we move into the computerized world of the twenty-first century, privacy will be one of our most important civil rights. But this right of privacy isn't the right of people to close their doors and pull down their window shades—perhaps because they want to engage in some sort of illicit or illegal activity. It's the right of people to control what details about their lives stay inside their own houses and what leaks to the outside.

Most of us recognize that our privacy is at risk. According to a 1996 nation-wide poll conducted by Louis Harris & Associates, 24 percent of Americans have "personally experienced a privacy invasion." In 1995 the same survey found that 80 percent felt that "consumers have lost all control over how personal informa-tion about them is circulated and used by companies." Ironically, both the 1995 and 1996 surveys were paid for by Equifax, a company that earns nearly $2 billion each year from collecting and distributing personal information.

Today the Internet is compounding our privacy conundrum—largely because the voluntary approach to privacy protection advocated by the Clinton Administration doesn't work in the rough and tumble world of real business. For example, a study just released by the California HealthCare Foundation found that nineteen of the top twenty-one health websites have privacy policies, but most sites fail to follow them. Not surprisingly, 17 percent of Americans questioned in a poll said they do not go online for health infor-mation because of privacy concerns.

✦

But privacy threats are not limited to the Internet: Data from all walks of life are now being captured, compiled, indexed and stored. For example, New York City has now deployed the Metrocard system, which allows subway and bus riders to pay their fares by simply swiping a magnetic-strip card. But the system also records the serial number of each card and the time and location of every swipe. New York police have used this vast database to crack crimes and disprove alibis. Although law enforcement is a reasonable use of this data-base, it is also a use that was adopted without any significant public debate. Furthermore, additional controls may be necessary: It is not clear who has access to the database, under what circumstances that access is given and what provisions are being taken to prevent the introduction of false data into it. It would be terrible if the subway's database were used by an employee to stalk an ex-lover or frame an innocent person for a heinous crime.

"New technology has brought extraordinary benefits to society, but it also has placed all of us in an electronic fishbowl in which our habits, tastes and activities are watched and recorded," New York State Attorney General Eliot Spitzer said in late January [2000], in announcing that Chase Manhattan had agreed to stop selling depositor information without clear permission from customers. "Personal information thought to be confidential is routinely shared with others without our consent."

Today's war on privacy is intimately related to the recent dramatic advances in technology. Many people today say that in order to enjoy the benefits of modern society, we must necessarily relinquish some degree of privacy. If we want the convenience of paying for a meal by credit card or paying for a toll with an electronic tag mounted on our rearview mirror, then we must accept the routine collection of our purchases and driving habits in a large database over which we have no control. It's a simple bargain, albeit a Faustian one.

This trade-off is both unnecessary and wrong. It reminds me of another crisis our society faced back in the fifties and sixties—the environmental crisis. Then, advocates of big business said that poisoned rivers and lakes were the necessary costs of economic development, jobs and an improved standard of living. Poison was progress: Anybody who argued otherwise simply didn't understand the facts.

Today we know better. Today we know that sustainable economic development depends on preserving the environment. Indeed, preserving the environment is a prerequisite to the survival of the human race. Without clean air to breathe and clean water to drink, we will all die. Similarly, in order to reap the benefits of technology, it is more important than ever for us to use technology to protect personal freedom.

Blaming technology for the death of privacy isn't new. In 1890 two Boston lawyers, Samuel Warren and Louis Brandeis, argued in the *Harvard Law Review* that privacy was under attack by "recent inventions and business methods." They contended that the pressures of modern society required the creation of a "right of privacy," which would help protect what they called "the right to be let alone." Warren and Brandeis refused to believe that privacy had to die for technology to flourish. Today, the Warren/Brandeis article is regarded as one of the most influential law review articles ever published.

Privacy-invasive technology does not exist in a vacuum, of course. That's because technology itself exists at a junction between science, the market and society. People create technology to fill specific needs and desires. And technology is regulated, or not, as people and society see fit. Few engineers set out to build systems designed to crush privacy and autonomy, and few businesses or consumers would willingly use or purchase these systems if they understood the consequences.

⚬◈⚬

How can we keep technology and the free market from killing our privacy? One way is by being careful and informed consumers. Some people have begun taking simple measures to protect their privacy, measures like making purchases with cash and refusing to provide their Social Security numbers—or providing fake ones. And a small but growing number of people are speaking out for technology with privacy. In 1990 Lotus and Equifax teamed up to create a CD-ROM product called "Lotus Marketplace: Households," which would have included names, addresses and demographic information on every household in the United States, so small businesses could do the same kind of target marketing that big businesses have been doing since the sixties. The project was canceled when more than 30,000 people wrote to Lotus demanding that their names be taken out of the database.

Similarly, in 1997 the press informed taxpayers that the Social Security Administration was making detailed tax-history information about them available over the Internet. The SSA argued that its security provisions—requiring that taxpayers enter their name, date of birth, state of birth and mother's maiden name—were sufficient to prevent fraud. But tens of thousands of Americans disagreed, several US senators investigated the agency and the service was promptly shut down. When the service was reactivated some months later, the detailed financial information in the SSA's computers could not be downloaded over the Internet.

But individual actions are not enough. We need to involve government itself in the privacy fight. The biggest privacy failure of the US government has been its failure to carry through with the impressive privacy groundwork that was laid in the Nixon, Ford and Carter administrations. It's worth taking a look back at that groundwork and considering how it may serve us today.

The seventies were a good decade for privacy protection and consumer rights. In 1970 Congress passed the Fair Credit Reporting Act, which gave Americans the previously denied right to see their own credit reports and demand the removal of erroneous information. Elliot Richardson, who at the time was President Nixon's Secretary of Health, Education and Welfare, created a commission in 1972 to study the impact of computers on privacy. After years of testimony in Congress, the commission found all the more reason for alarm and issued a landmark report in 1973.

The most important contribution of the Richardson report was a bill of rights for the computer age, which it called the Code of Fair Information Practices. The code is based on five principles:

- There must be no personal-data record-keeping system whose very existence is secret.
- There must be a way for a person to find out what information about the person is in a record and how it is used.
- There must be a way for a person to prevent information about the person that was obtained for one purpose from being used or made available for other purposes without the person's consent.
- There must be a way for a person to correct or amend a record of identifiable information about the person.
- Any organization creating, maintaining, using or disseminating records of identifiable personal data must assure the reliability of the

data for their intended use and must take precautions to prevent misuse of the data.

✦

The biggest impact of the Richardson report wasn't in the United States but in Europe. In the years after the report was published, practically every European country passed laws based on these principles. Many created data-protection commissions and commissioners to enforce the laws. Some believe that one reason for Europe's interest in electronic privacy was its experience with Nazi Germany in the thirties and forties. Hitler's secret police used the records of governments and private organizations in the countries he invaded to round up people who posed the greatest threat to German occupation; postwar Europe realized the danger of allowing potentially threatening private information to be collected, even by democratic governments that might be responsive to public opinion.

But here in the United States, the idea of institutionalized data protection faltered. President Jimmy Carter showed interest in improving medical privacy, but he was quickly overtaken by economic and political events. Carter lost the election of 1980 to Ronald Reagan, whose aides saw privacy protection as yet another failed Carter initiative. Although several privacy-protection laws were signed during the Reagan/Bush era, the leadership for these bills came from Congress, not the White House. The lack of leadership stifled any chance of passing a nationwide data-protection act. Such an act would give people the right to know if their name and personal information is stored in a database, to see the information and to demand that incorrect information be removed.

In fact, while most people in the federal government were ignoring the cause of privacy, some were actually pursuing an antiprivacy agenda. In the early eighties, the government initiated numerous "computer matching" programs designed to catch fraud and abuse. Unfortunately, because of erroneous data these programs often penalized innocent people. In 1994 Congress passed the Communications Assistance to Law Enforcement Act, which gave the government dramatic new powers for wiretapping digital communications. In 1996 Congress passed two laws, one requiring states to display Social Security numbers on driver's licenses and another requiring that all medical patients in the United States be issued unique numerical identifiers, even if they pay their own bills. Fortunately, the implementation of those 1996 laws has been delayed, thanks largely to a citizen backlash and the resulting inaction by Congress and the executive branch.

✦

Continuing the assault, both the Bush and Clinton administrations waged an all-out war against the rights of computer users to engage in private and secure communications. Starting in 1991, both administrations floated proposals for use of "Clipper" encryption systems that would have given the government access to encrypted personal communications. Only recently did the Clinton Administration finally relent in its seven-year war against computer privacy. President Clinton also backed the Communications Decency Act (CDA), which made it a crime to transmit sexually explicit information to minors—and, as a result, might have required Internet providers to deploy far-reaching monitoring and censorship systems. When a court in Philadelphia found the CDA unconstitutional, the Clinton Administration appealed the decision all the way to the Supreme Court—and lost.

One important step toward reversing the current direction of government would be to create a permanent federal oversight agency charged with protecting privacy. Such an agency would:

- Watch over the government's tendency to sacrifice people's privacy for other goals and perform government wide reviews of new federal programs for privacy violations before they're launched.
- Enforce the government's few existing privacy laws.
- Be a guardian for individual privacy and liberty in the business world, showing businesses how they can protect privacy and profits at the same time.
- Be an ombudsman for the American public and rein in the worst excesses that our society has created.

Evan Hendricks, editor of the Washington-based newsletter *Privacy Times*, estimates that a fifty-person privacy-protection agency could be created with an annual budget of less than $5 million—a tiny drop in the federal budget.

Some privacy activists scoff at the idea of using government to assure our privacy. Governments, they say, are responsible for some of the greatest privacy violations of all time. This is true, but the US government was also one of the greatest polluters of all time. Today the government is the nation's environmental police force, equally scrutinizing the actions of private business and the government itself.

At the very least, governments can alter the development of technology that affects privacy. They have done so in Europe. Consider this: A growing number of businesses in Europe are offering free telephone calls—provided that the caller first listens to a brief advertisement. The service saves consumers money, even if it does expose them to a subtle form of brainwashing. But not all these services are equal. In Sweden both the caller and the person being called are forced to listen to the advertisement, and the new advertisements are played during the phone call itself. But Italy's privacy ombudsman ruled that the person being called could not be forced to listen to the ads.

There is also considerable public support for governmental controls within the United States itself—especially on key issues, such as the protection of medical records. For example, a 1993 Harris-Equifax survey on medical privacy issues found that 56 percent of the American public favored "comprehensive federal legislation that spells out rules for confidentiality of individual medical records" as part of national healthcare reform legislation. Yet Congress failed to act on the public's wishes.

The Fair Credit Reporting Act [FCRA] was a good law in its day, but it should be upgraded into a Data Protection Act. Unfortunately, the Federal Trade Commission and the courts have narrowly interpreted the FCRA. The first thing that is needed is legislation that expands it into new areas. Specifically, consumer-reporting firms should be barred from reporting arrests unless those arrests result in convictions. Likewise, consumer-reporting firms should not be allowed to report evictions unless they result in court judgments in favor of the landlord or a settlement in which both the landlord and tenant agree that the eviction can be reported. Companies should be barred from exchanging medical information about individuals or furnishing medical information as part of a patient's report without the patient's explicit consent.

⋅⟨⊙⟩⋅

We also need new legislation that expands the fundamental rights offered to consumers under the FCRA. When negative information is reported to a credit bureau, the business making that report should be required to notify the subject of the report—the consumer—in writing. Laws should be clarified so that if a consumer-reporting company does not correct erroneous data in its reports, consumers can sue for real damages, punitive damages and legal fees. People should have the right to correct any false information in their files, and if the consumer and the business disagree about the truth, then the consumer should have a right to place a *detailed* explanation into his or her record. And people should have a right to see all the information that has been collected on them; these reports should be furnished for free, at least once every six months.

We need to rethink consent, a bedrock of modern law. Consent is a great idea, but the laws that govern consent need to be rewritten to limit what kinds of agreements can be made with consumers. Blanket, perpetual consent should be outlawed.

Further, we need laws that require improved computer security. In the eighties the United States aggressively deployed cellular-telephone and alpha-numeric-pager networks, even though both systems were fundamentally unsecure. Instead of deploying secure systems, manufacturers lobbied for laws that would make it illegal to listen to the broadcasts. The results were predictable: dozens of cases in which radio transmissions were eavesdropped. We are now making similar mistakes in the prosecution of many Internet crimes, going after the perpetrator while refusing to acknowledge the liabilities of businesses that do not even take the most basic security precautions.

We should also bring back the Office of Technology Assessment, set up under a bill passed in 1972. The OTA didn't have the power to make laws or issue regulations, but it could publish reports on topics Congress asked it to study. Among other things, the OTA considered at length the trade-offs between law enforcement and civil liberties, and it also looked closely at issues of worker monitoring. In total, the OTA published 741 reports, 175 of which dealt directly with privacy issues, before it was killed in 1995 by the newly elected Republican-majority Congress.

Nearly forty years ago, Rachel Carson's book *Silent Spring* helped seed the US environmental movement. And to our credit, the silent spring that Carson foretold never came to be. *Silent Spring* was successful because it helped people to understand the insidious damage that pesticides were wreaking on the environment, and it helped our society and our planet to plot a course to a better future.

Today, technology is killing one of our most cherished freedoms. Whether you call this freedom the right to digital self-determination, the right to informational autonomy or simply the right to privacy, the shape of our future will be determined in large part by how we understand, and ultimately how we control or regulate, the threats to this freedom that we face today.

Adam L. Penenberg

 **NO**

The End of Privacy

The phone rang and a stranger cracked sing-songy at the other end of the line: *"Happy Birthday."* That was spooky—the next day I would turn 37. "Your full name is Adam Landis Penenberg," the caller continued. "Landis?" My mother's maiden name. "I'm touched," he said. Then Daniel Cohn, Web detective, reeled off the rest of my "base identifiers"—my birth date, address in New York, Social Security number. Just two days earlier I had issued Cohn a challenge: Starting with my byline, dig up as much information about me as you can. "That didn't take long," I said.

"It took about five minutes," Cohn said, cackling back in Boca Raton, Fla. "I'll have the rest within a week." And the line went dead.

In all of six days Dan Cohn and his Web detective agency, Docusearch.com, shattered every notion I had about privacy in this country (or whatever remains of it). Using only a keyboard and the phone, he was able to uncover the innermost details of my life—whom I call late at night; how much money I have in the bank; my salary and rent. He even got my unlisted phone numbers, both of them. Okay, so you've heard it before: America, the country that made "right to privacy" a credo, has lost its privacy to the computer. But it's far worse than you think. Advances in smart data-sifting techniques and the rise of the massive databases have conspired to strip you naked. The spread of the Web is the final step. It will make most of the secrets you have more instantly available than ever before, ready to reveal themselves in a few taps on the keyboard.

For decades this information rested in remote mainframes that were difficult to access, even for the techies who put it there. The move to desktop PCs and local servers in the 1990s has distributed these data far and wide. Computers now hold half a billion bank accounts, half a billion credit card accounts, hundreds of millions of mortgages and retirement funds and medical claims and more. The Web seamlessly links it all together. As e-commerce grows, marketers and busybodies will crack open a cache of new consumer data more revealing than ever before.

It will be a salesman's dream—and a paranoid's nightmare. Adding to the paranoia: Hundreds of data sleuths like Dan Cohn of Docusearch have opened up shop on the Web to sell precious pieces of these data. Some are ethical; some aren't. They mine celebrity secrets, spy on business rivals and track down hidden assets, secret lovers and deadbeat dads. They

From *Forbes* Magazine, November 29, 1999. Reprinted by permission of Forbes Magazine, © 1999 Forbes Media Inc.

include Strategic Data Service . . . and . . . and Dig Dirt Inc. (both at the PI Mall, . . .).

Cohn's firm will get a client your unlisted number for $49, your Social Security number for $49 and your bank balances for $45. Your driving record goes for $35; tracing a cell phone number costs $84. Cohn will even tell some-one what stocks, bonds and securities you own (for $209). As with computers, the price of information has plunged.

You may well ask: What's the big deal? We consumers are as much to blame as marketers for all these loose data. At every turn we have willingly given up a layer of privacy in exchange for convenience; it is why we use a credit card to shop, enduring a barrage of junk mail. Why should we care if our personal information isn't so personal anymore?

Well, take this test: Next time you are at a party, tell a stranger your salary, checking account balance, mortgage payment and Social Security number. If this makes you uneasy, you have your answer.

"If the post office said we have to use transparent envelopes, people would go crazy, because the fact is we all have something to hide," says Edward Wade, a privacy advocate who wrote *Identity Theft: The Cybercrime of the Millennium* (Loompanics Unlimited, 1999) under the pseudonym John Q. Newman.

You can do a few things about it. Give your business to the companies that take extra steps to safeguard your data and will guarantee it. Refuse to reveal your Social Security number—the key for decrypting your privacy—to all but the financial institutions required by law to record it.

Do something, because many banks, brokerages, credit card issuers and others are lax, even careless, about locking away your records. They take varied steps in trying to protect your privacy. Some sell information to other marketers, and many let hundreds of employees access your data. Some workers, aiming to please, blithely hand out your account number, balance and more when-ever someone calls and asks for it. That's how Cohn pierced my privacy.

"You call up a company and make it seem like you're a spy on a covert mission, and only they can help you," he says. "It works every time. All day long I deal with spy wannabes."

I'm not the paranoid type; I don't see a huddle on TV and think that 11 football players are talking about me. But things have gone too far. A stalker would kill for the wealth of information Cohn was able to dig up. A crook could parlay the data into credit card scams and "identity theft," pilfering my good credit rating and using it to pull more ripoffs.

Cohn operates in this netherworld of private eyes, ex-spooks and ex-cops, retired military men, accountants and research librarians. Now 39, he grew up in the Philadelphia suburb of Bryn Mawr, attended Penn State and joined the Navy in 1980 for a three-year stint. In 1987 Cohn formed his own agency to investigate insurance fraud and set up shop in Florida. "There was no shortage of work," he says. He invented a "video periscope" that could rise up through the roof of a van to record a target's scam.

In 1995 he founded Docusearch with childhood pal Kenneth Zeiss. They fill up to 100 orders a day on the Web, and expect $1 million in business this year. Their clients include lawyers, insurers, private eyes; the Los Angeles Pension Union is a customer, and Citibank's legal recovery department uses Docusearch to find debtors on the run.

Cohn, Zeiss and 13 researchers (6 of them licensed P.I.s work out of the top floor of a dull, five-story office building in Boca Raton, Fla., sitting in cubicles under a flourescent glare and taking orders from 9 a.m. to 4 p.m. Their Web site is open 24 hours a day, 365 days a year. You click through it and load up an online shopping cart as casually as if you were at Amazon.com.

The researchers use sharp sifting methods, but Cohn also admits to misrepresenting who he is and what he is after. He says the law lets licensed investigators use such tricks as "pretext calling," fooling company employees into divulging customer data over the phone (legal in all but a few states). He even claims to have a government source who provides unpublished numbers for a fee, "and you'll never figure out how he is paid because there's no paper trail."

Yet Cohn claims to be more scrupulous than rivals. "Unlike an information broker, I won't break the law. I turn down jobs, like if a jealous boyfriend wants to find out where his ex is living." He also says he won't resell the information to anyone else.

Let's hope not. Cohn's first step into my digital domain was to plug my name into the credit bureaus—Transunion, Equifax, Experian. In minutes he had my Social Security number, address and birth date. Credit agencies are supposed to ensure that their subscribers (retailers, auto dealers, banks, mortgage companies) have a legitimate need to check credit.

"We physically visit applicants to make sure they live up to our service agreement," says David Mooney of Equifax, which keeps records on 200 million Americans and shares them with 114,000 clients. He says resellers of the data must do the same. "It's rare that anyone abuses the system." But Cohn says he gets his data from a reseller, and no one has ever checked up on him.

Armed with my credit header, Dan Cohn tapped other sites. A week after my birthday, true to his word, he faxed me a three-page summary of my life. He had pulled up my utility bills, my two unlisted phone numbers and my finances.

This gave him the ability to map my routines, if he had chosen to do so: how much cash I burn in a week ($400), how much I deposit twice a month ($3,061), my favorite neighborhood bistro (the Flea Market Cafe), the $720 monthly checks I write out to one Judith Pekowsky: my psychotherapist. (When you live in New York, you see a shrink; it's the law.) If I had an incurable disease, Cohn could probably find that out, too.

He had my latest phone bill ($108) and a list of long distance calls made from home—including late-night fiber-optic dalliances (which soon ended) with a woman who traveled a lot. Cohn also divined the phone numbers of a few of my sources, underground computer hackers who aren't wanted by the police—but probably should be.

Knowing my Social Security number and other personal details helped Cohn get access to a Federal Reserve database that told him where I had deposits. Cohn found accounts I had forgotten long ago: $503 at Apple Bank for Savings in an account held by a long-ago landlord as a security deposit; $7 in a dormant savings account at Chase Manhattan Bank; $1,000 in another Chase account.

A few days later Cohn struck the mother lode. He located my cash management account, opened a few months earlier at Merrill Lynch & Co. That gave him a peek at my balance, direct deposits from work, withdrawals, ATM visits, check numbers with dates and amounts, and the name of my broker.

That's too much for some privacy hawks. "If someone can call your bank and get them to release account information without your consent, it means you have no privacy," says Russell Smith, director of Consumer.net in Alexandria, Va., who has won more than $40,000 suing telemarketers for bothering him. "The two issues are knowledge and control: You should know what information about you is out there, and you should be able to control who gets it."

How did Cohn get hold of my Merrill Lynch secrets? Directly from the source. Cohn says he phoned Merrill Lynch and talked to one of 500 employees who can tap into my data. "Hi, I'm Dan Cohn, a licensed state investigator conducting an investigation of an Adam Penenberg," he told the staffer, knowing the words "licensed" and "state" make it sound like he works for law enforcement.

Then he recited my Social Security, birth date and address, "and before I could get out anything more he spat out your account number." Cohn told the helpful worker: "I talked to Penenberg's broker, um, I can't remember his name. . . ."

"Dan Dunn?" the Merrill Lynch guy asked. "Yeah, Dan Dunn," Cohn said. The staffer then read Cohn my complete history—balance, deposits, withdrawals, check numbers and amounts. "You have to talk in the lingo the bank people talk so they don't even know they are being taken," he says.

Merrill's response: It couldn't have happened this way—and if it did, it's partly my fault. Merrill staff answers phoned-in questions only when the caller provides the full account number or personal details, Merrill spokesperson Bobbie Collins says. She adds that I could have insisted on an "additional telephonic security code" the caller would have to punch in before getting information, and that this option was disclosed when I opened my CMA [cash management account]. Guess I didn't read the fine print, not that it mattered: Cohn says he got my account number from the Merrill rep.

Sprint, my long distance carrier, investigated how my account was breached and found that a Mr. Penenberg had called to inquire about my most recent bill. Cohn says only that he called his government contact. Whoever made the call, "he posed as you and had enough information to convince our customer service representative that he was you," says Russ R. Robinson, a Sprint spokesman. "We want to make it easy for our customers to do business with us over the phone, so you are darned if you do and darned if you don't."

Bell Atlantic, my local phone company, told me a similar tale, only it was a Mrs. Penenberg who called in on behalf of her husband. I recently attended a conference in Las Vegas but don't remember having tied the knot.

For the most part Cohn's methods fly below the radar of the law. "There is no general law that protects consumers' privacy in the U.S.," says David Banisar, a Washington lawyer who helped found the Electronic Privacy Information Center (www.epic.org). In Europe companies classified as "data controllers" can't hand out your personal details without your permission, but the U.S. has as little protection as China, he contends.

The "credit header"—name, address, birth date, Social Security—used to be kept confidential under the Fair Credit Reporting Act. But in 1989 the Federal Trade Commission exempted it from such protection, bowing to the credit bureaus, bail bondsmen and private eyes.

Some piecemeal protections are in place: a 1984 act protecting cable TV bills; the 1988 Video Privacy Protection Act, passed after a newspaper published the video rental records of Supreme Court nominee Robert Bork. "It's crazy, but your movie rental history is more protected under the law than your credit history is," says Wade, the author.

Colorado is one of the few states that prohibit "pretext calling" by someone pretending to be someone else. In July James Rapp, 39, and wife Regana, 29, who ran info-broker Touch Tone Information out of a strip mall in Aurora, Colo., were charged with impersonating the Ramseys—of the JonBenet child murder case—to get hold of banking records that might be related to the case.

Congress may get into the act with bills to outlaw pretext calling. But lawyer Banisar says more than 100 privacy bills filed in the past two years have gone nowhere. He blames "an unholy alliance between marketers and government agencies that want access" to their data.

Indeed, government agencies are some of the worst offenders in selling your data. In many states the Department of Motor Vehicles was a major peddler of personal data until Congress passed the Driver's Privacy Protection Act of 1994, pushing states to enact laws that let drivers block distribution of their names and addresses. Some states, such as Georgia, take it seriously, but South Carolina has challenged it all the way up to the U.S. Supreme Court. Oral arguments are scheduled. . . .

As originally conceived, Social Security numbers weren't to be used for identification purposes. But nowadays you are compelled by law to give an accurate number to a bank or other institution that pays you interest or dividends; thank you, Internal Revenue Service. The bank, in turn, just might trade that number away to a credit bureau—even if you aren't applying for credit. That's how snoops can tap so many databases.

Here's a theoretical way to stop this linking process without compromising the IRS' ability to track unreported income: Suppose that, instead of issuing you a single 9-digit number, the IRS gave you a dozen 11-digit numbers and let you report income under any of them. You could release one to your employer, another to your broker, a third to your health insurer, a fourth to the firms that need to know your credit history. It would be hard for a sleuth to know that William H. Smith 001–24–7829–33 was the same as 350–68–4561–49. Your digital personas would converge at only one point in cyberspace, inside the extremely well guarded computers of the IRS.

But for now, you have to fend for yourself by being picky about which firms you do business with and how much you tell them. If you are opening a bank account with no credit attached to it, ask the bank to withhold your

Social Security number from credit bureaus. Make sure your broker gives you, as Merrill Lynch does, the option of restricting telephone access to your account, and use it. If a business without a legitimate need for the Social Security number asks for it, leave the space blank—or fill it with an incorrect number. (Hint: To make it look legitimate, use an even number between 10 and 90 for the middle two digits.)

Daniel Cohn makes no apologies for how he earns a living. He sees himself as a data-robbing Robin Hood. "The problem isn't the amount of information available, it's the fact that until recently only the wealthy could afford it. That's where we come in."

In the meantime, until a better solution emerges, I'm starting over: I will change all of my bank, utility and credit-card account numbers and apply for new unlisted phone numbers. That should keep the info-brokers at bay for a while—at least for the next week or two.

POSTSCRIPT

Can Privacy Be Protected in the Information Age?

When issues of privacy originally surfaced during the formation of the United States, the key features had to do with what people did in their own homes as opposed to in public. The Bill of Rights and our Constitution guarantee "security of person" to everyone. But when our country was formed, no one could have foreseen the type of technologies we have today that are capable of processing information for individuals in any private or public setting, through terminals and other technologies that blur the distinctions between what goes on in the privacy of home, and what private activities can actually take place in a public arena.

Today the issues of privacy have attained greater complexity. For example, who owns your e-mail? If you're sending personal messages through a system that is owned and maintained by an employer, a school, or even a subscription system provider—does the system administrator have access to your personal messages? Almost universally, the answer is "yes" because the administrator needs to be able to monitor the system. When you use a computer in a public library, do you create a record of messages and deletions that can be tracked by someone else? Again, the answer is usually "yes."

Without a doubt, different cultures have various attitudes, laws, and values with regard to issues of personal privacy. In the United States, the definition of privacy has been handed down from the Supreme Court. Challenges to privacy often are debated in our highest court, and therefore, are influenced by legal precedent. New technology challenges the court to examine those precedents and see if a balance among the right to know, the right to privacy, and the technological capability to share information can coexist.

In many other countries, however, there are different cultural attitudes and concepts of what is "private" and what is not. Both the UN Declaration of Human Rights and the World International Property Organization (WIPO) have considered the right to privacy as a basic human need for all people. It is the role of governments then, to come up with national and regional policies to enforce these various beliefs with regard to their specific cultures. An excellent collection of issues such as these can be found in James R. Michael's *Privacy and Human Rights: An International and Comparative Study With Special Reference to Development in Information Technology* (UNESCO, 1994).

A number of studies further illuminate how broad a concept privacy may be for individuals. Ann Cavoukian's *Who Knows: Safeguarding Your Privacy in a Networked World* (McGraw-Hill, 1997) takes a practical approach toward understanding how we can control information about ourselves.

402

ISSUE 19

Are People Better Informed in the Information Society?

YES: Wade Roush, from "The Internet Reborn," *Technology Review* (October 2003)

NO: Matthew Robinson, from "Party On, Dudes!" *The American Spectator* (March/April 2002)

ISSUE SUMMARY

YES: *Technology Review* senior editor Wade Roush reflects on the way we currently use the architecture of the web. He outlines the likely scenario for the future of the Internet, with global networks connected to "smart nodes" that will be able to store all of our files, and allow us to access them from remote sites with only small, handheld devices. The improvements in technology will then lead to a more dynamic use of the web, and will make the Internet more user-friendly, as well as more secure.

NO: Author Matthew Robinson warns that no matter what technologies we have available, human beings seem interested in fewer subjects and know even less about politics and current events. He warns that even though we may call it an "information" society, there is evidence to suggest that we actually know less than in earlier years. His examples are humorous as well as sobering.

Many people feel that as we move toward a more technologically oriented lifestyle, we, as a nation, and as participants in the new information society, are inevitably moving toward a better quality of life. It almost seems logical that better technology is the result of moving from more primitive forms of communicating to more sophisticated, faster, and efficient means. But an age-old question is whether the ability to communicate equals a quality communication experience. Without a doubt, messages that can be sent, retrieved, and enhanced may all appear to be technological breakthroughs, and positive transactions. But there is another side to this scenario in which we must address whether an excess of information truly informs.

In this issue we examine two selections that ask the same question, but propose different ways to answer the question. The Roush article challenges our assumptions about the Internet as we now know it. Despite the rapid growth of the Internet, Roush compares it to a "1973 Buick refitted with air bags and emissions controls." Because the basic infrastructure of the Internet was built on trust and was originally designed to serve fewer people, it is vulnerable to viruses and worms caused by pranksters who hack into services and disrupt operations. The Roush article also reminds us that even though we may think that our current technologies are "state-of-the-art," they too may have structural limitations.

But Roush does not necessarily criticize the developers of our current Internet—instead, he describes how computer scientists and engineers have begun to design and implement an overlay to help protect computer users by better, more sophisticated nodes that will not only improve the Internet's functions, but will provide a plethora of new services that will indeed help the average user. His article, while critical of the original architecture of the Internet, is very optimistic about overcoming our current problems and embracing the freedom provided by a stronger, more flexible system that will enhance information flow and storage. In many ways, he looks optimistically toward improvements that perpetuate the argument that more technology equals better services.

Matthew Robinson, on the other hand, tackles the question of whether people are more informed today, despite the number of sources and technologies available to them. His statistics are at the same time humorous yet frightening. If Robinson is correct, there is much evidence to support the idea that as time goes by, the public's knowledge of basic civics and politics becomes even weaker. If this is the scenario of the future, we must question whether the information society really does represent a better world, or a world in which we've lost much of what we already have.

Robinson's article is reminiscent of the predictions of many forms of media. When radio was invented, some predicted that people would stop reading newspapers and magazines; when television was invented, some feared that people would stop going to films, listening to radio, and reading newspapers or books. And in many ways, there is evidence to demonstrate that *some* of these predictions were at least partially true.

As a concluding issue to this book, these selections ask the reader to make real decisions about how they feel about new technologies and the quality of our lives. The author Neil Postman wrote about predicting what our future would be like in his book, *Amusing Ourselves To Death* (Penguin, 1985). Postman recalled earlier authors, like George Orwell, who, in 1949, wrote a futuristic book called *1984* (Harcourt, Brace), and Aldous Huxley, who, in 1932, wrote *Brave New World* (London, Chatto, & Windus). Each of these authors focused on the most common form of media available to them—print media in the form of their book, and each dealt with the future in a different way. Orwell foretold of a time in which people couldn't read because they had no books. Huxley's world envisioned a world with books, but the people chose not to read. We will conclude this volume by asking you, our readers—does a new, improved Internet help transfer and store information that helps you lead a better quality of life?

YES

Wade Roush

The Internet Reborn

If you're like most cyber-citizens, you use the Internet for e-mail, Web searching, chatting with friends, music downloads, and buying books and gifts. More than 600 million people use these services worldwide—far more than anyone could have predicted in the 1970s, when the Internet's key components were conceived. An estimated $3.9 trillion in business transactions will take place over the Internet in 2003, and the medium's reach is increasingly global: an astonishing 24 percent of Brazilians, 30 percent of Chinese, and 72 percent of Americans now go online at least once per month.

Still, despite its enormous impact, today's Internet is like a 1973 Buick refitted with air bags and emissions controls. Its decades-old infrastructure has been rigged out with the Web and all it enables (like e-commerce), plus technologies such as streaming media, peer-to-peer file sharing, and videoconferencing; but it's still a 1973 Buick. Now, a grass-roots group of nearly 100 leading computer scientists, backed by heavyweight industrial sponsors, is working on replacing it with a new, vastly smarter model.

The project is called PlanetLab, and within the next three years, researchers say, it will help revitalize the Internet, eventually enabling you to

- forget about hauling your laptop around. No matter where you go, you'll be able to instantly re-create your entire private computer work-space, program for program and document for document, on any Internet terminal;
- escape the disruption caused by Internet worms and viruses—which inflicted an average of $81,000 in repair costs per company per incident in 2002—because the network itself will detect and crush rogue data packets before they get a chance to spread to your office or home;
- instantly retrieve video and other bandwidth-hogging data, no matter how many other users are competing for the same resources;
- archive your tax returns, digital photographs, family videos, and all your other data across the Internet itself, securely and indestructibly, for decades, making hard disks and recordable CDs seem as quaint as 78 RPM records.

These predicted PlanetLab innovations—with the potential to revolutionize home computing, e-commerce, and corporate information technology practices—can't be incorporated into the existing Net; that would be too disruptive. Instead, the PlanetLab researchers, who hail from Princeton, MIT, the University of California, Berkeley, and more than 50 other institutions, are building their network on top of the Internet. But their new machines—called smart nodes—will vastly increase its processing power and data storage capability, an idea that has quickly gained support from the National Science Foundation and industry players such as Intel, Hewlett-Packard, and Google.

Since starting out in March 2002, PlanetLab has linked 175 smart nodes at 79 sites in 13 countries, with plans to reach 1,000 nodes by 2006. It's the newest and hottest of several large-scale research efforts that have sought to address the Internet's limitations. . . . "The Internet has reached a plateau in terms of what it can do," says Larry Peterson, a Princeton computer scientist and the effort's leader. "The right thing to do is to start over at another level. That's the idea behind PlanetLab."

The Network *Is* the Computer, Finally

Like many revolutions, PlanetLab is based on a startlingly simple idea that has been around for a long time, advanced most notably by Sun Microsystems: move data and computation from desktop computers and individual main-frames into the network itself.

But this can't be done with today's Internet, which consists of basic machines, called routers, following 1970s-era procedures for breaking e-mail attachments, Web pages, and other electronic files into individually addressed packets and forwarding them to other machines. Beyond this function, the routers are dumb and inflexible: they weren't designed to handle the level of computing needed to, say, recognize and respond to virus attacks or bottle-necks elsewhere in the network.

PlanetLab's smart nodes, on the other hand, are standard PCs capable of running custom software uploaded by users. Copies of a single program can run simultaneously on many nodes around the world. Each node is plugged directly into a traditional router, so it can exchange data with other nodes over the existing Net. (For that reason, computer scientists call PlanetLab an "overlay" network.) To manage all this, each node runs software that divides the machine's resource—such as hard-drive space and processing power—among PlanetLab's many users. . . . If the Internet is a global, electronic nervous system, then PlanetLab is finally giving it brains.

The payoff should be huge. Smarter networks will foster a new genera-tion of distributed software programs that preempt congestion, spread out critical data, and keep the Internet secure, even as they make computer com-munications faster and more reliable in general. By expanding the network as quickly as possible, says Peterson, the PlanetLab researchers hope to restore the sense of risk-taking and experimentation that ruled the Internet's early days. But Peterson admits that progress won't come easily. "How do you get an innovative service out across a thousand machines and test it out?"

It helps that the network is no longer just a research sandbox, as the orig-inal Internet was during its development; instead, it's a place to deploy services that any programmer can use and help improve. And one of the Internet's original architects sees this as a tremendously exciting trait. "It's 2003, 30 years after the Internet was invented," says Vinton Cerf, who codeveloped the Internet's basic communications protocols as a Stanford University researcher in the early 1970s and is now senior vice president for architecture and technology at MCI. "We have millions of people out there who are interested in and capable of doing experimental development." Which means it shouldn't take long to replace that Buick.

Baiting Worms

The Achilles' heel of today's Internet is that it's a system built on trust. Designed into the Net is the assumption that users at the network's endpoints know and trust one another; after all, the early Internet was a tool mainly for a few hundred government and university researchers. It delivers packets whether they are legitimate or the electronic equivalent of letter bombs. Now that the Internet has exploded into the cultural mainstream, that assumption is clearly outdated: the result is a stream of worms, viruses, and inadvertent errors that can cascade into economically devastating Internet-wide slow-downs and disruptions.

Take the Code Red Internet worm, which surfaced on July 12, 2001. It quickly spread to 360,000 machines around the world, hijacking them in an attempt to flood the White House Web site with meaningless data—a so-called denial-of-service attack that chokes off legitimate communication. Cleaning up the infected machines took system administrators months and cost businesses more than $2.6 billion, according to Computer Economics, an independent research organization in Carlsbad, CA.

Thanks to one PlanetLab project, Netbait, that kind of scenario could become a thing of the past. Machines infected with Code Red and other worms and viruses often send out "probe" packets as they search for more unprotected systems to infect. Dumb routers pass along these packets, and no one is the wiser until the real invasion arrives and local systems start shutting down. But in theory, the right program running on smart routers could intercept the probes, register where they're coming from, and help administrators track—and perhaps preempt—a networkwide infection. That's exactly what Netbait, developed by researchers at Intel and UC Berkeley, is designed to do.

This spring, the program showed how it can map a spreading epidemic. Brent Chun, Netbait's author, is one of several senior researchers assigned to PlanetLab by Intel, which helped launch the network by donating the hardware for its first 100 nodes. Chun ran Netbait on 90 nodes for several months earlier this year. In mid-March, it detected a sixfold spike in Code Red probes, from about 200 probes per day to more than 1,200—a level of sensitivity far beyond that of a lone, standard router. The data collected by Netbait showed that a variant of Code Red had begun to displace its older cousin.

As it turned out, there was little threat. The variant turned out to be no more malignant than its predecessor, for which remedies are now well known. But the larger point had been made. Without a global platform like PlanetLab as a vantage point, the spread of a new Code Red strain could have gone undetected until much later, when the administrators of local systems compared notes. By then, any response required would have been far more costly.

Netbait means "we can detect patterns and warn the local system administrators that certain machines are infected at their site," says Peterson. "That's something that people hadn't thought about before." By issuing alerts as soon as it detects probe packets, Netbait could even act as an early-warning system for the entire Internet.

Netbait could be running full time on PlanetLab by year's end, according to Chun. "Assuming people deem the service to be useful, eventually it will get on the radar of people at various companies," he says. It would then be easy, says Chun, to offer commercial Internet service providers subscriptions to Netbait, or to license the software to companies with their own planetwide computing infrastructures, such as IBM, Intel, or Akamai.

Traffic Managers

Just as the Internet's architects didn't anticipate the need to defend against armies of hackers, they never foresaw flash crowds. These are throngs of users visiting a Web site simultaneously, overloading the network, the site's server, or both. (The most famous flash crowd, perhaps, formed during a 1999 Victoria's Secret lingerie Web broadcast that had been promoted during the Super Bowl. Within hours, viewers made 1.5 million requests to the company's servers. Most never got through.) Such events—or their more malevolent cousins, denial-of-service attacks—can knock out sites that aren't protected by a network like Akamai's, which caches copies of customers' Web sites on its own, widely scattered private servers. But the question is how many copies to make. Too few, and the overloads persist; too many, and the servers are choked with surplus copies. One solution, described in papers published in 1999 by the researchers who went on to found Akamai, is simply to set a fixed number.

In the not-too-distant future, PlanetLab nodes will adjust the number of cached copies on the fly. Here's how it works. Each node devotes a slice of its processor time and memory to a program designed by Vivek Pai, a colleague of Peterson's in the computer science department at Princeton. The software monitors requests for page downloads and, if it detects that a page is in high demand, copies it to the node's hard drive, which acts like the memory in a typical Web server. As demand grows, the program automatically caches the page on additional nodes to spread out the load, constantly adjusting the number of replicas according to the page's popularity. Pai says that simulations of a denial-of-service attack on a PlanetLab-like network showed that nodes equipped with the Princeton software absorbed twice as many page requests before failing as those running the algorithms published by the Akamai founders.

This new tool, known as CoDeeN, is already running full time on PlanetLab; anyone can use it, simply by changing his or her Web browser's settings to connect to a nearby PlanetLab node. It's a work in progress, so service isn't yet fully reliable. But Pai believes the software can support a network with thousands of nodes, eventually creating a free "public Akamai."

With this tool, Internet users would be able to get faster and more reliable access to any Web site they chose.

But banishing flash crowds won't, by itself, solve Internet slowdowns. Other PlanetLab software seeks to attack a subtler problem: the absence of a decent "highway map" of the network. Over the years the Internet has grown into an opaque tangle of routers and backbone links owned by thousands of competing Internet service providers, most of them private businesses. "Packets go in, they come out, and there's very little visibility or control as to what happens in the middle," says Thomas Anderson, a computer scientist at the University of Washington in Seattle.

One solution is software known as Scriptroute. Developed by Anderson and his colleagues at the University of Washington, it's a distributed program that uses smart nodes to launch probes that fan out through particular regions of the Internet and send back data about their travels. The data can be combined into a map of the active links within and between Internet service providers' networks—along with measurements of the time packets take to traverse each link. It's like having an aerial view of an urban freeway system. Anderson says operators at Internet service providers such as AOL and Earthlink, as well as universities, could use Scriptroute's maps to rapidly diagnose and repair network problems in one to three years.

Sea Change

Keeping data intact can be just as tricky as transmitting it: ask anyone who has left a personal digital assistant on a train or suffered a hard-drive crash. What's needed, says Berkeley computer scientist John Kubiatowicz, is a way to spread data around so that we don't have to carry it physically, but so it's always available, invulnerable to loss or destruction, and inaccessible to unauthorized people.

That's the grand vision behind OceanStore, a distributed storage system that's also being tested on PlanetLab. OceanStore encrypts files—whether memos or other documents, financial records, or digital photos, music, or video clips—then breaks them into overlapping fragments. The system continually moves the fragments and replicates them on nodes around the planet. The original file can be reconstituted from just a subset of the fragments, so it's virtually indestructible, even if a number of local nodes fail. PlanetLab nodes currently have enough memory to let a few hundred people store their records on OceanStore, says Kubiatowicz. Eventually, millions of nodes would be required to store everyone's data. Kubiatowicz's goal is to produce software capable of managing 100 trillion files, or 10,000 files for each of 10 billion people.

To keep track of distributed data, OceanStore assigns the fragments of each particular file their own ID code—a very long number called the Globally Unique Identifier. When a file's owner wants to retrieve the file, her computer tells a node running OceanStore to search for the nearest copies of fragments with the right ID and reassemble them.

Privacy and security are built in. An owner who wants to retrieve a file must first present a key that has been generated using now common encryption methods and stored in a password-protected section of her personal computer. This key contains so many digits that it's essentially impossible for others to guess it and gain unauthorized access. The key provides access to OceanStore directories that map human-readable names (such as "internet.draft") to fragment ID codes. The ID codes are then used to search OceanStore for the nearest copies of the needed fragments, which are reassembled and decrypted. And there's one more layer of protection: the ID codes are themselves generated from the data's contents at the time the contents are saved using a secure cryptographic function. Like encryption keys, the codes are so long (160 binary digits) that even today's most advanced supercomputers can't guess or fake them. So if data retrieved from OceanStore has an unaltered ID, the owner can be sure the data itself hasn't been changed or corrupted.

Kubiatowicz would like to see OceanStore become a utility similar to DSL or cable Internet service, with consumers paying a monthly access fee. "Say you just got back from a trip and you have a digital camera full of pictures," he suggests. "One option is to put these pictures on your home computer or write them to CDs. Another option is that you put those pictures into OceanStore. You just copy them to a partition of your hard drive, and the data is replicated efficiently on a global scale." That option could be available within three to five years, he predicts, but in the interim, two things need to happen. First, his team needs to produce sturdier versions of the OceanStore code. Second, someone needs to provide enough nodes to enlarge the system to a useful scale. That someone is likely to be a private company looking to enter the distributed-storage business, predicts Peterson. "I could imagine OceanStore attracting the next Hotmail-like startup as its first customer," he says.

Beyond providing distributed, secure storage, OceanStore could eventually make every computer your personal one. At its next level of development, it could store your entire computing environment—your PC desktop, plus all of the applications you're running and all the documents you have open—across the network and reconstitute it on demand, even if you popped up at an Internet terminal halfway around the world. This capability would be useful to the businessperson on the road, to a doctor who suddenly needs to review a chart, or to a contractor who wants to tweak a blueprint from home. Several companies are working to realize this vision. Intel calls it Internet Suspend/Resume, and Sun researchers are testing several approaches to "desktop mobility." But PlanetLab could provide the infrastructure that makes such technology possible, by offering a means to manage the large amounts of data—perhaps tens of gigabytes—that personal-computer users might regularly rely on.

Laundry List

Such ideas may seem radical. Then again, just a decade ago, so did e-commerce. The question now is which big idea will evolve into the Google or Amazon.com of the new, smarter Internet. By charter, PlanetLab can't be used for profit-making enterprises, but businesses may soon spring from the platform it provides. "We want it to be a place where you leave services running long-term—which brings us much closer to the point where someone commercial might want to adopt it or replicate it for profit," Peterson says. That could happen if the experiments running now, along with the methods being developed to keep the network operating smoothly, provide a reliable model for future intelligent networks. "We don't know where that next big idea is going to come from," says Peterson. "Our goal is just to provide the playing field."

PlanetLab's early industry sponsors, such as Intel and Hewlett-Packard, may be among the first to jump in. HP Labs in Palo Alto, CA, for example, installed 30 PlanetLab nodes in June and plans to use the network to road-test technologies that could soon become products. One example: software developed by researcher Susie Wee that uses a CoDeeN-like distribution network to deliver high-resolution streaming video to mobile devices. The goal is to avoid wasting bandwidth, and Wee's software would do just that by streaming, say, video of a major-league baseball game to a single local node, then splitting the data into separate streams optimized for the screen resolutions of different viewers' devices—whether desktop PCs, wireless laptops, PDAs, or cell phones. HP or its licensees could bring such a service to market within two years, Wee says. Projects like this one, says Rick McGeer, HP Labs' scientific liaison to a number of university efforts, means that PlanetLab is "not only a great experimental test bed, it's a place where you can see the demonstrable value of services you don't get on today's Internet."

Of course, researchers' enthusiasm about smart networks doesn't keep them from pondering the new problems they could create. Until now, viruses and worms have always been launched from machines at the Internet's edges; imagine how much more damage an attack could do if it originated from a trusted node inside the network. And there's no centralized authority to force local PlanetLab machines to meet security standards, as there is with Akamai and other private networks. But researchers at Princeton and other PlanetLab member institutions say they're already working on ways to avoid these hazards.

While it's impossible to know which blockbuster new technology and business paradigms will emerge from smarter networks, projects like PlanetLab virtually ensure that the Internet will eventually fulfill some of its long-unrealized potential in areas like broadband access, security, shared storage, and reliable video, text, and other content delivery. "There is a long laundry list of things we can and should do better on the Internet," Internet pioneer Cerf says. "Why didn't we do it before? Well, some of it is that they are hard problems; some of it is because the technology wasn't capable enough—we needed more brute-force computing capability than we had 20 years ago. And in some cases, it's because nobody cared."

That's now changing. Peterson expects that ultimately PlanetLab and similar networks will bring about a wholesale reinvention of the Internet. As smart nodes are installed at more of the Internet's existing hubs, these networks could multiply to the point that they cease to be add-ons at all and simply *become* the next generation's Internet. As Peterson puts it, "This is exactly the Internet all over again." The results could be as different from e-mail and Web browsing as those technologies are from the telephone—or a 1973 Buick is from a low-emissions, fuel-efficient Toyota—with impact to match.

N. Abramovitz and
Guilio A. De Leo

PARTY ON, DUDES! Ignorance Is the Curse of the Information Age

Almost any look at what the average citizen knows about politics is bound to be discouraging. Political scientists are nearly unanimous on the subject of voter ignorance. The average American citizen not only lacks basic knowledge, but also holds beliefs that are contradictory and inconsistent. Here is a small sample of what Americans "know":

Nearly one-third of Americans (29 percent) think the Constitution guarantees a job. Forty-two percent think it guarantees health care. And 75 percent think it guarantees a high school education.

Forty-five percent think the communist tenet "from each according to his abilities, to each according to his needs" is part of the U.S. Constitution.

More Americans recognize the Nike advertising slogan "Just Do It" than know where the right to "life, liberty and the pursuit of happiness" is set forth (79 percent versus 47 percent).

Ninety percent know that Bill Gates is the founder of the company that created the Windows operating system. Just over half (53 percent) correctly identified Alexander Hamilton as a Founding Father.

Fewer than half of adults (47 percent) can name their own representative in Congress.

Fewer than half of voters could identify whether their congressman voted for the use of force in the Persian Gulf War.

Just 30 percent of adults could name Newt Gingrich as the congressman who led Republican congressional candidates in signing the Contract with America. Six months after the GOP took congress, 64 percent admitted they did not know.

A 1998 poll by the Pew Research Center for the People and the Press showed that 56 percent of Americans could not name a single Democratic candidate for president; 63 percent knew the name "Bush," but it wasn't clear that voters connected the name to George W. Bush.

According to a January 2000 Gallup poll, 66 percent of Americans could correctly name Regis Philbin when asked who hosts *Who Wants to Be a Millionaire*, but only 6 percent could correctly name Dennis Hastert when asked to name the speaker of the House of Representatives in Washington.

Political scientists Michael X. Delli Carpini and Scott Keeter studied 3,700 questions surveying the public's political knowledge from the 1930s to

From *The American Spectator*, March/April 2002, pp. 68–71. Copyright © 2002 by American Spectator, LLC. Reprinted by permission.

the present. They discovered that people tend to remember or identify trivial details about political leaders, focusing on personalities or simply latching onto the politics that the press plays up. For example, the most commonly known fact about George Bush while he was president was that he hated broccoli, and during the 1992 presidential campaign, although 89 percent of the public knew that Vice President Quayle was feuding with the television character Murphy Brown, only 19 percent could characterize Bill Clinton's record on the environment.

Their findings demonstrate the full absurdity of public knowledge: More people could identify Judge Wapner (the long-time host of the television series *The People's Court*) than could identify Chief Justice Warren Burger or William Rehnquist. More people had heard of John Lennon than of Karl Marx. More Americans could identify comedian-actor Bill Cosby than could name either of their U.S. senators. More people knew who said "What's up, Doc;" "Hi ho, Silver;" or "Come up and see me sometime" than "Give me liberty or give me death;" "The only thing we have to fear is fear itself;" or "Speak softly and carry a big stick." More people knew that Pete Rose was accused of gambling than could name any of the five U.S. senators accused in the late 1980s of unethical conduct in the savings and loan scandal.

In 1986, the National Election Survey found that almost 24 percent of the general public did not know who George Bush was or that he was in his second term as vice president of the United States. "People at this level of inattentiveness can have only the haziest idea of the policy alternatives about which pollsters regularly ask, and such ideas as they do have must often be relatively innocent of the effects of exposure to elite discourse," writes UCLA political science professor John R. Zaller.

All of this would appear to be part of a broader trend of public ignorance that extends far beyond politics. Lack of knowledge on simple matters can reach staggering levels. In a 1996 study by the National Science Foundation, fewer than half of American adults polled (47 percent) knew that the earth takes one year to orbit the sun. Only about 9 percent could describe in their own words what a molecule is, and only 21 percent knew what DNA is.

Esoteric information? That's hard to say. One simple science-related question that has grown to have major political importance is whether police ought to genetically tag convicted criminals in the hopes of linking them to unsolved crimes. In other words, should police track the DNA of a convicted burglar to see if he is guilty of other crimes? Obviously, issues of privacy and government power are relevant here. Yet how can a poll about this issue make sense if the citizenry doesn't understand the scientific terms of debate? Asking an evaluative question seems pointless.

The next generation of voters—those who will undoubtedly be asked to answer even tougher questions about politics and science—are hardly doing any better on the basics. A 2000 study by the American Council of Trustees and Alumni found that 81 percent of seniors at the nation's 55 top colleges scored a D or F on high school-level history exams. It turns out that most college seniors—including those from such elite universities as Harvard, Stanford and the University of California—do not know the men or ideas that have shaped American freedom. Here are just a few examples from *Losing America's Memory: Historical Illiteracy in the 21st Century*, focusing on people's lack of knowledge about our First Citizen—the man whose respect for the laws of the infant republic set the standard for virtue and restraint in office.

Barely one in three students knew that George Washington was the American general at the battle of Yorktown—the battle that won the war for independence.

Only 42 percent could identify Washington with the line "First in war, first in peace, first in the hearts of his countrymen."

Only a little more than half knew that Washington's farewell address warned against permanent alliances with foreign governments.

And when it comes to actually explaining the ideas that preserve freedom and restrain government, the college seniors performed just as miserably.

More than one in three were clueless about the division of power set forth in the U.S. Constitution.

Only 22 percent of these seniors could identify the source of the phrase "government of the people, by the people, and for the people" (from Lincoln's Gettysburg Address).

Yet 99 percent of college seniors knew the crude cartoon characters Beavis and Butthead, and 98 percent could identify gangsta rapper Snoop Dogg.

Apparent ignorance of basic civics can be especially dangerous. Americans often "project" power onto institutions with little understanding of the Constitution or the law. Almost six of 10 Americans (59 percent) think the president, not Congress, has the power to declare war. Thirty-five percent of Americans believe the president has the power to adjourn Congress at his will. Almost half (49 percent) think he has the power to suspend the Constitution (49 percent). And six in 10 think the chief executive appoints judges to the federal courts without the approval of the Senate.

Some political scientists charge that American ignorance tends to help institutions and parties in power. That is hardly the active vigilance by the citizenry that the founders advocated. Political scientists continue to debate the role of ignorance and the future of democracy when voters are so woefully ignorant. As journalist Christopher Shea writes, "Clearly, voter ignorance poses problems for democratic theory: Politicians, the representatives of the people, are being elected by people who do not know their names or their platforms. Elites are committing the nation to major treaties and sweeping policies that most voters don't even know exist."

Professors Delli Carpini and Keeter discovered, for example, that most Americans make fundamental errors on some of the most contested and heavily covered political questions. "Americans grossly overestimate the average profit made by American corporations, the percentage of the U.S. population that is poor or homeless, and the percentage of the world population that is malnourished," they write. "And, despite 12 years of anti-abortion administrations, Americans substantially underestimate the number of abortions performed every year."

With most voters unable to even name their congressperson or senators during an election year, the clear winner is the establishment candidate.

Studies by Larry Bartels at Princeton University show that mere name recognition is enough to give incumbents, a 5-percentage-point advantage over challengers: Most voters in the election booth can't identify a single position of the incumbent, but if they've seen the candidate's name before, that can be enough to secure their vote. (In many cases, voters can't even recognize the names of incumbents.)

Media polls are typically searching in vain for hard-nosed public opinion that simply isn't there. Polls force people to say they are leaning toward a particular candidate, but when voters are asked the more open-ended question "Whom do you favor for the presidency?" the number of undecided voters rises. The mere practice, in polling, of naming the candidates yields results that convey a false sense of what voters know. When Harvard's "Vanishing Voter Project" asked voters their presidential preferences without giving the names of candidates, they routinely found that the number of undecided voters was much higher than in media polls. Just three weeks before the 2000 election, 14 percent of voters still hadn't made up their minds.

Even when polling covers subjects on which a person should have direct knowledge, it can yield misleading results because of basic ignorance. The nonpartisan Center for Studying Health System Change (HSC) found that how people rate their health care is attributable to the type of plan they *think* they are in, more than their actual health insurance. The center asked 20,000 privately insured people what they thought of their coverage, their doctor and their treatment. But instead of just taking their opinions and impressions, the center also looked at what coverage each respondent actually had.

Nearly a quarter of Americans mis-identified the coverage they had. Eleven percent didn't know they were in an HMO, and another 13 percent thought they were in an HMO but were not. Yet when people believed they were in a much-maligned HMO (even when they actually had another kind of insurance), their perceived satisfaction with their health care was lower than that of people who believed they had non-HMO coverage (even when they were in an HMO). Similarly, on nearly all 10 measures studied by the center, those HMO enrollees who thought they had a different kind of insurance gave satisfaction ratings similar to those who actually had those other kinds of insurance.

Once center researchers adjusted for incorrect self-identification, the differences between HMO and non-HMO enrollees nearly vanished. Even on something as personal as health care, citizens display a striking and debilitating ignorance that quietly undermines many polling results.

After looking at the carnage of polls that test voter knowledge rather than impressions, James L. Payne concluded in his 1991 book *The Culture of Spending:*

Surveys have repeatedly found that voters are remarkably ignorant about even simple, dramatic features of the political landscape. The vast majority of voters cannot recall the names of congressional candidates in the most recent election; they cannot use the labels "liberal" and "conservative" meaningfully; they do not know which party controls Congress; they are wildly wrong about elementary facts about the federal budget; and they do not know how their congressmen vote on even quite salient policy questions. In other words, they are generally incapable of rewarding or punishing their congressman for his action on spending bills.

Ignorance of basic facts such as a candidate's name or position isn't the only reason to question the efficacy of polling in such a dispiriting universe. Because polls have become "players in the political process," their influence is felt in the policy realm, undercutting efforts to educate because they assume respondents' knowledge and focus on the horse race. Is it correct to say that Americans oppose or support various policies when they don't even have a grasp of basic facts relating to those policies? For instance, in 1995, Grass Roots Research found that 83 percent of those polled underestimated the average family's tax burden. Taxes for a four-person family earning $35,000 are 54 percent higher than most people think. Naturally, when practical-minded Americans look at political issues, their perceptions of reality influence which solutions they find acceptable. If they perceive that there are fewer abortions or lower taxes than there really are, these misperceptions may affect the kinds of policy prescriptions they endorse. They might change their views if introduced to the facts. In this sense, the unreflective reporting on public opinion about these policy issues is deceptive.

The Wall Street Journal editorial page provides another example of how ignorance affects public debate. Media reports during the 1995 struggle between the Republicans in Congress and the Clinton White House continually asserted that the public strongly opposed the GOP's efforts to slow the growth of Medicare spending. A poll by Public Opinion Strategies asked 1,000 Americans not what they felt, but what they actually knew about the GOP plan. Twenty-seven percent said they thought the GOP would cut Medicare spending by $4,000 per recipient. Almost one in four (24 percent) said it would keep spending the same. Another 25 percent didn't know. Only 22 percent knew the correct answer: The plan would increase spending to $6,700 per recipient.

Public Opinion's pollsters then told respondents the true result of the GOP plan and explained: "[U]nder the plan that recently passed by Congress, spending on Medicare will increase 45 percent over the next seven years, which is twice the projected rate of inflation." How did such hard facts change public opinion about Medicare solutions? Six of 10 Americans said that the GOP's proposed Medicare spending was too *high*. Another 29 percent said it was about right. Only 2 percent said it was too *low*.

Indeed polling and the media may gain their ability to influence results from voter ignorance. When a polling question introduces new facts (or any facts at all), voters are presented with a reframed political issue and thus may have a new opinion. Voters are continually asked about higher spending, new programs, and the best way to solve social ills with government spending. But how does the knowledge base (or lack of knowledge) affect the results of a polling question? That is simply unknown. When asked in a June 2000 *Washington Post* poll how much money the federal government gives to the nation's public schools, only 31 percent chose the correct answer. Although only 10 percent admitted to not knowing the correct answer, fully 60 percent of registered voters claimed they knew, but were wrong. Is there any doubt that voters' knowledge, or lack thereof, affects the debate about whether to raise school spending to ever higher levels?

Reporters often claim that the public supports various policies, and they use such sentiment as an indicator of the electoral prospects of favored candidates. But this, too, can be misleading. Take, for instance, the results of a survey taken by The Polling Company for the Center for Security Policy about the Strategic Defense Initiative. Some 54 percent of respondents thought that the U.S. military had the capability to destroy a ballistic missile before it could hit an American city and do damage. Another 20 percent didn't know or refused to answer. Only 27 percent correctly said that the U.S. military could not destroy a missile.

What's interesting is that although 70 percent of those polled said they were concerned about the possibility of ballistic missile attack, the actual level of ignorance was very high. The Polling Company went on to tell those polled that "government documents indicate that the U.S. military cannot destroy even a single incoming missile." The responses were interesting. Nearly one in five said they were "shocked and angry" by the revelation. Another 28 percent said they were "very surprised," and 17 percent were "somewhat surprised." Only 22 percent said they were "not surprised at all." Finally, 14 percent were "skeptical because [they] believe that the documents are inaccurate."

Beyond simply skewing poll results, ignorance is actually amplified by polling. Perhaps the most amazing example of the extent of ignorance can be found in Larry Sabato's 1981 book *The Rise of Political Consultants*. Citizens were asked: "Some people say the 1975 Public Affairs Act should be repealed. Do you agree or disagree that it should be repealed?" Nearly one in four (24 percent) said they wanted it repealed. Another 19 percent wanted it to remain in effect. Fifty-seven percent didn't know what should be done. What's interesting is that there was no such thing as the 1975 Public Affairs Act. But for 43 percent of those polled, simply asking that question was enough to create public opinion.

Ignorance can threaten even the most democratic institutions and safeguards. In September 1997, the Center for Media and Public Affairs conducted one of the largest surveys ever on American views of the Fourth Estate. Fully 84 percent of Americans are willing to "turn to the government to require that the news media give equal coverage to all sides of controversial issues." Seven-in-10 back court-imposed fines for inaccurate or biased reporting. And just over half (53 percent) think that journalists should be licensed. Based on sheer numbers—in the absence of the rule of law and dedication to the Bill of Rights—there is enough support to put curbs on the free speech that most journalists (rightly) consider one of the most important bulwarks of liberty.

In an era when Americans have neither the time nor the interest to track politics closely, the power of the pollster to shape public opinion is almost unparalleled when united with the media agenda.

For elected leaders, voter ignorance is something they have to confront when they attempt to make a case for new policies or reforms. But for the media, ignorance isn't an obstacle. It's an opportunity for those asking the questions—whether pollster or media polling director—to drive debate. As more time is devoted to media pundits, journalists and pollsters, and less to candidates and leaders, the effect is a negative one: Public opinion becomes more important as arbiter for the chattering classes. But in a knowledge vacuum, public opinion also becomes more plastic and more subject to manipulation, however well intentioned.

Pollsters often try to bridge the gap in public knowledge by providing basic definitions of terms as part of their questions. But this presents a new problem: By writing the questions, pollsters are put in a position of power, particularly when those questions will be used in a media story. The story—if the poll is the story—is limited by the questions asked, the definitions supplied, and the answers that respondents are given to choose from.

The elevation of opinion without context or reference to knowledge exacerbates a problem of modern democracies. Self-expression may work in NEA-funded art, but it robs the political process of the communication and discussion that marries compromise with principle. Clearly "opinion" isn't the appropriate word for the mélange of impressions and sentiment that is presented as the public's belief in countless newspaper and television stories. If poll respondents lack a solid grasp of the facts, surveys give us little more than narcissistic opinion.

As intelligent and precise thinking declines, all that remains is a chaos of ideologies in which the lowest human appetites rule. In her essay "Truth and Politics," historian Hannah Arendt writes: "Facts inform opinions, and opinions, inspired by different interests and passions, can differ widely and still be legitimate as long as they respect factual truth. Freedom of opinion is a farce unless factual information is guaranteed and facts themselves are not in dispute."

If ignorance is rife in a republic, what do polls and the constant media attention to them do to deliberative democracy? As Hamilton put it, American government is based on "reflection and choice." Modern-day radical egalitarians—journalists and pollsters who believe that polls are the definitive voice of the people—may applaud the ability of the most uninformed citizen to be heard, but few if any of these champions of polling ever write about or discuss the implications of ignorance to a representative democracy. This is the dirtiest secret of polling.

Absent from most polling stories is the honest disclosure that American ignorance is driving public affairs. Basic ignorance of civic questions gives us reason to doubt the veracity of most polls. Were Americans armed with strongly held opinions and well-grounded knowledge of civic matters, they would not be open to manipulation by the wording of polls. This is one of the strongest reasons to question the effect of polls on representative government.

Pollsters assume and often control the presentation of the relevant facts. As a blunt instrument, the pollster's questions fail to explore what the contrary data may be. This is one reason that public opinion can differ so widely from one poll to another. When the citizens of a republic lack basic knowledge of political facts and cannot process ideas critically, uninformed opinion becomes even more potent in driving people. Worse, when the media fail to think critically about the lines of dispute on political questions, polls that are supposed to explore opinion will simplify and even mislead political leaders as well as the electorate.

When the media drives opinion by constant polling, the assumption of an educated public undermines the process of public deliberation that actually educates voters. Ideas are no longer honed, language isn't refined, and debate is truncated. The common ground needed for compromise and peaceful action is eroded because the discussion about facts and the parameters of the question are lost. In the frenzy to judge who wins and who loses, the media erodes what it is to be a democracy. Moments of change become opportunities for spin, not for new, bold responses to the exigencies of history.

Not only are polls influenced, shaped, and even dominated by voter ignorance, but so is political debate. The evidence shows that ignorance is being projected into public debate because of the pervasiveness of polls. Polls are leading to the democratization of ignorance in the public square by ratifying ill-formed opinions, with the march of the mob instigated by an impatient and unreflective media. Polls—especially in an age marked by their proliferation—are serving as broadcasting towers of ignorance.

Political science professor Rogan Kersh notes, "Public ignorance and apathy toward most policy matters have been constant (or have grown worse) for over three decades. Yet the same period has seen increasing reliance on finely tuned instruments for measuring popular opinion and more vigorous applications of the results in policy making." And here is the paradox in the Age of Polls: Pollsters and political scientists are still unclear about the full consequences of running a republic on the basis of opinion polls. The cost of voter ignorance is high, especially in a nation with a vast and sprawling government that, even for the most plugged-in elites, is too complicated to understand. Media polling that does not properly inform viewers and readers of its limitations serves only to give the façade of a healthy democracy, while consultants, wordsmiths and polling units gently massage questions, set the news agenda and then selectively report results. It is like the marionette player who claims (however visible the strings) that the puppet moves on his own.

POSTSCRIPT

Are People Better Informed in the Information Society?

It would be wonderful if we could predict the future with certainty, but unfortunately, even predictions are subject to change. It is interesting to note that virtually every new form of technology, especially media, has often been greeted with a mixed sense of optimism and pessimism. New technologies challenge us to think of new practices, new values, and new structures. Sometimes the combination of those elements suggest comfort, ease, and security—other times the threat to what we already know can be a disconcerting feeling of change, without control. We might be able to look back at the evolution of media and think that the variety of content available is great, but it would also be possible to see how our media forms have changed in negative ways too. Your parents were of the generation who knew free television and radio—when media in the airwaves was delivered to the home without a hefty cable bill. Today, unless you live in a part of the country where broadcast signals can still be received in your home, you may not have any choice in your delivery service, or the charges affixed by your program provider.

One of the pleasures of science fiction is that there is usually enough evidence in any portrayal of the future that elements of the story appear to be plausible. There are many futuristic novels like *1984* and *Brave New World* which, in their day, sent chills down the spines of readers. Today's equivalent of these novels would be a film like *The Matrix*.

To read more accounts of how media and technology can and do affect the quality of our lives by facilitating changes within our major institutions—such as education, government, and through popular culture, we suggest a number of readings from a variety of viewpoints. As mentioned above, Neil Postman's classic, *Amusing Ourselves To Death* looks at the impact of television on our lives. His thesis is that even news has to be packaged to be entertaining, and the desire to be entertained stretches to other institutions as well, like schools and within our political arena. Postman's later books, *Technopoly* (Vintage, 1992) and *Building a Bridge to the 18th Century* (Alfred A. Knopf, 1999) also deal with the subtle changes we often experience, but never critically question, as we venerate science and technology, and exclude very human traits such as morality and common sense.

Former Secretary of Labor, Robert Reich has written a very enjoyable, readable book focusing on social change in America, with some reference to the role of media and technology. See Reich, The Future of Success (Alfred A. Knopf, 2001). And for more specific references to media, see John Naughton's *A Brief History of the Future: From Radio Days to Internet Years In a Lifetime* (Overlook Press, 1999).

Contributors to This Volume

EDITORS

ALISON ALEXANDER is professor of telecommunications and senior associate dean at the Grady College of Journalism and Mass Communication at the University of Georgia. She is the past editor of the *Journal of Broadcasting & Electronic Media*, and past president of the Associate for Communication Administration and the Eastern Communication Association. She received her Ph.D. in communication from Ohio State University. She is widely published in the area of media and family, audience research, and media economics.

JARICE HANSON is professor of communication at the University of Massachusetts, Amherst, and the current Verizon Chair in Telecommunications at the School of Communications and Theater, Temple University. She was the founding dean of the School of Communications at Quinnipiac University from 2001 to 2003. She received a B.A. in speech and performing arts and a B.A. in English at Northeastern Illinois University in 1976, and she received an M.A. and a Ph.D. from Northwestern University in Radio-TV-Film in 1977 and 1979, respectively. She is author or editor of 18 books and numerous articles. The most recent books include *24/7: How Cell Phones and the Internet Change the Way We Live, Work and Play* (Praeger, 2007), and *Constructing America's War Culture: Iraq, Media, and Images at Home* (co-edited with Thomas Conroy) (Lexington Books, 2007). She lives in Massachusetts with three furry creatures: Dewey, Xena, and Frank.

AUTHORS

CRAIG A. ANDERSON is a professor in the department of psychology, University of Iowa. He has written extensively on human behavior and violence.

SPENCER E. ANTE has been the computer department editor for *Business-Week* since 2000. He has specialized in writing for online publications, including *TheStreet.com*, *Wired News*, *Business 2.0*, and *The Web* magazine.

STEPHANIE C. ARDITO is the principal of Ardito Information & Research, Inc., an information firm based in Wilmington, Delaware.

ERICA WEINTRAUB AUSTIN is a professor in the Edward R. Murrow School of Communication at Washington State University. She received her Ph.D. from Stanford University.

ERIC BOEHLERT is a journalist who most often writes about media, politics, and pop culture. His book, *Lapdogs: How the Press Rolled Over for Bush* (Free Press, 2006) addresses how the press has been used by politicians.

JOHN E. CALFEE is a resident scholar at the American Enterprise Institute in Washington, D.C. He is a former Federal Trade Commission economist, and he is the author of *Fear of Persuasion: A New Perspective on Advertising and Regulation* (Agora, 1997).

EDISON MEDIA RESEARCH is an organization that conducts survey research to develop strategic information for media organizations. The company is based in Somerville, New Jersey.

THE FIRST AMENDMENT CENTER is a project of Vanderbilt University in Nashville, Tennessee, and Arlington, Virginia. The organization sponsors a Web site on which issues of the First Amendment are featured, including commentary and discussion items. The site can be located at `http://www.firstamendmentcenter.org/`.

JIB FOWLES is professor of communication at the University of Houston-Clear Lake. His previous books include *Why Viewers Watch* (Sage Publications, 1992) and *Advertising and Popular Culture* (Sage Publications, 1996). His articles have also appeared in many popular magazines.

JULIA R. FOX is an associate professor of telecommunications at Indiana University–Bloomington. Her research interests include television news coverage and how people process and remember television news messages.

KIMBERLY GAMBLE was a doctoral student at the time she contributed to this article. She has a master's degree in clinical/community psychology, and conducts research on the HIV/AIDS epidemic in minority communities.

SIMSON GARFINKEL is a columnist for the *Boston Globe* and fellow at the Berkman Center for Internet and Society at Harvard Law School. He is author of *Database Nation: The Death of Privacy in the 21st Century* (O'Reilly & Associates, 2000).

DINYAR GODREJ is an editor with the *New Internationalist*. Recent books include the *No Nonsense Guide to Climate Change* (2006), and *Peace (Books to Go)* (2005), both published by New Internationalist Publications.

PAUL M. HIRSCH is a professor at the Kellogg School of Management at Northwestern University. He is the author of many articles on management practices and mass media organizations. His research interests include organization theory and media industries.

BARRY A. HOLLANDER is an associate professor of journalism at the University of Georgia. His research interests include the political effects of new media and the interaction of religious and poltical beliefs.

JANIS SANCHEZ-HUCKLES is a professor at Old Dominion University and the Virginia Consortium Program in Clinical Psychology. Her research involves the power of media images and how they distort social images of the lives of people.

PATRICK S. HUDGINS is a graduate of the Virginia Consortium Program in Clinical Psychology. He specializes in child and family therapy, and prevention programs to help children become more resilient.

ERIC KLINENBERG is an associate professor of sociology at New York University. He is author of *Fighting for Air: The Battle to Control America's Media* (Metropolitan, 2007). He writes on media production, urban studies, and disaster and social violence.

GLORY KOLOEN was a Ph.D. candidate in political science at Indiana University–Bloomington when this article was written. She studies political communication via mass media and political psychology.

ROBERT KUTTNER is a columnist for the *Boston Globe*, co-editor of *The American Prospect*, and the author of seven books. His most recent book is *The Squandering of America: How the Failure of Our Politics Undermines Our Prosperity* (Knopf, 2007). He has previously worked at *BusinessWeek* and the *Washington Post*.

RUTH ANN WEAVER LARISCY is professor of public relations at the University of Georgia. She studies political campaigning, with a focus on negative advertising.

TRUDY LIEBERMAN directs the health and medical reporting program in the graduate school of journalism at City University of New York, and is a longtime contributing editor to *Columbia Journalism Review*.

JEFFREY J. MACIEJEWSKI is an associate professor of advertising in the journalism and mass communication program at Creighton University. He writes about the implications of natural law for mass communication.

THOMAS A. MASCARO is an associate professor at Bowling Green State University who specializes in documentary history. His work analyzes documentary television programs, producers, and the contexts and consequences of those documentaries.

HORACE NEWCOMB is director of the Peabody Awards and Lambdin Kay Professor at the Grady College of the University of Georgia. He is the editor of *Museum of Broadcast Communications Encyclopedia of Television* (Fitzroy Dearborn, 1997).

DAVID T. OZAR is a professor of philosophy and past director of the Center for Ethics and Social Justice at Loyola University of Chicago. His areas of research include health care ethics, professional ethics, normative ethics, social/political philosophy, and philosophy of law.

ADAM L. PENENBERG writes for *Forbes*. He is a journalist who writes on issues of privacy and security.

BRUCE E. PINKLETON is an associate professor in the Edward R. Murrow School of Communications at Washington State University. He received his Ph.D. from Michigan State University.

JAMES PONIEWOZIK writes about television for *Time Magazine* and *Salon*. He also has a blog on which he comments about television and society.

W. JAMES POTTER is a professor of communication at Florida State University. He has conducted research on media violence and has served as one of the investigators on the National Television Violence Study. Recent books include *Media Literacy* (Sage Publications, 1998) and *An Analysis of Thinking and Research About Qualitative Methods* (Lawrence Erlbaum, 1996).

MICHAEL K. POWELL is the ex-chairman of the Federal Communications Commission (FCC). He was designated chairman by President Bush. Mr. Powell, a Republican, was nominated to the FCC by President Clinton.

PUBLIC RELATIONS SOCIETY OF AMERICA (PRSA) is an organization representing more than 20,000 public relations professionals. Its mission is to advance the profession of public relations and public relations professionals through education, innovation, and adherence to a strong code of ethical behavior.

RHODA RABKIN as an adjunct scholar at the Enterprise Institute for Public Policy and Research.

MATTHEW ROBINSON is managing editor of *Human Events* and the author of *Mobocracy: How the Media's Obsession with Polling Twists the News, Alters Elections and Undermines Democracy*.

WADE ROUSH lives in San Francisco and is a senior editor of *Technology Review*.

MICHAEL RYAN is a professor in the school of communication at the University of Houston. He writes about journalism practice and ethics, and has worked as a news reporter.

VOLKAN SAHIN was a Ph.D. student in curriculum and instruction at Indiana Unviersity–Bloomington when this article was written. His research interests include media literacy, critical viewing skills, and children's television.

CHUCK SALTER is a senior writer for the magazine *Fast Company*. The organization also sponsors an online resource, *FastCompany.com*.

HERBERT I. SCHILLER was Professor Emeritus of Communication at the University of California, San Diego upon his death in 2000. He was the author of a dozen books on the media, information and culture, and a foremost proponent of the critical/cultural perspective in the United States.

DANIEL SCHULMAN is an investigative fellow at *Mother Jones*. A former assistant editor at the *Columbia Journalism Review*, his work has appeared in the *Boston Globe Magazine*, the *Boston Phoenix*, the *Village Voice*, and other publications.

DAVID TALBOT is chief correspondent for *Technology Review*. He specializes in issues of energy, transportation, and communication.

SPENCER F. TINKHAM is a professor of advertising at the University of Georgia. He studies political campaigns and negative advertising.

TED TURNER is a businessman, entrepreneur, and philanthropist. Among his many media holdings, he was the founder of Turner Broadcasting, which originated CNN, TBS, and TNT. As one of the first entrepreneurs to challenge traditional media network dominance, he has become a major critic of the FCC's lifting of ownership restrictions.

NAM-HYUN UM (MA, Washington State University) is an account executive for Cheil Communications in Seoul, Korea.

SIVA VAIDHYANATHAN is an associate professor of culture and communication at New York University. He is the author of *Copyrights and Copywrongs: The Rise of Intellectual Property and How It Threatens Creativity* (NYU Press, 2001).

EUGENE VOLOKH is an attorney and professor at UCLA Law School in California.

DATE DUE

NOV – 8 2008	OCT 2 6 2013
DEC 2 2 2008	NOV 0 1 2014
MAY 1 3 2009	
NOV 4 2009	
NOV 5 2009	
NOV 2 7 2009	
JAN 1 7 2010 DISCARDED	
JAN 2 0 2010	
03/03/10	
MAY 0 1 2010	
MAY 1 9 2011	
NOV 2 5 2011	
MAR 2 4 2012	
MAY 3 1 2012	
OCT 2 8 2012	
MAR 1 6 2013	
MAY 2 4 2013	Printed in USA